Withdrawn

A HISTORY OF THE
BRITISH   CAVALRY
1816 to 1919
VOLUME II
1851 to 1871

By the same author

THE CAPEL LETTERS, 1814–1817 (CAPE, 1955)
ONE-LEG (CAPE, 1961)
SERGEANT PEARMAN'S MEMOIRS (CAPE, 1968)
LITTLE HODGE (LEO COOPER, 1971)
A HISTORY OF THE BRITISH CAVALRY, 1816–1919:
  VOLUME I: 1816–1850 (ARCHON BOOKS, 1973)

A HISTORY OF THE BRITISH CAVALRY

1816 to 1919

by

THE MARQUESS OF ANGLESEY

F.S.A.

VOLUME II
1851 to 1871

ARCHON BOOKS

Library of Congress Cataloging in Publication Data

Anglesey, George Charles Henry Victor Paget, 7th
   Marquis of, 1922–
   A History of the British cavalry, 1816–1919.

   Includes bibliographical references.
   CONTENTS: v. 1. 1816–1850. v. 2. 1851–1871.
   1. Great Britain. Army. Cavalry—History.
I Title.
UE57.A65   357'.1'0942   73–8663
ISBN 0–208–01468–3

Published in Great Britain 1975
by Leo Cooper Ltd, London
and in the United States of America
as an Archon Book
by The Shoe String Press, Inc.
Hamden, Connecticut
Printed in Great Britain

DEDICATED, WITH PERMISSION, TO
FIELD-MARSHAL SIR GERALD TEMPLER
K.G., G.C.B., G.C.M.G., K.B.E., D.S.O., D.C.L.
WHO HAS DONE SO MUCH TO FOSTER THE
STUDY AND APPRECIATION OF THE ARMY'S
HISTORY

CONTENTS

Contents

Contents

Contents

Contents

A list of abbreviations used in the footnotes and in the
source notes (p. 470) appears on p. 462

ILLUSTRATIONS

Illustrations

Illustrations

TEXT ILLUSTRATIONS

Text Illustrations

MAPS

ACKNOWLEDGMENTS

Without the invaluable aid of the Ministry of Defence Library and its Chief Librarian, D. W. King, Esq., O.B.E., F.L.A., now retired, this volume, like its predecessor, could not have been written. My gratitude to him and his staff knows no bounds.

The India Office Library, the Library of the Royal United Service Institute for Defence Studies, the National Army Museum, the Royal College of Veterinary Surgeons' Wellcome Library, the Royal Army Medical Corps Historical Museum and the London Library have all placed me in their debt by providing me, unstintingly, with books and information.

Amongst those who have allowed me to borrow, to keep for lengthy periods and to quote from original letters, diaries and other papers in their possession, I should like to thank especially Mrs L. S. Bickford, Miss G. M. Biddulph, Brigadier R. G. S. Bidwell, James Blake, Esq., John A. W. Bush, Esq., Mrs L. M. Chesterton, Colonel Henry Clowes, D.S.O., O.B.E., Major T. L. Fletcher, Honorary Curator, Army Physical Training Corps Museum, F. R. Hodge, Esq., Miss M. S. Lightfoot, E. A. Lucas, Esq., E. A. K. Patrick, Esq., the late Robert Poore-Saurin-Watts, Esq., L. Potiphar, Esq., the late Lord Raglan, Hugh E. Sutton, Esq., Miss Beryl A. Sylvester Hodder, Mrs B. Walker-Heneage-Vivian and Captain V. M. Wombwell.

Helpful advice and comments have been given to me by, among others, Brian Bond, Esq., Roger Fulford, Esq., C.V.O., Mrs Charles Morgan, Messrs Boris and John Mollo and Esmond Warner, Esq. To them and to my long-suffering wife, I make warm acknowledgment.

Patrick Leeson, Esq. has once again produced first-class maps out of my rough scribblings. To him, to my patient publishers, to Mrs H. St G. Saunders of Writer's and Speaker's Research and to Mrs Pat Brayne, for her swift and splendid typing, I am deeply thankful.

'A soldier,
... Jealous in honour, sudden and quick in quarrel,
Seeking the bubble reputation
Even in the cannon's mouth.'

—SHAKESPEARE, *As You Like It*
(Act ii, sc. 7)

'In the Cavalry, above all other branches,
each man, whether he be officer or trooper, gets
exceptional chances of personal distinction.'

—MAJOR-GENERAL R. S. S. BADEN-POWELL,
Inspector-General of Cavalry, in
1906. ('What Lies Before Us',
Cavalry Journal, Vol. I, p. 11)

PREFACE

For almost forty years after Waterloo, the British Army was in a state of near stagnation. A modern commentator has well described its pre-Crimean condition.

> 'In an age pulsating with commercialism and social unrest, it was taken for granted that the army were simply the caretakers of a vast economic empire, or the policemen of unruly industrial districts at home. They had no strategic role, and in the frequent protective or punitory clashes with tribes or mobs, the Brown-Bess tactics were considered and proven sufficient. These duties involved, both at home and abroad, a permanent tactical dispersion which prevented the experimentation of doctrine in large-scale manoeuvres.'[1]

In most of the tasks set it between 1815 and 1850 the army was successful in the end. Of the nine Indian campaigns described in the first volume of this work, the most testing were the two Sikh Wars. Both were won by troops armed and deployed in much the same way as Wellington's had been in the Peninsular War and at Waterloo. From the cavalry point of view, even more than from the infantry's, much the same could be said of the Crimean War and the Indian Mutiny, which dominated the twenty years covered by this second volume. The part played by the mounted branch of the army in both conflicts is here given at some length, using as much as possible first-hand accounts of persons actually present, a number of which have not before been published.

As a result of these two traumatic experiences numerous reforms came about both in the army at home and in India. The most far-reaching of these at home affected the day-to-day life of the rank and file, changes which were 'more momentous than the more dramatic but more remote ones wrought by Cardwell a few years later'.[2] An important part of this volume is devoted, therefore, to the details of barrack room existence during the 1850s and 1860s. Most of them have emerged as a result of extensive quarrying in Blue Books, of which there was a spate during the period. As far as I am aware much of the information thus gained has lain hidden from view during the century or so which has passed since the evidence was given. I hope that readers of this book will find it as fascinating to read about as it was to discover. It certainly paints an intriguing picture of an important section of mid-Victorian society.

*   *   *

The difficulties which I experienced in the first volume of separating the activities of one branch of the army from those of the others, especially when describing battles, have not lessened in the second. I have been ruthless in cutting out all details of the parts played by the artillery and the infantry, except where I have seen them as vital to an understanding of what happened. In the battle of Balaklava, for instance, I have treated the horse artillery's actions as fully as that of the two cavalry brigades, yet in many of the Mutiny engagements I have hardly mentioned what was being done by the other arms.

*   *   *

My claim to produce a definitive account of the life and actions of the British cavalry at home and overseas is tempered by the obvious limitations imposed by time and space. Those incidents which seem to me to illustrate particularly well the outlook or capacities of the officers and men have been dealt with fully. Others have been neglected altogether. Numerous engagements during the suppression of the Mutiny, for example, have had to be left out as if they had never taken place. I hope that my selections and omissions have not distorted the overall picture too much. On the other hand I have seen fit to enter into the cavalry's part in the battle of Balaklava as fully as has ever been done before. This I excuse on the grounds that inaccuracies of detail and of interpretation have, in my view, created myths which needed, if not exploding, at least revising so as to resemble more closely what actually happened and to explain 'the reason why'.

*   *   *

In the Preface to the first volume I wrote that each of the four which were planned to follow it was to be designed so as to be read independently of its companions, 'each seeking to present a more or less complete image of the period covered'. The chief exception which I then made applies equally to the present volume: all reference to South African campaigns has again been excluded. These will form the prelude to the larger conflicts which took place in the last quarter of the century, and will therefore appear in the next volume.

*   *   *

My debt to the works of Sir John Fortescue is as great in the case of this second volume as it was in the first. My task in the third and fourth volumes will be neither as easy nor as pleasant, for the last volume of his *History of the British Army* does not bring the story down beyond 1870. I shall sorely miss, as I expressed it in the Preface to the first volume, 'his grasp of the broad sweep of events and his capacity for condensing a vast mass of facts into highly readable prose'. I can only hope that my researches into the final fifty years of the cavalry arm will be of service to whatever brave men may attempt in the future to bring Fortescue's great work up to date.

*   *   *

In the spelling of Indian proper names I have adopted no set principle except that which appears to me to be generally acceptable to the average reader. I have rejected such scholarly affectations as would have Cawnpore spelled Kahnpur and Lucknow, Lakhnau, but where faced with alternatives for less well known names, I have usually selected the more modern or scholarly. When quoting from contemporary documents I have generally kept the original spelling.

*   *   *

As in the first volume I have not described in any detail the uniforms of the cavalry except where the temptation to do so has been overwhelming because of their special significance or eccentricity.

A HISTORY OF THE
BRITISH CAVALRY
1816–1919

VOLUME II
1851–1871

'[As a result of the Crimean War] the aristocracy no longer appeared as born war leaders free from middle class materialism, but as out-of-date privileged bunglers who should make way for the efficient, self-reliant men of the age.'

MRS O. ANDERSON, *A Liberal State at War*, 1967, 109

'In respect of engendering a false confidence, our latest great military achievement, the splendid, brilliant, but comparatively easy reconquest of India in 1859, has done us harm rather than good.'

SIR HENRY M. HAVELOCK, bart,
Three Main Military Questions of the Day, 1867, 1

'An English schoolboy would probably write a much better copy of Latin verses than a Prussian cadet, but Latin verses are not very much required in war.'

CAPTAIN HOZIER, 3rd Dragoon Guards, in evidence before the Royal Commission on Military Education, 1870, 246

'From 1860 to 1890 may be called the dark days of our cavalry.'

FIELD-MARSHAL SIR EVELYN WOOD, V.C.,
'British Cavalry, 1853–1903', *Cavalry Journal*, I, 1906, 147

1

'The Novelty of the proceeding excited great
interest.'

FORTESCUE[1]

(i)

'Camp of Exercise' at Chobham, 1853

In June, 1853, there was held on Chobham Common in Surrey,
about ten miles north-east of where Aldershot Camp now stands, a
divisional 'Camp of Exercise'. This experiment, proposed by the
Duke of Wellington before his death the previous year, had never
before been tried in time of peace. It was an event of national importance, for the country as a whole through the publicity given to
the manoeuvres was made aware after nearly forty years that an
army still existed. Further, the various branches of that army saw
each other, in many cases, for the very first time. Hitherto there had
been nowhere in the United Kingdom, except near Dublin, where
sufficient men could be collected together for the manoeuvring of
even a single brigade.

Some 8,000 men took part, including four regiments of cavalry.
This force, which also included a troop of Royal Horse Artillery,
was formed into one cavalry and three infantry brigades. For five
weeks of chiefly wet weather the troops were reviewed and exercised.
Punch commented that 'the men showed that they could not only
stand fire but water too'.[2] A second rather smaller force repeated the
process in late July. On both occasions the horses were housed in
large tents, thirty yards long and fifteen broad. Each held thirty
horses, standing in two ranks face to face with a four-foot passage
between their heads.[3]

Amongst other arrangements made by the Assistant Quartermaster-General, according to Sir Evelyn Wood, were shallow ponds
prepared in the peaty soil for watering the cavalry horses. 'It is
perhaps not remarkable', wrote Wood many years later, 'that the
commanding officers of cavalry regiments, accustomed to the con-
venience of a barrack – indeed as they had never been in camp it is
not strange that it was so – protested', fearing that their precious
horses 'would get bogged and drowned'. The Assistant Quarter-

27

master-General, objecting to this criticism of his arrangement, went up to General Lord Seaton, who was in command of the camp of exercise, and said: 'My Lord, will you order them to ride alongside of me, and we will gallop through every pond?' 'The order was given', says Wood, 'and executed, to the great detriment of the officers' tunics, for in those days full dress was worn in camp.'[4]

Numerous shortcomings were revealed in the course of the mock battles which were staged at Chobham, but attempts to right these had not borne fruit before the army at home was sent to war.

'Is it peace or war? better war!'
TENNYSON, *Maud*[1]

(ii)

Crimean War, 1854: origins and start – cavalry available – embarkation and passage out – Constantinople to Varna – 'Sore-Back Reconnaissance' – life at Varna

Lord John Russell told the Commons in 1852 that 'any territorial increase of one Power, any aggrandisement which disturbs the general balance of power in Europe . . . could not be a matter of indifference'[2] to Britain. For more than a hundred years this had been, and was to remain till the middle of the twentieth century, the corner stone of British foreign policy.

Only once in the ninety-nine years which followed Waterloo did the nation go to war on the continent of Europe in defence of that policy. Once only did 'national self-restraint, respect for the public law as defined in treaties, and willingness to enforce its observance by concerted action'[3] fail to keep the peace. The result was the Crimean War of 1854–1856.

By the 1850s the Turkish Empire, which for over three hundred years had dominated the Eastern world from the Adriatic to the Persian Gulf and from the Caspian to Algiers, seemed on the point of dissolution. Its Sultans and their advisers, through corruption and decadence, seemed no longer capable of governing or defending their vast territories. Russia, already a great Asiatic power, appeared to be set upon stepping into the imminent vacuum, and upon seizing the Black Sea, the Danubian lands, and, above all, Constantinople. Neither the British nor the French (who had ambitions in the Near East) were prepared to remain impassive in face of such a menace.

The immediate cause of the war between Turkey and Russia which broke out in 1853 was a dispute between the Roman Catholic and Greek Orthodox Churches respecting the custody of certain shrines in Jerusalem, which was, of course, within the Turkish

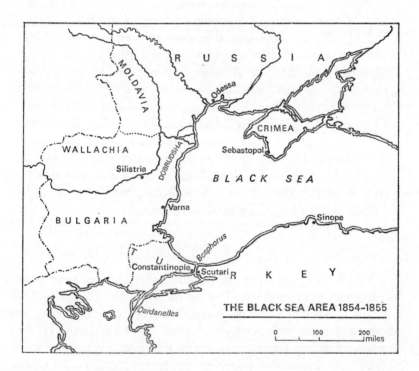

THE BLACK SEA AREA 1854–1855

Empire. The Emperor Napoleon III of France championed the Catholics. The Emperor Nicholas I of Russia championed the Greeks. This squalid squabble, in which blood was shed, resulted in the Russians demanding a general protectorate over the many millions of Christians living under Turkish rule. The Turks decided to reject these demands out of hand, rather than to negotiate. This action they took believing, with justice, that Palmerston, the most powerful member of the British cabinet, would persuade the Prime Minister, Aberdeen, and the Foreign Secretary, Clarendon, to stand by them in the last resort.

In June, 1853, a British fleet, supported by a French squadron, was posted outside the Dardanelles. In July, the Russians invaded Turkish Moldavia. The brink had nearly been reached. Though Lord Stratford de Redcliffe, the influential and usually pro-Turkish ambassador in Constantinople, advised the Sultan to accept an offer of mediation by a council of ambassadors, the Turks refused to do so. Even now

'war', as Churchill has put it, 'was not yet certain. The Czar, alarmed at Turkey's resistance, sought a compromise with the help of Austria, but by September Aberdeen and his Cabinet had become so suspicious that they rejected the offer. On October 4 the Sultan declared war on Russia, and soon afterwards attacked the Russians beyond the Danube. Such efforts as Aberdeen and Stratford could still make for peace were extinguished by a Russian onslaught against the Turkish Fleet off Sinope, in the Black Sea. Indignation flared in England, where the action was denounced as a massacre. . . . Thus England drifted into war. In February, 1854 Nicholas recalled his ambassadors from London and Paris, and at the end of March the Crimean War began, with France and Britain as the allies of Turkey.'[4]

* * *

The British Army at home was in almost every respect unprepared for an European conflict. The embarrassments experienced in attempting to scrape together an expeditionary force of some 27,000 officers and men, with twenty-six guns, were formidable. To find thirty-one infantry battalions at war establishment, it was necessary to draft large numbers of volunteers from other battalions into those chosen for service.

The same applied to the cavalry. The maximum force which could be put into the field was one heavy and one light brigade. To produce the twenty squadrons of which these were made up, ten regiments were required to furnish two squadrons apiece. Each of these 'service squadrons' consisted of only about 155 of all ranks, with 140 horses, yet extraordinary measures were necessary to find even that modest number. To make up the two squadrons of the 5th Dragoon Guards, for example, fifteen volunteers had to be taken from the 7th Dragoon Guards.[5] The band of the 8th Hussars had to be broken up so that the musicians could be put into the ranks. Even then the regiment set out two men short. Twenty-five of its horses were too young for service and had to be exchanged for the same number of seasoned ones from the 3rd Light Dragoons.[6] The 4th Dragoon Guards took fifteen horses from the King's Dragoon Guards and five from the 3rd Dragoon Guards. In return, their commanding officer 'gave them twenty young ones – as great a set of brutes as ever I saw. I felt quite ashamed of the transaction',[7] wrote the colonel of the 4th. Each regiment left at home two troops to form a recruiting depôt. In fact some of the regiments,[8] and probably all of them, left behind far fewer men than the number stipulated.

The mounted force which left the shores of Britain for the seat of war between mid-April and mid-July, 1854, numbered, at the most, 3,100 officers and men, and 3,000 horses. By the time that force was called upon to meet the enemy its numbers were considerably smaller.

*　　*　　*

It was at first proposed to march the cavalry regiments across France and to embark them at Marseilles. Lieutenant-Colonel Hodge, commanding the 4th Dragoon Guards, thought it a very bad plan. He feared that his men would get drunk and their clothing spoiled. But he was able to note in his diary on 12 April: 'The march through France is quite given up, I am glad to say.'[9] Instead the various regiments were embarked at the ports nearest to their home stations and made the voyage by sea all the way.

The ships which conveyed them were of all sorts, their variety well demonstrating the transitional period between sail and steam. At one end of the scale was the 3,438-ton screw-steamer *Himalaya*. In her were embarked all the 314 officers and men and 295 horses of the 5th Dragoon Guards, a larger number than had ever before been carried in one ship. She arrived in the Bosphorus after a voyage of only sixteen days from Queenstown, including a call at Malta.*

---

* The *Himalaya* was one of the earliest screw propelled steamships of the P. & O. Line. When she was launched she was the biggest steamer in the world, but the Company operated her at a loss. Consequently the Admiralty's purchase

The 1st Royal Dragoons, on the other hand, left Liverpool in six small sailing-vessels, the largest of which held only sixty men and as many horses. One of these ships left on 20 May, and did not arrive till 14 July. Off New Brighton, Lieutenant-Colonel Yorke, commanding the regiment, found his men 'a pattern of good behaviour. [They] create quite a sensation . . . Great cheering takes place when the river steamers pass, and sometimes the Band plays "God Save the Queen" . . . The *Gertrude* is the first ship with cavalry for a foreign land which has ever sailed from L'pool.'[10]

Trooper Mitchell of the 13th Hussars described the 'sea kit' with which his regiment was issued: 'A canvas slop [loose jacket or tunic] and trousers, a red worsted nightcap, two blue striped shirts, a large piece of waterproof to lay beneath us when in camp or on deck (this last was a present from the head colonel of the regiment, General Lygon) . . . soap, needles, thread, &c.'

He gives a vivid picture of the embarkation at Portsmouth:

'Our adjutant was there ready to receive us, and give us our orders. In a few minutes every man was dismounted, and his saddle and accoutrements neatly stowed in his corn-sack, and then I saw a sight I had never seen before. Each horse was led up to the ship's side (which lay close alongside the quay); a sling was placed beneath the horse's belly, and fastened to the tackling on the main-yard.

'The word was then given to "hoist away", when about a hundred convicts manned a large rope, and running away with it, the poor trooper was soon high in the air, quite helpless. He was then gradually lowered down the main hatchway (which was well padded round to prevent accidents) until he arrived at the hold which was fitted up as a stable, each horse being provided with a separate stall. They were placed with their heels towards the ship's side, and heads towards each other, with a passage between them. There were strong mangers fixed beneath their heads, to which they were fastened

of her as a troopship came as a welcome relief. She was eventually sunk by German bombers in the Second World War whilst serving as a hulk in Portland Harbour. (Rogers, Col H. C. B. *Troopships and Their History*, 1963, 105–6.)

The *Himalaya* also transported the whole of the Scots Greys, which left later than the 5th.

The 4th Light Dragoons, which was the last of the ten regiments to sail, was carried in the P. & O. steamer *Simla*, of 2,400 tons. She had only been completed earlier in the year.

1. 'The Plunger in Turkey. "I say, Old Fellah! – Do you think it pwobable the Infantry will accompany us to Sebastopol?"'

2. Private Sealey, 11th Hussars, 1854

3. The charge of the Heavy Brigade. 'Inniskilling Dragoons, 25th October, 1854.' Some of the Greys are shown on the left. (See p. 70)

4. General Sir James Yorke Scarlett leading the charge of the Heavy Brigade. (See p. 70)

by double halters, so that when once they were fastened there was no chance of lying down while they were on board.'[11]

This arrangement was not always as fool-proof as Trooper Mitchell supposed. Troop Sergeant-Major Cruse of the 1st Royal Dragoons, who was aboard the sailing ship *Arabia*, tells in a letter home how, in the Bay of Biscay, he found

'four or five of the horses in a horrible plight, loose, down under the other horses, who were all plunging dreadfully at every lurch of the ship. It took me the whole night up to 10 o'clock the next morning before I could get them all secured, some of them dreadfully bruised.

'I am sure', he told his wife, 'you will be grieved when I tell you that I have lost *poor Fanny*. I had been boasting all along how well she stood it, and how nicely she kept her legs, but on the morning of the 29th [May], just as I went down to stables, she had slipped down, and with all our efforts we could not get her up again. I was several hours before I could shift upwards of 30 horses, so as to get a spare stall next to her, and she had nearly exhausted herself with plunging. We got slings under her, and tried to raise her up, but the ship was too unsteady, and at last we got her to lay flat down, and I saw at once she had so injured herself that she could not live. She struggled very hard till seven in the evening and then died very easy, and was immediately thrown overboard in the Bay of Biscay. I went to my Cabin and had a good cry over her, and it will be some time before I recover [from] the shock.'[12]

The men of the 13th Hussars, according to Trooper Mitchell, from whose ship only one horse was lost during the whole passage, 'would spend all their spare time coaxing their horses to eat, bathing the face and nostrils with vinegar and water or salt water'. Some of the food for the men, he wrote in his *Recollections*, was decidedly antique. 'Barrels of peas there were with the date 1828 plainly marked on them.' It was impossible to boil them. Much the same applied to the salt pork and beef, portions of which had made numerous voyages to India and back before being returned to store.[13] Captain Cresswell of the 11th Hussars wrote home that the men were 'badly and insufficiently fed'.[14]

The officers, on the whole, did much better. 'Our feeding is pretty good,' wrote Colonel Hodge of the 4th Dragoon Guards, 'fresh bread and fresh meat nearly every day. I cannot manage the butter, but the cooking is tolerable, rather greasy, and the dirt I am getting accustomed to. The men are all on salt provisions, but I hear of no complaints.' He himself paid 7s 6d a day for four meals 'and a pint of wine'.[15] Cornet Clowes of the 8th 'got most *capitally* fed' and was 'always hungry'. He reported that in the Bay of Biscay 'everybody was dreadfully sick in all directions', and that he was 'obliged to stop below with the horses, who could not keep their legs and were down on the ground in heaps, lashing out at each other, mad with fright and screaming like children'.[16]

The captain of the ship carrying the headquarters of the 4th Light Dragoons, (known as 'Paget's Irregular Horse'), told Lord George Paget, commanding the regiment, that the storm in the Bay was so severe that 'if it did not abate in a $\frac{1}{4}$ of an hour, he would be obliged to throw the horses overboard. The characteristic reply,' according to Trooper Farquharson, 'was "Do what you like with the horses, but save my men".' It did not, however, come to that.[17]

In fact, though numbers of horses were lost, only one really serious mishap befell the cavalry transports. The *Europa*, on which were the headquarters of the Inniskilling Dragoons, caught fire 200 miles from Plymouth. The commanding officer and eighteen other men and women were lost. So were all the horses, equipment and baggage.[18]

On the other ships, once the Bay of Biscay was passed, both men and horses picked up their spirits. 'Our band', wrote Captain Wombwell of the 17th Lancers, 'consisting of a clarionet [*sic*], tambourine, bones and a fiddle, played hornpipes, etc., to which the men danced and sang.'[19]

Perhaps the worst trial for the horses came when the ships encountered the heat of the Mediterranean. On 25 July, Captain Portal of the 4th Light Dragoons, aboard the steamship *Simla*, wrote home that two horses of his troop

'on the main deck got perfectly mad from the heat, and at last became so dangerous to all the horses near them that they had to be destroyed. I am afraid that we shall lose many more from the intense heat. Those poor beasts who stand below close to the engines are in perfect steam all day and night too. We ought not to have any horses there at all.'[20]

*　　*　　*

When they got near to Constantinople some of the sailing transports were becalmed for as much as a fortnight. Others were given tows by passing steamers. In one ship of the Royal Dragoons there was a spot of trouble on arrival off Scutari. 'Some of our blackguard fellows', wrote Sergeant-Major Cruse to his wife, 'went to the captain of the ship and asked for grog before they would help to get the anchor up. The Major was in a great rage, and I thought there would have been a precious row, but it passed pretty quietly.'[21]

Everyone agreed that Constantinople was a superb sight from the sea. 'The view by moonlight is very lovely', thought Colonel Hodge, 'but I have no heart to enjoy it. I feel I am going into this business quite ignorant of what I have to do.'[22] Some of the officers, but not many of the men, landed in the great city, only to be gravely disappointed. Captain Portal of the 4th Light Dragoons could 'compare it to no Irish village for filth'.[23] This was the view universally held by all who entered the Turkish capital.

But few of the cavalry, most of which arrived some time after the mass of the infantry, had to stay long. At the end of May it had been decided that the British and French expeditionary forces should move to the Bulgarian port of Varna, 160 miles by sea from Constantinople, and from there make a demonstration in support of the Turks. The Russians had at this time crossed the Danube and were investing Silistria, fifty-five miles north of Varna. Humphry Sandwith, an army physician, when he heard of the move, wrote that the port was 'a notoriously unhealthy spot, and it is pretty certain that our full blooded troops will soon sicken under malarious fever.'[24] He was soon proved right. Though the authorities were told that the area was 'a very healthy spot',[25] Devna, some miles from Varna, where the Light Brigade was encamped, was known by the natives as ' "the Valley of Death", from it being', as Lieutenant Wombwell wrote in July, 'such an unhealthy place'.[26]

The unloading at Varna was 'a difficult and dangerous operation as the horses had to be lowered into boats and rowed ashore, and many were very restive and frightened.'[27] Thus wrote Mrs Henry Duberly (nicknamed 'Jubilee' by the troops), wife of the Paymaster of the 8th Hussars. She, like a few other officers' wives, travelled out with her husband and remained with him till the end of the war. In 1855 she published her *Journal*, which enjoyed a considerable success. Lieutenant-Colonel Shewell of the regiment was wont to refer to her as 'that nasty dirty Creature', while an officer of the 4th Dragoon Guards found her 'an odd woman. The French', he heard, 'have dedicated a Polka to her, as "The Amazone". I do not believe she is guilty of that which many say she is, but of course she has many "Followers" as the servant girls say, and her vanity causes her to encourage them.'[28] In 1856, Lieutenant Heneage of the 8th wrote: 'We have not yet got Mrs Duberly's Journal – the price ought to pay her well, as it is pretty certain to have a large circulation, but I don't expect there is anything but nonsense in it, and probably a good deal about herself.'[29] This was not quite fair. The book is very readable and full of interesting details.[30]

*   *   *

The 8th Hussars and the 17th Lancers were the first to arrive at Varna. They reached the port in late May and early June. Six other regiments were landed by mid-July, and the 4th Light Dragoons in early August. The Scots Greys left home so late that they only joined the army after the battle of the Alma. (See p. 50.) Before little more than half the cavalry had arrived, there came the news that the Russians had raised the siege of Silistria and were retreating in disorder. Lord Raglan, the British commander, at once ordered the Earl of Cardigan, commanding the Light Brigade, to carry out a reconnaissance 'in order to ascertain the movements of the enemy'. For this purpose a squadron from the 8th Hussars (121 horses) and another from the 13th Light Dragoons (75 horses) were selected. The men were in complete marching order, such as they would have worn at home, which meant that each horse carried about twenty stone. On top of this, two blankets, three days' barley or oats (36 lbs), two hay-nets (about 20 lbs), three pounds of biscuits, three pounds of salt beef or pork, a three-pint keg of water and extra ammunition were carried. A great deal of this was unnecessary lumber. The officers and men took no tents, though Cardigan himself had a small one 'about six feet square, just large enough to cover a spring sofa bed'.

For seventeen days no one took off his clothes (except Cardigan, once). From dawn till dusk, in very great heat, the little force marched relentlessly on. Cardigan said that it was necessary to perform these killing marches because of lack of water. 'No fountains were to be found at any intermediate places.'[31] Day by day the condition of the men, and particularly of the horses, deteriorated. 'The fitting of saddles to meet the decreasing girth', wrote Captain Tremayne of the 13th, 'was of necessity a very perfunctory business.'[32]

Five horses died and seventy-five were never again fit for anything but light work. A number of men collapsed, but none, luckily, was permanently disabled. 'You have ascertained for me', wrote Raglan to Cardigan, 'that the Russians have withdrawn from this end of the Dobrudsha and that the country between this and Trajan's Wall is not only clear of the enemy, but is wholly deserted by the inhabitants. These are important facts.'[33]

This first foray of the mounted arm in the Crimean War sheds some light on the character and abilities of the commander of the Light Brigade. It is too easy to condemn Cardigan out of hand. Neither he nor his officers and men had any experience of active service whatever. It was natural, perhaps, that overkeenness and inefficiency should have marked the 'Sore-Back Reconnaissance', as it came to be called.

In the course of it, Cardigan had an attack of dysentery. He sent for the 8th Hussars' doctor who expressed his anxiety about the declining health of the men. He replied, according to Mrs Duberly: 'Yes, Mr Somers – *I* am a brigadier, I may say a major-general; for I conclude the brevet is out by this time, and yet, sir, *I* can feel for the men.'[34] It is natural to sneer at such a remark, but not everyone thought Cardigan a foolish ogre. Captain Jenyns of the 13th, on his return from the reconnaissance, wrote home: 'We got tremendous praise from Lord Cardigan, who is a capital fellow to be under at this work.'[35]

Nevertheless, Jenyns' view was the minority one. More typical was that of Captain Cresswell of the 11th Hussars. 'The Major-General', he wrote home, 'amused us by giving us regulation Phoenix Park Field days – such a bore he is – comes round stables just as if he was Colonel instead of Major-General.'[36] Captain Shakespear of the Royal Horse Artillery, attached to the Light Brigade, thought Cardigan

'the most impracticable and most inefficient cavalry officer in the service. . . . He may do all very well when turned out by his valet in the Phoenix Park, but there his knowledge ceases. We are all greatly disgusted with him . . . He is every grade of rank between a Major-General and a Private . . . We have field days every other day now. Cardigan kills the horses with pace . . . We wish we were with Scarlett and his Heavy Cavalry.'[37]

*   *   *

After raising the siege of Silistria, the Russian commander, Prince Gortschakoff, had been routed by the Turks, without the aid of their allies. By mid-July his army was in full retreat north-westwards. Before long it had evacuated Wallachia and Moldavia. The declared objects of the war seemed to have been gained. But no one in Britain and France cared a fig for the official *casus belli* – the saving of Turkey. Only a crushing military defeat, it was felt, would teach Russia – 'this semi-barbarous nation, the enemy of all progress'[38] – the lesson she deserved. So the war went on.

Meanwhile life in the various cavalry encampments in and near Varna was proving far from comfortable. Captain Wombwell's thermometer in his tent registered 105°F in early June. 'This camp life', he wrote in his diary, 'is most wretched – nothing to be obtained to eat for any money. All we get is our ration of coarse brown bread, and $\frac{3}{4}$s of a lb. of mutton, miserably thin and hardly fit to eat – the same that is served out to the men.'[39] One of the men, Trooper Lucas of the Inniskillings, confirmed the Captain's view: 'What they called mutton', he declared, 'was like something between a dog and goat. They scarcely weighed more than about 10 pounds each. It took about 6 of them for a Troop's ration.'[40]

'Imagine', wrote Lieutenant-Colonel Hodge upon arrival at Varna in early July, 'an arid sandy shore covered with horses and soldiers picketted and encamped all about it. Twelve men lie in a tent, the saddles are in the open air, the burning sun is on the horses all day, and for one hour in the evening there comes a plague of cockchafers from the land side that regularly drive the horses mad.'[41]

The poor beasts suffered dreadfully. So strong was the sun at times that their eyes had to be bandaged with wet cloths.[42] Cornet Grey Neville of the 5th Dragoon Guards reported that the horses were 'getting very thin with bad forage, exposure to the most tremendous heat of the midday sun, and the severe dews of the cold nights.'[43] The highly contagious equine diseases of glanders and farcy* became common. The moment either was diagnosed, the infected horse had to be destroyed. In the 1st Royal Dragoons alone thirty were shot, twenty-three of them in one troop.[44]

The inadequacy and inefficiency of the supply services, which

* Both diseases are caused by the micro-organism *Bacillus mallei*. The symptoms are inflammation of the mucous membranes, especially of the nose, with a constant discharge of sticky matter, and ulcerating enlargement and hardening of the glands below and inside the lower jaw, and, in the case of farcy, of the head and legs.

were to bedevil the early stages of the war, already became apparent at Varna.

'I wanted coal for my farriers to heat the horse shoes with', wrote one commanding officer. 'I was told that I could not have it from the Commissariat but that I must get it where I could, as the Commissariat coal belonged to Government. It so happens that the only coal to be got is from the Commissariat, and it is not to be found here, therefore the cavalry are not to be shod, because John Bull who pays for both Cavalry and Commissariat has got all the coal in his possession. I offered to pay for the coal, but nothing could be done. Officers commanding regiments must, they said, buy it for their regiments where they could. Was ever such a system heard of?'[45]

A similar problem was facing the troops. After three months away from home, most of the men of the Royal Dragoons, according to one of their sergeant-majors, were 'going barefoot. How they will get reshod', he added, 'I do not know.'[46] Forage for the horses was another shortage problem which was hard to overcome. 'We hear', wrote an officer of the 4th Light Dragoons on arrival, 'that Lord Raglan would give anything that we had remained in England, as we are not wanted, and they have already immense difficulty in providing forage for the cavalry that are already here.'[47]

The moment a horse died or was shot, it was dragged out to the hills and left there. 'In less than twelve hours', noted Captain Wombwell, 'he is a perfect skeleton, being entirely eaten up by vultures, dogs and other carnivorous animals, with which this country abounds. You can see as many as thirty vultures standing on a horse at one time.'[48]

The loss of horses soon became very serious. On 11 August the 17th Lancers, for instance, reported that thirty out of their 250 had died, or been destroyed, since leaving home. More important, thirteen of their men had died from different illnesses.[49]

On 19 July it became known that a serious outbreak of cholera had occurred in the adjoining French camp. Within three days it had spread to their British neighbours. Deaths were soon mounting. The 5th Dragoon Guards seem to have suffered most of all the cavalry. One report said that twenty-nine of their men had died within a ten hour period.[50] This was probably an exaggeration, though by 28 August, three officers and thirty-four men of the regiment had died. The other regiments averaged less than that number of deaths during the whole of their stay in Bulgaria. By the end of the month 'cholera belts' had been served out to the men. As is now known, these were totally useless in preventing the fell disease.

By 19 August the 4th Dragoon Guards had buried twenty-three men, and their colonel remarked that it was 'difficult to find a spot here where burying has not been'. He had spent a whole morning

'on this Board about the Ambulance Corps; which is quite inefficient. Large Wagons with little harness, with heavy old Pensioners riding little Ponies of the Country, are expected to draw these machines. Anything so shameful as the way this Corps has been sent out cannot be conceived. It cannot be made serviceable as at present constituted, and has been sent out a mere clap trap to please the newspapers and House of Commons.'[51]

An infantry colonel reported that every case taken in at the notorious General Hospital in Varna had 'gone to the grave'.[52] The 8th Hussars had 'just one fourth' of their men in hospital, 'so you may fancy', wrote a major of the regiment, 'what work the healthy ones have to go through – every man has to look after 2 horses, and it seems quite a shame to get them up in the morning, they look so tired and wretched.'[53]

Indeed, even before the cholera struck, the men had been harassed by a number of other troubles and restrictions. When bathing, for instance, they were not allowed to move about without their swords, for fear of being attacked by Greek and other marauders.[54] Much unnecessary spit-and-polish was also imposed upon them as so often happens before keen officers get used to being on active service and away from barracks. Sergeant-Major Cruse of the 1st Royal Dragoons reported 'a great deal of grumbling among the men about one thing or another', while their commanding officer found them 'most indolent. I am greatly disappointed', he wrote home to his sister, 'with the English Dragoon. The fact is, he misses his Public House and friends.'[55]

Drink was unfortunately all too easily available. 'We have sad drunkenness amongst our men', declared Lieutenant-Colonel Hodge. 'The fools drink raw spirits, get horribly drunk and then wonder that they are ill; they do not give themselves a chance.' On 15 July he had seen a boat come on shore to sell rum to the men. He had made a rush at it, seized the whole crew and cargo, and taken them up to Lord Lucan, the commander of the cavalry division, who 'had caused the spirits to be spilled, but let the crew go. I would have burned the boat', Hodge added, 'and flogged the crew.'[56]

One of Hodge's officers, Cornet Fisher, confirmed that the men of the 4th Dragoon Guards were behaving very badly. He thought his colonel 'not fit to manage them. Privates and non-commissioned officers get drunk on escort duty, and the non-commissioned officers are not broken or the Privates flogged.'[57] In fact, Hodge had already applied for 'two Courts Martial on men for getting drunk on duty', and though Cornet Fisher might consider him slack, this was not the view of the Commander-in-Chief. On 24 August Lord Raglan, at Lord Lucan's prompting, found great fault with the 5th Dragoon Guards. He ordered them to be placed under Hodge 'to restore their discipline'. This Hodge thought 'a high compliment' to him, 'but a most severe and unjust act' towards Brigadier Scarlett, who was lieutenant-colonel of the 5th, though not, since he had been appointed commander of the Heavy Brigade, personally in charge of the regiment. Lieutenant-Colonel Le Marchant had thrown up command of the 5th and gone home on half-pay, leaving Captain Burton 'a very gentlemanly like young officer, but too young', in charge. Cornet Grey Neville of the 5th Dragoon Guards considered that Le Marchant was 'spoiling the regiment, not being either gentleman-like, or in the least understanding soldiering'.[58] He left the army later in the year. Cholera had left only seven of the regiment's officers fit for duty, and the grooming state of the regiment was down to one man for four or five horses. Hodge seems to have tackled his task of commanding two regiments (the combination was known jokingly as 'the 9th (4 & 5)') satisfactorily, for no further complaints are recorded. In fact, the arrangement did not last very long, Captain Burton proving himself adequate till a new commanding officer took over the 5th in December.[59]

For the officers the months of inactivity in Bulgaria were not at all up to expectation. 'They all complain', wrote an officer of the 4th Light Dragoons, 'that they are brought out here to do nothing but die of cholera.' He had heard it said that Lord Raglan had expressed wonder that 'more officers who can get away', should remain at all 'in such a vile country.'[60] 'I hope the good people at home', wrote an officer of the Royal Horse Artillery, 'do not fancy that the Army is full of enthusiasm, for it is a great mistake: it is full of grumbling and disappointment: there are very few who do not repent coming out.'[61]

The officers' food was, of course, infinitely better than the men's.

'What with chickens, ducks, etc. and lambs, we manage to get very fair food', reported an officer of the 'heavies'.[62] Personal standards of smartness quickly fell off. The commanding officer of the 1st Royal Dragoons had 'not shaved or changed his shirts', wrote Sergeant-Major Cruse, 'since he went on shore, and looks like an old Jew.'[63] Numbers of officers went about with buttons undone and open necks, many 'having nothing perceptible but their noses which appear from a dense forest of beard and whiskers.'[64]

Wild-dog hunting with lances and pony races for the officers, and foot races for the men, all accompanied by heavy betting, were the chief recreations to start with. Later on, as the heat and the cholera progressed, all such activity died out. Under the overwhelming lethargy which settled down on the army, even such matters as elementary sanitation were apt to go by the board.

'The migration to the Crimea saved our force; and was only just in time . . . In another month not a man would have remained alive.'

HARRIET MARTINEAU in 1859[1]

(iii)

Crimean War, 1854: embarkation for Crimea – landing at Kalamita Bay – Bulganak – battle of the Alma

From the very earliest days of the war there had been an assumption in many quarters that the capture of Sebastopol was a desirable, almost inevitable, objective, both politically and militarily. This assumption finally crystallized in the last days of June, when Lord Raglan was informed that the cabinet and the French had decided upon a siege of that great naval base. Reluctantly, since very little was known or could be found out about the enemy's strength in the Crimea, Raglan agreed to undertake it. Marshal St Arnaud, the ailing French commander, with equal misgivings, concurred. Consequently, orders were given for a survey of possible landing places;

a vast fleet was speedily assembled in Varna Bay, and before the end of August, embarkation had begun.

The effect of the news on the spirits and health of the army was wonderful. Apathy and indiscipline gave way, almost overnight, to a sense of purpose and something approaching energy. Above all an intense feeling of relief pervaded all ranks. 'I am so glad to leave Bulgaria,' wrote an aide-de-camp of Lord Lucan's. 'I never was so glad to leave any place in my life, not even the West Indies.'[2]

'Hurrah for the Crimea!' exclaimed a cornet of the Heavy Brigade. 'Take Sebastopol, in a week or so, and then into winter quarters.'[3] Other officers had reservations. 'I wish I could believe,' wrote Captain Portal of the 4th Light Dragoons, the first regiment to embark, 'that we are, in our present state, strong enough for this tremendous undertaking.'[4] His misgivings were not entirely unjustified. The 8th Hussars, for instance, since its arrival three and a half months before, had ninety-five men ineffective or dead at the time of its landing in the Crimea.[5] 'The sick, of whom there were many,' wrote a trooper of the 13th of the move down to Varna, 'were placed in arabas (small four-wheeled wagons), drawn by two bullocks or water buffaloes. There were a few poor fellows who were past recovery, yet not dead. These were left behind to die, a party of hospital orderlies being left with them to see the last of them and bury them. A surgeon was also left in charge of them.'[6]

On 24 August the loading of the ships started. There was room for all except the Heavy Brigade. This was to follow as soon as the transports returned from the Crimea. By last light on 6 September virtually all the other troops, British, French and Turkish, were safely aboard. At dawn next day the fleet weighed anchor and on 13 September came to rest off the Old Fort in Kalamita Bay, some twenty miles north of Sebastopol. The following morning, which was fine and calm, saw most of the infantry ashore. The landing was totally unopposed. Indeed, the local Tartars were more friendly by far than the Bulgarians had been at Varna. They brought supplies without stint. The local headmen, indeed, offered to lend the army their carts and animals. During the day the weather deteriorated and the swell increased so much that it was thought wiser to postpone the disembarkation of the cavalry till next morning. The Light Brigade therefore escaped the wet, tentless night ashore which was the infantry's lot.

In the course of the next four days, the difficult task of getting the horses ashore was completed.

'It is distressing', wrote Lord George Paget in his journal on the 16th, 'to see the poor horses, as they are upset out of the boats, swimming about in all directions among the ships. They swim so peacefully, but look rather unhappy with their heads in the air and the surf driving into their poor mouths. Only one has been drowned as yet, to our knowledge. We get on but slowly with our disembarkation.'[7]

The regiments took ashore three days' corn and cooked provisions, as well as three days' rum. The men's valises, pelisses, second overalls and second shoes were all left on board, and the men

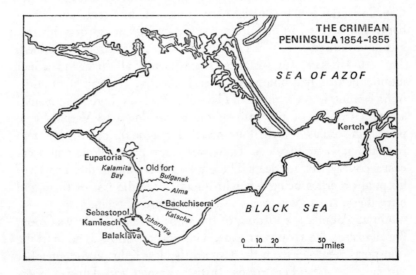

THE CRIMEAN
PENINSULA 1854-1855

SEA OF AZOF

Kertch

Eupatoria
Kalamita • Old fort
Bay Bulganak
• Alma
•Backchiserai
Sebastopol Katscha
Kamiesch Tchernaya
Balaklava

BLACK SEA

0 10 20 50 miles

did not see them again until well into December. With them they took only a shirt, a pair of socks and a towel wrapped in their 'man's blanket'.[8] This in the event meant that they had no other change of clothing for close on three months. Not more than three bat horses were allowed for regimental transport, the regulation number being fourteen. The officers' bat horses were also left behind at Varna. Spades, pickaxes and other tools for entrenching, camp drainage and wood cutting were issued on board ship, but as there were no means of carrying them, they were not taken ashore. Colonel Shewell of the 8th Hussars says that 'repeated requisitions were made for them without success until 14th December.'[9]

'All my detachment landed safe,' reported a lieutenant of the 17th, 'and after having to take them six miles to the nearest fresh water, we picqueted them for the night on the beach, and luckily found a tent into which we all crept for the night.'[10] Trooper Mitchell found it very difficult to get the pegs by which the horses were tethered to hold in the sand.[11]

The allied armies were in a precarious position. They had no base except the fleet, with which communication might at any time be cut off by rough seas. They had no ambulances and no land transport. They had no idea of the size or dispositions of the enemy. An enterprising enemy could have had them at his mercy. Fortunately the Russians were not an enterprising enemy.

By great exertions surprisingly large numbers of baggage-animals, wagons and drivers were collected. One of the expeditions which was sent off into the interior for this purpose was led by Lord Cardigan. An infantry officer who accompanied it thought it 'the most absurd expedition' he had ever had the ill-luck to be engaged in.[12] 'The cavalry,' wrote an officer of the 4th Light Dragoons, 'have been busy driving in bullocks, sheep, ponies, etc., all of which we pay for at our price, which is a very fair one.'[13]

In spite of means adequate to carry only a part of their essential supplies, the armies marched off towards Sebastopol on 19 September. For ten hours, under a hot sun, they kept going southwards. Hundreds of men from the infantry fell out on the way, some from thirst, for many had not been able to fill their water bottles before setting off, others from cholera which was still striking its sudden and lethal blows. The French were on the right with the fleet covering their right flank. The British, on their left, were in close columns, two infantry divisions in the first and two in the second line. The French had no cavalry to speak of, so the Light Brigade, supported by two troops of horse artillery and detachments of the Rifle Brigade, were responsible for covering the front, the exposed left flank and the rear.

Lord Raglan led the way with Lord Cardigan and the 11th and 13th. Lord Lucan with the 8th and 17th was on the left, while Lord George Paget with the 4th Light Dragoons brought up the rear. The ground was 'as green and smooth as a racecourse'.[14] It reminded many of Salisbury Plain. It was perfect cavalry country. Lord Raglan no doubt wished that it were not so, for no one was more aware of the allies' pitiably weak mounted arm. He was therefore determined not to waste what he had of it. 'In a phrase that ran through the army he declared that he would "keep the cavalry in a band-box".'[15]

* * *

In the afternoon the river Bulganak was reached. It was no more than 'a small sluggish stream, which had at that time a greater depth of mud than water'.[16] While most of the infantry broke ranks at the sight of it, and rushed forward to slake their thirst, Lord Cardigan with the advance guard was sent ahead to reconnoitre. When he was about a mile and a half beyond the river, he caught sight of a body of some 1,500 Russian horse. 'I threw out skirmishers from the 13th Light Dragoons,' he wrote, 'and the cossacks did the same.'[17] To his intense irritation, Lord Lucan joined him at this moment, and of course automatically took the command out of his hands. To add to his annoyance, Lord Raglan soon sent off a request (which was wisely converted into an order by its bearer) that the cavalry should retire.

His reason for doing so was that he had seen what Lucan and Cardigan, too close under the next ridge, could not, namely that well behind the Russian cavalry was a mass of their infantry. These were in fact some 6,000 men of the 17th Division. In the exhausted state of his army the last thing Lord Raglan wanted was to get embroiled with a fresh and numerous enemy. To support the withdrawal of his advance guard, he brought the 8th and 17th from the left to form a second line, and assembled two of his infantry divisions on the southern side of the river. 'We then retreated,' records Lord Cardigan, 'by alternate squadrons in one line, which was performed with great steadiness.'[18]

Before this took place, a battery of Russian guns was brought up and opened fire on the 11th and 13th.

> 'I shall never forget the sensation,' wrote a trooper of the 11th, 'of sitting perfectly inert on my horse . . . as long as I remember anything. There is nothing more trying. . . . I recall how when some of us more nervous fellows, bowing our heads down to our horses' manes . . . how angry and indignant was the tone of Major Peel's remonstrance: "What the hell are you bobbing your heads at?".'[19]

'Several shells burst close to us,' remembered Trooper Mitchell years later. 'One struck a troop horse . . . in the side, and bursting inside the horse, cleaned him out as though a butcher had done it. . . . Our Horse Artillery now galloped up and quickly came into action.'[20] An officer of one of the gun troops tells what happened next:

> ' "C" and "I" Troops opened fire immediately and soon

silenced the battery; before however this was done effectually, we, "I" Troop, were drawn away to the left to attack the cavalry moving towards our left flank. This cavalry moved in single file in parallel lines. We opened fire with shrapnel shells and soon turned them. We fired 80 rounds, 55 round shot, 25 shrapnel shells. And so our first skirmish ended.'[21]

"C" Troop, meanwhile, had taken some men of the 2nd battalion, Rifle Brigade, on to their guns, to act as sharpshooters. These were stationed on the axletree box, one on each trail, with three more on each limber box.[22]

The sole casualties (none of which was fatal), in what came to be known as 'the affair of the Bulganak', were five men. One of these was Paymaster-Sergeant Priestley of the 13th, who had no right, of course, to be under fire. His regiment credited him with being the first British field casualty of the war.[23] The same was claimed for Trooper Williamson of the 11th. He, according to his troop commander, 'rode out of the ranks, his leg shot off and hanging by his overall. Coming up to me he said, quite calmly, "I am hit, may I fall out?".'[24]

The light cavalrymen not realizing that it was Lord Raglan who had sent the order for them to retire, nor for what compelling reason, were very sore at having to do so, especially as the Russians jeered and, worse, the British infantry laughed at them. 'Serve them bloody right, silly peacock bastards,' wrote a private of the 41st Foot.[25] The blame for their humiliation was very unfairly laid on the commander of the cavalry division.

*   *   *

The following day, 20 September, the allied armies again moved forward, in the same formation as before, to attack the enemy immediately south of the River Alma. Prince Menschikoff, the Russian commander, had chosen the obvious place from which to destroy the invaders. Properly defended, the six miles of his position must have proved all but impregnable. Over-confidence, however, bred carelessness. Because the rocks on his left, adjoining the sea, were steep, he assumed that they were unassailable. He placed in their defence, therefore, only one battalion. Had he bothered to make an elementary reconnaissance, he would have noticed that a track wide enough for carts, and therefore for guns, ran through them. This the French used in an effort to turn the Russian left flank. Menschikoff, on perceiving this, lost his head, ordered large numbers of battalions over from his right, and when they had arrived marched most of them back again, thus effectively keeping them out of the battle for most of the day. The French, meanwhile, without good reason, believed themselves unable to advance and threatened to retreat if the British, who faced the strongest and steepest part of the Russian position, did not attack at once. Lord Raglan, therefore, launched his leading infantry divisions, (which for an hour and a half had been lying down under the fire of the enemy's guns), across the river with absolutely no cover whatever. After a period of heroic fighting on both sides, the Russians were forced to retreat in confusion. The British suffered some 2,000 casualties, the French only 550, and the Russians about 5,700.

Menschikoff's second blunder, as extraordinary as his first and more unaccountable, was to allow his sixteen squadrons of regular cavalry and his eleven squadrons of cossacks, 'drawn up in a curve from his extreme right flank to his right rear',[26] to remain inactive throughout the battle. The first and only order they received was the one which bade them retreat. Opposite them, as Menschikoff cannot have failed to see, guarding the British left flank, there was nothing but the Light Brigade with two troops of horse artillery. One of these, "C" Troop, which, surprisingly, was attached to the Light Infantry Division, not to the cavalry, became engaged before the final stages of the battle, but the other, "I" Troop, and the 900 men of the Light Brigade received no orders at all. 'We were in a position,' wrote Lord George Paget in the diary which he kept for his wife, 'to see the whole as if we had taken an opera box.'[27]

The mental tortures suffered by the cavalry commanders as they sat their horses, inert throughout the struggle, especially after their mortification of the previous day, were excruciating. When the Highland Division, immediately to their right, reached the Kourgane Hill, and the enemy was already in flight, Lord Lucan, still without orders, took his men across the river to join the victorious Scotsmen. Sir Colin Campbell, their commander, suggested that six of the horse artillery guns should pursue the fleeing hordes. This, for a while, they did.

'We opened a most tremendous fire of shell upon them,' wrote an officer of "I" Troop, 'and hundreds fell. However a Russian battery of 12 prs opening on us, and the enemy being out of range, we limbered up and retired 50 yds down the hill, out of fire. It was now about 5 o'clock. The Russian army was in full retreat, and the battle was over. If we had had 5000 cavalry [which was about the number at the disposal of the Russians], not a gun could have been carried off; but as it was, we only captured two. These were cross [?] howitzer guns, about 32 prs.'[28]

At about this time, General Estcourt, the Adjutant-General, was sent by Lord Raglan with the first of three orders to Lord Lucan. These further enraged a man who was already speechless with frustrated anger. The Light Brigade, he was told, was under no circumstances to pursue since the Commander-in-Chief felt sure that the enemy would make a stand. Instead, Lord Lucan was to escort the field guns on the left, and Lord Cardigan those on the right, to positions ahead of the army. General Estcourt is believed to have finished his message with the words: 'Mind now, the cavalry are not to attack.'[29]

Neither of the cavalry generals could bear this. Leaving a few troops to carry out what they considered a servile duty, both generals led the rest well beyond the guns.

'We went forward at a gallop, cheering and halloaing as loud as we could,' wrote an officer of the 17th Lancers. 'We could see the enemy running as hard as they could go, throwing away their knapsacks, arms and even their coats [the Russian infantry, though the day was very hot, were all wearing their long yellowish-grey greatcoats] to assist them in their flight. Morgan's Troop of my regiment were sent out to pursue and bring in prisoners, in which they succeeded very well, bringing in a good many. On coming up with the poor fellows they dropped on their knees and begged for mercy.'[30]

Lord Raglan, seeing that his first order was not obeyed, sent a second. This too was ignored, and a third, even more peremptory, was needed before the cavalry was stopped. In a boiling frenzy, Lord Lucan ordered the prisoners to be released, and at last desisted from the pursuit.

Whether Lord Raglan was right thus to restrain his small mounted force is still the subject of controversy. In face of the fact that some two miles beyond the battle-field 'an immense force of cavalry', as Lieutenant Wombwell of the 17th reported, 'came advancing towards us,'[31] and seemed prepared to make some sort of a stand, and aware as he was that the French refused to support him in following up the routed enemy, his decision was probably a wise one.

When Lord George Paget asked Lord Raglan two days later 'whether the cavalry might not have been of more use (in reply, by the bye, to a joking remark he made to me, "Well, George, you see I thought of Agnes in the battle")', he received the answer that 'his object all day had been to – what he called – "shut them up" (those were his words), the enemy's cavalry being so superior in numbers.'[32]

In the evening of the battle the commander of the cavalry, still fuming, conveyed a message to the Commander-in-Chief, to which Lord Raglan did not deign to reply. It ran thus: 'Lord Lucan trusts that Lord Raglan has that confidence in him, as commanding the cavalry, that he would allow him to act on his own responsibility, as occasion should offer and render advisable, for otherwise opportunities of acting will frequently be lost to the cavalry.'[33]

'Cardigan was annoyed, Lucan was furious, Raglan and Airey were irritated by both of them. Everyone seemed to be in a bad temper.'

CHRISTOPHER HIBBERT

in *The Destruction of Lord Raglan*[1]

(iv)

Crimean War, 1854: flank march – army enters Balaklava – Heavy Brigade joins from Varna

After the battle of the Alma, Marshal St Arnaud, in the last stages of a fatal disease, firmly refused to follow up the routed enemy, much to Lord Raglan's chagrin. Not till 24 September did the two armies come in sight of Sebastopol. The previous day they had been reinforced by an infantry regiment and the Scots Greys, which, though it had been the last heavy cavalry regiment to leave England, was

the first to arrive in the Crimea. This was because it came direct
from Constantinople and never went to Bulgaria at all. It disembarked at the mouth of the Katscha river, having sailed direct
from Scutari, 'horses and men', according to one who saw them
land, 'looking as clean as if they were going to review in Hyde Park.
They were greatly cheered.'[2]

The French declined to attack the almost defenceless town and
port from the north without a proper siege train, thereby, for the

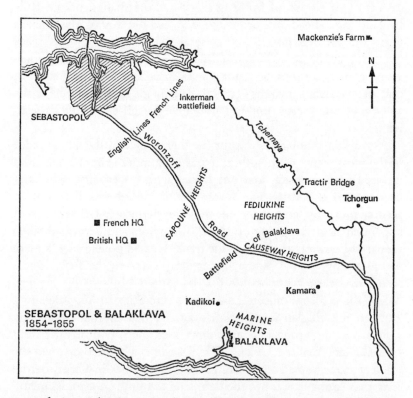

second time, almost certainly throwing away a chance of speedily
finishing the war. Menschikoff used the breathing space thus afforded
him to good effect. He took two actions which were little short of
brilliant. First, on 22 September, he sank a number of naval ships in
the harbour mouth, thus effectively closing it. Second, he decided
to withdraw his main army from Sebastopol towards Bakhchiserai
so as to maintain communication with the interior, and to be able to
threaten the allied rear, should an attack on Sebastopol be attempted. This flank march of the Russians coincided with the more famous
flank march of the allies. Raglan, faced with the blocking of the

harbour and the obstinacy of the French, conceived the highly audacious plan of marching both armies round to the south of Sebastopol. This would place them in a position to take it from the supposedly less well defended side, and at the same time secure the ports of Kamiesch and Balaklava.

His way lay through thick, almost trackless scrub and oak forest. If attacked, his troops, spread out in columns of route over a number of miles, would be extremely vulnerable. Lord Lucan with the cavalry, two troops of horse artillery and a battalion of the Rifle Brigade went ahead. His orders were to lead the way to Mackenzie's Farm on the Sebastopol-Bakhchiserai road.* It was at this place (named after the Scottish admiral who had lived there whilst supervising construction of Sebastopol's defences half a century earlier), that the two flank marches came into contact. Fortunately for the allies, they came across nothing more than the tail-end of the Russian rearguard.

Astonishing though it was that neither army had the faintest idea of the movements of the other, it was even more extraordinary that it was Raglan himself, and not Lucan with his cavalry, who first encountered the Russians. What had happened was that Lucan, accompanied by an officer of the Quartermaster-General's staff appointed as guide, going on ahead of the horse artillery, had taken the wrong turning at a fork in the track. He had gone down 'a mere wood-cutting road'.[3] When the artillery came to the fork, it was seen to be clearly impossible for the guns to follow the cavalry. While the artillery officers halted for more than an hour debating what to do, Raglan appeared. He agreed that the path taken by Lucan was the wrong one, and himself led the way down the right one. Captain Walker, Lucan's aide-de-camp, who accompanied the artillery, rode immediately behind the Commander-in-Chief. Before long they 'came in sight of the farm, and to our great astonishment,' as Walker reported, 'found a Russian rearguard, and an immense train of baggage and ammunition, directly in our front.'[4]

Captain Shakespear of "I" Troop, Royal Horse Artillery, tells what happened next:

* The wording of the order to Lord Lucan was in part as follows: 'The Cavalry Division supported by the second battalion Rifle Brigade will proceed on reconnaissance in a direction S.S.E., towards a spot marked on the map "Mackenzie's Farm", on the great road leading to Sebastopol. This road will be watched both ways, and reported on. . . . An officer will be sent back as soon as possible with the Earl of Lucan's report.' (Kinglake, III, 495.)

'Instantly the words "Get Lord Raglan out of the way" were said by everyone – and away he went [very reluctantly] with his Staff of course. Maude [commanding "I" Troop] and I instantly saw that . . . nothing could save us but a dashing action. . . . He accordingly took 4 guns to the right road: I took two howitzers to the left.* We unlimbered and fired shells at the shortest range. Capt. Walker had been sent back to hasten up the cavalry.'[5]

Walker eventually found some of the missing cavalry. 'I despatched the 17th one way,' he wrote three days later, 'and brought up the Greys another (having missed Lord Lucan), and we immediately pushed on to a height overlooking a great plain in which the small town of Batchi Serai is.'[6] The cavalry, according to Shakespear, were so slow that Maude and he, 'impetuous for the fight', rushed ahead,

'wheeled to the left and came into action, the enemy flying before us. We limbered up and pursued as hard as our guns would go for 10 minutes. Suddenly the road turned to the right (two guns were now abreast) and to our astonishment a regt. of infantry was formed across the road, front ranks kneeling within 30 yards of us. They fired a volley, but were so bewildered *nothing* touched us. . . . They then bolted into the bush. We came into action to the left and poured in common case.'[7]

Walker, meanwhile, was sent off 'with a dismounted troop [of the Scots Greys][8] to the left, to skirmish through the wood, and after I had posted them, I rode down into the plain to catch Lord Lucan and the staff, whom I saw going down the hill.'[9]

When, at last, the commander of the cavalry appeared before the Commander-in-Chief, he was met with an icy: 'Lord Lucan, you are late!' to which there was no reply. Raglan then gave an order that the cavalry was to pursue no further. Beside artillery and commissariat wagons, a considerable number of other wagons and carts were captured. These, according to an officer of the 8th Hussars on the Staff,

* The two horse artillery troops in the army of the Crimea at this time were equipped with two 12-pounder howitzers each as well as four standard horse artillery guns. (See Jocelyn, 14.)

'the troops were allowed to pillage. . . . In a few moments the ground was strewed with every sort of thing – handsome Hussar uniforms, rich fur cloaks, every kind of undergarment, male and female. Several wigs I saw being offered for sale, amidst the laughter of the men. French books and novels of an improper kind were not infrequently met with in the baggage of the Russian officers. All these were offered for sale and disposed of to the highest bidder. A gold Hussar pelisse would sell for about 30s or £2.'[10]

Lord Cardigan, at this moment, turned up. When Lord Raglan, in no good temper, said to him, 'The cavalry were out of their proper place. You took them much too low down,'[11] Cardigan, to use his own words, 'simply reminded his Lordship' that he 'did not command the cavalry.'[12]

The following day, 26 September, the British army, to Lord Raglan's intense relief, entered the port of Balaklava, against almost no opposition. The French, who had followed the British, moved further west, and established their sea base at Kamiesch.

* * *

The remainder of the heavy brigade left Varna for Balaklava between 24 and 27 September. The Royals embarked in three sailing vessels towed by steamers. Scarcely had they left port when a violent gale struck them.

'If I live for a century', wrote Sergeant-Major Cruse, 'I shall never forget the terrible sights [of the night of 26 September]. The *Jason* [steamer], finding that she could not tow us longer with safety to herself, cut us adrift without notice at midnight, and the ship being left all at once to the mercy of the raging of the Black Sea, soon became in an awful plight. The whole of the stabling on deck broke adrift & the officers' horses [nineteen of them] were dashed from one side to the other.'[13]

The scene was ghastly. A captain of the regiment saw 'horses that had cost hundreds lying with broken backs and legs. . . . Horses and saddles, carbines and swords mixed up like as they had been shook up in a bag.'[14]

One of the three transports, the *Wilson Kennedy*, failed to make the Crimea and was forced instead to run before the storm to the Bosphorus. On arrival there, Sergeant-Major Cruse 'found that out of all our splendid stock of horses, the finest in the whole Brigade, we had only 1 charger left and *11 troopers*, having lost 81 troopers, 16 chargers and two ponies. The history of the whole wars will not furnish such a fearful loss.'[15] A steamer took the remnant of the horses, and the men, none of whom had been badly hurt, on to Balaklava where they arrived on 4 October. A civilian who was with them before they left the Bosphorus found the men, despite their ordeal, in good heart.

> 'Our evenings', he wrote, 'have been enlivened with music. . . . I wish you could see one of these moonlight concerts. The men come out in every variety of dress and undress – some with the brass helmet on; some wearing over it the white linen cover, with loose side-flaps; others with their heads tied up in red handkerchiefs, their tall figures wrapped in military cloaks, or yet more picturesquely, draped in blankets. The officers gather near, on the poop, and join heartily in the plaudits; but it is a point of etiquette for the men to ignore their presence. Presently a song is called for; and a huge mustachioed giant advances to the window of the steward's cabin, and clears his voice. He is the *gran tenore* of the regiment. . . . He sings some tyrtaean strain, darkly alluding to the Czar, under threats of "driving aback to his mountains the grizzly old bear"; and each verse closing with the refrain –
> "Then come along – come along – drink while you may!
> Tomorrow we fight, boys (*bis*) – let's be happy today." '[16]

'I take my place in the brigade', wrote Lieutenant-Colonel Yorke, soon after arrival at Balaklava, 'as a single squadron, instead of two. . . .* On that fearful night . . . the Regt lost more horses than at Waterloo. . . . Total loss, 150.'[17]

Two troops of the Inniskilling Dragoons, which sailed early on 27 September, also suffered in the storm, their sailing transport being forced to put back into Varna. When, eventually, they reached Balaklava on 7 October, they disembarked only six out of the seventy-five horses with which they had started off.[18]

In all, the Heavy Brigade lost 226 horses on its passage to the

---

* A little later, seventy-five horses were transferred to the Royals from the Light Brigade. (Atkinson, 327.)

Crimea. The remainder, according to Lucan, were 'in such a con--
dition that I should scarcely have recognized them, from what they
had suffered at sea.'[19]

'We are commanded by one of the greatest old
women in the British Army, called the Earl of
Cardigan. He has as much brains as my boot. He
is only to be equalled in want of intellect by his
relation the Earl of Lucan. . . . Without mincing
matters two such *fools* could not be picked out of
the British Army to take command. But they are
Earls!'

CAPTAIN PORTAL, 4th Light Dragoons[1]

(v)

*Crimean War, 1854: siege of Sebastopol starts – Lucan
versus Cardigan: 'Lord Look-on' versus 'the Noble
Yachtsman'*

The twenty-eight days which followed the occupation of Balaklava
were anxious ones for the allies. For the Russians they were a god-
send. By 9 October some 28,000 reinforcements had been poured
into Sebastopol from the north. By heroic exertions the southern
defences, which were negligible at the time of the flank marches,
were daily made stronger.

At Balaklava, a port which soon proved inadequate for the weight
of traffic it was made to bear, the unloading of siege guns went
slowly ahead. The task of hauling them up to within range of
Sebastopol, seven miles distant, was an infinitely laborious one. For
three weeks not an allied gun was fired. Even the digging of trenches,
parallels and zigzags, essential for a siege *en règle*, was only started
on 9 October.

On the 17th the bombardment began. For over a week it continued. A. H. Layard (later Sir Henry), famous already as the exca-
vator of Nineveh, who was present in the allied camp, experienced
such a roaring of cannon in his ears 'as has not been heard since the
Creation'.[2] But the noise was all to no purpose. The fleet co-operated
half-heartedly, and its guns made little impression; the French be-

came demoralized by a lucky Russian hit which blew up a magazine with fearful loss of life, and Raglan, faced for the third time with his ally's *non possumus*, felt unable to make the assault on his own. 'The safety of the Alliance', wrote Fortescue, 'was a deity that, Saturn-like, devoured its own children.'[3] The first attempt at taking Sebastopol, while it was still comparatively easy to do so, fizzled out for lack of a single commander of the allied armies.

To start with the weather was balmy, and rations were supplemented by large quantities of grapes and other fruit. But the abundance and warmth of September soon gave way to the scarcity and cold of October. This did not affect the spirits of the young and fit. Cornet Fisher, for instance, reported on 8 October: 'We are living almost entirely on our rations – of which the mutton is first-rate. This is a glorious life.'[4]

It was the middle of October before everyone was housed in a tent (one for fourteen men or two officers). By then cholera and other diseases had again become rampant. By the end of the first week, twenty-five men a day were dying in the makeshift hospitals of Balaklava.

The war between Lucan and Cardigan, meanwhile, was being waged *con brio*. The day after the battle of the Alma Cardigan wrote a lengthy letter to Raglan seeking in his querulous manner to establish for the Light Brigade an independent existence free from Lucan's interference. A week later the Commander-in-Chief replied, stating that he considered Cardigan 'wrong in every one of the instances cited', and adding that the judgments of a general of division 'may be right or wrong; but the General of Brigade should bear this in mind, that the Lieutenant-General is the Senior Officer; and that all his orders and suggestions claim obedience and attention.' He added:

> 'The Earl of Lucan and the Earl of Cardigan are nearly connected. [They were brothers-in-law.] They are both gentlemen of high honour and elevated position in the country independently of their military rank. They must permit me . . . earnestly to recommend them frankly to associate with each other, and to come to such an understanding as that there should be no impression of the assumption of authority on the one side, and no apprehension of undue interference on the other.'[5]

This appeal was, of course, fruitless. On 4 October Lucan wrote a directive to Cardigan, in which he laid down, amongst other things equally calculated to irritate his insubordinate subordinate, that it was not the duty of the light cavalry 'needlessly, without authority, to engage the enemy' and that 'on no account should any party attack or pursue, unless specially instructed to do so.'[6] This was clear enough, and one of the few occasions on which Cardigan decided to abide by it came exactly twenty days after he had read it, with, as we shall, see far-reaching consequences.

On 5 October the commander of the Light Brigade 'being', as he said, 'very unwell with diarrhoea',[7] was ordered aboard ship by the cavalry division's medical officer. Two days later what seemed to Captain Shakespear of the Horse Artillery 'the finest opportunity for thrashing the Russian cavalry, was *thrown* away',[8] by Lucan. A large force of enemy horsemen cavorted about in the plain, seeming to invite a charge, but though urged on by some of his officers, 'the cautious ass', as Lucan had recently been christened by his officers, refused to charge – probably with wisdom as there were enemy infantry and artillery in support. When Cardigan heard of it he exploded, and called the officers of his own regiment, the 11th, 'a d——d set of old women' for not charging on their own and against orders. He later apologized to the commanding officer for his 'hasty expressions'. It was as a result of this day's work that Lucan acquired the punning sobriquet of 'Lord Look-on'. Inevitably the nickname stuck.[9]

A few days later Cardigan returned to duty, but on the 13th his private yacht, the *Dryad*, sailed into Balaklava harbour. So, 'having received Lord Raglan's permission to live on board and do duty from thence',[10] 'the Noble Yachtsman', as he at once became known, slept aboard for some weeks to come, dining each evening upon delicacies prepared by his French cook. 'This is the way to make war' commented Lieutenant-Colonel Hodge. 'I hope he will take compassion on me sometimes.'[11]

' "The charge of the heavies", said one of the
French generals, . . . "was the most glorious
thing I ever saw" .'

WILLIAM CATTELL, medical officer
of the 5th Dragoon Guards[1]

(vi)

*Crimean War, 1854: defences of Balaklava – battle of
Balaklava: Russians attack – charge of Heavy Brigade*

The British, during these anxious weeks, had to attend, not only to
the siege of Sebastopol, but also to the defence of Balaklava. For
this latter purpose the cavalry was kept perpetually on the alert. 'We
are worked dreadfully hard here looking out for the rear', wrote
Major Phillips of the 8th. 'Alarms night and day; horses kept
saddled for three days at a time, and ever ready.'[2] Lucan's A.D.C.
also found the work very hard, 'but I love it, and am never happier
than when I hear the bullets singing,' he wrote.[3] In the early morning Cornet Fisher of the 4th Dragoon Guards found it

'most awfully cold. . . . Two pairs of drawers, two pairs socks,
two jerseys, a red flannel under stable-jacket, and thick stable
jacket, which I bought at the auction of Pitcairn, the doctor of
the 5th, who died of cholera and weighed 18 stone, keep me
just comfortable. Horses have got coats like sheep, and are
never groomed.'[4]

On one significant occasion, the cavalry was kept out all night,
'neither officer nor man being allowed to leave his horse or his place
in the regiment',[5] in expectation of an attack which never materialized. 'If you keep a cabman out all night', complained Captain
Stocks of the Royals, 'he charges you double fare, whereas a Heavy
gets nothing extra but a cold.' This was on 20 October. The alert
had been given as the result of intelligence from the Turks that an
attempt upon Balaklava was imminent. Not only had the cavalry
been turned out, but at the same time the 4th Infantry Division had
been marched down from the heights before Sebastopol. This false
alarm, as will be seen, had its repercussions four days later. By day
cossack patrols were constantly encountered. Their sudden appearances and equally sudden disappearances reminded Captain Stocks
'of rabbits, only not quite so harmless!'[6]

On 14 October, Sir Colin Campbell, a brigadier in the Highland Division, was placed in command of the defences of Balaklava. Until then, Lucan, much senior in rank to Campbell, had been entrusted with these, such as they were. Campbell was willing to serve under Lucan, but it was said that 'Lord Raglan would not trust Lord Lucan to defend Balaklava',[7] so Campbell was given a separate command. The two men, to their credit, hit it off very well.

Beside some large guns placed immediately above the harbour, which were manned chiefly by Marines, the resources devoted to the defence of Balaklava consisted of the cavalry, with "I" Troop of the Horse Artillery, some 500 men of the 93rd Foot (later part of the Argyll and Sutherland Highlanders), one battery of foot artillery, and about 2,500 Turkish infantry, said to be mostly 'recruited from the lower trading class, aged-looking, but almost raw recruits'.[8] These last were stationed in the forward defences, which consisted of redoubts constructed on six high points along the Causeway

---

This map and the maps on pp. 66 and 81 are not to scale. The contours as well as the positions of the six redoubts are based upon a map produced by French army engineers at the time. This map, discovered in Paris, was the prototype for the topographical model now in the National Army Museum. The distance, as the crow flies, between Kadikoi and the centre of no. 1 redoubt is about $1\frac{3}{4}$ miles.

The locations of the redoubts on this map differ from those on virtually all other maps published; so do most of the roads and tracks. The present author has a hunch – no more than that – that they are more likely to be correct: not that their exact situations make any material difference to a clear understanding of the different phases of the battle.

The locations of the various troops at different stages of the battle are no more than 'intelligent guesswork'. They are probably within a hundred yards or so of the actual positions in most cases. Some of them differ from those generally accepted.

A. Possible position of Russians when first seen by the British

B. Approximate position of I Troop, R.H.A., when it fired the first shots of the battle

C. Probable position of the Heavy Brigade during the first hour or so of the battle

D. Possible positions of the 93rd Foot, Turkish infantry and Pipon's and Barker's guns just before the Russian 'left column' attacked

E. Probable position of the Heavy Brigade as a result of Raglan's 'first order'

F. Probable site of the Light Brigade camp

G. Probable line of march of the Heavy Brigade as a result of Raglan's 'second order'

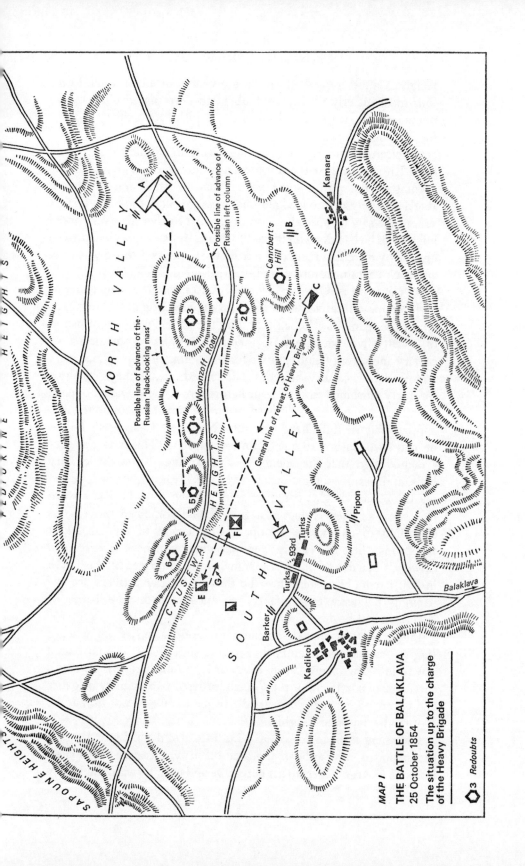

SAPOUNE HEIGHTS

FEDIOKINE HEIGHTS

NORTH VALLEY

Kamara

Possible line of advance of
Russian left column

Canrobert's
1 Hill

B

Possible line of advance of the
Russian 'black-looking mass'

3

2

C

Woronzoff Road

General line of retreat of Heavy Brigade

4

CAUSEWAY HEIGHTS

5

SOUTH VALLEY

Pipon

F

Turks

6

93rd

E

G

Turks

D

Balaklava

Barker

Kadikoi

MAP I

THE BATTLE OF BALAKLAVA
25 October 1854

The situation up to the charge
of the Heavy Brigade

3 Redoubts

Heights on the crest of which ran the vital Worontzoff road. In the four most easterly of these redoubts had been placed nine twelve-pounder guns, with a few men of the British foot artillery to assist the Turks in working them.

Between 18 and 24 October there were unmistakable signs of a large Russian force gathering for a swoop upon Balaklava. On the evening of the 24th a spy reported that an attack was imminent. Raglan merely acknowledged the message, and took no further action. He saw no special reason to exhaust further his overworked infantry as he had done on the 20th when a similar report had proved untrue, by marching them down from the trenches before Sebastopol and back again next morning. But this time the report was true.

At 5 a.m. on 25 October General P. P. Liprandi, a commander of high reputation, moved forward from the direction of Tchorgun to attack the redoubts. He had with him the 12th Division, consisting of twenty-five battalions of infantry, thirty-five squadrons of cavalry and seventy-eight guns, a force totalling perhaps 25,000 men.

The British cavalry brigades had turned out, as they had done for many mornings past, an hour before dawn. They waited outside their lines while Lucan, as usual, went forward to reconnoitre. On approaching the right-hand redoubt – No. 1, on 'Canrobert's Hill' – he saw two ensigns flying from its flagstaff. This was the pre-arranged sign that the enemy was advancing. From the cavalry lines, at the same moment, just as light was breaking, the vedettes on the Causeway Heights could be seen 'circling to right, and also to left, some of them being at a trot. These combined movements signalling to us', wrote Trooper Farquharson of the 4th Light Dragoons, 'that the enemy were showing with both *infantry and avalry*.'[9] In a few seconds these signals were confirmed by the Turks in No. 1 redoubt opening fire. To this the Russian artillery accompanying the assaulting infantry at once replied. The battle of Balaklava had begun.

Lucan sent off an aide-de-camp to headquarters, from whence Raglan ordered two infantry divisions to start their two-hour march down into the plain. Soon afterwards, Canrobert, St Arnaud's successor in command of the French, ordered two infantry brigades and two regiments of Chasseurs d'Afrique to take up position at the foot of the Sapouné Heights.

Galloping back to his troops, Lucan ordered the Light Brigade (commanded, till Cardigan appeared off his yacht some hours later, by Lord George Paget) to act in reserve and took forward the Heavy

Brigade with "I" Troop of the horse artillery. This troop, commanded by Captain Maude, rushed ahead to give the 500 Turks in No. 1 redoubt the only support their allies could provide. It came into action on the ridge 'to the right of the Redoubt, firing on the enemy's artillery in the plain below. The right half-Troop soon changed position to the right and fired shrapnel on the enemy's advancing skirmishers.'[10] The troop answered the Russian guns to the best of its limited capacity, 'being *ordered* to do so', according to one of Maude's officers; 'but what', he asked, 'could 6-pounders do against 18-pounders at 1800 yds? However, Maude stuck to it, and fell severely wounded in the first twenty minutes. He has since said he would have retired but feared the Turks would then retire also.'[11] As Maude's guns were hit, 'a sort of "Spread Eagle" was seen against the horizon, the splinters of broken guns, horses' legs, etc., shooting up into the air.'[12] The heavies also suffered some casualties.

'We were placed', wrote the commanding officer of the Royals, 'directly in the line of fire. . . . All the very large shot that over-crowned the heights naturally bowled like cricket balls into our ranks. . . . The officers could easily escape: we had only to move our horses a few yards to let the shot pass, which movement I effected frequently, but when a shot came opposite the closely packed squadron it generally took a front & rear rank horse, and sometimes a man or a single horse. In this foolish manner we lost 7 horses and 2 men.'[13]

Fighting against at least ten times their number and enormously out-gunned, the Turks put up an heroic resistance which gave the allies more than an hour's invaluable breathing space. After suffering 170 casualties, they were driven from the first two redoubts, but not before the Royal Artillerymen had spiked their guns. On seeing their comrades' flight, the Turks in the next two redoubts evacuated them before they were assaulted; though here, too, the twelve-pounders were spiked. Numbers of cossacks pursued these unfortunate Turks until Lucan, by showing a front, checked them. The Russians now poured infantry into the first three redoubts, and brought up to them a number of field-pieces.[14]

All this time Lucan could do nothing but make threatening de-monstrations whilst falling back before the slowly advancing Russians and firing at them with the remains of Maude's Troop, eventually assisted by the guns of Barker's foot battery. Paget found this retrograde movement 'by alternate regiments (which must have occupied more than an hour), one of the most painful ordeals it is possible to conceive – seeing all the defences in our front successively abandoned . . . and straining our eyes in vain all round the hills in our rear for indications of support.'[15]

'At this time', wrote Captain Shakespear, of Maude's Troop, 'A.D.C.s came to me one after the other: "Bring forward the guns to support the Scots Greys!" My answer was: "No ammunition". I had retired the Troop below the crest of a hill and let shot and shell fly over our heads there, waiting for ammunition.' This lack of ammunition at so vital a moment came about because "I" Troop's wagons had been sent as usual before daybreak to help in bringing up siege-gun and other ammunition from Balaklava to the trenches. Only the limber ammunition was therefore available, and this was quickly expended.[16]

On Sir Colin Campbell's advice, Lucan now withdrew to the left so as to be out of the line of fire of both the Russian guns and the 93rd, and in a position to attack the flank of the Russians should they charge the Scottish infantry. Scarcely had he taken up this new and sensible position when Lucan received his first order from the Commander-in-Chief. This reflected Raglan's anxiety that the cavalry should not become engaged until it could do so in conjunction with the infantry, still well over an hour's march away. The order, known in the controversy which followed the battle, as 'the First Order', read (according to Lucan): 'Cavalry to take ground to left of second line of redoubts occupied by Turks.'[17] This had the effect of removing the cavalry even further to the west, right under redoubt No. 6, where the squadrons were 'packed in enclosed vineyards'.[18] The order was received and most reluctantly acted upon.

Shakespear describes what happened next:

'Suddenly the whole plain we had left swarmed with cavalry. . . .
The left column charged the 93rd Highlanders, who, under Sir Colin, stood on some rising ground with Turkish infantry on both flanks [about 300 in number – some of the survivors from the redoubts], the whole flanked by Pipon's entrenched battery of position guns on the right and Barker's Battery on the left. The Highlanders ruined the charge in line, the guns worked them with grape and case; the enemy fled in great confusion.'[19]

Thus, laconically, does Shakespear describe the successful action of Campbell's 'thin red line'.[20]

5. (*above*) Field-Marshal Lord Raglan, 1855.

6. (*above right*) The Earl of Lucan, commander of the Cavalry Division in the Crimea, attending the Board of General Officers at Chelsea 1856

7. (*right*) Caricature of Sir George Wombwell, bart, veteran of the charge of the Light Brigade. (See p. 93)

8. (*below*) Captain Louis Edward Nolan, 15th Hussars. (See p. 83)

9. (*below right*) The Earl of Cardigan in the uniform of the 11th Hussars, wearing the Crimean medal

10. A heavy cavalryman conveying a sick infantryman from the front to Balaklava, early in 1855

Our Cavalry Dec 1854

11. 'Our Cavalry, Dec. 1854'

The 'left column' of Russian squadrons which attacked Campbell was only a small part of Liprandi's mounted arm. A competent eye-witness put their strength at 'not more than 400 sabres in all'.[21]* They had debouched into the so-called South Valley – that part of the Plain of Balaklava which lies south of the Causeway Heights. At the same time, the main mass of enemy cavalry, numbering not more than 2,000 'at the very outside, probably less',[22]† supported by artillery, was advancing unopposed along the North Valley. The Russian horsemen, commanded by General Rikoff, all of them 'light' hussars or lancers, 'had black horses, wore a black oilskin cover over a very broad-topped old-fashioned shako, and a dark grey overcoat. They were altogether a black-looking mass,'[23] but a mass that could not be seen by Campbell and Lucan, because the Causeway Heights intervened.

For the same reason, the British in the South Valley could not be seen by 'the black-looking mass' in the North Valley. On the other hand, Raglan, from his post high up on the Sapouné Heights, was in a position to see all the troops of both sides. In this he was aided by the exceptionally clear weather which had succeeded the early morning mist. His control of the battle, nevertheless, was gravely inhibited by his physical distance from it. The very fastest horseman could not convey an order to the commanders in the plain in much less than half-an-hour. 'Unless', as Mrs Woodham-Smith puts it in *The Reason Why*, 'Lord Raglan could put himself in the place of his generals 600 feet below, and could perpetually bear in mind when issuing orders that what was clear to him would by no means be clear to them, his position high above the battle was dangerous indeed.'[24] This was amply demonstrated by his 'Second Order' which followed closely on the first. It desired Lucan to detach eight

* Russian authorities put the number higher, but Campbell himself estimated it at only 400. One Russian historian says that the force consisted of 'four squadrons of the Saxon-Veimarsky (Ingermanland) Hussars'. The approximate minimum establishment of a Russian squadron was 120. (Kinglake (6th ed.), V, 1877, 79; 'A Russian Account of Balaklava' [translated from Bogdanovich, M. I. *Vostochnaia voina 1853–56*, 1876, by Cromie, W. H.], *United Service Magazine*, 1882, 196; Curtiss, J. S. *The Russian Army under Nicholas I, 1825–1855*, 1965, 131.)

† Kinglake, after exhaustive argument, makes the number 'about 3,000'. (Kinglake, V, 418–21.) This is certainly far too high. One of the difficulties in assessing the true figure is that the various authorities are unsure as to whether the 'left column' rejoined the main mass which was attacked by the Heavy Brigade, or retired separately.

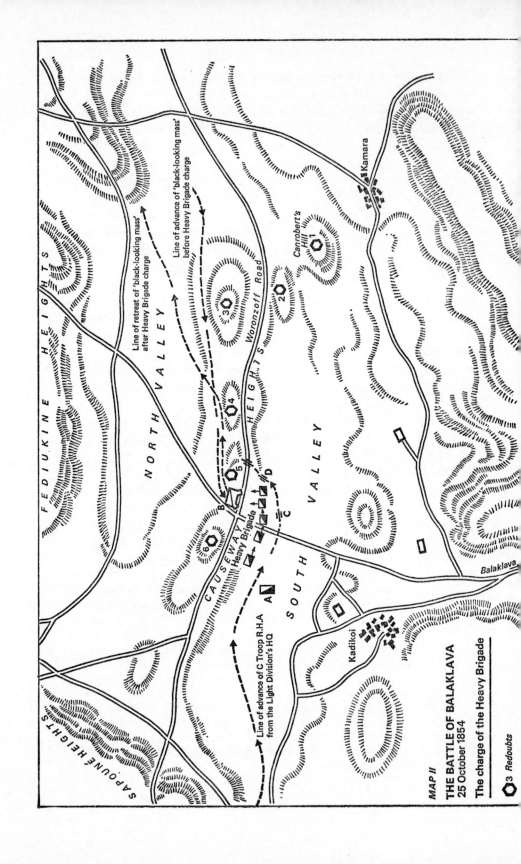

FEDIUKINE HEIGHTS

SAPOUNE HEIGHTS

NORTH VALLEY

Line of retreat of 'black-looking mass' after Heavy Brigade charge

Line of advance of 'black-looking mass' before Heavy Brigade charge

Kamara

Canrobert's Hill

Woronzoff Road

HEIGHTS

3

2

1

4

5

B

D

C

6

CAUSEWAY

Heavy Brigade

SOUTH VALLEY

Balaklava

A

Line of advance of C Troop R.H.A from the Light Division's HQ

Kadikoi

MAP II

THE BATTLE OF BALAKLAVA
25 October 1854

The charge of the Heavy Brigade

3 Redoubts

of his ten squadrons of heavies towards Balaklava to support the wavering Turks. By the time the order was received and acted upon the Turks had long since fled, and the 'left column' of Russian cavalry had already been repulsed by the 93rd.*

In compliance with the order, Lucan sent the Heavy Brigade back. Scarlett duly marched eastwards, in open column of troops with the 5th Dragoon Guards leading, and the Greys and the Inniskillings following. The 4th Dragoon Guards were ordered to follow, while the two squadrons of the Royals were left behind. Meanwhile the Russian 'black-looking mass' was moving in the opposite direction immediately north of the heights. Before long it wheeled to its left and began to cross them.† It did so, as it happened, at the very point which Scarlett had just reached. Neither now, nor earlier, had either side thrown out flankers or scouts.‡ Had this

* There is conflicting evidence about the 'Second Order'. One account states that the withdrawal of the cavalry westwards which resulted from the 'First Order' was closely followed by a number of cossacks, and that when these reached the site of the Light Brigade's camp, they set about killing the sick horses and laying waste the impedimenta which had been left there. Raglan, observing this, sent down an order 'to take some cavalry forward and protect the camp from being destroyed.' (Forbes, 76.) This was the purport, it is argued, of the order which set Scarlett moving eastwards again. The point is not vital, but if this version is the correct one, it shows that the time which elapsed between the sending and receiving of the 'Second Order', was not as great as is usually supposed.

† Some authorities say that the Russian cavalry was fired upon by French and Turkish guns sited on the Sapouné Heights, and that it was this which induced the left wheel. It seems more likely that it was the Russian intention from the start to turn southwards towards Balaklava, which was, presumably, their objective, at about the point where they did so.

‡ Kinglake states that the British cavalry regarded themselves 'within our own lines', and that 'Scarlett did not apparently entertain an idea that Russian cavalry could come so high up the North Valley as the "Number Five" Redoubt.' (Kinglake, V, 87.) This may account for the lack of precautions on the British side. No such excuses can be made for the Russians.

A. Possible position of the Light Brigade

B. Approximate position of the 'black-looking mass' just before the Heavy Brigade charged

C. Probable position of "C" Troop, R.H.A., at the start of the Heavy Brigade charge

D. Possible positions of "C" Troop, R.H.A., at the end of the Heavy Brigade charge

precaution been taken, their mutual surprise on seeing each other for the first time at a distance[25] of something like 500 yards would never have occurred.*

At this moment, quite unsuspecting, the British heavy squadrons were threading their way through and around vines and orchards which obstructed their path and were about to enter the camp of the Light Brigade. Lieutenant Alexander Elliot, one of Scarlett's aide-de-camps, happened to 'cast a glance', in Kinglake's graphic words, 'towards the ridge on his left, and saw its top fretted with lances. Another moment and the sky-line was broken by evident squadrons of horse.'[26]† Elliot pointed these out to his chief, whose short-sightedness made him at first doubtful. When he had been convinced, he decided at once to charge.

Closest to him was the second squadron of the Inniskillings, followed by the two squadrons of the Greys, just emerging from the confines of a ruined vineyard. To these he called out: 'Are you right in front?' and as soon as he received the reply 'Yes, sir!', he ordered: 'Left wheel into line.'[27] When this operation had been concluded – and it took some time – it became necessary for these three squadrons (Tennyson's 'three hundred') to take ground to their right, so as to make room for the 5th Dragoon Guards to come up between the left of the Greys and the wall of the vineyard.‡ This entailed

* In an 'explanatory statement' for Kinglake, Lucan declared that the 'advance of the Russian cavalry was *no* surprise. . . . From the time that they descended into the valley they moved very slow, and should have been seen by General Scarlett when still one mile distant. I saw them before they crowned the heights, and found time to travel over double the extent of ground, and to halt, form, and dress the attacking line before it had traversed more than half the breadth of the valley.' (Kinglake, V, 403.) Lucan may have convinced himself that all this was true, but it conflicts with virtually all other evidence, and cannot therefore be taken seriously.

† At about this moment Cardigan, too, saw the enemy for the first time. He allowed "I" Troop to fire a few shots into its right flank. Simultaneously, Barker's field battery, which had just supported the 93rd in repulsing the Russian 'left column', also saw the 'black-looking mass'. About twenty rounds were fired at it before the heavies began to cross the line of fire. Some of the guns on the Marine Heights also opened up. Further, just before the charge started, it is believed that three heavy guns, 'firing from the Upland [Sapouné Heights] hit the rear of the Russian mass.' (Wood, 111.) All this cannonading must have had some effect upon the steadiness of the enemy cavalry, though how much it is hard to say. (Jocelyn, 203, 204; Wood, 110.)

‡ Elliot, it seems, gave the 5th an order which was interpreted as meaning that it was to act in *support* of the Greys, and not in *line* with them, though Scarlett

breaking again into 'column of troops' followed by a second 'left wheel'. These manoeuvres took some minutes.

Meanwhile, Lucan, who had remained with the Light Brigade, received news of the presence of the enemy from an aide-de-camp sent down to him from Raglan. He at once galloped off to warn Scarlett. Finding most of the brigadier's troops marching westwards, he assumed they were still unaware of the enemy's proximity. Consequently he began yelling orders and causing the divisional trumpet to be sounded. Fortunately, neither orders nor trumpet were heeded. The squadrons calmly went about their business of dressing, in readiness for the charge, their officers supervising with their backs to the enemy. Lucan then went up to Scarlett and ordered him to charge, which, of course, the Brigadier was anyway about to do. Only when he was sure that all were properly aligned did he order his trumpeter to sound the 'charge'.

When the Russian commander first topped the ridge and saw Scarlett's men below him at the foot of the heights, he took ground to his left, (possibly because of the vineyard wall which he saw to his right front). All witnesses agree that this manoeuvre was effected with admirable skill. When it was completed, the Russian cavalry resumed its advance down upon Scarlett – but for only a short distance. Its commander, according to Kinglake, 'slackened the pace. He still slackened – his trumpets were sounding – he slackened, and came to a halt.'[28] An eye-witness says that 'many drew carbines and fired,* and Griffiths of the Greys was disabled by a shot in the head.'[29] Paget noticed 'the Russians halt, look about, and appear bewildered, as if they were at a loss to know what next to do! The impression of which bewilderment is forcibly engraven in my mind.'[30]

The obstructed ground in their front may well have bewildered the Russians. It is possible, too, that their morale was shaken by the slow deliberation of the Heavy Brigade's parade-ground preparations. What is certain is that the Russian commander decided to

had no recollection later of this having been his intention. (Kinglake, V, 91.) In the event, the 5th was a little to the left rear of the Greys when the charge was made.

* This reminded some old soldiers of the affair at Aroya-Molinos in 1811, when the French cavalry halted to receive the British charge with pistol fire. There are few known instances of British cavalry committing this particular error, so alien to what was known and enshrined as 'the true cavalry spirit'. The French cavalry repeated the mistake at Sedan in 1870, and so did the Austrian cavalry on more than one occasion in the War of 1866.

effect a partial deployment. He ordered the prolongation to right and left of his first two ranks, providing thereby two all-enveloping pincer arms. This was apparently a text-book manoeuvre in the Russian cavalry. It alone would account for the Russians' halt.

On the British side, when at last all were properly aligned, Scarlett himself led off. He rode well ahead, wearing a blue coat over his uniform, and his 5th Dragoon Guards helmet. Beside him were Elliot, a staff-officer's cocked hat on his head, the brigade trumpeter, and Trooper Shegog who was Scarlett's orderly and a skilled swordsman. All four quickly covered the short distance which lay between them and the enemy. They were 'several horses' lengths'[31] ahead of the troops at the moment of impact. The reason for this was that Scarlett's anxiety to get at his passive adversaries before they started moving again induced him to order the charge from a standstill. Such an unorthodox movement, known as the 'direct gallop depart', demands an 'extraordinarily high degree of collection', which his men were not quite capable of achieving.[32]

Scarlett's little group of four horsemen now forced its way into the centre of the Russians, who were either still halted or advancing at a walk. Wielding their swords to good effect, Scarlett and his companions were well enfolded by the 'black-looking mass' before the Greys and the second squadron of the Inniskillings had picked their way over the pegs, ropes and vines in their path, and had come in their turn to grips with the enemy. The ground in front of the Inniskillings was comparatively free of encumbrances, but their commander had, of course, to keep in line with the slower Greys on his left.

An eye-witness close at hand saw the first squadron of the Greys force their way in

'partly between the files, dismounting some of the Russians, and partly at the angles formed by the Russian centre checking. They then spread out something like a fan. . . . After the first crash our men knocked or pulled them off their horses in every conceivable way. Of course there were some of our own men knocked off also, who were staggering about with bleeding faces.'[33]

At the moment of impact the two extended wings of the Russians began to close in from both flanks. While this was happening the remaining seven squadrons of the Heavy Brigade came successively into action, all within a few moments of each other. From the left rear of the Greys, the 5th Dragoon Guards charged into the main mass of the enemy. An eye-witness says that the Russians at this moment had 'already wheeled round the Greys . . . and many of them had their backs turned'[34] as the 5th made impact. Into the inward-swinging Russian left wing charged the 1st squadron of the Inniskillings (which, it will be remembered, had been leading the brigade column at the time of the surprise). They went in 'at a splendid pace, the men sitting well down, and in good dressing . . . and catching [the Russians] as they did obliquely and on the bridle arm, unhorsed whole troops of them.'[35]

A little later, the 4th Dragoon Guards brought forward its left 'at a very slow trot till close' to the enemy and then charged it in its right flank, with considerable effect.[36]* The Royals too, though left in reserve, seem to have come forward on their own initiative and taken some small part in the action. Their commanding officer wrote that 'the Greys and Inniskillings did all, the 4th and 5th nothing more than us';[37] but, though it seems that the enemy horsemen began to break in places even before the 4th's flank charge, it was probably that charge, combined with the one made by the first squadron of the Inniskillings on the right, which ensured the retreat of the enemy cavalry only some eight minutes after Scarlett had first ridden into it.†

Though some eye-witnesses say that the British troopers penetrated right through to the rear of the 'black-looking mass', it seems much more likely (as stated by Lieutenant Fox Strangways, of "C" Troop, R.H.A., who was particularly well placed to observe) that

'the cutting and hacking was only carried on about as far as the fifth rank from the Russian front, and about as far inwards as the breadth of twelve horsemen on their flanks near the front. On the left flank [where the first squadron of the Inniskillings charged], which was in full view of "C" Troop, certainly two-thirds of the flank nearest the rear was quite untouched. . . . Probably on the Russian right flank [where the 4th Dragoon

---

* Lucan in his despatch, and elsewhere, claims to have ordered the 4th to effect the flank charge, but their commanding officer specifically refutes the claim. 'I do think', he wrote home, 'that Lord Lucan might as well have given me the credit of our flank charge, and not have told such a falsehood about it in saying that he ordered it when he never gave any orders to us at all. . . . It was quite my own idea.' (6 Dec 1854, 10 Apr 1855, Anglesey: *Hodge*, 49, 98.)

† This timing is a guess by Lord Lucan. (Kinglake, V, 165.)

Guards charged], the attack may have extended farther towards the rear, but the same rule holds good: only a certain number of horses standing sideways could have been ridden down or destroyed at the first crash, and the horses inside these would hardly feel it, or suffer inconvenience from it. Any of our men riding in between the Russian ranks would find it a losing game, for they must enter in single file or two abreast at the most, and then they would be cut at on both sides; from one rank by the men reaching back over their horses' croups, and from the other by the men merely leaning forward in their stirrups; but besides this, the Russians carried a large loaded pistol (which our people had not), and any number of men riding in single file between their ranks, would have been quickly disposed of.'[38]

There are conflicting accounts of the way in which both the British and Russian horsemen actually fought in the *mêlée*. An officer who took part in the charge said that 'it was just like a *mêlée* coming in or out of a crowded theatre, jostling horse against horse, violent language, hacking and pushing, till suddenly the Russians gave way.'[39] Speaking to Scarlett, Raglan said of the Greys, 'They knocked them over like the devil.'[40]

Casualties were surprisingly light. This was partly due to the inefficiency of the swords on both sides. 'Our swords', wrote Lieutenant-Colonel Griffiths, commanding the Greys, after the battle, 'are very defective. . . . When our men made a thrust with the sword, they all bent and would not go into a man's body. . . . Their arms are quite good enough for Home Service, but quite unfit for active service.'[41]

On the other hand, doctors of the Naval Brigade who attended the Russian wounded noticed that some of the dead had their 'head-dress and skull divided down to the chin'.[42] From this it can be inferred that when the edge was used against the head (the Heavies on their big horses being considerably higher from the ground than their opponents), the British sword was more efficient than when the point was used. The thick material of the Russians' greatcoats afforded very good protection for their bodies.

Sir Evelyn Wood tells a story which well illustrates the ill effects of a too slavish devotion to the text book: 'A doctor dressing a wound in one of our men's head, asked, "And how came you to get this ugly cut?" The trooper replied, with much warmth, "I had just cut five [a regulation 'body cut'] at a Russian, and the d——d fool never guarded at all, but hit me over the head!" '[43]*

There is evidence that the Russians had failed to sharpen their weapons. The few enemy swords picked up after the charge 'were as blunt as they could be'.[44] One trooper of the 4th Dragoon Guards had fifteen head cuts, 'none of which was more than skin deep'.[45] Numbers of brass helmets were stove in (including Scarlett's), without their wearers' heads being touched. As one officer put it, his 'brass pot stood well'.[46] Elliot, who was wearing only his staff officer's cocked hat, sustained fourteen sabre cuts, and was returned as 'slightly wounded'. His worst wound, above the ear, was in fact inflicted by a trooper of the Greys, who later admitted that 'he had done it striking about desperately . . . in attempting to cut his way out.'[47] He may have been indulging in what later came to be known as the *moulinet* – the 'almost ceaseless play of his sabre whirling round and round overhead'.[48] Many of the wounds inflicted on the heavies affected their sword hands. These would not have occurred had not the cavalry recently discarded the wearing of gauntlets in the field.

*　　*　　*

Another factor in the success of the Heavy Brigade charge – an important one which is seldom mentioned – was the action of "C" Troop of the Royal Horse Artillery. The moment news of the attack on Balaklava reached the camp of the Light Division on the Sapouné Heights, "C" Troop (which was attached, as we have seen, to that Division) started for the scene of action. Just as the 'black-looking mass' was throwing out its flank wings, the troop arrived about 150 yards in rear of the Greys and the Inniskillings. Its gun-horses were seen to be 'reeling and trembling' after galloping at top speed some five and a half miles. The Troop commander, Captain Brandling, placed his guns so as to be able to cover what, at that instant, seemed to be the certain defeat of the Heavies. When, a minute or so later, he saw the Russians waver and begin to retire up the incline to their left rear, he moved forward and to his right so as to be able to fire into them. This he did 'almost before some of the red-coats were clear of them'.[49] Brigadier-General Strangways, commanding the

---

* Another version goes: 'When he came at me, I gave right defend, but the fool gave cut seven, and hit me on the head, and down I went.' (Baker, 59.)

horse artillery, who had galloped down from the heights even before the troop arrived, observed what happened next:

'The Russians halted short of the ridge, and their officers could be seen holding their swords up and endeavouring to rally them, and get them into order, which they very soon would have done, but "C" Troop now came into action, and fired forty-nine shot and shell at them, at a range between 700 and 800 yards, with admirable results, the 24-pounder howitzers making splendid practice. This effectually prevented the Russians rallying, and they quickly retired, keeping a little inside the crest of the ridge, and thence over into the outer plain.'[50]

An officer of the 5th Dragoon Guards, going over the ground next day, saw that "C" Troop 'did good work'.[51]

An excellent illustration of the contrast between the characters of Lords Raglan and Lucan is the difference between their reactions to the success of the Heavy Brigade's charge. Raglan at once sent down a message saying: 'Well done, Scarlett!',[52] while Lucan, according to an officer of the 4th Dragoon Guards, 'blew up Scarlett as Lord Cardigan used to blow up a Captain, and with about as much reason.'[53] Another instance of Lucan's unpleasing character is afforded by his virtual suppression of Scarlett's report to him in his official despatch, and by his refusal to name Elliot in that despatch on the grounds that the consequences of indiscriminate recommendations of staff officers 'would be that but little value would be attached to general officers' requests'. This, however, did not prevent him commending his own first aide-de-camp who did not take part in any charge during the battle.[54]

A few individual men of the Light Brigade surreptitiously took part in the charge. Amongst them were two troopers of the 11th Hussars 'who must have been doing a bit on their own hook!', as one observer remarked.[55] The Light Brigade as a whole, however, remained immobile – some of the troops even dismounted – throughout the action, although within 500 yards of the nearest heavies. It also failed to pursue, although the Heavies were temporarily too disorganized to do so. Lord Cardigan is said to have exclaimed repeatedly: 'Damn those Heavies. They have the laugh of us this day.'[56] He justified his inaction thus: 'I had been ordered into a particular position [by Lord Lucan], with orders on no account to leave it, and to defend it against any attack of the Russians; they did not however approach the position.'[57] Lucan's version of the order he gave runs thus: '. . . You'll remember that you are placed here by Lord Raglan himself for the defence of this position. My instructions to you are to attack anything and everything that shall come within reach of you . . .'[58] Certainly the eruption of the Russian cavalry could be interpreted as something within reach of the Light Brigade.

Captain Morris, temporarily in command of the 17th Lancers – a man who had fought in at least three actions of the Sikh wars – went up to Cardigan at the moment when the Russians were seen to be breaking, and said:

' "My Lord, are you not going to charge the flying enemy?"
"No", replied Cardigan. "We have orders to remain here."
"But, my Lord, it is our positive duty to follow up this advantage."
"No. We must remain here."
"Do, my Lord, do allow me to charge them with the 17th. Sir, my Lord, they are in disorder."
"No, no, sir. We must not stir from here." '

Morris then turned to his regiment and said: 'Gentlemen, you are witnesses of my request.' A trooper of the 17th saw and heard all this, and records that Morris, angrily slapping his leg with his sword, shouted: 'My God, my God, what a chance we are losing!'[59]

Characteristically, Cardigan publicly denied that Morris had 'made any proposal of the sort'; that 'it was not his duty to do so', and that he 'did not commit such an irregularity'.[60] Cardigan nevertheless confided privately to Kinglake that Morris had in fact 'sought to push forward with his regiment' and that he (Cardigan) had prevented him from doing so, but 'at a moment when it had become too late to act with effect'.[61] The real blame seems to lie with Lucan. Why did he not order the Light Brigade at least to pursue? Because, he wrote, it 'had been placed in a position by Lord Raglan, [was] altogether out of my reach, and . . . to me . . . unavailable.'[62] It is difficult to view this excuse as anything but sheer nonsense.

It is possible that if the Light Brigade had in fact pursued the fleeing Russians the battle of Balaklava would have been a spectacular British victory. As it was, the Russian cavalry was suffered to return whence it had come together with the guns which had been following it. This may, though, have been inevitable, since any pursuers might before long have come under artillery fire from at least one side of the North Valley.

*   *   *

It is impossible to say what the casualties incurred in the charge amounted to. The Russians may have had 300 killed and wounded, but this figure is probably an exaggeration. The Heavy Brigade's total casualties for the day were ten killed and ninety-eight wounded, but more than half of these were almost certainly inflicted in passively supporting the Light Brigade later on. The 5th Dragoon Guards, for instance, suffered smaller losses in the former action than in the latter, whilst the Royals alone had about nineteen officers and men hit or dismounted by losing their horses at the time of the Light Brigade's charge. Lucan's aide-de-camp, Captain Walker, in the course of the Light Brigade charges 'saw one shot knock over 7 or 8 men and horses of the Greys'.[63] Further, a few casualties (included in the total figure) had occurred in the earlier stages of the battle.

One observer noticed that not long after the Heavy Brigade's charge there 'was no perceptible diminution' in its strength, and that it 'looked as quiet and as formidable as if no encounter had taken place'.[64]

'It is wonderful', wrote the colonel of the Royals, 'what a vast deal is said about this charge, and it is fortunate as it counterbalances the misfortunes of the Light Brigade, and affords satisfaction to the public, and brings honor on the Heavy Brigade; but there is, in truth, a precious deal of humbug even in battle, and the pen & fine language smooth the errors and make men appear great afterwards tho' their brains are in confusion during the affair.'[65]

The eye-witness account written by that very literate soldier Colonel Hamley in the *Edinburgh Review* is a good example of 'fine language' applied to the charge:

'All who had the good fortune to look down from the heights on that brilliant spectacle must carry through life a vivid remembrance of it. The plain and surrounding hills, all clad in sober green, formed an excellent background for the colours of the opposing masses – the dark grey Russian column sweeping down in multitudinous superiority of numbers on the red-clad squadrons, that, hindered by the obstacles of the ground on which they were moving, advanced slowly to meet them. There was a clash and fusion, as of wave meeting wave, when the head of the column encountered the leading squadrons of our brigade, all those engaged being resolved into a crowd of individual horsemen, whose swords rose and fell and glanced. So for a minute or two they fought, the impetus of the enemy's dense column carrying it on and pressing our combatants back for a short space; till the 4th Dragoon Guards, coming clear of a wall which was between them and the enemy, charged the Russian flank, while the remaining regiment of the brigade went in, in support of those which had first attacked. Then – almost, it seemed, in a moment and simultaneously – the whole Russian mass gave way and fled, at speed and in disorder, beyond the hill, vanishing behind the slope some four or five minutes after they had first swept over it.'[66]

Tennyson's little known poem 'The Charge of the Heavy Brigade' though not written till 1882, is another example of 'the pen & fine language' referred to by Lieutenant-Colonel Yorke:

I

The charge of the gallant three hundred, the Heavy Brigade!
Down the hill, down the hill, thousands of Russians,
Thousands of horsemen, drew to the valley – and stayed;
For Scarlett and Scarlett's three hundred were riding by
When the points of the Russian lances arose in the sky;
And he called 'Left wheel into line!' and they wheeled and
      obeyed.
Then he looked at the host that had halted he knew not why,
And he turned half round, and he bad his trumpeter sound
To the charge, and he rode on ahead, as he waved his blade
To the gallant three hundred whose glory will never die –
'Follow,' and up the hill, up the hill, up the hill,
Followed the Heavy Brigade.

II

The trumpet, the gallop, the charge, and the might of the
      fight!
Thousands of horsemen had gathered there on the height,

With a wing pushed out to the left, and a wing to the right,
And who shall escape if they close? but he dashed up alone
Through the great gray slope of men,
Swayed his sabre, and held his own
Like an Englishman there and then;
All in a moment followed with force
Three that were next in their fiery course,
Wedged themselves in between horse and horse,
Fought for their lives in the narrow gap they had made –
Four amid thousands! and up the hill, up the hill,
Gallopt the gallant three hundred, the Heavy Brigade.

III

Fell like a cannonshot,
Burst like a thunderbolt,
Crashed like a hurricane,
Broke through the mass from below,
Drove through the midst of the foe,
Plunged up and down, to and fro,
Rode flashing blow upon blow,
Brave Inniskillens and Greys
Whirling their sabres in circles of light!
And some of us, all in amaze,
Who were held for a while from the fight,
And were only standing at gaze,
When the dark-muffled Russian crowd
Folded its wings from the left and the right,
And rolled them around like a cloud, –
O mad for the charge and the battle were we,
When our own good redcoats sank from sight,
Like drops of blood in a dark-gray sea,
And we turn'd to each other, whispering, all dismayed,
'Lost are the gallant three hundred of Scarlett's Brigade!'

IV

'Lost one and all' were the words
Muttered in our dismay;
But they rode like Victors and Lords
Through the forest of lances and swords
In the heart of the Russian hordes,
They rode, or they stood at bay –

Struck with the sword-hand and slew,
Down with the bridle-hand drew
The foe from the saddle and threw
Underfoot there in the fray –
Ranged like a storm or stood like a rock
In the wave of a stormy day;
Till suddenly shock upon shock
Staggered the mass from without,
Drove it in wild disarray,
For our men gallopt up with a cheer and a shout,
And the foeman surged, and wavered, and reeled
Up the hill, up the hill, up the hill, out of the field,
And over the brow and away.

V

Glory to each and to all, and the charge they made!
Glory to all the three hundred, and all the Brigade!*

* This is the original version published in *Macmillan's Magazine*, March,
1882. It was begun in March, 1881, and was written at the request of A. W.
Kinglake, author of *The Invasion of the Crimea*. The version given here appeared
in *Tiresias and other poems*, 1885, and varies from the 1882 version in some
dozen minor ways. In 1885 a Prologue and an Epilogue were added. The
Prologue to General Hamley was written in 1883, because Edward Hamley, who
had served in the Crimea with distinction, was widely regarded as having been
given too little credit for the victory at Tel-el-Kebir. The *Epilogue*, also written
in 1883–4, was subtitled *To a Young Lady*, and deals with the morality of war.
(Ricks, Christopher (ed.) *The Poems of Tennyson*, 1969, 1304–10.)

'A sergeant of the old Cherry Pickers ... gave me
a warm shake of the hand, remarking, "Ah! my
old Fusilier, I told you a week ago we would
have something to talk about before long."
"But", I replied, "has there not been some
mistake?" He said, "It cannot be helped now; we
have tried to do our part. It will all come out
some day." '

SERGEANT GOWING, 7th Royal Fusiliers,
after the charge of the Light Brigade

'A child might have seen the trap that was laid
for us, as every private dragoon did.'

LIEUTENANT THOMAS HUTTON,
4th Light Dragoons after the charge[1]

(vii)

*Crimean War, 1854: battle of Balaklava: charge of
Light Brigade – Lord Cardigan's character*

The successful action of the Heavy Brigade had wrested the initiative
from the Russians, and dealt a blow to their morale. If Liprandi's
intention had been to make a dash for Balaklava, it had been firmly
frustrated.* His only gain was the capture of the first three redoubts,
and his position there was precarious. He at once made dispositions
designed to cover his retirement. Raglan, perceiving all this, realized
that only slight pressure would be needed to force the enemy out of
the redoubts. The battle would then be over, and the army could get
back to its chief occupation – the siege of Sebastopol.

Things, however, did not work out that way. The chief reason
for this was the obstinacy of Sir George Cathcart, who commanded
the 4th Infantry Division. When first ordered down from the
heights, he had been deliberately dilatory. It took time to convince
him that it was not another false alarm. His men, too, were tired out
from their day and night exertions in the trenches. Their progress,
therefore, was slow. The Duke of Cambridge's Guards Division

* The French commander however had apparently, from the very start of the
battle, believed that the Russian advance was 'a mere snare' to lure troops away
from the siege. (Kinglake, IV, 371.)

was less tardy. It had already reached the western end of the South Valley, ready, as planned, to support the 4th Division.

Raglan now ordered Cathcart to 'advance immediately and re-capture the redoubts.'[2] Reluctantly, and with maddening slowness, Sir George marched as far as No. 4 redoubt, which the Russians had never occupied, though they had dismounted the guns in it and

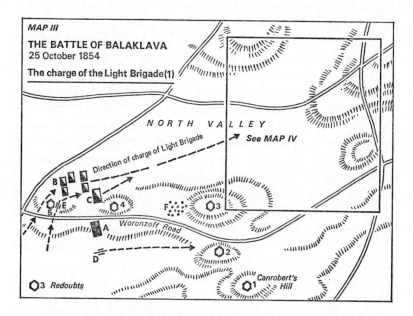

MAP III

THE BATTLE OF BALAKLAVA
25 October 1854

The charge of the Light Brigade(1)

NORTH VALLEY

See MAP IV

Direction of charge of Light Brigade

Woronzoff Road

Canrobert's Hill

3 Redoubts

A. Probable position of the vanguard of Cathcart's 4th Infantry Division at the start of the charge of the Light Brigade
B. Probable position of the Light Brigade as it set off
C. Possible position of the Heavy Brigade at the start of the charge of the Light Brigade
D. Possible line of advance of "C" Troop, R.H.A., at the start of the charge
E. Possible position of "I" Troop, R.H.A., at the start of the charge
F. Probable position of Cathcart's skirmishers at the moment when the Russians abandoned No. 3 redoubt

broken their carriages. This exercise of Cathcart's was futile since the range was too great; but closer to his objective Cathcart declined to go.

Since the infantry refused to respond, Raglan would have to resort to the only troops at hand – namely, the cavalry and horse artillery. He, therefore, sent off an order to Lucan ('the Third Order'). It read: 'Cavalry to advance and take advantage of any opportunity to recover the Heights. They will be supported by infantry, which have been ordered to advance on two fronts.'

On receipt of this order, Lucan did no more than mount his brigades and slightly alter their positions. For something between thirty and fifty-five minutes, he remained thus inactive.* From his experience in the campaign so far, he was totally incapable of believing that Raglan actually meant the cavalry to attack on its own, with only the distant prospect of being supported by the infantry. On at least four occasions between landing in the Crimea and that very morning, the cavalry had been 'restrained, recalled, forbidden to take the offensive, prohibited from engaging the enemy'.[3] It was surely not possible that he was now expected to attack infantry and artillery by charging uphill at the redoubts, even with the help of his horse artillery. He therefore interpreted the Third Order in exactly the opposite sense from that which Raglan intended. In his own words, he decided 'to give all the support possible to the infantry in the recapture of the redoubts'. Since the infantry 'had not yet arrived',[4] he would ignore the first part of the order which enjoined him to advance. He could hardly be expected, perhaps, to divine, as Raglan had, that the mere threat of the cavalry advancing towards them, would have been enough, as was later proved, to compel the Russians to retreat from the redoubts.

As the valuable minutes ticked by, a member of Raglan's staff suddenly exclaimed: 'By Jove, they're going to take away the guns!'[5] It seemed indeed that the Russians were bringing forward teams of artillery horses with lasso tackle to remove the guns from the three redoubts, prior to evacuating them. The thought of losing guns was anathema to Raglan. Wellington, it was believed, had never lost a gun in all his campaigns. Something, therefore, must be done – and quickly.

Another order, the famous 'Fourth Order', was, therefore, despatched to Lucan. It read: 'Lord Raglan wishes the cavalry to advance rapidly to the front – follow the enemy and try to prevent

---

* During the whole time between the two cavalry charges, the Russians 'never missed a chance of firing a shot, when they thought they could do so with advantage, up at "C" Troop and the Heavies, and every two or three minutes there was a quiet muttering in the ranks, "Look out! Here's another", when the smoke from the discharge of a gun on the ridge was observed, and the well-understood black spot was seen in the air coming towards our people. It was one of these that smashed a limber wheel in "C" Troop [R.H.A.], and another that landed in a remarkable manner on a dragoon's sword blade.' (Whinyates: Strangways, 195.)

the enemy carrying away the guns. Troop Horse Artillery may accompany. French cavalry is on your left. Immediate.' So as to get this order delivered as quickly as possible, Raglan entrusted it to Captain Nolan, instead of to the aide-de-camp next for duty. Nolan was known as a brilliant horseman, and so he proved himself. He charged straight down the precipitous hillside at breakneck speed, and reached Lucan in the shortest possible time. Before he set off, Raglan had called out to him, 'Tell Lord Lucan the cavalry is to attack immediately.'

Louis Edward Nolan, born in 1818, was serving at this time as aide-de-camp to Sir Richard Airey, Raglan's Quartermaster-General. Son of an Irish infantry captain, who had ended up as British vice-consul at Milan, his career had been very different from that of the average British cavalry officer. His first commission had been in the 10th Regiment of Austrian Imperial Hussars. By the age of twenty-one he had become its senior lieutenant. He was so anxious to serve in the British army, however, that he was very happy when his father bought him a cornetcy in the 15th Hussars. In 1840 he went with his new regiment to India. There four years later he was appointed regimental riding master, making his name as a superlative horse-master, swordsman and steeplechase rider. During the 2nd Sikh War he became aide-de-camp to the Commander-in-Chief, Madras. By 1851 Nolan had had enough of India and returned home on sick leave. The following year, on a continental tour, he visited a number of military establishments. 'In Russia he attended a review in the presence of the Emperor, and saw the Cossack and Circassian cavalry demonstrate their control of horse and weapon by charging, at the Emperor's signal, towards some pieces of paper scattered on the ground, which the horsemen shot to pieces as they went whirling into the air.'[6] When war broke out, he was sent ahead of the army to Turkey to purchase horses suitable for the cavalry. The drafts of Syrian horses which he bought were of high quality, and Raglan specially commended him for his efforts.

Nolan, who counted amongst his social accomplishments considerable musical talent, was a fanatical student of the cavalry arm. His enthusiastic faith in its capacities, properly exploited, knew no bounds. He published two books. The first was *The Training of Cavalry Remount Horses. A New System*, which was published in 1852. The second was *Cavalry: Its History and Tactics*, which caused a stir in military circles at the time of its appearance in 1853. His professionalism, zeal and vehemence did not endear him to the general run of his fellow officers, and he was apt to be dismissed as a bumptious prig. His contempt for Lucan, based on what he considered his culpable inactivity in the campaign so far, was unlimited and often expressed. Of Cardigan he did not think much better.

The success of the Heavy Brigade, and the inaction, so far in the battle, of the Light Brigade, can have given Nolan little pleasure, for one of his chief tenets was the superiority of light over heavy cavalry. It is easy, therefore, to imagine with what feelings he carried Raglan's order, for it must certainly cause Lucan to send the Light Brigade into action. In Kinglake's striking words, 'straight, swift, and intent – descending, as it were, on sure prey – he swooped angering down into the plain.'[7]

Lucan read the 'Fourth Order', as he himself expressed it, 'with much consideration – perhaps consternation would be the better word – at once seeing its impracticability for any useful purpose whatever.'[8] To Nolan he 'urged the uselessness of such an attack, and the dangers attending it',[9] to which the Captain replied, very correctly: 'Lord Raglan's orders are that the cavalry should attack immediately.'[10] Lucan then (as he later wrote to Raglan) 'asked him "Where, and to do what?" neither enemy nor guns being in sight.'* Nolan, (again according to Lucan), 'replied in a most disrespectful but significant manner, pointing to the farther end of the valley: "There, my Lord, is your enemy, there are your guns".'[11]†

Lucan's contention here is that Nolan was pointing at the guns, more than a mile and a quarter away, at the western end of the North Valley, behind which the 'black-looking mass' had withdrawn after its discomfiture at the hands of the Heavy Brigade. In fact, from where the two men stood, the angle between the distant guns and the redoubt guns was probably 'little more than twenty degrees'.[12]

---

* This admission seems to the present writer to be proof that Lucan *at this moment* had no thought that the guns at the end of the valley were to be attacked, for the distant guns *were* in sight from where Lucan and Nolan were standing, as Nolan's next words show.

† The only reliable first-hand evidence, other than Lucan's, that these words were used, comes from a letter written five days after the battle by his first aide-de-camp, Captain Walker, in which he says: 'an order . . . was brought [to Lucan] by an officer personally hostile to him, and received without the discretion fitting in an officer of high rank. . . . Lord Lucan, instead of taking the order, and exercising his own judgment as to how he carried it out, asked Captain Nolan what he was to attack, and was answered by his pointing to the Russians drawn up across the valley, with the words: "There, my Lord, is your enemy, there are the guns".' (29 Oct 1854, Walker.)

Further, though it is very likely that the guns in the redoubts were not actually in Lucan's view at this moment, it is quite certain that he knew to which guns the 'Fourth Order' referred, and where they were. He had, after all, been in command on the spot, when they were captured earlier in the day. If further proof were needed, it is contained in his despatch of three days later: 'Being instructed', he wrote, 'to make a rapid advance to our front, to prevent the enemy carrying the guns lost by the Turkish troops in the morning, I ordered the Light Brigade to advance . . .'[13]

How was it possible, therefore, that he should conceive the object of attack to be the distant guns, especially as he must have seen that to reach them it would be necessary to pass through artillery and infantry fire, not only in front, but also from at least one flank?*

If he had compared in his mind the order itself, and the interpretation of it which he believed Nolan to have given him, he should have seen that the latter was totally incompatible with the former, and must therefore be disregarded – particularly as the words of the order, though not the most precise ever written, were unambiguous when read in conjunction with the 'Third Order'. He doubtless still thought an unsupported attack upon the redoubts a dangerous, perhaps a reckless, idea; yet surely an equally unsupported attack upon the distant guns must have appeared very much more so.

The only answer which seems at all credible is that Lucan, under the accumulated frustrations of the campaign, resentment against Raglan, and anger at Nolan's insolence, temporarily lost his powers of reasoning. Lieutenant-Colonel Yorke of the Royals had noticed only five days earlier that when there was the least appearance of alarm Lucan became 'excited to madness and abuses everybody . . . We are consequently fearing his want of temper and judgement, should anything serious occur. He is sure to do wrong and then throw the blame on others.'[14]

Whether Nolan really thought the point of attack was the distant guns it is impossible to say, for he did not survive to give his version. It is conceivable that he had not read the 'Fourth Order', which he was carrying, and it is unlikely that he had seen the 'Third Order', of which, of course, he had not been the bearer. Some writers have believed that his resentment at seeing Cardigan inactive against the 'black-looking mass' after the Heavy Brigade charge may have predisposed him to assume that that same 'black-looking mass',

---

* It is conceivable that the men and guns on the Fediukine Hills had not been spotted by Lucan.

sheltering behind the distant guns, must in fact be the target now.[15] Yet the action which he was taking when he was killed (see p. 92) is difficult to explain unless he believed the redoubt guns to be the correct objective.

After his exchange with Lucan, Nolan went over to his friend, Captain Morris, commanding the 17th Lancers, and asked and received permission to ride in the impending charge. He appears not to have disclosed to his friend what he believed to be the goal of the attack, and Morris, who survived it, later said that he, himself, was never in any doubt that the distant guns were intended.

Lucan at once rode over to Cardigan, and ordered him to 'attack the Russians in the valley'.[16] Lucan later said that he thought that he had given him the actual contents, or at least the tenor, of the 'Fourth Order', and that he had directed him 'to advance', not 'to attack'. Cardigan denied both. The Commander of the Light Brigade now took the unusual step – especially unusual since the brothers-in-law were hardly on speaking terms – of making a sort of remonstrance. 'Certainly, sir', he said, 'but allow me to point out to you that the Russians have a battery in the valley in our front, and batteries and riflemen on each flank.' To which Lucan replied, 'I know it, but Lord Raglan will have it. We have no choice but to obey.'[17] Lest it be thought that Cardigan invented this exchange after the event, it should be pointed out that Lucan acknowledged that it took place, but believed that Cardigan's warning only applied to the men and guns on one flank.

The Light Brigade at this time was formed up, more or less in line with No. 4 redoubt and right on the edge of the Causeway Heights, as follows:

1st line (facing east):

Lt-Col Douglas *11th Hussars* (142 offrs & men)	Capt Morris *17th Lancers* (147 offrs & men)	Capt Oldham *13th Light Dragoons* (128 offrs & men)

2nd line (some way to the rear, facing north east):

Lt-Col Ld George Paget *4th Light Dragoons* (126 offrs & men)	Lt-Col Shewell *8th Hussars* (less 1 Troop, acting as escort to Lord Raglan; 115 offrs & men)

673 officers and men is the generally accepted figure for the total strength of the brigade in the charge. More likely to be correct is a very carefully compiled return which makes the total 661, including Cardigan and his two staff officers, Colonel Mayow and Captain Maxse.[18]

To the Brigade's right rear was the Heavy Brigade. Further back still, and to its left rear, was part of the French brigade of Chasseurs d'Afrique, which had recently come down from the Sapouné Heights.

Lucan, (according to his own version, which Cardigan denied), now told the commander of the Light Brigade to 'advance very steadily and quietly', and to narrow his front by removing the 11th Hussars from the first line. 'This', said Lucan, Cardigan 'strenuously opposed;* but I moved across his front and directed Colonel Douglas [commanding the 11th] not to advance with the rest of the line',[19] but instead to form, in effect, a sort of intermediate line between the first and second.† Lucan's intention seems to have been to narrow the brigade's deployment so as to expose as few men as possible.

Thus the formation was altered, somewhat as follows:

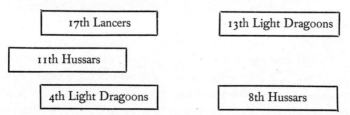

Each regiment was, of course, extended in line two deep.

Cardigan now rode back to Paget and said to him: 'You will take command of the second line, and I expect your best support – mind, your best support.'[20] He then returned to the head of his brigade and placed himself, alone, in front of his staff, who were about three horses' lengths in front of the two regimental commanders of the first line. Raising his sword, Cardigan gave the order: 'The Brigade will advance. First squadron of the 17th Lancers direct.'[21] From that moment on, as Captain Morris leading the 17th remarked,

* Particularly as the 11th was Cardigan's old regiment, while the 17th (which remained in the first line), was Lucan's!

† Lucan may have intended to place the 11th and 4th in second line, with the 8th in a final supporting line. If this was so, his orders were misunderstood or never conveyed.

the Brigade commander led 'in capital style'. Morris, when asked whether Cardigan had led 'quietly', answered: 'Quite so; just as it ought to be – in short, like a gentleman.'[22]

As the first line, followed by the 11th Hussars, moved off, Paget held back the second until it was the 'proper distance'[23] of 200 yards behind the 11th. Lucan followed some way further back, with Scarlett at the head of the Royals and Greys, in support.

For the first fifty yards or so, this splendid array of horsemen,* occupying, perhaps, less than one-fifth of the width of the valley,† advanced in perfect order, at a steady trot. Cardigan, at their head, erect, immaculately turned out, riding Ronald, his favourite chestnut charger, appeared to Wombwell, his aide-de-camp, 'the very incarnation of bravery'.[24] He kept his eyes firmly fixed upon the distant guns in his front.

Except for the jingling of bits, the clanking of accoutrements and the dull pounding of the horses' hooves, there was almost total silence. But it did not last long. Before many seconds had passed, the Russian artillery and the riflemen from the redoubts on the right, and from the Fediukine Hills on the left, soon joined by the distant guns in front, opened up. The Light Brigade was in the process of springing a deadly three-sided trap from which there was small chance of escape.

The first 200 yards or so of its progress would have followed the same route whether the distant guns, or the redoubts, had been its objective. After that an incline to the right would have been necessary, if it were to reach the redoubts. Immediately before this point had been reached, the Russians in numbers 2 and 3 redoubts (part of

* There was one jarring figure amongst the full-dress jackets and cased lance-caps of the 17th Lancers. At the last moment Trooper Veigh, the regimental butcher, rode up fresh from the shambles to join in the charge. Over his blood-stained canvas smock he had buckled the belt and accoutrements of one of the 'heavies' who had been killed in Scarlett's charge. Riding the dead dragoon's horse, he carried his poleaxe at the slope. In the charge his horse was shot, but Veigh himself returned unwounded. (Fortescue: *17 L*, 135; Wightman, 852.)

† The first line would have extended about 145 yards, at regulation intervals, *before* any casualties took place. (Whinyates, 164.)

This map is based on part of a plan referred to in the affidavit of George Mayow, Cardigan's Brigade Major, sworn in the Queen's Bench, May, 1863 (The Earl of Cardigan v. Lt-Colonel Calthorpe). The original is in the Public Records Office. It is likely to be as accurate as any other map and possesses the added interest of having been prepared by one of the participants in the charge.

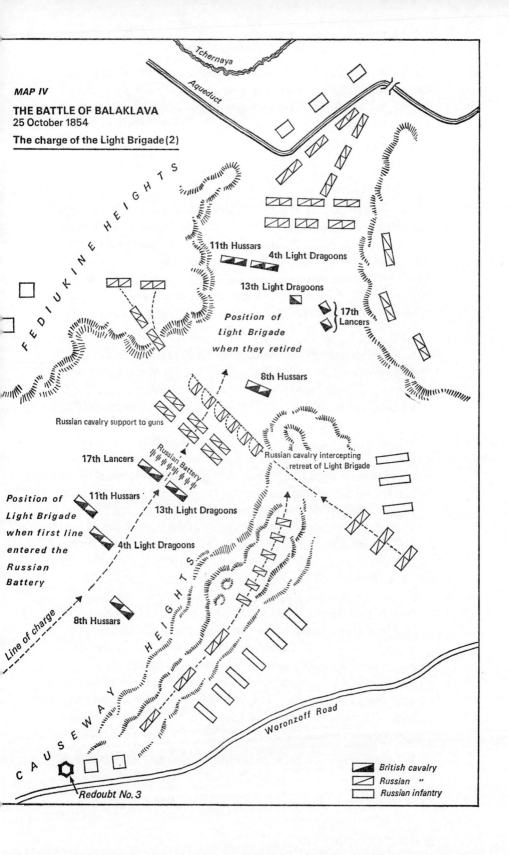

MAP IV

THE BATTLE OF BALAKLAVA
25 October 1854

The charge of the Light Brigade (2)

Tchernaya

Aqueduct

F E D I U K I N E   H E I G H T S

11th Hussars

4th Light Dragoons

13th Light Dragoons

17th Lancers

Position of

Light Brigade

when they retired

8th Hussars

Russian cavalry support to guns

17th Lancers

Russian Battery

Russian cavalry intercepting
retreat of Light Brigade

11th Hussars

13th Light Dragoons

Position of

Light Brigade

when first line

entered the

4th Light Dragoons

Russian

Battery

C A U S E W A Y   H E I G H T S

Line of charge

8th Hussars

Woronzoff Road

Redoubt No. 3

British cavalry

Russian   "

Russian infantry

the Odessa Regiment of Rifles), believing that the cavalry were in fact aiming at them, abandoned their guns, and formed square to the east of No. 2 redoubt. Thus, the mere sight of the advancing cavalry proved enough to effect part of Raglan's intention; but, in the event of course, only temporarily.

*   *   *

What, meanwhile, of the two troops of Horse Artillery? Before Nolan's arrival in the plain with the 'Fourth Order', the six guns of "I" Troop were with the Light Brigade in the South Valley, 'about 600 yards from the crest' of the Causeway Heights. Captain Shakespear, its commander, rode over the crest to see what was going on. There he met Lieutenant-Colonel McMahon, the Quartermaster-General of the cavalry.

'We were alone', Shakespear wrote later, 'and with our telescopes were examining the Russian artillery in the bush on the opposite [Fediukine] heights, across the second plain [North Valley]. The distance would be about 1500 yards. . . . Capt. Charteris rode up to us. . . . [He] said, "You will see something now! The Light cavalry are going to attack down the plain." I exclaimed, "You will all be destroyed. I will go and bring up the Troop and try and give assistance." I galloped back. I could not see Lord Lucan, but Maj.-gen. Scarlett being close at hand, I said, "Will you allow me to go to the support of the Light Cavalry?" His answer was, "Certainly". I moved off at a smart trot, seeing the rear regiments of the Light Cavalry just dip out of sight over the heights. My horses were tired and reduced in numbers, and I soon came to a walk. The Scotch Greys had moved before me and had halted in line just at the foot of the heights. I passed through their squadron intervals. At this time Major Walker, Lord Lucan's A.D.C., rode up to me. In a conversation I had with him afterwards, he said [that he had come] with "an order for me to advance". I perfectly remember his being with me, but have no recollection of this order. Had he brought me directions to do otherwise than I was doing, I should have probably paid more attention. Major Walker, in speaking to me afterwards, said, "My life was probably saved by being sent back for you." '[25]

Whether or not Lucan intended to give instructions to "I" Troop to support the cavalry's advance, it is certain that he gave "C" Troop no intimation that it was to take place. It so happened that Captain Brandling, its commander, (like Shakespear), had ridden over the crest of the Causeway Heights to reconnoitre. As soon as he saw the cavalry moving off, he galloped back to his Troop in the South Valley, calling out 'Mount! Mount!' The Troop then 'advanced rapidly into action in the direction of No. 2 redoubt'. One of its officers later wrote: ' "C" Troop naturally considered the front of the battle as being on the ground about No. 2 redoubt . . . from which there was then a Russian cannonade. The belief at the moment was that we were attempting to retake that part of the ridge.'[26] In the event neither Troop could do much that was useful to assist the Light Brigade. An highly-qualified first-hand observer believed that 'if before the Light Brigade attacked, both Troops of Horse Artillery had been ordered to make a vigorous advance into action towards no. 2 redoubt, to have distracted the enemy's fire, the losses to the Brigade, even going in the direction they actually took would have been less.'[27]*

* * *

At this time, Cathcart's main body of infantry was still halted before No. 4 redoubt, but his skirmishing riflemen were close to No. 3 at the moment when it was abandoned by the enemy. Here, then, was his opportunity to carry out the order to advance and 'recapture the redoubts'. When an officer of Raglan's staff, who had remained with the division, suggested to Cathcart that he should grasp the opportunity, the answer was a flat 'No'. Though, according to Kinglake, the General 'felt sure he could recapture all the redoubts, including even the "Number One" ', he thought that 'no advantage would accrue', because the position was 'much too extended' and the redoubts would have to be evacuated 'after dark'. His mind, he said, was quite made up, and he would write to Raglan about it.[28]†

* * *

The Russian guns had not been firing many seconds, when Captain

* Throughout the battle the expenditure of ammunition by "C" and "I" Troops, R.H.A. was, according to one return, 289 shot and shell. (Extract from Adye's Order Book, Jocelyn, 217.)

† No such letter survives in the Raglan papers.

Nolan, sitting beside his friend Captain Morris, at the head of the
17th Lancers, suddenly rode out in front of the first line. 'That
won't do, Nolan!' shouted Morris. 'We've a long way to go, and
must be steady.'[29] But Nolan paid no attention and to Cardigan's
amazement and anger overtook him, waving his sword and shouting
in front of the advancing brigade. Above the roar of the guns, no
one heard what he was trying to say. Nor will anyone ever know,
for almost immediately a shell splinter struck him in the chest,
piercing his heart. From his throat there came an unearthly shriek,
and as his frightened horse swerved back through the 13th Light
Dragoons, Nolan's sword arm, no less than his impeccably gripping
knees, remained uncannily frozen in the positions they had held at
the moment of death.

It can never be established whether Nolan, as seems likely, was
trying to change the direction of the Light Brigade's advance or not.
Captain Maxse, one of Cardigan's aides-de-camp, wrote ten years
later that he had 'no recollection of Nolan having attempted to
create a divergence either by deed or gesture'. From what is known
of Nolan's character, however, it seems unlikely that his actions were
inspired by nothing more than 'exhilaration at being at last in a Light
Cavalry charge and being impatient at the slowness of the pace set',
as has been suggested by one modern historian.[30]

*   *   *

The gauntlet of fire through which the Light Brigade now advanced
was formidable indeed. On the Causeway Heights to the right were
some thirty-two guns, as well as the rifles of eleven infantry battalions. Opposite, on the Fediukine Heights, were a further fourteen
guns and eight battalions. At the end of the valley was No. 3 Don
Battery, consisting of eight guns.*

'Grape, shells and minie balls', wrote an officer of the 4th Light
Dragoons, 'fell like hail all round us, to say nothing of 18 lb shot,
which whistled through our ranks, dealing death and destruction.'[31]

---

* It is generally held that there were twelve guns at the end of the valley (e.g.
Kinglake (1877), V, 194), but the official Russian version as well as that of
Strangways (Whinyates: Strangways, 176) that there were only eight seem more
convincing. The extent of a battery of eight guns would have been, most likely,
about 140 yards. The extent of the first line of the Light Brigade by the time it
arrived at the battery, would have been considerably less than 140 yards. (See
fn †, p. 88.)

Private Mitchell of the 13th, in the first line, prayed: 'Oh, Lord protect me, and watch over my poor mother.' He noted that 'oaths and imprecations might be heard between the report of the guns and the bursting of the shells, as the men crowded and jostled each other in their endeavours to close to the centre.'[32] Above everything else, as more and more gaps were torn in the ranks, could be heard the officers and non-commissioned officers yelling their orders: 'Close in! Close in to the centre!'[33]

Wombwell, who as extra aide-de-camp was riding immediately behind Cardigan, saw the men falling in heaps all round him, 'and every time I looked up I could see our line getting thinner.'[34] Cardigan himself found that 'the shower of grape shot and round shot . . . was awful, besides the flash fire of artillery and the flames which swept down the ranks every moment. . . . I considered it certain death, but I led straight and no man flinched.'[35]

The old grey mare of Trooper John Lee of the 17th, who was killed, kept alongside its neighbour for some distance, all the while 'treading on and tearing out her entrails as she galloped, till at length she dropped with a strange shriek.' Sergeant Talbot of the same regiment, 'had his head clean carried off by a round shot, yet for about thirty yards further the headless body kept the saddle, the lance at the charge, firmly gripped under the right arm.'[36]

Inevitably the pace quickened, 'every man feeling convinced that the quicker he rode . . . the better chance he would have of escaping unhurt.'[37] The fact that the valley sloped downwards towards the enemy did not make it easier to maintain a steady pace. 'We should all have been knocked over', wrote an officer of the 13th, 'only we went as hard as we could split, and they [the enemy] did not shoot forward enough from the flanks.'[38] Another witness states that 'luckily a great many of their shells burst too high'.[39] Early on, when Captain White of the 17th was about to overtake his brigade commander, Cardigan placed his sword across the Captain's breast to restrain him.[40] But before long even Cardigan himself, to avoid being engulfed by his men, was forced into a gallop. 'The Light Brigade', wrote a non-commissioned officer of the Heavy Brigade, 'went so rapid that we almost lost sight of them.'[41]

Lucan himself at this time was riding with his staff as link between the Light Brigade and Scarlett who was leading the Greys and the Royals.

'The rest of the Heavy Brigade', wrote the colonel of the

Royals, 'tho' stated to be likewise here in Ld Lucan's report were safe in the rear* shewing how inaccurate are these reports, for it was only Royals and Greys this time; and in a few moments we were in the hottest fire that was probably ever witnessed. The Regts were beautifully steady. I never had a better line in a Field Day, the only swerving was to let through the ranks the wounded & dead men & horses of the Light Brigade, which were even then thickly scattered over the plain. It was a fearful sight I assure you, and the appearance of all who retired was as if they had passed through a heavy shower of blood, positively dripping and saturated, and shattered arms blowing back like empty sleeves, as the poor fellows ran to the rear. During all this time there was a constant squibbing noise around me, proving even in these improved days of gunnery what numbers of shot do not take effect. However another moment & my horse was shot on the right flank. A few fatal paces further & my left leg was shattered.'[42]

Lucan himself was slightly wounded in the leg, an aide-de-camp was killed and two of his staff officers were wounded or unhorsed, before he made what was undoubtedly a wise and courageous decision. Remarking that the heavies 'were sufficiently close to protect the Light cavalry should they be pursued by the enemy', and that he 'could not allow them to be sacrificed as had been the Light Brigade', he ordered the two regiments to halt. Kinglake says that Scarlett, at this moment noticing that his men were retiring, and not realizing that Lucan had ordered the movement, 'sent back his trumpeter with orders to sound the halt. At the sound the brigade instantly halted, and fronted beautifully, as at a parade.'[43]

Writing some years later Lucan stated: 'Had not the Chasseurs d'Afrique at this time silenced one of these batteries, it is my opinion that the Heavy Cavalry would have been destroyed.'[44] This is very likely. The French help was both timely and substantial for all the British cavalry. Earlier in the day, as has been seen, General d'Allonville's brigade of two regiments of Chasseurs d'Afrique had been ordered down into the plain by General Canrobert. Conse-

* Nevertheless the 5th Dragoon Guards suffered more casualties at this stage of the battle than in the Heavy Brigade charge. Further, Colonel Hodge says of the 4th Dragoon Guards: 'We advanced to cover their [the Light Brigade's] retreat but the batteries got our range and began cutting us up terribly. I was not sorry when [we] were ordered to retreat.' (25 Oct, 1854, Anglesey: *Hodge*, 50.)

quently these regiments, consisting of French troopers mounted on Algerian horses, and with a distinguished fighting record in North Africa behind them, had for some hours been drawn up to the left rear of the British cavalry.*

General Morris, the commander of the French cavalry division, was himself present with them, and as soon as he saw that Cardigan was advancing straight down the valley, he decided to use two squadrons of one of d'Allonville's regiments (the 4th) to attack the guns on the Fediukine heights. After 'stealing up on them up the hill'[45] and charging over very rough ground, these 150 veterans under Major Abdelal, succeeded in dislodging and silencing the Russian battery. They were then attacked and forced to withdraw by two Russian infantry battalions, losing in the process ten men killed and twenty-eight wounded. By any standards Abdelal's action was brave and skilfully executed. It ensured that the remnants of the Light Brigade, as they returned from the charge, were only molested from one flank. There is evidence that some of the Chasseurs d'Afrique also deterred the cossacks who harassed the returning men of the Light Brigade. 'A party of Chasseurs d'Afrique', wrote Trooper Mitchell of the 13th of his return on foot, 'showed themselves menacingly. [This] had the desired effect of turning the cossacks from their purpose.'[46]

* * *

'We reached the battery', wrote Cardigan, 'in a very good line, and at the regulated charging pace; and here many officers and men were killed.'[47] Lieutenant Wombwell, immediately behind the Brigade commander, saw that 'just as he got close up to a gun, it went off [as did all the others, in a final salvo], luckily without touching him, and not being able to see from the smoke he rode right up against the gun.'[48] At this moment Wombwell's horse was shot under him. So was many another, including that of Captain Tremayne of the 13th. 'The last thing I heard', he wrote later, 'before I went down, was one man saying to his neighbour, "Come on; don't let those —— [17th Lancers] get ahead of us." '[49] Lieutenant Anstruther Thomson, also of the 13th, found it 'a fine sight to see the fellows sit down and put their heads straight at the guns.'[50]

As Cardigan led in, riding between two of the guns, he kept

---

* As is mentioned in Raglan's 'Fourth Order' (see p. 83).

'straight forward at the same pace', until, emerging from the pall of smoke, about eighty yards behind the guns, he came upon the first line of Russian cavalry. 'Being alone there', he wrote some years later, 'in consequence of the officers of my Staff being wounded or disabled, I was attacked by two Cossacks, slightly wounded [in the ribs], and nearly dismounted.'[51] Captain Percy Smith of the 13th, in the few seconds before he had to defend himself, noticed that Cardigan kept his 'sword at the slope and did not seem to take any trouble to defend himself.'[52] Cardigan's account continued:

> 'On being nearly surrounded by Cossacks [who probably wished to capture so glittering a prize], I gradually retreated until I reached the battery. . . . In that position . . . I could see none of the first line or of the supports. . . . The first line did not follow me. . . . They passed off to the left to avoid Russian limber-carriages, or retreated [because they were wounded or horseless].'[53]

This seems to have been the truth and in consequence Cardigan rode slowly back along the valley. Much ill-informed criticism was, for many years, levelled at him for 'not having brought his Brigade out of action'.[54]* His own view was that 'it is quite sufficient for a general of brigade to return with as well as lead the attack of the front line, unless he should by chance come in contact with his supports, in which case he would remain with them.'[55]

Since Cardigan found himself, through no fault of his own, virtually alone,† being chased by a number of cossacks, it is hard to see that he had any alternative but to retire as he did. 'What', he asked Kinglake, 'was the duty of the Brigadier under such circumstances? In such a desperate *mêlée* to remain to be taken prisoner, or was it his duty to retire?'[56]

It seems probable, too, that, as he claimed, he did not 'come in contact with his supports'. Paget, who was commanding them, had failed to control the 8th Hussars, (which regiment lost pace and disappeared to the right), and in trying to do so let the first line get

---

* Lord George Paget's *Journal,* published after Cardigan's death, revived the criticism; but many of Paget's strictures are too obviously 'interested' to be reliable.

† It is possible that with him, throughout, was Cornet Yates, Adjutant of the 11th Hussars. Yates had been acting as Brigade Major to the Light Brigade during the illness of Lieutenant-Colonel Mayow, the proper Brigade Major. Mayow in fact turned out that morning so as not to miss the battle. (See p. 87.)

12. Captain Brown, 4th Light Dragoons, with his servant in winter dress in the cavalry camp, Crimea

13. Captain Burton, commanding the 5th Dragoon Guards in the Crimea

14. The cavalry camp in the Crimea, looking towards Kadikoi

15. Officers and men of the 8th Hussars in the Crimea

too far ahead.* (See pp. 99–100.) Cardigan also believed that even if he had come upon parts of his brigade, 'No general officer could have been of any use. The feeble remains of the lines of the brigade could have done nothing more under a general officer than they did under their own officers.'[57]

* * *

Meanwhile the remnants of the first line had reached the guns under a pall of smoke from the gunners' final salvo. Some of the Russian artillerymen took refuge under their carriages and limbers, but most strove with magnificent courage to remove their guns. Some of these brave men were cut down or pierced by lances.

About twenty men of the 17th had, in fact, outflanked the battery on the left. Led by Captain Morris, they galloped beyond the smoke and found themselves facing a block of regular hussars. Morris at once attacked, shouting as he advanced: 'Now remember what I have told you, men, and keep together.'[58] Receiving the charge at the halt the Russians broke and fled in disorder; but some of them rallied and before long were joined by swarms of cossacks. The fate of this valiant little band of British Lancers was sealed. Morris himself, severely wounded in numerous places, was forced to surrender, but as it happened only temporarily. A very few others managed to escape back along the valley.

At the same time the rest of the first line who were still mounted and unhurt rallied under Lieutenant-Colonel Mayow, the Brigade Major. With them he charged at the Russian cavalry in rear of the guns. So, too, did Sergeant O'Hara of the 17th, with another group, and Corporal Morley, (who was heard bellowing in his Nottinghamshire accent: 'Coom 'ere! Coom 'ere! Fall in, lads, fall in!'), with yet another.[59] These three small parties kept the enemy horsemen at bay and even drove them back a considerable distance, until the 11th Hussars, followed by the 4th Light Dragoons, galloped through the battery.

* * *

* Kinglake says that 'an officer of great authority who was so placed in the field as to be highly capable of forming a correct judgment of the effect of the smoke and other baffling causes, believed that whilst the three supporting regiments were advancing, it would have been quite possible for Lord Cardigan to ride back between two of those regiments without seeing either of them.' (Kinglake (1877), V, 363.)

To Lieutenant-Colonel Douglas, commanding the 11th, as his regiment advanced, the first line had appeared 'to *dissolve*' in the smoke. A minute or so later, his right squadron crashed through the right of the battery, in the footsteps as it were of the 17th. Douglas, like Morris before him, then charged a body of Russian cavalry to his left front, thinking to '*jam* them into the gorge of the valley here forming a sort of cul-de-sac . . . as the Aqueduct and the river Tchernaya barred any hasty egress. I, strange to say, was all along impressed with the idea that we were being supported, and that shortly, both infantry and fresh cavalry would come up.'[60] But, since no supports materialized, and he was faced by large numbers of fresh horsemen, Douglas (again like Morris before him), having driven the enemy back in some disorder, was forced to retire. As he did so, he joined up with the 4th Light Dragoons under Paget, who had just led his regiment through the battery. Together they began slowly, and in as much order as could be contrived, to make their way back up the valley. The officers and men of both the 11th and the 4th found that those of the Russian gun teams who had escaped alive from the first line's onslaught, were attempting to drag their guns away. There followed, according to Paget,

> 'some fierce hand-to-hand encounters, and our fellows, in the excitement of the moment, lost sight, I fear, of the chief power of their sabres, and for the *point* . . . substituted the muscle of their arms, in the indiscriminate appliance of the cut, which generally fell harmlessly on the thick greatcoats of the Russians.'

Lieutenant Hunt of the 4th even jumped from his horse, amidst the *mêlée*, and tried to unhook the traces from one of the guns to prevent its removal.[61] Before the 4th had reached the guns, Trooper Mitchell of the 13th, whose leg was trapped beneath his dying horse, yelled, 'For God's sake don't ride over me!'[62] He was untouched, but others of the first line were trampled on by their comrades in the second.

Other hazards encountered by the second line were the crazed, bewildered, riderless horses of the first. Paget, riding alone in front of the 4th, was 'a marked object for the poor dumb brutes. . . . They made dashes at me . . . cringing in on me, and positively squeezing me . . . my overalls being a mass of blood from their gory flanks. They nearly upset me . . . and I had several times to use my sword.'[63]

*　　*　　*

The combined remnants of the 11th and 4th soon found their retreat barred by two squadrons of Russian Lancers.

'Helter-skelter then we went at these Lancers', wrote Paget in his *Journal*, 'as fast as our poor tired horses could carry us, rear rank of course in front (as far as anything by this time could be called a "front"), the officers of course in the rear, for it must be remembered that we still had our pursuers behind us. . . .

'A few of [the Russian Lancers] came into momentary collision with . . . our fellows, but beyond this, strange as it may sound, they did nothing, and actually allowed us to shuffle, to edge away, by them, at a distance of hardly a horse's length.'[64]

* * *

What, meanwhile, had been happening to the 8th Hussars? Paget states that, when the second line moved off, his order to Lieutenant-Colonel Shewell, its commanding officer,* had been '4th Light Dragoons will direct.'[65] If this order was in fact given, it was certainly not obeyed. Shewell not only kept his regiment's pace well down below that of the 4th on his left, but also veered so much to the right that visual connection between the two regiments was virtually severed. Paget was no doubt attempting to keep up with the first line so as to give it that 'best support' which Cardigan had asked for. Shewell, on the other hand, probably thought his first duty was to keep firm control of his men, which of course was

---

* Shewell, a very strict and religious man, rose from his sick bed to take part in the battle. When he was seen galloping up to take command one of his troopers exclaimed: 'Well, I'm d——d if it isn't the Colonel; what do you say to the "old woman" now?' Another of his men saw him, a few moments later, very angry.

' "What's this? What's this? – one, two, four, six, seven men *smoking*! – Swords drawn, and seven men smoking! – Why, the thing is inconceivable! Sergeant – Sergeant Pickworth", he calls out. And the truth is, we were warming our noses each with a short black pipe, and thinking no harm of the matter. "I never heard of such a thing", the Colonel said, "and no regiment except an 'Irish' regiment would be guilty of it. Sergeant, advance and take these men's names. . . . I'll have this breach of discipline punished." I understand that one [man] *was* punished next day.' ('The Charge . . . by one who was in it', Murray, I, 435–6.)

easier to achieve at a steady pace than at a headlong gallop. The result was that the first line was certainly not supported as it should have been.

The 8th, like all the other regiments, much decimated in the advance, bypassed the battery 'at a distance of a few horses' lengths from its (proper) left flank'.[66] Shewell then found himself in a vacuum, as it were, some 300 or 400 yards to his right rear of the silenced guns. He halted.

At this particular moment, Mayow and Douglas were still driving back the Russian cavalry, and Paget was not far behind them, all well to the left front of the 8th. But Shewell had not been halted more than a minute or two when he saw Mayow with his knot of 17th Lancers starting to retire. Taking these under his command, he set off back down the valley. At once he was faced with three squadrons of Russian lancers. These had debouched from under the Causeway Heights to cut off the British retreat. Before they had time to complete a line, Shewell 'charged bang through them', as one of his officers wrote, 'thus opening a way for the remnants of the first line'.[67] The enemy lancers were scattered.*

*   *   *

'A great many wounded and disabled had already passed to the rear by the left of "C" Troop [Royal Horse Artillery]', noted its commander, when Lord Cardigan 'rode up at a quiet pace' to one of the guns which was placed not far behind No. 2 redoubt. He had no one with him except Cornet Yates (see p. 96).

> 'His horse seemed to have had enough of it, and his lordship appeared to have been knocked about, but was cool and col-

* Lieutenant Edward Seager, adjutant of the 8th, wrote to his wife, two days after the battle:

> 'I suppose you would like to know what I had about me through all this danger. In my sabretash was your's and the darling children's picture, my dear mother's present (Prayer Book and Testament), very small writing case with a lot of letters in it, and in the pocket of my jacket was your letter containing dear little Emily's hair which has been there since I received it. In my haversack was some biscuits and a bottle with some whiskey and water in it, and very useful I find it. In my pocket some sovereigns and also some Turkish coins, and around my neck was the dear locket you gave me in Exeter. All these I turn out with, just the same as putting on my sword and revolver.' (Lt E. Seager, 8th Hussars, 26–27 Oct 1854, in Murray, II, 442.)

lected. He returned his sword, undid a little of the front of his dress, and pulled down his under-clothing under his waist-belt (military men who have even had a simple set-to at single-stick, mounted, with a sword-belt on, will easily understand this). He then in a quiet way, as if rather talking to himself, said, "I tell you what it is – those instruments of theirs", alluding to the Russian weapons, "are deuced blunt; they tickle up one's ribs! [referring to the slight wound given him by the cossacks]". . . . After this, he asked, "Has any one seen my regiment?" '

Being answered in the negative, he rode off 'in the direction of the enemy,* met the 8th Hussars, and returned with them. In passing the Heavies, the latter cheered. Lord Cardigan acknowledged it with his sword.'[68]

He then, according to his own version, spoke to Scarlett. 'What do you think, General', he said, 'of the aide-de-camp [Nolan], after such an order being brought to us which has destroyed the Light Brigade, riding to the rear and screaming like a woman?' Scarlett replied, 'Do not say more, for I have ridden over his body.'[69] Cardigan then rode on to where the survivors of the Light Brigade were assembling.

For most of these the ordeal had been ghastly. Those few who still had horses unhurt were best off, but even they could only move slowly, for their mounts were exhausted and they had to toil uphill. The rest, some 130 wounded and twice that number unhorsed, straggled along, some crawling, some limping, others running, some dragging loved horses bleeding to death behind them. At first they were harried by knots of cossacks and lancers, but these roving bodies of horsemen were soon obliged to retire so as to avoid the fire of their own guns and rifles from the Causeway Heights and (to a much reduced degree) from the Fediukine Heights.

As they reached safety, some of the men 'reeling in their saddles', called out to the horse artillerymen as they passed, 'Lads, look at my poor broken arm (or leg)'. The officers of "C" Troop 'held their flasks to these men's mouths as long as the contents lasted',[70] while Mr Cruickshank, a commissariat officer, arrived on his pony 'with saddle bags filled with bottles of rum'.[71]

* That Cardigan thus rode back towards the enemy to look for the remnants of his brigade is confirmed by other accounts. (For example: Thomson, 187; Mitchell, 79.)

Among so many grim and distressing sights, there were some touches of humour. For instance, Lieutenant Chamberlayne of the 13th was seen approaching with his saddle carried on his head. A fellow officer, finding him seated beside his dead horse, wondering what to do next, had told him: 'Another horse you can get, but you will not get another saddle so easily.' It was thought that Chamberlayne saved his life in this way, being taken for a fellow pillager by the marauding cossacks.[72] The same may have applied to others. When, for example, Colonel Shewell's Field Trumpeter's horse was shot dead, its owner stripped it of his kit and carried it on his arm all the way back up the valley, and was quite unhurt.[73]

*   *   *

Cardigan estimated that 'the whole affair, from the moment we moved off until we re-formed on the ground from which we started, did not occupy more than 20 minutes.' This was also Scarlett's guess.[74] 'On the troops forming up', Cardigan's account continues, 'I had them counted by my Brigade-Major, and found that there were 195 mounted men out of about 670.'[75] He then addressed the survivors, saying: 'Men! It is a mad-brained trick, but it is no fault of mine.'[76] To this some of the men replied, 'Never mind, my lord! We are ready to go again', Cardigan answering: 'No, no, men! You have done enough.'[77]

Next he sought out d'Allonville and thanked him warmly for his timely help, before riding off to report to Raglan who with his staff had descended into the valley. 'What did you mean, sir,' asked the Commander-in-Chief, 'by attacking a battery in front, contrary to all the usages of warfare, and the customs of the service?'

'My Lord', replied Cardigan, 'I hope you will not blame me, for I received the order to attack from my superior officer in front of the troops.'[78]

Not long after this exchange, an infantry lieutenant came across the commander of the Light Brigade, and declared that he had 'never seen a man so grieved'.[79] Later that evening, he wrapped himself in his cloak and lay down beside an aide-de-camp's camp fire, and soon fell asleep beneath the stars. He is said, later still, to have returned aboard his yacht to spend the night.

To Lucan that evening Raglan said: 'Lord Lucan, you were a Lieutenant-General and should therefore have exercised your discretion, and, not approving of the charge, should not have caused it to be made.' Lucan replied, in writing, before he went to bed: 'I gave the order to charge under what I considered a most imperious necessity, and I will not bear one particle of the blame.'[80]

*　　*　　*

The muster figure of 195 mounted men, given by Cardigan, bears no relation, of course, to the total number of officers and men of the Light Brigade who avoided being killed, returned wounded or were taken prisoner, many of whom turned up later. The figure for these has been computed at 416, which makes the brigade's total loss for the day, 245, or 37% of the 661 believed to have been present in the charge. Of this figure 118 were killed and 127 returned as wounded.[*] Kinglake's figures vary slightly from these (113 killed and 134 wounded). He adds that 475 horses were killed (including forty-three shot as unserviceable on account of their wounds), and forty-two wounded. This is almost certainly too great a number. Whinyates' figure of 362 seems more realistic.[81][†] Something like forty-five officers and men were taken prisoner. All of these were wounded or unhorsed. Paget's orderly, Parkes, who was awarded the Victoria Cross, was one of them. General Liprandi, when Parkes and other prisoners were brought before him, took some convincing that the whole brigade had not been drunk. He was astonished, too, at the size of the men before him. 'If you are a Light Dragoon', he asked Parkes, 'what sort of men are your Heavy Dragoons?!' After an initial roughness, the Russians treated their prisoners well, and respected them. 'Ay, my Lord,' Parkes told Paget on his return (by exchange in December, 1855), 'the officers were not ashamed of being seen walking about with us.'[82]

Another who was taken prisoner was Private Wightman of the 17th Lancers.

[*] For comparison, it is interesting to note that the generally accepted figure of casualties in the 23rd Light Dragoons in their charge at Talavera, is 207, which was nearly half the regiment's strength (see Vol. I, p. 50). Another charge which is more or less comparable, was that of the 3rd Light Dragoons at Mudki. The regiment is usually debited with ninety-six casualties out of the 497 men who took part (see Vol. I, p. 250). These figures have not, of course, been subjected to the minute scrutiny given to those of the Light Brigade charge, and may well be more than marginally inaccurate.

[†] The Russians killed and wounded for the whole day were about 627. (Kinglake (1877), V, 326, quoting Todleben, F. E. I. *Défence de Sébastopol*, 2 vols, 1863–70 (translated from the Russian).)

'My horse was shot dead', he wrote, 'riddled with bullets. One bullet struck me on the forehead, another passed through the top of my shoulder; while struggling out from under my dead horse a Cossack standing over me stabbed me with his lance once in the neck near the jugular, again above the collar bone, several times in the back, and once under the short rib; and when, having regained my feet, I was trying to draw my sword, he sent his lance through the palm of my hand. I believe he would have succeeded in killing me, clumsy as he was, if I had not blinded him for the moment with a handful of sand.'

Wightman and another prisoner, Fletcher, also wounded, were driven on by the application of the cossacks' lance-butts to their backs.

'With my shattered knee and the other bullet wound on the shin of the same leg, I could barely limp, and good old Fletcher said "Get on my back, chum!" I did so, and then found that he had been shot through the back of the head. When I told him of this, his only answer was, "Oh, never mind that, it's not much, I don't think." But it was that much that he died of the wound a few days later; and here he was, a doomed man himself, making light of a mortal wound, and carrying a chance comrade of another regiment on his back. I can write this, but I could not tell of it in speech, because I know I should play the woman.'[83]

Another prisoner who perhaps takes the prize for toughness was a man of the 11th Hussars. He received thirty-one lance and sword wounds, was two days without having his wounds dressed, and then spent three months in hospital before being taken north 800 versts. He was exchanged in November, 1855.[84]

*   *   *

One officer, four non-commissioned officers and one private of the Light Brigade received the newly instituted Victoria Cross for their bravery in the charge. The officer was Lieutenant A. R. Dunn of the 11th Hussars. Sergeant-Major Loy Smith saw him, behind the guns, 'a fine young fellow, standing 6 ft 3 inches, and mounted on a powerful horse, and wielding a terrific sword, many inches longer than the regulation. . . . He saved the life of Serjt Bentley when surrounded by Russians, by cutting them down right and left.'[85]

*   *   *

Raglan, it is believed, still wished to re-capture the three lost re-doubts. He certainly had to hand a sufficiently strong force of infantry to do so successfully; but Canrobert dissuaded him, on the grounds that to hold them it would be necessary to weaken the already inadequate force besieging Sebastopol. The chief immediate result of the battle, therefore, was that the Woronzoff road was denied to the British for communication between base and siege camp. Neither commander, it seems, appreciated the importance of the road. Without it only rough and sometimes precipitous tracks were available, and these were to form the bottleneck which so aggravated the cruel hardships of the winter ahead.

*   *   *

The moral effect of both cavalry brigades' actions in the battle was considerable. It is probable that, in Kinglake's words, 'for a long time afterwards it would have been impracticable to make the Russian cavalry act with anything like confidence in the presence of a few English squadrons.'[86]

The iron discipline of the Light Brigade, and the absolute steadi-ness of Cardigan's bearing at its head, rightly earned it immortality. The fact that a battery of guns had been totally silenced by a frontal assault, and that a vastly superior cavalry force had been, in Todle-ben's words, 'utterly overthrown',[87] was an astonishing achievement.

Of Cardigan's part, Raglan wrote privately that he had 'acted throughout with the greatest steadiness and gallantry, as well as perseverance'.[88] He called the charge 'perhaps the finest thing ever attempted', and in a General Order he spoke of the 'gallantry' dis-played by the officers and men, 'and the coolness and perseverance with which they executed one of the most arduous attacks that ever was witnessed.'[89]

It showed that under different circumstances − where supports could be provided − cavalry was still capable of performing a valu-able role, not only as advance and flank guards and reconnaisance patrols, but also in the charge.

*   *   *

It produced, too, the most famous poem about cavalry in action ever written. Tennyson wrote 'The Charge of the Light Brigade' on 2 December, 1854 'in a few minutes, after reading . . . *The Times* in which occurred the phrase "some one had blundered", and this was the origin of the metre of his poem.' In fact the *Times* editorial (13 November, 1854) spoke of 'some hideous blunder'. The poem was drastically revised in 1855, but Tennyson soon deplored the alterations which he had made, and reverted the following year to the 1854 version with only a few minor modifications. It was not, he declared, 'a poem on which I pique myself'.[90]

I

Half a league, half a league,
  Half a league onward,
All in the valley of Death
  Rode the six hundred.
'Forward, the Light Brigade!
Charge for the guns!' he said:
Into the valley of Death
  Rode the six hundred.

II

'Forward, the Light Brigade!'
Was there a man dismayed?
Not though the soldier knew
  Some one had blundered:
Their's not to make reply,
Their's not to reason why,
Their's but to do and die:
Into the valley of Death
  Rode the six hundred.

III

Cannon to right of them,
Cannon to left of them,
Cannon in front of them
  Volleyed and thundered:
Stormed at with shot and shell,
Boldly they rode and well,
Into the jaws of Death,
Into the mouth of Hell
  Rode the six hundred.

IV

Flashed all their sabres bare,
Flashed as they turned in air
Sabring the gunners there,
Charging an army, while
　All the world wondered:
Plunged in the battery-smoke
Right through the line they broke;
Cossack and Russian
Reeled from the sabre-stroke
　Shattered and sundered.
Then they rode back, but not
　Not the six hundred.

V

Cannon to right of them,
Cannon to left of them,
Cannon behind them
　Volleyed and thundered;
Stormed at with shot and shell,
While horse and hero fell,
They that had fought so well
Came through the jaws of Death,
Back from the mouth of Hell,
All that was left of them,
　Left of six hundred.

VI

When can their glory fade?
O the wild charge they made!
　All the world wondered.
Honour the charge they made!
Honour the Light Brigade,
　Noble six hundred!

*　*　*

The controversy which for many years followed the Light Brigade's action in the battle of Balaklava, took two main forms. The first, which has been dealt with, was the question of Cardigan's personal movements. The second was the question of who was responsible for the disaster. Cardigan, it is clear, can bear no part of the blame. Nolan may well have been intemperate in his language to Lucan, but at worst that cannot be held to have been more than a very minor contributory factor. Raglan's orders, by the standards of later generations, were far from being models of clarity. Nevertheless had Lucan remained calm, set aside his contempt for the Commander of the Forces, and applied his undoubted intelligence to trying to see what they meant, he would not have gone far wrong. There seems to be almost nothing to excuse Lucan's behaviour except his courage in stopping the Heavy Brigade when he did. He misinterpreted orders. He failed to use his discretion. He did not ask for the help of the French cavalry. He made no use of his horse artillery.

Raglan, in his despatch, tried to make his inevitable censure as mild as possible. He suggested that there had been 'some misconception of the order to advance' and that Lucan 'fancied he had no discretion to exercise'. With this Lucan was not satisfied. He wanted total exculpation, and wrote to the Duke of Newcastle, the Secretary at War, demanding it. This it was, of course, impossible to grant, and the Duke rightly decided that the commander of the Cavalry Division must be recalled. 'It is quite a relief to get rid of Lord Lucan', wrote Cornet Fisher of the 4th Dragoon Guards. 'Poor old man, he was a horrid old fellow.'[91]

The commander of the Light Brigade also went home. A medical board recommended that Cardigan 'be allowed to proceed to England' as he was suffering from diarrhoea which on occasion 'assumed a dysenteric form' and that he had 'for several years past been afflicted with pains and difficulty in voiding his urine, and that these symptoms in consequence of exposure and hardship have recently become much aggravated.'[92]

Neither Lucan nor Cardigan behaved, when at home, with discretion. Cardigan's head was soon turned by the excessive public adulation which he received, while Lucan first applied for (and was refused) a court-martial, and then abused his position as a peer by airing his grievances in the House of Lords. He died in 1888, aged eighty-eight, having risen, though he was never again employed, to the rank of Field-Marshal. Cardigan became Inspector-General of Cavalry in 1855, and died a Lieutenant-General in 1868, as the result of a fall from his horse. He was seventy-one.

His career and character have been written about so often that it has not been thought necessary to describe them yet again in detail.

The vast sums which he spent on his commissions and regimental commands have been referred to in Volume I. So has his notorious duel with Captain Tuckett. (See Vol. I, pp. 161, 175–6.) It is enough here to state that 'Jim the Bear', as the men of the 11th Hussars called him, was, as he showed at Balaklava, a superlatively brave soldier. He was also an insufferable cad. He behaved towards women like an insensitive, overbearing, over-rich, spoilt child. He was inexorably vindictive towards officers whose attention to the letter of military discipline was less than his own. Cardigan's self-confidence was almost inhuman. His pettiness knew no bounds. His persecutions of junior officers who got on the wrong side of him were numerous and vicious. In one famous case he made life hell for Captain Reynolds because he introduced a 'black bottle' to the immaculate table of the 11th. He received censure after censure from successive commanders-in-chief. But he treated his seniors with at least as much contempt as he did his juniors. To these censures he paid not the slightest attention.

Yet he had redeeming features. The rank and file who served under him mingled genuine respect with their deference. From their point of view he was a strict but just commanding officer. On one occasion he was much criticized for allowing a flogging on a Sunday. It so happens that the reponsibility for this was not his. His record as regards corporal punishment was in fact a good one. For instance not a single man was flogged in the 11th between 1839 and 1841.[93]

'Success has indeed been obtained, but its cost
has been great.'

W. H. RUSSELL, *The Times'* war correspondent

'After an army had sunk to the lowest degree of
misery and helplessness ever known, short of
extinction, it was lifted up into a condition of
high health and efficiency, with the lowest rate
of mortality on record.'

HARRIET MARTINEAU[1]

(viii)

*Crimean War, 1854–56: battle of Inkerman – great
storm – winter's hardships – cavalry employed on commissariat work – heavy losses of horses – death of
Raglan – Sebastopol falls – war ends*

Two nights after the battle of Balaklava, some hundred Russian
cavalry horses broke loose from their lines, and thundered into the
British camp. Though these provided extraordinarily welcome remounts for the Light Brigade, within three weeks most of them had
been transferred to the artillery whose need had become by then
operationally greater.

Five days later an officer of the Brigade reported that 'all the
chargers belonging to the poor fellows who were killed, were sold
by auction today and fetched very low prices.' This is not surprising
as the prospect of being able to maintain extra privately-owned
horses was not a bright one. On the other hand, the dead officers'
warm clothing and preserved fruits fetched fantastic prices. 'A
couple of cotton night caps', for instance, sold for a guinea; a pair of
'leather gloves lined with wool' for 33s, and 'two small pots of
cocoa' for 24s each. Useless clothing, however, went for a song: one
Hussar jacket, for example, worth £40 when new, though in good
condition, sold for only 46s.[2]

*   *   *

On 5 November, in a thick fog, the Russians, with very superior
numbers, tried and failed to overwhelm the British right at Inkerman. The rocky, confined nature of the ground made it impossible

for cavalry to operate, though the remnant of the Light Brigade was present, and for a time under fire. The battle, which consisted largely of a series of separate, heroically fought infantry combats, lasted eight hours. It was the bloodiest slogging-match since Waterloo. Though the Russians were everywhere repulsed with enormous casualties (which they could well afford), the battle from the Allies' point of view was negative. After it, there seemed even less hope of an immediate storming of Sebastopol, particularly as 2,500 of the army's best men had been killed or wounded. It was now certain that the winter would have to be spent in the Crimea.

It started with a bang. On 14 November a storm of major proportions overwhelmed the peninsula. 'Everything', noted one officer, 'went whiz bang in less time than I have taken to tell you.'[3] Tents went flying, so did anything which was not extremely well tethered. Even heavy wagons were lifted from the ground, dragging their oxen with them. 'Helmets, forage-caps, cocked hats, cork mattresses, air pillows, etc., were blown away through the air like feathers.' Every tent in the Heavy Brigade camp was blown down

'except', noted an officer of horse artillery, 'Lord Lucan's, which happened to be pitched in a sort of gully. . . . The hospital marquee was blown down first; it was full of sick men. Some were dying, and there were one or two dead bodies in the araba alongside waiting interment; the marquee was blown over the latter. . . . Many horses got loose, the picket posts of a whole squadron of the Greys gave way, and the animals started off still fastened to the lines and stumps of posts, going before the wind, to all appearance, as if they had no control over themselves, and were blown away in company with any amount of small stones and loose earth. . . . The only living things that seemed at all at home were Lord Lucan's pair of free-and-easy mules which he had for drawing his cooking-cart, etc., and which, according to custom, gave themselves up to plunder. These animals were not at all shy; when loose at night, as they usually were, they would silently poke their heads, ears and all into any tent not properly secured, and make free with the men's biscuit.'[4]

'A bloody battle, to perish by cold, or a Russian prison now seem our only prospects',[5] wrote Colonel Hodge of the 4th Dragoon Guards the day after the great storm. Certainly morale was low, and with good reason, for the loss of stores was well nigh catastrophic.

'Oh! that hurricane!' wrote an officer of the 8th Hussars. 'I can never forget the awful sight! Outside the harbour, *ten vessels* lost with nearly all hands.'[6] The greatest single loss was the screw-steamer *Prince* which was smashed up on the rocks in the outer anchorage. With her went to the bottom 'everything that was most wanted',[7] including boots for almost the whole army, and 40,000 greatcoats. 'With such another gale', wrote an horse artillery officer, 'we shall be eating our horses.'[8]

Even before the storm, Mr Filder, the Commissary General, was, as he wrote home to the Treasury,

'full of apprehension as to our power of keeping this Army supplied during the coming winter. . . . In this crowded little harbour . . . we can do little more than land sufficient supplies to keep pace with the daily consumption of the troops; and to add to our difficulties, the road from the harbour to the camp, not being a made one, is impassable after heavy rains.'[9]*

Now, after the storm, the supply difficulties were gravely increased. Already the inadequacy of the existing wharves at Balaklava was chronic. They had a frontage of not more than seventy-five feet for the landing of everything needed by 26,000 men. Once ashore, every pound of stores had to be transported along the one narrow road, for a distance of seven, eight or nine miles to the front. As the winter advanced, this muddy track quickly became impassable to all forms of wheeled traffic. The experience of Colonel Hodge of the 4th Dragoon Guards, who set off at daybreak on 29 November to post the vedettes, well illustrates what he situation on the road was like:

'I could hardly struggle thro' the mud', he wrote in his diary. 'I found several commissariat carts broken down upon the road. One had a barrel of rum in it, which had been tapped, and drunken infantry soldiers were lying about in every direction. Also many men from the Greys on picket were drunk. Some miserable recruits of the 97th [Foot] just landed were struggling up the muddy hill. . . . They had been all night trying to move up, but could not proceed, they were so overloaded and weak.'[10]

* * *

* When the roads became impassable for the arabas (bullock carts) these 'were turned into fuel and the cattle were eaten.' (Asst Comm. Gen. A. Crookshank, *Chelsea Board*, 224.)

The Light Brigade, at the special request of the French, was stationed between 30 October and 3 December on the heights not far from the Inkerman windmill, and eight miles from Balaklava.* It suffered therefore considerably more, during those first weeks of winter, from exposure and supply deficiencies than the Heavy Brigade, which quite soon moved much closer to Balaklava. During the last three weeks of November, the horses of the Light Brigade 'had on an average only about 1/5th of their regulated rations.'[11] In the course of their move 'from the heights to their present camp' stated Colonel Doherty of the 13th, 'although all the horses were led, about 17 fell dead on the road from sheer exhaustion.' He noted, incidentally, that 'the well-bred horses, especially the Irish, stood the work and exposure better than the low-bred horses, more particularly such as were of small size.'[12]

The Light Brigade suffered, also, in another respect from being so far from the source of supply. Even when their commissariat officer had transport available at the landing point, 'and a boatload of barley arrives, a dozen or more heavy dragoons, or so many artillerymen, jump in, carry out the sacks, load *their* transport – My few wretched Turks or Maltese having a very poor chance in the *mêlée*.'[13]

The cavalry brigades, once both of them were stationed below the windswept heights, and within a mile or two of the harbour, though very uncomfortable, were infinitely better served than the infantry. At least they were not killed off in their hundreds by exposure to wet and cold, by gross over-work, and by under-nourishment. 'We have every reason to be thankful', wrote Sergeant-Major Cruse of the Royals on 14 January, 1855, 'that our lot is not so bad as the poor infantry in the trenches.' A fortnight later, at the very height of the winter, he told his wife something which some historians tend to forget: 'Take it altogether', he wrote, 'I do not think the weather has been much more severe than it was in Manchester last January, but only fancy, dearest, a camp life, in such weather as that.'[14] On Boxing Day, Captain Portal of the 4th Light Dragoons, wrote: 'We certainly as yet have had nothing to complain of, and I have only just put on my great coat.'[15]

The chief hardships in the cavalry camps fell upon the horses. They could not be sheltered from the elements, and they could not

---

* Cardigan 'understood from General Canrobert personally that he considered it a great object to have the light cavalry brigade there.' (Cardigan's evidence, *Chelsea Board*, 213.)

be adequately fed. Of hay alone, twenty days' supply was lost in the great storm.[16] Already, only three days after that calamity, Captain Portal found his horses 'thin, miserable-looking brutes, covered all over with mud and dirt, the saddlery the same, a mass of mud'.[17]

The Heavy Brigade's first camp, at the same date, was so ill-drained that, according to the commanding officer of the Greys, 'there was a goose swimming in an officer's tent. That would show', he added, 'the quantity of water the horses were standing in.'[18] An infantry officer remarked a week later that the horses of the Light Brigade, in their hunger, were eating 'each other's tails off'.[19] Later on, as Trooper Mitchell, of the 13th, noticed, 'when a horse dropped dead in the lines, the others that could reach it would gnaw the hair off its skin. Saddlery, blankets, ropes, and picket pegs all were eaten by them, and we had to be careful on going near them, or they would seize us by the beard and whiskers for the same purpose.'[20] An officer of the 8th reported: 'They actually come, when loose of a night, and gnaw our tent ropes. . . . These tail-less, maneless, skinny brutes would never be recognised as the remains of five as fine Regts as ever left England.'[21] In early January, Sergeant-Major Cruse of the Royals wrote home that after the horses 'have had a good roll in the mud and after that a good fall of snow, and then the whole to be frozen on to them, it is enough to kill any animal except one cast in bronze.' By 1 February, they were so sore that they could 'scarcely bear to be touched. The mud, having frozen on to them, has taken the hair and in many instances the flesh off their poor bones.'[22]

The parsimonious attitude of peace time which the quarter-masters' departments carried into war did not help. Almost un-believably, in the first week of January, as Lieutenant Wombwell of the 17th wrote home, they 'made the officers give back the warm Turkish horse clothing they allowed them to have [for their own horses] a few days ago, and what is not used by the [troop horses] is to go into store. . . . When the authorities are spoken to about it, they answer, "The officers can buy clothing for their horses themselves. They can afford it." Now clothing is not to be bought or had for love or money.'[23]

*   *   *

'I have just seen', wrote an officer of the 4th Dragoon Guards on 12 December, 'the order for the cavalry to perform the work of the commissariat. 500 horses to be furnished every day. They will have to go down to Balaklava, procure the provisions, and go thence up to the front and back again.'[24] Considering how degrading the role of purveyor to the infantry must have been for the proud British cavalry, officers and men seeing the inescapable necessity for it took the affront to their dignity with resignation – if not with a good grace. Lucan, of course, protested as was his duty. On 17 January he represented to headquarters, not for the first time,

> 'the fearful consequence to the cavalry of having to continue in the discharge ... of duties so totally foreign to their profession. ... Feelings of ... dissatisfaction are felt by the officers ... and in addition, this army is losing a cavalry it will be difficult to replace. ... Since the 12th December, no less than 426 horses have died.*... A cessation of these duties ... might yet ... save 400 or 500 or more.'[25]

All the cavalry is 'used for now', complained one officer, 'is to carry meat (salt pork and beef) to the army on the heights. We call ourselves "the Butcher Boys".'[26] The usual method used was for one horse to be 'ridden by a man, and the other' to carry the supplies. There were no pack-saddles available. Had there been, 'nearly double' the weight which the ordinary regimental saddle would bear, could have been carried.[27]

'I must say', wrote Captain Shakespear of the horse artillery on 22 December, 'it was rather humiliating to the British Cavalry on the 20th to see the French Cavalry pass in front of Balaklava and reconnoitre the enemy.'[28] 'This then', lamented Colonel Hodge, 'is to be our end. ... When all our men's things are destroyed, saddles gone and horses killed they will tell us that we have neglected our regiments. It is too dreadful to think about.'[29]

---

* The loss of cavalry horses from sickness during the six months, October, 1854 to March, 1855, was as follows:

	Strength	Died by sickness	%
Heavy cavalry	1,055	493	47
Light cavalry	1,161	439	38
Total	2,216	932	

(McNeill & Tulloch, 20, 193.)

It took fifty-eight horses in one commissariat party loaded with biscuit for the Light Division, 'from 9 a.m. till $\frac{1}{2}$ past 3 p.m. to get there and back – a distance of nearly six miles. . . . It was most wretched to see the poor troop horses, so weak from cold and starvation. . . . We had to leave several on the road unable to move.'[30]

Initially, the cavalry had also, from time to time, to carry up ammunition for the artillery.

'They placed the shot and shell in sacks, two or four in each, according to size, and tied up the mouth; then, equalizing the weight to the extreme ends, the sack was lifted across the saddle seat, and the men walked on foot, leading their horses from Balaklava to the Right and Left Siege Train Depôts before Sevastopol. This very soon told on the horses' backs, for they were in such poor condition that the wooden arch of the saddle-tree was quite down on the backbone and withers; so after a time it had to be discontinued with the cavalry.'[31]

On their return from the front, they acted as ambulance men, carrying the sick and wounded to what real hospitals existed, and the worst cases to the ships for conveyance to Scutari.

'Just fancy', wrote Lieutenant Heneage of the 8th, 'what a mismanaged army is, when half-dying men have no other conveyance than a trooper to come seven miles to Balaklava in the bitter frost and snow. Constantly they die on the road, either frozen to death or exhausted by the exertion of sitting up on a hard saddle with no covering but a tattered coat and a thin blanket which they have not the strength to hold over their heads.'[32]

To the feelings of Major Forrest of the 4th Dragoon Guards, the sight of these miserable creatures was 'more horrible than the battle-field of Inkerman', many of them 'actually crying: men who probably had fought at Inkerman.'

'Many of these poor fellows', he wrote home, 'were scarcely able to sit on the horses, but were leaning down with their heads resting upon the horses' necks. The road was like a sheet of ice, and though our men led the horses of the most helpless, yet occasionally a horse would slip and fall. One poor creature's foot caught in the stirrup and he would have been dragged, but that I caught hold of the horse's head. The poor man wanted to walk the rest of the way, but he could not have walked 300 yards, so we had to lift him on to the horse again.'[33]

Another trying aspect of these duties was the certainty that there would not now be time, men or horses enough for the erection of shelter for horses and men, just at a moment when hutting material was on the point of arriving from home and elsewhere.* 'But for this constant occupation of the cavalry [in commissariat work]', wrote Lucan in mid-January, 'the hutting would ere this have been completed, and the horses all under cover.'[34] In fact no hutting for the horses was put up until the last days of January, though a sick horse depôt had earlier been established under cover near Lucan's headquarters. This, of course, was only large enough for a small number. According to Colonel Hodge, Lucan

> 'took all the Carpenters and Masons from the regiments and constructed stabling first for his own horses, then for those of his staff, and then he put ten horses a regiment into them as they were built. The situation and construction of these, however, was so bad that they were washed away, and some horses were drowned in them, and they were so close and damp that the glanders broke out amongst the horses he put in, and the last evil was worst than the first. We lost, I think, every horse that was put into them.'[35]

The erection of more makeshift shelter for the horses had been suggested to Lucan soon after the great storm by Colonel Griffiths of the Greys. Lucan's typical reaction was to threaten to place the colonel 'under arrest for presuming such a thing'.[36] Lucan's only justification must be that there was at that time uncertainty as to whether the cavalry camps would stay in the positions they then occupied.†

When the news of the catastrophic destruction of the cavalry reached home, many questions were asked. In reply to some such received by Captain Portal of the 4th Light Dragoons, he wrote:

---

* 'Contracts were entered into in England, about the middle of November, for wooden huts, of which the parts were so fitted that, with the aid of the printed directions and lithographed plans, which accompanied them, the whole might be put together, even by unskilled workmen.' The first cargo of these arrived at Balaklava on 25 December. It required from 250 to 300 men to carry up a single hut for twenty-five men. (McNeill & Tulloch, 33, 35–6.)

† Some officers obtained the services of French soldiers to build shelters for their own horses. (17 Jan 1855, Wombwell; 1 Jan 1855, Anglesey: *Hodge*, 72.)

'You say, "Why did you not skin the dead ones to cover the living?" This would have had no more effect in saving them after they had arrived at the state these were in than the Turkish warm clothing had, in which the horses were ultimately enveloped from their head to their heels. What happened then? Why, the animals lay down in the knee-deep mud and there froze, clothing and all. Then it is said, "You should not have allowed your horses to lie down!" How could you help it when they could not stand up? Then again, "Why did you not rub them with tar or grease?" A nice mess, supposing we could have got any of the former article, tar, than a layer of wet stiff clay freezing hard! Grease certainly could not have been got for love or money, as we could not even get enough to grease our boots with.'[37]

The Crimean Commissioners, who were sent from England in March, 1855 to inquire into the 'Supplies of the British Army',[38] censured the cavalry command for 'want of promptitude or ingenuity in devising . . . some means of temporary shelter, such as saved the baggage-horses of the Sappers and Miners at Balaklava.'[39] Lucan and Cardigan both objected to this and other animadversions in the Commission's report. Later, in 1856, both were exonerated by a Board of General Officers,[40] sitting at Chelsea, which came to be known as the 'whitewashing board'. Before that Board, Lucan gave a fascinating description of the duties of a trooper who was not engaged upon commissariat duties:

'He has to clean his own horse, appointments, arms, and clothing; he has to clean the horses and the horse appointments of the sick, and all men on dismounted duties, such as camp guards, hospital orderlies, cooks, prisoners, butchers, &c.; to attend three stable hours; to water the horses twice daily, a labour . . . sometimes of extraordinary difficulty, and at very great distances; he has to scrape and shovel away and remove to a distance all the dung, mud, &c. from the picket lines. . . . In bad weather he is constantly repitching tents and changing the ground for the picket lines. He has to attend his own or any spare horse when at the forge. He has to go upon divisional, brigade, regimental, and troop fatigues; to clean out the camp, draw provisions, fetch water and wood for the cooks, and carry out all requisitions, sometimes at great distances, for the different supplies for the use of the regiments, such as camp equipage, clothing, arms, and ammunition required for the equipment of man and horse, to bury dead horses of his own regiment and others found near his camp . . . and to attend funerals. To do all this, besides the stable hours, in the short days, he cannot be said to have more than three hours. . . . Those men . . . were still to have leisure to dig and build stables for the horses.'[41]

By the end of February, all the horses that had survived were at last under some sort of cover.

*   *   *

As for the men, as early as 17 November they appeared, according to an officer of the Light Brigade, 'with clothes all in patches, of every colour and size, all begrimed with mud; few have straps, and some no boots; these wear hay bands round their feet. Such is the present appearance of the once smart, clean Lancer, Hussar, and Light Dragoon.'[42] The surgeon of the 11th Hussars was shocked to see 'a man mounted with a boot on one foot only, and a part of a stocking on the other.'[43] In the Heavy Brigade the men were 'wretched objects in their tight coats. They cannot,' remarked Colonel Hodge, 'wear warm things under them.'[44] Sergeant-Major Cruse of the Royals wrote to his wife in early January: 'It is only *the drop of the creature* that keeps us in any sort of spirit now-a-days.'[45]

In the middle of December the cavalrymen received 'woollen Jerseys, which', noted Major Forrest of the 4th Dragoon Guards, 'are a great comfort to them. They were given draws [*sic*] at the same time, but they are so absurdly small that they are useless for any of our men, as are also the greater part of the boots and from the same cause, more particularly as our men are suffering much from swollen feet and legs.'[46]

Food for the men, besides being meagre in quantity, was, as usual, without variety. On 10 February, Colonel Hodge went 'round the men's dinner' and found 'all very beastly, mud and Salt Pork.' 'Wet feet and Salt Pork', he thought were the main causes of the men's sickness.[47] As a result of the great storm, supplies of rice were completely cut off. This deprived the men of 'the only vegetable food they had except biscuit'.[48] As for the salt beef, it was generally so bad that 'the greater part' of it had to be buried by the men.[49] When the supply position improved, in the hospital tent of the 4th Light Dragoons the salt beef that was not actually rotten was soaked 'for 48 hours and boiled with vegetables and spices. This made it', Surgeon Kendall found, 'much more palatable, and the men liked it.'[50] Coffee beans, until early in February, were issued green so that they should not be spoilt by getting wet. The only way to deal with them, Trooper Mitchell discovered, was to 'put the berries on the fire in a tin . . . keeping them stirred until they were brown, or more often black, then put them in a piece of rag and beat them between two stones.'[51]

The officers, of course, could afford to buy extra food when it was available, but until early in 1855, when certain ships were sent out with provisions to be sold at cost price, the men could not often supplement their rations. Three days before Christmas, an officer of heavy dragoons described the working of unrestricted free enter-prise. 'The Maltese and others having shops in Balaclava', he wrote, 'rush on board ship directly one comes in, and generally succeed in buying everything up, which they then retail to the soldiers at an immense profit.'[52]

The difficulties of the commissariat were immense, its inefficiency considerable. This was because, as Cornet Fisher of the 4th Dragoon Guards sagely observed, 'in time of peace we have no Commissariat at all, and the men are not trained to it.'[53] Kinglake gives an example of what was liable to happen. A cavalry regiment, he says, 'which obtained an order for 108 blankets on 2 December, did not fetch away any of them until the middle of January.'[54]

For the invalids in the cavalry conditions were bad. Throughout November, December and January, reported the 4th Dragoon Guards' doctor, 'the sick men were in bell-tents, lying without mattresses on blankets, empty bags and matting, on the bare ground, which was continually damp. No hay or straw could be obtained, as there was not sufficient for the horses.'[55] In the 4th Light Dragoons, the doctor had 'small twigs and branches' put under the blankets on which the men lay. These 'raised them a little from the ground.'[56] Only in the last week of January were wooden huts being put up for the invalids. In many cases they were not occupied till well into February. Dr Forteath of the Royals was 'in the habit of purchasing soft bread for the men in hospital from private funds, contributed by the officers and others.' At one time he was paying 'as much as 2s 6d for the two-pound loaf', which, after the winter was over, was selling for 1s in Balaklava.[57]

The drafts which arrived from home during the winter consisted largely of 'lads scarcely beyond the age of boyhood'. They succumbed quickly and in large numbers to the rigours which faced them. Surgeon Cooper of the 4th Dragoon Guards was very scathing about them. 'An army on active service', he said, 'needs other support than that derived from undeveloped youth.'[58] At home, in Burnley, a cavalry sergeant reported that his 'duty was very hard training recruits and young horses.' He had sixty old soldiers with him 'drilling all day. . . . Plenty of recruits, but we had to make soldiers of them in six weeks. Poor boys! They went out like lambs to be slaughtered.'[59] The standard of cavalry drafts did not improve as the war went on. A consignment for the 4th Dragoon Guards which arrived in mid-May, 1855, was described by their colonel as 'an ugly little scrubby lot of men. . . . Many of these recruits are terrible. Their clothes are made so tight that they cannot mount their horses.'[60] Another arrived 'with very good horses indeed, but miserable little boys'.[61] An earlier draft of horses for the 4th Light Dragoons, however, was very different. An officer described it thus: 'If you can picture . . . a very inferior "bus" horse (not a cab horse mind, but a "bus" horse) having been driven for six years between Hammersmith and Brentford, and then drafted into a Light Cavalry Regiment as a trooper, you have the nearest description I could give you of the draft sent out to us in the steamship *Arabia*.'[62]

The plight of the cavalry officers was never very serious. 'We are *capitally* fed', wrote Captain Jenyns of the 13th on 2 January, 'and I have no patience with grumblers on that score.'[63] The 4th Dragoon Guards' camp was beginning on 22 December 'to present quite a Christmas appearance'. One officer had got 'a turkey tied by the leg to his tent', another had 'a couple of geese fastened up in the same fashion'. On 1 January each cavalry officer was issued with a daily ration of six pounds of charcoal,[64] while a fortnight later he received a large fur coat, the back of which was 'white sheepskin worked all over with gay flowers in worsted work. They are Asiatic coats,' noted Colonel Hodge. 'They smell a little from not being properly cured.'[65]

One of the main hardships for the officers was boredom. Some, like Lord George Paget, who had married only a few days before leaving home, when he foresaw no further action for the cavalry, just went off back to England. This Paget did with the approval of Raglan and Lucan, particularly as he had been on the point of leaving the army when his regiment had been ordered overseas, and intended when he got home to carry out his earlier intention. Nevertheless there was 'much hostile criticism, both in the public journals and in the clubs'.[66] 'We hear', wrote home a young subaltern of the 8th Hussars, 'Lord George Paget was greatly snubbed at home for leaving this place. Everyone here thought him a most sensible man for leaving when he was tired of it, but the English people are such fools.'[67] But the weight of public opinion was such that Paget felt bound to return to the Crimea, while numbers of other less well-known officers, with smaller excuse, remained at home uncommented upon. When he returned to the seat of war he brought his wife with him.

A pleasure for the officers who remained at their posts was baiting the members of the headquarters staff. W. H. Russell, the famous correspondent of *The Times*, had been lashing out at Raglan and his staff officers for many weeks. 'It is great fun', wrote Lieutenant Heneage of the 8th, 'asking them whether they have improved themselves since the last article, and whether Raglan really receives his orders from the Editor.'[68]

By early April both officers and men were 'exceedingly well rationed. We now', exulted Major Forrest of the 4th Dragoon Guards, 'get maccaroni and cheese; preserved beet-root. In fact, I do not suppose that any army ever was so well cared for.'[69] Even as early as mid-January officers were writing home to stop the rapidly increasing flow of gifts for the men. 'They have now got everything they can possibly wish for', wrote Captain Portal of the 4th Light Dragoons. 'We have just received an enormous supply from England of every single thing, and they hardly know where to put them or what to do with them.'[70]

Just as the weather was becoming spring-like, the flow of supplies, particularly of warm clothing, publicly as well as privately provided, became a flood. On 13 February there arrived at Balaklava the schooner *Erminia*. Aboard her were a son of her owner, the Earl of Ellesmere, and an energetic giant named Tom Tower. These two men were the 'honorary agents' of the 'Crimean Army Fund' of which Lord Ellesmere was President. Within a fortnight the *Erminia* was followed by two steamers chartered by the Fund's London Committee. They carried enormous quantities of 'comforts' supplied by private charity at home. These ranged from '37,000 flannel shirts and jerseys, . . . brushes and combs, . . . wine, ale and meat, down to pepper, mustard and salt',[71] and large quantities of oranges against scurvy. The Fund also furnished its own transport. This included two Maltese carts, twenty-four transport animals, twenty porters and ten muleteers with their own provisions. Though it came too late, this effort of private enterprise was massive and superbly organized.

By 9 February Captain Portal of the 4th Light Dragoons declared that 'altogether we have more the appearance of a large party of emigrants who intend remaining here for life, what with railways making, houses building, electric [telegraph] wires laying down, etc.'[72] In early June, Colonel Hodge, who disapproved of officers' wives on active service, wrote home that there were 'a great many ladies' in the Crimea. 'I fully expect to see some excursion steamers come out from England soon, with Manchester, Birmingham and Liverpool on board.'[73]

*　　*　　*

On Lucan's recall, Scarlett succeeded to command of the Cavalry Division. 'We all like the change', wrote Colonel Hodge, who for a time took Scarlett's place at the head of the Heavy Brigade. 'Scarlett is most active. He does his work like a gentleman, and gives no unnecessary trouble. We all wish that he may be left here in command.'[74] Lieutenant Heneage of the 8th thought him 'a real old brick'.[75] In early April Scarlett went home because his wife was ill. He returned in July, but went back to England again when, in October, his own health was bad.

In April, May and June, while the siege of Sebastopol crept laboriously on, massive cavalry reinforcements landed at Balaklava. The 10th Hussars arrived first from the East, at full Indian establishment: '670 strong,' exclaimed Lord George Paget, 'about double what our 10 regiments muster!'[76] The 12th Lancers, also at full Indian strength, followed a month later.* From England, the Carabiniers (6th Dragoon Guards) disembarked between June and

---

* On 10 May an order was given to reduce the 10th and 12th to the Home Establishment.

'Now was ever such folly heard of', exploded Colonel Hodge. 'Here we are in the field. We want every man and horse we can get, and then they give out one of *General Routine's* orders. Besides the gross injustice to the officers, – the 2nd Lieut-Colonels, two Captains, and some subalterns will be reduced and put upon half pay – they have been put to the expense of coming from India, fitting themselves out for a campaign. They had to sell their bungalows and furniture at a great sacrifice in India, and had the trouble of coming here, merely to be placed upon half pay and sent home when they arrive.' (Anglesey: *Hodge*, 11 May 1855, 100.)

August, and the King's Dragoon Guards a little later. In July, the Division was expanded to three brigades. These came to be known as the 'Heavies', the 'Bashis' (Light Brigade) and the 'Dirties' (Hussar Brigade). The three brigadiers were, respectively, Lawrenson of the 17th Lancers, Paget of the 4th Light Dragoons, and Parlby of the 10th Hussars.

On 25 May, the ground lost at the battle of Balaklava was regained virtually without opposition and largely by the considerable Sardinian contingent which had recently joined the allied army. The next major attempt to take Sebastopol occurred on 18 June, the thirty-ninth anniversary of Waterloo. It was an expensive and depressing failure. About 800 of the British cavalry were made, as Mrs Duberly remarked, 'into special constables'[77] to keep the ground. They formed a chain just out of sight of the town. Their orders were to prevent anyone showing on the heights. Paget found the task a difficult one due to the 'very unruly people we had to deal with, from the general officer . . . down to the captains of transports, to say nothing of a whole army of travelling gents, with an occasional yeomanry officer in full canonicals.'[78] The same task was allotted to the cavalry during the final and successful assault on 8 September.*

Long before that, ten days after the abortive June attack, Lord Raglan had died, from, it was said, a broken heart. He was succeeded by General Simpson, who, in November, was himself succeeded by General Codrington. On 16 August an action, known as the battle of the Tchernaya, had been fought. The British cavalry's part in what was largely a French and Sardinian affair is summed up by Paget: 'This', he noted in his journal, 'may be called the poetry of battle to us – to ride out nearly three miles from one's house in the morning; see a general action; return home to a comfortable wash and breakfast, and then spend the afternoon on the battlefield!'[79]

In mid-September the Crimean medals arrived for distribution to all ranks. It was generally agreed amongst the officers that the medal was 'a vulgar looking thing', and that the clasps for the various battles looked like decanter labels. 'They call them here', declared

---

* In May, an Anglo-French expedition had been sent to destroy the defences at Kertch at the entrance to the Sea of Azov, thus opening up that sea to allied ships. In September a squadron of the 10th Hussars was sent as part of a reinforcement. At Seit Ali, on the 21st, together with the 2nd Chasseurs d'Afrique, part of the squadron twice charged a body of over 300 cossacks, supported by regular hussars, and dispersed them with heavy losses. The 10th lost two men killed and one wounded. (*J.A.H.R.*, XVII (1938), 125–6)

Paget, ' "Port", "Sherry" and "Claret".' 'How odd it is', complained Colonel Hodge, 'we cannot do things like people of taste.'[80]

The cavalry, early in November, began to go into winter quarters at Scutari.* Lieutenant Heneage wondered whether he would 'ever see the beautiful Crimea again. I am very sorry to leave it – after being here so long, one gets quite to look upon it as home.'[81] On arrival at Constantinople, Colonel White of the Inniskillings commented: 'If they had had the sense to have sent us here last year, what valuable soldiers would have been saved, and horses also.'[82]

Though the Treaty of Paris was not signed until the end of March, 1856, the war had in effect ended before winter set in.

* Early in October, 1855, Paget's brigade with one horse artillery troop was sent by sea to Eupatoria as part of an Anglo-French expedition. Its object was to harass the Russians, so as to hasten their evacuation of the Crimea. Early in December it returned after achieving little at small cost.

2

'Had we been stronger in cavalry, very few of the
Persian army would have escaped.'
CORNET COMBE, 3rd Bombay Light Cavalry,
after the battle of Khushab[1]

The Persian War, 1856–57

Like so many of the Indian campaigns of the nineteenth century the
little Persian War of 1856–57 was brought about by British fear of
Russia. It was supposed, probably correctly, that the Shah's preparations to seize Herat in western Afghanistan at the end of 1855 were
suggested to him by the Russians. In 1838–39 the British had invaded
Afghanistan largely because the Persians had besieged Herat in
1837 (see Volume I, p. 214). A Persian force had actually occupied
the place fifteen years later. In the following year, in consequence of
British protests, the Shah had agreed to withdraw. Now, for the
third time in twenty years the threat was renewed. On 1 November,
1856, the government of India declared war on Persia and decided
to assail her from the sea.

On 10 December, after a naval bombardment, Bushire on the
coast of the Persian Gulf was occupied by 4,000 men from the Bom-
bay army. In January, 1857, a second force commanded by Sir
James Outram arrived, for extensive operations were contemplated.
The cavalry element of the two divisions consisted of the 14th Light
Dragoons and part of the Scinde Irregular Horse, neither of which
saw much if any action, and the 3rd Bombay Light Cavalry and the
Poona Irregular Horse. All these came under Brigadier-General
John Jacob, one of the most distinguished cavalrymen of India (see
p. 242).

There was only one engagement of any consequence. It took place
at Khushab on 8 February, 1857, and is especially interesting to the
student of cavalry as will be shown. About 4,600 of Outram's men,
including 243 of the 3rd and 176 of the Poona Horse, faced some
6,000 Persians, only a few of whom were European-trained regulars
of any quality. The British troops came upon the field of battle after
a forced march of forty-six miles covered in forty-one hours during
which it rained 'cats and dogs all the time'.[2]

On the British side the battle was fought almost exclusively by a

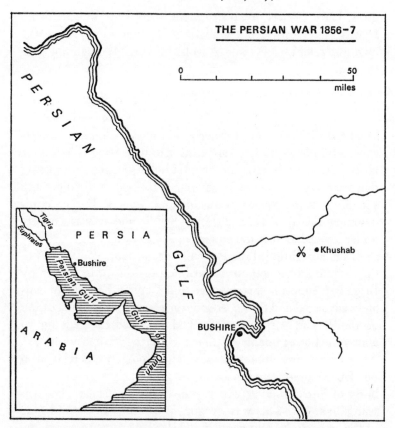

small part of the cavalry and some of the artillery. By the time the
infantry had completed the complicated manoeuvres needed to
bring them into line, the work had been done and the whole Persian
army had broken and fled. The ground was sandy desert 'most
favourable for cavalry'.[3] Just as it was becoming light, Captain J. C.
Graves of the 3rd galloped off with four sowars to reconnoitre the
enemy position. They rode 'along the front of the whole line of the
Persian army; escaping, in the most marvellous way, the hundreds
of shot fired at them.' Cornet Charles Combe of the 3rd describes
what happened next:

'By the time [Graves] returned it was pretty light, and we discovered the Persian army drawn up in "battle array" – in
line; their right resting on a village (Khooshab), their left
extending to a second village. . . . On their right front and flank
was a ditch, full of skirmishers, and in front of their centre
were two small mounds, which served as redoubts for their

guns. Large bodies of cavalry were formed up on each flank.
It was rather misty, but a sharp cold wind soon cleared the
mist away, and made us long to be moving. We had not long
to wait.'[4]

Captain Ross Moore, another officer of the regiment, takes up the
story:

'The 3rd Cavalry were formed up in close column of squadrons, left in front, facing the direction of the enemy. The Poona
Horse also in close column were on our right, the order being
that each regiment should have an attacking and supporting
squadron; as my squadron was in front, Captain Forbes, commanding the Regiment, accompanied it and it was entirely
under his orders that the squadron acted. . . .

'Brigadier Tapp [of the Poona Irregular Horse]* went off to
the right at a hand gallop. I heard no previous orders given by
Brigadier Tapp for this advance, but Captain Forbes immediately advanced and the squadron was soon employed in cutting
up the Persian skirmishers who had advanced close enough to
annoy the line of infantry [still manoeuvring into position]. . . .
After being thus employed for a few minutes we perceived to
our left what appeared to be in the grey of the morning . . . a
body of horse moving with a gun from the Persian right towards their left. This was a regiment of the Shah's guard [one
of the best regular regiments in the Persian army, known as the
1st Kushkai Regiment of Fars]. They halted on the rise of a
small hill and fired volleys at us; when we got close they formed
a solid square with kneeling ranks and awaited us most
steadily.'[5]

At this point, under artillery fire most of which went over the cavalrymen's heads, Captain Forbes, according to Cornet Combe, 'gave
the orders "The Line will advance". "Draw Swords". "Third
Squadron". "Walk". "Trot". "Gallop", and when within a hundred
yards of the enemy, "Charge!" '[6]
Another officer of the regiment tells how Forbes and his young
adjutant, Lieutenant A. T. Moore (brother of Captain Ross Moore),

'placed themselves in front of the 6th Troop, which was the one
directly opposite the nearest face of the square. The others,

* This officer, three years before, was responsible for trying to introduce a
primitive and painful method of sterilizing stallions. (See p. 434.)

16. Lieutenants Malcolmson and Moore at Khushab, 8 February, 1857. (See p. 129)

17. General Sir James Hope Grant in 1868. (See p. 148)

[Ross] Moore, Malcolmson and Spens, came the least thing behind, riding knee to knee, with spurs in their horses' flanks, as if racing after a dog. In rear of them rushed the dark troopers of the 3rd. . . . In spite of fire, steel and bullets, they tore down upon the nearest face of the devoted square. As they approached, Forbes was shot through the thigh, and Spens' horse was wounded; but unheeding, they swept onwards.

'Daunted by the flashes and the fire and the noise and the crackle of the musketry, the younger Moore's horse swerved as they came up. Dropping his sword and letting it hang by the knot at his wrist, he caught up the reins in both hands, screwed his horse's head straight, and then coolly, as if riding a fence, leaped him into the square. . . . Of course the horse fell stone-dead upon the bayonets; so did his brother's, ridden with equal courage and determination.

'The elder Moore – 18 stone in weight and 6 feet 7 inches in height, cut his way out on foot. Malcolmson took one foot out of the stirrup, when he saw his brother officer down and unarmed (for his sword had been broken to pieces by the fall), and holding on to that, the younger Moore escaped. (See illustration facing p. 128.)

'The barrier once broken, and the entrance once made, in and through it poured [our] Troops. On and over everything they rode, till getting out they re-formed on the other side, wheeled and swept back a second wave of ruin. Out of five hundred Persian soldiers . . . who composed that fatal square, only twenty escaped to tell the tale of its own destruction.'[7]

Captain Ross Moore believed that when the squadron charged it did not number quite 100 men 'from some having been wounded and several scattered after the skirmishers'. He believed that the square consisted of 800 men, but from other evidence it seems more likely not to have exceeded 500. Captain Ross Moore's account says that some guns had earlier separated the two squadrons of the 3rd, so that the right squadron was unable to support the left one when it charged the square. It apparently 'acted independently and equally distinguished itself by charging and routing large masses of the enemy'.[8] In the pursuit which followed, two Persian guns were captured. The regiment's total losses for the day were one sowar killed and Captain Forbes and fourteen sowars wounded. Lieutenants Moore and Malcolmson were awarded the Victoria Cross.

This small action has been given in some detail because it is one of the few examples in the history of the British cavalry of a perfectly formed square being broken. Indeed it was probably the only occasion when native troops performed the feat. The scale may have been small compared with Salamanca, Garcia Hernandez and Aliwal,* and the quality of the Persian infantry may have been inferior to that of the French and the Sikhs, but the performance of the left squadron of the 3rd Bombay Light Cavalry was nonetheless remarkable, especially in view of the odds against it and the light casualties which it suffered. In John Jacob's opinion, Khushab was 'the best Cavalry performance of modern times'.⁹ Hitherto it has been unjustly neglected by military historians.

Further operations involving very little fighting were put an end to on 4 April when peace was signed in Paris. Persia surrendered her claims to Herat and, not for the first time, agreed not to meddle again in Afghanistan's affairs. The war, the last to be fought by the Honourable East India Company, came to an end only just in time.¹⁰ The troops returned to face more important business in India.

* See Vol. I, pp. 55, 265.

3

'If our Indian Army became generally, seriously discontented, God help us.'

JOHN JACOB in 1842

'Hardly could the Bombay and Bengal men be kept from quarrelling. This enmity between the troops of the two presidencies is incomprehensible, but exists.'

SIR CHARLES NAPIER in 1842[1]

(i)

Indian Mutiny, 1857: causes of discontent in Bengal – cartridge grease question – Mangal Pande

'In India . . . our power does not rest on actual strength but upon impression', wrote Sir Charles Metcalfe, one of the finest early nineteenth-century Indian administrators. 'Our greatest danger is not from a Russian Army, but the fading of the impression of our invincibility from the minds of the Native inhabitants of India.'[2] In 1842, that 'handful of strangers from Europe', who had imposed their will upon some 130,000,000 Indians 'by sheer fighting power',[3] had suffered a crushing defeat at the hands of the Afghans. (See Vol. I, p. 223.) Further, in 1855, numbers of Queen's regiments had had to be withdrawn from India to reinforce the army in the Crimea. (See p. 123.) These two events had a profound effect on the Indian mind. Whatever the causes of the mutiny of the Bengal Army in 1857 – and they are complex – this evidence of the limits of the rulers' strength gave encouragement to the discontented.

Among the native rulers there was much cause for discontent. Many of them had recently been dispossessed of their domains and pensioned off. Some, like the royal family of Nagpur whose jewels had been publicly auctioned, had suffered humiliations. The Earl of Dalhousie, before he was succeeded as Governor-General by Lord Canning early in 1856, had added to Britain's possessions 250,000 square miles in eight years. The system of 'lapse', whereby a state became forfeit to the Company if there was no clear successor on the death of its ruler, certainly avoided the anarchy which so often occurred on these occasions, but it rendered numerous dissatisfied

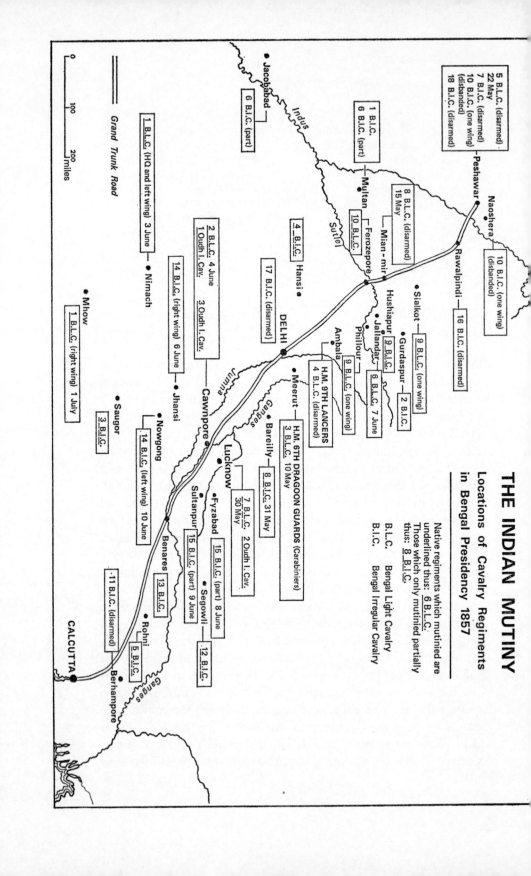

THE INDIAN MUTINY

Locations of Cavalry Regiments in Bengal Presidency 1857

Native regiments which mutinied are underlined thus: <u>6 B.L.C.</u> Those which only mutinied partially thus: <u>8 B.I.C.</u>

B.L.C. Bengal Light Cavalry
B.I.C. Bengal Irregular Cavalry

0   100   200
miles

Grand Trunk Road

5 B.L.C. (disarmed)
22 May
7 B.I.C. (disarmed)
10 B.I.C. (one wing)
(disbanded)
18 B.I.C. (disarmed)

Jacobabad

6 B.I.C. (part)

1 B.I.C.
6 B.I.C. (part)

Peshawar

Naoshera

10 B.I.C. (one wing)
(disbanded)

Multan

8 B.L.C. (disarmed)
15 May

Ferozepore

10 B.I.C.

Mian-mir

Rawalpindi

16 B.I.C. (disarmed)

Sutlej

Indus

1 B.L.C. (HQ and left wing) 3 June

Nimach

4 B.I.C.

Hansi

2 B.L.C. 4 June
1 Oudh I. Cav.

14 B.I.C. (right wing) 6 June

3 Oudh I. Cav.

17 B.I.C. (disarmed)

DELHI

Hushiapur

Sialkot

9 B.L.C. (one wing)

Gurdaspur

9 B.I.C.

Jallandar

6 B.I.C. 7 June

2 B.I.C.

Phillour

Ambala

9 B.I.C. (one wing)

Meerut

H.M. 9TH LANCERS
4 B.I.C. (disarmed)

Jhansi

Cawnpore

Jumna

Ganges

H.M. 6TH DRAGOON GUARDS (Carabiniers)
3 B.L.C. 10 May

Bareilly

8 B.I.C. 31 May

Nowgong

14 B.I.C. (left wing) 10 June

Lucknow

7 B.L.C. 30 May
2 Oudh I. Cav.

Mhow

1 B.L.C. (right wing) 1 July

Saugor

3 B.I.C.

Sultanpur

15 B.I.C. (part) 9 June

Fyzabad

15 B.I.C. (part) 8 June

Segowli

12 B.I.C.

Benares

13 B.I.C.

Rohni

5 B.I.C.

11 B.I.C. (disarmed)

Ganges

CALCUTTA

Berhampore

men dangerously idle. It is very probable that these resentful rulers exploited the religious doubts and fears which were increasingly besetting the people of Bengal.

No amount of assurances that there was no official intention to convert the peoples of India to Christianity, could eradicate the suspicion that this was in fact so.* Contributing to this belief were many factors. The British, at an increasing rate, were effecting a social revolution in India. Inevitably this entailed threats to religious scruples and caste taboos. The abolition of *sati* (widow burning); the increase of missionaries (sometimes thought, erroneously, to be maintained by government); the teaching of Christianity to prisoners in jail; the rare destruction of a temple to make way for a new road; the fact that in the carriages of the newly opened railway from Calcutta to Ranigani no caste distinction was made in the seating arrangements; the violation of *purda* in the new hospitals being built where none had been before; the discontinuance of Persian as the language of the law courts, and the use of English in the schools. These changes and many other results of modern progress sowed suspicion in the minds of the masses.

*   *   *

John Jacob, one of the finest leaders of *silladar* cavalry in the history of India and a persistent agitator for reform of abuses in the Bengal Army, declared that

> 'the natives of India are quite incapable of self government. . . . They cannot conceive that a subject can have any rights whatever not dependent on the favour of the sovereign. They expect their sovereign to govern them absolutely and according to his own superior knowledge and ability, and not according to their instructions.'[4]

Jacob and other thinking Englishmen in India believed that the slackening of the rulers' confidence in their moral right to govern absolutely – the gradually increasing belief that the governed should have some say in how they were governed – was a root cause of the discontent which flared up in Bengal. In particular it was thought that the sepoys and sowars of the Bengal Army were unduly pampered and their religious scruples paid too much attention to.

This view is in direct conflict with that of other respectable

* The same fears had been at the root of the Vellore Mutiny in 1806. (See Vol. I, p. 68.)

authorities who hold that threats to the men's religious scruples and taboos were the chief causes. The most important of these threats in a military point of view is instanced by the General Service Enlistment Act of September, 1856. This required every recruit to undertake to serve wherever he might be needed. Until it came into force his service had been restricted to within India's frontiers. The soldier saw this as an attack upon his caste feelings about travelling overseas. By crossing the *kala pani* (black water) the Brahmin was reduced to the same caste as a lascar.

There were other long-term causes within the Bengal Army. One of the more potent was the fact that a decreasing number of officers could speak the language of their men, either actually or metaphorically. Many commanding officers who had once been as fathers to their men had increasingly lost touch with them over the years. The advent in India of officers' wives in large numbers, facilitated by the speeding up of communications, had certainly ministered to this. Further, disciplinary powers within the regiment had been whittled down to almost nothing. Since 1853, for example, no commanding officer had been allowed to award a punishment more severe than five days' drill. The commanding officer of the 5th Bengal Native Cavalry told the Commission which inquired into the organization of the Indian Army in 1859 that commanding officers had 'no power at all; they can only reprimand a havildar-serjeant once or twice, and the third time bring him to a court-martial.'[5]

Nearly one-third of the Bengal soldiers came from Oudh, the central province of Bengal. These men, constituting a close-knit interest within the army, were in large part Brahmins. Others were Rajputs. Both were high-caste, full of bigotry and extremely resentful of any changes in the existing order. Three-fifths of the sepoys were high-born Hindus of one kind or another. Most of the sowars, on the other hand, came from good-class Mohammedan families.

As J. A. B. Palmer, the historian of the Meerut outbreak, has written:

> 'The soldiers of the Bengal Army were only an extract from the population of the North-West Provinces and Oudh. . . . The grievances and suspicions prevalent over that area worked continually in the minds of the sepoys and sowars. . . . They did not shed their religion, their caste, or their family ties when they enlisted: far from it; intercourse with their homes was ceaseless, social status all-important to them.'[6]

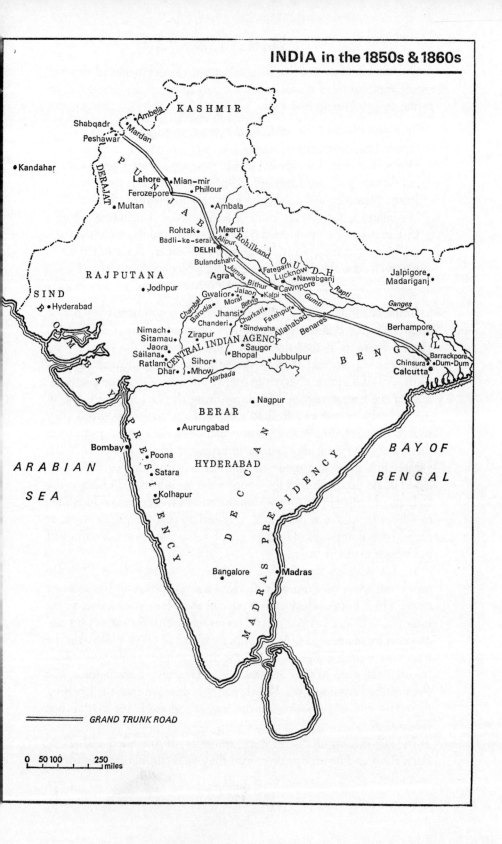

INDIA in the 1850s & 1860s

KASHMIR

Ambela

Shabqadr

Mardan

Peshawar

Kandahar

DERAJAT

P U N J A B

Lahore • Mian-mir

Ferozepore • Phillour

Multan

Ambala

Rohtak • Meerut

Badli-ke-serai • Alipur Rohilkhand

DELHI

Bulandshahr

O U D H

RAJPUTANA

Fategarh

Agra Jumna Bithur Lucknow • Nawabganj

Jodhpur

Jalpigore

Madariganj

SIND

Hyderabad

Chambal Gwalior • Jalaon Morar Betwa Kalpi Cawnpore Rapti

Gumti

Ganges

Barodia Jhansi Fatehpur

Nimach Chanderi Charkari Allahabad Benares Berhampore

Sitamau Zirapur Sindwaha

Jaora CENTRAL INDIAN AGENCY Saugor

Sailana Bhopal Jubbulpur B E N G A L Chinsura Barrackpore • Dum-Dum

Ratlam Sihor • Jubbulpur Calcutta

Dhar • Mhow

Narbada

B E R A R

Nagpur

Aurungabad

Bombay

ARABIAN

SEA

Poona

Satara

HYDERABAD

Kolhapur

D E C C A N

BAY OF

BENGAL

M A D R A S   P R E S I D E N C Y

Bangalore • Madras

GRAND TRUNK ROAD

0 50 100   250
                  miles

One senior officer of the Bengal regular cavalry believed that the recent annexation of Oudh had had a bad effect on the morale of the native troops in a special way.

'It deprived them', he said, 'of the great advantages which they before had. Formerly if a man had any complaint to make in Oude, that man's complaint was forwarded by the Commanding Officer to the resident at Lucknow, who made it over to the Prime Minister, and it was immediately listened to, free of all law charges, &c. When Oude was annexed, it became as other British provinces, governed by regulations, and the men had to appoint attorneys, petition on stamped paper, &c., and their plaints filed and settled in due course, which took months. The soldiers had no advantage over the other natives.'[7]

In the last thirteen years there had been four comparatively minor mutinies in the Bengal Army, all of which had been put down with vigour. In 1857, before the spark which exploded the powder-keg at Meerut was struck, there occurred a number of disturbing incidents. All of them resulted from increasing fears about the composition of the grease required for lubricating the cartridges for use in the recently introduced Enfield rifle, and the paper of which they were composed. For many years it had been the custom to bite off the end of the cartridge before inserting it in the weapon. If the grease now used was made of tallow from beef or pork fat there could be no doubt that its insertion in the mouth would outrage 'the feelings of both Hindus, to whom the cow was sacred, and Muslims, to whom the pig was unclean'.[8] It is certain that the grease made at Enfield was composed of such tallow. So also may have been some of the grease made in India.

In January, at the Dum-Dum arsenal, a high-caste Brahmin sepoy refused a labourer a drink from his water-pot on the score of caste. The labourer then said 'You will soon lose your caste, as ere long you will have to bite cartridges covered with the fat of pigs and cows.' This incident, one of a number which had taken place over the past two months, alerted the authorities to the men's suspicions. Shortly after it, Major-General J. B. Hearsey, commanding the Presidency Division, (see Vol. I, p. 198), directed that the greasing materials should be bought in the bazaar and made up by the men themselves.

In the meantime there were rumours of intended risings at Barrackpore. The sepoys there said they were afraid of being forced to relinquish their caste and become Christians. Hearsey, addressing the whole brigade in Hindustani, told them that forced conversion was against the tenets of Christianity itself, and that there was nothing of the sort to fear.

In February, at Berhampore, the 19th Native Infantry refused to take the cartridges for a firing practice, and got hold of their weapons by force. They were overawed by a Company of Bengal Artillery. As a result of a Court of Enquiry, the regiment was disbanded. What seemed to be an attempt to start a similar incident at Barrackpore took place on 29 March. An intoxicated sepoy of the 34th Native Infantry named Mangal Pande cut down two Europeans and tried to induce his comrades to rise 'for the sake of religion'. They refused to do so, and he was promptly cut down by General Hearsey himself. From his surname came the opprobrious term 'pandy' which the English later applied to the mutinous sepoys.

In a further attempt to allay the men's suspicions, the practice of biting off the top of the cartridges was discontinued, and that of tearing by hand substituted. This, combined with the order for purchase and mixing by the men, was almost certainly taken as proof that there had in fact been a plot to defile them.

'There are no people who are more amenable to tact and management than the natives of India; you can do almost anything with them by quietly explaining matters to them, and not enforcing anything violently.'

DR F. J. MOUAT, 1861[1]

(ii)

Indian Mutiny, 1857: troops at Meerut in May – trouble starts with 3rd Light Cavalry – outbreak at Meerut

At the end of May, 1856, the Carabiniers (6th Dragoon Guards) had arrived home from Scutari. (See p. 123.) At Canterbury they were ordered to prepare for service in India. In no more than two months they were expected to expand from less than 300 to something approaching the Indian establishment of 790 of all ranks. This meant that the majority of the men were raw recruits. Arriving at Chinsura in November and December, the regiment reached Meerut, where it was to be stationed, on 18 March, 1857. There it was provided with 305 unbroken countrybreds from government stud farms, and 316 discards from ten regiments of Bengal native cavalry. 'One cannot but feel sorry', writes the historian of the regiment, 'for Riding-Master Llewellyn, faced with 621 untrained or vicious horses, and no more than about 200 out of the 626 private men who could possibly be described as horsemen.'[2] The regiment's strength at the beginning of May, 1857, at the time of the outbreak which precipitated the Mutiny, was calculated at 652 officers and men,[3] but it would be surprising if their effective strength was in fact more than half that number, for many of the recruits would not have yet completed their elementary training. One of the Carabiniers' officers stated that only about twenty-five men per troop had passed riding school at that date.[4] Nor would most of the unbacked horses have been fully broken.

The other European troops at Meerut at the time of the outbreak were the 1st Battalion of the 60th Queen's Royal Rifle Corps with about 900 officers and men; a troop of Bengal Horse Artillery, with six guns; a company of foot artillery, and a light field battery with six guns. These were all below strength. The total number of European troops was probably not more than 1,700, of which quite a few were ineffective. This compared with a total of over 2,000 men in the three native regiments, the 3rd Bengal Light Cavalry (500), and the 11th (780) and 20th (950) Bengal Native Infantry, all of which were comparatively seasoned troops.

*   *   *

The trouble started with the 3rd Light Cavalry, a regiment of considerable distinction. It had fought under Lake at Delhi and Laswari in 1803 (see Vol. I, p. 66). For these actions it had been presented with an honorary standard inscribed 'Lake and Victory', and granted an extra Jemadar. It had been at Bhurtpore in 1825/6 and taken part in the 1st Afghan War (see Vol. I, pp. 209, 213). At Aliwal it had charged with the 16th Lancers, and it had also been present at Sobraon (see Vol. I, pp. 261, 267). Since then it had not been actively engaged. Lieutenant Hugh Gough relates that 'in the 3rd L.C. we used to pride ourselves on being steadier on parade than the British cavalry regiment then stationed at Meerut; and proud we were of the old regiment.'[5]

In 1857, the 3rd was commanded by Lieutenant-Colonel (Brevet Colonel) George Monro Carmichael-Smyth, a member of a numerous family well known in Anglo-India.* He had been with the regiment ever since he had arrived in India in 1819 or 1820. There is evidence that in the past, to alleviate the boredom of an undistinguished regimental career, he had meddled in semi-political affairs for which he was not well fitted. It is probable that he was a rather conceited man and not particularly beloved of his officers and men.

On 23 April, 'having learnt', as he afterwards wrote, 'that there was an order that men were now to load without biting their cartridges, and thinking they would be much pleased to hear of it',[6] he ordered for the following day a parade of the ninety regimental skirmishers (fifteen from each troop) who were armed with carbines.

Early in the morning of the fateful 10 May, Cornet John MacNabb of the regiment, aged eighteen, wrote the last letter of his life, for he was one of the first to be killed that evening.† In it he told his mother that he thought his colonel's action most injudicious.

'There was no necessity to have the parade at all or to make any fuss of the sort just now. No other Colonel of Cavalry thought of doing such a thing, as they knew at this unsettled time their men would refuse to be the first to fire these cartridges . . . and that next parade season, when the row had blown over, they would begin to fire as a matter of course, and think nothing of it. . . . The night before [23 April], Captn. Craigie, who knows everything that is going on in the regiment, wrote to the Adjutant to ask the Colonel to put this parade off, as he had got information that the men would refuse to fire.'

Craigie's letter ran thus:

* His grandfather was of the family of the Earls of Hyndford (extinct, 1817) and had married Miss Smyth, an heiress. Their son, James, added Smyth to his name under his mother's father's will. James had eight sons and two daughters – George Monro being the youngest of the family. The second son became the first Resident Superintendent of Addiscombe College in 1822, having served in India from 1797. He married W. M. Thackeray's widowed mother, and is possibly portrayed in part in Colonel Newcome. The third son became a major-general after long service in the irregular cavalry. The fourth and sixth sons were in the Bengal Civil Service. The family's span in India stretches from 1797 to 1939. (See Palmer, 148.)

† He spent the day with a friend in the Artillery lines. He was cut down whilst trying to get back to the 3rd Light Cavalry's lines.

'Go at once to Smyth and tell him that the men of my troop have requested in a body that the skirmishing tomorrow morning may be countermanded, as there is a commotion throughout the native troops about cartridges, and that the regiment will become *budnam* [disreputable] if they fire any cartridges. . . . We may have the whole regiment in mutiny in half an hour if this is not attended to. . . . We have none of the objectionable cartridges, but the men say that if they fire any kind of cartridge at present they lay themselves open to the imputation . . . of having fired the objectionable ones.'[7]

The men themselves also petitioned the Colonel to postpone the parade but, according to MacNabb, 'the Adjutant, who is always severe to the men, said it would look like being afraid of them.' So the parade was not countermanded, and all but five of the men refused to fire the cartridges

'as they did not want to be the first regiment who fired. . . . But the real case', continued MacNabb, 'is that they hate Smyth, and, if almost any other officer had gone down they would have fired them off. . . .

'The men of course had *no* real excuse for not doing what they were ordered, and they knew what these cartridges were made of, as they had fired them off privately in riding school since the 19th N.I. were disbanded, and they would have continued to do so if they had been left alone, instead of being paraded, and addressed, and all that humbug. . . . A day or two after, these 85 skirmishers were marched into an empty hospital and there confined. They were then tried by Court Martial [on 6, 7 and 8 May] and sentenced to 10 years on the roads in chains! They could not have hit upon a more severe punishment as it is much worse to them than death. . . . They will never see their wives and families, they are degraded, and one poor old man who has been 40 years in the regiment, and would have got his pension, is now thrown back the *whole* of his service. . . .

'It is a great pity that it has happened in my regiment, "The old and steady 3rd", and brought on us in such a useless manner. It is the *first* disgrace the regiment has ever had.

'The sentence was carried out yesterday morning [9 May]. We were paraded at 4 o'clock on foot, and marched up to the Grand Parade ground where all the troops in the station were assembled. The prisoners were escorted by a company of Rifles, and some of the 6th Dn. Guards [the Carabiniers]. . . . We reached the parade at 5, and there we *stood* for 2 hours and more, while the sentence was being read, and the irons put on. Didn't my long back ache neither! It was luckily a cloudy morning or we would have been grilled. When the sentence was read the men in the ranks behaved very well, with the exception of a few who wept for their brothers, and fathers among the mutineers. When the irons were put on they were marched past the whole parade, and when they passed us of course they began to cry, and curse the Colonel, and threw away their boots, almost at him, but they blessed Craigie, and called out that "they hoped he would be a Prince and a Lord".

'Some of our officers went down to the jail to see them, and pay them their wages, and they say it was heartrending to see them, but yet they accused no one, but thanked them for coming to see them. . . . When they were being paid, one man said, "Oh give it to my wife", another, "Oh give it to my brother; what good is it to me; I am a dead man now."

'. . . It is lucky that this had happened in Meerut where there are so many European troops, for if it had been at a small station I would not have given much for the officers' lives. But here there are Cavalry, Infantry and Artillery, all English, who would cut them up in no time.'[8]

Within a few hours of writing these lines, poor Cornet MacNabb was to be proved incredibly wrong. There were very few warnings of the holocaust. The most important occurred on the previous evening when Lieutenant Gough was visited by a Hindu native officer of his Troop

'under pretence of making up the accounts. After a time he made the following report: that a mutiny of the native troops at Meerut would certainly take place the next day, Sunday, May 10th, further stating that the Native Infantry were going to rise, that the 3rd Cavalry would also do so, and that they intended to release their comrades in gaol. . . . I went at once to my colonel and told him what had been secretly reported to me. He treated the communication with contempt, reproving me for listening to such idle words. I met the brigadier [Archdale Wilson] that evening, and told him the same story, but he also was incredulous. Such was our ill-judged confidence! But, indeed, few men would in those days have been inclined to believe in the "treachery" of our native soldiers.'[9]

*　　*　　*

Surprising as it may seem it was not the 3rd Light Cavalry which began the outbreak. It was the sepoys of the two infantry regiments. The trouble started around 5 p.m., an hour and a half before sunset, when an unfounded rumour was spread in the bazaar that the European troops were about to deprive the native regiments of their arms. This induced the sepoys to run back from the bazaar to their lines. They were followed by a crowd of the lower and more disorderly classes. There the uproar which was started brought the infantry officers to the scene. These tried in vain to restore order. Some of them were killed: the majority escaped. The sepoys and *badmashes* then began to plunder and burn the bungalows and to murder every European and Eurasian in sight.

The turmoil soon extended to the lines of the 3rd Light Cavalry, where the sowars mounted their horses and armed themselves with their swords. Amidst the pandemonium the officers, as they arrived on the scene, attempted to calm their men. A certain number of sowars rode off to release their comrades from the jail, upwards of three miles distant. Captain Craigie, a good linguist and very influential in the ranks, managed to gather behind him forty or fifty of those sowars who had hesitated to join in the commotion. With these and two other officers he set off to see whether he could stop the rescue. He was too late. He encountered some of the released men, mounted and armed by their rescuers, riding back to the regiment's lines. The rest were still having their fetters struck off by hastily summoned smiths.

Craigie now sent off one of his officers with four sowars to see what had happened to his wife and the other officers' ladies, who had been on their way to church. These were found and saved. Meanwhile, with the number of loyal sowars in his party swelled to eighty or ninety, Craigie returned to the regimental parade ground, recovered the colours and made for the European lines.

There he joined his commanding officer. When Carmichael-Smyth had first heard of the uproar, he had set off at once to warn first the Commissioner, Mr Greathed, and then the officer commanding the Meerut Division, Major-General W. H. Hewitt. He ultimately joined Brigadier Archdale Wilson, the Commandant of the station at Meerut who was also the Commandant of Artillery, on the Rifles' parade ground. As Field Officer of the week Carmichael-Smyth was quite correct in making these movements, instead of going to his own regiment's parade ground.

What action, meanwhile, was being taken by the European troops whom poor MacNabb supposed would have been able to 'cut up' the mutineers 'in no time'? The cavalry lines were the closest to the native infantry lines – about a mile away. An officer of the 11th Native Infantry alerted the commanding officer of the Carabiniers, Lieutenant-Colonel W. Neville Custance, in the bungalow which he occupied near his regiment's parade ground. He was at the time, as he later related, 'walking leisurely in his compound, on peaceful thoughts intent, when a panic-stricken individual rode in to order him to turn out immediately, as the troops were in arms, murdering every Christian they met.'[10] That part of his regiment which had horses and could ride, armed, saddled and mounted itself without delay, and the non-commissioned officers called the roll of the troops.* While this was taking place, an order came from Brigadier Wilson for the regiment to join the infantry and artillery on the parade ground of the Rifles. Before it could start off, darkness fell. It is not surprising, therefore, that it lost its way. What exactly happened it is impossible to know, but at some moment the regiment, having wasted time in retracing its steps, was diverted from the Rifles' parade ground to the native parade ground, where all the commotion was. There, in the dark, some time before 9 p.m., (at which hour the moon rose), nearly all the European troops were assembled. By then there were very few of the mutineers left in the vicinity. Nevertheless some volleys from the infantry and some rounds from the artillery were fired into the area of the burning bungalows. The whole force soon returned to the European lines where it bivouacked for the night.

Meanwhile the bulk of the mutineers had made their way, during the dark hours between 7 and 9 p.m., not as was to have been expected, to their homes, but along the road to Delhi, the ancient capital of India, thirty-eight miles away. At what precise point this fact was realized by the European troops is not clear. It is said that as soon as the Carabiniers reached the native parade ground, Captain Rosser of the regiment asked permission to pursue the mutineers

---

* Though this was later denied by Custance, it seems certain that it in fact took place; nor is there any good reason why it should not have done so. (See Palmer, 98–9.)

along the Delhi road. This, however, is doubtful, as it is almost certain that no one present could have known by then that Delhi was the men's objective.

Many writers have condemned the military authorities for dilatoriness in not speedily chasing and halting the mutineers. This view, under the glare of exhaustive research in recent times, can no longer be upheld. It was perhaps a mistake for Wilson to concentrate his force at the Rifles' parade ground, which entailed removing the Carabiniers further away from the native parade ground, instead of closer to it. Yet even had that small portion of the regiment which was mobile gone straight to the centre of the uproar it would have arrived just as darkness fell, and, (unsupported as it would have been by guns), it could at most have done little more than disperse and perhaps cut down some of the mutineers and *badmashes*. Later on it would certainly have been, as Lord Roberts put it, 'futile to have sent the small body of mounted troops available in pursuit of the mutineers'.[11] The right and only sensible thing was in fact done. Hewitt, who was old, fat and feeble, was rightly advised by Wilson to keep his force together for the protection of the station. Particularly was this necessary as the human contents of Meerut's two jails were, in the course of the night, set free.

Short of previous preparations being made in expectation of a mutiny, it is difficult to see that much blame can be attached to the European commanders at Meerut. It is clear that 'the mutineers chose their hour so that two hours of moonless dark would fall just as the European troops were getting ready to move, and a Sunday evening was chosen as the one when there would be the least readiness in the European lines.'[12]

Since the telegraph lines had been cut, it was not possible to send warnings to Delhi, Ambala or elsewhere, except by messengers. These were in fact sent off to both places. The Ambala one got through; the Delhi one did not.

*   *   *

Compared with the two regiments of native infantry (though there were a few instances of loyalty in both) the 3rd Light Cavalry emerges passably well from the Meerut outbreak. The sowars forebore to release any prisoners from the jail except the skirmishers of their own regiment. There was no attempt by the regiment as a whole to invade the European lines. No sowar killed or attempted to kill any of his officers or their families and there are well authenticated cases of sowars attempting to protect European women from the mob and of their warning individual European soldiers to escape to their lines. Above all, as has been shown, some eighty or ninety sowars remained true to their salt.

[Sir Henry Lawrence:] 'Give me plenary military power in Oude: I will not use it unnecessarily.' [Lord Canning:] 'You have full military powers. The Governor-General will support you in everything that you think necessary.'

Telegrams, 16 May, 1857[1]

(iii)

Indian Mutiny, 1857: Meerut rebels take over Delhi – Ghazi-ud-din Nagar – Badli-ke-serai – 'siege' of Delhi starts

The first of the mutineers to reach Delhi were, of course, since they were mounted, some of the sowars of the 3rd Light Cavalry. They killed the toll collector at the bridge of boats over the Jumna, and soon gained entry to the city. There they prevailed upon the ancient and reluctant Bahadur Shah, the pensioned-off last representative of the Mogul royal family, to lead them in their fight for the faith. In the course of the day, the sepoys from Meerut followed them in.

Though much treasure, a large arsenal and a vast magazine (a part of which was skilfully blown up by the British officer in charge of it) were kept within its walls, there were no European troops stationed in or near Delhi. Three regiments of native infantry and some native artillery were all that there were. These, except for certain guards drawn from them, were in the cantonments two miles to the north of the city. All of these mutinied, though many hung back till they were sure that there was to be no pursuit by the European troops from Meerut. By dawn of 12 May, after extensive plundering and the murder of many Europeans and Eurasians, not a vestige of British power survived in that great city of 150,000 inhabitants.

Many of the Europeans and Eurasians in the city were massacred, but numbers also escaped. Some thirty such fugitives were tracked down on 19 May, and brought to safety in Meerut by Lieutenants Gough and Mackenzie with a party of the loyal 3rd Cavalry sowars. They had been hidden in a village where the headman was an old German, called Cohen, who had gone native. Gough says that 'the zemindar Cohen received a very handsome reward from Government . . . and each man of our rescuing party received promotion or reward of some kind.' Among these were two who before long 'received commissions as native officers in Murray's Jat Horse', later the 14th Bengal Lancers.[2]

*   *   *

As soon as the news of the mutiny reached the Commander-in-Chief, Major-General the Hon. George Anson, he realized that the recovery of Delhi by European troops was the first essential. Upon this would depend whether the rest of the Bengal Army and the people generally remained staunch or not. Fortunately the three most important local rulers decided to support the British. With their help communications with the Punjab, where most of the European troops were stationed, were kept open. They also guarded the road to Delhi from Ambala, where Anson now began to collect his force.

His greatest difficulty in acting with speed was lack of transport. The permanent transport service had been abolished after the Second Sikh War, and 'there were', in Fortescue's words, 'no means of mobilising the troops for the field. Commissariat and Medical Departments were alike helpless. . . . The Bazaars were disorganized by the general unrest; provisions were difficult to collect; and contractors . . . were not easily to be found.'[3] Sufficient arms, ammunition, tent equipage, and a siege-train* had to be collected too. Delhi was, after all, a fortified city, seven miles in circumference 'defended by troops armed and trained by the best British officers.'[4]

Anson's plan was for the troops from Meerut under Wilson to join those from Ambala in re-occupying the cantonments north of Delhi. Before the junction could take place, Wilson, in whose force

---

* 'A third-class siege train' was ordered from Phillour. With it, as escort, came a wing of the 9th Bengal Irregular Cavalry. (Stubbs, III, 252.)

were two squadrons of the Carabiniers,* had to fight the first two actions of what came to be known as 'The Sepoy War'. On 30 May, at Ghazi-ud-din Nagar, about nine miles from Delhi, he was attacked by 'a large force of the mutineers, accompanied by heavy guns from Delhi'. One of the two Carabinier squadrons escorted four horse artillery guns, and one troop of the other escorted four guns of the Light Field Battery. These guns soon silenced the enemy's, and men of the 60th Rifles drove the mutineers from their pieces. They then retired, abandoning five guns. They were pursued by the Carabiniers 'for a considerable distance',[5] and some of them were cut down. The following day the mutineers attacked again and were again driven off. The extreme heat prevented any pursuit. In these two actions the Carabiniers lost six killed and eight wounded.

On 27 May Anson, like many of his men at this time, was struck down by cholera and died almost immediately. He was succeeded by the Crimean veteran, Major-General Sir Henry Barnard. On 6 June the siege-train arrived at Alipur, where next day Wilson joined Barnard.

The force now collected, perhaps 3,500 strong, was supported, as ever in India, by myriad camp followers. For every white man there were perhaps twenty natives. As Dr Sen, the official Indian chronicler, has put it 'It was the Indian cook who brought the white soldier his dinner . . ., it was the Indian bhisti who brought him his drink . . ., it was the Indian dooly-bearer who carried the wounded . . ., and the Indian servant who looked after his general comfort.'[6] Lord Roberts tells the story that when the men of the 9th Lancers were asked to name the man they thought most worthy of the Victoria Cross after the siege of Delhi, 'they unanimously chose the head bhisti.'[7]

The mutiny was condemned by numbers of Indians of all classes, on the ground that it was immoral to be faithless to one's salt. This widespread native condemnation ensured that the revolt could not develop into a nation-wide rising. It made it possible, too, to crush it within a tolerable period. Certainly without the natives' devoted service no European troops could have made a day's march towards Delhi.

As it was, the equivalent of three and a half infantry battalions,

---

* Under Lieutenant-Colonel Custance and Captain Rosser. The rest of Wilson's force consisted of 460 men of the 60th Rifles; 2nd Tp, 1st Bde, Bengal Horse Artillery; 3rd Coy, 3rd Bn, No. 14 Light Field Battery; 100 artillery recruits, with two eighteen-pounder guns, and two companies of Sappers and Miners. On 1 June the 2nd Gurkhas (only 490 strong) joined Wilson's force.

twenty-two field guns,* the 9th Lancers, the two squadrons of the Carabiniers† and the siege-train (another twenty-two guns) were now, less than a month after the Meerut outbreak, assembled before the city. Barnard grouped this force into one cavalry and two infantry brigades. The cavalry brigade was commanded by Brigadier Hope Grant, who had led the 9th Lancers so successfully in the Sikh Wars (see Vol. I, pp. 269–70, 280).

James Hope Grant, born of a good Scottish family in 1808, was one of the most remarkable cavalry officers of his age. He was a younger brother of the painter, Sir Francis Grant, but his own artistic bent was in the musical line. As a boy he had devoted a considerable portion of his time 'to the study of that noble instrument the violoncello'.[8] At eighteen he joined the 9th Lancers with which regiment he served for many years. In 1841, having muddled away most of a £10,000 patrimony in what was a very expensive regiment, he had almost decided to quit the army. His proficiency on what he called 'the big fiddle', however, procured him the post of brigade-major to Lord Saltoun, whose instrument was the guitar. Saltoun commanded the expedition to China in 1841–42 and Grant distinguished himself in the little war which followed, gaining the C.B. He was a resolutely religious man. His favourite maxim throughout life was 'Act according to your conscience and defy the consequences.' To this he lived up when he confronted his commanding officer with the charge of being drunk at the battle of Sobraon (see Vol. I, p. 269). Throughout the mutiny campaigns he was almost always accompanied, as one officer observed, 'by an enormous violoncello, carried on a camel. Natives ran away from it whenever it appeared, calling it "shaitan" (the devil).'[9]

* * *

* 60th; 75th; 1st and 2nd European Bengal Fusiliers; Simur (Gurkha) Battalion. 2nd Troop, 1st Brigade, and 2nd and 3rd Troops, 3rd Brigade, Bengal Horse Artillery: 3rd Company, 3rd Battalion, No. 14 Light Field Battery; 4th Company, 6th Battalion, Royal Artillery.

† Even before leaving Ambala, the 9th Lancers had lost twenty men from cholera. They had ninety-five men on detachment in the hills, and twenty-four officers were either detached or on leave. The regiment left Ambala with only sixteen officers and 493 men.

'The poor Carabiniers', wrote an officer of the 9th Lancers at this time, 'look dreadfully heavy and oppressed in their blue clothing and overalls. They envy us much our comfortable white clothing.' (Anson, 11.)

On 8 June, at Badli-ke-serai, six miles from Delhi, a large force of mutineers faced Barnard, entrenched with thirty guns. After a sharp engagement they were driven from their position with the loss of eleven of their guns: a remarkable instance of superior generalship triumphing over numbers. Cornet A. S. Jones, who gained in the action the first Victoria Cross ever to be won by the 9th Lancers, describes what happened:

'The niggers had not a large enough force for so extensive a position, and consequently we had the means of turning the position. For this purpose the 9th Lancers, with two troops of Horse Artillery, were . . . ordered to march at twelve o'clock on Sunday night [to the far side of the bank of a canal on the enemy's left flank], while the rest of the force was to attack the enemy in front at daylight. . . . About daybreak we [recrossed] the canal [and] astonished the enemy by appearing precisely in their rear when they were well engaged with our main column. . . . The enemy . . . poured in a good shower of grape. . . . I believe we none of us disgraced ourselves, though I was in great fear sometimes that the small numbers and inexperience of the officers we had would bring us to grief.'[10]

The 9th then charged with good effect, and Jones, with only a hand-ful of men, captured a nine-pounder, and, according to Grant, 'sabred its six gunners, turned the gun upon a village where the enemy had taken refuge, and dislodged them from it.'[11] The regi-ment's losses were fifteen killed and ten wounded. The total British losses were fifty-one killed and 132 wounded. Barnard immediately advanced to capture the old cantonments on the famous Ridge, and there he began to establish the equally famous Delhi Field Force.

'We are all delighted at the march the Guides
have been making. It is the talk of the border. I
hope the men will fill their pockets in the sack of
Delhi. . . . Bring back some standards from the
palace – especially Bahadur Shah's trousers.'
HERBERT EDWARDES to HENRY DALY,
8 June, 1857[1]

(iv)

*Indian Mutiny, 1857: Sir John Lawrence acts promptly
in Punjab – sends reinforcements to Delhi – Corps of
Guides arrives*

In the Punjab, meanwhile, the tension of the last three weeks had
been great. The province, as has been seen, had only been annexed
eight years before. How would its peoples react to the news from
Delhi? Fortunately the pick of the civil service was in charge of
affairs there and the ratio of European troops to native was higher
than in the older provinces. Swift action was taken by Sir John
Lawrence, the Chief Commissioner, and others. The most successful
instance of this was at Mian-mir cantonment outside Lahore, the
capital. On 13 May, 2,500 native troops, including the 8th Bengal
Native Cavalry, were at one fell swoop disarmed there, in the
presence of 600 Europeans with artillery. The pattern was much the
same, though not always so exceptionally speedy, thorough, or
lacking in bloodshed, in much of the rest of the province.

Lawrence saw at once that he must take a great risk and send away
to Delhi virtually every soldier upon whose loyalty he could count,
not only European but also native. The first to arrive, almost as soon
as Barnard himself, was the Corps of Guides. This famous corps had
been raised in 1846 after the First Sikh War 'for Police and General
Purposes' in the frontier districts around Peshawar. Its first Commandant was Lieutenant Harry Burnett Lumsden; one of its earliest
seconds-in-command and Adjutants was Lieutenant William Stephen
Raikes Hodson (see p. 154 below), two of the great names in Indian
cavalry history. To begin with, the Guides consisted of only ninety-
six cavalry and 184 infantry. After the annexation of the Punjab in
1849, the corps was expanded to 400 horse and 600 foot. The next
few years saw it engaged in countless further affairs.

'Men from every wild and warlike tribe were represented in its

ranks, men habituated to war and sport, the dangers and vicis-
situdes of Border life, Affredies and Goorkhas, Sikhs and
Huzaras, Wuziries, Pathans of every class, and even Kaffirs,
speaking all the tongues of the Border, Persian, Pooshtoo, etc.,
dialects unknown to the men of the plains; in many cases the
Guides had a camp language or patois of their own. Lumsden
sought out the men notorious for desperate deeds, leaders in
forays, who kept the passes into the hills, and lived amid inaccessible rocks. He made Guides of them; tempted by regular
pay and enterprise, many joined the Corps and became conspicuous for daring and fidelity.'[2]

Lumsden clothed his men in khaki, the first soldiers ever to be
dressed in uniform of this colour.* Inevitably they were soon nicknamed 'The Mudlarks'. The corps' transport was provided solely by
its own horses, mules and camels. It was this self-dependence which
enabled it to start off on its epic march to Delhi six hours after the
order was received. Lumsden himself, with an escort of forty-five
Guides, was on a mission to Kandahar, and so his second-in-
command, Captain Henry Dermot Daly, found himself in command
a bare two weeks after he had first joined. With 153 sabres and 349
rifles he marched out of Mardan at 6 p.m. on 12 May.

The Corps was at first intended to be part of the Movable Column
which Lawrence had just formed for nipping trouble in the bud at the
various military stations in the Punjab; but it was soon sent on alone
(to be followed much later by the Movable Column) to aid Barnard
before Delhi. There, a day late for Badli-ke-serai, it arrived on 9
June after marching 580 miles, chiefly at night, at the hottest season
of the year. In twenty-six days (including three days halted) the
Guides had performed a feat virtually unrivalled in the history of

* 'The clothing of the Guides was dyed by men regimentally employed,
each soldier contributing ¼ anna *per mensem* from his pay. This arrangement was maintained until early in the twentieth century, for quite twenty
years after the general adoption of fast-dyed khaki clothing; and its
abolition was agreed to with reluctance, as in addition to the khaki uniform
the dyers used to dye the brightly coloured pagris so popular among certain
classes of Indians when wearing plain clothes.' (*Guides*, 7.)

There is some doubt as to the original colour of khaki, the Urdu word for dusty.
One contemporary description calls it 'stone-coloured' (Lowe, 200), while another alleges that it was 'ash-coloured'. (Sherer, J. W. *Daily Life during the
Indian Mutiny: personal experiences of 1857*, 1898, 58, 93.) It was possibly more
grey and less yellow than it later became.

mounted troops. The foot managed to keep up with the horse because they were provided with camels: one for every two men.

As they approached the Ridge, a staff officer galloped up to Daly, asking, 'How soon can you be ready to go into action?' Without hesitation, he replied: 'In half an hour'.[3] That very afternoon, in support of the picquets, his men helped to drive off an enemy attack from Delhi. The Guides' arrival had been greeted by tremendous cheering. 'Their stately height and martial bearing', wrote one who welcomed them, 'made all who saw them proud to have such aid. They came in as firm and light as if they had marched a mile.'[4]

'Delhi has fallen to the Army of the North-West Provinces and Punjab alone.'
                    LORD CANNING tO VERNON SMITH,
                                        8 Oct 1857[1]

(v)

Indian Mutiny, 1857: 'siege' of Delhi: Punjab Cavalry arrives – Hodson and Hodson's Horse – Lind's Horse – Delhi recaptured – Hodson kills the Princes

As more and more regiments mutinied throughout the Ganges plain, in Rajputana, in the affected parts of Bengal, and in Central India, the number of mutineers in Delhi was constantly being added to. Opposed to them at the start of the so-called siege, as has been shown, was the Delhi Field Force, itself under siege. For three and a half months it kept a precarious hold upon the Ridge, sustained by the devoted services of myriad native camp followers. On 5 July, Barnard, its commander, died of cholera. His successor, Reed, who was an invalid, was superseded by Archdale Wilson on 17 July. Brigadier-General Neville Chamberlain, having organized the Movable Column and handed it over to Brigadier-General John Nicholson, arrived on the Ridge on 2 July as Adjutant-General.

The Force's losses from the mutineers' attacks (generally made,

with intent, at the hottest time of the day), and from disease and
exposure, were, for some weeks, not much more than equalled by
the reinforcements which from time to time came in from the Punjab. Amongst these there arrived on 23 June some infantry, six
horse artillery guns and a composite squadron of Punjab cavalry.
This last was made up of troops from the five regiments which
formed the mounted half of the Punjab Irregular Force, known from
its initials as 'The Piffers'.[2] Raised immediately after the annexation
of the Punjab, these regiments became in 1865 part of the famous
Punjab Frontier Force, immortalized by Kipling in 'The Lost
Legion':

> 'You must know that all along the north-west frontier of India
> there is spread a force . . . whose duty it is to quietly and un-
> ostentatiously shepherd the tribes in front of them. They move
> up and down, and down and up, from one desolate little post
> to another; they are ready to take the field at ten minutes'
> notice; they are always half in and half out of a difficulty some-
> where along the monotonous line; their lives are as hard as their
> own muscles, and the papers never say anything about them.'[3]

Lieutenant Daly, who as has been seen, brought the Guides down
to the Ridge, had raised the 1st Punjab Cavalry, 'unshackled by a
bank, unaided by a Government advance',[4] in May, 1849. During
1850, 1851 and 1852, he had commanded the regiment in four minor
but arduous frontier campaigns. The men were mostly of 'the fine
race of Eusafzai Pathans', and 'several of the native officers', wrote
Daly, 'are men of good family.' 'The regiment is armed, dressed,
and equipped in a style equal to the best irregular cavalry; all have
carbines; the horses are strong and hardy; they are purchased from a
subscription fund.'[5] The 2nd Punjab Cavalry was raised by Lieutenant Samuel Browne, who later gained the Victoria Cross and gave
his name to the sword belt which he invented.

Each of the five regiments had an establishment of 588 natives of
all ranks, in six troops, each man receiving twenty rupees a month.
There were, as was common in *silladar* cavalry, four British officers. 'In my regiment', noted Daly in 1850, 'each presidency has
furnished an officer. A strange combination. A lieutenant, Bombay
Army, commandant; a captain, Madras Army, 2nd in command; and
a cornet of Bengal Cavalry, adjutant.'[6] (See Appendix, p. 455.)

Daly was an Irishman from Galway, the son of a lieutenant-colonel of the 4th Light Dragoons, who had served in that regiment for twenty-four years. Born in India in 1821, he was commissioned at the age of nineteen as an ensign in the 1st Bombay European regiment, and in 1846 became its adjutant. He fought in the Second Sikh War at Multan and at Gujrat, distinguishing himself on both occasions. Daly, who spoke Hindustani, Maratha and Gujrati fluently, was a paragon amongst irregular cavalry leaders, appreciated equally, it seems, by his superiors and by his men. The care and interest which he applied to the individuals of the various regiments he commanded was both loving and unremitting. In 1856, on the annexation of Oudh, he had raised and commanded the 1st Oudh Irregular Cavalry; but he had scarcely completed that task when he was transferred to the Guides.

In the camp before Delhi was another, more controversial commander of irregulars. Born in the same year as Daly, Lieutenant William Hodson, the son of an archdeacon, had been educated under Dr Arnold at Rugby. Known to his intimates there as 'Larky Pritchard', he was probably the model for Harry East, the inseparable chum of Tom Brown in Thomas Hughes's *Tom Brown's Schooldays*. Arnold selected him to be praepostor in a house where disciplinary reform was urgently required and he fully justified the choice.[7]

After taking a degree at Trinity College, Cambridge, he joined the 2nd Bengal Grenadiers in 1845, and with that regiment took part in the battles of Mudki, Ferozeshah and Sobraon. Transferred to the 1st Bengal European Fusiliers, he became one of Sir Henry Lawrence's 'young men'. In 1847 he was appointed second-in-command and adjutant to the Guides. He took an active share in raising and training the regiment, and displayed exceptional daring and skill in irregular fighting during the Second Sikh War.

In 1852, aged thirty-one, after a spell as an assistant commissioner, he assumed command of the Guides when Lumsden went home on leave. Lumsden was lovable, gentle, rather easy-going. Hodson was none of these things. Overbearing and unconciliatory, contemptuous of 'proper channels' and almost devoid of tact, he made enemies both above and below him. His rapid preferment in itself was calculated to breed unpopularity. With only seven years' service it was, as he himself recognized, 'no small thing for a subaltern to be raised to the command of a battalion of infantry and a squadron and a half of cavalry, with four English officers under him.'[8] In his new command, as throughout his career, he seems to have been either worshipped or loathed.

'Lieutenant Hodson', wrote an admirer at this time, 'marvel-lously attaching the Guides to himself by the ties of mutual honour, mutual daring, and mutual devotion, has on every opportunity proved that the discipline of a public school and subsequent university training are no disqualification for hazardous warfare, or for the difficult task of keeping wild tribes in check.'[9]

Immediately on taking over the regiment, Hodson set about tightening up discipline. At the same time he showed himself ruth-less about dismissing those he did not instinctively trust. This led to his being much disliked in certain quarters, especially by his adjutant, Lieutenant Turner, who became an inveterate and implacable enemy. There soon arose, out of a minor dispute between Hodson and Turner over the price paid for a man's horse, doubts concerning the state of the regimental accounts. These, as in most *silladar* regi-ments, were extremely complicated, and neither Lumsden nor Hodson was very business-like. In short a Court of Enquiry was ordered. At the same time, Hodson was under another cloud. When he had been in charge of the civil administration of the Yusafzai, he had arrested their chieftain and kept him under arrest for instigating the murder of the Resident. The evidence had been circumstantial, and Hodson was now deprived of his command for an act which was officially labelled as one of high-handed oppression.

After many months, the Court of Enquiry reported that the state of the accounts was far from satisfactory. But, just when all seemed lost, things suddenly took a turn for the better. The new Comman-dant of the Guides, Major Reynell Taylor, was instructed by John Lawrence to carry out a full investigation of the accounts. In Febru-ary, 1856, after two months' painstaking work, Taylor completely cleared Hodson's honour.

Meanwhile he had been serving as an ordinary subaltern in the 1st Bengal European Fusiliers, practically beginning his military career all over again. To his credit, he performed his humble duties with exemplary dedication. His commanding officer, with whom he got on very well, was impelled, in January, 1857, to write to the Adju-tant-General that Hodson's 'numerous qualifications are virtually lost to the State by his being employed as a regimental subaltern, as he is fitted for, and capable of doing great justice to, any staff situa-tion.'[10] Hodson followed this up with a personal interview with Anson, the Commander-in-Chief. They rather took to each other, and it is no surprise that on 16 May, less than a week after the Meerut outbreak, Anson appointed him Deputy Assistant-Quartermaster-General at Ambala, and ordered him 'to raise 100 horse and 50 foot for service in the Intelligence Department, and as personal escort.'[11]

Two days later he was commissioned to 'raise and command an entire new regiment of Irregular Horse'.[12] To achieve this, since his duties with the Field Force prevented his returning in person to the Punjab, he called by correspondence upon his friend Robert Montgomery, the Judicial Commissioner of the Punjab, and upon the heads of the leading families in the province, with whom he had a close acquaintance. Between them, they raised seven troops, recruited for the most part from 'our old adversaries of the Khalsa'.[13] The first three troops of Hodson's Horse left for Delhi on 23 June, 235 strong, and arrived on 12 July. One of the last troops to be formed consisted entirely of Afghans, 'a counterpoise', as Hodson put it, 'to my Punjabees'.[14] (See Appendix, p. 455.)

The regimental uniform, like that of the Guides, was khaki-coloured. It was 'picked out with red, i.e. red puggrees and kummerbunds, and sash which was worn obliquely over the shoulder, and was meant to distinguish them from the "catch-'em-alive-ohs", which abounded both in our force and the enemy's.'* The men were armed 'with tulwar and matchlock, and an occasional long spear, according to each man's taste'.[15]

The first action in which Hodson's Horse took part occurred in mid-August forty-five miles from the Ridge at Rohtak, where a body of mutineers from Delhi had assembled in an effort to cut off communications with the Punjab. Hodson, who had temporarily assumed command of the Guides as well as of his own regiment, commanded on that occasion 361 irregular cavalrymen.† He employed an old ruse very successfully. Withdrawing his men a short distance, he lured the mutineers into the open.

'The enemy thought we were bolting', he wrote, 'and came on in crowds, firing and yelling, and the sowars brandishing their swords as if we were already in their hands, when suddenly I gave the order, "Threes about and at them." The men obeyed with a cheer; the effect was electrical; never was such a scatter.

---

* Hodson's Horse later adopted a salmon-coloured *alkalak* (long coat, fastened on the chest). From this the men acquired the nickname of 'The Flamingoes'.

† Guides Cavalry, 103; Hodson's Horse, 233; Jhind Horse, 25.

I launched five parties at them, each under an officer, and in they went, cutting and firing into the very thick of them. . . . We cut down upwards of fifty in as many seconds. The remainder flew back to the town, as if not the Guides and Hodson's Horse but death and the devil were at their heels . . .

'In three days', he claimed, 'we have frightened away and demoralized a force of artillery, cavalry and infantry some 2000 strong, beat those who stood or returned to fight us twice, in spite of numbers, and got fed and furnished forth by the rascally town itself.'[16]

On numerous occasions before that, the mutineers had sallied forth to harass the beleaguered men on the Ridge. Only when, as at Rohtak, engagements took place in the countryside, was there much scope for cavalry. Around the British camp itself the ground was broken 'and thick with gardens and trees'.[17] The most nearly successful of the many rebel attacks took place on 19 June. On that evening, the mutineers, tying down the infantry all round the camp perimeter, sneaked up in the twilight upon the right rear. With a small force which included two squadrons of the 9th Lancers, one Troop of the Carabiniers and some of the Guides, Hope Grant only just managed to beat the enemy off. 'We got into a fearful scrape', wrote Captain Anson of the 9th. 'Horse Artillery guns and Cavalry having to cope with the enemy's all arms, most strongly posted behind garden walls and villages and copses.'[18] Daly was severely wounded in the arm while leading the second of two desperate charges in a successful attempt to save some guns. At one point Hope Grant found himself

'unhorsed, surrounded by the enemy. . . . My orderly, a native Sowar of the 4th Irregulars* . . . rode up to me, and said, "Take my horse – it is your only chance of safety." . . . He was a Hindostanee Mussulman, belonging to a regiment the greater part of which had mutinied; and it would have been easy for him to have killed me and gone over to the enemy; but he behaved nobly, and was ready to save my life at the risk of his own. I refused his offer; but, taking a firm grasp of his horse's tail, I told [him] to drag me out of the crowd.'[19]

---

* Most of the 4th Bengal Irregular Cavalry mutinied, but about ninety of them remained faithful and served in the British camp till 9 July, when they were disarmed as a precautionary measure, and employed as unarmed police.

Brevet Lieutenant-Colonel R. A. Yule, who had succeeded Hope Grant in command of the 9th only twelve days before, was killed in another charge:

'My squadron', wrote Lieutenant A. S. Jones, who in the following year was to win the Victoria Cross, 'came down . . . in rear of a troop of Horse Artillery, who were nearly over-powered by a fire of musketry from two gardens and the road in front. The officer commanding the troop . . . cried out as we came up: "Get along to the front, you cavalry; I can't stand this!" and poor Colonel Yule, thus excited, brought us to the front, and before I had time to form the squadron on the road, cried out "Charge!" This order was impetuously obeyed by Lieutenant Blair, who rushed to the front, followed by the men. I had taken a look at the road and observed that it was not fit for a charge, so I watched Yule for an instant and observed his face change, so I tried to stop the men. I believe he also tried the same, but both of us were too late, and I gave way and went with the stream, getting as fast as I could to the front, where poor Yule was here shot. . . .'[20]

The 9th Lancers lost six killed and eight wounded on this day.

On 9 July there occurred a raid right into the centre of the British camp by two squadrons of the 8th Bengal Irregular Cavalry.* Their object was to induce the Native Horse Artillery to join them bringing their guns with them. 'The Native Artillerymen behaved admirably: they not only refused to respond to the call, but they begged the men of the European troop, which was unlimbered close by, to fire through them on the mutineers', which in the event proved unnecessary.[21] This bold incursion was thought at the time to have been aided by treacherous collusion between the 8th and the 9th Bengal Irregular Cavalry, the headquarters wing of which had arrived in camp a week previously. It is more likely to have been made easy by the fact that the uniforms of the rebel 8th were almost exactly the same as those of the loyal 9th. This led to the two horse artillery guns and the weak troop of thirty-two Carabiniers, which, with the detachment of the 9th Irregular Cavalry, formed the picquet, being completely taken by surprise. Indeed, the Carabiniers found themselves left 'to receive the first rush of the rebel Cavalry', unsupported by the guns.[22]

* This regiment had mutinied at Bareilly on 31 May. The men did not murder their officers, and twenty-one of them remained faithful.

'In the confusion, I am sorry to say', wrote General Reed, '... the Carabiniers gave way, in spite of the endeavours of their officers to stop them. These men I propose to dismount as a disgrace to them. It would appear that they are composed mostly of recruits, and, being mounted on half-broken horses, do not know how to manage them.'[23]

One of the guns also 'retreated into Camp'.[24] A very nasty situation was spectacularly saved by the gallantry and presence of mind of the two horse artillery officers, Major Harry Tombs and Lieutenant James Hills, both of whom received the Victoria Cross.[25]

The equivocal behaviour of the men of the 9th Irregular Cavalry decided the authorities to send them back to the Punjab in detachments. One of these mutinied en route. It was overtaken by a body of the 17th Bengal Irregular Cavalry, under its second-in-command, Captain Hockin. The 17th had been sent away from Delhi at the same time as the 9th. Hockin now called upon the sowars of the 9th to lay down their arms. This they refused to do. Hockin was on the point of charging them, when the leader of the mutinous detachment, Risaldar Wazir Khan, came forward and challenged Risaldar Ali Wardi Khan of the 17th to single combat. The men of both detachments then lined up to watch this rare engagement. It resulted in the Risaldar of the 9th killing the Risaldar of the 17th, but not before he himself had been severely wounded. Hockin's men then attacked the mutineers, killing, it seems, every one of them.[26]

*　　*　　*

On 14 August, part of the Movable Column under Brigadier-General John Nicholson, the 'Lion of the Punjab', arrived in camp. It included about 200 newly raised Multani irregulars, known from their Commandant's name as Lind's Pathan Horse, 'fine men, but totally undisciplined'.[27] These had been raised by Herbert Edwardes, Commissioner of Peshawar, and Nicholson immediately on news of the mutiny being received. The men were sent by the chiefs of the wild Pathan tribe which lived in and around Multan and in 'that portion of the trans-Indus country called the Derajat'.[28] Many of them had served on the British side in the Second Sikh War. In 1858, an irregular regiment was formed from a number of *ressalah*, each named after its commandant, e.g. Lind's, Cureton's. (See Appendix, p. 455.)

On 25 August, Nicholson defeated a large body of mutineers at Najafgarh, eighteen miles from Delhi. These had set out to intercept the thirty-four guns of the siege-train, which, heavily escorted and covering eight miles of road, had for weeks been lumbering towards Delhi from Ferozepore. In the night of 3 September they came safely into camp. By that date, the Field Force numbered more than 8,500, of which over 3,000 were Europeans; but because of sickness, the effective strength was only about 7,800. On 11 September, 618 of the 2,040 cavalry were reported as sick.[29]

During most of the siege there was little enough cavalry work to be done, and since trained artillerymen were scarce, men of the two European cavalry regiments were trained and employed as gunners. On 8 September Trooper Potiphar of the 9th reported that 'all our men working at the guns are to receive double pay and an extra portion of Grog and Beer, which is quite needful, as I can speak from experience by working in the Batteries since June last.'

The final preparations for the storming of the city entailed the erection of breaching batteries, under heavy fire, right close up to the walls. On the day before the assault, Trooper Potiphar described what hell it was to serve in one of them:

'The Battery I am in consists of 18 heavy pieces about 400 yards from the walls. We kept up a continual fire of salvos all night. . . . We were not long at work after daybreak before we had some casualties. . . . [Later] the cross fire from the enemy became so dangerous that our men were getting wounded in all directions. Out of 7 men who were posted at my gun only three were left, myself and two others, and we had to continue our fire as usual. I was now port fire man for a space of three hours, when our gun was returned disabled and we joined another gun's crew who had suffered much. . . . One good thing is we get a Dram about every two hours and much we need it. . . . At eight o'clock in the evening we were relieved by another troop of ours and we returned to our camp, but this was only for a few hours, as the storming commences at daybreak tomorrow, and we are to be in the saddle again by 3 a.m. . . . By the time I reached my tent I was pretty tired.'[30]

Of the four assaulting columns which set out at dawn on 14 September, that on the right, which had to contend with thousands of mutineers concealed in the suburbs outside the walls, was the

18. Sikh Horse, 1857–58, showing l. to r. Lieutenant C. H. Mecham and Assistant-Surgeon T. Anderson

19. The 14th Light Dragoons (Hussars) in India, 1857

20. (*above left*) Field-Marshal Lord Strathnairn (Sir Hugh Rose)

21. (*above*) General Sir Henry Dermot Daly. (See p. 153)

22. (*below left*) Major Hodson of Hodson's Horse. (See p. 154)

23. (*below*) Tantia Topi

least successful. Indeed, the enemy was about to overpower it, threatening the safety of the camp itself, when Hope Grant came to the rescue. With him he had 200 men of the 9th Lancers, 410 sabres from the Guides, 1st, 2nd and 5th Punjab Cavalry and Hodson's Horse, together with seven horse artillery guns. All these arrived on the scene, the 9th Lancers leading, 'at a gallop', as Hodson's second-in-command recorded, 'bang through our own batteries, the gunners cheering us as we leapt over the sandbags.'[31] The horse artillery then came forward, and suffering crippling casualties, attempted to hold the milling enemy back.

For two hours, under a horribly galling fire, mostly grape, the brigade sat motionless. 'It was necessary', wrote Hope Grant in his dispatch, 'to retain our position to prevent the enemy from taking our batteries. . . . Not a man flinched from his post . . . and when a poor fellow got knocked over it seemed to put the men in good spirits.'[32] One lancer was killed and forty were wounded. In the native cavalry two men were killed and twenty-three wounded. It had been a gruelling ordeal. 'There they sate, firm in their saddles, "ghastly motionless as if they slept," whilst the unerring grape-shot streamed upon them and made dreadful openings in their ranks.'[33]

It took six more days of street fighting before Delhi was finally recaptured; but the cavalry had little more to do.

With the fall of Delhi it seemed certain that the revolt had failed and that the mutineers would eventually be crushed. Yet further mutinies occurred in October. Even as late as the first week of December two detachments of the 11th Irregular Cavalry mutinied at the isolated stations of Jalpigore and Madariganj, not far from the Nepalese border.

*　　*　　*

On 20 September, Hodson, at considerable risk, sallied out to capture the King of Delhi, who had fled the city. Having guaranteed the old man's life Hodson with fifty men of his own regiment escorted him back to Delhi amidst large crowds of armed followers. Next day, again facing great dangers, Hodson rode out to make prisoner the King's three sons, the real directors of affairs in Delhi. They surrendered to him unconditionally, and as the procession approached Delhi, Hodson personally shot all three princes dead. In justification for this highhanded action he claimed that the mob was on the point of rescuing his captives. It is an unpleasing incident with which to close the remarkable history of the mounted arm at the siege of Delhi.*

> 'News from Lucknow. . . . Although the Garrison is saved – and just in time – it cannot be brought away.'
>
> LORD CANNING to VERNON SMITH,
> 8 Oct 1857[1]

(vi)

Indian Mutiny, 1857: situation in Oudh – siege of Cawnpore – Havelock enters Cawnpore – first 'relief' of Lucknow

Meanwhile, in Oudh, even more recently annexed than the Punjab, anxiety was widespread. There were very few European troops either at Lucknow, the capital; at Cawnpore, the military headquarters, forty-five miles away;† or anywhere else in the province. The Chief Commissioner, Sir Henry Lawrence, Sir John's brother, had for some time past been preparing the Residency at Lucknow for a siege. This started, in part, on 31 May, the day after the native regiments (including the 7th Bengal Native Cavalry and the 2nd Oudh Irregular Cavalry) had mutinied, though close investment did not occur for four weeks.‡ It lasted more than three and a half months.

Cawnpore rose on 5 June, the outbreak being led by the 2nd

---

* Hodson was killed on 11 March, 1858, during the final capture of Lucknow. He had attached himself to Colonel Napier of the Engineers (later Lord Napier of Magdala) in the course of the storming of the Begum Kothi. The story that he was struck down whilst looting has no basis in fact.

† Cawnpore was technically just outside Oudh, being on the south bank of the Ganges.

‡ Lawrence's careful preparations were put in jeopardy on 30 June when he sallied out ten miles to Chinhat with, amongst others, thirty-six Volunteer Horse, eighty-four Oudh Irregular Cavalry and eleven guns against a very superior force. Everything went wrong and Lawrence was lucky to be able to

Bengal Light Cavalry. General Sir Hugh Wheeler, in a previously prepared but sorely inadequate enclosure, was then besieged for twenty terrible days. The besieging forces were commanded by the Nana Sahib, the adopted son of the late Peshwa, Baji Rao (see Vol. I, p. 195) who had recently been deprived of his territories by the British. His skilful lieutenant was Tantia Topi, a Deshusta Brahmin, who had been brought up as a dependant of the Nana. Forced at last to surrender, most of the Europeans were massacred, possibly as the result of a tragic mistake. The women and children who survived were brutally murdered on 15 July, when news reached the Nana that a relief force was approaching the city.

From Calcutta, during these anxious weeks, Lord Canning, the Governor-General, knowing that no troops from England would reach India before October at the earliest, could do little more than dispatch north-westward whatever European reinforcements came to hand. Their quantity and speed of progress were equally pitiable.

On 4 June, the first men arrived at Benares under Colonel Neill, an infantry officer of iron determination. There, as elsewhere on his route, he subdued the surrounding area with extreme harshness. When he arrived at Allahabad on 11 June, with only forty-three of his own regiment, the 1st Madras European Fusiliers, he found a mutinous situation. It took him till 30 June to 'pacify' the environs of that great city. By then sufficient driblets had arrived from Calcutta to enable Neill to begin the advance towards Cawnpore. On that day he was superseded by Brigadier Henry Havelock, the famous brother of William Havelock, who died leading the 14th Light Dragoons at Ramnagar in 1848 (see Vol. I, p. 272).

Havelock had hurried back from Persia where he had held a command in Major-General Sir James Outram's expedition which had just returned to Bombay. The Persian War, as has been shown, had been short and sharp (see p. 126). It had removed from India, at this critical moment, three European infantry battalions, as well as the 14th Light Dragoons. These, as will be seen, were soon to be used in the suppression of the Mutiny.

In the extreme heat of July, Havelock, marching 126 miles in nine days, entered Cawnpore on the 17th, having fought four successful

save his troops. At one moment these were virtually surrounded, but a brave charge of the volunteer cavalry broke the encirclement enabling the survivors to escape. 'The enemy', he wrote to Havelock that evening, 'have followed us up, and we ... shall probably tonight be surrounded.' (Quoted in Morison, J. L. *Lawrence of Lucknow, 1806–1857*, 1934, 323.)

actions against enormous odds. These engagements were chiefly affairs of foot and artillery, for Havelock had virtually no cavalry.

On 28 June, while at Benares, he had wired to Lieutenant-General Sir Patrick Grant, whom Canning had just appointed as acting Commander-in-Chief, asking permission to form a corps of volunteer cavalry.* Such a body was quickly formed. It consisted of 'officers of regiments which had mutinied, or had been disbanded; of indigo planters, . . . of burnt-out shop-keepers; in short, of all who were willing to join him'.[2] When Havelock left Allahabad on 7 July, the Volunteer Horse, commanded by Captain Barrow, numbered only twenty. It served with distinction in the battles of Cawnpore, particularly in reconnaissance duties. In one charge, it lost a third of its number.† But by mid-August it had grown to eighty men, half of whom were individuals selected from the infantry.

Overcoming immense difficulties, Havelock, with his force much reduced by cholera, sunstroke and fatigue, began the first abortive advance to the relief of Lucknow. In nine well-fought actions he always defeated superior numbers; but in each case pursuit was impossible for lack of cavalry. The most serious result of this was that the mutineers were generally able to take their guns with them when they retreated.

On 17 August, Havelock, fearful for his communications, and beset by ever-increasing numbers of mutineers, was back at Cawnpore, waiting for reinforcements. There he learned that Outram, as had been expected, was to supersede him. Outram had just been nominated Chief Commissioner in succession to Lawrence, whose death, as the result of a wound, had taken place in the Lucknow Residency on 4 July. Chivalrously waiving his military command, he

---

* At this period, and later, a number of other bodies of volunteer horse were formed *ad hoc*. Major Vincent Eyre's unofficial 'Field Force' which restored order in Bihar, for instance, included a dozen mounted volunteers. Amongst the preparations made by Sir Henry Lawrence for the defence of the Residency at Lucknow, was the raising of 'a body of volunteer cavalry, consisting of fifty sabres – chiefly recruited from cavalry and infantry officers and clerks belonging to the public offices . . . under Captain Radcliffe of the 7th Cavalry'. (*Selections*, II, 39.) See Appendix p. 456 for a list of irregular regiments in 1858.

† The only other cavalry consisted of ninety-five men of the 13th Irregular Cavalry and the 3rd Oudh Irregular Cavalry. Havelock reported the disposition of these, at the engagement near Fatehpur, to be 'worse than doubtful'. (Havelock to D.A.G., 12 July, 1857, *Selections*, II, 88.) Two days later, on 14 July, they were quietly disarmed, and their horses appropriated 'for public purposes'. (Havelock to C-in-C, 15 July, 1857, *Selections*, II, 91.)

allowed Havelock the credit for the so-called relief of Lucknow. This, which was in effect simply a reinforcement of the defenders, was achieved with considerable loss on 25 September, some five months after the siege had begun.

In the course of the advance Outram twice put himself at the head of the Volunteer Horse, on one occasion killing over 100 mutineers and capturing two guns. By early September this body had grown to 109 men. It had been supplemented by the arrival of forty sowars of the 12th, as well as a handful of the 3rd Irregular Cavalry regiments. In the action at the Alambagh, outside Lucknow, on 23 September, Lieutenant W. T. Johnson, who commanded these loyal remnants, charged a particularly destructive gun 'which', as he wrote home, 'had been bowling 9-pounders at us for the last half-hour',[3] with twenty-five of his men, sabred 'the well-trained artillerymen of the Oude force'[4] and silenced it.

Outram now took over the command. He decided that the intention of evacuating the original garrison from the Residency was not possible. He determined, therefore, to await further reinforcements. Delhi meanwhile had been recaptured. This encouraging news meant that considerable forces would before long be released for what amounted to the second relief of Lucknow.

'Our old Commander, General [Hope] Grant has been very lucky up to the present time considering the number of actions he has been in. He is a brave man and deserves all he might get hereafter for his labours. . . .'
'Sir Colin's successes are continual.'
PRIVATE FREDERICK POTIPHAR,
9th Lancers, 23 March 1857

(vii)

Indian Mutiny, 1857–58: Bulandshahr – Sir Colin Campbell succeeds Sir Hope Grant – second relief of Lucknow – Narnul – Gangari – third battle of Cawnpore – Bays and 7th Hussars arrive from home – Lucknow recaptured

Within five days of the recapture of Delhi, a force numbering 2,800 men left the city to join in the second relief of Lucknow. It included two troops of horse artillery, 300 of the 9th Lancers and 400 irregular cavalry,* all under Major H. A. Ouvry of the 9th. Commanded from 19 October by Hope Grant, it arrived at Cawnpore on the 26th, having relieved Agra on its way.

Before that a number of minor actions had taken place. Chief of these was that of 28 September, when a force of mutineers was beaten off at Bulandshahr. Rather rashly, perhaps, Ouvry when the cavalry vanguard found the town occupied

> 'determined not to wait for the Infantry, but forming the 9th Lancers into threes, I ordered them to charge through the main street. . . . We passed through a shower of musketry. . . . We met with no loss till we got to the other side. . . . There the enemy made a stand for a moment, but the head of the column charging, the rebels took to flight. . . . We had no business to charge into the town, but I knew that unless we did so, they would have held the town against us.'

Four officers were wounded, and 'about ten men killed and wounded'. No less than five Victoria Crosses were gained that day by the 9th Lancers. Ouvry's account ends thus: 'The enemy's Cavalry were cut up splendidly by the Irregulars, who outstrip the Lancers in a swift pursuit.'[1]

On 9 November, Sir Colin Campbell, who had been sent out from home to assume the command-in-chief, arrived from Calcutta to supersede Hope Grant in personal command of the Lucknow Relief Force. At Cawnpore, he left Major-General Windham with a small force of infantry. Three days later, at the Alambagh, the large walled park and palace of the Kings of Oudh, a few miles to the south of Lucknow, the squadron of Hodson's Horse which formed the advance guard commanded by Gough, 'was attacked by two guns and a body of about 2,000 infantry'.[2]

> 'Hope Grant', wrote Gough, 'rode up to me and desired me to take my squadron and see if I could capture the guns. He further gave me an order to spike them if I found I could not get them away, and to carry out this order I was provided with a hammer and spikes or large nails. Of how I disposed of them I have not the slightest recollection, but I rather suspect I threw them away!

* Detachments of 1st, 2nd and 5th Punjab Cavalry and of Hodson's Horse.

'With my small body of men, my only chance of success was by making a flank attack, and if possible a surprise. With this object I made a considerable *détour*, and managed, under cover of some fields of growing corn or sugar-cane, to arrive on the left flank of the enemy perfectly unseen. The guns were posted on a small mound and a considerable body of the enemy had an admirable position in rear of this mound, in front of and amidst some trees and shrub. Between us and them lay a marshy jheel, with long, reedy grass – an unpleasant obstacle, but which served admirably to cover our movements. I then advanced my men through this . . . at a trot, and so concealed our movements till we got clear, when I gave the word "Form line" and "Charge". My men gave a ringing cheer, and we were into the masses. The surprise was complete, and owing to its suddenness they had no conception of our numbers, and so the shock to them and the victory to us was as if it had been a whole brigade. . . . The guns were captured, the enemy scattered, and the fight became a pursuit. Our loss was very trifling as is often the case in a sudden surprise.'[3]

Gough received the Victoria Cross for this little gem of a cavalry action.

On 16 November the whole force advanced to the relief of Outram and Havelock in the Residency. The cavalry's part in this hard fought operation was chiefly a passive one. The garrison was evacuated and Lucknow temporarily abandoned. Outram, with some 4,000 men, was left at the Alambagh.

*   *   *

At Narnul, some 150 miles to the north-west of Lucknow, a column from Delhi, 2,500 strong, defeated the mutinied Jodhpur Legion on 16 November. Parts of the Carabiniers and the Guides, under Captain Wardlaw of the former, distinguished themselves by a spirited and successful charge in open country, losing sixteen men and twenty-two horses. 'Never', wrote Malleson, 'were the British cavalry met so fairly by the rebel horse.' 'They [the enemy] fought in the most determined manner,' reported Wardlaw afterwards, 'but found their pluck of little avail against the swords of the Guides and Carabiniers. . . . The Guides wheeled to their left and charged the guns on the flanks.'[4] Malleson continues the story: 'The gunners who stood were cut down. Leaving the guns, the cavalry then went on to prevent any rally on the part of the enemy's horse.'[5] This seems to have been a well controlled, if expensive, cavalry engagement.[6]

A month later, on 15 December, at the crisis of a successful action at Gangari, Wardlaw charged an enemy battery over ground much intersected by nullahs. These, which held back the *troop* horses, unfortunately proved no obstacle to the *officers'* chargers. 'No doubt' writes the historian of the Carabiniers, 'the troop horses could have got over somehow had they been better ridden, but the men were mostly novices.'[7] The result was that Wardlaw and two of his lieutenants, not being supported by their men, were cut down and killed. Another version of Wardlaw's death, given by a civil servant who was in the Meerut Volunteer Horse, raised in June and July, states that 'on drawing up after riding through the enemy, he took off his helmet, and was calling on his men to give three cheers, when a bullet through the brain caused his instantaneous death.'[8] Whatever the truth about his death, Wardlaw seems to have been very rash in this engagement.

* * *

When Sir Colin marched south from Lucknow, he found the situation at Cawnpore almost desperate. On 28 November, Major-General Windham, whom he had left in charge, had been driven out of the city into the entrenchment by a very superior force under Tantia Topi, including much of the formidable Gwalior Contingent (see p. 206 below). Campbell arrived only just in time to secure the bridge across the Ganges. Over this he then led his troops from the Lucknow side. First he set about evacuating to safety the large number of women and children and sick and wounded with which he was encumbered. Then, on 6 December, though greatly outnumbered, he defeated Tantia Topi at the so-called Third Battle of Cawnpore, with very small loss to himself.

At one point in that action the 9th Lancers and part of Hodson's Horse, followed by a field battery, surprised a body of the Gwalior Contingent. This at once started to form square.

'The cavalry charged forward to within three hundred yards of their objective; then', according to the historian of the 9th

Lancers, 'Hope Grant's voice was heard thundering "Squadrons outwards!", and, when they had wheeled away to both flanks "as if at a review on the Calcutta parade-ground", as an eye-witness wrote, the guns were seen ready for action in rear. The first shots ploughed great lanes in the hostile squares, and as their serried array began to waver and break up, the Lancers crashed into them, and completed their dissolution.'[9]

At the end of the action, the cavalry* and horse artillery belatedly, having lost their way, pursued the main enemy force towards Kalpi. 'Sir Colin', wrote Private Potiphar of the 9th, 'who was with us . . . passed the remark that we should make good fox hunters as we bagged the game so well, meaning, I suppose, the 16 guns we had captured . . . also about 170 carts laden with ammunition and stores.'[10] Two days later Hope Grant captured fifteen guns which had been allowed to escape towards Bithur on the 6th.

* * *

After securing communications with the Punjab by clearing the Doab and capturing Fategarh, Campbell was reinforced by a column from Delhi commanded by Colonel Seaton. This had with it large quantities of transport, camels, tents and ammunition. By 2 January, 1858, Sir Colin had under his command some 10,000 men.

He now urged upon the Governor-General his preference for campaigning against the rebels in Rohilkand and Central India, while postponing the reconquest of Oudh until after the hot weather. Only then, he considered, would he have a force sufficient for the task. Canning overruled him on political grounds – 'Every eye in India', he wrote, 'is upon Oude, as it was upon Delhi.'[11] Further, unlike that of most other rural districts, the civil population of Oudh was chiefly on the side of the rebels. Campbell loyally accepted this decision and set about preparing for the final capture of Lucknow. For this he reckoned that he needed some 30,000 troops, and it took time for so large a force to assemble. Not till the beginning of March was all ready.

The 2nd Punjab Cavalry, commanded by Captain Sam Browne, was amongst the troops which came in from the north-west. It had taken only forty-eight days to cover over 900 miles. The regiment,

* 9th Lancers; detachments of 1st, 2nd and 5th Punjab Cavalry, and Hodson's Horse.

470 strong, arrived at Cawnpore with 'sixteen sore backs only, and most of those slight ones'.[12]

Among the reinforcements which arrived from home at this time were the 2nd Dragoon Guards (the Bays), on active service for the first time in forty years, and the 7th Hussars. Both regiments went out by the Cape route, carried in sailing transports. The Bays embarked on 25 July, and arrived at Calcutta on 27 November, 125 days later. The 7th arrived on the same date, having taken thirty-seven days less. Neither regiment brought its horses with it. The 7th obtained some from the remount depôt at Allahabad, where it arrived on 21 December. They were 'untrained'.[13] More fortunate were the Bays who were given 120 horses from the Governor-General's Bodyguard. Otherwise, good horses, as Captain W. H. Seymour of the regiment discovered, were 'exceedingly difficult to get. . . . Government are paying 1000 and 1500 rupees for our troopers.' The regiment, the same officer wrote home, had 'no less than 2000 *paid* camp followers'. His own establishment, he reported, consisted of 'a bearer (head servant and valet), a kitmutghar (cook and butler), a doby (washerman), a clashy (tent-pitcher), four syces (grooms) and four grass cutters.' He kept two chargers and two baggage ponies.[14]

As part of the build-up for the capture of Lucknow, a squadron of the 7th Hussars, soon after arriving at Cawnpore, was passed through to Outram at the Alambagh. There, surrounded since mid-November by vastly superior numbers, receiving reinforcements sufficient only to keep his numbers up, he had been holding out against numerous assaults upon his position.

The last and most determined of these was beaten off on 25 February. Engaged in the action were men of the Military Train, which had been temporarily converted into cavalry. This body had been sent out from England to form the transport corps of the China Expedition, diverted to Calcutta by Canning soon after the start of the emergency. Its 220 men comprised well over half Outram's cavalry. They soon became 'thoroughly efficient'.[15] They were mounted on the horses of the 8th Madras Light Cavalry. This regiment was to have formed part of a force which was sent by sea from Madras to Calcutta at the urgent application of Lord Canning to Lord Harris, the Governor of Madras. On their way to embark, the native officers of the 8th demanded, on behalf of the regiment, as a condition of its proceeding on service, 'the restoration of the old and superior rates of field *batta*'. There is no evidence that they were

being disloyal. It seems that they were merely taking advantage of
the crisis 'to secure some profit for themselves'.[16] The regiment was
summarily disbanded and its horses were shipped with the rest of
the force to Bengal. This is believed to have been the sole instance
of misconduct in the Madras Army during the whole of the Mutiny
campaigns.

Also taking part on the 25th, was Hodson's Horse, 'now',
according to Hugh Gough, the adjutant, 'a full-blown regiment,
men better equipped, clothed, and drilled, and the horses of a better
stamp, and with decent saddlery and accoutrements.' In the course
of the action, the regiment attacked a mass of infantry accompanying
two field-guns.

> 'We advanced and charged', wrote Gough. 'We got well into
> them, and the whole affair seemed over. The rearmost gun was
> in our possession; . . . but somehow, owing to the ardour of the
> charge and pursuit, our regiment got quite out of hand, lost all
> formation, and scattered; and they, seeing our condition . . .
> regained their formation as we lost ours. . . . It looked sadly
> probable that Hodson's Horse would in their turn retreat.
> Hodson at this crisis managed to get a few brave spirits to-
> gether – not more than a dozen. . . . Fortunately I [too] was able
> to rally our men to a certain extent, who seeing our supports
> coming up (7th Hussars and Military Train), now came on with
> a will, and charging the remaining gun, scattered the enemy in
> all directions.
>
> '. . . I was much pleased to think that our men had retrieved
> their previous discomfiture.'[17]

*   *   *

Sir Colin's siege of Lucknow, a city with a circumference of twenty
miles, was a methodical affair, designed to conserve the lives of his
own troops as much as possible. Its preliminaries started on 2 March
and its capture was not completed till the 21st. The Commander-in-
Chief had some 31,000 men at his disposal, including 3,500 cavalry
and two troops of Horse Artillery. The mutineers in the city
numbered over 100,000 organized troops 'beside the armed and turbulent scum of a population of 700,000 souls'.[18]

The cavalry division, under Hope Grant, divided into two
brigades commanded by Brigadier William Campbell of the Bays,

and Brigadier A. Little of the 9th Lancers,* though hard-worked in
patrolling and reconnaissance, saw little action. In a skirmish on 6
March, two squadrons of the Bays 'did not stop for three miles',
according to one of the squadron commanders, 'pursuing and
cutting up the pandies right up to Lucknow. . . . We are told the
most gallant, smartest, though somewhat rash thing that has been
done before Lucknow.'[19] Major Percy Smith, in command, as well
as two other ranks were killed, and six were wounded, in this unnecessary business. The truth is that the inexperienced young men
of these two squadrons got out of hand in broken ground over
which they should never have been led. A squadron of the 2nd
Punjab Cavalry, commanded by Captain D. M. Probyn (see p. 224),
charged on the right of the Bays. They had only three men wounded.
Beside capturing an elephant, they claimed to have killed 'sixty to
eighty' mutineers.[20]

It is estimated that some 20,000 rebels escaped from the city in the
concluding stages of the siege. To have allowed this was a grave
blunder, for these mutineers lived to fight again, (and during the hot
weather). Sir Colin was partly to blame. On 15 March he sent off
both cavalry brigades along two roads to pursue some of the fugitives. These had, in fact, scattered all over the countryside and very
few of them were discovered. Consequently, when next day, the
mounted arm was desperately wanted on the outskirts of the city to
destroy other rebels who had taken the opportunity of the cavalry's
absence to escape by different routes, it was not available. By the
time Grant (who had taken over Little's Brigade after its commander
had been wounded on 2 March) and William Campbell had returned on the 17th, they were too late.

On 19 March, after Outram's division had attacked the last major
stronghold four miles to the north-west of the city, the cavalry's
great chance arrived. It was not taken. Grant had been ordered,
pointlessly as it turned out, to remain on the north side of the River
Gumti, which ran along the north side of Lucknow. He could not,
therefore, pursue the mutineers who were escaping, some 9,000
strong, on the other side of the river. William Campbell, on the
other hand, who was on the south bank, remained unaccountably

---

* *1st Brigade* (Little): 9th Lancers; 2nd Battalion Military Train; 2nd Punjab
Cavalry; detachment, 5th Punjab Cavalry; Wale's (Sikh) Horse.

   2nd Brigade (W. Campbell): 2nd Dragoon Guards (Bays); 7th Hussars;
Hodson's Horse; detachment, 1st Punjab Cavalry; (Barrow's) Volunteer
Cavalry.

inactive. The Brigadier was, of course, new to India, and seems to have been obstinate and inefficient as well as inexperienced. He claimed to have lost his way, which is very probable. It seems that 'he moved his force in utter disregard of the statement of his guides, in opposition to the protestations and explanations of all to whose information and advice he was bound to listen.'[21] To be fair to him, however, the Commander-in-Chief's despatch states that he 'performed his detached duty with much vigilance and judgment', adding that 'his march round the city, which was a running fight for the greater part of the day, was a very difficult one.'[22]

Outram, it appears, took action over the Brigadier's head. He ordered Coles' squadron of the 9th Lancers to pursue. This it did to great effect showing what could have been done if the whole brigade had been employed. It captured twelve guns and killed something like 100 of the mutineers. Two men of the 9th won the Victoria Cross for their part in the fight.

'But midway in its victorious career the squadron was brought up short by a steep-sided nullah, from the far side of which guns sheltered in a village opened on it with grape at 200 yards' range. . . . It was only thanks to Coles's coolness', states the regiment's historian, 'that the men could be recalled and brought off without unduly heavy loss.'[23]

*　　*　　*

The record of the 9th Lancers in the Mutiny is very imposing. Though its strength never reached 500, its casualties amounted to five officers and 143 men. No other regiment in India was present at all three of the best known military episodes: the siege of Delhi (where it acquired from the mutineers the long-lasting nickname of the 'Delhi Spearmen'), the siege of Lucknow and its final re-capture. From first to last it marched more than three thousand miles. Fourteen Victoria Crosses were won by the regiment. In no other campaign up to the First World War was this record beaten by any unit of the British army.

'The villain Nanah Saheb still baffles all our ablest
Generals and I am afraid he will continue to do
so.'

PRIVATE FREDERICK POTIPHAR,
9th Lancers, 17 March 1857

(viii)

*Indian Mutiny, 1857–58: pacification of Rohilkand
and Oudh – Cureton's Multani Horse – Kukrauli –
Nawabganj – Rapti*

After the fall of Lucknow and during the hot weather, the Commander-in-Chief, aided by Hope Grant, continued the pacification
of Rohilkand and Oudh. Campbell got through the task, wrote
Fortescue, 'in his own rather heavy and methodical fashion',[1] in
contrast, as will be shown, to Sir Hugh Rose further south. He was
not always well served by his generals. Brigadier-General Robert
Walpole, for example, in whose force were part of the 9th Lancers,
was slow and unenterprising. Brigadier-General John Jones, on the
other hand, who commanded another of the three main columns
formed for the invasion of Rohilkand, was of higher calibre. His
'Roorkee Field Force', unlike Walpole's which suffered at least one
humiliating defeat, was nearly always successful, Jones himself acquiring the nickname of 'the Avenger'. He claimed to have captured
every rebel gun which was employed against him. His troops included, besides one squadron of the Carabiniers, Cureton's Multani
Horse.

The men of this irregular regiment were the very first to espouse
the British cause in the Punjab after the outbreak of the Mutiny.
They were formally constituted as a regiment at Lahore in January,
1858. Their Commandant was Captain Charles Cureton (1826–
1891), second son of Brigadier-General Cureton. He had fought at
Aliwal with the 12th Irregular Cavalry, and had been present as his
aide-de-camp when his father was killed at Ramnagar (see Vol. I,
p. 275).

The regiment consisted of five troops of Multani Pathans and one
of Multani Beluchis, over 600 men in all. Many of these had previously served as frontier police and, during the Second Sikh War, as

auxiliaries. They were wild, proud, fierce warriors, intensely loyal, but taking uneasily to discipline. 'When Cureton endeavoured to form them into two ranks, their pride took the alarm', according to a contemporary writer, 'and not a man would go into the rear rank. At length they arranged among themselves that it should be composed of men of inferior position and family.'[2]

In the course of the campaign, Cureton's Multanis suffered 136 casualties and lost 204 horses. They fought eleven distinct actions, besides undertaking numerous long marches. On many occasions they fought beside the Carabiniers. At Kukrauli on 30 April, 1858, for example, the Carabiniers foiled repeated attempts by a large body of rebels to capture the column's guns, by charge after charge, 'until it was with great difficulty that the horses could move, on account of the number of slain . . .' The Multanis then took up the pursuit in company with the Carabiniers 'until the horses were almost foundered . . .' Both regiments had been in the saddle for twelve consecutive hours.[3]

More often than not, Sir Colin's columns were greatly outnumbered, but the rebels were seldom led by resolute or skilful men. Their mounted troops almost invariably fled when opposed, but were very seldom successfully pursued. This was due in some cases to poor leadership on the British side, but also to the smallness of the mounted element and, as the season advanced, to the excessive heat. The frustrating nature of the operations is well illustrated by Sir Colin's complaint to Hope Grant, as late as 1 June, 1858: 'The march of a column, or even columns, through the country does not appear to produce any permanent result. The people hate us and our rule, and have in every instance risen against us immediately after our column has passed.'[4]

The chief engagement which took place in Oudh after Lucknow fell was the action at Nawabganj fought on 13 June at the height of the hot weather. Tantia Topi's seizure of Gwalior (see p. 206) encouraged the remaining rebels near Lucknow to reassemble. Hope Grant, therefore, after a twelve-mile night march, surprised a large rebel force (estimated at 15,000) with about 3,500 men. These included two squadrons of the Bays, the 7th Hussars, Hodson's Horse, a squadron of the 1st Sikh Cavalry, and 200 mounted police. Towards the end of the three hour action:

'A very large body of Ghazis and two guns advanced against Hodson's Horse and [some guns] on the British right. The onslaught of the fanatics, led by standard-bearers, was not to be checked by the small body of troops before them; but Sir Hope Grant, seeing the danger in time, brought up the rest of the battery and the 7th Hussars, and at length the enemy retreated, having lost nine guns and 600 men killed.'[5]

Major Daly had led the initial charges. The enemy's fire, he wrote, 'was good; the shot and shell fell thick among us, and the musketry reached us. . . . Grant came down and *joined* in two or three charges.[6]

'Many of the enemy stood to the last and received the [final] charge with musket and sword; they were sabred or shot.'[7]

By the time the action was over – at 8 a.m. – thirty-three men had died of 'sunstroke', none of them in the 7th Hussars. 250 men went into hospital at the end of the day. Three officers and fifteen men of the 7th were wounded. Hodson's Horse alone lost three men killed and twenty-three wounded. Grant's total battle casualties were sixty-seven.

Campbell's final subjugation of Oudh was postponed till October, after the hot months and the rains were over. He achieved it by driving the rebels north-eastwards, securing his conquests with a large body of police which he formed for the purpose. 'The movements were conducted according to a careful time-table',[8] and by the end of 1858, the task was more or less complete. Nana Sahib was never captured and his fate remains a mystery to this day.

A young officer of the Carabiniers describes what this campaign had been like for him:

'We certainly had our fill of marching, never having halted from the middle of September [1858] to the middle of February [1859] for more than two or three days. Of fighting we have had but little; that is to say I was only four times under fire during that time, but even the little experience I have had has not in the least increased my love of fighting, and my belief is that half of the people who talk of going into action as their greatest desire soon heartily wish themselves out of it. It sounds well at a distance to hear of tremendous fire, of intrepid advances and dashing charges, but you feel uncommonly uncomfortable when you are just coming within range of the enemy's guns and begin to think that the glitter and fun of a soldier's life is hardly worth the risk.

'It has been our luck to advance in support of artillery on two occasions, when of course we had nothing to do but sit still in our saddles to be fired at. It is I can assure you decidedly unpleasant to be calmly watching a lot of fellows loading and firing at you without the slightest chance of your personally doing anything to annoy them. This kind of work the niggers like immensely. They will hammer away with guns any length of time, and are very fair artillerymen. In the last brush we had with them, four guns of Horse Artillery with our squadron in support pursued them to the edge of a wood, where they turned and with two guns kept up a fire which four of ours could not silence, and it being impossible to come to close quarters we were obliged to retire till the rifles came up. As soon as the enemy even saw *them*, they bolted. While you are going full speed after them you never think of shot, but remaining stationary and inactive under fire is the most trying.'[9]

One of the last actions fought included the gallant but foolish charge of two squadrons of the 7th Hussars and part of the 1st Punjab Cavalry into the River Rapti on 29 December, 1858. Closing in on the fugitives of the Nana's army, the speed of the squadrons

'became tremendous as they neared the enemy', wrote an eye-witness. 'As the word "charge" was given, a cheer rose from the ranks, and they closed with a shock – men and horses rolled together into the river, which, running like a mill stream, was alive with rebels, trying to escape. . . . Major Horne, who led the leading squadron *most gallantly*, was last seen in the river, engaged with two sowars. . . . Later his body was found . . . with a dead sowar grasped in each hand.'[10]

An officer and three men whose horses had been drowned, and none of whom could swim, were rescued under fire from a sandbank by Major Charles Fraser who was himself wounded. He was awarded the Victoria Cross.

This charge shows a lamentable lack of restraint. To gallop into a fast-flowing river not knowing its depth or foundations must be foolhardy. It was lucky that only Horne was killed, as the river turned out to be full of hidden rocks, tree trunks and quicksands.

'The lack of cavalry has been the main cause of
the protraction of the struggle, and even now,
although so many regiments have been sent out,
one half are unavailable for want of horses.'

VALENTINE BAKER[1]

(ix)

Indian Mutiny, 1858: cavalry reinforcements from
home – Central Indian campaigns start – attitude of
Sindhia and Holkar – Dhar – Goraria

In May, 1857, there had been four European cavalry regiments on
the Indian establishment, only two of which, as has been shown,
were stationed in the Bengal Presidency. Now, at the end of March,
1858, there were eleven. With Sir Colin in Bengal were the Bays, the
Carabiniers, the 7th Hussars and the 9th Lancers. In the Bombay
Presidency were the 3rd Dragoon Guards, the 7th Dragoon Guards,
the 8th Hussars, the 14th Light Dragoons and the 17th Lancers. In
the Madras Presidency were the King's Dragoon Guards and the
12th Lancers.

A return of the effective state of these eleven regiments shows that
at one point in the summer of 1858 their combined strength was
7,720, which was 284 over establishment. Yet there were only 4,897
rank and file fit for duty in India. On the sick list were 653; on
passage out were 734 and under training at their depôts were 1,436.[2]

The King's Dragoon Guards and the 7th Dragoon Guards took
no part in the suppression of the Mutiny. This was chiefly due to the
almost total lack of horses in India large enough to mount the men,
who, particularly in the King's Dragoon Guards, were at this period
the heaviest of the 'heavies'.[3] The 3rd Dragoon Guards, however,
seem to have overcome the problem of mounts. The regiment was
employed, scattered about in troops and sub-troops, 'in very much
the same way as it had been during the years of industrial unrest at
home, being constantly on the march . . . through Central India and
Berar, without having any excitement, or finding any rebels.'[4] The
12th Lancers' tour of duty in India, which had only started early in
1854, was interrupted by the Crimean War (see p. 123). After a short
period at home, where it had arrived in June, 1856, the regiment was
ordered to complete its allotted time in India. With the exception of

one wing, which was stationed at Poona, it had returned to Madras by the beginning of 1857.

The 8th Hussars and the 17th Lancers, on their return from the Crimea, had been stationed in Ireland. On 2 September, 1857, both regiments received orders to embark for India. Each, leaving its horses at home, was to be remounted on arrival. The establishment was augmented, as usual for regiments in India, from six troops to nine, making the numbers of officers and men well over 700. In fact neither regiment had anywhere near reached that figure by the time it left home. On arrival in India neither numbered much over 500 officers and men. To reach even this total, the 8th had to take 108 volunteers, and the 17th 132, from five other light cavalry regiments. The historian of the 8th Hussars describes the changes made in equipment at this time:

'The Victoria percussion carbines, now nearly sixteen years in use in the regiment, were exchanged for Sharpe's breech-loading carbines. [See p. 419.] The shabraques were ordered to be given back to the War Department and abolished. White cotton covers with peaks, forage caps, and lassoes were provided: the eighty lassoes were never used. All old saddlery was given into store and 707 sets, principally new, were packed at Weedon (six in each deal case in linen), and put on board when the regiment embarked. The saddles were all Pannel ones of different kinds, and we thus finished with the old Hussar saddle and blanket which had been in use since 1823.'[5]

The 8th and 17th were carried in Brunel's famous *Great Britain*, then the largest iron ship in the world, and the first sizeable vessel in which the screw propeller was used. Sailing from Cork on 8 October, she reached Bombay on 16 December. On the voyage 'each cavalry regiment', wrote Mrs Duberly, once again determined not to miss a campaign with the 8th, 'had brought its band, refreshed with new instruments since their return from the Crimea; and from half-past two until four o'clock their music completed the luxury of the day.'[6] Neither regiment received its full complement of horses for some months to come, the 8th by the second week of February, 1858, and the 17th not until May. For the first part of the great Central Indian campaigns, therefore, these two regiments were too late. Their chance came, as will be seen, in the famous pursuit of Tantia Topi between June, 1858 and April, 1859. When new regiments and reinforcements for others arrived in Calcutta, they found that the chief mode of conveyance up country was 'by what is called bullock train, in bullock carts, each containing six men or two officers. We go up', wrote an officer who was joining the Carabiniers from home, 'in parties of about 120 at a time.'[7]

*   *   *

The sole European cavalry regiment employed in the earlier Central Indian campaigns was the 14th Light Dragoons, which had only returned from the Persian expedition (see p. 130) in May, 1857 and which before that had taken a prominent part in the Sikh Wars (see Vol. I, p. 271).* One of its troops was almost immediately sent 130 miles to the south of Bombay to help stifle an outbreak at Kolhapur, one of the few places in the Bombay Presidency (and the most southerly in all the sub-continent) where a dangerous rising was threatened. In the event the troop was not much needed, for the astonishing enterprise of Lieutenant W. A. Kerr of the Southern Mahratta Horse had already quelled the mutinous regiments which included a small part of his own. On learning of the revolt, he had set off with fifty men from Satara, eighty-one miles away. He marched without a halt, swimming several swollen rivers and flooded nullahs on the way. The journey took him only twenty-six hours. With assistance from some loyal sepoys he at once, on 10 August, the day of his arrival, attacked the rebels' extremely strong outwork. They made a determined stand, 'but a private entrance having been pointed out to Lieutenant Kerr, he got in [with seventeen of his men dismounted] unperceived till he reached the interior buildings, where a desperate conflict ensued.'[8] He himself was wounded and ten of his men became casualties. Of the forty or so rebels only three escaped. Kerr was awarded the Victoria Cross for this superb exploit.

Five other troops of the 14th formed part of a very small 'movable column' known at first as the Deccan Field Force,† under Major-General Alexander Woodburn, who, through ill-health, was

* Ever since their arrival in India in 1841, the 14th had worn *pagris* (light turbans, as worn by Indians) round their forage-caps. From this they had acquired the nickname of 'Puggrie Wallahs'. Now the regiment was given permission to wear turbans. The shako, which had been worn for some years only in full dress, and the forage-cap were abandoned altogether. So were gloves and stocks.

† Initially, the only other troops in Woodburn's column were the 25th Bombay Native Infantry, the 4th Company, 2nd Battalion Artillery, a company of the Madras Sappers and Miners, and a pontoon train.

soon succeeded by Brigadier-General C. S. Stuart. On 8 June, Lord Elphinstone, the Governor of Bombay, sent Woodburn off towards Mhow, where he was to establish a firm base from which to secure the great line of road connecting Bombay with Central India. He was instructed at the same time, and urgently, to relieve the Europeans who were holding out in a number of places where mutinies had occurred. The Deccan Field Force, which, as it moved northeastwards, was renamed, successively, the Malwa Field Force and the Nerbudda Field Force, was the nucleus of what was to become, many months later, the Central India Field Force.

Sir Colin's grand design, settled upon soon after his arrival in Calcutta, was that this Bombay force, supported on one side by a column from Rajputana, and on the other by one from Madras, should restore order in the areas south of the Jumna, and secure, as it were, the southern flank of his operations in Oudh and Rohilkand.

The states of Central India, mostly under indirect British rule, over which these campaigns were to be fought, were much the same as those involved in the Third Maratha War of 1817–1819. There were nearly 150 of them, of which only two were Mohammedan. All the others were Hindu. Their rulers, now as then (see Vol. I, p. 195), were not necessarily to be relied upon. Further, their troops, mostly trained and commanded by British officers, were much exposed to agents sent southwards by the Nana and Tantia Topi. Even a part of the 1st Cavalry of the Hyderabad Contingent ('little, if at all, less efficient than the Bombay Government's own native regiments'),[9] indulged in disaffection at Aurungabad. Woodburn's column made first, therefore, for that place, where it arrived in pouring rain, on 23 June, 1857. The incipient mutiny was speedily put down, and for the rest of the campaign the Contingent, half* of which was placed at the disposal of the British by the Nizam, served with conspicuous success. Throughout the campaign in Malwa, numerous other native troops of varying quality rendered more or less indispensable help.

* Cavalry: 1,200 sabres; infantry: 1,200; artillery: 12 guns. The four regiments of cavalry were the descendants of the Hyderabad Reformed Horse, which had taken part in the Third Maratha War (see Vol. I, p. 197). Lieutenant (later F-M Sir Evelyn) Wood, whilst marching with the 17th Lancers to Mhow in July, 1858, found that

'the men of the Hyderabad Contingent thought it beneath their dignity to work, and after crossing one of the rivers wished to wait until coolies were collected to carry their saddles and equipment from the edge of the water to the top of the bank; when, however, they saw me pull off my coat and carry my own saddle, they followed my example.' (*Midshipman*, 125.)

Beside some regulars of the staunch Madras Army, there were units from such loyal states as Ratlam, Sailana, Jaora and Sitamau. They kept open the vital lines of communication and often intercepted the rebels' supplies. In charge of them administratively was Mir Shahmat Ali, the Indian Assistant to the Governor-General's Agent.

The native troops chiefly employed by the British in these Central Indian campaigns were regulars of the Bombay Army. In spite of much temptation, these men remained staunch. Large numbers of them were Purbias, that is Brahmans and Rajputs, mostly from Oudh. Another considerable element, particularly in the cavalry, was composed of Hindustani Mohammedans, 'to whom the re-establishment of a Mogul Emperor at Delhi would naturally appeal'.[10] The largest single component was, of course, Maratha, and the proclamation made by the Nana that he would soon again become Peshwa might have been expected to influence Marathas. Further the three largest states which had recently been subjected to the doctrine of lapse, Nagpur, Satara and Jhansi, were all Maratha.

One reason why the Bombay Army remained loyal and the Bengal Army did not was that for many years there had existed jealousy, almost mutual contempt, between the men of the two armies. A more vital reason lay in a fundamental difference in morale and discipline. In the Bombay regiments, unlike those of Bengal, the question of caste had always been secondary.* Promotion was decided much more upon merit. Even men of the lowest caste were often made officers. In Bengal there had grown up an increasing tendency to select the native officers from the ranks on the sole ground of seniority, so that they were generally too old and inefficient to exercise effective discipline. Above all, the excessive control from headquarters, which had made commanding officers in Bengal (as one of them said) into mere sergeant-majors, had not been introduced to Bombay. The Bengal Army had been called the most expensive and inefficient in the world. The same could never have been said of the Bombay Army.

*   *   *

From Arungabad Stuart proceeded by forced marches to Mhow, which was reached, and its embattled Europeans relieved, on 2

---

* Typical of the difference between the spoiling of the Bengal sowars and the robust independence of his Bombay brothers is the fact that in Bengal they had horsekeepers to clean their horses, while in Bombay the men did it themselves. (Col Skeffington Poole, Bombay cavalry, *R.O.I.A.*, 115.)

August. There, because of the rains, it was forced to remain till late October. The men of the 14th at the start of this prolonged period of waiting for the roads to become passable, were, according to their medical officer, 'very sickly in appearance from the constant wetting'. Near the end of it, two months later, he reported:

> 'We had sports for the men, foot races, sack races. The heavy rain . . . very disagreeable. . . . 7th [October] More sports for the men, greasy pole, greased peg, &c. . . . It was capital fun. Sword exercise by natives. I did not remark', he added, 'a very friendly feeling to them by the Europeans, who cried out "Greased Cartridge Buckkers", &c.'[11]

Colonel Henry Durand, who had temporarily become head of the Central Indian Agency, and was therefore political chief where Stuart was military, summed up at the end of August the state of affairs in his vast district:

> 'The means of coercion at our disposal are extremely inadequate. . . . The Gwalior contingent* has wholly gone from our colours, and is now with its well-equipped artillery in Sindia's hands, and of course at his disposal. . . . The Malwa contingent has lost [to the mutineers] all its cavalry, a body of 800 good horse. . . . The Bhopal contingent . . . is now in open mutiny. . . . The Bheel Corps [the Malwa Bhil Corps] is in course of re-assembling, but with its character and influence deteriorated. . . . [With the exception of the 50th Bengal Native Infantry], from north to south of this charge, there is not a gun, there is not a sabre, there is not a musket, which can be called in aid . . . except Stuart's weak column. . . . The total of this effective force may amount to 700 Europeans of all arms, and 1,200 Native troops.'[12]

Meanwhile a large number of Sindhia's troops had revolted and, reinforced from far and wide, had occupied amongst other places the fort at Dhar. Outside it, on 22 October, a rebel force (including, as nearly always at this time, numbers of Arab and Afghan 'mercenaries') stood, briefly, to fight. It was driven into the fort by one

---

* The Gwalior Contingent consisted of 8,300 men and comprised two cavalry regiments, seven infantry battalions and four artillery batteries. Of all these no more than a handful of sowars of the 2nd Cavalry remained loyal.

Sir Hugh Rose thought the Contingent's men the 'best drilled and organized native troops of all arms in India. . . .' (Rose to Mansfield, 22 June, 1858, *Selections*, IV, 83.)

troop of the 14th and 350 men of the 3rd Cavalry, Hyderabad Contingent. The fort was then invested. Though it was supposed to be completely surrounded, and 'the officer commanding the Cavalry said not a mouse could get through his line',[13] the rebels evacuated it without being noticed on 31 October. They had created a small diversion which quite deceived the 14th's and 3rd Cavalry's outposts. Most of these had unfortunately been changed that morning 'and the men were scarcely acquainted with the ground'. In consequence, when they began to move, 'more than half became thoroughly bogged in the marshy ground'.[14] The rebels then 'passed by' the picquets 'wholly unobserved'. They were helped by the 'extensive plantations of high-grown sugar-cane and jewaree [millet] some 8 to 10 feet high',[15] which grew right up to the edge of the fort. This was typical of what happened time and again in the course of the suppression of the Mutiny. The ability of the rebels to melt away so as to fight another day was their greatest asset. The art of countering it was never fully mastered. 'How hard a thing it is to manacle your prey', bemoaned the medical officer of the Madras Sappers and Miners on this occasion, 'although you may have entrapped him.'[16]

In the course of the operations before Dhar, Sylvester, the Assistant-Surgeon of the 14th, reported that

> 'the men off duty and even some native soldiers, but chiefly the 86th and artillery, were frightfully drunk, having seized on native liquor shops. They then commenced looting and killed everything black. Old men and young. Women and Children!! This of course was to be deplored. . . . They shouted "Cawn-pore", "Delhi", and down they went. Strutt says he saw a room full of dead women with children sucking at their breasts. Other women brought out dead children supplicating for mercy; officers rushed down. Our provost marshal and some Dragoons very soon put a stop to it and destroyed all the liquor.'[17]

The enemy was again allowed to escape, though this time to a lesser degree, when Major W. A. Orr,* commanding 337 men of the

---

* There were three officers named Orr connected with the Hyderabad Contingent at this date: Surgeon John Orr, 4th Cavalry; Captain Sutherland G. G. Orr, commanding 3rd Cavalry, and Major William A. Orr, Commandant, 1st Company, Artillery. The last named was placed in command of what was now called the Hyderabad Contingent Field Force, attached to the Malwa Field Force.

1st, 3rd and 4th Cavalry, Hyderabad Contingent, fought an action on 12 November at Rawal, near Mehidpur, the scene of the battle in 1817 (see Vol. I, p. 201). Though he captured all the guns which had been taken from Mehidpur (after the mutiny there), and took seventy-four prisoners in a dashing two-pronged charge, the majority of the rebels melted away to fight another day.[18] Nor were Orr's casualties slight. One British officer was killed and nearly 100 men were killed or wounded.

Due to the gross inefficiency of the mutineers, who here consisted largely of men from Holkar's contingent, Stuart was able, on 19 and 20 November, to cross unopposed the Chambal River, the most powerful barrier yet encountered. Its banks were almost perpendicular, and the sappers had to cut a road down and up them. An eyewitness describes the scene at the crossing:

'The babble and yelling of men, the lowing of the cattle, the grunting screams of the camels, and the trumpeting of the wary heavily-laden elephants, the rattle of our artillery down the bank, through the river, and up the opposite side; the splashing and plunging of our cavalry through the stream – neighing and eager for the green encamping ground before them . . . formed a *tableau vivant* never to be forgotten.'[19]

The following day some 300 of the enemy's best infantry advanced boldly to threaten the British position. As they approached the right front, Lieutenant G. M. Dew's picquet of twenty troopers of the 14th made a furious onslaught upon them, driving them off with heavy loss. Dew was recommended for the Victoria Cross but did not in fact receive it.

*   *   *

Outside Mandisur, at Goraria, on 23 and 24 November, Stuart fought a considerable engagement against very determined resistance. In the course of it, Lieutenant C. M. Martin (late of the 1st Bengal Cavalry) with nineteen troopers of the 14th charged and captured five of the enemy's guns. This seems to have been a dashing if rash affair. Martin was severely wounded, and his men were forced to abandon the guns and retire under heavy infantry fire. Captain R. H. Gall, (see p. 290), however, coming to the rescue with two troops of the 14th, recaptured them, cut down the gunners and pursued and killed many of the rebel infantry. There were further charges made that day and the next both by the 14th and by the Hyderabad Cavalry. Stuart's total casualties for the two days were seven killed and sixty-nine wounded. Though Mandisur and Nimach were then relieved, thousands of the enemy were able, as usual, to escape, for the cavalry was too worn out to pursue them. The Malwa Field Force, nevertheless, had completed its task, against great odds, and without unacceptable casualties. India south of the Narbada River had been saved but the difficult country to the north of that river, largely jungle or mountain, dotted about with strong forts, was almost all in the hands of the enemy. Durand and Stuart between them had 'prepared the way for a decisive campaign'[20] in this vital part of Central India.

'Sir Hugh Rose. . . . I would follow him to the devil, if need be, and I know, also, it was the universal feeling of everyone under his command.'

CORPORAL GEORGE STENT,
14th Light Dragoons[1]

(x)

Indian Mutiny, 1858: Sir Hugh Rose – Central India Field Force – Saugor – Chanderi – Rani of Jhansi – siege of Jhansi – the Betwa – Kunch – Kalpi falls

Durand was now succeeded as Governor-General's Agent by Sir Robert Hamilton, who had been on leave. Stuart, whom Sylvester called 'a superannuated old fellow, good natured but useless' who used to approach Durand 'like a frightened schoolboy going to be flogged',[2] was succeeded by Major-General Sir Hugh Rose.

This remarkable man, aged fifty-six, certainly the finest general to emerge from the Mutiny, whose career hitherto had been as much diplomatic as military, at once set about welding into an efficient instrument the two brigades which formed his Central India Field

Force. At first Rose 'was laughed at and called a griff* by a good many'[3] as Dr Lowe records. Dr Sylvester's first impression of Sir Hugh was that he looked 'very effeminate, weak and I should think unable to rough it much'.[4] That could scarcely have been further from the truth. 'The General', Lowe soon discovered, 'not only displayed a polished *suaviter in modo* at once pleasing and attractive, but the *fortiter in re* that marked him as a man of promptitude, determination and vigour, and one in whom confidence could be reposed.'[5] Rose had been British representative at French headquarters in the Crimea, discharging a difficult task with skill.

On hearing of the Mutiny he had volunteered for service in India and, landing at Bombay on 19 September, had taken command of the Poona Division of the Bombay Army. His methods, when in mid-December he took over the force at Mhow, did not, of course, commend themselves to officers of the old India school. Nevertheless intense activity of body, will power of no common order, and the quickest of brains, made him ideally suited for the command of a series of flying columns, pursuing an enemy as tough and slippery as any ever encountered in India before or since.

Rose's 1st Brigade, commanded by Stuart, included the left wing of the 14th, one troop of the 3rd Bombay Light Cavalry, two regiments of the Hyderabad Contingent Cavalry, and the 1st Troop, Bombay Horse Artillery.† The 2nd Brigade, commanded by Brigadier Charles Steuart, of the 14th, contained the headquarters and the right wing of the 14th, the headquarters and part of the 3rd Bombay Light Cavalry, one regiment of the Hyderabad Contingent Cavalry, and a battery of Bombay Horse Artillery.‡

Under the Commander-in-Chief's master plan, the relief of Saugor, where 170 Europeans, mostly women and children, had been holding out in the mud fort for close on eight months, was to be undertaken by Brigadier-General George Whitlock's Madrasi

---

* Griff = griffin, Anglo-Indian word for an European newly arrived in India, and unaccustomed to Indian ways. The first year in India was known as 'griffinage'.

† The other troops in the 1st Brigade were: 86th Foot; 25th Regiment, Bombay Native Infantry; one infantry regiment, Hyderabad Contingent; one light field battery; two field batteries, Hyderabad Contingent, and some of the Madras Sappers and Miners.

‡ The other troops in the 2nd Bde were: 3rd Bombay European Regiment; 24th Bombay Native Infantry; one field battery, Hyderabad Contingent; one company, Madras Sappers and Miners, and a siege-train which joined a few days after the brigade started its march.

column. This, however, was much behindhand largely because a part of it, including the 12th Lancers, had to march more than 600 miles from Bangalore before it could start operations from Nagpur. Rose decided therefore to effect the relief himself. He marched with Steuart's brigade, followed by the siege-train, from Sihor, on 16 January. Amongst his transport animals were twenty-three elephants and numerous camels and oxen. On his way he picked up some 200 men of the loyal Bhopal Contingent. By the end of the month he had reduced the formidable fort at Rathgarh,* though once again its defenders and a large but ineffective relieving force, eluded effective pursuit. On 30 January they stood before Barodia and Rose, fighting his way 'step by step',[6] smashed them. He entered Saugor unopposed on 3 February. One of the garrison, describing the entry of the troops, wrote:

> 'Such a thing as a European regiment had never been seen in Saugor, and we certainly never expected to see Her Majesty's 14th Dragoons. These men, and the large siege-guns dragged by elephants, were a source of much curiosity and awe to the natives.'[7]

On 9 February, a detached force approached the immensely strong fort of Gathakot. The first shot fired from the British eight-inch howitzer was a lucky one. It blew in an embrasure, dismounted a gun 'and took off the head of a sepoy who was serving it, clad in a red jacket, with an English medal and two clasps.'[8] This so de-moralized the rebels that they at once evacuated their almost im-pregnable stronghold. This time the cavalry seems to have been quicker off the mark. Two troops of the 14th, some of the Hydera-bad cavalry and two horse artillery guns, pursued, and 'cut up 70 or 100' of the rebels. Captain Arthur Need of the 14th 'killed with his own hands five of the rebels . . . and pursued with his gallant troop till dark.'[9]

Before Rose could advance upon Jhansi, the mainstay of rebel power in Central India, which was his next objective, he had to wait at Saugor in accordance with his orders till he knew that Whitlock had started from Jubbulpur. But Whitlock was excessively dilatory. One officer likened him to 'a bad revolver, always going round but

---

* This fort was typical of the numerous hill fortresses scattered all over Central India. They are usually built on the summits of igneous rock formations which rise to great heights almost perpendicularly from the jungle plain.

never going off'.[10] There were other reasons for the delay. The country ahead was sometimes mountainous and, partly because it was in rebel hands, always inhospitable. Provisions would be scarce. Further, the hot season had already begun and 'not a blade of grass would survive a few weeks' of it.[11] Rose employed, therefore, his twenty-four days of enforced idleness, in collecting large quantities of grain, flour, sheep and goats, as well as transport animals, especially elephants and oxen. In this task he was much aided by a number of the loyal rulers of neighbouring states.

At this time it was estimated that, exclusive of the Hyderabad Contingent, there were 10,000 mouths to feed.[12] As usual very large numbers of these were camp followers and servants. Two cornets of the 3rd Bombay Light Cavalry, for instance, shared 'eighteen servants, five horses, two ponies, six bullocks and four carts!'[13]

Opposed to Sir Hugh when, on 26 February, he eventually got going again were increased numbers of rebels and mercenaries, whose morale had benefited from the respite. Time had been given to them to prepare strong defences in the forbidding passes which lay in Sir Hugh's path. These he overcame by a combination of skilful feinting and guile, and by hard infantry fighting and artillery pounding. By 5 March, he had compelled the enemy to abandon two major passes, five forts, and the line of the rivers Bina and Betwa, excepting the fortress of Chanderi. This important stronghold was taken by Stuart's 1st Brigade, (which had left Mhow on 10 January), after a four day siege, on 17 March. Except for incessant reconnaissance and rear-guard work, Stuart's cavalry was not much employed during these gruelling weeks, for the nature of the ground was unsuitable for mounted troops.

Cornet Charles Combe of the 3rd Bombay Light Cavalry gives a good idea of what the 'tails' of these columns were like on the march at this time. He also shows how important was the 'shepherding' role of the native cavalry:

'16th March. Our line of carts now extends 14 miles, cart behind cart, to say nothing of hundreds of elephants, camels, bullocks, led horses, mules, donkeys, &c, which go straggling all along the line. The rearguard has an endless job with them: "The 3rd Cavalry will do this or that" seems to be the everlasting order.'[14]

The heat was becoming daily more intense.

'The roads', records Dr Lowe, 'were dusty, the wells almost

dry, the grass bleached and withered away. . . . The winds began to blow as though they had just escaped from the hither-to-closed door of Pandemonium, and they swept over us, scorching up every pore of the body, and making the eyes feel as though they had been blistered. The thermometer stood in the shade of our tents at 110°, in the open at 130°! . . . Having our beer cooled for the evening became one of the great and momentous objects of our existence. Each bottle was carefully enveloped in a wet cloth and assiduously punkahed by a servant until required, or when a breeze blew was hung up and constant evaporation encouraged.'[15]

At this time Sir Hugh received orders from both Canning and Elphinstone to defer his attack on Jhansi. Some eighty miles away, the loyal rajah of Charkari was being besieged in his fort by the Gwalior Contingent under Tantia Topi. Rose was instructed to go to his assistance. Knowing that his chances of reaching Charkari in time were remote, Sir Robert Hamilton took it upon himself to relieve the General of the responsibility of obeying the order.* Sir Hugh therefore marched to Jhansi without delay. The city was about four and a half miles in circumference and surrounded by a wall never less than eighteen feet high and six feet thick. Within it was the granite fort, standing almost impregnable, on an elevated rock. The garrison, numbering nearly 11,000, included some 1,500 sepoys and 400 sowars, with thirty or forty guns. It was commanded by the Rani of Jhansi in person. This remarkable lady 'united the martial spirit of the Mahratta soldier with the subtlety of the Deccan Brahmin.'[16] 'She is a wonderful woman', wrote a Cornet of the 3rd Bombay Light Cavalry. 'Very brave and determined. It is fortunate for us that the men are not all like her!'[17] A non-commissioned officer of the 14th Light Dragoons thought she was 'just the sort of dare-devil woman that soldiers admire'.[18] She and Tantia Topi were without doubt the two most able leaders thrown up on the rebel side.

In 1817 Jhansi had become a Dependent Native State. In 1853 on the death of her husband without issue, the Rani had demanded the succession for an adopted son. This Dalhousie had refused and the doctrine of lapse being applied the state was annexed to the Raj. The Rani, young, proud and vigorous, though handsomely pensioned off, was bitter. It is not surprising that on the outbreak of the Mutiny she was tempted to throw in her lot with the rebels. Whether, early

* Sir Owen Tudor Burne contests the truth of this. (Burne, 112–13.)

in June, she had encouraged the mutiny of the native regiments (which included the 14th Irregular Cavalry), and whether she sanctioned the consequent massacre of Europeans in spite of a safe conduct, will never be known. What is certain is that now, eight months later, she managed the defence of Jhansi with skill and energy.

On 20 March, Sir Hugh sent forward the cavalry and horse artillery of the 2nd Brigade to start the investment of the city. The following day, Major Gall, having covered seventy miles in two days, arrived with the three troops of the 14th Light Dragoons of the 1st Brigade. Seven 'flying camps' of cavalry with horse artillery were now established around the perimeter of the city. From each of these were detached vedettes and outposts designed to ensure that the garrison could not leave the city unobserved. The roads were obstructed by abattis and trenches, and each camp was to call upon its neighbours, should an attempt be made to force its line. For the fifteen days which the siege lasted, the cavalry kept vigilant watch. The orders were 'to spare nobody over sixteen years – except women, of course', wrote Cornet Combe of the 3rd Bombay Light Cavalry.

'Our servants brought us out a few clean shirts, and we have a "mussuk" [a leather water-bag] of cold water poured over our head and shoulders by way of a bath, but we have not regularly undressed since the 19th ult. . . . At night we take turn about every two hours sleeping on the ground, wrapped in our cloaks. . . . My man brought out my desk, and I amuse myself scribbling.'[19]

Corporal Stent of the 14th wrote that his troop was

'never out of harness, sleeping in front of our horses, which were always ready saddled and bridled – never having the bits taken out of their mouths, night or day, except a few at a time for feeding purposes, or to give them a drink in comfort, so that it came harder on the horses than it did on us. . . . In spite of the dreadful heat, none of us fell sick, and all of us seemed to enjoy the life we led. . . . No quarter was given: those attempting to escape from the city were cut off. . . . There was not a night passed but a large number of prisoners were taken by our cavalry picquets, and many of these were summarily disposed of.'[20]

The cavalry also prevented any form of supplies from reaching the city.

The siege guns pounded away day and night and received spirited replies. Not till 30 March, when most of the enemy's guns had been dismounted, was anything like a practicable breach effected. This the besieged at once closed up with a stockade, which, in turn, Rose's gunners destroyed with red-hot shot. This fierce contest was still in full swing that afternoon when the General learned that a large enemy force had arrived at a point three miles beyond the River Betwa.* This was the 'so-called army of the Peishwa' under Tantia Topi, marching, at the Rani's urgent request, to the relief of Jhansi. After his victory over Windham at Cawnpore four months before, and his subsequent defeat by Sir Colin, (see p. 168), Tantia Topi had retired to Kalpi. From there he had taken Charkari (to the relief of which, as has been shown, Rose had been ordered but had declined to march), capturing twenty-four guns. Now, reinforced by further regiments of the Gwalior Contingent and by the levies of local rebel rulers, he commanded a formidable army of over 20,000 men, with twenty-eight guns.

A lesser man than Sir Hugh Rose might have quailed at such a crisis, but he was equal to the occasion.

> 'The fact is', he wrote in his despatch, 'that Jhansie had proved so strong, and the ground to be watched by Cavalry was so extensive, that my force had actually enough on its hands. But I relied on the spirit of British soldiers, which rises with difficulties, and resolved, whilst I fought a general action with the enemy, not to relax the siege or the investment.'[21]

Thus the troops which he could spare to oppose Tantia's 20,000 were pitiably few: 430 European infantry; 700 native infantry; 240 sabres from the 14th Light Dragoons and 200 from the Hyderabad Cavalry. That evening, after dark, he silently withdrew from the investment sixteen field guns and sent his elephants to collect three of the large siege guns. With these, having sent some of the Hyderabad cavalry ahead to watch the enemy's movements at the two fords on the River Betwa, he marched at 9 p.m. to the village of Bupoba,

---

* There is some confusion as to whether it was on 30 or 31 March that Sir Hugh learned of the presence of the relieving force. Most authorities telescope events by making the Battle of the Betwa, which took place, indisputably, on 1 April, follow the morning after Rose received his intelligence. His own despatch, however, leaves little doubt that a further day intervened.

24. The charge of the 8th Hussars at Gwalior, 17 June 1858. (See pp. 208–10)

25. A Sikh sowar, Punjab Irregular
Cavalry, in China, 1860

26. Fane's Horse on the 'Havoc'
gunboat, en route to China, 1860

six miles from Jhansi. He hoped next morning to force the enemy troops to cross the river, so that they would have to fight with it in their rear. Consequently, at first light, Sir Hugh feigned retreat. This succeeded in bringing part of the enemy over at the upper ford. After sunset on the 31st this part of Tantia Topi's first line was drawn up in order of battle on the Jhansi side of the river. Opposite it, Sir Hugh, after dark and in total silence, arranged his tiny force in two slender lines. 'Both ourselves and the Enemy', he reported,

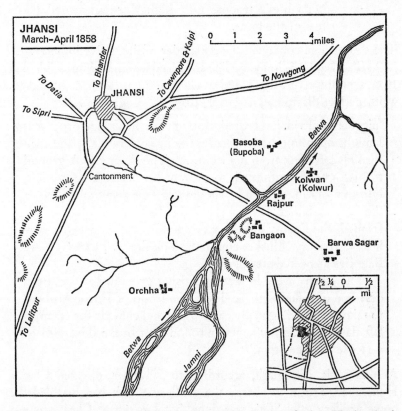

'slept on our arms.' During the night 'one of the Hyderabad Cavalry, left at the lower, the Kolwar, ford, came in as hard as he could, and reported that the enemy were crossing in great numbers.'[22] Tantia's object, it was clear, was to turn the British left flank. Rose at once despatched his second line, commanded by Brigadier Stuart, to 'oppose and outflank' the new threat, (which, in the course of the next day, he succeeded in doing). This left Sir Hugh even weaker than before. He meant, nevertheless, to seize the initiative by a dashing attack at first light next morning (1 April).

But the rebels, 'before daybreak', as Rose admitted, 'covered by a cloud of skirmishers, advanced against me.'[23]

His first line was now disposed as follows:

Right: Lieutenant Henry Clerk's troop, Hyderabad Cavalry; Captain Arthur Need's troop, 14th Light Dragoons; four horse artillery guns.

Centre: The heavy guns and most of the infantry.

Left: Captain R. B. Prettejohn's and Captain William McMahon's troops, 14th Light Dragoons, and the rest of the guns.

The second line contained the remainder of the native infantry.

As Tantia Topi's immense line advanced it seemed impossible that Rose's diminutive force could avoid being completely outflanked. With perfect discipline, however, Rose's

'picquets and videttes retired, closing to each flank, in order that I might open upon [the enemy] the fire of my guns, and then turn his left flank from my right. . . . The Enemy took ground to his right. I conformed, to prevent his outflanking my left, but very cautiously, lest he should draw me away too much to the left, and then fall on my right flank. . . . I halted and fronted; the Enemy did the same, and instantly opened a very heavy Artillery, Musket and matchlock fire . . . to which my Batteries answered steadily.'[24]

'The enemy were in rear of a rising ground. I ordered my first line of infantry to lie down, the troop of Horse Artillery to take ground diagonally to the right and enfilade the enemy's left flank. In this movement a round-shot broke the wheel of a Horse Artillery gun.'[25]

At this crisis, Sir Hugh, according to Sylvester, directed Clerk's Hyderabad Troop to charge the artillery which had disabled the horse artillery gun. 'This was done, but Lieutenant Clerk was not well followed, and had to retire severely wounded after three unsuccessful attempts.'[26] At nearly the same time Rose ordered Prettejohn, supported by McMahon, to charge the enemy's right flank, which gave way before it was reached. The General himself at the other end of the line 'dashed into the enemy's left'[27] at the head of Need's troop.

'It was a glorious sight', recorded Corporal Stent, 'to see them thundering along . . . One minute, and they were among the enemy, and all that was to be seen was a confused mass of flashing swords and bayonets, struggling men and horses, and hoarse shouts of rage. From this seething, struggling mass our men emerged victorious, for the result of the charge showed that an act of daring and personal bravery on the part of a leader (an act not often done – a Commander-in-Chief to lead a charge) will sometimes change defeat into victory as it did in this case.'[28]

'I believe I may say', wrote Rose in his despatch, 'that what Captain Need's Troop did on this occasion was equal to breaking a square of Infantry.'[29]

Sir Hugh immediately moved forward the cavalry and horse artillery in pursuit. In spite of the terrible heat the chase was fast and fierce. The enemy 'were rallied, formed again, to be again charged and routed; and yet again', in Stent's graphic words, 'only to undergo the same infliction, losing all their guns, and finally bolting in the greatest confusion, pursued by our men, who cut up great numbers of them.'[30]

Rose's despatch continues the grim story:

'The pursuit had now penetrated and cleared away the first line. A cloud of dust about a mile-and-a-half to our right, pointed out the line of retreat of another large body, the second line of the rebels, [commanded by Tantia Topi in person], which, by a singular arrangement . . . must have been three miles in rear of his first line.

'The whole force again went in immediate pursuit . . .

'Neither the jungle which was set on fire to stop the pursuit, nor difficult ground, could check the ardour of the pursuing troops . . .'

At Rajpore, the enemy made their last stand.

'The 14th Light Dragoons and Hyderabad Cavalry gallantly surmounted all opposition, and sabred the rebels who still held their ground.

'I detached parties in pursuit of the numerous fugitives who took across country; another body followed the road, and captured, a mile-and-a-half from the Betwa, the . . . 18th and last gun of the rebel army . . .

'Horses and men being completely exhausted by incessant marching and fighting . . . and being now nine miles from Jhansie, I marched the troops back to camp.'[31]

Thus ended the decisive Battle of the Betwa. It was an astonishing victory. Tantia Topi lost some 1,500 men, eighteen guns (some of them heavy) and quantities of ordnance and other stores. Rose lost nineteen killed and sixty-six wounded. Thirteen horses were killed and twenty-four wounded. The 14th suffered the heaviest casualties of any regiment engaged: five men were killed and twenty-five wounded.

Tantia Topi's intervention had only delayed the assault on Jhansi by forty-eight hours. It took two and a half days of hard fighting before the city and fort were finally captured.* At about 4 p.m. on the first of these, Cornet Combe of the 3rd Bombay Light Cavalry saw a large body of enemy horsemen suddenly issue forth and make a dash.

> 'We went at them', he wrote home, 'and drove many back; about 100, however, got through. A troop of ours, and some Irregular Cavalry [Hyderabad Contingent] pursued them seven miles, cutting up most of them. . . . All night we were on the move, cutting up parties of fugitives. Next morning our flag was flying from the highest tower, but we were very much disgusted to find the Queen [the Rani] had escaped; how, when or where we couldn't imagine. We were sent all over the country in pursuit, and one of our troops overtook her at a place called Banda [Bhander] 20 miles off. Her escort made a hard fight of it, and though our fellows did their utmost and

* As an example of how detailed casualty returns had become, here is that for the 4th Cavalry, Hyderabad Contingent. It refers to casualties sustained during the siege of Jhansi, exclusive of the Battle of the Betwa, and shows incidentally that the Hyderabad cavalry was actively engaged in the siege:

'Captain Commanding	W. Murray	Contusion from a musket ball.
Jemadar	Unooman Sing	Dangerously wounded.
Duffadar	Runjeet Khan	Killed.
Trooper	Ummeer Sing	Killed.
Trooper	Meer Hyder	Killed.
Trooper	Khyre Mohomed Khan	Severely wounded.
Trumpet Major	Mirza Soorab Beg	Severely wounded.
Trooper	Ahmed Khan	Slightly.
Trooper	Meer Ukbur Ali	Severely.
Trooper	Sheik Wuzzeer Ali	Severely.
Jemadar	Syud Noor Ali	Dangerously.'

(*Selections*, IV, 61.)

killed nearly every man, she got away, her smart saddle, etc., falling into our hands.'[32]

Some twenty hours later, the indomitable Rani, having ridden more than 100 miles, arrived safely at Kalpi. There, on the same day, she was joined by Tantia Topi. Both had survived to fight another day.

*   *   *

Kalpi on the south bank of the Jumna was only forty-six miles from Cawnpore. Besides being the headquarters of Rao Sahib, the self-styled Peshwa, it was also the rebels' arsenal. So long, wrote Sir Hugh, as it was in their hands they could 'say that the East and West of India might be British, but that the pivot of its centre was theirs.'[33] But before he could advance against it, Rose must replenish his supplies and ammunition. He must also be assured that a column marching from Rajputana was on its way to help in protecting his lengthy lines of communication. He was forced to wait nearly three weeks. During that time most of his cavalry was employed in keeping at bay the rebels of Kotah, Banpur and Shahgarh.

Meanwhile the main rebel forces under Tantia Topi, inspired by the Rani of Jhansi, marched out to Kunch, forty-two miles south of Kalpi, and took up a very strong position there. Before Sir Hugh could meet them, he had to traverse (his two brigades separated by two days' march) what was virtually a desert.

'Here and there', wrote Sylvester, 'a few dried-up cactus plants or bushes of camel thorn* scattered the plain, and how sustenance was found for the enormous train of ammunition and baggage animals, I cannot conceive. It is small wonder that they perished in numbers by the way . . .

'Water was confined to wells, 8 or 10 miles apart; these, moreover, were narrow and deep and the supply limited . . . The scene at a well was distressing: thousands of parched men each eagerly waiting his turn to drink from the leathern bucket as it came to the surface, longing too, as I have often done, to thrust in head and all.'[34]

On 6 May Rose's spies, confirmed by cavalry patrols, revealed that Tantia Topi's flank at Kunch could be turned. To effect this

* *Zizyphus nummularius:* a spiny rhamnaceous shrub used as fodder for goats and sheep, common in Indian desert areas.

Sir Hugh had to march his force a distance of fourteen miles. As a consequence there occurred that day forty-six cases of 'sunstroke', of which fourteen were fatal. In the battle that followed next day, after an artillery bombardment succeeded by hard infantry fighting, the rebels' 'line of defence was cut in two, and their right completely turned . . .' At a critical moment Captain Gordon's troop of the 14th made a spirited charge in support of the 1st Brigade. But the rebels retreated, as Sir Hugh wrote in his despatch, 'with resolution and intelligence. The line of skirmishers [observed] the rules of Light Infantry drill. When charged, they threw aside their muskets, and fought desperately with their swords.'[35] 'They fired and retired', says an eye-witness, 'in perfect order, and, at the first charge of the 14th, coolly knelt down and delivered their fire at two yards. Of course the whole of that line was cut up.'[36]

The horse artillery 'opened a hot fire'[37] in the centre, while Captain McMahon's two troops on the right, and Captain Blyth's troop on the left, charged the two mile long line of skirmishers simultaneously. The ground over which they rode was flat plain, intersected by heavy plough. At one point

> 'the ground was broken into rough clods, where the rebels stood and maintained a splendid front with fixed bayonets, and some hesitation at the critical moment seized the cavalry, many of whom, and a considerable number of horses, were killed and wounded.
>
> 'Again the guns opened, and a second time the cavalry charged, yet still the rebels maintained a steady front, facing about while retiring. . . . The Dragoon Troops . . . fought brilliantly and cut up a great many. A large number of officers, notably some of those on Sir Hugh's staff, used their swords to great advantage, but none made cleaner cuts than the sepoys.'[38]

Sergeant Wilson had his bridle arm completely severed above the elbow, which shows how sharp and strongly wielded were the native swords. By contrast, Dr Sylvester records that he saw 'the blunt sword of a dragoon bound off the skull instead of cleaving it'* and part of a dragoon's foot cut off, 'shoe, sole and all'.[39]

McMahon received in this charge three sword wounds, but continued at the head of his two troops. Blyth took one gun, and so did

---

* The same inferiority of the British cavalry sabre was remarked upon at the charge of the heavy brigade at Balaklava. (See p. 72.)

Captain Abbott with a troop of the 3rd Hyderabad Cavalry. The enemy, at one point, threw back the extreme right of his skirmishing line so as to enfilade the pursuing cavalry. Rose at once directed Captain Prettejohn's troop 'to form line to the left, charge, and cut off the enfilading skirmishers, which he did effectually. This officer, on the horses of his own Troop being knocked up, placed himself with well-timed zeal, at the head of a Troop with fresh horses which was without an officer, and continued the pursuit.'[40]

For eight miles the enemy kept his order. 'History', wrote a cavalry officer, 'does not record an instance of devotion superior to that displayed by Tantia's rear guard at Koonch – I should like to see a monument erected on the spot where they fell, all rebels as they were.'[41] They were not supported by their cavalry. Indeed, throughout the campaign, the rebel sowars made a very poor showing.

The 3rd Bombay Light Cavalry also joined in the pursuit. Cornet Combe of that regiment wrote home next day, 8 May, that they

'had nothing to eat from dinner on the 6th to this morning ... My sword was so hot yesterday, I really could hardly hold it; everything is hot – the water even in the wells. Even the flying rebels gave in yesterday, after running eight miles, begging for water.

'Sir H. Rose is suffering very much – he was lying in a dhoolie yesterday, covered with wet clothes, when the attack commenced; he insisted on getting up, and even joined in the pursuit, falling twice from his horse from the heat. He is a most determined, plucky fellow ...

'Our horses quite knocked up, and could pursue no further. They got no water all day.'[42]

'The 14th', wrote Sylvester, 'were never better than on this day. They charged like a body of demons straight into the huge masses ... until Scudamore [Major Arthur Scudamore, commanding the regiment] screamed "Halt! It is perfect madness".'[43] The 14th lost that day five men killed. One officer and seventeen men were wounded. Two officers and sixteen men went down with 'sunstroke', two of the men dying later. The rebels lost nine guns, but saved two. About 500 were killed and wounded. The exhaustion of the cavalry – some of the men had been in the saddle sixteen hours – prevented the massive slaughter which should otherwise have taken place.

The next day, which was one of rest, nearly 150 men (including the wounded) of the left wing of the 14th alone were under medical treatment.[44] During the seven days which it took to reach Golowli, six miles from Kalpi,

> 'the enemy', as Rose reported, 'continued their tactics of harassing unceasingly my troops, and forcing them into the sun, large bodies of cavalry hanging on my position, retiring when attacked, but ready to fall on escorts, which I was obliged to send to a distance to forage, the want of which was the cause of serious losses. Out of 36 men of the 14th Light Dragoons, forming part of one forage escort, 17 were brought back to the Camp in dhoolies after only two hours' exposure to sun . . .
>
> 'The prostration of the whole force had become a matter of arithmetical calculation. So many hours' sun laid low so many men.'[45]

The general made special mention of the 14th in his despatch, 'for the admirable order and celerity with which their in-lying and out-lying picquets mounted on the frequent occasions when I turned them out . . . Their videttes and patrols also were always watchful and intelligent.'[46]

Sylvester describes what the seemingly endless baggage train consisted of at this time:

> 'long strings of laden camels, ponderous elephants, thousands of bullocks laden with round shot and shell; bags of grain, spare stores of every description; led horses; trains of mules; huge pieces of cannon; unwieldy mortars; pontoon bridges; scaling ladders; sick in dhoolies; sick in wheeled ambulances; sick on camels; sick on foot; and, worse than all, an immense number of wheeled vehicles of the worst possible description, many broken down and all drawn by galled and exhausted cattle tended and driven by timid natives or unwilling agriculturalists pressed for service.'[47]

On 16 May a serious attack was made on the rearguard as the baggage train was negotiating a deep ravine. Over a thousand rebel cavalry, some 4,000 foot and a few guns were held off by Major Forbes of the 3rd Bombay Light Cavalry with 400 sabres, 200 infantry and two guns. For over two hours 'the enemy's cavalry', as Forbes reported that evening, 'made several advances, one or two at a rapid pace, but deceived, I imagine, by the perfect steadiness of the troops into supposing that a larger force was concealed in the broken ground in our rear, they did not close.' By a series of backwards and forwards movements, and the 'excellent practice' of his two guns, Forbes kept the rebel cavalry guessing, until time had been given

'for the baggage to get on a considerable distance. For the first three miles of the remainder of our march, we were almost surrounded by the rebel cavalry, and fired into by their artillery, but alternately halting and retiring, we succeeded in preventing any of the baggage from falling into their hands.'[48]

So dangerous was this attack considered by Sir Hugh that he himself brought up a considerable force to assist Forbes, but in the event it was hardly needed. This seems to have been a classic rearguard defence. 'It was most anxious work', wrote Cornet Combe, who was in command of his regiment's skirmishers, 'for we of course would not leave the baggage, which seemed to *creep* along!'[49]

*　　*　　*

The battle for Kalpi, fought near Golowli on the south bank of the Jumna, took place on 22 May. By then a force from the Bengal army which Sir Colin had sent to assist Sir Hugh was ready to co-operate with him. It was able to replenish Rose's almost exhausted ammunition supply, and with its twelve guns to bombard the city from the north bank of the Jumna. It included some 200 men of the Rifle Brigade, who, with a hundred Sikh police, formed a Camel Corps each man of which rode on a camel accompanied by a native driver. This corps of mounted infantry had been formed at Lucknow in early April. It was now sent across the river to help in the battle.

Tantia Topi, with his infantry completely concealed in a series of deep ravines running into the river on his left and centre, made a noisy feint attack with his right. Rose was not taken in. While holding it, he awaited the main attack from the ravines. When this came, Brigadier Stuart was almost overwhelmed by it. Just as his guns were about to be overrun – 'We have nothing to do but die like Scotchmen', he shouted[50] – up came Rose with the Camel Corps. 'The situation', wrote the general, 'was very critical. Volleys of musketry, which killed or wounded every horse of my Staff but one, were coming over the crest of the rising ground.' The men, who were dismounted from their camels, charged down from the crest, Sir Hugh at their head, 'giving one of those cheers which all over the world have been the heralds of British successes. The rebels wavered, turned and fled, pursued by the Camel Corps.'[51] The battle was won. Next day, as he expected, Rose found Kalpi evacuated.

In spite of the ever-increasing heat, Major Gall set off in pursuit of the rebels that same morning (23 May). With five troops of the 14th, reduced by illness to a total of 201 sabres, a few Hyderabad cavalry and six Hyderabad horse artillery guns, he took five guns and six caparisoned elephants amongst much else. Large numbers of demoralized rebels were killed, and what might have been an orderly retreat was converted into a rout. 'For once,' writes Fortescue, 'the enemy was not only defeated, but routed and heavily punished.'[52] On Gall's return, Rose sent off a more substantial 'column of observation and pursuit,' under Major Robertson along the Jalaon road.

'To overtake the enemy was hopeless', wrote Sir Hugh, 'because *firstly*, they had a start, and were not encumbered, like our troops, with baggage, tents, and Commissariat, or even the usual kit of rebels, which they had thrown away; *secondly*, their cavalry and infantry were in as good, as mine were in bad condition; *thirdly*, my European Cavalry riding 18 stone, could not catch Indian Cavalry, riding 10 or at most 11 stone.'[53]

'We have had a jolly fight with the rascals at last.'
LIEUTENANT KENNETH COFFIN,
after the battle of Banda[1]

(xi)

Indian Mutiny, 1858: Saugor Field Force – Banda

In contrast with Rose's lightning campaign are General Whitlock's snail-like movements with the Saugor Field Division. On the day that Sir Hugh relieved Saugor, a task which Whitlock had been meant to perform (see p. 187), the dilatory general at last set out from Jubbulpur. The cavalry with him, commanded by Major T. C. A. Oakes of the 12th, consisted of part of the 12th Lancers (227), the

4th, 6th* and 7th Madras Light Cavalry, and one squadron of the 2nd Cavalry, Hyderabad Contingent (136).

Moving roughly parallel to Rose, Whitlock at no point was quick enough to be able, as was intended, to co-operate with him. He seems, too, to have 'passed through the country without any

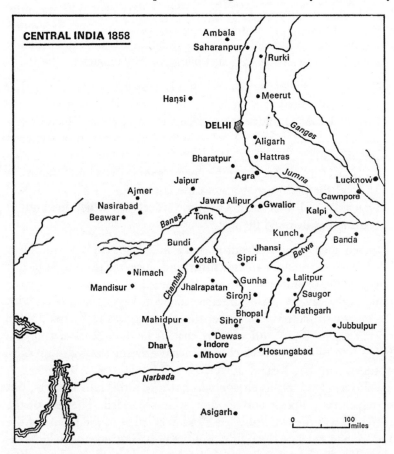

CENTRAL INDIA 1858

attempt at pacification'. His troops, though suffering as Rose's from the heat, and undergoing 'many months of severe and laborious work',[3] saw little action. At Jhigan on 10 April, nevertheless, Whitlock took a rebel force by surprise. Here it was that a trooper of the 12th was sent by the general, whose orderly he was, to deal with a troublesome sniper. He thrust his lance into the man who clung with

* These two regiments seem to have marched in February north east to Allahabad, and therefore played no part in the Central Indian campaigns. (*Revolt*, 171.[2])

both hands to the shaft. The trooper was then seen to be leaning over his dying victim, energetically shaking his fist 'in his face, with the words "G–d D—n your eyes, if you don't let that there go I'll get off my horse and punch your b——y head".'[4]

On 17 April Whitlock fell foul of an ambush at Kubrai, prepared for him by the Nawab of Banda, against whose capital he was now slowly marching. He extricated himself somehow and proceeded two days later to fight his only general action. The battle of Banda opened with the advanced guard being heavily engaged.

> 'No men', wrote the general in his despatch, 'ever charged more nobly than the squadron of the 2nd Hyderabad Contingent Cavalry, under their gallant leader Captain Macintire; one gun was captured, the other in the *mêlée* escaped for a time, but the object was effected. . . .
>
> '[Macintire's] charge on the enemy's guns (I had no infantry at hand for that purpose), was the admiration of all. . . . His men followed their leader with an order with which his high bearing has inspired them.'[5]

Seven men of the squadron were killed and fifteen wounded. These heavy casualties are not surprising since 'the ground to be got over', as the commander of the advance guard reported, 'was most difficult for cavalry, being intersected with deep nullahs filled with the enemy's infantry.'[6] Whether this sacrifice was really required is open to question. Whitlock says that 'it became necessary to dislodge' the rebel guns 'which would have swept through our skirmishers, had they further advanced.'[7]

Also engaged in this charge was a troop of the 12th Lancers, out of which two officers and six men were wounded. The rest of the regiment was then skilfully led by Major Oakes to the rescue of the Hyderabad cavalry. For four miles the fleeing enemy, which included men of the 3rd Bengal Irregular Cavalry[8] who had mutinied at Saugor nine months before,* were pursued by the lancers.

Whitlock halted at Banda for more than a month, awaiting reinforcements in the shape of his 2nd Brigade. On hearing that Rose

---

* Some of the sowars of this regiment had been in the Nana's army which was defeated by Havelock on 16 August, 1857. There was also a considerable loyal remnant of the regiment. Together with men of the 12th Irregular Cavalry, they 'served most creditably under Lieutenant Johnson of the 12th in all the engagements between Cawnpore and Lucknow, and subsequently at Alambagh.' (Gimlette, 226.)

had completed his campaign with the capture of Kalpi, Whitlock sent a message to him saying 'Really your motto seems to be *Veni, Vidi, Vici*, whilst my Second Brigade, with their snail's pace [as if his own had been much faster!], has prevented me leaving this place.'[9]

He was now ordered to march against the disloyal Raos of Kirwi. These rulers (one of whom was only nine years old) gave in at his approach. Whitlock's force then took possession of their vast treasure 'the biggest prize-money ever taken in India'.[10] After lengthy and expensive litigation, and in spite of support from Governor-General, Commander-in Chief and Prime Minister, Rose's force, which had done virtually all the fighting, received no part of the 4,300,000 rupees and numerous valuable jewels. The prize money which came to Rose's men, from their own efforts, totalled in all only R.400,000.

General Whitlock, with the 12th Lancers still in his force, continued '*going around*, marching and countermarching' throughout 1858, policing the area. 'No length of road was so intimately known to all in his force,' wrote Sylvester, 'as that about Saugor.'[11] He even became involved in the final stages of the hunt for Tantia Topi. His force was not finally broken up till the spring of 1860.

'There is no military prescription for the capture of a defeated general who is prepared to desert the stricken field in good time.'

MICHAEL MACLAGAN,
'*Clemency*' *Canning*[1]

(xii)

Indian Mutiny, 1858: Sindhia's troops take Gwalior – Kotah-ke-serai – Gwalior falls – Meade's Horse – Jowra-Alipur – Tantia Topi escapes

Rose and his indomitable Central India Field Force had, it seemed, completed their task. In five gruelling months, as Sir Hugh's stirring Order of the Day, issued on 1 June, proclaimed, they had 'marched

205

more than a thousand miles and taken more than a hundred guns.'
Sir Colin decided to break up the force, and Rose, after his fifth
attack of sunstroke, putting his camp equipage and horses up for
sale,[2] prepared to go home on leave.

But it was not to be. 'Scarcely', wrote Dr Lowe, 'had the sick been
sent away [to Cawnpore] ere the trumpets to arms were again
sounded.'[3] A totally unexpected development, 'almost as sensational, and ... certainly as potentially dangerous, as the first outbreak
of the Mutiny at Meerut',[4] was about to change the situation radically
and dramatically.

The Gwalior Contingent, as has been shown, had long since
joined the mutineers. Jiaji Rao Sindhia, whom the British had made
Maharajah of Gwalior in 1843 had himself remained loyal. So too, up
to the present, had his own small army. He was even now preparing
at Gwalior quarters and supplies for the victorious British troops,
who were much looking forward to them. But the rebel leaders,
after losing their last stronghold at Kalpi, and without funds, muni-
tions or provisions, believed that the Sindhia's nobles and troops
could be persuaded to revolt. Tantia Topi at once set about the task.
Though he could not shake the ruler himself, he was almost completely successful with his followers. On 1 June, as the rebel army
approached his capital, the Sindhia marched out to oppose it with what
he believed might still be his faithful troops. But, after no more than
a token resistance, they went over to Tantia Topi, and the Maharajah only just managed to escape to Agra with part of his personal
bodyguard.

Thus, at a stroke, the rebel army had gained not only reinforcements but also Gwalior, one of the strongest forts in all India, together with shelter, a substantial arsenal, a rich treasury and plente-
ous provisions. 'This is getting past a joke,' wrote a member of Sir
Robert Hamilton's staff. 'We all thought Calpee finished the campaign in these parts.'[5] But now an even greater challenge lay ahead.

Rose, when on 4 June he learned the astonishing news from
Major Robertson, (who had arrived within fifty-five miles of
Gwalior), acted swiftly. Not only were the rains about to come, but
the rebels must at all costs, he realized, be denied time in which to
recruit wavering rulers to their cause. His successor, Brigadier-
General Robert Napier (later Field-Marshal Lord Napier of Magdala) of the Royal Engineers, had not yet arrived. He therefore
telegraphed Canning offering his services once again. The offer was
accepted, and Sir Hugh at once resumed command.

Brigadier Stuart, with two troops of the 14th Light Dragoons, and some guns and infantry, was instantly sent off to reinforce Robertson. Rose followed on 6 June with a further two troops of the 14th, two troops of the 3rd Bombay Light Cavalry and the 1st ('Eagle') Troop of the Bombay Horse Artillery, leaving orders for the garrison left at Kalpi to follow as soon as troops from Bengal relieved it. It was to bring up 'all the spare ammunition, ordnance and commissariat stores'. When it left on 8 June, Cornet Combe of the Bombay Light Cavalry found himself 'the only cavalry officer in this force. I command', he wrote, 'the whole Brigade!! (about 130 men under Brigadier Combe!) I get off orderly officer, picquet, rear-guard and a variety of duties which would be "infra dig" for a Brigadier to perform!'[6] Combe was one of a number of junior officers who found themselves in commands well beyond their rank. More than forty officers of Rose's force had gone off sick to Cawnpore.

All marching was done at night to avoid the worst of the heat, which in the summer of 1858 reached exceptional intensity. In one officer's tent, indeed, the thermometer had burst at 130°. On the night of the third day Rose reported that the men of the outlying picquet of the 14th 'had fallen from their saddles from exhaustion. . . .'[7] They had had to be replaced by native troops.

Converging on Gwalior at the same time, at Sir Colin's instance, were a movable column from Agra, escorting siege guns (which in the event were not required), and a brigade of the Rajputana Field Force, under Brigadier M. W. Smith, 3rd Dragoon Guards, from Chanderi. At Rose's urgent request the men of the Hyderabad Contingent, who had already started for home, 'instantly counter-marched and moved against Gwalior',[8] in order to block any retreat southwards.

Rose arrived four miles east of the Morar Cantonments, which are five miles from Gwalior, on 16 June. Napier joined him there and took command of what had arrived of the 2nd Brigade, while Stuart, as before, commanded the 1st. The rate of advance would have been even speedier if more troops had been available 'to take care of our baggage, the dreadful impedimenta of every small force. The enemy', wrote one officer, 'are so strong in cavalry that it would take half our Brigade to protect the baggage.'[9] Before long, further troops despatched from those left at Jhansi, and others sent by Sir Colin from the north, relieved Rose of these anxieties.

Though the sun had been up some hours, Sir Hugh decided to

attack the strong force at Morar without delay. Thus he hoped to gain the shelter of the cantonment buildings before the rebels had time to burn them down. He advanced in two lines with wings of the 14th Light Dragoons on either flank. 'The enemy', wrote Captain J. G. Lightfoot, commanding the 'Eagle' Troop of horse artillery, 'did not make much of a fight, though they fought better when we were following them up, and driving them through the cantonments.'[10] Two troops of the 14th, under Captain P. Scott Thompson, caught the fleeing rebels 'in the plains, before they could reach the hills to which they were hurrying, and made', wrote Sir Hugh, 'great slaughter of them.'[11]

The following morning (17 June), at 7.30, Brigadier Smith's column arrived at Kotah-ke-serai, three miles south east of Gwalior. His force included most of the 8th Hussars, the 1st Bombay Light Cavalry (Lancers)* and the 2nd Troop, Bombay Horse Artillery.

He immediately attacked a very large force of rebels of all three arms. Employing first his horse artillery and then charging with infantry, he ousted the enemy from some hilly ground, much intersected by small ravines. Next, he fought his way through a narrow defile. On emerging from it, he was confronted by the rebels drawn up on an extensive plain not far from Gwalior, 'often used by the Maharajah's army as a parade ground. Nothing', wrote Sylvester, 'could have been more inviting for a charge.'[12] As the 8th Hussars were about to debouch from the mouth of the pass, the regiment was halted. The Brigadier was

'not quite sure', wrote Captain Robert Poore, who was present, 'whether they would send a Troop or a Squadron out. However the Squadron [of ninety-eight sabres] went eventually, covered till we got out of the pass by the fire of the 95th [Foot]. When we got clear we front formed and went at them, the Brig. leading for a short way. The enemy cut when we came up, and we pursued for a mile, or perhaps half, and then turned,

* This regiment had been stationed at Nasirabad, when, in late May, 1857, the rest of the garrison, all belonging to the Bengal Army, had mutinied. While these, more than 2,000 strong and with six guns, were plundering and burning the cantonment, the lancers (about 400 in number), 'detached one party to save the European officers of the mutinous regiments, which they succeeded in doing, while another party made a determined effort to deprive the mutineers of their guns.' Only eleven men of the regiment deserted. (*Blackwood's*, 184. A rather less flattering account of the regiment's actions is given elsewhere, see, especially, Cadell, 207.)

and came back, and got in among a lot of very deep nullahs, during which time it was precious lucky the enemy did not come down on us.'[13]

At the head of the squadron was its commander, Captain Clement Heneage. Accompanying him was Lieutenant-Colonel Hicks, commanding the artillery, who reported that they 'had advanced too far without any support'. When that support, in the shape of the 1st

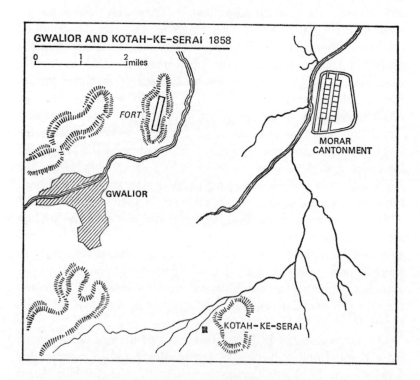

GWALIOR AND KOTAH–KE–SERAI 1858

0   1   2 miles

FORT

MORAR CANTONMENT

GWALIOR

KOTAH–KE–SERAI

Bombay Lancers did arrive, the 8th's 'horses were not fit for a second immediate attack. Captain Heneage was certainly quite black in the face and unable to speak, although [still] on his horse. It was a gallant charge.'[14] In it, five guns were captured, and large numbers of rebels were killed. Amongst these, at the head of her troops, was said to be the indomitable Rani of Jhansi. It is thought that she was cut down by an hussar, but there is much doubt about the circumstances of her death and the disposal of her body.

One officer of the 8th died of 'sunstroke', while seven were killed and seven wounded in the charge. Heneage and three other ranks were awarded the Victoria Cross. The Royal Warrant of

1856, instituting the decoration, laid down that it could be awarded by election. The practice died out later, but at this early date it was still in use – not always working smoothly: 'Morning spent', wrote Captain Poore, on 28 June, 'in trying to make the men recommend one of their number for the V.C., of which you have no conception of the difficulty, as they are so jealous of one another.'[15]

After the charge, the Brigadier 'retired the cavalry by alternative Troops, protected by the Artillery, during which movement both arms showed the greatest steadiness.'[16] They were under fire for some time while the captured guns were secured and the wounded removed. 'There was at this time', wrote Poore, 'a Squadron of the 1st Native Lancers who stood the fire as steady as could be. . . . We went back to the position . . . that we had started from and put up there for the night. It was by a well of splendid water.'[17]

That evening, with the rebels still threatening it, Smith's position was by no means secure. He asked for reinforcements. These Sir Hugh sent off to him without delay. 'A Squadron of the 14th Light Dragoons', wrote Poore, 'came in before dark. They are a fine looking lot, none of them under 7 years service, and they had been turned out so quick that nearly all were in their shirt sleeves.'[18] This was the first time the two regiments had met since the 8th had arrived in India. Both had marched vast distances and suffered enormous discomforts, but the 14th had been almost constantly in action, while the 8th had just fought its first engagement of any consequence. 'After all the marching and work we have had', lamented Captain George Clowes, 'it is the only time we have been engaged.'[19]

On the morning of 18 June, Rose received the rest of his troops from Kalpi. Leaving Napier to defend Morar and to organize his force so as to be able to pursue the rebels when he (Sir Hugh) had taken Gwalior, the indefatigable force commander set off to join Smith near Kotah-ke-serai. From there, next day, he advanced to the capture of the city. Towards the end of the battle, which was largely fought by the infantry and artillery, 'the 1st Bombay Lancers were to debouch', as Rose's despatch explained, 'from the entrance of the road on which I had placed them, charge the enemy on the grand parade [the same that the 8th had charged across two days before], and assist the 95th [Foot] in taking it.' This they did – and just at the right moment. The 1st Squadron, followed by the 2nd, charged 'most gallantly, in sight of the British troops', as Sir Hugh was careful to state, 'descending the slopes of the heights of

Gwalior into the grand parade, clearing all the right of it.' Unfortunately, 'carried away by their ardour',[20] as Rose kindly put it,
but in truth with what Sylvester called 'an illjudged zeal',[21] the 2nd
Squadron overtook the 1st and found itself in the narrow streets of
the city. By good fortune only one death resulted: Cornet Mills
received a musket ball through the spine.[22] But five of the men were
wounded, three of them severely. 'The rebel cavalry, as usual,
availing themselves of their horses, headed the retreat', wrote Sir
Hugh, 'instead of covering it.'[23] With them flew the Rao Sahib and
Tantia Topi. The city was now in Rose's hands, and next day by an
astonishing *coup de main* on the part of two infantry officers, the
almost impregnable fort also fell.[24]

On the morning of the day on which the fort was taken, Napier
set off in pursuit of the fleeing rebels. In his column, which, for the
first time, really was a 'flying' one, for it contained no infantry or
foot artillery, were 180 men of Meade's Horse.

A squadron of this newly formed regiment had escorted the
Sindhia into Agra on 1 June. Captain R. J. Meade, its founder, had
originally been in the Bengal native infantry. At the outbreak of the
Mutiny, he had been Brigade-Major of the Gwalior Contingent.
When the Contingent had revolted, he had escaped to Agra. There,
chiefly so as to deal with local marauding bands, he had been
ordered, on 31 October, 1857, to raise a body of irregular horse. By
early March, 1858, with the help of two other officers and Sergeant
Hartigan, 9th Lancers (who had won the Victoria Cross at Badli-
ke-serai), Meade's Horse was ready for service. Its organization and
clothing were based on those of the Corps of Guides (see p. 151).
In Agra Meade had found many men,

'faithful men from unfaithful regiments' as the regimental
historian has written, 'with very little to do. There were some
fifty or sixty Sikhs, for instance, and about the same number
of Panjabi Mahomedans. These he quickly enrolled, and so
made his 1st and 2nd Troops. A little later he was strengthened
by the arrival of a body of Jats from Rohtak, who became the
3rd Troop. The 4th Troop were Christians, bandsmen and
drummers whose regiments had mutinied or been disarmed.
The 6th was composed chiefly of Rajputs, both Hindu and
Mahomedan, but was classed as "Mixed".'[25]

The men of the Christian troop presented a special problem. Two-
thirds of them were penniless Eurasians.

'It was impossible to entertain them in a corps of Irregular
Horse without some modification of the Silladar system (see
p. 237). Meade therefore prevailed upon the Government of
India to advance them the price of their horses, which was to
be recovered by monthly cuttings from their pay. He tried also
to obtain special allowances for the Eurasian members of the
troop who were accustomed to a somewhat higher standard of
living than their purely Indian comrades; but here he was unsuccessful, and the result of all this was that these Christian
Sowars, like most paupers exceedingly improvident, were
nearly always in debt.'[26]

The 5th troop, which came later to be known as the 'Chambal
Horse', consisted of Brahmins from near Gwalior, who called them-
selves Dandotia Thakurs. Together with Mayne's and Beatson's
Horse, Meade's Horse became, in 1860, the famous Central India
Horse.

The wing of the regiment which now came under Napier had
escorted the Sindhia back to his territories. He and it had joined Sir
Hugh soon after the action at Morar. Napier's other troops consisted
of sixty-two sabres of the 14th; 104 of the 3rd Bombay Light
Cavalry; 245 of the Hyderabad Cavalry; the 3rd and the 'Eagle'
Troops of Bombay Horse Artillery. The first day's march was
twenty-five miles, and two days later the rebel army was caught up
with at Jowra-Alipur. Cornet Combe, of the 3rd, describes what
happened:

> [Captain Abbott's men of the Hyderabad] Cavalry 'discovered
> a large force encamped under some trees. Two camel-riders
> came out and enquired who we were. "Who are *you*?" said our
> men. "Tantia Topee and the Nawab's Army" was the answer.
> "Well, we are Sir Hugh Rose's army"; upon hearing which
> they hurried away. Our men killed one of them, the other got
> back; and from the commotion, etc. which followed his arrival,
> it was evident that his news was unexpected and disagree-
> able!'[27]

Captain Lightfoot, commanding the horse artillery, describes the
next move:

> 'Our small force . . . halted under a hill, out of observation,
> while the General and one or two of us went to the top to re-
> connoitre. On reaching the summit, we beheld an imposing

force . . . in line . . . so crowded together we could form no opinion as to their numbers. The artillery we could not see at all, and it turned out to be masked behind their infantry. The natives assured us that there were from 10 to 13 thousand with 25 guns, there. The General hesitated for some time before deciding to attack such odds. I urged the necessity of attacking at once before they had any means of ascertaining our numbers, and the General agreed with me, I am glad to say, and I was ordered to open the ball by a spirited attack upon their left flank.'[28]

Napier's own words tell what happened next:

'After a few rounds the enemy's guns were silenced and a rapid thinning and wavering of their ranks took place. Captain Lightfoot limbered up, and advanced at a gallop; and Captain Abbott with his Hyderabad Cavalry charged at the same moment, . . . instantaneously followed by the rest of the Cavalry, and the whole of the little force swept through the enemy's batteries and camp. . . . Wherever there was a body of the enemy collected in front, Lightfoot's guns opened and dispersed them.'[29]

One of the cavalry wrote: 'You cannot imagine the dash of the artillery: it was wonderful. We could scarcely keep up with them.'[30] Lightfoot's men, according to his own account, now

'set up a screech and a howl, which there was no resisting. I screeched and howled, too, and at them we went like a set of madmen. It was all very rash, I daresay, but I had my eyes open. . . . I do believe that when [the rebels] heard us screeching behind them, they thought the old Gentleman himself was at their heels. They just gave us one parting volley and fled. . . . We continued pursuing them until the General, seeing the smallness of our force, and the heat being most oppressive, ordered a halt.'[31]

Napier's despatch completes the story of what Cornet Combe modestly called 'this exciting little scrimmage': '25 guns had been captured [and] a considerable quantity of ammunition and elephants, tents, carts, and baggage fell into our hands. Never was the rout of an army more complete.'[32] Napier lost only three killed, and of the eight wounded all except one were returned as 'slightly'. The lowest estimate of killed on the rebel side was 200. But Tantia Topi, who had been in command, was not amongst them. Once again he had escaped, deserting his men. He had yet to be hunted down and captured.

'Our object was to try by sheer hard marching if we could not overtake and bring to action the mutineers under Tantia Topee, who kept up a perpetual dance all round the country.'

MAJOR LEOPOLD PAGET,
i/c "D" Troop, Royal Horse Artillery[1]

(xiii)

Indian Mutiny, 1858–59: chase of Tantia Topi – Bunas River – Zirapur – Sindwaha – Macaulay's Horse – Mayne's Horse – Beatson's Horse – Tantia Topi captured

The process was prolonged and hectic. It took nine months. The chase went on through the hot, rainy and cold seasons, covering an area roughly that of England proper. In the course of it, four major-generals, seven brigadiers, five colonels and one major led their 'flying columns' against the swift-moving guerrilla leader. These columns were usually composed of an *ad hoc* 'medly of detachments from various regiments'[2] and they changed with bewildering frequency. More often than not they were strong in infantry and weak in cavalry and horse artillery. The infantry generally acted as a brake on the mobility of the cavalry. Even without that brake the 'overworked irregular and the overweighted regular cavalry'[3] of the pursuers were no match for Tantia's light horse, while there was seldom sufficient of the mounted element to risk its employment unsupported. It is remarkable, in these circumstances, that on at least sixteen occasions, Tantia was brought to some sort of action. It was seldom more than what one who was there called 'the usual programme': 'Rebels drawn up on an eminence; parties pretend to threaten British flank; British advance in a steady line, capture rebel guns; *exeunt* rebels. . . . Our handful of cavalry had to rest content with seeing their enemies fly before them'.[4]

Co-ordination was not always all that could be desired. The officer commanding "D" Troop of the Royal Horse Artillery noted

'a peculiarity . . . about these detached columns. . . . They all wanted to be the one to catch Tantia Topee; and as each wanted his own column to do it without interference from another, in addition to chasing the rebels, the columns were often running away from one another, so that when the uninitiated thought they were in hot pursuit of the mutineers, it frequently transpired that it was only a rapid countermarch to get out of the neighbourhood of Brigadier Somebody else, who had been heard of within a few miles of the last halting-ground.'[5]

Before his eventual capture, Tantia covered more than 3,000 miles in his wanderings. He had enormous short-term advantages. For the most part he was operating in a friendly country. He looked to the co-operation of the rajahs of the Indian states. These, through sympathy or impotence, seldom failed him. They had 'as large a body of troops in their service as they could afford to pay; [and these] were entirely in favour of the mutineers'.[6] In the Maratha area, particularly, he found 'a mine of discontent hitherto unworked by any rebel leader – and no one could work it with such profit as a delegate of the Nana Sahib.'[7] Time and again he was able to replenish his forces with recruits, guns, remounts and supplies of all sorts.

Tantia's men, unlike his pursuers, were burdened with very few encumbrances. Their guides knew the country well and there was no difficulty about living off it. Much of it was roadless and deep forest or inhospitable desert where it was almost impossible for the pursuing troops to follow their quarry. Tantia's intelligence was, of course, consistently superior to that of his opponents. Further 'his outposts were always alert, and, if overtaken, he threw out a line of skirmishers to parry the impending blow while the main body decamped'.[8]

Of the Queen's regiments employed, the 14th Light Dragoons until well into the winter played a relatively unimportant part, enjoying a well earned rest. The 8th Hussars, on the other hand, came into their own. Usually split up into detachments of one or two troops, the regiment performed astonishing feats of speed and endurance. From the time of its landing in December, 1857, till 5

May, 1859, when it eventually went into cantonments, the regimental headquarters 'shifted camp 300 times'.[9] In the same period, Captain George Clowes's troop marched 3,365 miles. In one eleven day period, it covered 251 miles. Later it marched fifty-two miles 'through thick jungle, and very bad roads' in eighteen hours.[10]

In February, 1859, a column which, unlike most, was composed exclusively of mounted men, including infantry on camels and headed by 146 sabres of the 8th, marched 145 miles in four days. It then killed 'upwards of 200' rebels and captured a number of camels.

'A curious incident occurred on this occasion: Lieutenant Stourton of the 8th Hussars made desperate efforts to cut down, or rather to cut *up*, a rebel chief mounted on a swift Sandney camel, but his horse always swerved before bringing him within sword's length. A sergeant of the 8th coming up, exclaimed, "Why don't you try him with your revolver, sir?" Stourton, who had forgotten [about] his revolver, took the hint, and brought down both man and camel at the first discharge. On examination, the ball was found to have passed through the rider's body into the back of the camel's head, killing both outright.'[11]

This was one of the rare occasions when a cavalryman's firearm was of real use to him on horseback. There were others in this final phase of the suppression of the Mutiny. At the engagement of the Bunas River on 15 August, 1858, for example, Captain Clowes's troop 'found the rebels all about hiding in the bushes. We spread out in skirmishing order, got out the carbines (the new [Sharpe's] breech-loading ones) and shot every man of them we could see. The carbines were of great use for once in a way.' The rebels got themselves so far into the bushes that not even the lances of the 1st Bombay Lancers, who were with the 8th, could reach them.[12]

Of the last stages of this action, which was fought while the hot season was still at its height, Clowes says:

'At last the Artillery came to a dead stop. Their horses were completely pumped. Ours were getting very much done, but we had not got up to the elephants, so pushed on, killing the bushmen all the way, until at last . . . having gone over 15 miles from where the action commenced, we saw the elephants about a mile ahead with a mob of rebels. *Tremendous* was the excitement, the men yelling like a pack of hounds, and kicking away at their horses to raise a canter. The rebels were as much beat as we were though, and we soon caught them up. . . . Some of them stood firm and fought well. . . . If they had all fought as well, they might at any moment have cut us to pieces. We had not 100 men up, and about 30 of the Bombay Native Lancers and some of the Belooch Horse (sort of Bashi Bazouks, who plunder and nothing else much) were all that we had with us, while some thousands of rebels all well armed, and five or six hundred well mounted Cavalry, were bolting from us.'[13]

*   *   *

The 17th Lancers did not enter the chase till the autumn. 'They looked very smart indeed compared with all of us', wrote an officer of the 8th of one of their squadrons, 'having only just come up from Bombay. . . .'[14] Emulating the regiment's exploits in the same area forty years before (see Vol. I, p. 208), the 17th again performed with distinction. In December, 1858, for instance, 210 men of the regiment, accompanied by two horse artillery guns, marched 148 miles in 120 hours, before catching up with the rebels at Zirapur on the 29th. There followed a two hour engagement in which, as Fortescue, the regiment's historian, says:

'Colonel Benson advanced to the attack in columns of divisions, and, on the commencement of the rebel fire, moved the leading column to the right, thus uncovering his guns, which opened fire at 400 yards with grape and shell. The rebels soon gave way, and Benson then attacked with two divisions from his right, and drove them into the jungle. The 17th then pursued them through the jungle and across the ravine, and on emerging from the latter found them rallied and drawn up in a new position. The 17th then advanced in line, with the two guns in the centre, and after a vain attempt of the rebels to make a counter-attack, Sir William Gordon charged with his squadron and drove the enemy once more into the jungle and across the ravine. . . . After one or two more feeble attempts to rally, the rebels were dispersed and pursued in all directions. The action closed with the capture of four of Tantia's elephants by Captain Drury Lowe. . . . The whole affair lasted about two hours; and the distance covered before the day's work was ended was 36 miles, making a total of 178 miles, including the passage of two large rivers, in six days. . . . The casualties were as usual trifling enough. The Artillery and the 17th each lost one man wounded and two horses killed.'[15]

An officer of horse artillery complained that on some of these marches when the 17th was leading a column, it 'had a habit of marching at night by files, and whenever they came to a wet place, or broken ground, of crossing it in single file, and then closing up at a trot, and then they were easily lost in the darkness.'[16] On these marathon marches the columns were unaccompanied by their usual supplies: 'When a column started in rapid pursuit, the tents followed in charge of a small guard, and often did not come up for days, during which the troops had to shelter themselves under the forest trees from the sun and rain.'[17]

In the course of the campaign, all sorts of expedients were gradually developed. In Major-General Roberts' force, for instance, the method adopted for gaining information was

'to have about twenty cavalry in advance, close to the rebels. They left connecting links of two or three men at every few miles, so as to keep up the chain of communication. The advanced party was composed half of Belooch horse, who had no sympathy with the rebels, but could not communicate very well with the villagers, and half of horsemen belonging to the Rajah of Jyepore, attached to the suite of Captain Eden, the political agent, who were supposed, as Rajpoots, to be on good terms and able easily to communicate with the villagers, but not to be very warm partisans of the British. By this mixed party correct and immediate intelligence was constantly supplied.'[18]

To remedy in part the lack of cavalry, the use of infantry mounted on camels was resorted to. In addition to Captain H. Templer's 'Gwalior Camel Corps',[19] men of the 71st and 92nd Highlanders (like the Rifle Brigade at Kalpi), were placed on camels, under Lieutenant Barras. In one column all the infantry were thus carried.

It was found that it could march about twice as fast as the ordinary columns. The Scotsmen in their kilts were far from happy with the camel's action. It was apt

'to take the skin off a part of his person which is never turned towards the enemy. "I wunna mount the caemel, I wunna mount the caemel!" exclaimed more than one gallant Scotchman after a halt. "Weel, if you wunna mount the caemel, you'll stay behind and lose your head to the raebels," retorted Barras.'[20]

Lieutenant (later Field-Marshal Sir) Evelyn Wood, who won the Victoria Cross at the action of Sindwaha on 19 October, and commanded a troop of the 3rd Bombay Light Cavalry throughout the pursuit of Tantia Topi, wrote that when a body of European cavalry came up with the enemy rear guard it halted while a troop of native cavalry 'advanced in skirmishing order, firing while mounted, as was the custom. . . .'[21] He also tells a story which shows how much the mutinied cavalry lacked initiative. One day he was placing vedettes, when two enemy squadrons about 400 yards away advanced, conforming to his dispositions.

'As the Native officer opposite to me placed a pair of vedettes exactly opposite to mine, I got off my horse after I had gone about 500 yards, and sitting down, waited to see if he had sufficient self-confidence to choose a spot on his own initiative; this he did not do, however, and he remained sitting on his horse waiting for me.'[22]

*　　*　　*

Beside the Queen's and regular Bombay cavalry regiments a number of irregular bodies, some of them very ephemeral, helped in the hunt for Tantia Topi. From Bengal came the newly raised and shadowy Alexander's Horse, which was disbanded in 1861; from Gwalior came the 2nd Gwalior Mahratta Horse, which evolved into the 18th Prince of Wales's Tiwana Lancers; from Gujrat came the Gujrat Irregular Horse, formed in 1839 and disbanded in 1865, and from Sind came the Aden Troop, formed in 1855 of volunteers from the Scinde and Poona Horse. It had been intended for the protection of Aden's fortifications from marauding Arabs on the landward side, but it never reached its destination, being diverted en route to the Persian War.[23] In 1867 it was reconstituted, and served in many theatres of war until its disbandment in 1927.

The Baluch, or Macaulay's Horse, already mentioned, had been raised in 1857 from the tribes on the Afghan and Sind borders.

'These turbulent hordes', wrote an anonymous writer in *Blackwood's Magazine*, 'profess themselves followers of the prophet, but their practical tenets are to murder and rob mankind in general; that Hindoos especially are sent into the world for Beloochees to plunder, and Indian Mussulmans are little different from Hindoos. [Lieutenant] Macaulay had power of life and death over his followers, and certainly kept them in tolerable order; but they came to Rajputana with such a frightfully bad name, that it was scarcely possible to avoid hanging them. The presence of such convenient scapegoats was an incentive to crime. Every rascal among the camp-followers, when accused of pillage, threw it on the Beloochees. If a peasant missed his sheep or grain, he came straight to camp and confidently said, "A Belooch has done this thing." They were mounted on small ponies (chiefly mares), and their intelligence made them very useful as light cavalry.'[24]

In 1861, Macaulay's Horse became the 3rd Scinde Horse, and fought in a number of campaigns before being disbanded in 1882.

Another regiment which was raised especially for the suppression of the Mutiny was Mayne's Horse. Before Durand was replaced by Hamilton as Governor-General's Agent (see p. 186), he had ordered Captain H. O. Mayne to take in hand various detachments of native cavalry which had remained loyal. Captain Mayne, who had started his career in the 6th Madras Light Cavalry, had, at twenty-one, transferred to the Hyderabad Contingent, of which he became Brigade-Major. In the Second Sikh War he was aide-de-camp to Gough, becoming soon afterwards aide-de-camp to Lord Dalhousie, the Governor-General. In 1856, Canning, Dalhousie's successor, sent him to reorganize the 1st Cavalry, Hyderabad Contingent, which had shown signs of insubordination, the recurrence of which under Mayne's successor, had been the cause of Woodburn's detour to Aurungabad (see p. 181). In the early part of the Central India campaign, he had served as Stuart's intelligence officer. The nucleus of the regiment of irregular cavalry of which he now took charge, consisted of the loyal troop and a half of the Gwalior Contingent, a detachment of the Malwa Contingent Cavalry, and another of the Bhopal Contingent (see p. 188). From these he formed Mayne's Horse, which, in 1860, together with Meade's and Beatson's Horse, was to become the famous Central India Horse.

The two regiments of Beatson's Horse were raised between February and September, 1858. Their founder, Lieutenant-Colonel

William Fergusson Beatson, originally of the Bengal Native Infantry, was fifty-five, and had seen thirty-eight years of very varied service. Though he weighed fourteen stone, he was an exemplary horseman, and had been for some years in charge of the Hyderabad Contingent Cavalry. In the Crimean War, on Scarlett's Staff, he had commanded a corps of Bashi Bazouks.

The men of Beatson's Horse all came from Hyderabad. Mohammedans and Hindus were recruited indiscriminately. In each regiment there were six troops, four British officers, nineteen Indian officers, forty-eight dafadars and 500 sowars. Their uniform was green, with a red turban and cummerbund. Their arms were curved swords, 'hog spears', and carbines which they were taught to load and fire on horseback. The 2nd Regiment's mounts were all mares, except for a few geldings, while the horses of the 1st were all entire stallions.

On 26 October, the 1st Regiment went into action against Tantia Topi's men. Sylvester, who had been appointed its medical officer, describes this first charge of Beatson's Horse:

'We dashed off in line across country. . . . The pace was frightful, and six men out of eight had lost all control over their horses. Many had purposely from fear, or from bad riding, left their saddles [i.e. fallen off], while their now freed horses added to the excitement of the rest. . . .

'Just as we came up with the [rebel] cavalry, a deep dry nullah crossed our path, and into this fell more of our troopers, headlong, together with our second-in-command. Again more riderless horses were galloping amongst us. Fortunately, our Adjutant, Clay, a bold and intrepid pigsticker, was to the front, and by dint of much shouting at the handful of men who had kept pace, we dashed amongst the mounted rebels in some sort of line. They drew up into close order as though intending to receive our charge, but not liking the pace, broke and fled. Our men followed right well and the Adjutant and myself set to work with our hog spears in earnest while the troopers, with their sabres, almost brought to my mind General Beatson's vision of "cutting our way to Hindoostan"!'[25]

*   *   *

By the end of March, 1859, Tantia Topi's followers had dwindled to a mere handful. His own jungle hiding place was betrayed by

Man Sing an outlawed feudatory of Sindhia. On 7 April, he was surprised in his sleep and captured. A week later he was tried and hanged. To all intents and purposes the Great Indian Mutiny was over.

In the words of E. L. Woodward, the distinguished modern historian, it had

> 'scarcely affected more than a third of the area of British India. . . . No foreign power attempted to intervene. The frontiers were not disturbed; there was no trouble in Afghanistan. The Sikhs were quiet. . . . Sindhia's loyalty in Gwalior was of untold value. . . . Hardly more than a quarter of the sepoys of the army of Bengal took part in the fighting. There was no organized leadership. . . . Few Moslems and few peasants joined the rebels. Most of the population in the disturbed areas was disarmed, and only wanted peace. The rebellion was broken within four months, and during these months the civil administration was undisturbed south of the Narbada.'[26]

On the other hand the effect of the Mutiny upon the future outlook of the government and of parliament was considerable and long-lasting. Further, as Adrian Preston has put it,

> 'upon the evolution of the theory and practice of military authority and constitutional liberty, and of the relationship between them, the Indian Mutiny, like the English Civil War and the American Rebellion before it, had a profound and enduring effect.'[27]

The most obvious and immediate consequences of the 'Sepoy War' were the radical reassessments of the form and composition of the army in India which swiftly followed it. These, with especial reference to the cavalry, are discussed in a succeeding chapter.

4

'Our cavalry was of the utmost use to us throughout the whole campaign.'

LIEUTENANT-COLONEL GARNET WOLSELEY

in 1862[1]

China War 1860: causes – Probyn's Horse – Fane's Horse – Taku forts – Sinho – Palikao Bridge

In the early part of 1857, differences between Britain and China had come to a head over the seizure of a small sailing gunboat called the *Arrow*. At the time of the outbreak of the Mutiny, therefore, troops from England were on their way to exact compensation from and to enforce treaty compliance upon the Chinese. Canning, the Governor-General, declaring 'Canton will keep – India will not',[2] diverted this force to the defence of India. Thus it was that 'the Arrow War' had to wait till 1860 before it got under way in earnest. Lord Elgin was in diplomatic charge, and Lieutenant-General Sir Hope Grant, exercising chief command for the first time, was given charge of the British element in an Anglo-French expedition.

Unlike the last war with China in 1842, cavalry was included in the British part of the 'China Expeditionary Force' which sailed from Calcutta in February and March. Part of one Queen's regiment, the 1st King's Dragoon Guards, and two irregular Indian regiments, Probyn's and Fane's Horse, formed the cavalry brigade under the commanding officer of the King's Dragoon Guards, Thomas Pattle. The King's Dragoon Guards, it will be remembered (see p. 178), had been kicking their heels near Madras since early 1858. Only now had the regiment managed to horse itself adequately.

From headquarters in January, 1860, Hope Grant received at Lucknow the following telegram: 'Pass before you 1st Sikh Irregular Cavalry – Probyn's – and ascertain from each man individually his willingness to volunteer for service in China. Each man to sign or seal a paper.' The General at once ordered the regiment to parade before him at his quarters,

'and thither', writes the regimental historian, 'the men went, cheering throughout the three miles which lay between the

223

lines and the General's house. Every man in the Regiment, without exception, went up to the General and signed the required paper. They then cheered themselves all the way back to the lines.'[3]

This regiment was one of a number which Sir John Lawrence had raised at Lahore in the Punjab soon after the news of the Mutiny had reached him. Composed of loyal landowners and their retainers, these bodies of irregular horsemen were formed 'not upon written and published orders, but upon the verbal instructions of the Chief Commissioner.'[4] Captain Frederick Wale, an infantry officer who had been severely wounded at Aliwal, was told in July, 1857, to raise, organize and command the 1st Sikh Irregular Cavalry. By 1 October, Wale's Horse, as it was at first called, was ready. (See Appendix, p. 456.)

How 'irregular' the regiment was was described in later years by an officer who joined at this time:

'Every variety of bit and bridle, saddle and tulwar; every variety of horse, entire, mare and gelding – of all heights from fifteen hands to animals little bigger than ponies. . . . Our notions of drill were at first equally primitive. It was all we could do to form "threes right or left." The men, however, if no two of them rode alike and none of them had a "cavalry seat", were undeniable horsemen; and there was never any difficulty in getting them, when an enemy was before them, to form some sort of line to the front, and ride as hard and as straight, if not with quite as good dressing, as the better drilled troops of the present day.'[5]

With the 2nd Sikh Irregular Cavalry, raised a little later, Wale's Horse performed useful service as part of various flying columns scouring the United Provinces to the south of Delhi. In 1858, the regiment served at Lucknow, near which place, on 21 March, Wale was killed.

In January, 1860, Major Dighton Probyn, V.C., who had served throughout the Mutiny with the 2nd Punjab Cavalry, (see p. 172) assumed command of what now became known as Probyn's Horse. When the regiment reached Calcutta on its way to China, it was mounted and equipped by Government, thus temporarily lapsing from the silladar system.

*   *   *

27. A Pathan officer, Punjab Irregular Cavalry, in China, 1860

28. Brigadier-General John Jacob

The other Indian regiment employed in the China War was Fane's Horse. (See Appendix, p. 457.) It was specially raised for the purpose by Lieutenant Walter Fane, an infantry officer in the Madras Army, who had been given temporary command of the 4th Sikh Irregular Cavalry soon after its raising in 1858. Allowed a completely free hand, Fane started his work on 14 January in Cawnpore. By 11 March, he had arrived in Calcutta with four complete troops. He had gathered men from many sources. These included the 3rd Regiment of Hodson's Horse (see p. 156) and several regiments of Oude Police Cavalry, all of which were in the process of being disbanded. The organization was not wholly *silladar*, though many of the men came from *silladar* regiments.

'Any men who brought horses with them were paid Rs 150, [about £15 6s] the horses becoming the property of Government. To complete the number of horses', writes the regimental historian, 'Fane was allowed to draw on Government studs, spare horses of European cavalry regiments, and to purchase in the open market, the price, in this case, being an average of Rs 150.'[6]

Just over 300 of all ranks embarked for China. They were armed with sword and pistol, the flank men of troops being provided with lances.

*   *   *

The 'China Expeditionary Force' consisting of about 11,000 men with followers, left India in February and March, 1860. 7,000 Frenchmen joined at Hong Kong. The thirteen sailing ships which carried the native cavalry were towed by steamers. The passage from Calcutta to Hong Kong took, on average, thirty days, much of it in great heat. It produced two reports. One written by Lieutenant Allgood, the Deputy Assistant Quartermaster General, concerned native troops aboard ships.

'It is desirable', he wrote, 'that Native regiments proceeding on foreign service should be composed of either Sikhs or Mahomedans and not of mixed classes and castes where the prejudices of one sect interfere, on board ship, with those of another. Mahomedans and Sikhs both cook regularly on board and are not so particular about trifles of caste as Hindostanees are. The latter should not be sent on foreign service when the others are available, as their prejudices are obstructive.'[7]

The other report was written by Probyn and concerned conditions on horse-transports. Amongst other things he pressed for greater attention to be paid to ventilation, and for more space 'in rear of the stalls to enable the men to clean the horses properly.' He stated that 'a horse requires six gallons of water per day in hot weather; in cool weather, five.' He recommended that larger scuppers should be provided 'to carry off the urine'. Oats he found 'were superior to gram [the chick-pea, common as fodder in India], the latter frequently causing gripes.' 'Coir [coco-nut] mats', he observed, were most useful, but he recommended that they should 'only be used in rough weather as they are liable to stink and become full of insects if not taken up.'[8]

* * *

The campaign started with the taking of the Taku forts at the mouth of the Peiho River. It continued with a march along the river's banks to the outskirts of Pekin. It finished with the sacking of the Summer Palace as retribution for the treacherous capture, torture and murder of prisoners, (including eight men of Fane's Horse), during the advance. Lord Elgin's object was attained. The Chinese agreed to fulfil their treaty obligations and amongst other conditions to pay certain indemnities.

Soon after the landing at Pehtang, an eye-witness came across some of the native cavalry:

'The floor of the fort', he wrote, 'is entirely under water. On the right are encamped Probyn's Seikh Troopers, with their fine Arab horses, picketed in rows, hoof-deep in slush, notwithstanding the straw that is spread under each; the gay pennant-topped spears belonging to each Seikh standing fixed in the ground by the side of his horse. The men themselves are arranged in various groups, talking or carrying on their different avocations. Indian water-carriers and grooms are running to and fro, interspersed with here and there a British soldier or Frenchman in the uniform of his regiment, making a most curious and motley spectacle.'

The secretary of Count Ignatieff, the official Russian observer, was amazed in contemplating Probyn's Horse 'to think that from a country of black savages' there could be produced such fine mounted soldiers.[9]

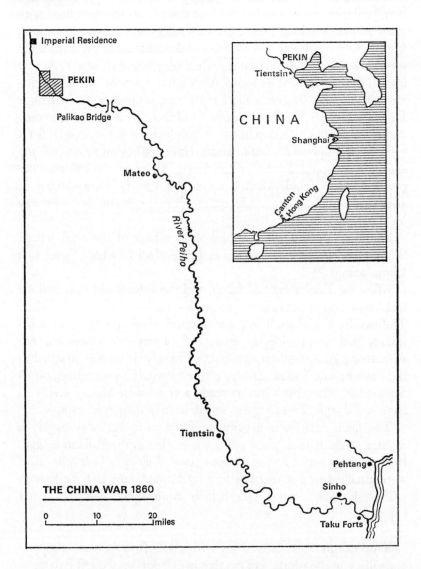

On 12 August, at Sinho, Sir Robert Napier's Division, to which the cavalry was attached, had its first important brush with the Tartar horsemen. These, mounted on tough little ponies, seated on high wooden saddles, and armed some with spears, others with swords, bows and arrows, and matchlocks, perhaps 3,000 in number,

advanced in irregular order, but with great spirit and steadiness. They were but slightly disorganized by the long-range fire of a battery of Armstrong guns. These breech-loading rifled twelve-pounders were here brought into action for the first time. Though they fired with great accuracy at long range, yet their effect was not very startling, for the Chinese horsemen in open order still came on undaunted until close to the British infantry when they began to waver. At that instant the cavalry was let loose. After a few moments of close fighting with some of Probyn's and Fane's men, supported by the King's Dragoon Guards, the Tartars turned and fled. Their ponies soon outdistanced the British troop horses which had not yet recovered from their long shipboard confinement. Nevertheless numbers of the enemy were toppled over or cut down. Amongst the officers, 'the performances of individuals', wrote a surgeon, 'were spoken of afterwards much as one would speak of the success on that same day on the moors.'[10]

Summing up the affair at Sinho, an officer of the Staff wrote: 'Plucky as the Tartars were, it was a case of all Lombard Street to a China orange.'[11]

After the Taku forts had fallen, and the subsequent negotiations had broken down, the allies resumed their advance on 9 September. The cavalry found itself in great demand. Probyn's Horse, for instance, had to provide an escort of twenty-five sabres for the Armstrong guns, whilst a squadron of Fane's Horse was attached to the French, who had no cavalry of their own. This squadron, on 18 September, when the Chinese made a stand near Matao, seems to have saved some French guns which were in danger of capture.

The final, decisive engagement of the campaign was largely a cavalry affair. It took place on 21 September at the Palikao bridge. Here some 15,000 Chinese troops extended along a four mile front were attacked in a strong position by Hope Grant and the French with only 4,000 men. The British commander describes what happened:

'Our troops were formed up with the infantry on the right, artillery in the centre and cavalry in echelon on the left [where they had been placed so as to make a wide turning movement designed to drive the enemy's right upon their centre, thus forcing them to cross the canal at those points which were the objectives of the allied advance]. I rode up to the French to reconnoitre the position of the enemy. As I was riding quietly

back, I saw some cavalry on the left front of our allies, which I
at first took for some of their skirmishers, when they suddenly
approached and I found that they were Tartars. I immediately
galloped off to Stirling's guns and opened fire with case at a
range of 200 yards, which quickly made them retire. The
King's Dragoon Guards and Fane's Horse, with Probyn's
Regiment in support, now advanced to the charge.'[12]

The story is taken up by one who took part in that charge, Major
Beauchamp Walker (see p. 52), Assistant Quartermaster General
to the cavalry:

'The Brigadier [Pattle] soon got his line in front of the enemy,
sounded the "trot", and swept down on them in a good line,
the Brigadier leading well to the front. As we drew near they
stood quite firm, and received us with a sharp but very ineffective fire from their matchlocks. The gallop sounded when we
were within eighty yards of them, and down we went, when,
to our great disgust, we found a drop of about four feet, then
a narrow road, and a bank of six feet to get up on the other
side. The *beauty* of our charge was quite spoilt.'[13]

Lieutenant-Colonel Garnet Wolseley, Deputy Assistant Quartermaster General to the Force, who witnessed the whole affair, explains exactly what happened:

'The men of the King's Dragoon Guards were then about the
biggest of our Cavalry of the Line, and as they went thundering
forward with loud shouts, their opponents may well have
thought their last hour had come. . . . What an inspiring sight
it was! My heart beat quicker as I watched it. Had the Chairman
of the Peace Society been there I am sure he would have
shouted in exaltation as he saw those lines of gallant horsemen
charge at full speed amongst the enemies' hordes. The Tartar
cavalry had, however, cunningly halted behind a wide ditch to
receive the charge, and delivered a volley when our horsemen
reached them. At that period our irregular cavalry always rode
with short, standing martingales, which prevented their
horses from jumping freely. Many accordingly went head over
heels into that ditch, their riders being unable to pull up in
time. Not so, however, the King's Dragoon Guards, whose
horses having free heads jumped or scrambled over safely.

'They got well in amongst the Tartars, riding over ponies

and men, knocking both down together like so many ninepins.
. . . In the short pursuit which then ensued the wild Pathans of
Fane's Horse showed well fighting side by side with the
powerful British dragoon. The result was most satisfactory.
Riderless Tartar horses were to be seen galloping about in all
directions, and the ground passed over in the charge was well
strewn with the enemy.'[14]

An account of what it was like to be in that charge is given by John
Goldsworthy of the King's Dragoon Guards, who was trumpeter to
the Divisional General Sir John Michel:

'Notwithstanding the difficult nature of the ground, I had disposed of some six or seven of the enemy, when I noticed that
Lieutenant W. S. McLeod of the Madras Cavalry, who was
attached to my Regiment for duty, was surrounded by seven
or eight Tartars, one of whom was preparing to give him a
final stroke, when I pierced him through the neck, killing him
instantly. I then turned my attention immediately to the
others, and succeeded in killing, or mortally wounding them all,
thus saving the officer's life. I followed in the pursuit and
managed to slay three Mandarins, and, catching the eye of
Lieutenant Marsland (now General and late Colonel 5th
Dragoon Guards), remarked to him: "That's the way to
polish them off, Sir!" He replied: "Well done, Trumpeter, go
on and polish some more off." I did so, but on coming to a
halt, as soon as the smoke had cleared away, found that I was
simply in the midst of the Chinese Army.

'I resolved to clear myself, so putting spurs to my horse I
made a dash and rode straight through them about a mile and a
half in the direction of my Regiment, which I found formed up
for the roll-call. I had to cut my way right and left to get through
the Tartar army as I did, and my trumpet was shot off my
back, but I calculated that forty-six fell to my sword that day.
. . . I recovered my trumpet next day, it having been found by
one of Probyn's Horse; and on unrolling my cloak from my
saddle four bullets rolled out.'*

Lieutenant McLeod presented Goldsworthy with a gold watch and

---

* This account should perhaps be taken with a pinch of salt. He does not, for
instance, explain why if he was the General's trumpeter, he was taking part in
the *mêlée*!

chain, and he was unsuccessfully recommended for the Victoria Cross. General Marsland tried for many years to obtain recognition for the Trumpeter. At last, in 1896, thirty-six years after the battle, Saddler-Sergeant Goldsworthy (as he had by then become) received an additional pension of sixpence a day![15]

The cavalry's total casualties in the engagement were two killed and twenty wounded. It was, of course, a very one-sided affair, in spite of the large numerical superiority of the Chinese. Lord Elgin who 'accompanied the army, and saw it all', wrote in his journal: 'Considering that the Tartars are so wretchedly armed and led, they did pretty well.'[16]

*   *   *

Hope Grant was full of praise for the way in which the cavalry throughout the campaign carried out 'numerous duties . . . of an infinitely harassing nature – patrols, escorts, reconnaissances, as well as the task of conveying letters almost daily between Tientsin and Pekin (a distance of 75 miles) for upwards of a month, during which they were frequently fired upon.'[17] Wolseley's views upon the cavalry's role are particularly worth noting, since his influence upon the army over the next thirty years was to grow steadily and in the end to be very great indeed.

'Some people', he wrote in his *Narrative of the War with China*, 'seem to consider that the military inventions of modern times have so changed the principles of war that cavalry can be of no further use, and, in fact, regard its existence now merely in the same light with many other relics of past ages. . . . The China campaign has taught us differently. Our two regiments and a half of cavalry there rendered most valuable service. With even that small force we were enabled to scour the country all round our camps to a great distance; and in action against an enemy whose mounted force was considerable, they gave us the power of following up by rapid charges the effect produced at long ranges by our Armstrong guns. In contending against an enemy similarly provided with a formidable artillery, its use would be all the more valuable, as by its rapidity in getting over the ground an onslaught might be effected upon the enemy's batteries which would so employ them and distract their attention that the infantry might have time for an advance in

line without incurring that heavy loss inevitable if they themselves had commenced the attack. In our actions in the field the
Chinese suffered but very little from our infantry, our cavalry
and artillery playing the principal parts, and inflicting almost
all the loss which the enemy sustained.'[18]

5

'[The objections of the men have been put forward] for the most part in a soldier-like and respectful manner, after the first excitement had passed away.'

Bengal General Order No. 883,
20 June, 1859

(i)

India: post-Mutiny alterations – the 'White Mutiny' – decision to amalgamate Royal and Indian armies

Long before the final suppression of the Mutiny, anxious thought was being given both in India and at home as to what shape the army of India should take in the future. Only two things were absolutely clear: first, after the passing of the Act of 1858 by which the Crown replaced the Company, all military forces in India would henceforth owe direct allegiance to the Queen. Second, since the Bengal Army had virtually ceased to exist in its pre-Mutiny form, there was now an excellent opportunity for complete reconstruction. To consider what all this meant in practical terms a Royal Commission was appointed at home, while Lord Canning set to in India to gather facts on which to base recommendations. Upon a wide range of obvious or minor matters nearly everyone was agreed. For example, no artillery and none of the arsenals were ever again to be in native hands. The future proportion of white to native troops was never to drop below a ratio of 1:2 in Bengal and 1:3 in Bombay and Madras. Promotion of officers at home was still to be by purchase,* and the prospects of officers of the old army in India were to be safeguarded. The major point of controversy was whether the defunct Company's forces could or should be amalgamated with the Royal army.

Before that great question could be settled an unexpected and

---

* It was laid down that 'the system of purchase, as practiced in the Queen's army, is not to be introduced into [any of the regiments in the new Indian army]. They will be seniority corps; but, in the promotion to field officers, the fitness and efficiency of the officers will be taken into account.' (*East India* (*Army Amalgamation*): *Return to an Address of H. of C.*, 17 June 1861). Within a decade, of course, the purchase system was abolished at home (see p. 379).

dangerous revolt took place among the European regiments which had been in the Company's employ. These numbered about 15,000 of all ranks. While Palmerston was still Prime Minister, (he resigned in February, 1858, but took office again sixteen months later), he had made a speech in support of a Bill which did not in the event become law. In the course of it he had said of the Company's troops: 'They will be transferred to the Crown . . . subject to the same conditions of service as those under which they were enlisted, and if they dislike the change, I think in common justice they will be entitled to their discharge.'[1] It should not therefore have come as a surprise that when the Queen's Proclamation transferring the Company's possessions to the Crown was made known, some of the Company's European troops, led by the 4th Bengal European Cavalry (only raised, as were the other four cavalry regiments, during the Mutiny), protested that they had enlisted solely for the service of the Company. They resented, they said, being 'transferred to that of the Queen as if they were so much livestock'.[2] They set up a claim for a free discharge (which, as it turned out, was what the majority of them wanted most), or a bounty on re-enlistment. Lord Clyde, as Commander-in-Chief, recommended some sort of concessions to the men, but Canning, standing on the letter of the law, overruled him and referred the question to London. After much deliberation it was decided that the men's claim was inadmissible.[3]

As soon as this news reached India, discontent flared up into what came to be known as the 'White Mutiny'.* Clyde received a telegram on 2 May, 1859, from Meerut (a month and a station of ill-omen indeed!) in which he was informed that the white troops there, headed by the 2nd Bengal European Cavalry, were evincing a bad spirit. On the walls of the rears and wash-houses appeared such inflammatory slogans as 'Unity is strength', 'John Company is dead: we will not soldier for the Queen' and 'Stick up for discharge or bounty: if refused immediately for Delhi.'[4] The 5th European Light Cavalry went so far as to give 'three cheers for the Company and three groans for the Queen'.[5] The manifestations of what was said to have been 'a widespread combination'[6] were not confined to the cavalry or to Meerut. Things were as serious at Allahabad where the general commanding actually asked permission, which was refused, to disarm the 1st Bengal European Cavalry.

* Not to be confused with the Madras officers' mutiny of 1809, which is sometimes referred to by the same name. (See Vol. I, p. 69.)

Courts of Enquiry were at once set up at the affected stations and the fullest possible investigation was made. Every man who wished it was called upon to state his grievance and the grounds for it. 'It is only by such means', the men were told, 'that the Commander-in-Chief can arrive at the merits of the case.'[7] Many of the men said that they wanted to return to England, but others seemed to expect some cash bonus and were prepared to soldier on if given that. Taking into account what the men said together with Palmerston's unfortunate speech, the Government came to the conclusion 'that the objections of the men are founded in the case of many of them, on an honest conviction that their rights have been overlooked'.[8] Every non-commissioned officer and man was therefore to be allowed to take his discharge should he want to. His passage home was to be free, and he was not to be allowed to re-enlist in any regiment in India ever again. This last condition was not likely to be a hardship!

As it turned out 10,116 men returned home – at a cost of £250,000. Of these only 2,809 re-enlisted when they got there. This small figure should not be taken as a general gauge of the army's unpopularity, for the men concerned were, in Canning's words, 'raw lads . . . landed in India and immediately marched to the Central Provinces, where . . . they were put to severe regimental training in the hottest part of the year.' Most of the European units involved in the 'White Mutiny', including all five of the cavalry regiments, had only been formed recently in the heat and hurry of the Mutiny, and the men were only partly drilled and 'unused to obey'.[9] Further they were commanded by officers, some of them no doubt demoralized, who had come from disbanded native regiments 'alike unacquainted with their men and inexperienced in dealing with European troops'.[10] That a full explosion did not take place was probably due to Clyde's prompt action in making known that he was setting up Courts of Enquiry at which the men would be fully heard. At one moment the situation was thought to be so grave that several Queen's regiments were prevented for a time from embarking for home, and reinforcements were ordered to the affected stations.

Even after the discharges had been granted, the state of discipline did not improve among the remains of the regiments. The 5th Bengal European Cavalry was the worst behaved. 'The state of the 5th is quite hopeless', wrote Sir Hugh Rose soon after succeeding Clyde as Commander-in-Chief. 'All the elements of order and discipline are the wrong way in them. . . . Nothing will stop the mutinous and insubordinate conduct of the 5th but capital punishment. They do not seem to care for Penal Servitude, even for life.'[11] One of the ringleaders, Private Johnson, was made an example of and shot. The regiment was disbanded forthwith. So also was the 4th Regiment.*

It is interesting to note that there was no sign whatever of discontent amongst the native regiments, although they were being transferred from Company to Queen on almost exactly the same terms as the European regiments.

*   *   *

The 'White Mutiny' had an important effect upon the great debate as to whether or not to amalgamate the armies of India with the Royal army. There were those, particularly Lord Clyde, who tended at first to favour a local force, but who now believed, as he wrote to the Duke of Cambridge and to Canning, 'that we can alone put faith in a discipline which is constantly renovated by a return to England', and 'that, after this most recent experience, it will be unsafe to have any European forces which do not undergo the regular process of relief, and that this consideration must be held to be paramount.'[12] The opposite view was baldly and erroneously expressed by Outram who said: 'The amalgamation of bodies so differently constituted as the British and Indian armies, I deem to be impossible.'[13] Lord Stanley, the first Secretary of State for India under the new dispensation, Canning and Sir John Lawrence, amongst many other distinguished men, not all of them 'Indians', were strong advocates, as Stanley put it, of 'a large, local European army in India'.[14] The Queen and the Prince Consort, the Duke of Cambridge, Sir Hugh Rose and General Peel, the Secretary of State for War, who presided over the Royal Commission, were staunch supporters of amalgamation. Their view prevailed when the question eventually came to be decided by the Cabinet. In India, needless to say, the decision was unpopular, particularly when it was fully realised that enlistment to serve solely in India was never again to be allowed. Lord Roberts, writing many years later, expressed the fear felt by many in the sub-continent at the time,

> 'that the change would result in a great increase to the military
> charges which the Indian Government would be called upon

---

* The nine European infantry regiments entered the Line taking the numbers 101 to 109.

to pay; that, notwithstanding such increase, there would be a serious diminution in the control exercised by that Government over the administration and organization of the British Army in India; and that, under the pressure of political emergency in Europe, troops might be withdrawn and Indian requirements disregarded.'

He thought that there was much to be said on both sides, 'but, although', he continued, 'it has been proved that the fears of those opposed to the change were not altogether without foundation, in my opinion it was unavoidable, and has greatly benefited both services.'[15]

'For purposes of active service, the regular cavalry are very superior to the irregular.'

LIEUTENANT-COLONEL HARINGTON,
5th Bengal Native Cavalry

'The irregular system is the best adapted for Native Cavalry in India.'

Report of the Commissioners appointed to inquire into the Organization of the Indian Army[1]

(ii)

India: regular cavalry abolished – silladar *system* – asamis – *death of John Jacob* – *comparative cheapness of irregulars* – *reorganization of cavalry promulgated, 1861* – *native cavalry uniforms* – *formation of Staff Corps*

The major change for the mounted arm was that the regular system was to be virtually done away with. All native cavalry, with the exception of that of Madras, where irregulars had always been unknown, was in future to be on the *silladar* or irregular system. The basis of this was much the same as that of the yeomanry in Britain and it has been expounded in detail in Volume I (see p. 179). In principle each man supplied his own mount as well as, amongst other things, his attendants, accoutrements, clothing and some of his weapons. In return he received a small monthly sum of money: twenty rupees in most regiments up to the early 1860s. His and his horse's 'berth' in the regiment, known as an *asami*, was looked upon as personal property. Subject to the Commandant's approval it could be sold or bequeathed. Should a man be deprived of his *asami* for misconduct, it became at the commanding officer's disposal. He sometimes gave it to a particularly deserving individual, but more often, which was the usual practice in the Scinde Horse for instance, it was

> 'put up to competition, all qualified Bargheers [see below] being allowed to race for it on bare-backed horses, and on a course appointed by the Commanding Officer. The Bargheers thus allowed to compete are started by batches of eight or ten, and the winners of each separate batch are then allowed to have a second competition, at "ball practice", the winner in this second test being considered the successful candidate.'[2]

The average value of an *asami* in mid-century was about 250 rupees. The whole system, unlike that of the regulars which was organized strictly on European models, was simple administratively and well understood by the natives.

Over the years it underwent numerous changes, but the basic principle was maintained. What this was has been well defined by Major-General Watson, an officer in and the historian of the Central India Horse:

> 'It was an ordinary bargain between the State and the individual, who gave his services and lent his property in return for a cash payment. . . . He might have much or little, the essential point being that he must have something to bring in to the service of the State beyond his own person and his own goodwill. If he were a large landowner . . . with men and horses at his command, he would bring in as many of these as he could muster. He then became a "Silladar" – or Sillah bardar, an armour-bearer, an esquire. . . . His men were called "Bargirs" [*Barghirs*: literally "rein-holders"] and were paid by Government at the same rate as infantry soldiers. A group of horses belonging to one Silladar was known as a "Paigah" [*paga*].'

On a barghir vacancy occurring, potential recruits applying for it, at any rate in the Scinde Horse, were first personally examined by the commanding officer 'to see that they have got good thews and sinews' and then were put on bare-backed horses and made to race each other. If a man covered the course in good time and went boldly round the sharp turnings which it included at a gallop, showed no hesitation and did not fall off, he was likely to be selected.[3] After the reorganization there were hardly ever again any cases where a *silladar* actually was 'a large landowner'. In almost every case the man who joined the irregular cavalry produced only cash,

> 'and the State, in the person of the Commanding Officer of the regiment, having purchased horses and equipment, sold the asamis to him, and enlisted the Bargirs where they could best be found. The purchase of a number of asamis was, in fact, regarded as a good investment; and it sometimes happened that such investments were made by civilians – rich merchants, for instance – who had no intention of performing military duty in their own persons, and were not compelled to do so. These men were known as "Be-nokar silladars". There were several of them in Beatson's Horse [raised in 1858, and incorporated into Mayne's Horse in 1860, which in the same year became the Central India Horse (see p. 220)]; but the arrangement was unsatisfactory, and when the crisis of the Mutiny was over, all "Be-nokar silladars" were persuaded either to pass on their asamis to fighting men or to resell them to Government, who then held them as "Government asamis" until soldiers of sufficient means or sufficient credit could be found to purchase them.'

As the true paga-owning *silladar* became extinct and men of lesser substance bought *asamis*, 'so by degrees the composition of the regiment changed, and, even before the Mutiny, we find Silladars in all ranks and the proportion of Silladars to Bargirs gradually increasing.' The 10th Bengal Lancers when it sailed for Abyssinia in 1867 was allowed only twenty barghirs although its strength in other ranks was 444.[4] By the early 1870s all barghirs had been abolished except for one each allowed to troop commanders and the Wurdi Major. From then onwards no man was enlisted who could not find at least 200 rupees in cash. He took over the asami of the man whom he replaced. This was valued by a committee of native officers.

> 'The price of the horse was, however, always the same, whatever its age or its service; for all transactions in relation to horses were carried out by the Chanda Fund, to which every man paid a small monthly subscription. The recruit paid Rs. 200 into this fund for his horse, or he brought in his own, which, if considered fit for service, the fund took over; and thereafter, in virtue of his monthly subscription, he was entitled to be remounted by the Chanda whenever his mount became a casualty.'*

Though regiments consisted of six troops formed into three squadrons for tactical purposes, the basic unit was the 'juri' or couple:

> 'In addition to their horses, arms, uniform and saddlery, every pair of men owned between them a pony and a tent, and employed a syce or grass-cutter. Thus the complete "Juri" was a small self-contained unit; and the obvious advantage of the system was that any portion of the regiment, from a couple of sowars to a squadron, or the whole, could march off at any moment to any place in India and remain there an indefinite time. This was not a mere theory: it was a constant practice. . . . For every two men, and for each officer, there was a pony loaded with the tent and baggage and a syce in charge of him.'[5]

* * *

Commanding officers of *silladari* regiments had a very special position of accountability. Beside their ordinary military duties they were responsible for buying and selling everything necessary for the life of their regiments. A commandant's first responsibility, after the welfare of his men, was the purchase of horses (see p. 435). He had also to make bulk purchases of material for clothing, leather for saddlery and such items as iron for horseshoes. The finished articles were nearly all made up in the regimental workshops. The carbine, indeed, was virtually the only item of any sort which was issued by Government. All other weapons, including swords, made mostly in Birmingham, were bought by the commanding officer and sold to the men. There was usually a fund into which the small profit

* For further details of the Chanda Fund see p. 436.

which was made on the sale of these items was paid. The monies from this fund were used for welfare purposes. There was also a 'Forge Fund' into which the men paid regular subscriptions covering the cost of shoeing their horses.

The most troublesome and time-consuming of the commandant's multifarious business concerns was the supply of food for the men and forage for the horses. Extended operations were involved, requiring, as Major-General Watson has put it,

'a sort of regimental Army Service Corps. [The business] was entrusted to a Committee of Indian officers, known as the "Afiseran Committee", of which the Risaldar Major was President, working always under the supervision of the Commanding Officer. The members of this Committee were usually able men, with a good knowledge of business as well as of agriculture, and they worked very hard indeed. The custom was, until the year 1885 or thereabout, [for] a member of the Committee, very often the Risaldar Major himself, to go out at seed-time to the districts . . . and negotiate with the farmers for the purchase of the crops when harvested. Large advances were made to the farmers to cover their intermediate expenditure, and as a result of these, the price agreed upon was considerably below the wholesale market price. At harvest-time the crop, being reaped, was buried in the villages until the grain was required, when it was brought to the Lines and handed over at wholesale price to the regimental banias [corn-dealers and money-lenders], who were allowed to make a small profit on retailing it to the men. The regiment made considerable profit in this way. . . .

'There was a bania to each troop. They constituted the regimental bazaar, and they supplied the men with most of their requirements and kept their accounts. Each regiment, too, had its own banker – the "Seth" as he was usually called. These seths and banias had other dealings than those with the men. They came to the assistance of impoverished British officers [who] could borrow money from them, plenty of it, at 7½ per cent on a simple note of hand . . . and many of us were in debt to them for years; but to the best of my belief no [seth or bania] was ever let down.'

The provision of grass for the horses was a major problem even when, as in the case of the Central India Horse, it did not have to be paid for:

'The stuff was there for the taking. The Maharajah of Gwalior placed large grasslands – "Birs" as they were called – at our disposal. All we had to do was to go and fetch it; but that is just where the trouble began. Immediately the rains had ceased the syces used to go daily to the bir to cut as much grass as the pony could carry and bring it into the Lines. So far all was plain sailing; but this could not go on for many months. It was necessary to cut all the grass on the bir before it withered, and to stack it within view of the Quarter Guard for consumption during the ensuing hot weather and rains. An army of coolies, many of them women, and a great number of bullock carts were employed on this service during the cold weather; but before they could commence operations a protracted altercation took place between the Gwalior officials and the "Afiseran Committee" – which demanded all one's sense of humour to endure without irritation – as to the hire of the carts and the weight to be carried by them, and the amount to be paid to the coolies for every thousand "pulas" cut. Now a "pula" has been aptly described as a bundle of grass as thick as a tree and as long as a piece of string. It was therefore necessary, before fixing the price of cutting, to agree upon some approximate size or weight. It is said that in olden times the thickness of the "pula" was deemed sufficient if it was equal to the girth of a sowar; and tradition had it that we enlisted a specially corpulent recruit for this purpose and fed him up annually to be at his fattest in October. . . . When the grass was stacked it was often found that there was more than the regiment required. The surplus was therefore sold to the local farmers and dairymen for their cattle.'[6]

*   *   *

On 5 December, 1858, there died at the early age of forty-five, a great leader of *silladar* horse. Brigadier-General John Jacob (see Vol. I, p. 229) was one of the brightest stars in that small but brilliant galaxy of soldier-administrators, including John Nicholson and the Lawrences, who served Victorian India so well. He had first made his mark in Sind after its conquest by Sir Charles Napier. In 1847, as a mere brevet captain, he had been appointed superintendent and commandant of the Upper Sind frontier. For fifteen years he waged successful campaigns on India's new western boundaries, striking terror into marauders and preventing their incursions into British territory. Among the wild Sind border tribes over whom he ruled 'his name only was known, feared and respected', wrote one of his officers, 'such as no other ever has been, or ever will be.'[7] 'This incomparable Captain and Administrator, a Murat in the saddle, a Lawrence in the tent', as he was described by the *Daily Telegraph*,[8] 'created', in the words of Lord Stanley in the Commons, 'a flourishing settlement out of a desert'.[9] He increased the area under cultivation enormously and he transformed an impoverished village of fifty inhabitants into a city which by the time of his death had 30,000 mostly prosperous citizens. In 1851, Lord Dalhousie decreed that it should henceforth be known as Jacobabad.

An unconquerable stammer partly accounted for Jacob's habitual reserve and his aggressive self-assertion. He made many enemies and more often than not failed to gain adherents to his tenaciously held and sometimes outrageous opinions. H. T. Lambrick in his brilliant biography of Jacob calls him 'acrimonious and intolerant, but warmhearted, generous and hospitable: almost inhuman in his utter devotion to efficiency and duty, but no enemy to fun in season and a lover of manly sport of every kind'.[10]

His passion for firearms led him to the invention of a new type of rifle with which he armed Jacob's Rifles raised by him in the year of his death. For the cavalry he developed a smooth-bore, double-barrelled carbine with which the Scinde Irregular Horse was armed as late as 1868 and probably even later. It was not a very satisfactory or up-to-date weapon being both heavy and expensive. 'Such success as it did enjoy', according to Dr C. H. Roads, the eminent historian of firearms of the period, 'was directly due to effective promotion by its inventor and excellent workmanship by its maker.'[11]

Jacob also had named after him a Mountain Battery and, most famous of all, Jacob's Horse or in other words the Scinde Irregular Horse. A modern historian has suggested that Jacob was 'perhaps the greatest British cavalry commander of the century'.[12] Certainly no cavalry officer in India approached him in intellect or influence. His horsemen were trained above all else always to act on the offensive. His detachments watching the frontier were often posted in the open plain and never allowed to depend upon defensive works

of any kind. In the organization of supply Jacob taught and practised that each unit – infantry as well as cavalry – should be equipped
with its own transport 'so as to be able to move far and fast at a
moment's notice, and to be as self-contained and independent of the
"regular" transport as possible'. In all modern armies the essence of
his organization – 'independence and mobility' – has become axio-
matic.[13] He was in this as in much else a prophet well before his
time. The principles of the irregular system as effected by him were
the basis on which the armies of India were reorganized after the
Mutiny.

Jacob believed in the 'natural and inherent superiority'[14] of the
white races, yet he was the leading practical exponent of 'Indianiza-
tion' in his day. He believed that

> 'to attempt to keep the natives of India or the soldier of the
> Indian Army', as he put it, 'in darkness and ignorance, in the
> hope of increasing our power over them, will be as contemp-
> tible and base as it would be unwise and useless. The better
> example we set them, the more we make them feel the value of
> truth and honesty, the more we can raise their moral and
> intellectual powers, the firmer we must stand as their rulers.'[15]

According to Lambrick, Jacob often asserted that

> 'no European subalterns could perform the duties of his Indian
> officers better than they did. And not only did his rissaldars
> command squadrons in battle, under the eye of the comman-
> dant or his lieutenants, but they were left in charge of isolated
> posts in the face of a watchful and bold enemy for weeks at a
> stretch, with no means of "reference to Headquarters" in an
> emergency. He once wrote, "I would give a year's life to be
> able to show my Native officers to the Governor-General." ...
>
> 'He held that the Indian character, under European control
> and guidance, was capable of far-reaching development. But to
> this development he seems, in his own mind, to have set a
> bound: nor apparently did he contemplate a time when such
> control and guidance would be unnecessary, at least in the army
> – in which the Indians were "the bones and muscles of the
> whole frame, of which the Europeans are the brains and
> nerves". Such a limitation modifies his general perfectibilian
> outlook.'[16]

Jacob was a prolific polemical writer. In many of his works published in the late 1840s and the middle 1850s, some of them unsigned.

he defined and attempted to propound remedies for the numerous defects which he saw in the Bengal army. With Henry Lawrence and a very few others he pointed out what were too soon seen to have been some of the predisposing causes of the Mutiny.

In 1938 the Scinde Horse was the first Indian cavalry regiment to be mechanized. The commandant at the time wrote: 'I believe that General John Jacob, whose mind was considerably in advance of the age in which he lived, would have welcomed the news that his old Regiment had been selected first for mechanization.'[17]

* * *

Before the decision to abolish the regulars was taken, much impassioned controversy took place. The advocates of the regulars were at a basic disadvantage, for all the Bengal regular regiments had either mutinied or had appeared to be on the point of doing so when they were disarmed – indeed, as has been shown, some of them were in the very van of the rebellion. On the other hand many of the irregular regiments had been conspicuously loyal.

There were other compelling reasons why the irregulars won the day. Chief amongst them was the comparative inexpensiveness of the *silladar* sowar. He cost the state about a third less than the regular. Lieutenant-Colonel Harington, a strong supporter of the regulars since he was one himself, admitted in evidence before the 1859 Commission, that

'for six years the regular cost the state upwards of £200 and the irregular £144. Thus:

Cost of an irregular and irregular trooper for six years:

Irregulars.

20 rupees a month, including every charge to the state	R. 1,440

Regulars.

Cost of horse (to last six years)	600
Nett pay, at 9 R.	648
Groom . . ., one for three horses	96
Grasscutter	252
Gram [chick-pea], 4½ seers, at 30 seers the rupee	328
Contract for shoeing; stable gear, &c.	216
Saddle, cost of	30
	R. 2,170

Clothing, arms, tents, pensions to syces (grooms), grasscutters, not included.'[18]

More important from the purely military point of view was the question of mobility. 'I think,' said Major Merewether, commanding the Scinde Irregular Horse, 'the regular cavalry are comparatively useless, there is so much trouble in moving them; the necessity of a commissariat makes it difficult.'[19] On the other hand, conventional discipline was not always the irregulars' strong point. 'It is no uncommon thing', declared Lieutenant-Colonel Harington, 'to see a corps of irregulars after a charge, spread over the parade like a flock of sheep, whilst the regular regiment pulls up in compact order.'[20]

One of the chief objections to the regular system in the minds of the commanders of the *silladar* regiments, was its tendency to make the sowars 'thorough dragoons, than which nothing can be more foreign to the Asiatic'.[21] Another telling argument used by the upholders of the irregulars was the fact that they attracted men who had some real stake and interest in their profession and their regiment: 'men of some money', as Major Daly of the Punjab and the Guides Cavalry put it, '– fond, too, of the position and importance which belonged to the irregular branch.' Brigadier Christie* pointed out that it was

> 'considered more honourable to ride one's own horse. [The irregulars] are altogether a more respectable class of men than those which enter the regular regiments, small zemindars [land owners], &c. Although the regulars are better paid, still the men that generally compose the irregular cavalry will not take service in the regular cavalry, disliking the constant parades, stable duty morning and evening, &c.'[22]

Lieutenant-Colonel Harington's view was precisely the opposite to Christie's. He believed that the men were

> 'exactly the same; and in many of the [irregular] regiments . . . inferior. In former years the irregular horsemen were enlisted from the cavalry of the armies of native chiefs, Mahrattas, etc., engaged in constant warfare, and trained to the use of arms from their birth. On the defeat of these native powers by the British, these men took service with us. . . . Since then they have been enlisted, and from the same class of men as the regular cavalry.'[23]

The officers of the Punjab irregular regiments made clear to the

* See Vol. I, p. 298.

1859 Commission their view that 'in critical times the trooper who rides a government horse has a direct inducement to desert. The trooper who rides his own has something to lose.' On the other hand, Lieutenant-Colonel Harington testified that 'irregular cavalry will save their horses in action. I have seen it', he added.[24]

*   *   *

The official reorganization of the confused mass of the Bengal regiments was promulgated in 1861. The General Order for the cavalry was dated 31 May. The total number of regiments was twenty-five, excluding such units as the Guides Cavalry, which still came into the category of local contingents (see p. 150). Each regiment, with a few exceptions,* was to consist of 420 sowars† in six troops (three squadrons). The pay of the sowars was to be twenty-seven rupees a month. The establishment and pay of the non-commissioned officers and trumpeters were first laid down as follows:

> '3 Risaldars, on R300, 250 and 200 a month, respectively
> 3 Ressaidars, on R150, 135 and 120   [Native officers]
> 1 Wurdi-Major, on R130
> 6 Jemadars, 2 each on R80, 70 and 60
> 6 Kot-Dafadars [Sergeant-Majors], on R47
> 48 Dafadars [Sergeants]
> 6 Nishanbardars [Standard Bearers]   } on R38
> 6 Trumpeters, on R34.'[26]

Though there were numerous alterations of detail in the establishments and pay rates of regiments in the next twenty years, by 1864 the main outlines had settled into the form which they retained up to 1914. The establishment of European officers with native cavalry regiments was finally agreed after much discussion. This was to be as a general rule: a commandant, a second-in-command, two squadron officers, an adjutant and a 'doing-duty' officer,

---

* The 2nd Bengal Cavalry for instance was one regiment that was reduced in 1863 from 420 to 384 sowars. (Whitworth, Capt. D. E. *A History of the 2nd Lancers (Gardiner's Horse)*, 1924, 9.)

† Of the sowars in the Scinde Irregular Horse from Bombay in 1867, twelve were farriers, three acting farriers, three acting trumpeters, six pay-dafadars [pay sergeants] and eighteen lance-naiques [lance-corporals]. (Holland and Hozier, I, 186.) In the Bengal regiments the proportions of such men were probably much the same as these.

as well as the medical officer. In practice, the number of 'doing-duty' officers varied considerably. In the Abyssinian expedition of 1867–68, for instance, the 10th Bengal Lancers had a total of eleven and the 3rd Bombay Light Cavalry ten European officers, while the 3rd Scinde Horse, typically, had only six.[27]

In the same year the 'class' composition of native regiments was formally laid down in the Bengal forces. This was a matter which had very little troubled the pre-Mutiny army. From now on, for obvious reasons, it was considered of very great importance. In future a much larger proportion of recruits was to come from the Punjab.

'The Purbiah soldier', as Sir George MacMunn has put it, 'had lost his place in the sun. No longer would the generations of a Purbiah village, the Brahmin and the Rajput of Oudh, serve the Crown as he had served the Company. . . . The Sikh, the Pathan, the Dogra, the Punjabi Moslem and the Gurkha had proved themselves the far better men, and therefore in the re-construction the number of Purbiahs was to be much re-duced.'[28]

The 1st Bengal Cavalry, originally Skinner's Horse, was to be the only regiment composed exclusively, as hitherto, of Hindustani Mussulmans. Four regiments (the 2nd, 3rd, 5th and 7th Bengal Cavalry) were to become 'General Mixture Regiments'. This meant that they were to be composed as soon as possible of equal numbers of Mohammedans, Dogras, Sikhs, Jats, Rajputs, Brahmins and Marathas. The 14th Bengal Cavalry, raised originally as the Jat Horse Yeomanry in 1857, was to remain, as formerly, a class regi-ment of Jats only. The 15th, which had been formed in 1858 from a number of volunteer troops of Pathan Horse, named after their commandants, 'Cureton's' and 'Lind's' amongst others, was to be composed as before of Pathans, Multanis, Duranis and Baluchis. The remaining eleven regiments were to have 'class' troops of various kinds. For example, the 6th Bengal Cavalry (the old 8th Irregulars) was to consist of one troop of Hindustani Mussulmans, one of the trans-Indus and border tribes, one of Hindus, one of Sikhs, one of Bundelas and one of Jats. The 11th, on the other hand, which had been raised as the 1st Sikh Irregular Cavalry ('Wale's Horse'), in 1857, was to have three troops of Sikhs, one of trans-Indus and border tribes, one of Punjabi Mussulmans and one of 'Dogras and Hillmen'.[29] The 10th Lancers went to Abyssinia in

1867 with one Sikh, one Mohammedan and one Hindu squadron. In the Hindu squadron, however, 'there were many Sikhs, supernumeraries in course of absorption.'[30]

*   *   *

In 1864 five of the Bengal regiments (the 10th, 11th, 13th, 14th and 19th) were made into lancers. Their lances, it was stipulated, were to be of bamboo with a bayonet-shaped head. They were not to weigh more than four pounds, and their length was to be not less than ten and not more than eleven-and-a-half feet.* The male bamboos for the shafts were cut by parties of sowars sent into the jungle at the right season. The heads and butts were made in the regimental workshops.[31]† Beside the lance the sowars were to be armed with sword and pistol. At the same time the regulation cavalry carbine was given to all those regiments which had formerly been armed with any sort of carbine. It was issued free to every man who gave firearms in exchange, and at half-price to others.[32] In the Bombay army none of the regiments became lancers officially until the 1880s.

*   *   *

The post-reorganization dress regulations of the Bengal native cavalry were numerous in the years to come. Those of 1863 laid down the basic form for the officers. That it was not slavishly followed is quite manifest. By the European officers in the first eight regiments (the 1st to 8th) an *alkalak* or loose frock was to be worn; in the last eleven (the 9th to 19th) a tunic instead. Shoulder cords were to be 'of curb-chain or chain-mail'; helmets of grey felt with bronze bars, binding, spike and chain; pantaloons of blue or green cloth with a double stripe the colour of whatever the regimental facings might be. Hessian boots and a forage cap of the colour of the facings completed the dress. Native officers were all to wear *alkalaks* and pyjamas 'the same as the British officers' pantaloons'. Five years later, amongst other changes, gilt was substituted for bronze in the

---

* For a full description of the lance see Vol. I, pp. 99–100.

† *The Times,* reporting the return from India of the 9th Lancers in 1859 noticed that 'many of the men have substituted the long bamboo used by the native lancers, instead of the ash shaft according to regulations.' (Quoted in Thomson, I, 79.)

helmet ornaments and white 'Melton'* pantaloons replaced the blue or green. In 1874 lancer officers were ordered to wear blue pantaloons and 'Napoleons' were substituted for jack-boots, which in 1868 had superseded Hessians.[33]

In the Bombay cavalry, when the three regular regiments were converted in 1862 to the *silladari* system, there do not seem to have been any important changes in their dress. The original irregular regiments, such as the Scinde Horse and the Poona Horse, appear to have been at least equally slow to change the type of their uniform. Not until the late 1870s and 1880s were the Dress Regulations of the early 1850s much altered. The Madras cavalrymen were even more conservative, but they were not numerous after the post-Mutiny reductions, and they remained on the old regular system, unlike the rest of the cavalry in India.

*   *   *

The change from regular to irregular meant that a large number of officers of the old Bengal regular army would henceforth be without a place in the new irregular regiments. These, as has been shown, were to have only six European officers.† The old regular cavalry regiments on the other hand had had a normal establishment of twenty-two European officers. Most of the surplus, after the dissolution of their regiments through disloyalty, proved or suspected, had been employed in the numerous *ad hoc* units, such as the five Bengal European regiments which were raised in a hurry during the suppression of the Mutiny. Now that most of these were to be disbanded the question was what to do with the spare officers thus thrown out of employment. Many schemes were put forward and rejected. The one which was finally accepted involved the creation in each Presidency of a so-called Staff Corps.‡ This was a misnomer as neither their constitution nor the training of their officers had any particular connection with the staff as such. They were to act in part as a replacement of the system under which, from the establishment of the old regular regiments, numerous officers had in the past been taken, without being officially seconded, to perform the ever-

---

* A stout smooth woollen cloth with the face finished without pressing or glossing and with the nap cut very loose.

† The pre-Mutiny irregular regiments had a basic establishment of only three European officers.

‡ These were amalgamated into a single Indian Staff Corps in 1891.

increasing extra-regimental duties which India's administrative machine demanded. These included beside quasi-military appointments, political and civil posts of all sorts with such bodies as the Public Works, Survey and Stud departments.

Those who did not wish to join the Staff Corps, and many of those officers who joined after their first formation, were placed on a separate list from which they were to be promoted after fixed periods of service. After twelve (later reduced to eleven) years an officer was to become a captain, after twenty a major and after twenty-six a lieutenant-colonel.

'Mounted men could not do much in such a hilly country.'

LORD ROBERTS[1]

(iii)

India: the north-west frontier – Ambela campaign, 1863–64 – 7th Hussars at Shabqadr, 1864

The amalgamation did not immediately affect the status of those local forces which were officered by Europeans but which were outside the Commander-in-Chief's control. The object of this system, which was to take a long time adying, 'was, or seems to have been', as Fortescue puts it, 'that civil lieutenant-governors or commissioners should have a military force at their disposal without inconvenient superintendence from the higher military authorities; and the practice helps to account for the readiness with which "politicals" interfered with the military operations of British armies also in the field.'[2] It is not always easy at this distance of time to distinguish between units which still came under the Commander-in-Chief and those which were still local 'contingents'. In 1860 certain regiments were transferred from the Punjab Government to the control of the Commander-in-Chief. These included the four regiments of Sikh Irregular Cavalry, one of which in the amalgamation of the following year became the 11th Bengal Cavalry known as

Probyn's Horse. Still left under the control of the Lieutenant-Governor of the Punjab was the Corps of Guides (see p. 150). Elements of both these units took part in the Ambela campaign of 1863–64, the first of any consequence in India since the Mutiny.

The campaign was one of the earliest of the many hundreds which were to be fought on the north-west frontier. British India had found itself saddled with this ill-defined, mountainous border on Central Asia as a result of the Second Sikh War (see Vol. I, p. 289). It was to become during the next hundred years the traditional training ground for generations of British officers and men. The fierce, intolerant, hardy and headstrong Pathan tribes were never totally subdued and still today remain free and unadministered. The essential problem which faced the Indian government was, in the words of Major-General Elliott, the historian of the frontier campaigns, 'to persuade a proud and warlike people, the independent tribes from across the administrative border, to live on neighbourly terms with the inhabitants of the settled and administered districts who were themselves Pathans and spoke the same language, Pashtu.'[3] In view of the nature of the terrain, cavalry seldom had much opportunity for action, but in the Ambela campaign, on 13 December, 1863, Lieutenant-Colonel Probyn, V.C., managed to lead 150 sabres of his regiment in one charge which was much praised at the time, and Sir Neville Chamberlain who commanded the expedition made use of the Guides' cavalry as well as Probyn's in defending static positions. He knew, he said, that 'in the event of a rush on a picket by the fanatics, the cavalry, with their drawn swords, would stand more steadily than any others'.[4]

* * *

There was only one other occasion before the very end of the century on which cavalry took part in any considerable action on the north-west frontier. Concurrent with the Ambela campaign, a large number of Mohmands, almost the worst troublemakers astride the administrative border, descended upon the fort of Shabqadr. On 2 January, 1864, about 5,000 of them faced the British garrison of 1,700. This included, beside European and native infantry, 145 of the 7th Hussars, 236 of the 2nd and 96 of the 6th Bengal Cavalry and three horse artillery guns. The Mohmands, ranged in a crescent, were enticed into pushing their right wing forward from the high ground to the edge of the plain.

Shabqadr, 2 January, 1864

'The cavalry', as the 7th's historian puts it, 'thereupon advanced, turned and gradually folded the enemy's right on the centre. . . . The 7th Hussars charged the enemy no fewer than three times. Colonel Macdonell [in command of the garrison] then sent forward the 3rd Battalion of the Rifle Brigade in skirmishing order. The enemy were driven across the border and the British returned towards evening to Fort Shabqadr.'

The 7th suffered nine casualties[*] and the 2nd Bengal Cavalry eight.

This was the sole engagement in which European cavalry had opportunities of regular charges in all the hundreds of operations on the frontier. In 1897 the 13th Bengal Lancers repeated almost the same tactics as those used by the 7th Hussars thirty-three years earlier, over exactly the same ground.[5]

[*] One report says that three hussars were killed and seven wounded. (Col J. M. Adye to Lieut-Col R. Biddulph, 19 Dec 1863, (ed.). Brig-Gen Biddulph 'The Umbeyla Campaign of 1863 and the Bhutan Expedition of 1865–66', *J.A.H.R.*, XIX (1940), 43.)

6

'Though a little war, it was a great campaign.'
H. M. STANLEY[1]

The Abyssinian campaign, 1867–68

The first substantial test of the post-amalgamation Indian army came
in 1867. At the end of that year there set out from Bombay and Calcutta Lieutenant-General Sir Robert Napier's Abyssinian expedition,
perhaps the most romantic and the most moral of all the 'little wars'
of the 'long peace'. It took 62,000 men and 290 ships, some from
Britain but most from India,* to rescue sixty European hostages from
the clutches of the mad Emperor Theodore at a cost of £8,600,000.
Fortescue thought it 'perhaps the most difficult and dangerous enterprise in which a British army was ever engaged.' Its base was on 'the
scorching shore of the Red Sea'.[2] The almost inaccessible mountain
fastness of Magdala where the captives were held was over 300 miles
inland. There were no roads: they had to be built. The mountains en
route rose to 11,000 feet. There were innumerable chasms where
neither man nor beast could get a foothold. Temperatures often
varied from 110° Fahrenheit at midday to close on freezing point at
night. There was very little water, even after wells had been sunk.
Virtually all provisions and forage had to be brought in by sea, and
to be carried inland. A complete port had to be built with a considerable railway leading from it. Above all, the whole operation had
to be completed within the period of the dry season or else the
rivers and tracks would be impassable. It in fact lasted, from first to
last, nine months. All these problems were more or less solved and
the objects of the expedition were gained. Casualties were minimal,
those of the Europeans from all causes numbering only thirty-five
dead and 333 seriously ill and wounded. Admittedly the enemy was
not very formidably armed and the people were on the whole well
disposed. Yet the *Illustrated London News* hardly exaggerated when
it hailed the Campaign as 'the most astonishing feat of modern days.
It was a triumph of which science may well be proud; and it shows

* Of the troop transports from India forty-five were sailing ships and thirty-
three were steamers. (Holland and Hozier, I, 230–1.)

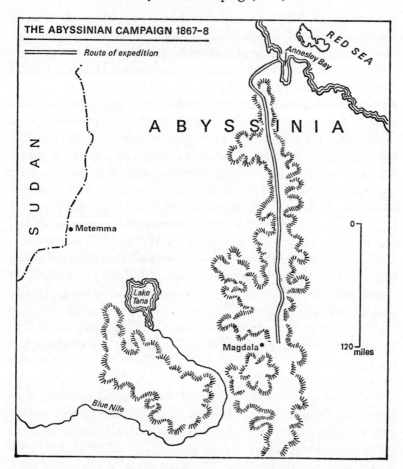

THE ABYSSINIAN CAMPAIGN 1867-8

Route of expedition

RED SEA

Annesley Bay

ABYSSINIA

SUDAN

Metemma

Lake Tana

Magdala

Blue Nile

0

120 miles

how large a part science will hereafter bear in military administration.'[3]

For the historian the campaign has a special fascination. Two large official volumes giving virtually every detail of the expedition's planning and progress were published in 1870.[4] These provide a vast amount of information unobtainable elsewhere referring not only to the campaign itself but also to life in the Indian army and the organization of regiments and commissariat.

It may be asked how cavalry fitted into such a campaign. With terrain so classically unsuited to mounted action, and with their horses to feed, were the 2,000 cavalrymen not more of an encumbrance than an asset? The answer is that this was the first campaign ever in which cavalry was specifically intended in the main for non-combatant duties. Its inclusion in the meticulous planning of Napier and his staff was probably justified, though it was undoubtedly expensive, especially as regards horses.

Three troops forming the right wing of the 3rd Dragoon Guards were the only European cavalry involved. They numbered 204 of all ranks with 224 horses and 257 native followers. An interesting sidelight on their passage from Bombay is that all the horseshoes were removed for the voyage. On landing at Annesley Bay the first task was to put them on again. As there was only one regimental farrier, it took some time. Nevertheless within a week they were on their way. On their heads the men wore cork sun helmets of the type later known as 'Wolseleys'. Their uniform consisted of the same types of loose blouses and khaki coloured country cloth overalls which had first become common in suppressing the Mutiny. This clothing was well suited to the heat but it did not wear well. Before long the men began to give the appearance of 'gangs of ruffians', particularly as the shortage of water limited their washing and shaving. 'In this matter', says the regimental historian, 'the British troops were in marked contrast to the Indians, whose officers generally insisted on a smart turn-out for reasons of discipline. . . . But so formidable was the reputation of the British soldier that it did not much matter what he wore, or how he looked.'[5]

Four native regiments completed the mounted element. Two came from Bengal: the 10th Lancers (2nd Hodson's Horse) and the 12th Cavalry; and two from Bombay: the 3rd Light Cavalry and the 3rd Scinde Horse. These comprised 1,821 of all ranks and 1,896 horses with 2,100 followers. 'The main point of our expedition', wrote Napier to the Governor-General, Sir John (later Lord) Lawrence, 'is carriage, as you know.'[6] The expedition's Transport Train employed throughout the campaign 41,767 animals. There were mules, ponies, camels, bullocks, donkeys and fourty-four elephants. It is recorded that the 3rd Scinde Horse had with it as regimental transport 339 ponies, 158 camels, 38 bullocks and 12 asses.[7]

The losses of horses in the course of the expedition were large. The 3rd Bombay Light Cavalry who were early arrivals, a few of them forming (with others of the 3rd Scinde Horse) an escort for the reconnaissance party which preceded the main force, suffered terribly whilst in the foetid plain behind the landing places. Their horses were killed by the Danakil equine typhus fever, 'at all seasons prevailing on the eastern coast of Africa'. It was a fatal, incurable

29. Headquarters detachment of the 5th Dragoon Guards at Athy on the line of march from the Curragh to Cahir, Ireland, June, 1863

30. Sergeant-Major Edwin Mole,
14th (King's) Hussars. (See p. 265)

31. Recruiting for the cavalry,
1855

disease, known as African glanders, and it struck with great suddenness. The first symptom was loss of appetite, the head and neck
then swelled obscenely and after intense pain death followed in a
matter of hours.[8] 367 of the regiment's mounts died: about 70% of
the strength. They were soon replaced by purchases made chiefly in
Egypt (see p. 437). The other regiments largely escaped the disease
by being sent straight away into the foothills. The 3rd Scinde Horse,
for instance, did not suffer a single death from this cause. During the
rest of the campaign numerous horses died from exposure and hard
work. The 10th Bengal Lancers, for example, returned to Calcutta
with only 191 of the 470 with which they had left it, and the 3rd
Scinde Horse landed back in Bombay with only 152 of their original
473.[9]

* * *

By the time Magdala was reached and stormed by the infantry using
breech-loading rifles for the first time in action, and supported by
Armstrong guns, only a fraction of the troops was present.* Most
of them were required to maintain and protect the lines of communication. The rations and baggage were successively cut down as the
objective was approached. So, too, was the number of both 'public
and private followers'. The 3rd Dragoon Guards, for instance, was
reduced to only seventy-eight followers.[10] About two-thirds of the
way all officers' servants were sent back and their masters 'were
obliged', as the official account puts it, 'to rely upon such assistance
as they might obtain from the soldiery'. At the same time the cavalry
troopers were deprived of their syces and grass-cutters. 'Their dismissal greatly assisted the rapid prosecution of the campaign.'

Throughout the expedition the cavalry was split up into detachments of various sizes at the numerous staging camps and posts,
often left in isolated positions, far from control. The 3rd Scinde
Horse, for example, beside providing the Commander-in-Chief's
escort was at one time divided into nine separate detachments, most
of them under native officers or non-commissioned officers. All
'postal duties', which meant the carrying of orders, messages and
indents as well as mail by two sowars at a time, up and down the
immense lines of communication, were given to the mounted troops.

* Of the cavalry: 173, 3rd Dragoon Guards under Lieut-Col Tower; 183, 3rd
Bombay Cavalry (Capt Macnaghten); 96, 12th Bengal Cavalry (Maj Gough,
V.C.). (Holland and Hozier, II, 459.)

On the return march which from bad weather and the activities of marauders was more hazardous than the outward one, a few postal sowars were ambushed and killed for the sake of their horses and arms. The cavalry officers and non-commissioned officers were also entrusted with commissariat 'purchases and issues to a very large amount; . . . in the aggregate many thousands of dollars passed through their hands.'[11] But the cavalry's chief task was the provision of guards and escorts for the endless convoys of men, guns and supplies. As Napier said in his despatch, 'the cavalry service has been such as to call for the fullest powers of that arm as Light Cavalry. . . . Seldom or never have Cavalry had such a variety of duties in maintaining communications for so many miles, climbing over mountains and through forest ranges, often benighted, where a false step would be destruction.'[12]

At the investment of Magdala on 13 April, 1868, the cavalry's part was to ring the vast hill. At one point it was rumoured that Theodore was on the point of escaping from it. Lieutenant William Scott, one of Napier's aides-de-camp, describes what happened:

'Sir Robert called me up, told me to take his escort and any Sowars I could find about, and to lose no time in circling to the rear of the enemy's position, to take prisoner, or to cut up any people trying to escape. My orders were to make them lay down their arms and to take them prisoners if possible; if any refused, to have at them at once. I accordingly got together with as little delay as possible, Sir Robert's and [Major-General] Sir Charles Staveley's* escort of the 3rd Bombay Cavalry, also a stray Sowar or two of the 12th Bengal Cavalry, making in all 35 sabres (the remainder of the cavalry were . . . on their way up), and started off with them round the hill. . . .

'I waited all that afternoon dismounting one-third of my men at a time, but nothing turned up and no orders were sent me; by the time I got back to my position [from watering his horse], I found Colonel Graves with a party of the 3rd Cavalry very little stronger than mine, had passed and taken up a position about three miles to my right. Between us a squadron of the 3rd Dragoons had taken up the ground; and beyond the 3rd Cavalry again, and completely round Magdala, the 12th Bengal Cavalry occupied the ground, so we were in force by the time the storming began, and well able to stop anybody bolting. . . .

* Commanding the assault.

'The enemy lay very close, but as soon as our men got well in they bolted as hard as they could, and over the far side of Magdala, where I suppose the rock is not so precipitous as it was on my side; anyhow, they came yelling down to where the 12th Bengal Cavalry were in position, who advanced to meet them; our men shot at them all the way down, and those who reached below were taken prisoners by the 12th Cavalry and made to lay down their arms. . . .

'When the country people found out that Theodore was done for [he committed suicide], they turned out below Magdala, where the cavalry were, kissed our feet and skipped about for joy: the women singing and chanting and clapping their hands; they took the Sowar's leather choggles [water bags],* went a long way for water, and brought them back full. It was quite a sight to see how overjoyed they were.'[13]

On the return march, the cavalry had the added burden of escorting not only the hostages and their belongings, but also large numbers of Christian Ethiopians who had been in Magdala and whose enemies, the Gallas, were out for their blood. The whole march was an epic race against time which was only just won. Indeed the cavalry were ordered to make especial speed towards the coast so that the vessels waiting to convey them to India 'might reach their destination without encountering the heavy gales of the monsoon'.[14] A few of them in fact did not succeed in doing so, losing as a result a number of horses' lives during the voyage.

Napier was promoted and given a peerage as Lord Napier of Magdala. He well deserved both. 'The honour of England', as a modern historian has rightly written, 'had been vindicated, and the martial qualities of the post-Crimean and post-Mutiny Army had been tested and not found wanting.'[15]

* Most native cavalry carried 'chaguls', sometimes called 'mussacks', slung underneath each horse's stomach. These were water-bags, generally made of some sort of animal's skin, and they held about a gallon of drinking water. They were attached by straps running parallel to the girths. (Holland and Hozier, II, 192, 195.)

7

'You get the refuse of the population . . . men
who have no other option left them than to go
into the army.'
          A brigade commander at Aldershot, 1866[1]

(i)

Rank and file: types of recruits

In 1859, the Adjutant-General of the Army told a Royal Commission on Recruiting that there were 'very few men who enlisted for the love of being a soldier; it is a very rare exception.'[2] Seven years later his successor told another Royal Commission: 'I am afraid that it is drink and being hard up which lead a great many to enlist.'[3] Recruiting Sergeant William Knibbs of the 17th Lancers found that of the many hundreds of recruits he had enlisted between 1851 and 1859 'not one in fifty has money in his pocket when he comes to us – and then I must ask him, "Have you a bed to go to?" "No." "Well, I will find you a bed." Sometimes I must find him his food.'[4]

Colonel Thomas Oakes, commanding the 12th Lancers, gave the reasons which he believed induced men to enlist in the cavalry:

'Sometimes it is really because he wants the food; he knows he will be fed when he gets there. There are other causes, such as taking a fancy to a soldier's life, the pretty part of it; at other times a man has quarrelled with his friends and wants to get away. [Some men] said they had been told exaggerated things by the recruiting serjeants; that they were to get a good deal which they had really no chance of getting. . . . Many men enlist in the cavalry just to get their education in riding and in the management of horses; they come prepared just to get this and are ready to pay their £30 for it. [£30 was the discharge purchase price in the cavalry during the first seven years of a man's service (see p. 331).]'[5]

The Adjutant of the London recruiting district in 1859 found that very few of the recruits for the cavalry had 'ever groomed a horse in their lives before. I do not suppose', he said, 'that one in ten has done so; some of them come forward with as white hands as possible.'[6]

'I have heard mothers solemnly declare', said Mr Samuel Haden, Secretary to the Army and Navy Pensioners Employment Society, 'they would prefer to hear that their sons were dead, rather than that they were enlisted.'[7] Eleven years later, in 1877, after numerous reforms had been effected, a parent confirmed Samuel Haden's statement. The mother of the seventeen-year-old future Field-Marshal Sir William Robertson, when he exchanged his job as footman for that of cavalry recruit, asked him: 'What cause have you for such a Low Life? . . . There are plenty of things Steady Young Men can do when they can write and read as you can. . . . I would rather Bury you than see you in a red coat.'[8]

Colonel Frederick FitzWygram of the 15th Hussars thought, as had many others for centuries past, that there was 'a general feeling abroad among the middle and lower classes that soldiering is not a good trade.'[9] But this applied very much less in the cavalry than in the infantry. Colonel Russell, the Superintendent of Recruiting in 1859, thought that 'the cavalry men are generally a more intelligent and better educated class of men and with better connections. A cavalry soldier will be well received in a county town or in a public house, where they would look down upon an infantry man.'[10]

Since the 1840s there had been a marked decline in the number of real country recruits. 'I never see what I used to see', said the Inspecting Field Officer of the London Recruiting District in the mid-1860s, 'namely the chaw-bacon* fellow in a smock frock.'[11] But though more and more men came from the industrial areas, they were often ex-countrymen. 'The men who are got in London', thought the Adjutant-General, 'are chiefly men who come up for work and do not get it.'[12]

'Labourers, husbandmen and servants' accounted for much the largest proportion of army recruits. Of the men examined in 1864, those three classes accounted for 59%. Of these 46% were rejected, chiefly on medical grounds. A long way behind came 'mechanics employed in occupations favourable to physical development (as carpenters, smiths, masons, &c.)'. These supplied 17% (of which 42% were rejected). 'Manufacturing artisans (as clothworkers, weavers, lace makers, &c.)' furnished 14% (48% rejected); 'shop-

---

* *Chaw-bacon:* 1822, formed from *chaw,* to chew, a country bumpkin. (*O.E.D.*)

men and clerks': 6.5% (41% rejected); 'professional occupations and students': 0.6% (50% rejected), and boys, chiefly from the Royal Military Schools at Chelsea and Kilmainham: 2% (18.5% rejected). Unfortunately, separate figures were not kept for the different arms of the service, so it is not possible to say whether these percentages applied equally in the cavalry and in the infantry. About 6% of all recruits were classified in 1864 as 'well educated'; 24.5% were unable either to read or write, while just under 10% could read but not write.[13]

In the post-Crimea period the men coming forward were often inferior in physique to those recruited before the war. The head of the army medical department put this down to better civil employment prospects 'and also to the decrease of population in Ireland' consequent on the great famine of the late 1840s.[14] Witnesses giving evidence before the 1861 and 1867 Recruiting Commissions were nearly unanimous in saying that the classes as well as the physiques of post-Crimea recruits were lower. Colonel Hodge of the 4th Dragoon Guards gave the chief reasons: 'The introduction of the railway system and the introduction of the police throughout the country have certainly taken from my own regiment the men that formerly came into it.'[15]

'When a recruit joins, things are not explained to him.'

An old soldier of the 12th Lancers[1]

(ii)

Rank and file: means of recruiting − regimental basis − an enlistment − smart money − age limits − height standards

There were four chief ways of obtaining recruits for the army, each of them in some measure competing with the others: at regimental headquarters; 'line parties', usually headed by sergeants seconded from their regiments; the Militia* Staff (mostly army pensioners), and, finally, pensioners, often working only part-time, supervised

* The militia had originally been the basis of Britain's home defence force. It had once been on a compulsory basis, men being found by a system of ballots

by half-pay officers known as staff officers of pensioners. The pensioners were 'quite inefficient generally speaking; they are old and worn out', said the Inspecting Officer of the London Recruiting District in 1866, 'and more likely to deter from joining from their appearance than to induce a recruit to join.'[2] Nevertheless they were not entirely unsuccessful. In 1865, a typical mid-century peace-time year, 207 line parties brought in 6,179 approved recruits, and 704 pensioners brought in 4,265.[3]

With the exception of recruiting at regimental headquarters, men were almost always enlisted in public houses. Recruiting sergeants often lived for years on end in them. 'You must go', declared a senior recruiting staff officer, 'where you can find the material'.[4] To these ale houses potential recruits were often brought by 'bringers'. In theory these were any members of the public who brought men to enlisting parties; but in practice they were generally crimps, men 'of the very worst character, touting about in the lowest haunts of every town'.[5] They were remunerated at a fixed rate. In 1859, for example, the bringer was given 7s 6d for each cavalry recruit for whom he had been responsible and who was finally approved.[6]

The best men were often obtained by regiments recruiting directly. Before a regiment started home after its tour of duty in India, its men were usually allowed and often encouraged to volunteer for other regiments remaining in that country. Considerable numbers did in fact do so. For instance, 193 men of the 8th Hussars volunteered for other cavalry regiments before the regiment went home in 1864.[7] This meant that on their arrival in Britain regiments were instructed to take immediate steps to refill their ranks. Recruiting parties were dispatched to likely places and posters were printed and distributed. The 7th Hussars, for example, on its arrival in York from Bombay in 1870 received its 'Recruiting Orders' on 20 July. By 17 December it had raised 187 recruits. Of these, eighty-one were enlisted direct at regimental headquarters.[8]

and substitutes. From 1815 it had been virtually in abeyance, the volunteer movement, including the yeomanry (see p. 443), more or less, taking its place. In 1852, this change was officially recognized, and recruiting for the militia was effected by bounty as in the regular army. It was embodied during the Crimean War and the Indian Mutiny in an effort to replace the regulars withdrawn from Britain. Militiamen were allowed to join the regular army, and the militia staff, unlike that of the yeomanry, was used to assist in recruiting for it. Until 1871, when it was taken over by the Crown, the militia was controlled by the Lords-Lieutenant. It then became a national rather than a purely local force.

Commanding officers sometimes used unconventional methods. Colonel Oakes of the 12th Lancers, for instance, on one occasion got hold of a good man from a village near Sheffield. 'I was anxious', he told the 1866 Recruiting Commission, 'to get some more and I sent him away after a few months to go and see if he could get any recruits, giving him a little money to spend, and he got me 18 boys out of that village.'[9]

Staff officers of pensioners were paid 1s a day, provided they obtained at least twenty approved recruits a year. Sixpence a day was paid to each pensioner who brought in six or more recruits per annum, and fourpence a day if he only raised four. In addition from 1861 onwards he received half the 'smart' money, if this was paid (see p. 267), and so long as he recruited at least two men a year he was allowed an annual suit of clothing.[10]

The number of recruiting parties of the line employed at any one time varied largely. At the beginning of 1858, for example, the number of parties from cavalry regiments was seventy-eight. By March, 1859, it had dropped to forty-two, reflecting the decline in the pressure for men exerted by the Mutiny.[11]

By law, all recruiting ceased when the establishment of the army was complete. This happened chiefly when Parliament decreed sudden reductions, as at the end of a war or in a peace-time fit of economy, or when economic recessions leading to low wages and under-employment quickly filled the ranks. Because so many were laid off during the cold winter months, these were usually the most fruitful for recruiters.

Until the late 1860s there was no general recruiting for the army. Every recruit not only had the right to choose which regiment he wished to join, but had to specify which it was to be. Whenever systems of general as opposed to regimental recruiting were proposed, it was always pleaded that the cavalry should be excluded from them.

> 'Almost all the cavalry recruits that we get in London', said the adjutant of that recruiting district in 1859, 'have a particular feeling for a particular corps. . . . They are a very much better class of young men than those who enlist in the infantry; they are generally clerks, shopmen and that class of men . . . and if they go into the 10th or 11th Hussars they say "I must see the serjeant before I enlist to see the clothes they wear".'[12]

A charming account of an enlistment in the 14th Hussars comes from the pen of Edwin Mole, son of a small farmer, who retired from his regiment in 1888 as a Troop Sergeant-Major. In 1863, when a lad of seventeen, Mole was working as a labourer on the building of the Charing Cross Hotel. After a row with his employer he walked off the site and met up with Sergeant Gibbs of the 14th, one of 'the great number of recruiting sergeants who hung about the locality'. Mole was taken first to the Ship ale-house in Charles Street, Westminster, and then to Gibbs' lodging, where he was shown 'several pictures of soldiers in different army uniforms'. Pointing to his own uniform, Gibbs exclaimed: 'there's none to beat this one in the Service! And, do you know, I think you'd look a rare treat in stable dress.' Mole asked what stable dress was. He was told that it was 'the walking-out costume, consisting of a dark blue shell jacket, overalls cut tight to show off the figure to advantage, Wellington boots with jingling spurs, a small cap "on three hairs", and a whip'. Attracted though he was, Mole was still uncertain about joining up.

' " Look at me, lad," said the sergeant, "I've done sixteen years of it, and the best part of them in Kalapoosh [army slang for India];* but I don't seem any the worse, do I? I tell you, it's the finest life out."

' "I don't doubt that", answered Mole, "but I'm earning good money, and I've no mind to 'list just now. At least, not without a chum of mine."

' "Why, lad, you've only to 'list, and once your chum claps eyes on you in the Hussar uniform there's nothing'll stop him from coming after you. As for your earning good money, see the mucking work you have to do for it. And you'll never want money in the 14th Hussars. If you only keep yourself smart and your eyes purling, you'll get your fun and plenty to drink free gratis; for the girls will fight for you, and you'll always find a Christian ready to stand treat. The Fourteenth", he added, with a wink of his eye and a cock of his head, "get the pick of the girls wherever they go".'

Gibbs and Sergeant Hudson of the 60th Rifles then took their half-willing victim to the theatre. On the way Mole asked Sergeant Hudson:

' "Do you really like the Service?"

* *Kalah-posh*. The word, meaning hat-wearers, occurs, applied to Europeans, in the *History of Hydur Naik*, 1842, by a Persian author.

' "What a question to ask!" he responded. "I have only one wish, and that is that I had entered it four years sooner; and a man can't say more than that, can he?"

'. . . As Sergeant Hudson had seventeen years' service, and four more would have completed his time, there were two ways of interpreting his reply.

'I then asked him if he knew anything about the 14th Hussars.

' "They have not been home long," he answered, "but they are a smart corps, and will always get first-class stations. A young fellow like you, if he only keeps himself clean and on the right side of the booze, is bound to get on in the Fourteenth."

'This pretty well decided me.'

To make sure, however, Gibbs got him drunk that evening, and put him to bed in his lodgings.

'Next morning, when I awoke,' wrote Mole, 'my head was very lumpy. The first thing I saw was Sergeant Gibbs, sitting up in bed, smoking.'

' "Hel-lo!" he cried. "You've woke up, have you? Could you do a drop of beer?"

' "No beer for me," I answered, "but I'd like some tea or coffee."

' "Coffee you shall have and that directly, for you'll have to go before the doctor this morning, and as it's rather late I think you had better get up at once."

' "What have I to go before the doctor for?"

' "Why, because you 'listed last night, of course; and there's the medical to pass. You're a soldier now. If you feel in your pocket you'll find the bob, and if you want any luck you'd better come down-stairs and break it, for that's the custom and according to the Articles of War."

'This information staggered me, for I had no recollection of taking any shilling. Thinking Sergeant Gibbs was only joking, I said: "Don't talk silly. If I had 'listed last night I should have remembered it."

' "Not by the way you looked when you went to bed," he replied. "Why, you drank me and Hudson blind, toasting your new regiment; and it was as much as we could do to carry you upstairs and sling you on to your cot. But just look in your pocket."

'I had my trousers on, and I slipped my hand into my pocket and pulled out what there was there. All my money, I found, was gone, except a few coppers and –

' "The Queen's Shilling," put in Sergeant Gibbs, with a knowing nod of his head, as I picked out a solitary one and held it in front of me, between finger and thumb.

'It was just the same as any other shilling – yet I could not help looking at it with a bit of awe, and wondering if I had gone and 'prenticed myself to twelve years' soldiering for this little bit of silver.

' "Come on, my tulip, buck about," cried the sergeant, breaking into my reflections; "You've done it now and Parliament itself can't undo it. Get on your clothes or we shall be all behindhand."

'I felt in no mood to argue, and after all, it was a relief to me to know I had "gone and done it", and that it was all over.'[13]

It need not in fact have been all over. Had Mole been able to raise £1 before the time came for him to be attested, he could have procured his release by paying what was known as 'smart money' (one half of which was allowed to the enlisting party). In 1858, about 10% of recruits paid it.[14]

There was nothing to stop boys of seventeen enlisting,* but years of service could not be reckoned for good-conduct pay or pension before a man's eighteenth birthday. This led to much abuse. The recruiting sergeant would say to a lad of sixteen or seventeen, 'Now my lad you are of the standard height, you can pass in as eighteen, and you will save two years' service by attesting yourself as eighteen years of age.'[15] The reverse fraud was also practised: 'By close shaving, a comparatively youthful appearance is given to a man, who is then instructed to state his age as seventeen or less . . . thus to pass in as a growing lad. Hundreds of men upwards of 25 years of age are thus received into the service.'[16] The point here was that men who were below the height standard could only be accepted if they were not fully grown.[17] At one time the upper age limit had been thirty, but by the late 1850s it was fixed at twenty-five.[18]

* A percentage of boys aged 14 and 15 (usually 1%) was enlisted. These were trained as drummers, trumpeters and buglers. 'A boy much above 14 can never learn to drum,' declared Col Russel in 1859. 'His wrists get stiff. Fifteen is rather old.' (R.C., 1861, 24.)

There were both height and chest standards which every recruit had to attain. These were varied from time to time, depending on the greater or lesser need for recruits. In the cavalry the height standard was always greater than in the infantry. In 1859, for instance, men of less than 5ft 8ins could not be enlisted for the 4th and 5th Dragoon Guards and the 1st and 2nd Dragoons. At the same time the 6th Dragoon Guards, four regiments of Light Dragoons and five of Hussars accepted a minimum of 5ft 4½ins.[19] But many cavalry officers believed that men of 5ft 6ins, which was the minimum for four regiments of Dragoon Guards, one of Dragoons and all of the lancers, were 'too short and that they could scarcely get on a horse'.[20] When he joined the cavalry after the Crimean War, Field-Marshal Sir Evelyn Wood found that 'commanding officers had a mania for tall men'. He tells a story of how

'when Lord George Paget, the Inspector-General [of Cavalry], remarked on the excessive height of a Light Cavalry regiment he was inspecting at Brighton, he was gravely assured by the colonel that the men had all grown since they enlisted. As the General passed on for a moment out of hearing, the colonel observed in an undertone to a friend, a former comrade, who was looking on: "I have sent half a dozen of my tallest men to bed in hospital, there to remain until the General leaves".'[21]

Sometimes, if a recruit was slightly below the standard, the recruiting sergeant, 'by bathing and stretching him' was able to increase his stature to some extent.[22]*

* Out of 3,279 men enlisted for all branches in the London Recruiting District during the first four months of 1859, only 1,112 were 5ft 6ins and more in height. Only six of these were 6ft and over. (*R.C.*, 1861, 23.)

'Which is the better off, they or the convicts?
The soldier gets £1 to take him home; the convict, after the same period, will have his £15 to
£20, has been well fed, warmly clothed, has had
no hard work, and every night in bed.'

A veteran of the Crimea, speaking in 1860,
of men leaving the army after their
first period of service[1]

(iii)

Rank and file: limited service

Since 1847, when the Limited Service Act was passed, men instead of
signing on for one engagement of twenty-one years, joined for an
initial twelve years (ten in the infantry until 1867). At the end of the
first period cavalrymen could either engage for a further twelve
years (in the infantry, eleven), taking two months' furlough and a
fresh bounty, or be discharged without pension. This meant that the
earliest age at which a cavalryman could retire with a pension, unless
he was discharged for disability, was forty-two while in the infantry
it was only thirty-nine. At one period men could be retained for up
to two years beyond either term of service when serving overseas.*
There were a number of reasons why the mounted arm was treated
differently in this respect. One of them never had had much substance and was out of date by mid-century. It was that the wear and
tear on an infantryman was greater than that on a cavalryman.
Corporal George Hollis, who as a farrier in the 8th Hussars had won
the Victoria Cross at Gwalior, explained to the Dalhousie Commission why cavalrymen considered twenty-four years too long:
'When the 24 Years' Act was brought in the infantry used to have to
march from one station to another, but now they go by railway, and
they have no more arduous duties to perform than a cavalry
soldier.'[2] Another reason was more telling: it took longer and cost
more to train a trooper. It was seldom less than a year before a
dragoon recruit was first sent out on a field day, and it took 'much

---

* Sir Hugh Rose lamented in 1866 that men were 'not sent out [to India] with
their regiments (and we all know that old soldiers are the best men) if they are
eighteen months short of their term, in consequence of the expense.' (*R.C.*,
1867, 177.)

longer than twelve months', according to the commanding officer of the 12th Lancers, 'to make a good lancer. That', he added, 'is a particular branch.'[3] Colonel FitzWygram of the 15th Hussars imagined that the twenty-four years were fixed 'on account of cavalry regiments doing less colonial service in former days than infantry'.[4]

For both branches it caused great hardship that at the end of the first term, men could be set adrift pensionless. Under the old single-term system the soldier was certain of a pension at the end of his twenty-one years. Now, when he wished to re-enlist for a second term, his commanding officer could say: 'No. You have been a troublesome fellow. I will not have you.' Or, alternatively, the regimental medical officer might say: 'No. You have not another twelve years more service in you. I cannot pass you.' In either case the man would be 'thrown upon the wide world' without any pension whatever. One brigadier was so incensed by this injustice that he considered that the Act 'was virtually abolishing the pension list'.[5]

From the efficiency point of view, of course, there was much to be said for the arrangement. Regiments were able to rid themselves of bad characters and incompetent or broken down men at a much earlier stage. Colonel FitzWygram of the 15th Hussars told the Dalhousie Commission in 1866 that he would like to see every man leave the regiment at the end of twelve or fourteen years.

> 'We find that, practically, the old soldiers do all they can to get out of riding. . . . We get good work out of our men up to four-teen years' service, but after that time they will get into any berth in order to get out of riding. Officers may get perfectly good and broken horses, but we are obliged to put our men on to such troopers as there happen to be, and some of them are rough and some are vicious. Most soldiers, long before they have completed twenty-four years' service, get nervous, and, if possible get out of all duties on horseback.'

He gave another reason for wishing men to serve for only twelve or so years: 'I think it very necessary', he said, 'for adjutants and riding-masters and commanding officers to have a number of men to train every year.' Colonel FitzWygram found that with the exception of two troop sergeant-majors not a single man of the twenty-eight who had more than twelve years' service in the regiment was at his ordinary troop duty. One was regimental sergeant-major, one was farrier major, one was sergeant i/c young horses, one was saddler sergeant, one was a recruiting sergeant, one was the sergeant tailor, one was corporal i/c sick horses, one was orderly room clerk, one was hospital orderly, one was regimental policeman, one was librarian, one was an officers' mess waiter, four were bat-men, four were in the band, three were farriers and three were away at Sandhurst.[6]

For obvious reasons the 1847 Act took a considerable time to come into full effect, but it was possible to get some idea of how it was working by the 1860s. In the first five years of that decade, for instance, there were 1,572 men in the cavalry entitled to discharge on completing their first twelve years. Of these, 668 re-engaged, and 904 left voluntarily or were got rid of. Eighty-seven of this last number re-enlisted after being discharged.[7] This figure is surprisingly large when it is considered that these men were not allowed to count their previous service for pension or for purchase-of-discharge purposes.

*　　*　　*

Much suffering occurred upon the reductions of establishment which took place from time to time. Regiments had then to be 'weeded' to the prescribed limits with the consequence that many men were 'unexpectedly turned out of the army, for a time, to certain starvation, complaining bitterly of what, though strictly within the conditions of the soldier's engagement, [was] nevertheless looked upon as injustice.'[8]

'I   do make Oath
that I will be faithful and bear true allegiance to
Her Majesty, Her heirs and successors, and that
I will, as in duty bound, honestly and faithfully
defend Her Majesty, Her heirs and successors,
in person, crown and dignity, against all
enemies, and will observe and obey all orders of
Her Majesty, Her heirs and successors, and of
the generals and officers set over me. So help me
God.'

The soldier's Oath of Allegiance
signed on attestation[1]

(iv)

*Rank and file: medical examination of recruits –
attestation*

The first thing a recruiter did after dispensing the 'Queen's Shilling',
officially known as Enlisting Money, and possibly making the recruit spend it on toasting his new regiment, was to take his catch to
a doctor, either a military surgeon or a private practitioner, for what
was known as the primary inspection. For each man finally approved
the doctor received 4s. He lost this fee if the man was rejected at the
secondary inspection (see below). If passed medically fit, the recruit
was then taken before a Justice of the Peace or a magistrate (to be
attested). It was illegal for less than twenty-four hours or more than
four days to elapse between the enlistment and the attestation.
Edwin Mole, for example, was marched with a squad of recruits the
day after his enlistment 'to Bow Street Station, where', as he put it,
'we each nipped a thumbful of prayer book, and took the oath of
allegiance to Her Majesty.'[2]

Recruits were next sent off either to the headquarters of one of the
eighty-two recruiting districts or direct to regimental headquarters
or depôt. It would sometimes take a month or six weeks to get them
through the various channels to their regiments.[3] During this period,
though paid and fed, the recruit hung about doing nothing, without
either uniform or 'necessaries'.

Mole, after being locked for the night into an overcrowded room
filled with recruits for other regiments, and having been forced to
hand over his watch and purse to Sergeant Gibbs for 'safe-keeping',
was taken to Euston by an old pensioner, so as to catch the train for

Manchester, where the regiment had a temporary depôt. 'When we arrived at the station, he took a ticket for me, and then explained he ought by rights to travel with me, but his wife being ill, he did not like to leave her, and thought he could trust me to go to Manchester by myself.'[4]

The secondary medical inspection which now took place was carried out by the district staff surgeon or the regimental surgeon, or by both. Sometimes, where there was a conflict between the primary and secondary examinations, a two- or three-man medical board made the final pronouncement. The proportion of rejections was apt to vary from year to year depending upon the demand for men. The official standards were extremely high, and when rigorously applied led to nearly half of all recruits being rejected. In 1864, for example, over 45% of those for the cavalry of the line were refused as unfit.[5] Special care was taken by staff surgeons when examining cavalry recruits. Good, strong arms, a well formed chest and straight legs were considered important. The chief London staff surgeon told the Hotham Commission that he often passed men fit for the infantry whom he would have rejected for the mounted branch.[6]

During a period of crisis, such as that of the Mutiny, instructions were issued to relax the regulations, especially with respect to varicose veins, flat feet, 'relaxation of abdominal rings' and loss of teeth.[7] Consequently for the period January, 1858 to March, 1859, the rejections in the army as a whole averaged as little as 28.5%. Faulty vision and eye diseases were usually a total bar to enlistment. On average they accounted for over 4% of rejections.[8]

Commanding officers, if they were keen, took a personal interest in seeing that they accepted only physically fit recruits. Lord William Paulet, for instance, used to see the men for his regiment 'stripped and put through all sorts of gymnastics, and the inspection used to be very minute.' When asked whether the men did not object to this, he replied 'They do not know what is to take place until they are brought into the room, and then they go through it and it is all over.'[9]

When recruits were sent to large depôts they were often kept there for a couple of days before joining their regiments. They were housed at Chatham, for instance, in 'recruit receiving rooms'. Whilst there every man was sent to the depôt hospital where he was given a warm bath before being issued with his regimentals, and where he disposed of his civilian clothing. 'A very respectable person' attended at the hospital, 'and the recruit, in presence of a non-commissioned officer makes his own bargain. If he is not satisfied with the price which is offered by this party, he is at liberty to go into the town and dispose of his clothing himself, in the presence of the recruit serjeant.'[10] He was then handed over to a pay-serjeant of his regiment and his life as a soldier began in earnest.

'It is usually considered that the cavalry should be better paid than the infantry, inasmuch as it is supposed to be a finer service and to be composed of a superior class of men.'

COLONEL RUSSELL in 1859[1]

(v)

Rank and file: bounty money – pay – re-engagements extended – good-conduct pay, badges and medals – military savings banks

One of the inducements to men to join the army, and to many others to desert (see p. 281), was the payment of 'bounty' money. The sum varied over the years. In 1854, for instance, when the demand for recruits for the Crimea was pressing, the bounty was raised to £7 15s 6d, and in 1855 to £10. In 1859 a recruit received 2s 6d on attestation, 7s 6d on final approval, and £2 10s on joining his regiment.[2] In the mid-1860s the total bounty was reduced to £1. An additional bounty was given to men in India who volunteered for other regiments which were remaining there when their own was ordered home. It was calculated on a sliding scale based on the payment of £1 for every unexpired year of service.[3] Until 1856, when the principle of a free kit was first applied, the stoppages from the bounty money were generally heavy. (See p. 304.)

The 1866 Royal Commission on Recruiting recommended that the bounty should be increased and this was eventually effected. It also advocated the completely free renewal of necessaries and that the meat ration should be increased. It was in lieu of these two recommendations that the first addition to pay for seventy years was made by Royal Warrant in 1867. The cavalry trooper's pay was thereby increased from 1s 3d to 1s 5d a day (including the long-standing 1d beer money). It was still, as it always had been, higher than that of the foot soldier.*

This increase still left the soldier with little enough spare money. In 1859 a good careful cavalry soldier, according to Sergeant James Macneff of the 8th Hussars would seldom have as much as 7d a day to spend. The Commandant of the Cavalry Depôt at Canterbury thought that the average there was about 3d to 4d. Sir William Robertson, when he joined the cavalry as a trooper in 1877, considered himself lucky if he was left with 5d a day actual cash.[4] More generally the trooper was in debt to such a degree, chiefly due to stoppages from his pay (see p. 301), that he received only the 1d which by regulation he had to be paid each day, whether he wished it or not.[5] 'It is well known', said the Chatham barrack-master, 'in every hamlet throughout the Kingdom that the soldier's shilling a day is only a fallacy.'[6]

Until 1867 the pay of a soldier was thought to have been rather smaller than the average wages of an agricultural worker. In that year the position was said to have been reversed. The War Office calculated that the average weekly pay of a country labourer in England was 1s 7½d less than that of an infantry private. A town labourer, however, received 5s 10¼d more in London and 1s 11¼d more elsewhere.[7]

In 1867, too, an extra 1d a day was granted to each man who re-engaged for a second term of service. At the same time re-engagements were extended up to a total of twenty-one years' service, with indefinite extension thereafter, subject only to three months' notice.[8]

*   *   *

In the Crimea during the autumn of 1855 a field allowance of 6d a day was granted to every man. There was in consequence an immediate increase in intemperance. Lord George Paget found his whole time 'taken up with courts-martial, chiefly for drunkenness'. He

* Trumpeters, drummers, buglers and fifers received extra pay: in the Life Guards 10d, in the Royal Horse Guards 7d and in the line 2d. (*Royal Pay Warrant*, 1850). In the cavalry of the line there were three other specialist grades below the rank of non-commissioned officer. The 1870 *Royal Pay Warrant* gives their pay as: Saddler and Saddle-Tree Maker, 2s 0½d; Shoeing Smith, 2s 1d.

commented on the foolishness of giving out the extra money on service 'when the only possible way for the loose ones to spend it is on drink. Had they been given this boon to be accumulated on discharge (the single ones), or to be remitted to the families of the married ones, it would have been a beneficial measure; as it is, it is the reverse.'[9]

*   *   *

Since 1836, troopers and corporals had received good-conduct pay and badges. By 1870 an extra 1d a day and a badge, which consisted of a stripe or ring sewn on to the jacket sleeve, were awarded after two years' service with a clean sheet. After six years a man received an extra 2d a day and a second badge (so long as he had been receiving his first good-conduct 1d uninterruptedly for the previous two years). After twelve years he received 3d and three badges; after eighteen, 4d and four badges; after twenty-three, 5d and five badges, and after twenty-eight years 6d and six badges. From sixteen years upwards there were accelerated rates for continuous good conduct.[10]

There was also a Long Service and Good Conduct Medal accompanied by a gratuity, known as 'the Medal with Gratuity'. This was only available to limited numbers of men below the rank of sergeant. The periods of service required to qualify were, up to 1854, twenty-one years in the cavalry (eighteen in the infantry), and after 1866, eighteen years for both branches. From 1875 onwards, the value of the gratuity was £5, and the limit set to the numbers of men eligible was removed.[11]

For a very limited number of sergeants and sergeant-majors there had been since 1843 a Meritorious Service Medal, known familiarly as 'the Sergeants' Medal', with which went an annuity of £20.[12]

*   *   *

When soldiers managed to save any money they could put it in the Military Savings Bank which had branches in each regiment. This had been established by Macaulay in 1842. An annual rate of interest not exceeding £3 16s % was guaranteed to the non-commissioned officers and men who deposited. 'The chief people who put in the savings bank', said Colonel Hodge in 1859, 'are farriers, servants, mess waiters, people of that kind. Very few of the men have much money in it.'[13] Colonel Oakes, seven years later, found that many of the troopers in the 12th Lancers preferred to use the Post Office Savings Bank which had been founded in 1861.[14] This may have been in part because of the comparative inefficiency of the military banks, especially when it came to withdrawals, there being complaints from time to time about the length of time it took to effect these. The preference for the Post Office may also have risen from the men's desire to keep the amounts of their deposits confidential.

'Men enlist into the cavalry for the jingling of the spurs and sabre, but they never take into calculation the extra labour of cleaning their horses.'

COL RUSSELL in 1859[1]

(vi)

Rank and file: 'swaddies' – the recruit's day – physical exercise – furloughs

When a cavalry recruit eventually joined his regiment, unless the percentage of recruits was abnormally large, he was handed over individually to a veteran soldier, known as an 'old swaddy',* who was held responsible for his charge's behaviour in barracks. Trooper Mole's swaddy was called Harris. He

'at once proceeded to introduce me to the horses, and putting a brush and curry-comb into my hand, told me "to have a go at old Balaclava", pointing out a big bay trooper, with a terrible rough coat, which stood in one of the stalls. This animal had been through the Crimean war, and bore the marks of active service in the shape of a deep sabre scar on his forehead, and half of his left ear missing.

'Pulling off my coat, I hung it on the bail, or bar between the stalls, and started to groom old Balaclava. But no sooner had I touched him with the brush than he made a sort of half-rear in

* Or *swad*. The word seems to have been applied at one time to a discharged soldier. It may have come from *shoddy*, which was woollen yarn obtained by tearing to shreds soldiers' (and others') worn-out coats.

the stall, and threw his sound ear back in a way that induced me to chance the character of the trooper in the next stall by scuttling under the bail and against its feet, which made it nearly jump into its neighbour's premises. There was a roar of laughter from all the men, and it was some time before I plucked up courage to face old Balaclava again who now stood looking as meek as a towel-horse.'[2]

In most regiments the recruit went into the riding school the day he joined. Many men deserted in their first few weeks, largely because 'they find themselves worked too much' as Colonel Hodge of the 4th Dragoon Guards put it. For those who were accustomed to the care of horses and to riding before they joined, 'not more than one in ten' according to Sergeant Knibbs,[3] life was of course easier. Yet Lord Cardigan could say that even a fully trained 'cavalry soldier has no leisure hours'.[4] Colonel Oakes of the 12th Lancers declared that the recruits in his regiment were 'at work from 5 a.m. till $6\frac{1}{2}$ p.m.' every day. There was only half-an-hour for breakfast and just over half-an-hour for dinner.[5] 'From 2.15 to 4', according to a sergeant of the 17th Lancers, the recruit 'goes to drill; he then goes to his barrack room till 5.45; he then goes to stables again; he leaves at seven; from seven till ten he has to himself.'[6] As soon as he was finished with his initial weeks of drill, the newly-joined trooper had to attend school, though at certain periods this was only optional. (See p. 288.)

*   *   *

The question of physical exercise was a subject which the Sanitary Commission discussed. Considerable evidence was given to show that mortality rates increased in both civil and military occupations where exercise was seldom taken or of a monotonous nature. One of the reasons why cavalrymen were healthier than foot soldiers, it was argued, was the greater variety of exercise which they took. It was recommended that far more facilities should be provided in the army 'for all athletic games, such as fives, cricket, quoits, single-stick and for gymnastic exercise'.[7]

In 1860 action began to be taken to implement these recommendations. In that year a school was established at Aldershot under a Major Hammersley, who became its first Superintendent of Gymnastic Exercises, 'a situation' according to his horrified father, 'which seems hardly fit for a gentleman, much less an officer.' Two years later gymnasia were ordered to be built in every garrison, and in 1865 one of the earliest sets of regulations was issued. These decreed that physical training was to take precedence over all other forms of training during the first two months of every recruit's service, and, among other things, made fencing drill compulsory in the cavalry. Two years earlier, it had been officially recommended that every trooper, once trained, should undergo 'a course of Fencing and Sword exercise [see p. 414] in lieu of Gymnastic training' which last was to be 'considered voluntary'. In the following year *The Times* reported that classes were to be formed 'for the practice of Fencing in the Cavalry, in accordance with the established system of Fencing for instructors in the Army'.[8] Fencing was considered by some to be the basis of all good swordsmanship. Its chief value was in giving the cavalryman 'quickness of eye and coolness in watching the expression, demeanour and play of his opponent'.[9]

By the early 1870s Hammersley had become Inspector of Gymnasia with the rank of lieutenant-colonel, and had established himself as a highly respected and successful pioneer. In 1885, the Army Gymnastic Staff was officially recognised as an important 'School of Instruction' in the army.[10]

At home, commanding officers had power to grant furloughs to non-commissioned officers and men, not as of right but only as an indulgence. Except in special circumstances these could not be granted 'during the season for reviews, field exercises, and inspections', which lasted from 10 March to 25 October.[11] The numbers allowed on leave at any one moment were controlled by general orders issued from time to time, and depended on how many men there were in relation to the establishment. In the early 1870s, for instance, 12% of all ranks were allowed to be away at once. The usual length of furlough was four weeks and it had to start on the 1st or 15th of the month. Young soldiers were not permitted leave until they had been 'dismissed recruit drill'. Men who were in debt, whose kit was incomplete, or who were defaulters were denied it. A man might take his greatcoat with him, but no part of his accoutrements.[12] A proportion of the men's pay was kept back by the regimental paymaster to be 'applied to the provision of such articles of necessaries as they may require on rejoining the regiment'.

Since, for many years, men were not given a railway warrant for their return journey, quite a few became deserters because they could not raise the necessary fare. The 1859 *Queen's Regulations* laid down that when men returned from furlough they were to be 're-drilled until reported fit to rejoin their troops; . . . but they are not to be required to "bring up" missed duties, nor, in the cavalry, to pay for the charge of their horses during their absence.'[13]

When men who had completed their first term of service (time-expired men) returned from abroad intending to leave the army, it was customary to grant them two months' furlough before their discharge so as to give them a chance to change their minds.[14]

*   *   *

From time to time the question of employing soldiers on extra-military work was brought forward. At harvest time especially, when there was an acute shortage of labour, men were occasionally allowed to help out. Lord William Paulet said in 1866 that 'some-times when a farmer applies wanting to get in a crop quickly, one turns out the married people who would turn their pay to good account. . . . But if you allowed all the men to go and work, you would have the civilians saying that you were ruining the trade of the place; it would be unpopular.'[15] In 1867 Lord Hardwicke tried, without success, to get established some kind of industrial employ-ment for soldiers 'so that their general health would be better and their pay subsidized'.[16]

'Desertion is thought so trifling a thing at the present time.'

SERGEANT KNIBBS,
17th Lancers in 1859[1]

(vii)

Rank and file: absconded recruits – desertion – 'bounty jumping' – apprehension of deserters – crime and punishment – lock-ups – military prisons

Desertion had been for many years a regular and disturbing feature of the army scene. Throughout the period covered by this volume the figures remained high.

Very considerable numbers of men deserted immediately after receiving the Queen's shilling. They were known as 'absconded recruits'. Colonel Leslie, who commanded the East India depôt at Warley thought that the country was 'beset by a class of men who make a living by robbing recruiting serjeants'.[2] This was made easy by the law which laid down that twenty-four hours must elapse between the moment at which the recruiter handed over the shilling and the serving by him of the written notice telling the recruit to report for attestation. 'What can I do?' asked Recruiting Sergeant Knibbs of the 17th Lancers. 'All that I can do is to take his name and residence, and in the last few days I have had several who gave a false residence. I have had the trouble of walking several miles, and when I have arrived there, have not been able to find the man.'[3] The financial loss fell entirely upon the sergeants, most of whom, according to a Westminster police magistrate, were 'very respectable men'.[4]

That same magistrate well described in 1859 an important change which had taken place in the middle decades of the century. In earlier years, he told the Recruiting Commission,

> 'the recruit was an ignorant and often half-intoxicated lad, the serjeant an unscrupulous deceiver, and the army generally was then an unpopular and jealously watched service. This state of things has silently changed. The recruit is commonly sharp and cunning, and far less scrupulous than the serjeant, who is bound to good behaviour and the strict discharge of duty by many responsibilities to which the recruiting officer of former times was a stranger; so that it is, in fact, more necessary now to protect the serjeant against the wiles and frauds of the recruit, than to guard the latter against any abuse of authority by the former. Instances are of constant occurrence where one recruit fraudulently obtains the enlisting shilling from two, three, four, and sometimes five or more serjeants, and the difficulty is, not to obtain by craft or deception, a recruit of some sort, but to select from the numerous applicants those most worth acceptance and least likely to run away as soon as the enlisting shilling is obtained.'[5]

Out of 11,328 men returned as deserters from the army in 1859, 'absconded recruits' accounted for 2,482. Desertions after attestation and between final approval were about the same in number (2,516). Those who deserted after joining their regiments and before they had served six months* numbered 2,820. 3,510 men were returned as having deserted after becoming trained soldiers. Quite large numbers of this last category were recovered to the service.⁶ The desertions which took place within the first six months occurred after the bounty, uniform and necessaries had been received. It was often the temptation which these offered which induced men to desert.† When from 1856 onwards part, and later all, of the clothing and necessaries were given free, the rate of desertion accelerated noticeably. 'It appears', declared Sir Alexander Tulloch in 1859, 'that desertion has materially increased in the cavalry. . . . They get the bounty, and then they get a large kit in addition, much larger than in the infantry.'⁷

In 1858 desertions from the cavalry ran at about 14%, while in the infantry the figure was about 11%. This higher percentage was partly due to the re-forming of two cavalry regiments in that year. These were the 5th (Royal Irish) Lancers, which had been disbanded in 1799, and the 18th Light Dragoons (Hussars), which had been disbanded in 1821. Both regiments were re-raised within a very short period of time, by means of special inducements including special bounties. 'These men', said a senior clerk in the War Department, 'were very glad to get what money they possibly could', and then to desert. During the year over 500 recruits deserted from the two regiments. In the following year the figure had fallen to less than 120.⁸

'Bounty jumping' was a common practice whereby a man deserted after receiving his bounty and kit in one regiment and then enlisted in another, repeating the process again and again. Colonel Gibsone, Commandant of the Canterbury Cavalry Depôt, had heard of a man of the 7th Dragoon Guards who boasted aboard ship on his way to India 'not vaingloriously or anything like it, for he was only telling it as a good story, that he had taken twenty bounties, the first and last of which were in the 7th Dragoon Guards.'⁹ 'Desertion', declared Colonel Russell in 1859, 'has now become such a profitable trade.'¹⁰ There was some profit, too, in apprehending deserters. The reward for handing one over to the authorities was £1. But, in fact, no very large proportion of them was ever caught. There was often great legal difficulty in establishing the identity of the deserter.¹¹ The mere confession by a man that he was a deserter

---

* A man was normally classed officially as a deserter when he had been absent without leave for twenty-two days. (Clode, II, 42).

† It was a penal offence to buy any of a soldier's kit.

was not sufficient for him to be committed. This rule had been made because it was not uncommon for a civilian to confess to being a deserter when he was nothing of the sort. A man would give himself up at, say, Maidstone, declaring that he had deserted from a regiment stationed at Manchester. He would thus achieve his object in getting free transport to Manchester. There, on it being established that he was not a deserter, the local magistrate as likely as not would merely remit the penalty.[12]

As for the motives, other than the obviously fraudulent ones, which moved soldiers to desert, diverse opinions were held. They ranged from the inadequacy of rations, of pay, of freedom, to mere boredom. Overwork and the irksomeness of drill during the recruit's first months of service were held by many to be responsible for most desertions. Especially was this so in the cavalry where the hard work in stables and riding school came as a grave shock to many young men (see p. 278). To remedy this the Hotham Recruiting Commission recommended that where a man's 'physical inaptitude' or 'disinclination to the care and maintenance of horses' made him ill-fitted for the mounted branch, he should be transferred if he were willing, to the infantry within six months of his joining. This reform was carried out immediately.[13] Another common cause of desertion was said to be that men overstayed their pass and were afraid to return to face the punishment which awaited them.

'Absconded recruits', that is men who deserted before attestation, unlike deserters proper, came under the civil law. In London in the 1850s the punishment usually awarded was three months' imprisonment; but in the country, especially where there were few absconders, as little as fourteen days were sometimes given.[14]

The punishments for post-attestation desertion could be severe. The Mutiny Act of 1859 re-introduced the power to inflict corporal punishment for this crime, and it was in fact used. In 1865, for instance, six men were flogged for desertion in the cavalry, and in the following year, nine: four of them in the 10th Hussars.[15] Indelible branding with the letter 'D' was often awarded by court-martial in the case of habitual offenders. 'The spot for marking', as laid down in *Queen's Regulations*, was 'to be about two inches below and one inch in rear of the nipple of the left breast.' Sometimes this was effected by a bunch of sewing needles. More often a brass instrument specially designed for the purpose was used. Into the punctures which it made gunpowder was rubbed, so as to make the tattoo indelible.[16] The whole operation was no more painful than any other tattooing. The Duke of Cambridge, the Commander-in-Chief, went so far as to recommend that after the first offence, each time a man re-deserted he should be re-branded. 'I am convinced', he told the Hotham Commission, 'that a confirmed deserter escapes detection by not having plenty of marks on him.'[17] Incorrigible bad characters were also sometimes branded. In their case the letters used were 'B.C.'. In the cavalry alone 489 men were branded with the letter D, and 30 with the letters B.C. during the three years 1865, 1866 and 1867.[18]

Both flogging and branding were abolished in 1868. One young soldier much regretted this. Writing in 1873 he said: 'Now in compassion for *their* [deserters' and bad characters'] tender feelings they are just left alone, and able at any time to come back and corrupt the young recruits, and be a perpetual trouble to the whole regiment, and worry the very life out of the NCOs.'[19]

*   *   *

The period covered by this volume saw a considerable reduction in the severity, but not much in the frequency of punishments in the army. Fines increasingly replaced imprisonment for drunkenness. Flogging virtually disappeared. Branding of deserters and bad characters was abolished. But there was no compensating decrease of the most common crimes. Desertion and drunkenness remained at a very high level. For some years after the introduction of short service, indeed, crime increased alarmingly. This was almost certainly due to the greatly increased turn-over of men, and the consequent lowering of the proportion of old soldiers, especially among the non-commissioned officers. The class of offence which included violence to superiors, drunkenness on duty and making away with necessaries, for example, increased 37% in the army at home between 1872 and 1882.[20] Over the long term, however, serious crime was on the decrease. In 1838 there were 103 courts-martial per 1,000 men; in 1884 only seventy-three.[21]

Death remained, of course, the ultimate punishment for such crimes as mutiny, misbehaviour before an enemy, 'making known the watchword' and 'throwing away arms in face of the enemy'.[22] The penalty was very rarely exacted. The next most severe punishment was penal servitude in a civil prison to which a man could not be sentenced for less than five years and which meant automatic dismissal from the army. The worst sentence which could be passed on men who remained in the army was two years' imprisonment with or without hard labour in either a civil or military prison.[23]

In 1868 flogging, which from the middle years of the eighteenth century till the 1850s had been the foundation upon which discipline rested, was prohibited in time of peace, the limit of fifty lashes being retained for service in the field. In the cavalry only fifty floggings were administered in the three years 1865, 1866 and 1867, years for which very comprehensive figures are given in the *Report of the Courts-Martial Commission* of 1869. Eighteen of these floggings were for violence to superiors or insubordination, and fifteen for desertion.[24] Out of a total effective cavalry strength of some 17,000[25] this was a very small proportion.

In the same period thirty men were discharged from the cavalry with ignominy, while pay stoppages with or without other punishment progressed from 480 in 1865 to 577 in 1867.[26] Imprisonment of one sort or another accounted for over 71,000 days in each of the three years.[27] From the point of view of efficiency this taking of men away from duty on so large a scale was deplorable. It was also very hard upon the well-behaved, sober men upon whom so much extra duty fell. When, therefore, the system of fines for drunkenness was instituted in 1869 it was universally welcomed.

There were three main types of military court. The General Court-Martial was made up of not less than nine officers of at least three years' standing, with a Deputy Judge Advocate as legal adviser. Unlike the inferior courts, it could deal with officers, and it alone had the power to pass sentences of death and penal servitude. The District or Garrison Court-Martial consisted of seven officers and did not require the services of a Deputy Judge Advocate. The lowest court of all was the Regimental Court-Martial, which was convened by the commanding officer and consisted of three or more officers who themselves sometimes took on the rôle of prosecutor as well as of judge. In the cavalry during 1865, 1866 and 1867 2,541 Regimental Courts-Martial took place. In the same period there were 1,377 District and twenty-five General Courts-Martial. Of the crimes tried, absence without leave was the most common at 1,092. Desertion accounted for 594 and habitual drunkenness (which, since 1866, was calculated from the fourth offence) accounted for 535.[28] There was much more habitual drunkenness when regiments were in India. Colonel Oakes of the 12th Lancers found that when his regiment was there he had seventeen cases in a year because, comparatively, 'the men had nothing to do', whereas at home in 1865 he had only three cases.[29]

The powers of a commanding officer were limited. For instance any crime which called for more than seven days' imprisonment had to be tried by regimental court-martial. Longer periods of confinement to barracks and a number of other minor punishments could, of course, be awarded by him. Some of these carried concomitant penalties which were much disliked by the men. Any punishment beyond seven days' confinement to barracks, for example, entailed the loss of one good conduct badge.

> 'I have known', said one colonel, 'a man with three or four badges for good-conduct brought up before some commanding officer, who takes a severe view of the case, and perhaps without thinking gives the man a punishment, which he cannot withdraw afterwards, of 10 days' confinement to barracks. That takes away 1d a day for a year, and the man may not be able to get it restored.'[30]

Samuel Haden knew of cases in which

> 'men who have been absent without leave for two or three days have been awarded for that a full stoppage of 1s for each of those days, in addition to an imprisonment of seven days in the cells, with 14 days' marching order drill and confinement to barracks for another period, making altogether thirty days. . . .
>
> 'I have known instances . . . in which men who have been undergoing long sentences of that sort for two or three offences following each other have again committed offences and asked for courts-martial in order to get rid of an accumulation of minor punishments while undergoing the sentence awarded by such court.'[31]

Another punishment for another crime which was within the commanding officer's jurisdiction was described in *Queen's Regulations*: 'Soldiers', says regulation No. 29, 'who have been convicted of making an improper use of their belts, as weapons, in brawls in public houses, and in disturbances in the street, and who are of disreputable and disorderly character, are to be deprived of the privilege of wearing their belts when out of barracks.'[32]

*   *   *

In the temporary lock-ups attached to the guard-rooms, the 'regulation number of inmates' provided as little as 140 cubic feet per man, and seldom exceeded 360. When, as was too often the case, the regulation number was exceeded, the degree of overcrowding was, according to Dr Sutherland's Committee,

> 'almost incredible. It reminds us of the Black Hole of Calcutta. . . . We were not at all surprised on being informed that when these lock-up rooms happen to be crowded, the men break every pane of glass to obtain fresh air. . . . We have met with instances where there are no lock-up rooms at all, the prisoners being crowded with the soldiers on guard into the already overcrowded guard rooms.'[33]

Conditions in military prisons were in many respects better than in barracks. As regards space per man, Dr Sutherland's Committee found in 1861 that improvement had 'indeed gone a long way ahead of improvement in barrack rooms.'[34] The food was less palatable, consisting chiefly of American corn meal made into a pudding, with meat provided only on Sundays, but as regards washing, for instance, a jug of water and a wash basin were part of the equipment of every cell. So were individual chamber pots, made of gutta-percha or earthenware. In nearly all military prisons there were baths, many of them large enough for the prisoners to lie down in.[35] 'It ought not to be possible', commented the Commissioners' Report, 'to say, as was said by a witness whom we examined, that a soldier never knows a healthy home, as regards air and space, till he commits some crime which brings him into the thoroughly ventilated cell of a military prison.'[36]

Further, even in civil prisons, as Sir Joseph Paxton pointed out in the Commons in 1856, the cost of maintaining a convict was greater than the sum allowed for housing the soldier.[37] 'It was very characteristic of Parliament', wrote Sir John Fortescue, 'to take better care of convicts, who were public enemies, than of soldiers who were a public safeguard.'[38]

'I am convinced that much of the dissipation and consequent irregularity of the troops has been owing to the absence of any opportunity for mental occupation.'

LORD HILL, Commander-in-Chief,
in *Report of Committee on Military Punishments*, 1838[1]

(viii)

Rank and file: education

In 1858 a report upon military illiteracy showed that one fifth of the troops could neither read nor write, that another fifth could read but not write, and that only 5% of the men possessed 'a superior degree of education'. Within ten years of that report, the Council of Military Education, which had been set up under Sidney Herbert in 1857,* was able to show that the first two categories (classed as 'uneducated') had been halved in numbers, but that the 'superior degree' class had only increased by 1%.

For the background to this situation it is necessary to go back to 1812. In that year schools for soldiers and their children were first included in the Army Estimates. Until then regimental schools had been run 'by the zeal, intelligence and liberality of the officers. . . .' In 1846, the Rev. G. R. Gleig, a friend of the Duke of Wellington's, and already Chaplain-General to the Army, was appointed the first Inspector-General of Army Schools. At the same time official Army Schools were set up in every regiment and in many detachments, and, more important, the Corps of Army Schoolmasters was established. Three years later it was made compulsory for recruits to attend school until their primary training was completed. This placed a considerable strain upon men whose time (in the cavalry at any rate) was already very fully occupied, and by 1859 the regulations had been amended so as to reverse the position, school attendance beginning, not ending, when recruit training was over. But dis-

---

* In 1870 the Council was abolished and a Director-General of Military Education created. His duties were 'much the same as those of the Council, but the office, from being a consultative one . . . became an executive branch of the War Office under the Department of the Commander-in-Chief.' (*First Report on the Education of Officers*, 1873.)

cretion was given to commanding officers as to whether to order men to attend school or not. The Article of War which made it a court-martial offence for any soldier to absent himself from school if ordered to attend by his commanding officer had become almost a dead letter by the late 1860s. In practice only if a man had put his name down to attend could he be ordered to;[2] and this was not often done. In 1869 a member of the Council of Military Education stated that out of 200 to 300 men's names on the school books of a regiment 'there would not probably be an average attendance daily of more than thirty men.' In 1867, there were 37,840 adults on the army's school books.[3]

Seven commanding officers of cavalry regiments were asked by the Royal Commission on Military Education whether they favoured compulsory education for their men. A majority of them were doubtful whether recruits, until they had been dismissed drills, would not find daily forced attendance too much, but most of them agreed that compulsory education for those who could not read or write was essential once the recruit stage was passed. Others, like Brevet-Colonel Soame G. Jenyns of the 13th Hussars, thought that

'a cavalry soldier has so very little time to himself that compulsory attendance at school would make men discontented; but I think', he added, 'the attendance of recruits on *joining* should be compulsory. I have always compelled men who cannot read or write fairly to attend on joining. . . . There are sixty-two recruits now attending school in the regiment under my command; of these eight cannot read or write. After they are dismissed drills I do not make school attendance compulsory.'

Brevet-Colonel E. B. Cureton, Commandant of the Cavalry Depôt, whose distinguished father had been killed at Ramnagar in 1848 (see Vol. I, p. 275), believed that 'every soldier should be compelled to attend school and to learn to read and write, but . . . the time should not be taken from his recreation hours.' Regimental Sergeant-Major Andrew Moreton of the Inniskilling Dragoons was absolutely certain that no cavalryman could attend school on more than two days a week without neglecting his other work.

'During the drill season', he told the Royal Commission in 1870, 'the regiment has to attend three field days a week, on neither of which days could he attend school without neglecting his horse or appointments. Guard would take him from school another day. . . . Even in the winter months the absence of men on furlough leaves spare horses, and the extra labour required to keep the horses and appointments clean would, in my opinion, prevent his attendance on more than two days weekly.'[4]

In India, Colonel Gall of the 14th Light Dragoons described the regimental schools in 1861 as 'very good. . . . There are men', he added, 'who have been educated in the schools of the 14th entirely, men who could not write before. The late Regimental Sergeant-Major was, I believe, entirely educated in the regimental school.'[5]

In the early 1860s considerable strides were made in the soldier's education. In 1861 for instance there were 191 masters and 99 trainees. Five years later there were 238 masters and 326 trainees.[6]* This increase, and much else that was achieved in military education during this period was largely due to the reforming zeal of Lord de Grey (later 1st Marquess of Ripon) when he was first Under-Secretary and later Secretary of State for War.

* * *

There were three 'certificates of education' which could be issued to soldiers by commanding officers on the recommendation of the regimental schoolmaster through the Inspector-General of Army Schools. To gain the third class certificate, a man had to pass an examination in 'reading easy narratives, simple writing from dictation, the four compound rules of arithmetic and of the reduction of money.' For the second class certificate a greater facility in reading and writing, 'an acquaintance with regimental accounts, and the power of working questions in practice, simple interest and proportion' were demanded. The qualifications for a first class certificate included a fair knowledge of two out of ten more advanced subjects. These ranged from English history, through algebra and plane trigonometry to fortification, drawing and chemistry.[7]

Though it was not a legal necessity,[8] it was rare for a man to be promoted to corporal unless he had achieved at least a third class

---

* 'This was a considerable achievement at a time when "payment by results" was in full swing in elementary education at large, and when the education grant to the voluntary schools dropped from £813,441 in 1861 to £636,806 in 1865.' (Denholm, 60.)

certificate. A regimental order was published in the Scots Greys in 1868, which probably reflected most cavalry commanding officers' views on the matter. It laid down the qualifications required for promotion:

'From private to lance-corporal'

'To read the second school book, to write an easy passage from the same (from dictation), and in arithmetic to work simple multiplication.*

'*From lance-corporal to corporal* – 3rd class certificate.

'*From corporal to serjeant* – 2nd class certificate.

'*From serjeant to higher rank* – 1st class certificate.

'An examination of candidates for certificates will take place once a quarter. The names of non-commissioned officers and men holding certificates will be entered in a book kept for the purpose.'[9]

The Inspector of Army Schools in 1869 found that there were still

'a great many commanding officers who do not lay themselves out to foster the school in an especial manner. At one time it was quite a common thing for the serjeant-major (a very influential person in the regiment) rather to put down the school, and to let every duty which he could get in the way. That is no longer the case as a rule, and I know many adjutants who encourage the schools by all means in their power. But there are great difficulties in the way of making suitable arrangements.'[10]

One of these was the question of where the school should be held. It seems that as often as not a barrack room was misappropriated for the purpose, though sometimes the regimental chapel was used.[11]

In some progressive regiments special classes of about twenty-five to thirty men were formed for limited periods, usually during the winter months. The men who attended these were taken off all duties except guards, and they spent as much as five hours a day in class.

As for extra-mural activities, evening lectures given by school-masters or by officers, often with the help of magic lanterns, proved

* The 1870 Royal Commission recommended (and the recommendation was acted upon) that a fourth class certificate should be introduced to mark the stage at which the recruit was exempt from compulsion. The requirements for this certificate were much the same as the first test described in the Scots Greys order.

generally unpopular. Much better attended were 'penny readings', sometimes 'accompanied by music', at which officers, including quite often the commanding officer, read aloud to the men.[12]

*   *   *

In 1867 there were 19,025 soldiers' children under instruction in the army schools. For them, from about the age of two or three, attendance was compulsory. But unlike their fathers' their education was not free. For a single child 2d a month and for two or more children 3d a month had to be paid. The sole exception was the children of soldiers serving abroad who were left at home on their fathers' embarkation. These were educated free. The infants and girls were usually taught by the regimental schoolmistress.

For both children and adults there were, in 1869, 272 properly trained and certificated schoolmasters and 218 trained school-mistresses (most of these last paid £30 a year), pupil-teachers and 'monitoresses'. As well as these there were about 500 assistant teachers. Depending on the numbers of pupils, there were usually about three or four in each regiment. They were appointed by the commanding officer on the recommendation of the schoolmaster, and they were usually no more than superior troopers drawn from the ranks of the regiment. They received 3d a day extra pay.

The schoolmaster generally ranked immediately below the regi-mental sergeant-major. His pay was 3s a day with a 6d increase every two years up to 6s 6d at fourteen years. After twenty-one years' service he was entitled to retire on a pension of 3s a day. He wore the blue uniform with chevrons of the Corps of Army School-masters. He was also required to wear a sword. Brevet-Colonel Shute of the 4th Dragoon Guards thought that the reason why many of the schoolmasters complained of both chevrons and sword was that the result was 'too military in appearance. . . . I think', he added, 'that for teaching infant children what they are now required to wear is out of character.' The Regimental Sergeant-Major of the Innis-killings, asked by Dr Butler, the headmaster of Harrow, whether the schoolmaster was looked up to or looked down upon, replied: 'I will tell you candidly that they are not popular. . . . I believe the reason is that they consider themselves altogether separated from the regiment. . . . Upon the old system, a serjeant of the regiment was the schoolmaster; but now a man is trained at a regular college and is attached to the regiment, and therefore a good many men do not like the schoolmaster.'[13]

There were twelve Superintending Schoolmasters stationed in the large garrisons. Their tasks were to make annual inspections of all army schools in their areas, and to conduct examinations. They were all men who had risen from being regimental schoolmasters. They were commissioned officers ranking as cornets and receiving 7s a day, rising to 8s after five years.[14]

A certain number of army schoolmasters were trained at the Royal Military Asylum at Chelsea. Since 1846 a Normal School had been established there for the purpose, alongside the Duke of York's School (see below). Candidates for places, up to forty in number each year, were admitted by competitive examination. They had to be between twenty and twenty-five years of age and 'not under 5ft 5in in height'. If they were not non-commissioned officers or privates, they were required to be 'either pupil-teachers who have completed their apprenticeship or else certificated schoolmasters' from National schools or elsewhere.[15] Their course lasted two years, during the second of which they were pupil-teachers. Civilian candidates, who were usually more numerous, received no pay during their training, though their rations and clothing were free. They had to pay a £58 deposit which was only returnable when they had become fully fledged army schoolmasters. Student teachers from regiments received the pay of their rank with a 6d stoppage for rations.[16]

The main part of the Royal Military Asylum at Chelsea was the Duke of York's School which had been founded in 1801. It was chiefly designed for the education of orphan sons of non-commissioned officers and privates born whilst their fathers were serving. The Asylum's Commissioners were responsible for selecting the boys to fill the vacancies. These numbered about eighty a year in the 1860s. Applications always greatly exceeded the vacancies. The establishment varied over the years from about 400 to 500 pupils and the average course lasted from four-and-a-half to five years. From 1869 no boy under seven or over twelve could be admitted.

Though the proportion of soldiers educated at Chelsea was small, it was generally agreed that the standard of the men produced from there was high. Of 616 boys who were reported upon by the regiments in which they were serving in 1866–67, only 1.4 % had bad characters, while 88.5 % were stated to be 'very good' or 'good'. Two had become officers and 122 were non-commissioned officers.[17]

In Phoenix Park, Dublin, a similar institution had been in existence since 1769. Known from 1846 onwards as the Royal Hibernian Military School, its object was to maintain, educate and apprentice 'the orphans and children of soldiers in Ireland'. Not all, but the vast majority, of the boys went into the army. The establishment was just over 400 pupils. They were admitted from seven to twelve years of age, and usually left at fourteen. The Governors were not allowed to know the boys' religions when selecting them. The standard of ex-pupils serving in the army was high and the demand from commanding officers for boys from the Hibernian was greater than could be met. A considerable majority of them became members of regimental bands and were thus virtually ineligible for promotion to non-commissioned rank. In 1870, of the 169 men and boys who had been at the school and who were in the cavalry, 116 were band members and six were boys training as trumpeters. Twenty-seven of the remainder were non-commissioned officers and only twenty were mere privates. The Chaplain-General thought that the course of education was not as good as at Chelsea:

'the influence of the Romish clergy', he told the Royal Commission, 'hampers the freedom of choice in subjects to be taught. . . . It strikes me that the absolute severance of one section [of boys] from another, whenever certain subjects are approached, has a tendency to perpetuate ideas in the army which should, as much as possible, be got rid of – religious antipathies.'[18]

'In the cavalry service the life of a serjeant is a very onerous one.'

COLONEL HODGE,
4th Dragoon Guards, 1859[1]

(ix)

Rank and file: non-commissioned officers

In effect no trooper who could not read and write was eligible to become a non-commissioned officer. No man could become a corporal until he had been certified as 'sufficiently advanced in reading, writing and arithmetic',[2] or, in other words, had passed the lowest standard in the regimental school (see p. 290). It was usual for any recruit who could read and write fluently to become an unpaid* lance-corporal within two years of joining.[3] In that probationary rank he might remain for a further three or four years. When he became a full corporal his pay in the cavalry was 1s 7½d, and a very careful man could clear 1s 1½d after his main stoppages.[4]

Before a corporal could become a sergeant (*via* the unpaid* rank of lance-sergeant) he had to obtain a second-class certificate of education. This, as Sergeant Acland-Troyte discovered, consisted of

'two pieces of writing from dictation, including a lot of orders with officers' names, etc., reading prose and poetry – difficult examples of the elementary rules in arithmetic up to vulgar fractions – balancing a Dr. and Cr. account – keeping an imaginary savings bank account for a year, and making up the accounts of a mess for one day, i.e. all about the groceries, vegetables, etc.'[5]

When a corporal was promoted to sergeant he generally discovered that the extra work and responsibility were scarcely compensated for by the extra comforts and the increase in his pay which his position afforded. Though this came to 2s 6d a day (after 1867), he found that he had to spend at least £5 a year on extra clothing.[6]† He was also bound (as, too, were farriers) to pay the old soldier who looked after his horse and appointments 1s 6d a week.[7] Colonel Hodge thought the cavalry sergeants and sergeant-majors were not paid 'in a corresponding manner' to what they would have received had they been 'out of the service'. They were overworked because the establishment allowed too few of them. In his own regiment, the 4th Dragoon Guards, he told the Hotham Commission in 1859, 'I have one of my troop sergeant-majors who is a band-serjeant; another is employed in the riding school; another is at Maidstone. All this throws extra duty upon the men who remain.'[8] Seven years later the commanding officer of the 12th Lancers went so far as to record his belief that the money sergeants had actually to spend was 'less than a private without a good-conduct badge has to spend'.[9]

* Lance rank was paid at a lower rate than the full rank from 1878 onwards.

† Every cavalry sergeant was issued with a free copy of *Regulations for the Instruction, Formations, and Movements of the Cavalry*. If he lost it, he was required to pay 3s for a replacement. (*Q.R.*, 1859, 127.)

In these circumstances it is a wonder that any man sought the rank of sergeant. Yet there were considerations other than financial ones. Prestige and exemption from menial tasks were among them. Membership of the sergeants' mess was another. Commanding officers had the duty to provide such a mess in every regiment. A description of one of the most modern, that at Anglesea Barracks, Portsmouth, comes from the pen of a sergeant writing in the mid-1870s:

'It consisted mainly of one large room, and leading out of it two smaller ones, which served as a kitchen and bar for sale of liquors respectively. The kitchen was well supplied with all necessary articles, and in it everything was cooked for our meals, the sergeants' rations, etc., being kept quite distinct from the men's. At the bar we could buy beer, porter, and various spirits, everything being paid for on the spot; but, according to regulations, the bar was not open for the sale of spirituous liquors at an earlier time of day than the canteen, viz. 12 noon. At "tatoo" the canteen was shut up, but the sergeants' mess had the privilege of keeping open till 11 p.m. These rules were, however, often broken, and sergeants used not unfrequently to "get a glass" at very early hours, and I have known cases of the mess being kept open long after the proper time.

'The large room was used as general sitting-room, dining room, and billiard-room, half the space being occupied by a good full-sized billiard-table, which was generally being played upon by somebody, the sum charged being twopence for a game of fifty, paid only by the loser.

'The other half of the room was taken up with a large table for meals, and several small tables, on which were a good supply of weekly and daily newspapers, magazines, etc. There were a few low arm-chairs, and a number of common wooden kitchen chairs. We had a comfortable carpet or druggett, hearth-rug, etc., and pictures on the walls, besides a large mirror over the chimney-piece. This was a vast improvement on the barrack-room, where I had been accustomed to use my bed for chair, and my knees for writing-table; but without doubt my greatest gain was at meal times. The table was laid quite nicely with a tablecloth, which seemed to me a real luxury, and the places all properly arranged with knives and forks, glasses, etc. Instead of the tin cans of soup, we had an ordinary tureen, and soup plates took the place of basins. A bountiful supply of vegetables was brought in steaming from the kitchen in proper dishes, and an unmistakable sirloin or round of beef was a matter of common occurrence, and it was always carved quite *à la mode*, not hacked up into so many portions, and seized on indiscriminately. To give an idea of a day's food in the sergeants' mess, I must quote from a letter written soon after my promotion: – "For breakfast we had sausages, an unlimited supply of bread and butter, and very fair coffee, which was brought in to the table in coffee-pots, but already mixed with milk and sugar. At dinner we were given a nice soup, round of beef, plenty of potatoes, and cabbages; and at 4.30, tea, placed on the table already mixed in the teapots, as the coffee was in the morning, and again abundance of bread and butter." There was no "meal" after this; but there was always bread to be had, and, with some cheese from the canteen and a glass of beer, one could make a very passable supper.

'It was also a very pleasant change to be "waited on", for, although the men employed did not actually hand the plates round at meals, there was always some one present to get anything we wanted. The soldiers regularly employed in the mess were – one man as cook, and sometimes an assistant; one waiter, who had to lay the cloth, bring in dinner, etc., wash up, and get from the bar anything we wanted. A sergeant was selected to act as caterer. His duty was to sell the beer, etc., at the bar, to provide generally for meals, and was responsible for all stores of eatables and liquors. He was exempt from all other duties while acting caterer, and it was considered by the sergeants as a lucrative post. . . .

'Every sergeant on first joining had to pay an entrance fee of about five shillings, and, besides a small monthly subscription, every dining member had to pay a sum of about ninepence per day for messing, which made a considerable hole in the pay of a poor lance-sergeant.'[10]

Among the advantages enjoyed by non-commissioned officers was their immunity from minor punishments. 'They can only have such offences recorded against them,' decreed *Queen's Regulations*, 'as may have undergone *judicial* investigation. Corporals cannot forfeit their claim to, or be deprived of, good conduct pay, except as a consequence of conviction by court-martial, or before a civil court, or a magistrate.'[11] When a corporal was promoted to sergeant he lost his good-conduct pay altogether. This was meant to be compensated for by his sergeant's pay, but as has been shown this was very far from being the case.

Under the Mutiny Act no non-commissioned officer could be subjected to any punishment by court-martial without being reduced to the ranks. This automatically made it impossible for him to gain his gratuity and medal on discharge, even though he were restored to his former non-commissioned rank. This was a grievance which was not remedied for many years to come.[12]

The most oppressive task which fell to sergeants was that of squadron orderly-sergeant, which was taken in turn a week at a time. During their week they were virtually on duty every waking hour, and could not leave barracks at any time, except on duty.

The 1870 and 1878 Royal Pay Warrants give the daily pay rates of non-commissioned officers of the cavalry of the line as:

	1870	1878
Regimental Sergeant-Major	3s 10d	4s 1d
Bandmaster; Farrier-Major	3s 10d	3s 9d
Saddler Sergeant	3s 6d	3s 5d
Troop Sergeant-Major; Quartermaster Sergeant	3s 4d	3s 3d
Sergeant Instructor in Gymnastics and Fencing	3s 2d	3s 1d
Farrier (Farrier-Sergeant in 1870)	2s 8d	2s 7d
Sergeant; Paymaster-Sergeant*; Orderly Room Clerk*; Trumpet, Drum, Pipe or Bugle Major	2s 6d	2s 5d
Armourer Sergeant (non-interchangeable arms)	2s 4d	–
Armourer Sergeant (interchangeable arms)	5s 0d	5s 1d
Corporal	1s 9½d	1s 7½d

*with increases after varying years of service in the rank.

'The soldier who saves a nation free should have
a ration savoury.'

Punch, 1855

(x)

Rank and file: rations – stoppages – means of cooking

The soldier's daily ration supplied by the commissariat at home was
the same in 1858 as it had been when last fixed forty-five years
before: 1 lb of bread 'of the quality denominated "best-seconds" ',[1]
and ¾ lb of meat (ox beef or mutton) (1 lb in camp, and in India).
When cooked and with the bone taken out the meat ration seldom
weighed as much as seven ounces per man. 'A mess of sixteen men',
wrote an officer who had closely examined the subject in 1859, 'gets
twelve pounds of meat, three pounds of that is bone, add fat and
gristle and it will be found that six to seven ounces of meat is a
flattering representative of the soldier's ¾ of a pound of meat; no
wonder they look for soup to fill them out.'[2]

For these meagre supplies the *commissariat* stoppage had been
fixed in 1854 at 4½d from the trooper's pay of 1s 3d a day (which
included 1d beer money). Not until 1873 was this daily ration for
the first time issued free. At the same time the 1d beer money was
abolished but ½d a day extra pay was granted. All other food, including vegetables and potatoes, had to be bought by the men, and
it was virtually compulsory that a further 3d should be paid for it.
This *regimental* stoppage included 1d for an extra ½ lb of bread.

In 1858, as it had always been, the sole method of cooking both in
barrack and regimental hospital cookhouses, with very few exceptions, was by boiling in large coppers. These were usually designed
to hold twenty-five gallons and to cater for from thirty to forty men.
They were used 'for making coffee, boiling tea, preparing hot water',
as well as for boiling the men's dinners. Being of very simple design,
these boilers were 'not liable to inadvertent damage'. This was about
their sole merit, for the thickness of their cast-iron walls (⅜ths of an
inch) and the arrangement of the fire-grates beneath them ensured
enormous waste. 'Count Rumford's* standard consumption of fuel
for cooking,' states Dr Sutherland's Committee's 1861 Report, 'is

* (1753–1814) American physicist and adventurer whose real name was
Benjamin Thompson. In 1795 he introduced into England improvements in
heating and cooking equipment for houses.

one-fifteenth part of the weight of the food', whereas the barrack cookhouse boilers consumed 'from a pound to a pound and a half, or upwards, of coal per man per day.'[3] Only gradually was more sophisticated cooking apparatus introduced into barracks. Nothing meanwhile could be roasted, stewed, baked or fried, and men often left part of their meat ration, 'their stomachs loathing the constant repetition of the same food in the same form'.[4]

William Rhys, a troop sergeant-major in the 11th Hussars, under examination by the Sanitary Commissioners in 1858, described the situation in his regiment. A trooper's messing cost him 8½d a day, of which 6d a week was for washing his clothes. The troop sergeant-major was responsible for buying his troop's food, and for choosing the tradesmen from whom it was bought. The men themselves decided what it should be. For breakfast, they generally had coffee, milk and sugar as well as bread. Asked whether they got anything else for breakfast, William Rhys said, 'Yes, they buy it and pay for it themselves out of their daily pay.'

'Do they generally buy it?'

'Some of the men – most of them are under stoppages and cannot afford to buy it.'

The midday meal consisted of a pint of meat soup per man, mutton twice a week, and beef for the other five days.[5] Rhys said that the quality of the meat was good, but that the quantity of it was far too small.

Trooper Mole of the 14th Hussars, eating his first midday meal in barracks in 1863, describes how at the start

'there came a shout of "Look out for scaldings!" and a man ran up with a large dish of meat and a round tin of potatoes. Lumping them down on the table, he cried: "Come on; bring your *churries*!" whereupon some of the soldiers produced knives and began to cut up the meat into lots according to the number in the mess. Then each soldier took the portion that suited his fancy; but at least half-a-dozen men, after a look at the dish, lit their pipes and went off to the canteen. . . . The meat and potatoes were both bad, and I made my dinner off bread. . . .

'After a bit the men who had gone to the canteen began to return, a few not quite so steady as they might be, and by three o'clock all the room was asleep except myself. . . .

'There were fifteen men in my mess, fourteen of whom wore three or four medals. They were good-natured fellows in the main, though a little short-tempered; and all bore signs of their long residence in India, where the regiment had been for nineteen years without coming home. They used many queer Hindustan names and terms, which it took me some time to get the hang of. For instance, they never spoke of knives, or salt, or bread, but always "Give me a *churrie!*" "Pass the *neemuck!*" or "Sling over some *rootee!*" '[6]

In the 11th Hussars, according to William Rhys, on Thursdays and Sundays there was 'a baked dinner'.[7] On these days the ration was sent out of barracks, as was noted in the Report, 'to be dressed by a baker', whom the men 'find means to pay by diminishing their allowance of vegetables, a practice which, looking to the composition of the ration, may be prejudicial to health.'[8] For the third meal, the provision of which had been made compulsory in 1840, the men usually had tea, milk, sugar and bread.

The Commissioners recommended that means of roasting, baking, frying and stewing should be introduced into the kitchens of all barracks and hospitals, so that when a soldier entered the service, he should no longer have 'the prospect of dining on boiled meat every day for 21 years'.[9] The Barrack Committee had suggested the provision of kitchen-cum-dining rooms for every fifty men.[10]

It was also recommended by the Sanitary Commission that the commissariat stoppages and the regimental stoppages should be consolidated. The need for this was highlighted by the evidence of an assistant commissary-general in the Crimea. He stated that in one month of 1855, his voucher for settling the ration stoppages in the Royal Artillery, 'when rendered in quadruplicate as required by regulations, comprised no less than 348 half sheets of foolscap paper. The compilation and examination of this voucher occupied the whole time of one person for at least a week.'[11] The Commissioners further recommended that in future the commissariat should be responsible for the provision of all supplies to the men, including vegetables, tea, coffee and sugar.[12]

By the early 1870s, the quality and variety of the food had been so much improved that a recruit who joined in 1873 was 'rather surprised by its goodness: for breakfast as much bread and coffee as could be desired; for dinner a good stew or baked meat, with plenty of potatoes, etc., and for the evening meal bread and tea.'[13] He added two interesting sidelights:

'Whatever a man leaves of his dinner or bread, he puts away on the shelf, sticking his fork into it so that he may recognise it again.'[14]

'The refuse of the food of the whole regiment, which comes to a considerable amount each day, is sold to a man who contracts for it; and the money obtained from this source is . . . sometimes saved up with a view to help the Christmas Dinner; but generally spent in buying nets for cooking,* and for providing smocks for the cooks' wear.'[15]

'Stoppages . . . the great grievance of a soldier's life.'

COLONEL RUSSELL in 1859[1]

(xi)

Rank and file: 'necessaries': stoppages – clothing – free issue

The Sanitary Commissioners also recommended that the commissariat should be responsible for the provision and renewal of the soldier's 'necessaries', hitherto obtained, like so much of his food, by regimental contract.[2] When he enlisted, the soldier was required to pay for his necessaries out of his bounty. This system led to much complaint, for the recruit was often charged such a high price for the articles that he seldom received more than a small part of his bounty. It was more common, as has been shown, for men to join their regiments in debt. In 1857 the system was changed. The bounty was then reduced and was to be paid in cash supposedly without deduction, while the initial supply of some of the necessaries was made free from the commissariat.[3] For their renewal, as well as for a number of other contingencies, such as cleaning materials, barrack-room damages and 2d a month for the washing of

* 'The meat is taken from stores to cook-house in a net, which is marked in some way, so that it may be distinguished from the various other messes.' (Acland-Troyte, 44.)

his sheets,[4] the browning of his arms, alterations to his clothing, the 'branding' of his shako and boots, the marking of his clothes and necessaries, and 1d a month for the cutting of his hair,[5] he had to provide out of the balance of his pay: that is, what was left after the deduction for rations, groceries and vegetables.

The Clothing Regulations of 1862 laid down that every recruit was to 'receive a complete kit of necessaries, free of all charge, as a single issue, to be kept up by him at his own expense.' In the cavalry the necessaries which at that date were issued free to recruits, but which he had to replace as time went on, were one Bible and Prayer Book, for each man who could read and asked for them, and:

'1 bag, stable
1 pair braces

Brushes
- 1 brass
- 1 clothes
- 1 hair
- 1 shaving
- shoe { 1 blacking / 1 polishing }
- 1 lace

1 tin blacking
1 brass ball
1 forage cap, and strap*
1 hair comb
1 pipe-clay sponge
1 button brass
1 stock
2 towels
1 pair stable trousers
2 pairs cotton drawers
1 girdle for Lancers only
1 pair gauntlets for Heavy Cavalry and Lancers
1 pair gloves for Hussars
3 pairs socks
1 holdall
1 horse rubber
1 stable jacket†
1 knife fork and spoon

* The 1866 Recruiting Commission recommended that these items should be replaced free. (*R.C.*, 1867, x.)   † See footnote on p. 304.

1 razor and case
3 cotton shirts*
2 flannel vests
1 valise
1 oil can
1 mess tin and strap
1 plume case
1 cake of soap.'⁶

Though all these items were issued free, there were other items which the unsuspecting recruit found to be less 'free', though equally 'necessary'. Trooper Mole who joined the 14th Hussars in 1863, for instance, received his £1 bounty and a supposedly 'free kit'. Nevertheless when he went to collect them, he was handed only 5s 9d. The sergeant-major explained: 'Bounty, one pound. Deductions: one whip, so much; one cap for walking out, so much; one dandy brush [made of split whalebone, and used for cleaning horses], so much; one sponge, so much; one burnisher, so much. Total, fourteen three. . . . There you are, you toad; and see you don't make a fool of yourself.'⁷ Mole's civilian clothes he never saw again. They were probably put into store or else they were burned.

Towards keeping up both his clothing and necessaries, each trooper was 'liable to' a weekly stoppage of 2s 7½d; the stoppage was not to be made in advance 'before the necessaries are required'. The free clothing consisted of a tunic, one pair of 'overalls (unbooted [without leather 'bootings' around the lower part of the leg and up the inside])', one pair of 'boots (ankle)' [known as highlows], and one pair of gloves: all to be supplied annually; one pair each of cloth trousers, bootings and Wellington boots to be supplied every two years. Dragoon Guards and Dragoons were issued every sixth year with one helmet and holland bag (in the Greys 'one bear skin cap'). Hussars received 'one busby and holland bag, quadrennially', while Lancers had 'one cap, quadrennially' and 'one oilskin cap cover and cap lines, biennially'.⁸ But regulations, of course, were not always sacrosanct. 'At present', an ex-orderly room clerk told the Dalhousie Royal Commission on Recruiting in 1866, 'what a soldier wears depends very much upon the opinions which his commanding

---

* The fact that the price of cotton shirts had risen between 1862 and 1865 as a result of the American cotton famine consequent upon the Civil War was recognized both in the Navy and in the police. It took a further three years for an increase in pay to cover this in the army.

officer entertains as to how soldiers should be dressed. In some regiments men are oftener under stoppages for periodical supplies . . .
than in others.'[9]

Recruiting Sergeant Knibbs found that the first question which
men wanting to enlist in the 17th Lancers asked of him was 'What is
the clothing which will be supplied to me? Am I to wear the same as
you wear?'[10] Trooper Mole reported with pride that his uniform on
joining in 1863

> 'consisted of a pair of blue cloth overalls with yellow stripes
> down the sides, a tunic of blue cloth with six cross rows of
> yellow braid in front, and two straight ones down the back, a
> stable jacket, which fitted as tight as a glove, and a second pair
> of overalls, called leathers. My arms and accoutrements were a
> muzzle-loading carbine, a sword, a pair of spurs, pouch and
> belt, and last, but to my thinking best of all, a bearskin busby,
> with a yellow bag and lines of yellow cord hanging over one
> side, and a white plume in front.'[11]

In 1858 Lieutenant-Colonel Valentine Baker thought that

> 'the present light stable jacket on service wears very badly, is
> sure to get torn and soon looks old and dirty. No troops in the
> world are so unserviceably dressed as the English. As long as
> they remain in quarters, the men are dressed strictly alike, and
> look very well. But the moment they have real work in the
> field, all uniformity immediately disappears. . . . After three
> months of real hard service, an English regiment has the
> appearance of a mob.'[12]*

* See p. 256 for the short-lasting qualities of the khaki uniforms of the 3rd
Dragoon Guards in Abyssinia in 1868.

> 'There is something in the trappings of the
> horse, the spur, and the jingle of the sabre,
> which takes young men, but there is nothing to
> render the dress of the infantry soldier attrac-
> tive.'
>
> COLONEL RUSSELL in 1859[1]

(xii)

*Rank and file: clothing regulations – off-reckonings –
clothing factories – uniform reforms*

From the time of James II until 1854, the 'Clothing and Equipments'
for the army were supplied to each regiment by its Colonel (not its
commanding officer). He was given a fixed sum for every man on the
establishment. These sums were known as off-reckonings. A Board
of General Officers appointed by the Sovereign decided on the
details of the men's clothing, and the Colonel was bound to supply
it according to the Board's 'sealed patterns'.* It was the large augmentations in establishments at the opening of the Crimean War
which at last brought about a reform of this system. 'The off-
reckonings were granted upon the increase of Establishment, without any reference to the numbers actually effective, and these being
considerably below the Establishment, it became apparent that the
public were paying the Colonels to clothe men who were never in
existence.' Consequently Sidney Herbert abolished off-reckonings,
and gave the Colonels 'a fixed sum in lieu of any profits upon
clothing'. In the 1st Dragoon Guards this was £800 a year; in the
rest of the cavalry of the line the sum was £450.[2] They still appointed
the clothiers and were responsible for the supply, but the public
paid only the cost price charged by the clothiers to the Colonels.

Within a year of this major reform, the Board of Ordnance was
abolished, and the different departments which had hitherto ad-

---

* The Household Cavalry's system was, as ever, different. A Royal Warrant
in 1780 ordained that a fixed sum should be granted for every man, 'which
forms a fund, out of which the Clothing and Equipment is supplied by the
Lieutenant-Colonel, acting under the orders of the Goldstick, who is Colonel of
the Regiment. The whole fund is expended upon Clothing and Equipment; no
profit is derived by the Colonel, who receives a fixed annual rate of pay.'
(Clode, II, 568.) Thus had the Household Cavalry pioneered a reform which
did not occur in the rest of the army until seventy-four years later.

ministered the army were consolidated. At the same time, and in consequence of that consolidation, a Clothing Department was set up in the new War Office. A Royal Warrant abolished the old Clothing Board and removed the Colonels' responsibility for clothing once and for all. In 1862 the Royal Army Clothing Factory at Pimlico was built. From then on an increasing amount of soldiers' clothing was manufactured by the Government. It proved much cheaper. In 1869 a tunic made at Pimlico cost 16s 6d. The same garment made by contract in 1857 had cost £1 1s 6d.[3]

As for reforms in the clothing itself, the Sanitary Commissioners were able to report in 1858 that there had been in recent years an improvement in the quality of the materials used. The greatcoat, though, was still made 'of very bad material, of little use against the cold, while it readily imbibes and retains wet'.[4] This did not apply to Hussars, for until after the Crimea, they had no greatcoats at all. Their pelisses, slung in warm weather, were worn as rather inadequate top coats in winter.[5]

The Commissioners also found that the balance of evidence was in favour of flannel rather than cotton or linen for shirts and vests, though the non-commissioned officers and men complained of the extra expense, and the comparative difficulty of keeping flannel garments clean.[6]

'The fashion of tight clothing is for the present at least', said the Report, 'discarded.'[7] No longer were cavalrymen to be killed in action because their overalls were so tight as to make it impossible for them when surprised on foot to mount their horses unaided (see Vol. I, p. 125). In the late 1850s, for example, the tight short jacket of the light cavalry was replaced by the wide-skirted tunic. So was the tight coatee of the heavies, with its cutaway front and whimsical tails behind. Thus, for the first time for many decades, some sort of protection from cold and wet was afforded the man's middle and loins.

Some of the earliest glimmerings of concession to the Indian climate for European troops were to be noticed in the late 1850s. Khaki, and loose clothing made their first appearances in the irregular cavalry of the East India Company in the late 1840s (see p. 151). Now for undress wear in India, the Inniskillings were provided with 'a grey or brown Karkee tunic made of some thin stuff and edged with white cord and braided down the front like a Hussar tunic', and on their heads they were to wear white pith helmets.[8] At home, the brass helmet remained for many years the head-dress of the heavy cavalry regiments. An officer writing from the Crimea described it as

'the most comfortable head dress – the weight being low on the head, the peak in front is quite sufficient for the eyes and that in the rear not only keeps the neck dry but is a great protection from a sword cut. As a proof of its serviceable qualities, no Dragoon is ever seen with any other head dress on, not even a forage cap, whereas scarce a shako is now to be found in the army. I remember men throwing them away as soon as we landed.'[9]

For the light dragoons, from 1857, a new shako, rather like a French *képi*, was worn for a few years.[10]

The whole question of military head-dress both in India and at home much exercised the Sanitary Commission of 1858:

'Formerly it was a *sine quâ non* that the head-dress should protect the head of the wearer from a sabre cut. . . . The altered system of warfare, from the daily increasing range of the weapons used, renders the attempted protection of particular parts of the body more than ever useless; and it becomes the more important to consider what character of head-gear will afford the best protection to the head, not from sabre or bullet, but from heat, cold and wet. . . .

'We are satisfied that the shako is, from its colour, weight, material, and form, altogether inapplicable to tropical climates. . . . There is no head-dress giving so efficient a protection to the head, face and neck as a light cap covered by wadded linen, with a flap hanging down behind, or else a few yards of linen rolled, turban-fashion, round the forage cap; we recommend the adoption of some such head-dress in India.'[11]

From the middle of the 1840s the process of simplification had begun in a modest way. The elaborate, expensive fancy dress which was the joy of George IV and William IV had been slowly amended in the first decade of their niece's reign; but it took the Crimea to show how necessary it was to make fundamental changes. These were less sweeping for the mounted than for the other arms, and, though on active service they produced more practical clothing, on parade the cavalryman still cut a spectacular figure.

'Our soldiers enlist to death in the barracks.'
FLORENCE NIGHTINGALE

'At present [1858] the army stands almost at the
head of unhealthy occupations in the United
Kingdom.'

The Sanitary Commission[1]

(xiii)

*Rank and file: mortality rates – venereal disease –
hospital stoppages – major causes of death*

The extraordinary difference between the mortality rates of civilian
males and soldiers at home was dramatically tabulated in the Report
of the Royal Commission on the Sanitary Condition of the Army,
which began its hearings in May, 1857. Presided over by Sidney
Herbert, the great Secretary at War, who had left office when
Aberdeen's Government fell in 1855, the Commission had been set
up by Lord Panmure, his successor, largely as a result of pressure
from Florence Nightingale. Behind the scenes day after day she fed
its members with facts and figures and told them what questions to
ask. Its report, written almost entirely by her, appeared in 1858 and
is unquestionably one of the great State Papers. It set the scene for
major reforms in the living conditions of the rank and file of the
army at home. Amongst the mass of statistical information contained
within its nine hundred closely printed, double-columned pages,
was a table which showed that between 1839 and 1853 the rates of
mortality per 1,000 per annum were as follows:

'Effective men of all ages of the Army at home:

Total	17.5
Household Cavalry	11.0
Dragoon Guards and Dragoons	13.3
Foot Guards	20.4
Infantry of the Line	18.7

Population of England and Wales, army ages

Town and Country population	9.2
Country alone	7.7

One of the unhealthiest towns, army ages

Manchester	12.4'

Other figures drawn chiefly from the Registrar General's returns showed that if the army at home had been as healthy as the population from which it was drawn, soldiers 'would die at one half the rate at which they die now'.[2] The Report went on to point out that these figures were even worse than at first glance appeared, for 'all men offering to enlist, who bear signs of physical weakness or of tendency to disease, are rejected [see p. 261], and even after acceptance can be discharged on the representation of the regimental surgeon at any period within three years from their admission; and all these rejected lives are thrown back on the civil population.'[3] Figures covering the years 1842 to 1852 show that 335 out of every 1,000 recruits examined were for one reason or another rejected. In later years the proportion was often considerably higher [see p. 273].

Further, rates of mortality represented only a part of the annual loss caused in the ranks of the army by disease. Discharge by invaliding was also an important factor. Many men died of diseases resulting from service after their discharge. Indeed it was calculated that among men discharged on temporary pension in the 1850s the deaths numbered no less than 119 per 1,000 each year.[4]

The alarming extent of the unhealthiness rampant in the army was revealed by the fact that while 10.3 out of every 1,000 men working in the mines between the ages of twenty and forty died at this mid-century period, the figure for the cavalry of the line of the same ages was 13.5. As always, the figures for the infantry of the line were worse: in this case 17.8. A chief reason for this marked difference between the two arms was said to be

'the greater number of hours passed out of doors on duty by the trooper, the variety of exercise which he takes, – part of his duty being on horseback, part on foot, – and the amount of muscular exertion required of him in grooming his horse, which is far greater than any exacted of the infantry soldier. His stable duty, as well as his sword exercise, calls into activity a different set of muscles to those exercised by men in marching. Indeed, all the attitudes of the foot soldier on parade, at drill, and on the march, are singularly monotonous and constrained, and it is rare to see an infantry soldier whose figure is as fully developed or as well set up as that of the cavalry soldier.'[5]

Neither 'night duty' nor 'intemperate and debauched habits' (by which were meant drunkenness and sexual profligacy), were thought by the Sanitary Commissioners to be important causes of the excessive mortality in the army. They conceded nevertheless that soldiers'

> 'residence in towns offers great facilities for sexual debauchery; and the diseases which are thereby generated, – the existence of which the soldier, from one cause or another, frequently conceals, thereby greatly adding to the intensity of the malady, and the difficulty of cure, as well as to the necessary severity of the treatment, – no doubt have a most injurious effect on his constitution.'[6]

Police regulation and inspection of prostitutes, which was the norm in the armies of Europe, was introduced at home in 1864 and repealed in 1883. Many reformers disapproved of the measure. One of these was Florence Nightingale who believed that the way to improve the soldier's morals and thus cut down the incidence of venereal disease was to improve his living conditions. 'In civil life you don't expect that *every* workman who does not marry before he is 30 will become diseased', she wrote in 1861. 'In military life you do. Why? Because a workman may have occupation and amusement and consort with honest women. . . . Every time you provide a hospital for sick wives and children, means for making marriage respectable, for making the soldier's life comfortable you are doing something towards [prevention].'[7]

When a soldier went into hospital he was put under a stoppage from pay of 10d a day towards the cost of his food, washing and treatment. 'A man who is on spoon diet', said an ex-hospital sergeant in 1866, 'pays just the same as a man who has fowls and port wine.'[8] This applied equally to the man who was ill through no fault of his own, and to the man who was suffering from venereal disease or *delirium tremens*.*

Such a large stoppage ensured that men did not go into hospital except in the last resort, and it accounted for the strenuous efforts which they made to conceal their illnesses, thus contributing to the unhealthiness of the army in no small degree. The married man had a particular aversion to reporting sick, for his family was totally unprovided for whilst he was in hospital. Further, when his wife or

---

* It applied also to a man who was hurt accidentally. The risk of accidents was higher in the cavalry than in the infantry. Cavalry regiments' sick lists were often swelled by casualties resulting, as Colonel Oakes of the 12th Lancers put it, 'from horses' kicks and chafes and so forth'. (*R.C.*, 1867, 115.)

children needed treatment nothing whatever was done to help them financially. When a soldier died in hospital the proceeds from the sale of his necessaries was used to defray the funeral expenses. If this was insufficient, his captain had to find the difference from his own pocket![9]

*   *   *

The major causes of deaths in the army at home were 'consumption, chronic catarrh, spitting of blood, asthma, and difficulty in breathing,' all of which have an obvious connection with 'the impurity of the atmosphere'. In 1853, for instance, 6.6 out of the 13.6 deaths per 1,000 in the cavalry of the line, resulted from these diseases.[10] It is no surprise, therefore, that overcrowding, poor ventilation, defective sewerage and 'other noxious agencies of analogous character in barracks' came in for the largest share of the blame.

What is both surprising and gratifying is that by the early 1860s the sanitary improvements at home stations which resulted from the Commission's recommendations had reduced the mortality rate to an annual average of about 1%.[11]

'It would never be pleaded as a reason for reducing the soldier's ration of bread and meat that a larger number of men had joined the regiment than the commissariat could provide for. Why should the soldier's air ration, which is equally important to his health and efficiency be differently dealt with?'

Barrack and Hospital Improvement Blue Book, 1861[1]

(xiv)

Rank and file: barracks: overcrowding – hospital conditions – ventilation – heating – ablution rooms

The Sanitary Commissioners were impressed by the evidence that in the native army in India, the mortality rates were 'slightly lower than those of the native civil population': the only army in the world, it was believed, where this was so. Why? Because it was not barracked. Usually the native soldier received 'hutting money, with which each man erects for himself a rude construction with mats and other articles of a similar character; and he frequently sleeps outside of the hut so erected.'[2] At home, at stations where the troops were encamped chiefly in huts in open country as at Shorncliffe and at the new camp of Aldershot, the deaths per thousand for 1857, 1858 and 1859 averaged only 4.7 each year.[3]

The cavalry was less crowded in barracks than the infantry. This was, in part, because the reduced establishments of regiments in recent years left greater space for each man. Even so, the 1855 Barrack Committee saw fit to recommend that the cavalryman should be allotted more space than the foot soldier, 'on account of the increased space occupied by his accoutrements'.[4] By a General Order of 1845, a space of not less than from 450 to 500 cubic feet per man had been directed to be provided in all new barracks on home stations.[5] Yet in 1848 and for many years afterwards, even in those nineteen barracks which were exclusively used by cavalry, much less than this very inadequate cubic space per man was often to be found. In some of the twenty-four barrack rooms of the depôt at Maidstone, for instance, where conditions were notoriously bad (see Vol. I, p. 104), only 174 cubic feet were provided. The 196 troopers accommodated at Brighton had to make do with 412 cubic feet per man, while the forty-four quartered in Kensington Barracks were given only 363 each. Even in the hospitals attached to cavalry barracks, many of the rooms provided less than the regulation space. Some of the beds at Norwich, for example, allowed as little as 325. Only six of the sixteen cavalry barracks with hospitals, including all three of those in Scotland, provided more than the regulation space per man in both barracks and hospitals.[6]

Queen Victoria was deeply shocked after a visit to a hospital in England during the Crimean War

'The buildings', she wrote to Lord Panmure, 'are bad – the wards more like prisons than hospitals, with the windows so high that no one can look out of them; and the generality of the wards are small rooms, with hardly space for you to walk between the beds. There is no dining room or hall, so the poor men must have their dinners in the same room in which they sleep, and in which some may be dying, and, at any rate, many suffering, whilst others are at their meals.'[7]

Some idea of how much hospital and the other medical services were improved in mid-century is given by the fact that in 1853 £97,000 was spent on them, while eleven years later the sum was £295,000.[8]

*   *   *

The Sanitary Commissioners recommended a minimum cubic space of 600 feet per man in barrack rooms, and that an interval of at least three feet should in future be allowed between each bed. In 1861 it was calculated that the deficiency in barrack accommodation, if these recommendations were to be carried out, would be over 32%. It would therefore be necessary, concluded Dr Sutherland's Committee, 'to add about a third part to the permanent barrack buildings of the United Kingdom'.[9] It took many decades, of course, before anything like this could be achieved. In 1870, a lieutenant stationed in Portsmouth always began his route march reports thus: 'Starting from Clarence Barracks, long since condemned as unfit for habitation. . . .'[10]

One of the most sensational revelations of the Sanitary Commission's Report emerged from the examination of Sir John McNeil, who had been one of the Crimean Commissioners (see p. 118). He was now Chairman of the Board for the Relief of the Poor in Scotland. He told the Sanitary Commissioners that the minimum allowance of space in the poor-house dormitories was 484 cubic feet, thirty-four more than that in barracks. It was a regulation, he added, 'which we never permit to be transgressed'. The dormitories were seldom full, and Sir John pointed out that the paupers were never in them during the day, if they could be moved. 'The windows are opened and the bed clothes are all thrown back, so that the whole atmosphere of the place is completely renewed.' The inmates were 'not permitted', he added, 'to enter the dormitory during the day.'[11] How different was the situation in barracks! Even the regulation space of one foot between beds was very seldom attained, much of the allotted cubic space being between bed and ceiling.

As to ventilation, windows at opposite sides or ends of rooms were rare. Where they, or other forms of ventilation existed, they were 'frequently stopped up by the men themselves, who come from a class very little persuaded of the advantages of ventilation, and whom poverty accustomed from their youth up to look to the exclusion of external air, in the absence of fuel, as the best mode of securing warmth.'[12] There was another reason, especially in winter. If at home the soldier found an 'absence of fuel', in barracks he was not much better provided for. The Barrack Committee, set up by Lord Panmure when he succeeded Sidney Herbert at the War Office in 1855, thought that at least one third more than the existing allowance of fuel was necessary for adequate heating.[13]

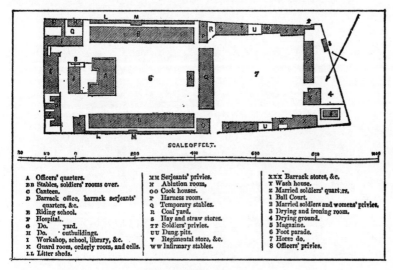

SCALE OF FEET.

A	Officers' quarters.	MM	Serjeants' privies.	XXX	Barrack stores, &c.
BB	Stables, soldiers' rooms over.	N	Ablution room,	Y	Wash house.
C	Canteen.	OO	Cook houses.	Z	Married soldiers' quarters,
D	Barrack office, barrack serjeants'	P	Harness room.	1	Ball Court.
	quarters, &c.	Q	Temporary stables.	2	Married soldiers and womens' privies.
E	Riding school.	R	Coal yard.	3	Drying and ironing room.
F	Hospital..	S	Hay and straw stores.	4	Drying ground.
G	Do. yard.	TT	Soldiers' privies.	5	Magazine.
H	Do. outbuildings.	UU	Dung-pits.	6	Foot parade.
I	Workshop, school, library, &c.	V	Regimental store, &c.	7	Horse do.
K	Guard room, orderly room, and cells.	WW	Infirmary stables.	8	Officers' privies.
LL	Litter sheds.				

Hulme Cavalry Barracks

One sergeant, giving evidence before the Barrack Committee, said that he often found it too nauseating to enter the barrack rooms in the morning. He first had to call 'to the orderly man to open the windows. The air was offensive both from the men's breath and from the urine tubs in the room; and, of course, some soldiers do not keep their feet very clean, especially in summer time.'[14] Another sergeant said that as a consequence of the atmosphere in which the men were shut up at night, 'there was a good deal of coughing, and it used to cause a phthisicky [wheezy] sensation in the throat, and spitting in the morning.'[15]

In the cavalry the barrack rooms were frequently over the stables, which added a new source of foul air and a further offence to the nose.[16] Dr Sutherland's Barrack Improvement Committee which reported in 1861 found most cavalry barracks 'saturated throughout with ammonia and organic matter; and in cases where the barrack rooms have been shut up and unoccupied for some time, the putrescent odour experienced on entering them is indescribably offensive.'[17]

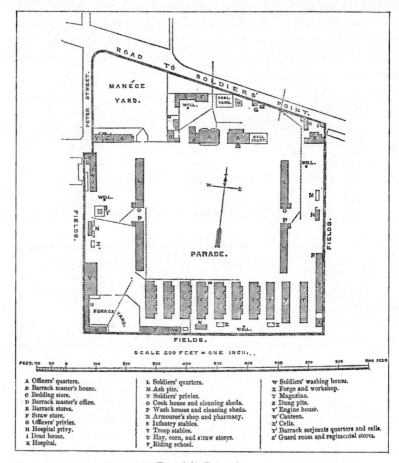

A Officers' quarters.	L Soldiers' quarters.	w Soldiers' washing house.
B Barrack master's house.	M Ash pits.	x Forge and workshop.
c Bedding store.	N Soldiers' privies.	Y Magazine.
D Barrack master's office.	o Cook house and cleaning sheds.	z Dung pits.
E Barrack stores.	P Wash houses and cleaning sheds.	v' Engine house.
F Straw store.	R Armourer's shop and pharmacy.	w' Canteen.
G Officers' privies.	s Infantry stables.	x' Cells.
H Hospital privy.	T Troop stables.	y' Barrack serjeants quarters and cells.
I Dead house.	u Hay, corn, and straw stores.	z' Guard room and regimental stores.
K Hospital.	v Riding school.	

Dundalk Barracks

Hulme Cavalry Barracks in Manchester were quoted as an example of bad design. Not only were the men's rooms over the stables, but right up against the boundary walls was 'a closely peopled district of houses', the smell from 'the privies and midden-steads of which pervades the rooms at certain times, much to the annoyance of the men'. The cavalry barracks at Dundalk in Ireland, on the other hand, were excellent. The Committee found that they 'presented a remarkable contrast in the cleanliness both of stables and quarters, as compared with barracks where the stables with their litter, filth and foul air are placed under the barrack rooms.'[18] The space, ventilation and daylighting of many a barrack room were further restricted by the boxing off of a non-commissioned officer's bunk in a corner of it, often cutting off one of the windows from it.

From the late 1850s onwards, great attention was paid to the question of ventilation in the building of new barracks. In those put up at Chelsea, indeed, it 'was carried to such an extent', as Lord Dalhousie* said, almost disapprovingly, 'that in the winter months the soldiers were obliged to be supplied with an extra blanket in order to keep them from being starved with cold during the night.'[19]

*   *   *

Considerable improvements in washing accommodation took place in the 1850s and 1860s. Numerous ablution rooms were then built in barracks. No longer was it the rule for the urine tub to be used, when emptied, for personal washing in cold weather. Nor did men in most barracks have any more 'to wash at pumps in the open air or under any convenient shed'.[20] The ablution room at Anglesea Barracks, Portsmouth, in 1874 was described by one recruit as being fitted up

'with stone slabs all round, and also down the middle, at which I suppose 50 men could stand and wash at the same time. Large tin basins were supplied in quite sufficient quantity, and water pipes running all round, just above the stone slabs, with taps at intervals, and always a good supply of water.

'Besides this "Ablution Room" there was a bath-house with four or six baths, in which a man could lie at almost full length. Cold water was laid on as a permanency, and in the winter hot water also.'[21]

Such luxury as this was of course limited to the most modern barracks. It was by no means universal.

*   *   *

One of the more trying deficiencies in barrack rooms was referred to by General Codrington in a Commons debate on the army's sanitary condition in 1858. 'At present in a barrack-room', he pointed out, 'there is not even a place for soldiers to lock up their

---

* In 1860 Lord Panmure had succeeded his cousin, the 10th Earl of Dalhousie, Governor-General of India.

things, whilst in every foreign barrack each soldier has a cupboard over his bed.' This lack was gradually remedied over the next decade or two.[22]

'There is an orderly every day; it is the custom of the service to have one.'

An old colour-sergeant in 1860[1]

(xv)

Rank and file: barrack-room orderly's duties

The soldiers took it in turn to be barrack-room orderly. The tour of duty lasted twenty-four hours. After opening the windows at 'reveille', and, in winter, lighting the fire, he set about sweeping the floor and arranging the tables and forms. These functions he performed whilst the other men were at first parade, which he was excused. At about 7 a.m. the bugle or trumpet, which regulated all movements in barracks, would sound 'rations'. On hearing this, the orderly man would go to the store and draw the meat and bread for his 'mess'. He and the squadron orderly corporal, who supervised the issues, were jointly responsible for seeing that the quantity was correct. The bread was left in the barrack room, while the meat was taken to the cook house in the squadron net (see p. 302).

At the next bugle or trumpet call, he went to fetch the coffee from the kitchen, which he would then pour in equal portions into the men's basins. After breakfast he brought hot water from the cook house, washed up the basins, scrubbed the tables, and swept up the crumbs. The same procedure occurred for each meal. While he was engaged in his post-prandial clearing up, the rest of the men peeled the potatoes and prepared whatever vegetables were supplied for dinner. These he would have collected the previous evening before tea time at the call for 'groceries'. His final duties of the day were to bring in fresh drinking water, a can of which was always kept in the room, and to prepare the kindling wood for next morning's fire.[2]

All the barrack-room utensils were in his charge during his tour of duty. 'If there are any deficiencies', said one barrack-master, 'either an urine tub is mislaid or . . . any utensil, he immediately looks about the barracks and very soon finds it.'[3] If he failed to do so, he was placed under stoppage to pay for it.

'There is no cure for the misery which is occasioned by the movement of a body of troops from a station where they may have induced a great number of girls to marry them whom they cannot provide for when they move.'

THE EARL OF DALHOUSIE in 1866[1]

(xvi)

Rank and file: barracks: married men – married quarters – laundry – lighting – libraries – reading rooms – canteens

Except in the case of the post-Mutiny Indian Army, into which married men were enlisted at the rate of 6%, only bachelors were accepted as recruits. Yet, as the Commandant at Chatham told the Hotham Commission in 1859:

'It is astonishing what a number of married men enlist. It is well known that the recruiting parties in many instances are aware of this, and tell them to swear they are single, and in the end the wife and children appear. You can send them before a magistrate, who has power to treat a man as a rogue and vagabond for having declared himself as a single man when in reality he is married.'[2]

Once a man had joined he found that the regulations regarding marriage (up to the 1870s) laid down that, beside the regimental staff and a certain proportion of the sergeants, only 6 or 7% of the men and corporals in the cavalry were allowed to marry; but, as Colonel Oakes of the 12th Lancers observed, 'a great many men were married without leave that I know of, and a great many that I do not know of.'[3] For 'unofficial' wives and children no sort of provision was made, (except very rarely),[4] and this, of course, caused real hardship. In certain circumstances even the 'official' wives were shabbily treated. 'We turn our soldiers' families adrift in the event of the soldiers themselves being killed upon active service, or dying in the service; they go away,' as an old officer said with feeling in 1860, 'without the slightest remuneration or hope of an allowance from Government.'[5] No wonder that commanding officers 'who have ample experience of the very great inconvenience arising to the service, and to the public, from the improvident and injudicious marriage of soldiers', were exhorted by *Queen's Regulations* to 'discountenance such connexions, and to explain to the men that their comforts, as soldiers, are in a very small degree increased by their marriage, while the inconvenience and distress naturally accruing therefrom are serious and unavoidable, particularly when regiments are ordered to embark for foreign service.'[6]

When regiments went to India they were allowed to take with them twelve wives to every hundred men of all ranks. For example the actual number of women who accompanied the 513 other ranks of the 5th Lancers on passage to India in 1863 was sixty-nine. The number of children who went with their mothers was ninety-three.[7] Those wives who were left behind received nothing beyond what would take them to the place in which they were to live during their husbands' absence overseas. In the 1870s the proportion of official wives at home was raised to one to every eight troopers.

The reasons for so severely restricting the numbers of married soldiers, which seems so harsh by modern standards, were the 'inconvenience of having a large train attached to a regiment',[8] the expense of moving that train from station to station, and above all the lack of married quarters.

In 1856 at only twenty of the 251 home stations were there separate rooms for married soldiers,[9] and in each of these lived several couples. In most cases only a hanging blanket divided the married couple and their young children from the bachelors in the common barrack rooms. As late as 1861 Dr Sutherland's committee members could report that they had 'seen married men's beds in the men's barrack rooms without any screens', while at Chatham barracks 'there was a married non-commissioned officer or soldier in every barrack room among the men; and not unfrequently girls from 14 to 16 years of age were thus accommodated.'[10]

The presence in the barrack room of families, according to one sergeant who was examined, 'is quite as objectionable on one side as it is on the other. . . . A soldier will sometimes say foolish things, and let words slip that, perhaps, are not fit for a married person to hear, and they consider that it is a sort of restraint upon them.'

Then again the married couples who were allowed to live in barracks were apt to take up much of the limited space. Amongst other things, they did their cooking in the barrack room, 'and in the summer time', said the same witness, 'the heat is very great, and the slop and one thing and the other about the fireplace is sometimes very disagreeable to the men; and there are the children also.'[11]

An important function of the wives was the washing of 'the men's body linen'. Primitive wash-houses existed in most barracks. These were 'much behind similar establishments connected with work-houses, prisons and other public establishments'. They were provided with boilers, to which in most cases water had to be carried by hand. The only means of drying were outdoor posts and lines, 'and as a necessary consequence wet linen is secreted by the women in barrack rooms until an opportunity occurs of drying it at the barrack room fire. This is against order, but it is nevertheless done from sheer necessity. Ironing is also done on the tables in the men's rooms, for there is no other place for it.'[12] These deficiencies were remedied in some barracks over the next decade or two. In the same period, too, the building of separate married quarters was pushed ahead, a specific annual sum being allocated for the purpose.

In the meantime the Barrack Committee recommended either that married women should be excluded from barracks altogether (which was quite out of the question); that decent accommodation beyond the barrack walls should be provided for them, or that married quarters 'should be in a part of the barrack distinct from the quarters of the unmarried men, and that no other women beyond the number provided with such quarters should be allowed to live in the barrack on any pretence.'[13] It was pointed out that though this recommendation would increase the initial building expense, the cost of lodging-money given to that proportion of 'officially' married soldiers not allowed in barracks in or near towns would be saved. This, at the rate of 1s 2d a week, amounted to £8,000 a year. Nevertheless, as one officer witness averred, 1s 2d was insufficient to procure good lodgings for married soldiers and their wives. They were often 'a class of tenants that landlords do not like having, so that the rent which they have to pay is considerably more than the rent that ordinary mechanics and labourers of the town have to pay. That,' the witness suggested, 'could be brought down very much by the Government either hiring or building houses for the purpose.'[14]

* * *

If the commanding officer happened to be a rich man he could some-times ameliorate the plight of the regimental women and children. In 1872, for instance, Lieutenant-Colonel W. H. Seymour of the Bays 'further enhanced his popularity with all ranks', as the regi-mental historians have put it, 'by donating a sum of 200 guineas – in commemoration of his fourteenth year as Commander of the Regi-ment – for the purchase of warm clothing for wives and families of men of the Bays.'[15]

* * *

The fact that men, whether married or unmarried, were confined by day to the same ill-lit, ill-aired, ill-heated room in which they slept, with a row of tables down its centre at which they ate, leaving little space for movement, was one of the worst aspects of barrack life. After dark, too, the barrack room must have been gloomy indeed. The weekly allowance of candles was fixed at only $2\frac{1}{2}$ lbs for every eight troopers. This, though, was vastly better than the $1\frac{1}{4}$ lbs allowed every twelve infantrymen. The reason for this preferential treatment was the extra amount of equipment and accoutrements which the cavalryman had to clean and maintain.

* * *

Where libraries and reading rooms were provided, they were more often than not sited in misappropriated barrack rooms. This often applied, too, to the tailors' and shoemakers' shops, and sometimes to the forges and armourers' shops. Even some of the regimental schools were only made available by this parsimonious method, which of course further reduced the space per man in his sleeping quarters.

The provision of a day room, with tables and benches as well as adequate lighting, was forcefully advocated by the Sanitary Com-missioners.

'We may observe', said their Report, 'that the cost of the accommodation for the men in a barrack amounts but to one-

fourth of the whole. Thus, if a barrack with all its appurten-
ances cost at the rate of £100 per man, £25 would be the sum
appropriated to the barrack-rooms, the remaining £75 being
devoted to officers' quarters, offices, canteen, library, guard-
room, punishment cells, parade ground, fives court, boundary
wall &c, none of which things, except for a proportion of the
offices, would be necessary to the lodging of a man of the same
class in civil life. It is only upon this fourth part of the whole
cost of a barrack, that any increase of outlay would be required to give the additional or better-arranged accommodation which the health of the men imperatively requires. . . .
Nothing is more costly to the public than the annual loss of men
from ill health and mortality. . . . We feel satisfied, looking at
the question as a matter of finance alone, that money judiciously
laid out in promoting the health and comfort of the soldier
makes an ample return to the public.'[16]

*   *   *

In each barracks with only a few exceptions there was an official
canteen. It usually consisted of a bar, store rooms, a room for the
non-commissioned officers, and a tap room for the men. Canteens
varied much in character and accommodation. 'Some', reported Dr
Sutherland's Committee, 'are small, confined and wretched, many of
them having merely flagged floors. A better class resemble the ordinary public-houses or shops frequented by working people.' A
very few had 'light airy cheerful rooms, and verandahs running
along the front for shelter in wet weather'.[17] Not so very long ago
the lessee of a canteen had been allowed to sell nothing but spirits
(nearly always of very inferior quality). Thus the Government
actively encouraged drunkenness amongst soldiers, although it was,
of course, a crime for a man to be drunk. In recent years, the sale of
other goods, such as groceries and vegetables had been permitted.
Then, in 1847, under parliamentary pressure, it was announced that
when the existing contracts had run out, spirits (though not beer)
would no longer be sold in canteens. In fact their sale by no means
ceased altogether, 'though it was *controlled* by posting non-commissioned officers to stop drinking after the dinner hour.'[18] The
really vicious aspect of the system was the fact that whatever was
sold the Board of Ordnance made a large annual profit out of the
canteens. This profit came straight from the soldier's pocket.

'The practice at present', states the 1855 Barrack Committee Report, 'is to lease canteens to a capitalist, who pays the Government a fixed rent for the house in which he lives, and in addition, a fluctuating sum, called privilege or head money, regulated by the number of men occupying the barracks. . . . The canteen lessee is merely a shopkeeper, who speculates on the possibility of making the usual profit. . . . He is not permitted to deal in the canteen with civilians living without the barrack walls, and the soldiers are not obliged to make their purchases at his shop.'

The system put him at an obvious commercial disadvantage compared with tradesmen outside barracks. He therefore either charged his military customer 'a higher price for an equally good article as that which he can purchase outside the barrack, or the same price for an inferior article. In either case the soldier suffers.'[19]

As a result of the Barrack Committee's recommendations, privilege money was soon abolished; but this meant merely that the contractor or tenant, instead of the Government, profited at the cost of the soldier. New regulations were therefore promulgated in 1863. These established the canteen as a regimental affair.

'The commanding officer selected a canteen-committee, consisting of a president, and two subordinates, and purchased his goods for the canteen in the open market from any tradesmen selected by that committee. The steward, waiters, and barmen were generally drawn from the regiment; and the whole of the retail profits went to the regiment . . . for the benefit of the men.'

In practice there were numerous faults to this new system, but it was a great improvement on the old one, and it lasted for nearly forty years.[20] 'It is splendid', declared a corporal in 1866. In the old canteen he had been 'robbed, as a regular thing. I being a married man lay out 6s every Saturday for the coming week's wants.' Of this, in the new canteen, where he got 'more and better things', he now each week took '1s 6d away in my pocket.'[21]

'Could there be worse economy, Lord Ebrington
asked, than to give bounties to recruits in order
to kill them off prematurely twice as fast as the
rest of the population?'

FORTESCUE, quoting his father in 1858[1]

(xvii)

*Rank and file: barracks: urinals – latrines – cesspools –
drains – a barrack-room in 1873*

More vital to the soldier's health than anything else was 'the state of
the latrines, the cesspools and the drains'. Until cesspools were done
away with and drains properly constructed, the high military death
rate would not be diminished, nor the consequent excessive charge
upon the public purse.

Without exception in barracks not situated in the middle of
towns, the only means of latrine and urinal drainage was by 'the
use of cesspits within the barrack enclosure and immediately connected with the privies'.[2] The obvious need for more healthy and
sophisticated sewerage was stressed by the Sanitary Commission
and Dr Sutherland's Committee. The total abolition of cesspits, 'the
application of the sewage to agriculture', and drainage into existing
sewers were recommended. An essential precondition was the re-
construction of the barrack privy 'so as to admit of the soil being
received and conveyed away in water'.[3] The Committee's report
enthused over the new latrines and urinals in Glasgow barracks.
These had

'two latrines, one on each side of the entrance gate. There were
originally cesspits under them, which were a source of great
nuisance, and as a large sum was asked for permission to drain
into the town sewers, the following plan was resorted to. The
buildings were fitted up with Macfarlane's iron latrines, the discharge pipe of which was carried out directly behind the latrine.
The earth was cut away to enable a water-tight cart to be
backed down the slope under the pipe, and every day the
sewage matter is discharged into the cart, and removed. The
cart has a lid for admitting the discharge pipe, and also a valve
for emptying it at the manure depot. In order to save the urine

325

for manure, the urinals can be drained into a urine tank, to be discharged into the cart, together with the contents of the latrine. It is advisable to keep the two separate, on account of the great increase of nuisance from admitting urine into the latrines.'[4]

Macfarlane's Iron Latrines

Nearly all urinals in barracks were made of brick or stone, the porous nature of which was the cause of much 'nuisance'. Slate, glazed earthenware or cast iron were the substitutes recommended. The slate urinal 'made by Mr Jennings of Blackfriars',[5] with water basins and overflow, was among those recommended.

Much more intractable was the problem of the urine tubs which were introduced nightly into the barrack rooms. These abominations were strongly condemned by the Sanitary Commissioners. 'Besides the indecency generated by their use, the stench proceeding from a wooden vessel saturated with urine is most prejudicial to health.'[6] Between 1858 and 1861 earthenware chamber pots were tried in a number of barrack rooms. They were a total failure. This was because of

'the amount of cleaning required to prevent them becoming a greater nuisance even than the urine tubs, the number of cloths, &c., required for cleaning, the large amount of breakages charged against the men and occasioned not so much by carelessness as by accident in putting up and down the iron bedsteads, the want of any place to keep the utensils – leading to their being kept under the beds or on the shelves with food, &c., the dislike the men had to bringing their friends into their rooms when so many of these utensils were about. For these reasons, indeed, the men in one barrack preferred going out during the night to using them. Altogether both officers and men were glad to get quit of them, and to have the urine tubs back.'[7]

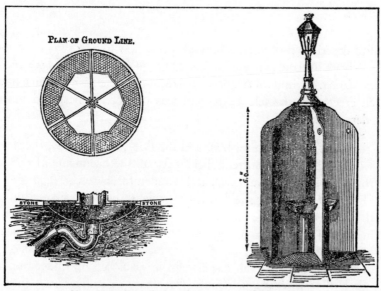

Slate Urinal 'made by Mr Jennings of Blackfriars'

The barrack-master at Chatham who had charge of the accommodation for nearly 6,000 men, 'only found two or three instances throughout the whole barracks where they were used, and those', he added, 'only by some old Indians, soldiers who had been long in India who said "Really, sir, I do confess to you that I use mine because I should be obliged to go too far to enable me to do what I require".'[8]

A temporary amelioration of the urine tub problem was the coating of them with coal tar, but though this made the smell less loathsome it caused extra trouble and did not provide a real solution.[9] Next was tried 'the conversion of the urine tub into an iron urinal, with an enamelled or white stone-ware hood', but 'it was found that no improvement in material and no amount of care could prevent such utensils from becoming receptacles of the vomit of drunken men, or even worse nuisances.'[10] The mind boggles at what these might have been!

The only other resource seemed to be water urinals outside the rooms; but there was generally no available space on the landings or in the passages. They were tried, therefore, in one corner of the barrack rooms, with a door for decency's sake. This proved a successful experiment, and at long last one of the great sanitary problems had been solved.

*   *   *

A full description of what a barrack-room was like in 1873 is given by Private Acland-Troyte in his book, *Through the Ranks to a Commission*. Writing of Anglesea Barracks at Portsmouth, which had been erected in the late 1850s and was one of the best and most modern, he says:

'the walls were whitewashed, and the floor, bare boards; there were tables in the centre sufficient for all the occupants of the room to sit down to at once, and wooden forms to correspond. Generally a hanging shelf over the table, on which are kept all the plates and basins, one of each being provided for each man in the room. The iron bedsteads are arranged all round, the heads against the wall, and they are made in two parts, so that during the day one half can be run in or closed up under the other, thus giving much more free space to move about in. The mattress is rolled up, pillow inside, and kept fastened with a strap, the two blankets and two sheets folded up very neatly, and placed on the top of the rolled mattress, which is stood against the head of the bed, occupying about half of the bedstead when closed up. The remaining half (on which the rug or counterpane is laid) serves for the men to sit on. As a rule there is a space of about three or four feet between the bedstead, and a man next a window is generally best off.

'All round the rooms, over the heads of the beds, are iron shelves, and hooks just below, each man having that part of the shelves immediately over his own cot. All the soldiers' worldly possessions are kept on these shelves, and have to be arranged with scrupulous tidiness. The knapsack and other accoutrements are put on the hooks. . . . Very often if a man has near his cot a piece of spare wall he will hang up pictures or photographs, which gives the room a more comfortable appearance, and provided it is done tidily, it is never objected to. The other articles of common property in the room are a hair broom, mop, long-handled scrubber (for cleaning the wood floors), a hand scrubbing brush (for cleaning tables and forms), two tin dishes, on which the dinner is brought in, two tin pails, two wooden buckets and a big iron coal box, also two coal trays, i.e. square wooden boxes used for carrying coal about in, but generally kept in the room for throwing any litter into. . . .

'The tables are often quite beautifully white; and without plenty of hand-scrubbing they soon get a very different colour; for all the meals take place on them without tablecloths, and ink may be spilt, etc., or they may be soiled in many ways. As a rule the men keep one side of the table extra clean. To explain this I ought to say that the regulation barrack-room table is made in 6-foot lengths, each length being supported by and merely resting on two iron trestles; so that the tables can be used with either side uppermost, or can be taken off the trestles and stood against the wall, which would be done always when the floor was swept or washed. The "extra clean" side of the table would only be seen on special occasions, such as the officer's visit to the room, and kit inspections, etc. At all meals the side least clean would certainly be used.'[11]

'The purchase of 10,000 acres at . . . Aldershot would enable the military authorities to concentrate a large body of troops in the best possible position, and to a certain extent correct the danger of dispersion by a cheap and useful system of concentration.'

LORD HARDINGE, 1853[1]

(xviii)

Rank and file: founding of Aldershot camp – Mrs Daniell's reforms

Forty miles from London, near Farnham, there once were (and in some degree still are) wide expanses of gorse, heather and sand. In the year before the Crimean War, Lord Hardinge, as Commander-in-Chief, recommended that a permanent encampment for the army should be placed in this wilderness. Thus with the enthusiastic help of Prince Albert came into being the place that now advertises itself as 'Home of the British Army', the world famous Aldershot camp.

In 1851 the town which gave it its name had a civilian population of 900. Ten years later this had risen to 8,000, with 25,000 soldiers in camp. Within twelve months of its birth the number of public houses had grown from two to sixty. Most of them were shanties. So were the proliferating dancing saloons with brothels attached. Provision was speedily made for indulgence in 'the unblushing vice that tracks the everyday life of the poor soldier'. The 'wicked panderers' swooped down from London, and the moment the poor soldier, 'tired with the forced inaction of camp life', set foot beyond the lines, his case was desperate. These quotations are from Mrs Louisa Daniell, a middle-aged widow, who aided by her equally fanatical daughter, used persuasion, persistence and prayer to achieve a revolution at Aldershot. Her Soldiers' Home and Institute, forerunner of the N.A.A.F.I., opened in 1865. Cups of tea, coffee and cocoa, and slabs of cake could be bought for a penny each. Cheap, wholesome meals were served in the dining-room. Georgina Daniell was a tiresome woman at times, an extreme Protestant and full of prejudices, but she served the soldier well at Aldershot.[2]

'When a man seeks his discharge from the Army, his motive may reasonably be assumed to be his distaste . . . for the occupation of soldier (in which he has been trained, and in which he has become a proficient), or he would never leave a certain for an uncertain future subsistence.'

C. M. CLODE in 1869[1]

(xix)

Rank and file: discharges

The cost of buying his discharge from the army had been graduated, since 1829, according to the years a soldier spent with the colours.

But after fifteen years' service, he received a free discharge. After sixteen years, if he wished to leave the army, he obtained a bonus of six months' pay, and so on, on an ascending scale. This bonus system was abolished in 1866. At the same time the rates of discharge-purchase money were altered, and linked to the possession of good conduct badges. Thus, for example, in the cavalry, it cost a man with under seven years' service £30 to buy his discharge if he was without a badge (£20 in the infantry), and £25 if he had gained one badge.* After ten years' service it cost him £10 if he had two badges; after sixteen years, £5 if he had no badges, and nothing if he had two or more badges.[2]

The Commander-in-Chief possessed the power to prevent a man taking his discharge. The Duke of Cambridge stated in 1866 that if a regiment was not up to establishment, the rule was that consent to the discharge was withheld, 'but of late', he added, 'there have been so many regiments under their establishment that we have been constantly obliged to relax that rule. Some officers are of opinion (and I believe that to a certain extent it is the right one) that when these men have put down their money they have a right to get their discharge, and they grumble if they do not get it.' Usually, in practice, unless the commanding officer could show good cause why a man should not take his discharge, 'he must be discharged according to law if he lodges his money.'[3] In fact, *Queen's Regulations* specifically stated the reverse: 'No soldier can *demand* his discharge as matter of right, either with or without pension, until the expiration of his engagement.'[4] Thirty days had to elapse between the application for discharge and its sanction, so as to give the man 'sufficient time to reconsider the step he is about to take'.[5]

As has been shown (see p. 260), considerable numbers of young men, especially in the cavalry, bought their discharge within the first few years of their service. Not only did they get valuable training with horses of great use to them in civil life, but they also learned, amongst other things, 'to keep accounts, and', as Colonel Oakes of the 12th Lancers found, 'they are taken away for [civilian] clerks.' In one year, 1865–66, he had lost twenty-one men who bought their discharge at the full £30; five at £25 and one each at £20 and £10.[6] Colonel Hodge thought that in nearly every case the young men who left his regiment, the 4th Dragoon Guards, did

* Armourer-Sergeants in view of their special skills and training were not normally allowed to purchase their discharge until they had served at least seven years. (*Q.R.*, 1859, 143.)

so at the persuasion of their friends and even sometimes against their own wishes. 'Many', he said, 're-enlist afterwards'. In a period of seven months of 1859, he told the Hotham Commission, thirty men in his regiment had purchased their discharge at £30, and he had a further nine registered to do so. One of the chief reasons for these early discharges, thought Colonel Hodge, was that men soon discovered and did not relish the fact that 'the soldier is a mere machine: he has no liberty of his own.'[7]

Most men, of course, could not afford £30. There were still in the 1860s cases, certainly more frequent in the infantry than in the cavalry, of soldiers wilfully maiming themselves or their comrades (particularly tampering with the eyes) so as to obtain discharge by invaliding. This was one of the numerous crimes for which the soldier automatically forfeited all claim to reckon his service for pension or for discharge up to the date of his conviction.[8]

Free discharges could be granted at any time if the Commander-in-Chief saw fit to allow them. These were sometimes given on compassionate grounds, at other times because 'experience has proved', as *Queen's Regulations* put it, 'that the army derives great advantages from the occasional discharge . . . of men of indifferent character, and whose habits may have rendered them permanently inefficient, as well as men who have been too long in a state of desertion to be again fit for the ranks.'[9] On discharge for any reason other than a dishonourable one, twenty days' pay and a railway warrant were usually provided.

In the six years 1860 to 1865, 6,803 cavalrymen were discharged for reasons other than the completion of their service. Of these 2,867 were invalids, 2,147 purchased their discharges, 1,049 were discharged 'by indulgence' and 740 went from 'other causes',[10] chiefly because they were incorrigible 'bad characters', or because of reduction of establishments. 'I believe,' said the Secretary of the Pensioners Employment Society in 1866, 'that the destitution into which men are driven when discharged on a reduction of establishment is very prejudicial to the public interest.' Such men were very bad advertisers for the army. They were found 'in every village of the Kingdom, and their stories of military life and their complaints . . . have a greater effect upon the young men, their associates, than all the Royal Warrants ever issued.'[11]

'A man who serves his 24 years in the cavalry
gets very little pension on his discharge; he must
be a man of good character, and a well-conducted
man to receive 1s a day, and it is not enough to
keep him in his old age.'

EX-TROOPER GEORGE TOWNSEND,
12th Lancers, in 1866[1]

(xx)

Rank and file: pensions

Pensions for other ranks were of four chief kinds: those awarded for
length of service, known as Service pensions; disability pensions;
'Meritorious Service Rewards', and Victoria Cross pensions. Service
pensions were only awarded after twenty-one and more years'
service, and they varied in value according to how many good
conduct badges a man possessed. Since 1848 the regulations had
laid down that if a trooper possessed none, he received 8d a day. For
each badge he earned, an extra 1d a day was added. When he had the
maximum number of five badges, he was granted a pension of 1s 1d.
To this there was added $\frac{1}{2}$d a day for each year of service beyond
twenty-one. But no matter how long he served beyond twenty-one
years the service pension was not allowed to exceed 1s 2d a day. In
1864 this was increased to 1s 3d. For sergeant-majors the maximum
was 2s 6d, for quartermaster-sergeants and sergeant instructors (a
new class of non-commissioned officer created in 1864) it was 2s 3d,
for colour-sergeants and sergeants 2s, and for corporals 1s 6d.[2]

By Royal Warrant in 1848 troopers who were discharged with
disabilities caused by their military service were entitled to receive
up to 1s 0d a day disability pension (1s 6d from 1864) if partially
incapacitated, and up to 2s 0d (2s 6d from 1864) if wholly so. Non-
commissioned officers received proportionately higher sums. To
these rates in cases of extreme suffering from wounds, or, from 1870
onwards, of gallant conduct in the field, 6d a day could be added.
For disabilities caused as a result of military service other than
wounds in action, 3d a day above the service pension was granted
after twenty-one years' service and lower rates for lesser terms of
service. Very unfairly and parsimoniously, it seems, the total
pension, adding together both service and disability pensions, was

not allowed to exceed the maximum rates laid down for service pensions. This meant, in effect, that a man who through impeccable good conduct over more than twenty-one years had achieved the highest possible pension was debarred from receiving any disability pension, although he might have suffered grievous wounds in the field.[3] For disabilities which arose during a man's service but which were not caused by it, there was no regular pension till the 1880s. From 1876 special additions to the maximum pension 'where the soldier's service or the incidents thereof' merited it, were granted, subject to Treasury consent.[4]

'Meritorious Service Rewards', consisting of not more than £20 a year could be granted to soldiers and ex-soldiers of the rank of sergeant or above who had rendered specially distinguished service. In 1870 £5,000 a year was set aside for these rewards. The Victoria Cross, instituted in 1856, carried with it an annuity of £10 a year, with an extra £5 for each bar.[5]

* * *

The Secretary of the Pensioners Employment Society in 1866 was much concerned about what happened to pensioners when they left the army.

> 'The public', he said, 'look upon pensioners in a great many instances as a bad lot altogether. . . . A great many who come from the army with the best characters turn out very badly indeed. . . . Men who have always been accustomed to discipline and to be constantly looked after, when they get into civil life will very often fall into bad habits from having no one to look after them.'[6]

'[The men] fade away in the prime of life; leave few children; and have to be replaced, at great cost, by successive shiploads of recruits. . . . It is at that expense that we have held dominion [in India] for a century.'

Report of the Royal Commissioners on the Sanitary State of the Army in India, 1863

'Meerut, one of the largest and best stations in India. . . . The men are splendidly put up, with swimming baths and every possible comfort. It is a pity the barracks at home are not built something like these Bengal ones.'

CAPTAIN HENEAGE, 8th Hussars, in 1861[1]

(xxi)

Rank and file: India: mortality and sickness rates – sewage disposal – bazaars – water supply – baths and tanks – overcrowding in barracks – married quarters – hospitals

If the mortality rate of the troops at home had been in the first half of the century alarmingly large (see p. 309), among the white troops in India it was in mid-century even larger. Once again Florence Nightingale was the chief moving force in exposing a great evil. The massive report of the Royal Commissioners on the Indian Army's sanitary state which eventually came out in 1863 was largely based on many hundreds of reports received from stations in India as a result of circulars initiated by her in 1859. They showed that over the first half of the century an average of sixty-nine white other ranks died each year out of every 1,000.* In the ten years 1847–56 the mortality rate of men 'of the age 20 and under 25' alone was 56.4 per 1,000. Since 'mortality of men of the corresponding age in England', the Commissioners go on to say, 'is at the rate of 8.7, the excess of the mortality in India is 47.7 per 1,000.'[2]†

---

* In Bengal 'the usual proportion' for white women was 44 deaths per 1,000 per year, and 84 for their children. (*I.S.R.*, I, lvi.)

† The casualties of the cavalry at home and in India for the six years 1860 to 1865 are shown in the Appendix, p. 458.

The rate varied from over 11% in the most unhealthy to about 2% in the most healthy stations. The proposed post-Mutiny establishment of European troops was 73,000 men. It was reckoned that unless the mortality rate decreased, just over 5,000 recruits would be required each year to fill the vacancies caused by death alone. If, however, the rate could be reduced to 2% (double, incidentally, what it had become by 1862 at home), it was estimated that taking the cost of recruiting, training and landing each man in India at £100, the taxpayer would be saved nearly £1,000 a day.[3] It is pleasing to note what actually happened: in 1864, out of a mean European strength of 65,102 only 1,428 men died: just over 1.9%; whereas the average for the years 1860–63 had been just over 3%.[4] These remarkable improvements can hardly be wholly accounted for by the advances made as a result of the Commissioners' recommendations. It was more a reflection of the gradual amelioration of sanitary conditions which had been taking place over the past two or three decades.* This is well illustrated by the case of the 14th Light Dragoons. In the nine years ending in 1857, out of an average strength of about 700, the regiment lost 161 men. The deaths in the first four years of that period were 35, 28, 31 and 22 respectively, while in the last five years of the period, the deaths numbered only 12, 12, 11, 6 and 4 respectively.[5]† Even more revealing are the figures of dead in the 4th Hussars spanning a much longer period. In the eleven years ending 1833, 671 other ranks of that regiment died in India. In the eleven years ending 1878 the number was only eighty-six.[6] Even allowing for the caution with which such comparative figures must be treated, they show a very remarkable improvement. These statistics incidentally tend to show what is confirmed elsewhere that in cavalry regiments the mortality rate in India, as at home, was generally less high than in the infantry.

Another reason for the speedy improvement in the health of the army over the immediate post-Mutiny years was the closing down or reduced occupation of the unhealthier stations. This had become increasingly possible because as Sir Hugh Rose put it in 1866: 'The railroads and the lateral lines of communication, some of which I believe are to be tramways, would enable a large force to be concentrated at the unhealthy localities very rapidly, and instead of

* For the mortality and sickness rates of Royal cavalry regiments during the ten years immediately before the Mutiny, see Appendix, p. 457.

† For further statistics referring to the 14th, as well as to the 9th Lancers and the 15th Hussars in India, see Appendix, pp. 457–8.

having a sickly garrison there would be fresh men, with good health, from the mountains or healthy stations.'[7]

The sickness rate among the white troops in India was not surprisingly about twice what it was at home. 'An army of 70,000 British in India', said the Sanitary Commissioners in 1863, 'has so to speak a vast hospital of 5,880 beds constantly full of sick.'[8] The causes of the high death and sickness rates were much the same on an enlarged scale as they had been at home. Between a half and two thirds of deaths and more than three quarters of admissions to hospital were a result of the zymotic or infectious diseases. The rates were much increased by the climate and, of course, by heat apoplexy and 'the great endemic diseases of India . . . fevers, dysenteries, diseases of the liver and epidemic cholera, which has for many years engrafted itself on the endemics of the country.'[9]*

The chief trouble was sewage disposal. The state of the drains in Indian barracks was found to be almost beyond belief. It was the same in barracks as it was in the civilian native quarters. Nowhere were either latrines or urinals properly drained. 'Sometimes', the Commissioners were told, 'the fluid refuse of stations is passed into deep cesspits, at no great distance from the barrack, with the view of its draining into the subsoil; the water from the subsoil being, at the same time, the source which supplies the wells.'[10] In Madras a high wall had been built between the grounds of Government House and the town, 'expressly for the purpose of excluding the noxious smell' from the drains. The trouble there was a deficiency of water for flushing the open drains which were 'of the most offensive and scandalous description'.[11]

Latrines and urinals were usually placed in outbuildings not far from the barrack rooms. Sometimes they were connected with them by covered passages. Most of them were fixed over 'cesspits cleansed from outside'. But in the more modern ones metal pans had been introduced 'to facilitate the operation of removal. There is no drainage of any kind, and the arrangements altogether are very offensive. The only object attained is rapid removal of excreta to be

---

* There were other diseases peculiar to hot climates. Amongst these was one which attacked men who were subjected to great exertion during the heat of the day. It was the guinea worm, very thin and often several feet long, which lived under the skin causing painful and dangerous sores chiefly on the legs and feet not only of men but also of horses. More than half the officers and men of the 8th Hussars who survived the Central Indian campaign of 1858–59 were thus afflicted. (Murray, II, 470.) Though men did not die from this torturing worm, it often weakened their constitutions.

buried or otherwise disposed of at a distance. . . . None of the latrines have the recent improvements of divisions and doors which
have been introduced of late years at home.'[12] Colonel Greathed
found that 'the great disadvantage in barracks in India' was the
stink from what he called the 'urinaries'. 'As you ride through the
barracks', he complained, 'you go through those places in going to
the general parade ground – and it is invariably most offensive.
There is never any time of the day or night that you do not smell
them.'[13]

At Cawnpore is the singular statement, that the drains are "not intended" for draining cookhouses, privies, &c. Here, as elsewhere, the drainage is effected *by hand*; that is, everything that will not evaporate or sink into the ground is carried away to a distance in pails, skins, or carts, and emptied out.

INDIAN DRAINAGE SYSTEM.

From the *Indian Sanitary Report*, 1863

At night urine tubs such as had virtually disappeared at home were
still universally used in India. They remained in the barrack rooms
or on the verandahs outside them 'until the sweepers were allowed
to come in. In using large bamboos to remove a heavy tub, they
would splash it over, and the offensive smell would remain . . . for
some time afterwards.'[14] Not even in the hospitals was there a single
water closet. The usual arrangement was 'to have night-chairs
placed in a small room adjacent to the ward, or to have privies at a
distance of from 30 to 80 feet' connected by a covered way. These
privies were placed over cesspits which were emptied once a day.[15]

One of the least hygienic aspects of cantonment life was the close
proximity to the European lines of the bazaar. This consisted of
masses of huts and houses 'arranged on no general plan, and without
any regard at all to sanitary conditions. . . . There are generally no

> In Dinapore some streets were impassable dunghills "last year," "until cleared." The elephant sheds and all the south of the station in a state disgraceful to any cantonment. The drains, deep holes of festering mud. No latrines, although "the population is as thick as can be;" until lately, only one filth cart, now three. At a neighbouring village the dead are buried within the huts.
>
> FEMALE SWEEPER.
>
> At Agra it is a proof of "respectability" to have cesspools. The inhabitants (152,000) generally "resort to the fields."
>
> English works, treating of sanitary improvement, insert sections of the bad drainage arrangements. But none contain such an illustration as this of how a woman is made to supply the place of a drain tile.
>
> At Berhampore "nothing can be worse than the sanitary condition " of bazaars." The native houses are dirty in the extreme. Dungheaps or deep holes full of stagnant water, the common cesspit of the houses, are close to them. The nuisance is felt even at barracks. The "Conservancy" establishment is quite unequal to its work.
>
> At Muttra the bazaar is an accumulation of huts without order. "Drainage bad; ventilation worse; water supply execrable." "All the wells brackish, from nitre," the earth being contaminated with all sorts of impurities. Latrines "hardly known." "In short, the " bazaar is a mass of filth."
>
> At one hill station, Nynee Tāl, where *men are sent for their health (!) the stench is at times overpowering,* from both bazaars being in a filthy and crowded state, no proper drainage or latrines, no means of preserving cleanliness, which causes nuisance even in the barracks. At another, Darjeeling, among other defects, the native villages, writes the medical officer, " are the most filthy " he has " ever entered, and " it is quite sickening to walk through them."
>
> At Jubbulpore, where every hut is crowded, where there are no latrines, where cleanliness is almost impossible, the same causes produce the same results.
>
> At Cannanore the native houses have dungheaps and cesspits within the compounds. Owing to the want of latrines, the "filth and indecency" are described to be what it is impossible to repeat. The dead are buried within the compounds of houses.

Extract from 'Observations by Miss Nightingale' in the *Indian Sanitary Report*, 1863

public necessaries. There are often open cesspits among the houses.' The practice was to 'dig the mud for the huts close by' and then not to fill in the hole thus made. 'And then the hole serves to throw all the filth' into it. The bazaars had grown up anyhow, increasing as the military population increased. At Bangalore, for instance, where in 1860 the barracks housed 1,700 European and 2,600 native troops, there were 93,000 people living in the adjoining bazaar.[16] An European bazaar-master with the powers of a magistrate was responsible for law and order. Colonel Gall of the 14th Light Dragoons thought that 'great attention was paid to cleanliness' and that the bazaars he had seen presented 'a favourable contrast with any native town, but where the natives are concerned', he added, 'there is great difficulty in overcoming their habits; they give offence.'[17] Dr Mouat pointed out that the native population was 'like the Israelites of old: they go and deposit their excreta on the plain; but they do not bury it as the Israelites did.'* 'A heavy shower of rain washes down all

* 'The ground so defiled', said Mr Dempster, late Superintending-Surgeon, Bengal Establishment, 'is generally quickly cleared by the herds of swine,

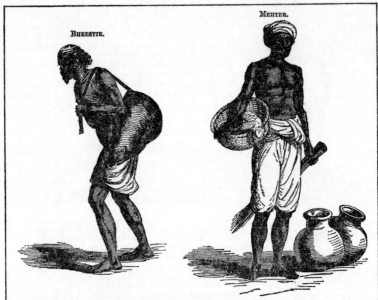

BHEESTIE.

MEHTER.

THESE TWO OFFICIALS REPRESENT THE SYSTEM OF WATER SUPPLY AND DRAINAGE IN INDIA FOR GARRISONS
AND TOWNS.

Drainage, in the sense in which we have found it necessary for health in this colder climate, is by no
means considered necessary for health in the hot climate of India; for, as in the case of the water supply,
most of the reporters consider *no drainage* a sufficient guarantee for health.

From the *Indian Sanitary Report*, 1863

soluble matter through the natural percolation of the soil, and it
must find its way to the tanks.'[18]

Sir John Lawrence pointed out that

'in India one great point upon which good health depends is the
water. Our people', he told the Sanitary Commission, 'very
seldom look to the water in choosing a locality. . . . I have seen
positions which were considered unexceptionally good by
Englishmen, but if you asked natives about one of them, they
would say that it was very bad on account of the bad quality of
the water.'[19]

Yet the natives seldom took any personal sanitary precautions. 'For
instance', a distinguished doctor told the Commission, 'a man will
eat and drink and perform his evacuations actually on the very same

literally fed upon human ordure, which they devour with surprising greediness.
. . . A number of these disgusting country pigs have sometimes been permitted
to follow in the rear of a British regiment as part of its "flocks and herds".'
(*I.S.R.*, I, 466.)

340

foot of water standing in it, or close to it; he has no idea of impurity as long as it happens to be Ganges water.'[20] From water supplies thus tainted drank both Europeans and natives. Water for all purposes was drawn from the 'tank' or well by dipping goat skins and other vessels into it. These were then carried by the water carriers (*bhistis*) to the barracks, where the water was poured either into wooden casks 'with a square hole cut in the top' or into large earthen jars.[21]

From the *Indian Sanitary Report*, 1863

At every cantonment there was at least one tank. These were of considerable size and depth, larger and deeper than the horse ponds of England. Many of them were ancient and lined with dressed stone, but the modern ones were 'simply excavated. In some places they are puddled with clay to prevent leakage, and there are generally brick steps constructed, ghauts as they are called, leading down to them to enable the men to bathe and take water at all times.' There was often a special tank meant to contain purer water, set aside for drinking. A guard was placed over it to prevent bathing and to stop dogs and other animals being washed in it.[22]

Archibald Stewart, the Deputy Inspector-General of Hospitals in India, who had served as surgeon to the 9th Lancers and later to the 14th Light Dragoons, told the Sanitary Commissioners that he had never seen a single instance in India 'in which anything like adequate means for the purposes of ablution existed'.[23] He was referring chiefly to conventional ablution rooms and bath accommodation, for as Colonel Greathed told the Commission, there were generally one or two tanks or 'plunge baths' provided at each station for the non-commissioned officers and men 'in which they can bathe as much as they like. . . . Where gardens are provided for the troops, the waste water runs off to supply the gardens. . . . They are always full; there is always a surface water running through them.' They were expensive to keep filled, 'because you must always keep bullocks at work, and you have to pay the men who work the bullocks.' There were no compulsory bathing parades, but these outdoor baths were much used, according to Colonel Greathed, yet 'some men will never wash if they can help it'. When asked whether 'a soldier, if he likes it, may go without washing from one year's end to another', he replied 'Yes.'[24]

* * *

As at home there was overcrowding in badly sited, poorly designed barracks. The medical authorities were nearly unanimous in condemning the practice which was prevalent in the middle decades of

'Daily means of occupation and amusement. India *passim*': from the *Indian Sanitary Report*, 1863

the century of 'erecting costly palaces for troops'. These were so expensive to build 'that Government', one doctor asserted, 'grudges the space required for the men.'[25] Further, in a misguided attempt to reduce the effects of heat, double verandahs had been built around many of the newer barrack rooms. In fact, this form of construction made ventilation more difficult and enabled 'the inner verandah to be appropriated as extra sleeping space. The double verandah is at the same time', the Sanitary Commission report stated, 'an unnecessary cost.'[26]

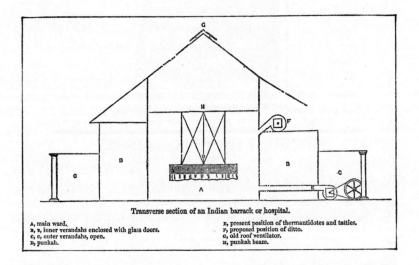

Transverse section of an Indian barrack or hospital.

A, main ward.
B, B, inner verandahs enclosed with glass doors.
C, C, outer verandahs, open.
D, punkah.

E, present position of thermantidotes and tatties.
F, proposed position of ditto.
G, old roof ventilator.
H, punkah beam.

During the hot season, there were punkahs in every barrack room the cord of which was pulled like a bell-rope by the punkah-coolies or -wallahs. Tatties were also used for keeping the temperature down. These were screens or mats made from the roots of a particular type of grass, placed in a frame against doorways and windows. They were kept wet by what Archibald Stewart called 'an establishment furnished at the expense of Government to water them'.[27] Tatties were also a part of the increasingly used thermantidotes. These were rotating fans, modelled on the ordinary winnowing machine, fitted in window openings and encased in tatties so as to drive a current of cooled air into the barrack rooms.

A very few of the most recently built barracks, such as those at Moulmein, consisted of detached bungalows 'well raised from the ground and with roof ventilation,' conforming more or less to the model which the Commission laid down: huts 'with doors on opposite sides, which are protected by verandahs'.[28] But there were objections to this detached system from regimental officers on the grounds that the sergeants could not 'look so well after the men'.[29]

'Kus kus' tattie applied to common doorway

Nevertheless the trend as the years went by was to concentrate on this cheaper, more healthy system.

In the meantime, though in the majority of barrack rooms the regulation 1,000 cubic feet per man was provided, the great height

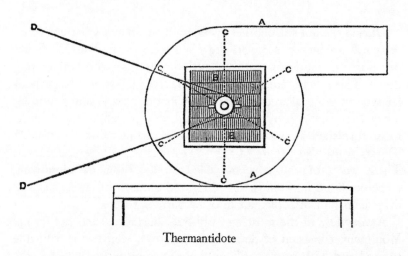

Thermantidote

of the rooms in Indian barracks meant that the superficial area per bed by no means corresponded to the cubic contents.[30] In nearly every case there was no more than a foot between beds. Yet to young Lieutenant Alexander Tulloch, arriving from Ireland at

Secunderabad in late 1857, 'the men's barracks, after the huts at the Curragh, seemed spacious enough.'[31]

There was considerable controversy about the best form of flooring in barrack rooms. Colonel Greathed favoured 'that which the natives use, which is rammed earth washed over with cowdung. . . . It keeps away fleas and bugs', he thought, 'better than anything else.' Many of the older barrack room floors were thus treated. Alexander Stewart, being a modern medical officer, deplored this 'filthy nauseating process called "cow-dunging".' The floor, he explained, was 'varnished over' with a mixture of cowdung and water. 'The effect, for the time being, is to render the rooms damp and offensive.' He recommended stone flags where available, other-wise burnt brick.[33]

Another practice which Stewart complained of in cavalry regi-ments was the keeping of saddles, valises, bridles and 'the different accoutrements of a dragoon suspended in the room where the men sleep . . . in the space of seven feet . . . immediately over the beds. I have seen a man's saddle hung close by his ear. The saddles are often foul from being saturated with the horses' perspiration', so that beside the misuse of limited space, there was the evil of the men breathing 'over and over again an impure atmosphere'.[34]

Overcrowding was still sometimes aggravated by lack of married quarters, though there had been a great improvement in recent years. In 1859 only about 20% of Indian stations reported that they possessed no separate accommodation.[35] There had been none at Meerut when the 14th Light Dragoons were there between 1851 and 1854. The families of married men had then lived, 'screened off in compartments, in the enclosed verandahs on each side of the central room occupied by the men.'[36] Elsewhere families were sometimes lodged in barrack rooms set aside for them, divided by hanging blankets. There were still a few instances, as had been the case in England, in which married people occupied 'the same rooms as single men, separated from them by mats'. The newest married quarters usually consisted of 'separate huts or bungalows, of two or three rooms, built in the patchery, a court belonging to the barracks'. The Sanitary Commissioners found that the men living in the pat-cheries with their families were 'much more healthy than men living in barracks'.[37] Other married quarters, such as those newly built at Poona, consisted of 'one long building divided into contiguous rooms'.[38]

On the whole the lot of the married man in India, at any rate by the mid-1860s, was a happier one than elsewhere. This seems to be confirmed by the large proportion of them who when their regiments were ordered home volunteered to remain in the country. Indeed, as Sir Hugh Rose said in 1866, the service in India generally was not at all unpopular, 'it is merely the serious diseases which make it so'. He had

> 'heard a case the other day when a recruiting sergeant was bringing 13 recruits and passed some men who had come from India; they fell in with the recruits and talked with them, and told them that they might go to India, and that they would get sick of cholera and diarrhoea, and would come home with broken health and have nothing for it. I believe that every one of those men left the recruiting sergeant.'[39]

Corporal Hollis of the 8th Hussars, when asked whether service in India was not a favourite one, replied, 'Yes, while you are out there.' When his regiment was sent home over 200 of the men volunteered to stay in India. 'We filled up the 19th and 21st regiments', he said.[40]*

A witness, giving evidence before the 1861 Recruiting Commission, thought that there was

> 'something peculiar to the East Indies, because young men think that it is a country paved with gold, and that if they go out there they are sure of some appointment, so that there is no difficulty in raising recruits [for the Company's regiments]. . . . Young men have an impression . . . that the Indian force holds out more chances of promotion than the line. . . . They are a superior class to those who go into the line.'[41]

There were other less admirable reasons for joining the army in India. As Sir Alexander Tulloch said in 1861 many young men 'who have run away from their parents and misconducted themselves go into [the Indian] army . . ., in order that they may not be likely to meet any of their acquaintances.'[42]

* * *

* The Hon. East India Company's 1st Bengal European Cavalry and the 3rd Bengal European Cavalry, both raised in 1858, became in 1861–62 the 19th and 21st Hussars respectively. 133 men of the 8th Hussars volunteered for the 19th and 54 for the 21st. (Murray, II, 472.) (See p. 234.)

The hospitals in India, like every other organization in the army there, were what is today known as labour-intensive. The establishment of a regimental hospital at home was in the region of ten men, including two sergeants, one for general discipline and attendance upon the sick, the other in charge of the purveyor's department (supplies, care of stores and cooking). In India the same regiment would find that its hospital establishment numbered seventy-nine native 'officials' over and above the European hospital sergeant and 'the orderlies taken from the regiment, who are supplied in all serious cases or at the request of the sick'. There was a native steward and there were native apothecaries, tailors, barbers, cooks, dressers, sweepers, bearers, nurses, ward coolies, water-carriers and washermen. In the hot weather 104 punkah-wallahs, '23 coolies for throwing water on tatties' and 34 extra water-carriers were added, making a grand total of 240 'native assistants'.[43]

Hospital stoppages for the European troops were very much lower in India than they were at home. Consequently, as Colonel Greathed put it, 'a man may go in for a finger ache in India, but he would not do it in England.'[44]

'. . . Anything that would keep them out of idleness and out of the grog shops would be conferring a benefit upon them. They are never so healthy as when undergoing the fatigues of a long march.'

DR J. MCCOSH, in evidence before
the Indian Sanitary Commission[1]

(xxii)

Rank and file: India: Company's European recruits during the Mutiny – drunkenness – spirits, chiefly arrack – canteens – the canteen fund – beer – refreshment rooms

At the time of the Mutiny when the Company was raising European cavalry regiments, recruits were assembled at the depôt at Warley, near Brentwood in Essex, given some very elementary training and then rushed out East. 'It happened occasionally that men were embarked for India on the day of their arrival at Warley.' The normal recruiting age was between twenty and thirty-five, but 'a great many', the Sanitary Commissioners were told, 'have entered under twenty.' Much concern was expressed in the Report that recruits for the Indian army were sent out too young and raw, often even before their basic training had been completed. This was no doubt a chief reason for the 'White Mutiny' of 1859 (see p. 234).

Arrived in India the recruit for both the Royal and the Company's regiments was dependent, much more than at home, upon the wisdom of his commanding officer, a thing, as was stressed by Colonel Durand,

'of very immense importance in India, for almost everything is in his hands: he must maintain the state of efficiency of his corps, and in a climate of that kind, unless he does so having paid great attention to the times at which it is best to carry on his drills, and to all those internal arrangements which rest entirely with him . . . his regiment may very likely suffer severely.'[2]

Sir John Lawrence believed that much of the ill health of both the Royal and the Company's troops was due to 'the habits of their lives, want of care for themselves, particularly when they first go out [to India]. . . . No man will believe that the sun will hurt him, and even the officers will not believe it.'[3] But Sir Charles Napier found that 'in most parts of India the effects of man's imprudence are attributed to climate! If a man gets drunk', he wrote in 1853, 'the sun has given him a headache, and so on.'[4]

Excessive drinking by white troops in India was becoming less common by the early 1860s. Stricter regulations and the increasing substitution of beer for spirits were the chief reasons for this. The sale of spirits, chiefly arrack,* to the troops in the bazaars had for many years been totally prohibited. Colonel Greathed told the Sanitary Commissioners that regimental police were selected for their sharpness. 'They assist the cantonment magistrate in putting down the illicit sale of liquors, and generally speaking I should say with success.' The temptation to the '40 or 50 men'[5] in every regiment who were heavy drinkers was a real one, for 'the very deleterious kind of spirit which is to be procured all over India' was so cheap,

---

* The name for any locally distilled liquor: usually made from the fermented sap of the coco-palm, or from rice and sugar, fermented with the coco-nut juice.

as Colonel Gall of the 14th Light Dragoons pointed out, 'that a man may get drunk upon it for a halfpenny'.[6] In every regiment there was, as at home, a canteen. Arrack, rum and malt liquors, (chiefly porter), were all available. Unlike the spirits, the malt liquors, which included a variety of beers, ales and stout, could be drunk away from the canteen bar. Sergeant-Major William Walker of the 8th Foot described the routine in the infantry, which was doubtless much the same in the cavalry:

'A non-commissioned officer will go round to each company and collect the names of the men who require beer for their dinner; a man may put himself down for a quart of beer, and the money is collected at the same time from the men and handed over to the non-commissioned officer; he then goes with a written pass signed by the senior non-commissioned officer of the company to the canteen sergeant, draws the liquor and brings it to the barrack, and issues it to the men at the dinner hour.'[7]

Each man was rationed to two drams of spirits (roughly a quarter of a fluid ounce)* per day. To prevent multiple issues a non-commissioned officer kept a tally. The arrack was always watered down to a regulation extent, and an officer of the canteen committee was responsible for seeing that this was done in his presence every day before issue.[8]

'Each soldier who avails himself of his privilege of dram-drinking to the fullest extent', stated the Sanitary Report, 'will consume $18\frac{1}{4}$ gallons of raw spirit per annum; but most men content themselves with one dram and an equivalent of malt liquor. Throughout the whole of India, it has been considered advisable to permit the sale of ardent spirits, under restriction as to quality and amount in all canteens; because bad, un-adulterated and, in some cases, poisonous spirits only could be otherwise obtained by the soldiers.'[9]

Another reason or excuse for continuing the sale of spirits in canteens, though perhaps on a smaller scale, was the maintenance of the canteen fund. This was chiefly raised

'by putting 1s on every gallon of spirits. The canteen fund, for instance, under regulations of the Government, pays for the

* The Bengal dram differed a little from the English one. Forty Bengal drams equalled one gallon.

cap covers of the men, which are very necessary, and a constant expense; it also pays for all his amusements – the fives court and the theatre; the skittle ground and the gardens. In fact any reasonable request which the commanding officer makes is always granted.

'The canteen fund', said Colonel Greathed, 'accumulates in a wonderful way; in fact the great difficulty in a regiment was to keep it down. After 3,000 rupees are accumulated the Government may lay its hands on the fund, and it is the object of the C.O. to spend it as quickly as he can.'[10]

The canteen fund was also used to help soldiers and their families when ill 'and on the line of march'.[11]

Sir Charles Napier when he was Commander-in-Chief had laid down that no man should be allowed any form of alcoholic drink before midday, and that in the hot weather, from May to October, the canteen was not to open until sundown.[12] Also obtainable at the canteen were brandy, gin, port and sherry; but these were only 'for particular occasions' and were not, according to Colonel Stewart 'so commonly used'.[13]

He also believed, as did numerous other witnesses, that most soldiers would have much preferred beer to spirits, 'and the only reason for their not using beer almost exclusively is their means being insufficient to procure it.' Draught porter cost in 1861 about threepence a quart, and no type of malt liquor sold for more than sixpence a quart.[14] The trouble of course was that beer was an expensive and bulky article to bring all the way from home. For instance, it was reported in 1861 that large quantities had gone bad and become undrinkable by the time they reached the commissariat stores at Meerut. The advent of railways soon put an end to this difficulty and the price of beer was not long in reaching an acceptably low level. At the same time 'a good wholesome beer was being brewed in the hills', but it took some years before its price and quantity brought it into general regimental use.[15] To encourage beer drinking the Government started to subsidise it. Consequently beer became cheaper in India than at home. It was sold 'at a rate low enough', it was said, 'to place it within the means of the private soldiers.' In the three years 1855 to 1857 the loss to Government in Bengal alone was £109,671.[16]

By the mid-1860s an increasing number of cantonments could boast a refreshment room as well as a canteen.

'At the end of the recreation room, or in a separate room', said Sir Hugh Rose in 1866, 'there is a refreshment place with rolls of bread, butter, tea, coffee, ginger beer (made on the best receipt), cold meat, &c. The men are extremely fond of this system. The money which they used to spend in drinking in the Indian liquor shops they now spend in the refreshment room. They very often do not go out of their barracks at all after dark, and they then have all sorts of games in the recreation room.'[17]

It took some years before such regimental refreshment rooms became common in the cantonments of India. For instance it was not until the end of 1875 that the 9th Lancers stationed at Sialkot was provided with its first regimental institute in the shape of a room designed 'to supply to the men the best articles that can be procured at low prices, and to provide a place where every man can at any time in the day procure a good and comfortable meal'.[18]

'The men of course are more careless in every
respect than the officers, and their habits of life
are very inimical to health in India.'
                    SIR JOHN LAWRENCE before the
                    Indian Sanitary Commission, 1863[1]

(xxiii)

*Rank and file: India: venereal disease – prostitutes –
'lock hospitals' – married soldiers – official treatment of
wives – native wives of white soldiers*

Nearly 25% of the cases of sickness constantly in the hospitals of the European part of the Indian army were accounted for by the venereal diseases, chiefly syphilis. In the 1850s and 1860s there was a steady increase in the number of cases. In 1860 there were reported 345 cases 'of venereal affections' per 1,000 men in Bengal, 314 in

Bombay and 249 in Madras.* Dr W. C. Maclean, giving evidence before the Indian Sanitary Commission, believed that the loss of efficiency from syphilis in India was 'becoming quite a state question'. In the 1830s, he pointed out, there had been at every station a 'lock hospital' for prostitutes, but prejudices against them had led in time to their abolition. 'The consequence is now that the prostitutes . . . are under no control whatever.' He knew of one Queen's regiment in which it had recently been 'ascertained that one woman had in the course of two nights utterly destroyed ten men. These men were so injured by her that they were no longer fit for duty, their efficiency was completely destroyed by a malignant form of syphilis.' Dr Maclean recommended the revival of properly organized lock hospitals, believing that, with the help of the police magistrates at stations, all the prostitutes could be brought completely under control. If there were two or three annual examinations, the diseased women could be 'taken and confined in the lock hospitals'. Asked whether such women had any means of subsistence other than prostitution, he replied: 'Perhaps not; but it is better . . . to maintain them while sick than leave them at large. It would cost very little compared with the destruction that one infected woman is sure to work in a regiment.'[2]

Among the native troops generally the incidence of the venereal diseases was small, since most of them lived with their wives. The Sikhs were an exception. One medical authority stated that they were 'eaten up with syphilis. They do not carry their families with them; they are just as gregarious in their amours as the British soldier, and in that way one woman who is popular among them, may affect a whole company.'[3]

The obvious if not complete solution to the problem among the white troops was to allow a higher proportion of married soldiers; but there were very real obstacles in the way. Excluding sergeant-majors and sergeants about 12% of other ranks in India were allowed official wives – that is wives with 'a claim for accommodation in barracks', each receiving five rupees a month.[4] This number of 'legal' wives was about double that permitted at home. It led not only to much expense but, more important in modern eyes, it was the cause of shocking suffering. The practice when regiments went

* In 1842–46 'the English troops of the Madras army sent 189 cases per 1,000 annually to hospital for syphilis, while the native troops sent 31. Colonel Sykes says "*only* 31", and adds, "as might be expected from the majority of the men having families with them." ' (*I.S.R.*, I, xxiii.)

32. Private George Payne, 14th Light Dragoons, *c.* 1851, off duty in India

33. Private George Payne, 14th Light Dragoons, c. 1851, on duty in India

into the field was for soldiers' wives to be as good as abandoned. 'If', said Colonel Greathed, 'the women were properly cared for when they were left behind, and had money enough given to them to provide themselves with food, a great deal might be done to remedy the present evil.'[5] Sir John Lawrence declared that the system produced 'terrible results':

'I would take care,' he said, 'of the wives and children of the soldiers who went into the field. I would do what the natives do. When a regiment is going on service, the first thing that respectable natives do, is to go to the officer and make some arrangement by which their women are to be looked after, and taken care of, and we ought to do that; it is constantly the case in a regiment in the service that there are women going to the bad for want of a little care. In a cantonment I would leave a picked officer to look after them, a married man who had sympathy with the women.

'In the height of the mutiny officers of native regiments at Delhi used to write to me to look after the wives and children of the men who were in the Punjab, and supposing that I had neglected them, it might have just turned the scale against us. I recollect an officer of the Guides writing to say: "There are such and such women in Lahore belonging to the Guide corps, several of their husbands, men of rank," have been killed. "Mind you look after those women carefully, and do not let them be in distress." I did so just as if they had been some of my own people, and of course that went down to the corps, and the men all heard of it, and felt it very much. This you do with the foreigner and the stranger, why not do it with your own countrymen?'[6]

When in barracks, if he was lodged in married quarters, the married man could eat his meals with his family. He could either fetch his food from the commissariat, or he could draw, in lieu, $6\frac{1}{2}$ rupees a month and provide his own. 'Some', said Sergeant-Major Walker, 'prefer that, as they can get meat so very cheap.'[7]

It was always an object of importance to the widow of a soldier in India to get herself re-married as soon as possible. Otherwise, after a certain period she would be left destitute. General Sir Neville Lyttelton tells of one specially speedy re-marriage:

'In India', he wrote, 'burials follow death very rapidly, and in one instance at all events a widow's re-engagement was equally hasty. She attended her husband's funeral the day after he died, and on the same day the Colour Sergeant of the company proposed to her. She burst into tears, and the N.C.O., thinking perhaps that he had been too hasty, said he would come again in two or three days. "Oh, it isn't that," said the bereaved one, "but on the way back from the cemetery I accepted the Corporal of the firing party", by no means so good a match.'[8]

European soldiers were permitted to marry native women, who received from Government $2\frac{1}{2}$ rupees a month, half the European allowance. How often such marriages occurred it is difficult to establish. The Sanitary Commissioners' report says that 'sons and daughters of the two races, known as Eurasians, or East Indians, or half-castes, amount to considerable numbers'.[9] Colonel Gall of the 14th Light Dragoons found that the native wives of troopers very seldom went home to England with their husbands, though they had the right to do so. 'I think', he said, 'that the general result of a man marrying a native woman would be that he would remain in the country, and volunteer into another regiment.'[10]

'The same diet which may be consumed in the cold season with safety cannot be the most suitable for heat.'
> The Report of the Indian Sanitary
> Commission, 1863[1]

(xxiv)

Rank and file: India: diet – soldiers better fed than at home – cookhouses – 'back-ration money' – meal times – fatigue duties – native followers – sports and games – clothing and uniforms

In mid-century responsible administrators, officers and doctors were beginning to show concern about the unsuitability of much of the soldiers' diet in India. For instance, meat was eaten two and often three times a day all the year round. Sir John Lawrence did not 'believe that any officer does, and if he does he gets sick too. . . . The natives', he added, 'who are accustomed to the climate eat very little animal food, particularly in hot weather.'[2]* 'Of the recruits drawn from Ireland and Scotland', declared one medical man, 'it is certain that the majority must eat in the hot weather in India *many times the bulk of animal food* ever consumed in their native country while working hardest in the coldest season of the year.'[3] The daily ration included one pound of beef, for which mutton was substituted twice a week. Contrary to the usual practice at home, the large bone was separated from the meat before it was weighed for issue by the Commissariat.[4]† If they had any spare cash the men would often spend it on bacon and pork, thus adding to the quantity of animal food they consumed.[5]

Though the diet was undoubtedly ill-suited to the climate, Sergeant-Major Walker voiced an opinion universally held in the ranks when he said that

'the soldier in India is better fed than he is in England. . . . Every soldier in England must confine himself, at the most, to two descriptions of food, either boiled meat, or, if he chooses to pay for it, he may have a baked dinner; but every soldier in India can order his own dinner to be prepared by the native cook, and the cook is bound to bring him that dinner; some get curry, some get baked meat, some get stews, and some get food of other descriptions; the soldier may make his choice of 20 different dinners.'

Pilaus of rice boiled with fowl, meat or fish, and spices and raisins, were popular dishes. Carrots, onions and pumpkins were plentiful, and the troops got 'oranges in abundance, and also plenty of mangoes in the season, and custard apples.' The potato, said Sergeant-Major Walker, which had been 'considered a dainty 20 years ago in India', was now 'served out to a regiment in plenty'.[6]

Private Hyom of the 10th Hussars, writing in the early 1850s, found that all provisions were 'wonderful cheap'. When he arrived

---

* The native soldier's diet was entirely of his own choice. Dr Mouat told the Sanitary Commission that 'no influence is exercised over him . . ., but the Government try to procure for him the largest quantity and best quality of the food to which he has become accustomed.' (*I.S.R.*, I, 331.)

† The offal from the slaughter and preparation of the cattle and sheep seldom caused a nuisance as it was at once 'eaten up by innumerable kites and vultures.' (*I.S.R.*, I, 202.)

at his first barracks in India he was 'astonished to find' that he could get

> 'a pound of good steak for three farthings . . ., vegetables, as many as you can eat for ¼d . . ., butter, 4d per lb . . . but cheese is very dear, about 2s 6d per lb. . . . The fruit is also very cheap . . . grapes about 3 lbs for 2d – bananas 4 for a farthing, plantains 5 for a farthing, pomegranates a farthing each, figs a double handful for ½d, cocoanuts ½d each. . . . You also get poultry very cheap, a very good fowl for 3d, and hares, if the natives ask more than 6d each they are ordered out of barracks, the average price being 4½d.'[7]

The means of cooking and the utensils used were very simple. The barrack cookhouses were usually small detached sheds without chimneys and ill-lit. Along the walls there were 'low platforms of masonry, with square holes to hold the fire'. There was a large consumption of fuel, 'the smoke from which fills the kitchen and blackens its walls'. There was no water-supply except, as everywhere, by water-carriers. The refuse water was generally 'allowed to escape the best' it could. Sometimes it ran into a cesspit and was removed by hand labour.[8]

The troop commanders engaged the native cooks, 'just as they would engage washermen',* and the charge for cooking was 10 to 12 annas a month. In spite of their limited means, they cooked, according to most authorities, extremely well and imaginatively, though from the health point of view Dr Dempster was possibly right to describe the cookery as 'generally of a very objectionable character, all meat being made into rich pies, or hot curries, or fried with fat in common frying pans.'[9] What a delightful contrast, though, to the soup and boiled beef at home!

The full daily ration consisted of:

Meat, 1 lb.	Rice, 4 oz.
Bread, 1 lb.	Sugar, 2½ oz.
Vegetables, 1 lb.	Tea, $\frac{5}{7}$ oz. *or* Coffee, $1\frac{3}{7}$ oz.
Salt, 1 oz.	

---

* 'In every troop', said Colonel Gall, 'a man is engaged as washerman, and he engages his own servants, and he washes for the men. The captain contracts on the part of the men for the washing generally. The men pay a certain sum per month, and the captain is the person who is responsible for the payment of the washermen.' (*I.S.R.*, I, 77.)

The men were subject to a ration stoppage of 3 annas, 4 pie (about
4½d or 5d) a day. If it actually cost more than that, the public bore
the loss. If it cost less, the soldier received the difference. When this
'back-ration money' was issued to a man, 'which', said Colonel Gall,
'it is sometimes after a lapse of two months, it has accumulated to a
rupee or more. On those occasions he is likely to exceed a little', or,
in other words, to go and get drunk! For an extra anna a day the
native cook would supply 'some trifling articles' in addition to the
rations, such as 'meat for breakfast, milk and sometimes butter, &c.'

The Commissioners pointed out that the soldier normally had
breakfast at seven or eight in the morning; dinner at one o'clock;
tea 'about five, sometimes with meat too. The dinner is therefore
eaten just before the hottest part of the day; and all the meals are
crowded into nine or ten hours of inaction.'[10]

*   *   *

During the hot weather in the plains the European soldiers were
confined to their barrack rooms during the eight hottest hours of the
day. 'They may not go out to walk in the sun', said Colonel Gall.
He found that the men of the 14th Light Dragoons 'were surprisingly healthy at Meerut when confined to the barracks from 9 a.m.
to 5 p.m.' 'Some go to sleep', said Sergeant-Major Walker; 'some
play at dominos, but they are not allowed to gamble. Cards are
never allowed, but they may play at dominos or chess, and back-
gammon.'[11] According to Archibald Stewart 'soldiers of late years
read a good deal. . . . They obtain books, &c. from the library, and
lie upon their beds and read during the day.'[12] Whatever they did,
there were few who would not have agreed with Private Blatchford.
'What can you do', he asked, 'with the prickly heat? You must
swear!'[13] As for the soldier who could not read or write, or who
could only do either with difficulty, he, thought Colonel Greathed,
'must be a very miserable fellow if he is shut up in a room'. Such
men, he noticed, liked to be read aloud to 'and they like men to tell
stories to them.'[14]

Sir Hugh Rose was certain that in India the men had 'far greater
comforts with regard to reading, refreshment rooms, &c. than they
have elsewhere. Almost every regiment there', he told the 1867
Recruiting Commission, 'has its regimental cricket club. The men
play till it is quite dark.'[15]

In the cavalry, as always, there were many more chores to occupy the men than in the infantry, the cleaning of elaborate accoutrements being the chief of them. But life as a whole was wonderfully easy in Indian cantonments. There were very few fatigue duties compared with those at home. Sweeping out the barrack rooms, cooking, carrying dinners to the men on guard ('which is the most cruel of all the duties thrown upon the soldier' in England) – all these tasks were performed by native labour. In short the soldiers in India were waited upon instead of as at home waiting upon themselves. Efforts were sometimes made to reduce the number of followers, but they seldom succeeded.

'We employ the barber', wrote Private Hyom of the 10th Hussars, 'giving him at the rate of 6d per month each man, and they can shave you almost when you are asleep. The Dhobie or washerman we also employ at the rate of 1s 3d per month and you have a clean shirt and sometimes two every day besides trowsers, jackets, etc. all as white as snow. You would see numbers of washermen by the side of the river making such a noise and beating the clothes that you would fancy there would not be a thread left but they do not wear them out more than they do in England. I always employed one shoemaker while I was in India and used to give him 12 annas (1s 6d) for my Bluchers and 5s for Wellington boots and very good they were for the Country. Of course they would not do for England being too slight.

'You also can get the Native Tailor to work for you at so much per day, 6d to 9d being the average price.'[16]

In some regiments native barbers and boot and accoutrement cleaners were for a time dispensed with, but especially in the cavalry such economies were neither encouraged nor welcome.[17]

For many years to come in the European cavalry regiments of the Indian army, 'the number of horsekeepers, grass-cutters, water-carriers, &c., &c., and other native followers, a large proportion of them paid for by Government, sometimes amounted to nearly the number of the corps themselves.' Their health was a perpetual problem, for every follower, 'by the usages of the service', was entitled to medical aid when ill. But adequate accommodation was never officially provided. At Kirkee, for instance,

'when native followers came under treatment, it was necessary, from want of any other accommodation, to put them into the "deadhouse"; and when they exceeded a certain number', remembered Archibald Stewart, 'into the open verandahs of the men's hospitals, where, besides being exposed to the weather, their presence often proved inconvenient. Even the "deadhouse" was not always available, as when any casualty occurred in hospital it became necessary to remove the native patients, who often could not be afterwards prevailed upon to return.'[18]

* * *

Attempts were made from time to time, especially during the cold season, to provide the troops with work of a non-military nature. They generally failed. Gardens and allotments were made at some stations, but the men did not take to looking after them. 'I do not think', said Sir John Lawrence, 'that any Englishman likes working in India. They like throwing great balls of iron, and playing football in cold weather, but I do not think they like work.'[19] Colonel Greathed found that

'the great game for soldiers in India is what they call long bullets; that is the game they play at in all stations; it is more of the nature of golf than any other game, only it is played, not with a bat [sic], but with the hand. They also play at quoits, cricket and fives. Those are the usual games; but the best of all recreations was this: we encouraged them to go out shooting when it could be done with safety.'[20]

Some of the men of the 14th Light Dragoons, according to Colonel Gall, did 'do work as tinmen, curriers, carpenters and turners', but only 'occasionally'.[21]

* * *

The traumatic experience of the Mutiny had gone some way towards altering the official attitude towards soldiers' clothing. 'The attempt to secure uniformity in all climates, the standard type being the moist raw, variable atmosphere of sea-girt England,'[22] was gradually abandoned. Hot, heavy, ill-ventilated headgear was on the way out. The 14th, for instance, wore 'on the late campaign the turban and forage cap. We left the shako behind us in quarters. The turban', reported Colonel Gall, 'was bound round anything that fitted the head the best, with a flap at the back which was merely the end of the turban.'[23] The experience of the Mutiny veterans, however, did not prevent the King's Dragoon Guards and the 7th Dragoon Guards bringing out from England their brass helmets. Not long since, Archibald Stewart had seen one regiment on afternoon parade on the Queen's birthday in May wearing its brass helmets 'without any cover whatever to guard against the effects of the scorching sun.'[24] Lord Clyde, when Commander-in-Chief, had introduced wicker helmets with quilted coverings, and these soon became universal.

The Sanitary Commissioners could report in 1863 that 'the soldier now wears habitually a Khakee (dust-coloured) cotton tunic and trousers', showing how quickly the example of the Corps of Guides set in 1857 had caught on (see p. 151). His shirt was usually made of flannel.[25] His greatcoat, according to Dr Mouat, writing in 1859, was 'a ponderous sponge, which, by keeping moisture long in contact with the body, is, in wet weather, productive of far more evil than good.'[26]

*　　*　　*

When European troops took the field in India, free carriage was allowed at a rate of forty pounds of baggage for each non-commissioned officer and man. On all normal peacetime movements, the men's kit was carried by camels supplied at the public expense, in the proportion of one to every seven cavalrymen (or five infantrymen). Married soldiers who required additional carriage had to arrange and pay for it themselves. For the kit which a man did not carry on his back or on his horse, such as his bedding and many of his necessaries, there was provided a kit-bag made of canvas or network known as a *sulleetah*. The weight of such kit was meant not to exceed fifty-four pounds for the cavalryman (and seventy-five for the infantryman). The weight of baggage 'considered sufficient' for officers, exclusive of camp equipage, ranged from 2,880 pounds for a general of division to 480 pounds for a subaltern or an assistant surgeon. Over and above these quantities, 320 pounds for each officer was allowed for the mess baggage.[27]

'The ratio of the cost of the Europeans to that of natives may be set down as 289 to 100, or nearly 3 to 1. Consequently the cost of 235,221 native soldiers is equivalent to the cost of 81,349 European soldiers.'

Indian Sanitary Report, 1863[1]

(xxv)

Rank and file: India: native soldiers: mortality – pay – huts – recreations – food, drink and drugs – promotion – uniforms

It is impossible to compare the mortality rate of the native troops of the Indian army with that of the Europeans. It was said in 1859 not to exceed 2%, but this figure did not mean much when numbers of men were discharged as soon as they became ill 'to go home', as Dr Mouat put it, 'to die from diseases contracted in their regiments.' These deaths were not, of course, recorded.

The native soldier's pay was about a third of the European's, but it generally well exceeded the earnings of his civilian counterparts. The army was therefore an extremely attractive profession. Since, consequently, the supply of recruits was virtually unlimited, commanding officers could select 'the finest, the strongest, the healthiest and the handsomest fellows'. The medical examination of recruits was very thorough, 'all physical blemishes and defects were carefully examined', and the proportion of rejections was high. At first, it was noticed, the recruit was 'rather lean and hungry-looking; but the improvement in his physical condition when he once gets upon pay is remarkable.'[2]

Most of the native troops were married men. The Brahmins of Bengal and the Sikhs were apt to leave their wives and families at home, visiting them periodically on furlough. The vast mass of wives and children, however, lived in the native lines of the cantonments with their husbands in small huts. These were built by the men themselves with the help of a small Government grant. Each of them was made with considerable skill and very little labour. The materials were invariably bamboo and straw matting 'with a little mud put over it at times'. The cost of each hut seldom exceeded two rupees.[3] They were of various dimensions. Those for single men were about ten feet long by seven-and-a-half wide, seven feet high and contained not more than 525 cubic feet. A married soldier's hut was some fifteen feet long, eleven wide and nine high. The floors were generally raised with earth excavated from a hole made close to the door 'in which all manner of filth was deposited'.[4] Except during the rains, the men slept on their *charpoys* (cots or bedsteads) outside their huts. There was seldom any order or regularity in the placing of the huts. Officers sometimes induced the men to arrange them with a decent space separating them, but more often they were huddled as close together as they could stand, 'without drainage or attention to ventilation. . . . It is usually considered', reported the Commissioners, 'that little or no sanitary improvement can be carried out among natives on account of caste prejudices'.[5]

It is clear that men living in these primitive native lines enjoyed healthier conditions than men herded together in barrack rooms. Indeed the native had 'an instinctive horror of barracks'. When he came off duty he retired to his hut 'into which not even the doctor dares to penetrate. . . . His hut is his home. There he enjoys quiet [and] the society of his wife and children. . . . In a hut which costs two, or it may be four rupees, [he] appears to live three times as securely [from the health point of view] as the English soldier in barracks, which cost 131 rupees per man annually.'[6]

When off duty most of the native soldiers' time was 'occupied in lying on their backs upon their charpoys at the doors of their huts, smoking and sleeping. They are fond of gossiping', said Dr Mouat, 'and have no great occupation. . . . Once or twice a week they wrestle, and play among themselves.' In the lines of nearly every native regiment there was a building set aside as a gymnasium. It is an interesting commentary on contemporary standards that no such thing existed for the white troops.[7]

Many of the native troops chewed opium and smoked 'intoxicating drugs', but they were proverbially sober. The chief exceptions to this were the Sikhs who were 'quite as fond of drink as the Europeans. The low caste Hindoos', added Dr Mouat, 'are also rather fond of it. The so-called Christian drummers were scandalous in that respect; they were usually low Portugese.'[8]

The higher classes of Hindus never allowed meat, fish or spirits to pass their lips. They lived (almost exclusively) upon 'leavened cakes of wheat flour, daily baked upon an iron dish, and washed down with water.'[9] On the other hand, Mohammedans and low caste Hindus, such as the Marathas, had no aversion to animal food. They drank ardent spirits and consumed opium and *ganja* which was made from cannabis.

Before the Mutiny more than three-quarters of the Bengal Army consisted of Hindus, chiefly high-class Brahmins and Rajputs. The Bombay Army was also made up chiefly of Hindus of one sort or another, while in Madras about 60% of the soldiers were of that religion, the lower castes predominating.[10] The 'class' regulations which were introduced in 1864, after reorganization, are detailed on p. 248.

* * *

Promotion of native soldiers in the regular regiments was based most rigidly on seniority. There was always a seniority roll of troopers, and 'the senior man, if he can write and is a well-conducted man, and there is nothing against his character, is promoted. I am sorry to say', declared Lieutenant-Colonel Harington of the 5th Bengal Native Cavalry in 1858, 'that a man generally fulfils twenty years' service before he becomes a non-commissioned officer.' This extreme slowness of promotion also meant that no man gained the rank of native officer before he had reached the age of at least fifty-five and often sixty or over.[11]

In the *silladar* regiments up to the early 1860s the basis of promotion was, as might be expected, much more irregular. In a small number of regiments, chiefly the numbered ones, promotion was based on seniority very much tempered by merit, but, at the other extreme, in the Punjab cavalry and particularly in the Scinde Horse, as Brigadier-General Jacob stoutly declared in 1858, 'promotion by merit alone is the rule, and the commandant is the sole judge of such merit.'[12]

* * *

In 1864 good conduct pay was first introduced into native regiments. The scale was one, two and three rupees per month after six (later three), ten (later nine) and fifteen years' service.[13]

Six years later a very novel order was issued. Every Thursday was henceforth to be a holiday 'on which no field days or parades, except musketry, should take place, nor general, district or regimental court-martials should sit, unless the exigencies of the public service absolutely required it.'[14]

* * *

Elaborate Dress Regulations for the Bengal cavalry regiments came out in 1863. They were certainly not closely adhered to by the older commanding officers, but as the years went by standardization gradually increased. The sowars were to wear *alkalaks* or loose frocks made of serge in the cold season and of white American drill in summer. 'The frock to open to the waist and be fastened with round buttons. . . . The skirts . . . to reach to within three inches of the knee.' The head-dress was to be a turban or *loongee* of the same colour as the regimental facings. The men were to wear on their legs pyjamas 'of Loodianah Dussootee loose above the knee, and fitting tight below, dyed "Mooltanee Muttee" colour.'[15] There were many changes in the regulations over the next couple of decades – too numerous to be detailed here.[16]

Even before the Mutiny Lieutenant-Colonel Harington (an officer of regulars and rather prejudiced against irregulars) accused the commanding officers of some of the *silladar* regiments of introducing 'a system of spoiling the irregulars by aping the dragoons – making the men purchase Nolan's bridles, shabracques, brass-mounted pouch and belt. . . .'[17] After re-organization this process was increasingly but gradually applied not so much by the commanding officers as by the military bureaucrats at much higher levels.

As might have been expected the alterations in the dress regulations of the Bombay and Madras cavalry were fewer and applied more slowly than in that of Bengal.

8

'The class of officers that you get in the cavalry
are generally speaking from the wealthier classes,
are they not? – Yes.'

MAJOR-GENERAL SCARLETT under
examination by the *Royal Commission
on Purchase of Commissions in the
Army*, 1856[1]

(i)

*Officers: classes and types – mode of living – pay and
allowances*

In the 1844 edition of *Queen's Regulations* it is stated that the chief
object of the officers' 'Mess Allowance' was

> 'to enable Regimental Officers of every rank, but more
> especially of the junior ranks, to enjoy the comfort and
> advantages which it is calculated to afford, by placing it in the
> power of every individual to drink a moderate quantity of
> wine daily at or after dinner, on reasonable terms, and such as
> his rate of pay may fairly justify.'

A dozen years later the 1856 edition had been altered to read:

> 'The principal object of this Allowance is to enable the Officers
> of a regiment, of every rank, but more especially of the junior
> ranks, to enjoy the comfort and advantages of a mess, without
> incurring expenses which their pay is not calculated to meet.'[2]

This seemingly trivial change of wording typifies the alteration of
official outlook regarding the British officer which had come about
after the Crimean holocaust. Yet it was little enough reflected in
cavalry regiments, especially the smarter ones. In the late 1860s
Sergeant-Major Mole of the 14th Hussars found that numbers of the
young gentlemen who entered the regiment 'belonged to wealthy
families and had plenty of money at their command, which they
freely spent'.[3] Drinking and betting, both on an ample scale, ensured that generally speaking only the richer man found place in
most cavalry officers' messes. 'It was the common practice in the

9th [Lancers]', wrote Lieutenant (later Major-General Sir) Hugh McCalmont in 1867, 'to drink claret at breakfast in the mess almost as a matter of course'.[4] But the 9th was very much a rich man's regiment and therefore something of an exception. Taking the army as a whole, Lord Panmure, when he was Secretary of State for War in 1856, believed that 'now an officer . . . does not at all suffer in the opinion of his brother officers because he cannot drink wine, or does not choose to drink it.'[5] Nevertheless it was 'more difficult for a poor man to live and maintain his position in the army' in the post-Crimean period 'than it was at the end of the Peninsular War'. 'The pay is the same,' admitted that arch-reactionary General Sir George Brown, 'but things are not any cheaper and habits are more expensive.'[6]

An amusing account of how his fellow officers appeared to him was given in letters home from a young subaltern of the Carabiniers during the suppression of the Indian Mutiny. Lieutenant W. G. Blake's descriptions are not untypical, perhaps, of the types to be found in the less smart regiments of the line in mid-century.

'Colonel Jones', he wrote, 'is a stupid harmless old fellow, very fond of good living and telling stories over and over again. [He is] generally very kind, but exceedingly irritable if anything crosses him. He is however always gentlemanly. Major Bickerstaff, a most odious man, is egotistical to an extent I could never have believed possible in a man possessing good sound sense and military talent which he does; rude in his manner and constantly giving flat contradiction. He is one of those men who would be if it were not for education very vulgar. Wetherby is not a bad kind of fellow but rather too patronising in his [*illegible*] connection with nobility and his talk is constantly about them. He is married to a very flashy little woman who he informs you has a brother in the Guards and whose father he represents as a great swell, but I have not been able to ascertain his name. He takes her about in the march with him. She rides very well, carries a revolver and uses her whip on the natives and though very diminutive is very masculine. . . . Capt. Betty is a conceited, good-looking, rich nonentity; Burder, a bubbling, foolish, tittering boy; Graham, a man who rose from the ranks who seems to think it necessary to preserve his position by a saturnine solidity; Turner, an uneducated boy, curiously ignorant. . . . Beside these we have an exceedingly disagreeable, sneering, scandal-loving Pay-master, and an old excessively conceited, disobliging and un-gentlemanly Quartermaster.'[7]

*   *   *

Field-Marshal Sir Evelyn Wood gives a good picture of his life as a subaltern in a line regiment immediately after the Crimean War.

'Life was easy', he wrote fifty years later. 'The residents in the neighbourhood of barracks showed the young cavalry officers great hospitality, and they spent a considerable proportion of their time in winter in hunting and shooting. This, though pleasant, and, as regards hunting, good educationally for officers, was not sufficient. . . .

'[In 1856] I found the regiment [13th Light Dragoons] in Ireland, with a pack of harriers hunted by the senior subaltern and managed, as were the regimental funds, by the medical officer. The most wealthy officer then with the regiment had about £500 a year, £300 being sufficient to meet all regimental subscriptions and to keep a third horse for hunting, which in-deed was practically enforced by public opinion. Those who, like myself, were anxious for more hunting than they could afford often obtained a mount of a subaltern who, though he had a third horse as a hunter, did not care to ride it. . . .

'We dined at seven o'clock . . . and were never allowed to leave the table until the senior officer got up, the cost of all wine being shared alike. Our senior was often a Cavalry general, living in barracks, and besides marching us past every Sunday before church, he frequently honoured us with his presence at mess, and seldom left the table before half-past ten. There were no billiard-rooms in those days, and smoking was not permitted in the mess, and only cigars in the ante-room after dinner, the cheapest being at sixpence; and as cigarettes were not then invented the effect of these rules was to drive all the officers, who wished to smoke a pipe, off to their rooms.

'The power of the senior lieutenant, commonly called "the mother of the subalterns", was unquestioned. In the summer of 1857 that officer looked up at breakfast time and said to me, "You are for a ball at Dundalk next Tuesday." I demurred, saying, "But I don't want to go," to which he replied severely, "You are to go, I want to hear no more about it," and I went.'[8]

In 1864, when the 10th Hussars were in Ireland, a pack of hounds, known as the Rock Harriers, was purchased from Cashel, 'and', says the regimental historian, 'with Captain the Hon. C. C. Molyneux as huntsman, Lord Valentia and Private Thomas Bowkett as whips, capital sport was shown in the Golden Valley of Tipperary.'[9] Clearly hunting was one sphere in which familiarity between officer and man could exist even in a notoriously 'exclusive' regiment.

In his famous *Soldiers' Pocket Book*, first published in 1869, Colonel (later Field-Marshal) Sir Garnet Wolseley made a plea for a radical change in officers' bearing towards their men.

'To officers brought up in regiments, accustomed to see the ordinary routine of military life go on as a machine, it seldom occurs that any change could be made for the better. In fact', he wrote, 'many pass their lives without discovering that the military career has any higher aim than that of moving men on parade by a most complicated process called drill, and that of keeping order amongst them at all times by a rigid system of espionage, which is believed to be discipline. . . . In our intercourse with the rank and file, we must make them realise that all our interests are identical. . . . Let us sink as far as possible the respective titles of officers, sergeants and privates. . . . Let us give up the phrase "officer and gentleman", substituting that of "soldier" for it; let the word officer be used as seldom as possible, so that the private may really feel that there is no gulf between him and his commander, but that they are merely separated by a ladder, the rungs of which all can equally aspire to mount. . . .

'Study to be familiar without being vulgar, and habit, if not intuition, will soon enable you to be gracious and intimate with your men without any loss of dignity. . . . Cease to treat them as unreasoning children.'[10]

*   *   *

The Commander-in-Chief had discretion as to who should purchase commissions in the army. There can be little doubt that in peacetime at least, when the army was small and applicants were numerous, he sometimes gave preference to so-called gentlemen and to those who 'made interest' successfully. 'If you see a horsedealer's son or a shopkeeper's son in the army', declared a radical civilian witness before the 1857 Royal Commission, 'you may be certain that . . . his father had contrived to ingratiate himself with the class above his own.' Asked whether 'any county attorney or any person who has a little money may put his son into the army and purchase his commission', the same witness replied: 'Certainly not; not unless he has interest to get his name down.'[11] In spite of this probably prejudiced statement, the fact is that the majority of officers were sons of merchants, doctors, clergymen, lawyers and 'little country gentlemen'.[12] Yet it was certain, as Sir Charles Trevelyan, the Assistant Secretary to the Treasury, declared, that 'the large and important class of well-educated young men, who depend for their advancement in life upon their own exertions, and not upon already accumulated means, and who constitute the pith of the law, the church and other active professions, are [by the purchase system] ordinarily excluded from the army.'[13]

It was virtually impossible for a young gentleman to become a cornet of cavalry with a capital sum of less than £1,350. His cornetcy cost him 800 guineas* and he would need £500 to £600 for his initial outfit. Once he had joined, he needed a minimum of about £250 a year, beyond his pay of 8s a day, if he were 'a prudent man', to be able to compete in the mess.[14] The basic messing cost in the cavalry was about 3s 6d a day, but the Duke of Cambridge in the year that he became Commander-in-Chief, believed

'that the least extravagance of officers is in the mess. They are very fond', he told the Purchase Commission in 1856, 'of putting it forward as an excuse to their parents and guardians to get their bills paid, because they are considered legitimate bills; but the real extravagance . . . is in betting and other amusements unconnected with their regiments.'[15]

There were other 'contributions' required from officers. These included an initial payment as well as an annual subscription 'not exceeding twelve days' pay' towards the maintenance of the band ('essential to the credit and appearance of a regiment' according to *Queen's Regulations*).[16]† Further, on joining, the cornet had to pay

---

* Before 1860. After that year until abolition eleven years later, cavalry prices were reduced to those in the infantry. A cornetcy then cost £450. A cornetcy in the Life Guards cost £1,260 and in the Royal Horse Guards £1,200.

† In the cavalry of the line the regimental band consisted of a sergeant (bandmaster), whose pay equalled that of the regimental sergeant-major (3s 10d in 1866), one corporal and fifteen privates (musicians). The 1859 *Queen's*

the riding master three guineas for riding instruction, two guineas for 'breaking horses' and a further guinea for each horse subsequently broken.[17] There were also certain stoppages from an officer's pay. For instance, when he went into an army hospital he was stopped 2s 6d a day, and on board ship when his passage was at the public expense he was stopped 3s 'if supplied with wine and beer' or 2s if not.[18]

On the other hand, beside the mess allowance already referred to, which had first been granted in 1811, and which was refused to officers on overseas stations where the local duty on wine was low, there were certain other officers' allowances. For example, £7 per troop each year was allowed to the regimental riding master to enable him to pay, amongst other things, 'for rough riders'. Then there was the 'Contingent Allowance to Captains' which cost the State over £50,000 a year in 1856. This had been instituted in 1783 and was paid to every captain of a troop. The sum varied according to the number of men in the troop, but it was never less than £18 a year. The object was 'to indemnify the officer for his liability to pay for the repair of arms, for the burial of soldiers, and to pay their debts when their effects are insufficient' (see p. 312). When a man deserted, his captain also had to bear some of the expenses connected with the desertion. The captain usually managed to make a small profit out of this allowance.[19]

The commanding officer and the senior major of a regiment had been granted, since 1803, an annual allowance of £20 each 'in lieu of non-effectives',[20] the origin of which need not be gone into here. It was calculated in 1857 that with this 'Non-Effective Allowance' added to his pay a cavalry lieutenant-colonel received £339 15s a year. However, income-tax, forage for four horses (at $8\frac{1}{2}$d a day each) and mess and band subscription of £104, considerably reduced that figure.[21]

Officers' pay was much the same in 1870 as it had been in the reign of William III. A lieutenant-colonel of the cavalry of the line received £1 3s a day, a major 19s 3d, a captain 14s 7d and a lieutenant 9s.* These sums represented scarcely more and often less than the

Regulations stated that instruments could be 'obtained through the Commandant of the Military School of Music cheaper than if procured direct from the instrument makers, and of one uniform pitch for the whole army.' (*Q.R.*, 1859, 136.)

* In the Household Cavalry (Life Guards and Royal Horse Guards) a lieutenant-colonel was paid £1 9s 2d; a major £1 4s 5d; a captain 15s 1d; a lieutenant 10s 4d, and a cornet 8s.

interest upon the capital which officers laid out in buying their commissions and promotion. In 1854 it was calculated that 'in many cases officers receive less than the annuities they might have purchased for the money they have paid for their commission.'[22]

'There is no doubt that the system of purchase is to a certain degree a protection against favouritism; but if you had a system of distributing commissions by lot or by dice, you might say the same of it.'

M. J. HIGGINS ('Jacob Omnium'), 1856

'In the cavalry a vast number of officers come in who never intend to remain beyond a certain period. . . . When they arrive at the rank of captain they then begin to think whether they will pursue the profession as a profession or not, or whether they are ambitious of higher rank, and they will sell at that time.'

GENERAL SCARLETT in 1856[1]

(ii)

Officers: purchase and sale of commissions: 'over-regulation' prices – half-pay – advantages and disadvantages of system – abolition

Until 1871 when the system of buying and selling of commissions was abolished, the normal way of becoming an officer in the cavalry and infantry was by purchasing a cornetcy or ensigncy. In most cases, too, all promotion up to and including the command of regiments was bought. The system had been in operation from the beginning of the standing army in the seventeenth century. At that time each regiment was formed and maintained by some man of substance to whom his officers stood, as it were, in the relation of 'shareholders' in the venture.[2]

By the time it was abolished the system's ramifications had become prodigious. Most of them have been dealt with more or less exhaustively in volume I (pp. 155–67). In outline it worked in its final form as follows: Except for certain free commissions,* including those given to cadets at the Royal Military College, Sandhurst (see p. 389), which accounted in the 1850s for about one in sixteen, all first commissions were conferred on the nomination of the Commander-in-Chief, except for those in the Household troops to which their Colonels nominated. In the case of about three-quarters of the whole in peace time, when cornetcies became vacant the Commander-in-Chief's nominees purchased them at the regulation price.

As for promotion up to the rank of lieutenant-colonel, when a vacancy arose by the sale of a commission, the senior officer of the next rank below who was prepared to buy received the vacant commission on payment of the regulation price,† if he was 'deemed qualified' by his commanding officer. In practice, of course, only some flagrant misconduct or notorious incapacity would induce a commanding officer to withhold the necessary certificate.‡ If no qualified officer in the regiment presented himself for purchase, an officer who was prepared to pay was brought in to fill the vacancy from another regiment or, as frequently happened, particularly during the 1850s and 1860s, from the half-pay list (see p. 376). The Commander-in-Chief could and sometimes did interfere with this rule. If, for instance, on a major wishing to sell out, only the junior

---

* During the Crimean War those who could raise a certain number of recruits were given free commissions. In the cavalry six such gentlemen, each of whom raised fifty men, obtained cornetcies thus. (*R.C.*, 1861, 87).

† Regulation prices of commissions in the cavalry of the line before 1860 were:

	Full price	Difference in value between the several commissions in succession
Lieutenant-Colonel	£6,175	£1,600
Major	4,575	1,350
Captain	3,225	2,035
Lieutenant	1,190	350
Cornet	840	–

After 1860 the prices were reduced to those of the infantry:

Lieutenant-Colonel	£4,500	£1,300
Major	3,200	1,400
Captain	1,800	1,100
Lieutenant	700	250
Cornet	450	–

‡ To become a captain, two years', and to become a major, six years' service were required.

captain in the regiment was prepared to purchase, an older captain might be brought in from another regiment.[3] The prices of all steps of promotion were fixed by regulation, but more often than not 'over-regulation' prices were also paid (see p. 375).

When an officer exchanged from one regiment to another, he was automatically placed at the bottom of the list of those of his rank in his new regiment. The Duke of Wellington had adopted a rule, which succeeding Commanders-in-Chief continued, never to allow an officer to exchange, as the Duke of Cambridge put it, 'at the moment his regiment was under orders for foreign service, except on medical grounds'.[4] What often happened, therefore, was that in the case of cavalry regiments going out to India, officers with money and influence would wait for about eighteen months to two years before exchanging to regiments at home.

> 'They do not come immediately', as an influential journalist told the 1857 *Royal Commission on Purchase and Sale*, 'because those who are pretty nearly at the top of their grades wait until they get their step, and then exchange back to England, and leave the poorer men to do the duty.
>
> 'I recollect perfectly one man on the staff whom I met in Dublin, who had exchanged so often that it had become quite a joke. When his friends asked him what regiment he was in, he used to call his servant and say, "What regiment are we in now?" He was a man of very good interest, or he could not have done it.'[5]

There were only two ways in which promotion within the regiment could be achieved without purchase: when augmentations of establishment were authorized and when vacancies were created by death. Captains, majors and lieutenant-colonels were nevertheless eligible for promotion for distinguished services without reference to seniority, but such promotion was nearly always to 'army rank' and in no way affected regimental rank, and was therefore unconnected with the purchase system.

An officer who had purchased any of his commissions was normally permitted to retire from the army at any time, without reference to the period of his service. He then received from his successor the regulation value of the commissions which he had bought, provided he had not been guilty of misconduct. About 300 officers sold out each year in the 1840s and 1850s in peacetime.[6] The element of chance came in most strongly when an officer died in the service. The whole of what he had invested in his commissions was then lost. A warrant of 1856, however, sanctioned the repayment of the price of his commissions to an officer's widow, children or other relations, if he had been killed in action or had died of wounds within six months of being wounded. According to the Military Secretary in 1856, there were 'no cases on record of officers in ill health being permitted to sell out in immediate anticipation of their decease'.[7]

Those comparatively few officers who had not bought any of their commissions were usually allowed to retire by selling them after a certain period of service. Lieutenant-colonels and majors were allowed the full price after serving twenty years. Officers who had served a shorter time, so long as it exceeded three years, received back £50 for every year of home service and £100 for each year of foreign service, as well as whatever they might have paid for any step.*

On promotion to major-general an officer lost everything he had invested in his commissions. Lieutenant-colonels after serving as such for three years became from 1854 onwards entitled to the *army* rank of full colonel. From the list of these colonels major-generals were normally selected by seniority as vacancies occurred.

The purchase system thus cursorily described, which the Royal Commission, sitting fifteen years before abolition, condemned as 'vicious in principle, repugnant to the public sentiment of the present day, and equally inconsistent with the honour of the military profession and with the policy of the British empire',[8] prevailed in peace time considerably more in the cavalry than in the infantry. This was largely because, since the cavalry did not go abroad except to India, and never to the really unhealthy climates, there were fewer casualties to create 'death vacancies'.

Another reason, as has been shown, was that more rich men entered the cavalry. This meant that 'over-regulation' prices for promotion were higher than in the infantry. These illegal over-payments were an unavoidable and generally acknowledged part of the purchase system. They could arise thus: an officer, being usually the senior of his rank in a regiment, would announce to his juniors that he would sell out so as to recover the value of his commission,

* The number of officers in the line cavalry who were allowed to sell out, though they had bought none of their commissions, was only eight in the three years immediately preceding the Crimean War. Six of these were lieutenants receiving £1,190 each. (*P.&S.C.*, 364.)

thereby giving each of them who could pay for it a step in promotion. This, however, he would only do if they offered him a good price above the regulation. The juniors would then get together and those who would especially benefit because they were at the top of their rank would offer higher sums than the others. Mr Hammersley of Cox & Co, the army agents, found that 'very frequently perhaps half of the officers will contribute to make up the sum that is called for. A great many of them will pay, particularly among the subalterns. They will each contribute something, £100 or £50 or £10 if there is a sum to be made up.'[9] Before commissions by purchase were gazetted the regulation sum of money was usually lodged with one of the firms of Army Agents, of which Cox & Co was the most famous,* but of the over-regulation payment no official record was ever made and it always took place after the gazette announcement. It was, as Mr Hammersley pointed out, 'a matter of private arrangement. The money generally passes through the agent's hands, but there is no explanation of it. It is subject to the orders of the officer who lodges it.'[10] Thus was the Act which forbade over-payment and prescribed severe penalties on conviction evaded.

The other chief way in which over-payments came about was more complicated. To understand it a word about half-pay is necessary. Up to the early eighteenth century when provision was first made for wounded or disabled officers, half-pay was designed to act as a form of pension for them, as well as a sort of retainer for future service when officers were temporarily unemployed as a result of reductions. When, however, as Sir Charles Trevelyan put it, 'half-pay was brought within the operation of the purchase system, . . . it became impossible . . . to prevent effective officers from receiving an annuity from the public without performing any

---

* In 1827 there were thirteen firms of army agents; in 1878, eight and in 1891, three; in 1923, only two. They acted in effect chiefly as 'Attorney to the Colonel' of each regiment, as well as a sort of financial go-between with the War Office. (Turner, J. D. 'Army Agency', *Glyn's Christmas Annual*, Dec 1933, 59.) The issue of all pay, and such matters as soldiers' remittances, distribution of effects, claims for pensions and, up to 1854 (see p. 306), supply of clothing and accoutrements went through their hands. Apart from often acting as bankers and dealing with purchase transactions, their private work for officers included the dispatch of articles required while on service, and receipt of allowances from relatives. The agency system was said to save the War Office work and money. It seems that virtually all their profit came from their private business. Some aspects of the system continue today, particularly in the Cox and Kings Branch of Lloyds Bank.

service.'[11] Rates of half-pay were always well below half of full pay.*

The most common way in which half-pay was abused so as to effect an overpayment is best understood by a fictional example. Let it be supposed that there are two lieutenant-colonels. One of them, Lieutenant-Colonel Jones commands a regiment. He wishes to stay in the army but he does not want to risk losing the value of his commission by death or by promotion to major-general. In other words he wishes to go on to half-pay but at the same time to ensure that he can ultimately realize the *full* regulation value of his investment. The other lieutenant-colonel – let him be called Williams – is anxious to sell out altogether and to recover at once the full value of his commission. They agree to effect an exchange. Williams comes from half-pay to take Jones's place in the regiment on full pay. To achieve this he pays Jones, who now goes on half-pay, the sum laid down in the Pay Warrant as the difference in value between a half-pay and a full pay lieutenant-colonelcy (£1,314).† Williams then sells at the regulation price (£4,500) the lieutenant-colonelcy which he has just bought, to the senior major next in line for promotion in the regiment. So far all is above board, but Jones is left short of the value of his full pay commission by £1,186. This he now proceeds to obtain as illegal over-regulation payment from the major who has succeeded him in command of the regiment and from the captain, lieutenant and cornet who are at the top of their respective ranks, and each of whom gains a step as a result of Williams's retirement.

*　　*　　*

* Half-pay rates in the cavalry of the line were:

	Up to 1866	After 1870
Lieutenant-Colonel	10s 0d	12s 6d a day
Major	8s 0d	10s 0d a day
Captain	5s 6d	7s 6d a day
Lieutenant	3s 0d	4s 8d a day
Cornet	2s 6d	3s 6d a day

† The differences in value between full and half-pay commissions in 1870 were:

Lieutenant-Colonel	£1,314
Major	949
Captain	511
Lieutenant	365
Cornet	150

In the cavalry over-regulation prices were often outrageously high. Mr Hammersley stated in 1856 that 'anything under double the regulation is considered very reasonable; for instance, in the case of a lieutenant-colonel of the cavalry, the regulation is £6,175; the common price is £14,000 . . . I have heard of £16,000; indeed one very remarkable instance of £18,000.'[12] After 1860, when regulation cavalry prices were reduced to those of the infantry, over-regulation prices declined absolutely; but their proportion of the whole was sometimes even greater than before the decrease. As late as 1869, less than two years before abolition, Lieutenant McCalmont bought his captaincy in the 9th Lancers for £5,125, paying over-regulation of £3,325. He had only joined the regiment in 1865, having already spent £1,550 on his first commission and lieutenancy.[13]

During the Crimean War and to a certain extent during the Mutiny, over-regulation prices, like all other aspects of the purchase system, were virtually suspended. 'The War', said Mr Hammersley, 'has brought everything down to regulation.'[14] Sir Charles Trevelyan asked why an officer in the Crimea should 'lay out hundreds and hundreds for promotion when he may be shot the next hour, and when the casualties of warfare may give him promotion without any cost.'[15] There was also, of course, 'the feeling of officers', as Earl Grey pointed out, 'that they ought not to sell out when the country was engaged in war.'[16] Field-Marshal Sir Evelyn Wood joined the army towards the end of the war.

'The supply of cavalry officers', he wrote many years later, 'did not equal the demand, for some having been killed and others having died, parents were no longer willing to pay £800 for a cornetcy; and when I joined on October 1st, 1855, the depot of the regiment [13th Light Dragoons] in which I had been given a commission was commanded by a Riding-master. The other officers were three subalterns, the senior having six weeks' service. We breakfasted in our rooms, dined at an hotel in the town, and learnt our duties as best we could.'[17]

The Military Secretary prophesied correctly when he said: 'The difficulty in obtaining promotion immediately after peace, from the reductions that must take place, will encourage the practice of giving more than the regulation price.'[18] In peacetime, too, there was generally a sharp up-surge in over-regulation payments when a regiment was ordered for India.

* * *

A number of advantages were claimed for the purchase system. Chief among these was the indisputable fact that by facilitating the retirement of officers, it accelerated promotion which would otherwise, it was asserted, have stagnated in peacetime. Such stagnation had certainly taken place in the non-purchase parts of the army, particularly in the ordnance corps, during the years between Waterloo and the Crimea. In the artillery, engineers, marines and ordnance the system of seniority prevailed pretty well exclusively. Their officers, having no inducement to retire, 'remained in the service far beyond the age which was desirable for the efficiency of the corps.' As the Report of the 1857 Royal Commission put it:

'A lengthened period of peace renders it difficult to keep any military corps in a state of efficiency; a scheme of retirement, therefore, which induces old officers to withdraw from the army, and which replaces them by younger men, must, it is said, be beneficial to the country; and this benefit is still greater if it is effected without any cost to the country.'[19]

The chief argument of the reformers was that purchase was not the only system which could be devised to bring about the required beneficial result. They were also in some doubt as to whether the apparent financial saving was as great as it was made out to be. If it was, they contended, then the state was getting its officers on the cheap which was reprehensible. Among the many objections to the system, there was one put forward by Trevelyan which illustrated a typically unjust and inefficient aspect of the system.

'There is, undoubtedly,' he told the Royal Commission, 'one mode in which promotion is accelerated by purchase, but it is anything but conducive to the efficiency of the army, namely that married officers, however zealous and efficient they may be, are often obliged to sell out in order to avoid risking, by the contingencies of foreign service, the fortune of their families, which have been invested in their commissions.'[20]

The strongest objection to abolition was that under any system other than purchase, such as one of seniority tempered by selection, officers would have, it was said, no security against 'the influence of favour'.[21] One distinguished politician member of the Royal Commission suggested that gentlemen with '£2,000 or £3,000 at their command to provide for younger sons, send them into the army, with the assurance that no officer can be put over their heads, on account of his influence as belonging to an aristocratic family, or his connection with a member of the legislature.'[22]

The advantages and disadvantages of the system have been looked at at some length in volume I. It is sufficient here to say that what was called by Sir Henry Bentinck 'the leap-frog system'[23] was condemned by the 1857 Royal Commission as a 'military policy irreconcileable with justice'.[24] Nevertheless a majority of officers, even including many non-purchase officers, such as the few non-commissioned officers who had been given commissions (see p. 382), thought that the advantages outweighed the disadvantages. General Scarlett, for instance, thought that 'very probably those who cannot purchase derive an advantage by the purchase of others . . . by being moved up in rank.'[25] On the other hand, a case such as that of Riding Master Chamberlain of the Royals, shows how the poor officer could be left behind. He obtained his cornetcy in 1832 and his lieutenancy in 1835. By 1842 he had become senior subaltern and in that position he remained for twelve years, being 'bought over' by nearly twenty officers, including some who entered the regiment after he had reached the head of the subalterns' list. In December, 1854, because of the augmentation which was made at the height of the Crimean War, Chamberlain at last obtained a troop.[26]

That abolition was delayed as long as it was was chiefly due to the cost which it entailed. Parliament felt disinclined to put an end to a system which seemed to save the taxpayer money. The opponents of the Bill, which was introduced by Edward Cardwell, Gladstone's great War Minister, proved formidable. It scraped through the Commons only to be virtually thrown out by the Lords. The Government then discovered that, by an Act of 1809, the whole system was illegal except in so far as it was 'fixed by regulation made . . . by the Crown.' A new Royal Warrant was therefore issued which forced Parliament's hand, and the Act providing the necessary finance was in due course passed.

The Regulation of the Forces Act, 1871, which included other major reforms which will be discussed in the next volume, provided that no new commissions might be purchased after a certain date. 'You may buy your commissions in the Army', exulted *Punch* in a notice to 'gallant but stupid' young gentlemen, 'up to the thirty-first day of October next. After that you will be driven to the cruel necessity of deserving them.'[27] Commissioners were appointed to ascertain the over-regulation prices in every regiment, and to stand in the place of purchasers, with money provided by Parliament. The

Commissioners obtained from every officer above the rank of cornet a statutory declaration of the over-regulation prices paid by him for each rank he had bought. Eliminating fancy prices, they then decided on fair prices for each rank and regiment. In the cavalry of the line over-regulation prices paid varied from £619 for a lieutenant to £6,702 for a lieutenant-colonel. The agreed arrangement was that when an officer, whether he had originally bought his commission or not, wished to retire, he received both regulation and over-regulation price. The eventual cost was £6,150,000. Parliament was persuaded to face this vast expenditure because Cardwell managed to make cuts in other directions. A million pounds a year was saved, for instance, by the withdrawal of troops from Canada.[28] Moreover, the short service system in the ranks (see p. 454) reduced the large expenditure which went into the provision of pensions for old soldiers. The last officer with a vested right in the over-regulation price of his commission retired from the active list in 1909.*

The abolition of purchase was not immediately followed by any great change in the type and quality of officer. Still, of course, if the Commander-in-Chief 'deemed any candidate unfit to serve the Queen, no one would question his right to withdraw him from the competition'.[29] His powers of selection were, if anything, increased. Yet as late as 1903, after the Boer War, a War Office committee judged it 'deplorable that an officer who goes through his career in a dilatory, slovenly, unenterprising manner should be permitted, as he is now . . ., to rise to positions of trust and responsibility as long as he does not commit any grave error or show marked incompetence.'[30] How the surviving hankerers after the vanished system must have relished that remark!

A full account of the ways in which the new system affected the officers and the efficiency of the army will be given in volume III of this work. Here it is sufficient to say that the Royal Commission on Army Promotion and Retirement which reported in 1876 found that the system of promotion at that date was 'as a rule, governed by seniority, tempered by rejection'.

'We find', the Report continued, 'a system now in existence which has been much developed since 1871, under which the lieutenant-colonel in each regiment makes what is called a confidential report at stated intervals upon the conduct,

* Officers were still allowed to arrange exchanges between themselves, with the permission of the War Office, until after the First World War.

abilities and military qualifications of the officers under him, and this report is submitted to the inspecting general for his approval and remarks, and forwarded to the Commander-in-Chief.'

The Commissioners suggested an improvement upon this system which they believed would add to its flexibility. They recommended

'that one unattached promotion to lieutenant-colonel, two to major and ten to captain be placed at the disposal of the Commander-in-Chief annually for the purpose of pushing forward individual officers, whether serving with regiments or on the Staff, who, on the reports of their commanding officers or otherwise, are made known to him as officers of special merit and promise, using these terms in their wide and general sense, and by no means confining them to the possession of mental acquirements.'

This recommendation was put into effect and with minor adjustments remained in force for many years to come.[31]

'An excellent thing for the Army would be promotion from the ranks. Get a few good sergeants made officers, and the "gentlemen" will have to wake up, or be left.'

SERGEANT BLATCHFORD,
late nineteenth century

'Can it be imagined that a man of the class our recruits come from, would be comfortable in gentlemen's society, and having to conform to society manners?'

SERGEANT ACLAND-TROYTE, a 'gentleman' who went through the ranks in the 1870s[1]

(iii)

Officers: commissioned from the ranks – adjutants – paymasters – quartermasters – riding masters – chaplains – surgeons – veterinary surgeons

The ending of the purchase system helped to make possible an increase in the number of officers who rose from the ranks. Yet it is surprising to discover that it was many years before this actually happened. It took a long time for what Samuel Haden, Secretary of the Pensioners' Employment Society, called 'prejudices in the highest quarters' to be worn down. These, he lamented in the mid-1860s, 'are effectual in so limiting the number of commissions [from the ranks] as to prevent any inducement being offered to the young men of Great Britain, as is the case in other nations with no better material, to enter H.M.'s service with the reasonable prospect of attaining commissioned rank.'[2] It was a vicious circle, for only if more non-commissioned officers could become officers would the ranks become more attractive to a higher class of men; and unless they did, there would be too few non-commissioned officers willing and able to become commissioned officers.

In 1866 the Duke of Cambridge declared that he was 'always too happy to promote an intelligent and good non-commissioned officer, but I think', he added, 'I am often doing him a much greater injury in so promoting him than were I not to do so.'[3] This was chiefly because of such a man's inability to compete financially. Although in 1845 Sidney Herbert had arranged that every cornet on promotion from the ranks should receive £150 'by way of outfit', still in the mid-1860s many a non-commissioned officer was refusing a commission rather than face a life of 'perpetual struggle to free himself from the incumbrances . . . imposed upon him as a reward for his good conduct'. 'In this struggle', wrote Herbert, 'he is frequently exposed to temptations which end in his disgrace; at best he must lead a life of self-denial and privation.'[4]

It was unusual for a non-commissioned officer on promotion to cornet to have had less than fifteen years' service – often he had twenty-one or more. His pay, nevertheless, was exactly the same as for a young gentleman of seventeen. Further, any pension or distinguished conduct annuity to which such a non-commissioned officer was entitled, and most of them were, ceased on his becoming an officer. A sergeant-major receiving about 4s a day with free clothing, rations and education for his children, was much better off than a cornet paid 8s a day with his mess bills and band subscription, uniforms, horses and accoutrements to find. In one regiment, a commission was offered to and declined by eight non-commissioned officers in succession.[5]

*　　*　　*

In the ten years 1858 to 1867, 258 non-commissioned officers were promoted from the ranks of the cavalry and infantry. All but twenty-nine of them were appointed to posts on the regimental staff.[6] There were four such posts which were traditionally filled by officers promoted from the ranks. These were the adjutant, paymaster, riding master and quartermaster. During the period covered by this volume an increasing number of adjutancies and paymasterships went to officers other than ex-non-commissioned officers. This change – in a sense a retrograde one – came about in the case of paymasters because there was increasing competition for what was thought to be 'one of the best appointments in the service'[7] from a financial point of view. In the case of the adjutancy, 'gentlemen' officers were beginning to compete for it because the more ambitious ones had begun to recognize that its work was a good training for staff officers. Indeed in a number of regiments there was what was known as a 'sucking adjutant' who looked 'to filling the position of adjutant when it becomes vacant'.[8]

Adjutants received 3s 6d a day extra pay, but even with that General Scarlett did not think that their pay was sufficient to enable those who had risen from the ranks to live in the mess. Most of them, however, were married and did not do so anyway. In 1856, Lord Panmure could say that in many regiments it was very difficult to get any gentleman subaltern 'to take the office of adjutant from the arduous character of its duties and the constant confinement it requires to barracks.' General Scarlett at that date thought adjutants 'to be the most hard-worked and most ill-used men in the service of the cavalry'.[9] But Lord Panmure believed that the labour and trouble which the job entailed meant little to an ex-non-commissioned officer. 'The men who are promoted to that situation from the ranks,' he said, 'come from a much more troublesome situation [i.e. that of senior non-commissioned officer].'[10] Ten years later, Samuel Haden was deploring that adjutancies were 'at present much sought after by subalterns, and but very few of those from the ranks now obtain the appointment.'[11] This was a significant alteration of outlook: a beginning of increased professionalism; a part, too, of the mid-Victorian trend towards serious-mindedness in the upper classes. It was reflected in the remark of Colonel Cameron Shute, 4th Dragoon Guards, who told the Military Education Commission in 1870: 'Now, I am glad to say, military subjects are frequently discussed in the mess room.'[12]

*   *   *

Regimental quartermasters and riding masters* were almost always promoted non-commissioned officers. The posts generally figured prominently on recruiting placards, being held out as within the reach of every recruit. In fact they were arduous positions, not particularly well paid. Their commissions, unlike those of adjutants and others, were unsaleable, and there was no question of promotion. Neither quartermasters nor riding masters could get beyond the relative rank of lieutenant, though quartermasters did sometimes become paymasters and could rise to the rank of major. In all these respects they were treated as inferior to other non-combatant commission holders such as paymasters, surgeons, veterinary surgeons and chaplains. A quartermaster in the cavalry of the line received 8s 6d a day on first appointment. He had to serve thirty-two years, including twelve as quartermaster, before he achieved 13s 6d. This contrasted unfavourably with the pay of a paymaster who started with 12s 6d and received 17s 6d after ten years in the post and £1 2s 6d after twenty.[13] These comparatively high rates were accounted for by the fact that large sums of money were constantly passing through the paymaster's hands. For the same reason the War Office demanded a sizeable security from non-commissioned officers who were to be promoted to the paymaster's department.[14]

Chaplains, medical officers and veterinary officers were paid less than paymasters. On first appointment each category received 10s a day, but whereas assistant surgeons and chaplains after fifteen years' service rose to 17s 6d, veterinary surgeons achieved only 14s. This reflected the continuing derogatory attitude towards 'vets' which has been discussed in detail in volume I (see p. 111). They were still not treated as 'gentlemen'.† Until Lord Gough presented Mr

---

* The historian of the 16th Lancers tells a charming story concerning that regiment's riding master:

'In July, 1858, HRH the Prince of Wales [aged sixteen] was attached to the Regiment for a course of equitation. Colonel Keppel, the equerry-in-waiting, went through the usual course in the riding school with the Prince, and the Riding-Master, T. Brown, caused great amusement by using Colonel Keppel as a sort of Royal "whipping boy", and corrected him for HRH's faults in riding, as he was afraid to speak to the Prince himself.' (Graham, 124.)

† Some of them were nevertheless highly respected. Mr Thacker of the 10th Hussars for instance was 'not only remarkable as a professional man of the greatest ability, but was one of the finest horsemen that ever got into a saddle'. (Liddell, 336.)

Sir Frederick FitzWygram, bart, who at one time commanded the 15th

34. (*inset*) Sir Dighton Probyn, V.C. in the uniform of the 2nd Punjab Cavalry,
c. 1859

35. Captain F. J. Craigie and Lieutenants F. Lance and R. Clifford, 2nd Punjab
Cavalry, 1859

36. Risaldar Shahzada Wali Ahmad (centre) and Jemadars Ali Ahmad and Jowahir
Singh (later Risaldar Major), 2nd Punjab Cavalry, 1859

Cullimore, the veterinary surgeon of the Bengal Horse Artillery in 1850, there was a rule which specifically excluded them from Court! Until 1891 they were condemned to remain, however long their service, the juniors of the relative rank in the army, except for choice of quarters. Minimal improvements in pay and pensions remained consistently behind those of the other regimental staff officers. In the 1850s the average remuneration of a veterinary officer was only £135 a year for the first twenty years of his service.

A committee of the War Office reaffirmed in 1859 that it was right 'to make a distinction between the pay of the horse doctor and the doctor of human patients', and that the relative rank of veterinary officers ought always to be kept low 'as these officers serve with regiments and corps [the cavalry and the artillery] where it is important to prevent any approach to the rank of the Commanding Officer'. The first full-time, non-civilian Principal Veterinary Surgeon of the Cavalry was not appointed until 1839. He was succeeded in 1854 by John Wilkinson who had served as veterinary surgeon of the 17th Lancers for some years. He became the first Principal Veterinary Surgeon of the army as a whole in 1859 and died in harness twenty-two years later. Wilkinson, although he was entitled to, never wore uniform, always appearing instead in frock coat and tall hat. He did his best to improve the status and authority of the officers in his service. The Warrant he obtained in 1859 laid down various grades of officers. The highest, Staff Veterinary Surgeon, was equivalent to a major, the first time that that rank had been attainable by veterinary officers. For the first time, too, retiring ages were laid down.

Very little was done in Wilkinson's time to improve the standard of professional competence or the effectiveness of supervision of the regimental farriers. Nor was the chronic shortage of medicines and means of caring for sick horses remedied. The first serious attempts to establish 'Sick Depôts' for animals on active service were made during the Abyssinian campaign of 1867–68, but these were 'necessarily crude, being improvised in the Field instead of being an integral part of the Expedition.'

In the Crimean War the number of veterinary officers, all of them

Hussars, did much to make the veterinary art more esteemed. He even, when a subaltern, graduated as a veterinary surgeon – a very unorthodox thing for a cavalry officer to do. (Tylden, 143.) He never in fact practised professionally, but he wrote a number of text books, the most widely known of which, *Horses and Stables,* ran into many editions.

regimental, in March, 1855, was only eighteen out of a total of forty-four in the whole army. By the war's end in 1856, there were forty-three, only twenty-five of them being more than temporaries, out of sixty-four in the army. The Crimean army had no Principal Veterinary Surgeon until January, 1856. Not till ten years later was the first Principal Veterinary Surgeon appointed in India, and even then he had no jurisdiction over the government studs or the veterinary officers attached to them.[15]

'Eventually, I suppose [the officer] feels an interest in his profession, and desires to have a knowledge of it? – I think not in the English army, because we do not desire to make our officers more than serjeant majors.'

CAPTAIN H. M. HOZIER, 3rd Dragoon Guards, in reply to Earl de Grey, Chairman of the 1870 Military Education Commission[1]

(iv)

Officers: examinations for commissions – junior department, Royal Military College, Sandhurst – examinations for promotion – Staff College, Sandhurst – other specialist instruction

'In order to have some certainty that the applicants for commissions . . . have been educated as gentlemen',[2] the Duke of Wellington in 1849 introduced a qualifying examination. With the exception of university graduates, no one from that year onwards could become an officer without passing it.* The examinations were always held by the professors of the Royal Military College at Sandhurst (see below). At first they were very elementary affairs carried out to a

* For six months in 1857–8, because of the pressing need for expansion due to the Mutiny, a circular was in force permitting commissions 'without examination on the condition of the applicant raising a certain number of recruits'. How many availed themselves of this is not clear. (*M.E.C.*(1), lxix.)

large extent *viva voce*. In the only part of them which had a military character, namely fortification, it was authoritatively stated that 'the knowledge required would easily be mastered in a week.'[3] In early 1854 Sidney Herbert found that it was 'too technical, too limited, and within its limits too severe'. It led to candidates 'cramming up a few books which happened to be in use at Sandhurst, without affording any test of general education.'[4] The examination became a little more sophisticated as the years went by. In 1867 it consisted largely in demonstrating a knowledge of 'arithmetic, including vulgar and decimal fractions, proportion, extraction of the square root, and simple interest. Algebra, including fractions, simple equations, and questions producing them: Euclid, the first three books.' The candidate was required, too, to write English correctly and 'in a good legible hand from dictation, and to compose grammatically.'[5] Major-General Sir Owen Tudor Burne, who took his examination in 1855, found that candidates also had to 'translate parts of Livy's *History of Rome* and Virgil's *Aeneid* with parsing and prosody; to show a fair knowledge of French and German; to answer questions in history and geography, and to make tracings of fortifications in presence of the examiners.'[6] According to the Royal Commission on Public Schools of 1864, the examination required nothing that was 'beyond the reach of any boy of moderate industry and ordinary capacity'.[7] Nevertheless it was sufficiently taxing for the failure rate to be 25% over the four years 1866 to 1869. This was in spite of the growth, in considerable numbers, of private tutors, known as 'army crammers', some of them pretty disreputable. The most famous establishment was that of Captain Lendy at Sunbury who concentrated on the memorizing of facts.[8] In 1869 Colonel Valentine Baker, commanding the 10th Hussars, roundly condemned the cramming system. The young men who go through it, he told the Military Education Commission, 'forget what they have thus superficially learnt as quickly as they attain it ... They associate together in numbers at a most dangerous age without any decided control, and often acquire bad and desultory habits which affect the whole character of their after lives.'[9] The Army Class at Eton and 'the military and civil department' at Cheltenham College were both instituted in part to prevent the need for crammers. In 1859 a new public school, named Wellington College as a memorial to the great Duke, was opened. It was intended partly for the education of army officers' sons at reduced fees. Initially about twenty of these entered the army every year.[10]

Though it had not always been the case, the numbers of public-school boys who went into the army in the 1860s and 1870s were not large. Within a three year period, only 122 out of 1,975 candidates for commissions (besides those from Sandhurst) had been at public schools other than Cheltenham or Wellington. Nor was the number of public-school candidates for Sandhurst very great. During 1868 and 1869 out of 320 admissions only 16 came from the regular public schools, but from Cheltenham and Wellington the admissions were more numerous.[11]

*   *   *

The junior department of the Royal Military College at Sandhurst was founded in 1801. Its chief purpose was 'the instruction of those who from early life are intended for the military profession', especially 'the sons of meritorious officers'.[12] From the late 1850s onwards there had been suggestions from high quarters that Sandhurst should become the sole avenue to a commission.[13] The report of the military education commission of 1870, however, concluded that an exclusive military college 'would not harmonize with the general feeling of the country or with the views of parliament'.[14] Nevertheless, from 1874 onwards, as a result of a Royal Warrant of 1871, virtually all officers for line regiments passed through Sandhurst.

From 1832 till 1855 the junior department had been entirely self-supporting, the fees of the 'gentlemen cadets' covering all expenses. In 1858, this and many other aspects of the institution were changed – indeed its whole character underwent a radical transformation. Up to that year cadets had been admitted at thirteen to fifteen years of age for an average of three and a maximum of four years. The course they took was intended to complete their general education while at the same time giving them some military instruction. Now the establishment had been converted from a school for boys into a college for young men. The minimum age of admission was raised to sixteen, and (from 1862) the maximum to nineteen. The course was limited at first to two and, in 1865, to one and a half years, and it became almost exclusively professional. Another major change was that the principle of competition for admission replaced, with only a few minor exceptions, the Governor's list and the 'rule of rotation' which had hitherto been strictly adhered to.[15]

Up to 1855 there had been places for about 180 boys; in 1865 the number of young men was 300. This expansion was chiefly accounted for by the increased number of non-purchase commissions arising from the amalgamation of the Indian with the Imperial armies (see p. 236). From 1862 onwards, except for a dozen or so given each year to non-commissioned officers and to 'gentlemen who have held the appointment of page to Her Majesty', all non-purchase commissions were reserved for Sandhurst cadets. These were thrown open to competition amongst them, excepting those which were reserved for Queen's and Indian cadets. Both these classes of cadets were entitled to receive free commissions on passing a qualifying examination.[16]

Though semi-adult cadets had replaced the military schoolboys of earlier days, the regulations and conditions at Sandhurst, always pretty strict and spartan, were not changed until the cadets staged a revolt in 1862. For instance, the feeding arrangements as described by Cadet Tulloch in 1852 were in no way altered till four years after the great change had come about.

'For breakfast', wrote Tulloch, 'a cadet had a bowl of boiled milk, as much bread as he wanted, and a pat of decidedly nasty butter, which had to be macerated in some of the milk to make it palatable.

'Dinner consisted of a leg or shoulder of mutton for each table of ten cadets, with an unlimited supply of waxy potatoes in their skins, and as much bread and small beer as was wanted. . . . The second course on alternate days consisted of boiled rice-pudding, which was very fair, or baked plum-duff, known as stick-jaw, so badly cooked that few could eat it.

'Such necessary articles of diet as green vegetables or fruit-tarts were quite unknown.

'On Sundays the cadets had ribs of beef instead of mutton. . . . The evening meal, tea and bread and butter.'[17]

The revolt which succeeded in improving matters did not come to an end until the Commander-in-Chief himself intervened. Hugh Thomas in his *Story of Sandhurst* tells how His Royal Highness went towards the 'redoubt' in which the rebel cadets had installed themselves armed with loaves of bread,

'accompanied only by his A.D.C. He was permitted to approach very closely to the rebel headquarters. Here he made a short speech in ". . . his own inimitable manner." This meant a large number of "damns" and other swear words, all delivered in terms of the utmost solemnity. No one perhaps even in the history of the British Army has had quite such a strong sense of personal dignity as Cambridge. In his speech to the mutineers, nevertheless, he undertook to review personally all their grievances. . . . He added, however, a strict homily on the disgraceful nature of the rebels' action, adding that severe punishments could only be avoided, whatever the justice of their cause, on the assumption that such an occurrence was never repeated. . . .

'The mutiny thus came to an end. And the food and general conditions of the cadets were generally improved without delay. Sofas were even ordered; and the following extraordinary minute was penned in Horse Guards parade: "it is very important that a sofa should be supplied, in order that weakly and young cadets may repose upon them instead of being obliged to sit all day in armchairs." A canteen, an anteroom, a billiard-room and a reading-room ("equipped" with books) were put in at Sandhurst in 1864. The food was greatly improved, three normal large Victorian meals being provided every day.'[18]

* * *

Amongst the many criticisms of the training at Sandhurst was one made by Major-General H. D. White, commanding the Cavalry Brigade at Aldershot in 1869. He declared that the Sandhurst course did not even pretend to give a knowledge of cavalry drill to the cadets. On hearing this evidence at the military education commission, one of its members, Lord de Ros, muttered: 'Have you not heard of "killed before drilled"?'

In General White's experience the best cavalry officers that he had seen were 'Eton boys or Harrow boys'. 'As far as the cavalry is concerned', he added, 'the cadets and young officers who come from Sandhurst are not better than those who come from a good public school. . . . In the cavalry we have not so many Sandhurst cadets as the infantry have, in proportion to those who come from public schools and other schools.'[19]

* * *

Examinations for promotion to the ranks of lieutenant and captain were first introduced in 1850. Conducted regimentally by the commanding officer and the two next senior officers, they were rather a farce even when carried out conscientiously. But 'little attempt was made, even nominally, to enforce the regulations.'[20] In practice therefore they had no value whatever. Completely new regulations were promulgated in 1858. The regimental examinations, which had included geography and history, were abolished, and the new ones were made entirely professional. A board appointed by the officer commanding the district was set up to examine candidates for promotion. It consisted of three field officers selected so far as possible from regiments other than the candidates'. It reported on each one direct to the Military Secretary. As well as all the usual matters such as drill and the duties of orderly officers, candidates had to show a good knowledge of *Queen's Regulations*, especially in regard to the pay and messing of troops. In the cavalry a prospective lieutenant had, amongst other things, to 'be able to put a troop through carbine, lance and sword exercise, and to exercise both a squad and a troop in the drill and evolutions prescribed in the Cavalry Exercise Book.' He had also to show himself master of 'the detail of saddlery, the mode of fitting the saddle, bridle, &c.' Cornets were expected to pass the examination for promotion to lieutenant before completing eight months' service.[21] The Commander-in-Chief made it clear that he would 'not hesitate to promote (either regimentally or from other corps) officers who may have passed the required examination, in place of the idle and incompetent.' By Royal Warrant of 1871 the rank of cornet was abolished. It was replaced by that of sublieutenant. Another, more important, provision was that if within three years of first appointment a sub-lieutenant had not qualified for promotion to lieutenant, he was compelled to resign.

*   *   *

Up to the early 1850s, beyond the mere routine of drill and regimental duties, officers received no instruction in any subjects whatever. The only exceptions were those very small numbers who passed through the senior department at Sandhurst. From 1820 till 1858 there had never been more than fifteen officers there at a time. In 1854, indeed, there were only six. The 1808 Royal Warrant laid down that the purpose of the department was the instruction of officers

'in the scientific part of their profession, with the view of enabling them better to discharge their duty when acting in command of regiments (the situation in which they can best recommend themselves to us, and be entitled to hope for advancement in the higher stations of our service), and at the same time of qualifying themselves to be employed in the Quartermaster-general and Adjutant-general's departments.'[22]

In 1858 the senior department was converted into the Staff College. Its standards began to improve. The range of subjects taught and the number of students gradually increased. Yet in the late 1860s the number of officers allowed to go on the staff was limited to two per regiment.[23] Between 1856 and 1881 – a quarter of a century – only thirty-eight cavalry officers passed out successfully.[24] By no means were all staff officers products of Sandhurst. 'All the personal appointments', pointed out Captain Hozier of the 3rd Dragoon Guards in 1869, 'and the appointments of military secretaries or assistant military secretaries, which are the best appointments of any, are given to men who have never passed through the Staff College.'[25]

Generally speaking, officers were not selected for the Staff College. They volunteered. 'Consequently', as the Military Secretary put it, 'it would be bold to say that there are not officers who are not better qualified in some respects than those who go there, for there are many officers of independent fortune who would rather remain with their regiments than qualify for the staff.'[26] Colonel Valentine Baker of the 10th Hussars thought that officers often got themselves into the Staff College 'to escape regimental duty, or because they are going to be married. . . . Men of a studious, quiet turn of mind prefer the hard mental work of the Staff College to the active habits of real military life.'[27] The Deputy Adjutant-General told the military education commission that 'the most active, energetic and practical officers, both in the field and in quarters, prefer remaining with their regiments. . . . Officers', he added, 'who dislike the restraint of discipline, who are married, who wish to avoid foreign service, in many instances compete for admission.'[28] The root of the matter, as Captain Hozier remarked, was that 'commanding officers only care to have their officers to know their regimental drill, and do not care to have them more highly educated.'[29] This parochial attitude, which was probably even more strongly entrenched in the minds of junior officers than in their colonels', took many years to die out. In 1875, for example, Lieutenant George

Gough of the 14th Hussars could say that there was a 'very strong feeling indeed' against officers of his regiment going to Sandhurst, 'because', he said, 'it throws the duties on others, and of course they go to the Staff College for their own advancement and not for the good of the regiment in any way.'[30] The army in Gough's view and in that of most officers was still, it seems, no more than a collection of autonomous regiments!

From time to time there were criticisms of the type of teaching at the Staff College. One such concerned military drawing. It came from Sir Hope Grant when he was Quartermaster-General:

> 'It appears to me', he said, 'that those drawings are . . . very beautifully done. . . . Some of the officers have told me that they have taken three or four months to make one drawing; that appears to me to be time and trouble thrown away. I should like an officer to be taken out to ride, and to draw a sketch of the country from his eye rather than from measurement.'[31]

The same subject, as it affected regimental officers, was touched upon by Colonel Cameron Shute of the 4th Dragoon Guards. Writing in 1870, he said 'The chief want I have found amongst the officers of the two cavalry regiments I for some years commanded, is a knowledge of military drawing.'[32] In 1857, Survey Classes had been started for the instruction of officers quartered at Aldershot camp. Twelve years later Colonel Baker reported that 'the officers do not attend them in any numbers. They do not like leaving their regiments for many reasons. In the first place if they do so it throws the duties upon other officers.'[33] In an effort to improve the standard of military drawing and observation, commanding officers were directed in 1859 to require from their officers 'reports, and, if possible, sketches of the roads traversed when route marching in winter.'[34]

For the first eleven years of the Staff College's existence officers passing out of it had to spend some months with units of those branches of the army in which they had not served. Amongst those infantrymen attached in 1863 to the 10th Hussars, for instance, was Major Pomeroy Colley, whose brilliant career and tragic death at Majuba will be discussed in the next volume. From 1870 on, this practice was stopped and instead 'p.s.c.'s* were attached during the

* These letters after an officer's name meaning 'passed staff college' first appeared in the Army List in 1864.

'summer drill season' to a general's staff at a camp where all three arms were represented.[35]

* * *

What was virtually the first specialist training centre in the army's history was established in 1853. It was the School of Musketry at Hythe which came about so as to satisfy the need to train a proportion of all officers and men in the new systems of musketry which had followed the introduction of rifled arms. Even officers from cavalry regiments as well as troopers underwent courses there. From 1869 onwards some also attended the School of Engineering at Chatham, where they learned the elements of military signalling.[36] One of the first to do so was Cornet H. S. Gough of the 10th Hussars. Whilst marching to a royal review that year he supervised 'the system of signalling with flags . . . for the first time'. Communication was 'maintained between the columns as they advanced on the opposite banks of the river Thames.'[37]

These were some of the early, cautious steps on the long road towards the production of a larger number of officers acquainted at least with the rudiments of the higher military sciences. But, as Valentine Baker put it in a memorandum for the military education commission in 1870:

'Nothing is more difficult . . . than to carry out any sound system of military education in the British army. Military education has for its object the fitting of an officer for a state of war; but in time of peace in our service there is little that in any way represents war. . . .

'In foreign armies at the present time the officers have very superior advantages. During the comparatively short time their camps are formed, war is as nearly represented as it can be in time of peace. Bodies of men are moved as in a campaign, and on ground not perfectly well known to them; combinations and strategical movement are practised, and consequently, the powers of staff and other officers are more or less tested, and their theoretical military education is brought into practical use.

'With us, from the nature of the ground selected, its limited extent, and certain routine customs which apply only to peace, officers have little chance of acquiring or utilizing any real military education.'[38]

More pithily if with some exaggeration, Captain Hozier put his finger on the chief difference between the British and the continental officer when he said: 'A Prussian officer knows perfectly well the whole of the art of war, whereas an English officer may be for years and years in our service, and only see one regiment or one battalion.' He added another important consideration: 'A young officer in our service has a great deal to do in the way of amusement; he has plenty of hunting and shooting and things of that kind to attend to, which are more amusing at the moment than instruction in military subjects.'[39]

'[Sir De Lacy Evans:] There is a publication by Lord de Ros, in which he says that the officers in the Company's service may be considered ... to be a rather more educated or professional body of officers than those in the British army, and ... that the officers do instruct themselves? – [Philip Melvill, Secretary, Military Department of HEIC:] Many, no doubt, do pursue their studies after joining their corps. They are found for the most part to be highly qualified for their duties. They are placed in responsible charges at an early period of their career, and thus gain experience and self-confidence which are of the greatest value.'

Royal Commission on Purchase and Sale, 1857[1]

(v)

Officers: India: 'direct' appointments to Company's regular regiments – pre-amalgamation: promotion by seniority – making up a purse – mortality rates – retirement system – pay, allowances and deductions – batta *– examinations – accommodation – servants – the Crawley affair, 1858–63*

In the Honourable East India Company's regular regiments, there was no purchase system for the European officers. Instead, young gentlemen wishing to join did so on what were called 'direct' appointments. They went before a board of examiners and if they passed the prescribed test they were sent out to India direct without passing through any military college in Britain. Once allotted a regiment they were not allowed to exchange into another until they had gained a lieutenant-colonelcy.[2] Most officers were very young when appointed, many of them being no older than seventeen years of age.

Promotion was governed almost entirely by seniority. Consequently it took a cornet, on average, fifteen years to become a captain, twenty-nine to reach the rank of major and over thirty to become a lieutenant-colonel. To command of a regiment a lieutenant-colonel had no automatic claim. Seniority then no longer counted. Selection by the Commander-in-Chief took its place.[3] In spite of quite liberal pensions (see below), the financial inducements to retire were not as great as under the purchase system at home. Consequently, in an attempt to ameliorate the stagnating effects of strict adherence to the seniority rule, a practice had grown up whereby regimental officers subscribed amongst themselves so as to add 'to the comforts', as a memorandum of the Court of Directors put it, 'of a senior officer on his retirement from the service upon the pension to which he may be entitled'. The practice, which seems to have applied chiefly to the rank of major and not at all to lieutenant-colonels, was 'permitted by the authorities though not sanctioned by law'. Contributing was, of course, optional, but as the report of the Purchase and Sale Royal Commission stated a trifle disingenuously, 'In most cases a young man would sooner incur pecuniary inconvenience than withhold his aid from a scheme so popular in the regiment.'[4] This in fact often meant that poorer officers were forced to raise money at a high rate of interest, thereby in some cases seriously embarrassing themselves. Philip Melvill, the Secretary of the Company's Military Department, believed that 'very few officers retire without being induced to do so by their brother officers.' He gave an example of how the system worked:

'[A senior officer] is entitled to claim his pension, which cannot exceed £456 a year, and he says to his brother officers, I cannot live upon my pension. [It] will not maintain me and my family, but I am ready to accept it if you can make up a purse for me. . . . All officers of the regiment contribute . . . in proportion to their proximity to the step (i.e. in proportion to their rank). . . .

He who gets the step will contribute perhaps one half, and the others in proportion down to the last.'

The total sums subscribed varied considerably. In one case as much as £6,000 was believed to have been paid, but this was an exceptionally high figure.[5] The average for a majority was about £2,500 to £3,000. The arrangements were usually made through 'an office of agency'.[6]

There were two other factors which helped to speed up promotion under the heavy hand of the seniority rule. First was the high mortality rate. This had averaged out at 38 deaths per year per 1,000 for officers of both the Royal and the Company's officers over the twenty years ending 1833: between three and four times the rate at home. Though there had been some improvement over the years, the rate was still exceptional thirty years later as was shown by the high premium which the officer going out to India had to pay for life insurance. At the age of thirty the annual premium on a life in England was £2 4s 10d to insure £100[7] whereas on an officer's life in India it was £4.

The other factor which helped to accelerate promotion was that numerous officers were tempted away from their regiments 'to supply', as General Vivian put it, 'the necessary auxiliary troops',[8] to join the various staffs or to take up other para-military and even civilian posts such as were provided by the surveying and public works departments. Almost invariably too the officers who were selected to raise irregular troops and command them were drawn from the Company's regular regiments. This was probably the greatest attraction which service in the Company's regular armies afforded the ambitious young man. The extra-regimental opportunities which opened up for him were often lucrative and absorbing. 'Every young officer', said Lieutenant-Colonel Harington of the 5th Bengal Native Cavalry in 1858, 'who comes out now says, "My father is a director [of the Company]" and so and so, "directly I have passed my examination I shall be off, and care nothing for the regiment". And no wonder, when the threat of being sent back to one's regiment is held out as a punishment for misconduct or misbehaviour.' This drain had increased very considerably of recent years with every new acquisition of Indian territory.

Handsome allowances were provided for officers who went on to the staff. How they got there and of what calibre they were much exercised Lieutenant-Colonel Harington: 'Regimental officers', he said, 'are constantly taunted with the remark "that the best and most intelligent officers are selected for the staff." Officers *are* selected', he added, 'but the *rule* is interest, and merit the *exception* that guides these selections. . . . Commanding officers are seldom or ever asked the character or fitness of an officer for staff employ.'[9]

Officers of the Royal army invariably took precedence over Company's officers of the same rank. This sometimes caused much ill feeling and jealousy. It also indicated the lower social status accorded the Company's officers. They were not normally allowed to serve outside the Company's domains, which automatically prevented the only British officers who had recent experience of war from taking part in an European conflict such as the Crimean War.

*   *   *

There was no half-pay system as at home. Officers in poor health were allowed to retire after a certain period of service on the actual half-pay of their rank, but they could never thereafter return to the active list on full pay as in the Royal Army. An officer in good health, *whatever his rank*, was permitted to retire on the full pay of a captain after twenty years' service, on that of a major after twenty-four years, on that of a lieutenant-colonel after twenty-eight years, and that of a full colonel after thirty-two years.[10] This was a quite different and more generous pension arrangement than in the Royal Army.

Pay was much the same but, so far as it is possible to judge, allowances were rather more liberal than at home. The Company did not furnish forage, fuel, tents or lodgings as the British Government did. Money allowances were paid instead. Philip Melvill believed that these were ample. The tent allowance he thought was 'more than the officers could spend'. In the regular cavalry, troop commanders had 'very advantageous' contract allowances for saddlery and other equipment for the troop horses. The command of a regiment was worth at least £1,700 a year on full *batta*, and about £1,450 on half *batta*. *Batta* was an extra payment much the same as the field allowance at home, except that it was paid whether the army was in the field or not. All officers who were stationed within 200 miles of the capital of a Presidency received half *batta*. Beyond that radius they were paid the full allowance.[11]

As at home, there were numerous 'contributions' required from officers of the Company. 'Out of my 300 rupees' pay', wrote Cornet Combe of the 3rd Bombay Light Cavalry in 1856, 'I receive 10! So many deductions now for horses, mess, band etc. funds, and expenses.'[12] If for the ranks life in India was a good deal cheaper than at home it was probably not so for the officers. The ordinary necessities of life were much less dear than in Britain, but the luxuries, 'which for the most part to the British officer are necessaries',[13] were considerably more expensive.

The only examinations which an officer had to pass before being promoted were in languages. Command of a troop, for instance, depended upon proof of ability to 'converse freely in the Hindustani language with the men'. No officer could qualify for the staff unless he had passed 'a superior examination in Hindustani',[14] or in some cases another native language.

*　　*　　*

Lieutenant Blake of the Carabiniers gave in 1858 a good description of a typical Indian station. He found that at Dum Dum there was 'no town whatever, but large barracks and around in every direction numerous villas generally of one storey only in pleasant gardens and connected by numerous accommodation roads which intersect each other in every direction.' 'Officers', he wrote in another letter, 'do not live in barracks with the men, but rent bungalows, or what we should call villas . . . distant from the barracks from a mile to a mile and a half. I can assure you I felt very unsafe at the idea of sleeping with open doors and windows a mile and a half distant from the men.'[15]

General Sir Bindon Blood, when he was a young subaltern in the early 1870s, found that

> 'in the "compound" or garden of every house . . . apart from the servants' huts, [there was] a set of rooms used as a guest house, but styled the "bibi khana" – ladies' quarters – and originally built to accommodate native ladies. I was told that the custom which gave rise to the building of these quarters had disappeared soon after the Mutiny.'[16]

The Indian Sanitary Commission reported that the 'great advantage, as regards health, possessed by officers, is living in detached buildings, with free external ventilation. But their quarters', the report added, 'partake of the general sanitary disadvantages of the station as to drainage, water supply, &c.' Generally speaking, officers lived in great luxury. A junior officer of the 8th Hussars for example, found himself in 1861 sharing with a fellow officer 'a very fine house. . . . We have five rooms each on the flanks of the building and two large reception rooms in the middle, with a kind of ante-chamber between the big rooms and the front door.'[17]

The leisurely formality of life in a native regiment's mess is conveyed by Bindon Blood's account of his time with a Bombay regiment in 1871: 'I found that we all took our three principal meals together at the mess at fixed hours, and each meal finished with pipes and cigars in the mess-room.'[18]

Even the most junior officers were attended upon by large numbers of native servants. Lieutenant Blake believed that fewer were considered necessary in Bombay and Madras than in Bengal,

> 'as caste is not so strictly carried out. You require in the first place a bearer, who is your valet and body servant, who dresses you, takes care of your clothes, money and looks after the other servants and pays them. This man could not be induced under any circumstances to touch a plate or anything beyond tea or coffee. The next man is a Rhitumdgar. . . . If you go out either to mess or to dine out he accompanies you and I dare say you will laugh when I tell you that he takes with him your chair, your knife and fork, spoon, glasses, etc. All [that is] provided by your host being the food itself. . . .'

He also cooked and waited at table when his master was at home. The general servants included 'a water-carrier, a gardener, a watchman to keep away jackals at night, for they abound in this neighbourhood and are very partial to boots, and as we sleep with doors and windows open they might easily help themselves.'[19] A Royal Warrant of 1852 had laid down that under no circumstances were European soldiers to be 'employed in any way as servants in hot climates.'[20]

When the Carabiniers settled down for the hot weather at Muttra in 1859, after the northern campaigns against the rebels were over, Blake wrote home giving a description of how his day was usually spent:

> 'On parade at five, at which hour it has just become light. I think you wished to know the length of the day in India. It varies from the longest day – light about five in the morning

and dark about half past six in the evening, to the shortest: light about half past six in the morning and dark about half past five in the evening, and as you know there is hardly any twilight. . . . On parade for riding drill at five which continues till half past six, then we remain at stables till half past seven to superintend the cleaning and feeding of the horses. We then have to inspect the men's horses and breakfasts which takes up till about a quarter to eight, by which time the sun is getting dangerous. Home to a bath and breakfast, etc.; then we have a long day before us of heat and languid attempts to read and fighting against drowsing till five in the afternoon, when another bath brings you to half past five at which hour we can again safely go out. We have either parade or evening stables till half past six at which latter however the attendance of one officer only a troop is required, so if it is not your turn for duty a ride round the station carries one on to mess at seven. We do not remain long there, as it is in a tent, air very hot and uncomfortable, and by nine we are all in bed with a nigger and a fire (*sic*) to keep away insects and ourselves cool. We roll about trying to sleep till morning when *da capo*.

'There is not the slightest society here, for though we have three married officers, no visiting goes on at all. If you call they are not visible and we can only know that they still exist by seeing a languid face under the hood of a buggy taking its evening drive. Besides there are only the wives of the two magistrates here and of the other civilians, in all not half a dozen who all seem to live in the same secluded way. The only two unmarried ladies are two so exceeding plain and vulgar that even in this solitude they attract no attention. They are the nieces of an officer of the customs.'[21]

*　　*　　*

Life during the hot season must often have been unbearably trying. There is much evidence to show that tempers became frayed, prejudices magnified and that unsavoury rows developed, often bringing to the surface the less pleasing traits in men's characters. Sometimes the results hit the headlines and turned into national scandals. Such a one was the notorious Crawley affair. Lieutenant-Colonel Thomas Crawley took over command of the 6th Inniskilling Dragoons not long after the regiment arrived in India at the end of 1858, just too late to take part in the Central Indian campaigns. In the days of his predecessor, Lieutenant-Colonel Shute, who had been recommended for the Victoria Cross after Balaklava, actual fighting had broken out in the mess between the 'gentlemen' and the ex-rankers. The last included Cornet Robert Davies, who as a sergeant in the 11th Hussars had been wounded in the charge of the Light Brigade, as well as the Riding Master, Joseph Malone, and the Quartermaster, Charles Wooden, both recipients of the Victoria Cross after Balaklava. When Crawley took over from Shute, therefore, he found a state of social anarchy reigning in the mess. He was a strongly opinionated man, zealous and pernickety, totally insensitive and lacking in tact to an abnormal degree. His ineffectual efforts to put things right ended in his taking sides most violently in the officers' petty squabbles. He soon became obsessed with the notion that the Paymaster, Captain Thomas Smales, was opposing his every scheme and action. He therefore tried to provoke him into some indiscretion upon which to base a charge against him. In this he succeeded. Smales was arrested for not providing cash when ordered to do so at an entirely unreasonable hour, and for a mildly insubordinate letter explaining why he could not do so.

From this small beginning emerged first a court of inquiry, then a court-martial held at Mhow where the regiment was stationed, with Crawley as prosecutor! Finally, after agitation in the press in India and at home, Crawley faced a court-martial on a grand scale at Aldershot. The first court-martial found Smales guilty. He was cashiered, both verdict and sentence being of very dubious justice. So much was this so that later on he was given a free pardon though not reinstated. Eventually, he was placed on half-pay and given the pension that would have been due to him had he not left the army: a tacit acknowledgement by the War Office that he had been unfairly condemned.

Crawley's court-martial came about because, believing or pretending to believe that his regimental sergeant-major and two of his troop sergeant-majors were conspiring against him during Smales' trial, he had placed them in close arrest. No charge was ever preferred against them, but they were confined for many weeks with sentries posted to watch their every movement day and night. Regimental Sergeant-Major Lilley was at the time caring for his wife who was dying of consumption. But he himself died before her – of apoplexy whilst still under close arrest during the height of the hot season. There is good reason to believe that the conditions of his confinement were the chief cause of his death. Crawley, in a totally unscrupulous manner, tried to make out that Lilley was an habitual drunkard, a view not supported by any reliable evidence.

To cut short a long, complex and squalid story, Crawley was totally exonerated in what was clearly a gross miscarriage of justice. Sir Hugh Rose, as Commander-in-Chief in India and Sir William Mansfield, as Commander-in-Chief, Bombay come out of the business with reputations scarred and the Duke of Cambridge only just escapes posterity's condemnation. A modern writer has summed up Crawley as 'a charlatan' and his 'full and honourable' acquittal as a classic case of the establishment 'protecting its own out of self-interest'.[22] The establishment's defence would have been that in the interests of discipline, the commanding officer had to be supported even if the ends of justice were not well served. Crawley was a persistent man who managed to manipulate the faulty court-martial system shamelessly. The case pointed to the need for reforms in the administration of military justice and over the next few decades some of these were quietly brought about.

9

'When we come to the Cavalry, we find not only
a theory of action, and consequently of instruction, apparently behind and at variance with the
spirit of the times, but symptoms, only too evident, of an intention to shut the eyes to the
manifest direction in which all progress in military practice and art is tending.'

MAJOR SIR HENRY HAVELOCK in 1867[1]

(i)

*Field movements – non-pivot drill – 'Fours' replace
'Threes' – annual manoeuvres started*

The *Cavalry Regulations* of 1865 run to 224 pages: the edition of
1876 runs to 327. It would be trying the modern reader's patience
beyond endurance to detail the contents of these expanding volumes.
They governed most aspects of training and military equitation as
well as the formations and movements of troops, squadrons and
regiments in every conceivable combination and situation. There
were over twenty basic field movements, many of them complicated
and some difficult to execute quickly, even with the fullest training.
There was a good deal too much attention paid to tidiness and regularity so that all would look impressive on the parade ground at the
expense of pliability and speed.

Some progressive commanding officers from time to time made
alterations to the official systems. The most thoughtful and vigorous
of these innovators was Valentine Baker of the 10th Hussars. He was
the first, incidentally, to practise cavalry in the art of travelling by
train. In 1860 he exercised one saddled and one unsaddled squadron
in entraining and detraining between Islington and Holloway,
proving thereby the practicability of moving mounted troops by
this new and speedy means of transport and at the same time learning
about the special equipment and techniques needed. But his most
controversial reform resulted from a visit which he made to the
Austrian cavalry in the early 1860s. He introduced into the 10th
their system of non-pivot drill. This was undoubtedly a simpler

method of manoeuvring troops and squadrons because it reduced both the number of movements required and the time taken to make them. Above all it was easier to learn both for the commanders and the troops.[2] Other regiments, notably the 13th Hussars, under Lieutenant-Colonel Jenyns [see p. 37],[3] soon followed suit, but there was much opposition to the method from traditionalists, and it was not until the 1870s that pivot-drill, the complexities of which when well performed must have looked beautiful on the parade ground, was officially abolished.

The most important official alteration in cavalry drill which was made during the period covered by this volume appeared first in the *Cavalry Regulations* of 1865. Before that date the ranks had been told off by threes for the purposes of manoeuvre,

'an arrangement', as Fortescue puts it, 'which made the movements particularly neat, for the breadth of three horses was just the length of one horse. It was found, however, on active service that, if two men out of the three were struck down, the moral effect upon the third was too severe to be borne by ordinary soldiers; so the ranks were now told off by fours. Thus the word "Fours right" took the place of the old word "Threes right", and the taunt of "Threes about" which, if addressed to members of one or two regiments, almost sufficed at one time to cause a military riot, became obsolete and meaningless. The change usefully anticipated the time when cavalry should be largely employed on foot; for under the old system it was possible only to dismount two men in three, whereas, under the new, there were dismounted three out of every four, the fourth man sufficing to hold three horses.'[4]

*　　*　　*

The provision of 'eyes and ears' in the field, which in reality was the most important function of the mounted arm in an age when artillery and small arms were being speedily improved, was still given much lower priority in training than was shock action. Most cavalrymen still placed preparation for the charge, the charge itself and its aftermath in the forefront of their minds. The rôles of reconnaissance, of patrolling, outposts, pickets and vedettes, of skirmishing and the escorting of stores and baggage, of advance and rear guards and of employment with horse artillery were generally treated as secondary and often despised as menial. As for the concept of 'mounted infantry' it was anathema to the true cavalryman. It was to be many years before the lessons of the American Civil War were to be taken to heart. In that conflict the traditional shock action of cavalry was largely abandoned in the face of increased weapon-power. In its place came 'flanking approaches or strategic raids by mounted riflemen'. One unofficial observer from the British army found the actual cavalry engagements

> 'miserable affairs. Neither party has any idea of seriously charging with the sabre. They approach one another with considerable boldness, until they get to within about forty yards, and then, at the very moment when a dash is necessary, and the sword alone should be used, they hesitate, halt, and commence a desultory fire with carbines and revolvers. . . . It can hardly be called cavalry, in the European sense of the word.'[5]

* * *

In the sphere of field training large strides were taken between the early fifties and the early seventies. The Prince Consort was perhaps the greatest single innovating influence. It was largely at his instigation and with his tireless encouragement that the habit of annual camps became a normal part of British army life. It took some time before these grew into anything at all like the continental system. They were usually held at or near Aldershot [see p. 330]. For the first time in the army's history during each year of peace hitherto isolated regiments were brought together and actually brigaded. Officers and men were taught the rudiments of a soldier's life in the field. Except for the Chobham Camp of Exercise in 1853 [see pp. 27–28], 'prior to 1855', as Sir Hope Grant's biographer has put it, 'the principles of route-marching, encamping, bivouacking, field-cooking, early-dawn attacks, and rapid construction of earthworks . . . were by many regarded as the pedantic arcana of a secret guild.' As the years went by bodies of troops, sometimes consisting of more than one brigade, were exercised against each other as opposing forces. Yet, till 1871, these manoeuvres were

> 'practically restricted', as one observer reported, 'to a change of front on a bare plain . . . with skirmishers thrown out, and batteries at carefully calculated intervals, cannonading an imaginary enemy. . . . Next came a charge of cavalry, with

horse-artillery galloping furiously on the flanks. . . . Operations were concluded with a very lengthy march past, and the proceedings were carried out with the undeviating regularity, and even the harmony, of a musical snuff-box, not materially impaired on certain occasions by a never-failing regulation allowance of expletives.'[6]

It was not only at manoeuvres that regiments were increasingly coming together. The ever-increasing network of railways made it possible for Lord Hardinge to decide in 1856 'that the army should no longer be scattered in battalions or detachments, but that it should as much as possible, for the sake of discipline and exercise, be brigaded and habituated to act together. This decision was founded' according to the report of a commission of 1858, 'on the axiom that no army can be fit for war which has not in peace been prepared for the duties of war.'

'The difference between a school-rider and a real horseman is this: the first depends upon guiding and managing his horse for maintaining his seat; the second, or real horseman, depends upon his seat for controlling and guiding his horse.'

CAPTAIN NOLAN in 1853[1]

(ii)

The cavalry seat – the English trot versus *bumping*

On the vexed subject of the cavalry seat, the conflict between the two main schools of thought was only partially resolved during the period covered by this volume. The more obviously uncomfortable, impractical, insecure, stiff and tiring positions, as imported from Europe by the Prince Regent early in the century, were finally abandoned after the Crimean War. The advocates of 'the fork seat', 'the scissors', 'the tongs across a wall' and 'the balance without clinging' methods were finally routed. At last men were no longer forced to ride like unrealistic dummies with straight legs, sitting on their forks (often causing ruptures) and not on their buttocks. By the late 1860s something like the normal hunting seat had become standard, 'with the knees tight to the saddle flaps and the legs taking their natural place, the feet not thrust quite so far into the stirrups as in hunting, but far enough to afford a good hold, differing again from the old seat where the point of the toe was only just allowed to touch it.'[2]

* * *

Still controversial for many years to come was the question of the 'English Trot' *versus* 'bumping'. The 'English Trot' was the name given to the process of rising in the stirrups at the trot. It was the ordinary way in which civilians rode. 'Bumping' was the opposite: sitting as if glued to the saddle without moving up and down. Until the late 1870s bumping was officially taught by Riding Masters both at the Maidstone Riding Establishment and in regiments. Later it was kept only for formal parades. Like so much that was traditional in the cavalry, 'bumping' was a matter not of efficiency but of regimentation and appearance. It was 'not only excruciating to [the men] but ruinous to their unfortunate animals',[3] being a major cause of sore backs. But 'a body of troops looked much smarter sitting down to the trot. . . . If they rose, the effect of each man bobbing up and down in time to his own horse's movements' did not look at all well.[4]

'I have for long past had not a doubt but that the cutting sword is by far the most formidable weapon for the hands of the cavalry soldier.'

MAJOR JOHN JACOB in 1854

'Why keep the cut – is it any good for cavalry? I answer with an emphatic "No".'

STAFF-SERGEANT-MAJOR INSTRUCTOR-OF-
FENCING J. E. WILLIAMS in 1906[1]

(iii)

Types of cavalry sword – the pros and cons of cut and thrust – training in the use of sword and lance – sword versus lance

Until 1853, the types of sword* issued to other ranks of heavy and light cavalry differed from each other. The 1834 heavies' pattern, which had a broad, very slightly curved blade thirty-six inches long was not thought much of by those who had to use it. (See the comments of the Colonel of the Greys at Balaklava.) The Household Cavalry sword was a much more efficient affair – Valentine Baker called it 'a very perfect weapon'.[2] It was a good deal more expensive and this accounted for its not being adopted for line regiments. The less ponderous, rather more curved blade of the light cavalry pattern introduced in the 1820s was half an inch shorter and much more effective than the heavies' for both cutting and thrusting. The 'Sword, Cavalry, Pattern –/53', which was the first to be issued for use by all branches of the cavalry except the Household Cavalry, had a slightly curved blade the same length as the old light pattern. Its hilt was divided into three steel bars 'which brought the tang [the extension of the blade to which the grip was attached] through the guard to the full width of the blade and formed the grip by riveting to it two side pieces or scales of leather'.[3] The sword was housed in a steel scabbard† with one ring at the mouthpiece and another eight

* The word sabre was used in the past in a loose way, meaning any type of cavalry sword. It should be applied strictly only to the curved cavalry sword specially designed for cutting as opposed to pointing.

† Nolan had tried to get wooden scabbards substituted for metal ones, not only to prevent blunting of the swords, but also to stop the clatter made by the rattling of the sword against the inside of the scabbard. (See Vol. I, p. 97). He

inches below it, so that it could be carried from slings. This sword, like most new weapons, took some years to replace its predecessors. There is no evidence that it was used either in the Crimea or the Mutiny. In 1864 a slightly shorter version with a bowl hilt pierced in the shape of a Maltese cross replaced the 1853 pattern. It did not have a successor until 1882. Officers had regulation swords which differed in some respects from those of the men, especially in the shape and decoration of their hilts and grips, but in practice many officers, particularly the more senior ones, still wore swords of whatever design took their fancy.

Sword knots were essential adjuncts to sword fighting. They attached the weapon to the wrist thereby preventing the swordsman from being disarmed should he have to let go of it to control his mount. They also made sure that it was not knocked out of his hand by an enemy. In the nineteenth century they were often extremely colourful with elaborate tassels attached. The standard issue for Hussars, for instance, was made of crimson cord with a large gold acorn.

In mid-century, sabretaches, those decorative leather satchels suspended on the left side of the rider by long straps from the sword-belt, were, except for the Hussars, done away with in the ranks. They were thought to be of little use except for their inner pockets in which messages could be carried. In 1858, Valentine Baker questioned the wisdom of this reform.

> 'As the sword is at present slung', he wrote, '[the sabretache] is very useful, for without it there is no possibility of keeping the sword steady; and if a horse is at all fidgetty or irritable, it is sure to madden him by knocking against his sides, or occasionally flying right over his back. It also jingles and makes a noise; and the march of even a small body of cavalry may be heard a long way at night from the rattling of their swords.'[4]

In the early 1850s Henry Wilkinson, the great designer and manufacturer of swords, wrote scathingly, as also did Captain Nolan and Colonel Baker, of the cavalry regulation sword. Amongst other observations he wrote: 'A young gentleman going to India is presented with a *regulation* sword, purchased along with his shirts and stockings and he only discovers, when opposed to some sturdy

failed, but certain of the irregular Indian regiments had wooden scabbards. Those of the Scinde Horse were covered with black leather and had a metal boot at the point. (Holland and Hozier, I, 189.)

foe for the first time, that the hoop of an ale-cask would have been equally serviceable.' Wilkinson put succinctly what were the properties essential to a good sword:

> 'Every swordsman knows', he wrote, 'that a thrust is always more efficient than a cut; and a sword that is too elastic vibrates in the hand, and is more inconvenient to use than one that is firm. An old officer of the 11th Dragoons told me that it was proverbial through all the Peninsular War that our Dragoons who were mostly brought into the hospital with slight punctured wounds in the chest or abdomen almost invariably died. The French Dragoons on the contrary had mostly cut or incised wounds and almost all recovered.'[5]

Throughout modern times there had been two schools of thought on this subject. Wilkinson's exaggerated statement that 'every swordsman' preferred the thrust was merely a shot in a running battle which was still raging passionately right up to the end of the mounted arm. By 1914 there seems to have been a clear majority against the cut accompanied by a tendency to teach recruits only the use of the point for thrusting. Certainly the manufacture of regulation swords over the last few decades of the nineteenth century was increasingly directed towards a decline in elasticity and away from curved blades. They were designed essentially for pointing and not for cutting. In 1854 John Jacob, the great commander of the Scinde Irregular Horse, who had had recent experience of fighting against skilled riders and swordsmen, was asked by the Commander-in-Chief in India for his views on the matter. He replied:

> 'The straight sword, and the use of its point, are far more formidable than the cutting sword in the hands of men on foot, and I was myself strongly prejudiced in their favour for use on horseback also, until many trials in the field quite convinced me of the contrary.
>
> 'On horseback, when moving at a rapid pace, as the cavalry ought always to be in attacking, the arm, after a home-thrust, cannot be drawn back sufficiently quickly; the speed of the horse carries all forward with great velocity, and the blade runs up to the hilt, or breaks before it can be withdrawn.
>
> 'I have had my own sword forcibly struck from my hand in this manner, the hilt striking with the greatest violence against a man's breast after the blade had passed through his body.

The blade happened to be very good and strong, and the hilt was attached to my wrist by a stout leather strap; neither gave way, but as the horse passed on at speed, the body of the tall heavy man who had assailed me was turned completely round and over by the blade of the sword in it, before the weapon could free itself.

'The violence of the shock, and the concurrent circumstances attending this and hundreds of other somewhat similar circumstances, perfectly convince me that on such occasions the chances are ten to one that the sword will break or the Cavalry soldier be torn from his seat; or both these accidents may occur. . . .

'I have never used any sword exercise with the men of the Scinde Irregular Horse, thinking that it is not required;* but I have myself witnessed very many instances of the terrible power of their cutting weapons, and those of the enemy. . . .

'At the battle of Meeanee [Miani],† a well-mounted Belooche warrior was flourishing his sword and challenging all comers. A sowar of the Scinde Irregular Horse rode at him at speed, and in an instant cut the man's head off at one blow. In the same battle, a sowar of the Scinde Irregular Horse, riding hard at the man opposed to him – a stout, able-bodied Belooche on foot, armed with sword and shield – the latter was knocked violently down by the horse's shoulder, but as he lay on his back on the ground, the Belooche warrior struck upwards so violent a blow with his heavy curved blade, that the sword cut completely through both branches of the under jaw of the sowar's horse, and the front part of the animal's lower jaw, with all its incisor teeth, remained hanging by a piece of skin only.

'The force of this blow appeared to me so extraordinary, that I for long preserved the skull of the horse on which it took effect.'[6]

* Captain Nolan when he asked an old trooper of the Nizam of Hyderabad's Horse 'How do you strike with your swords to cut off men's limbs?' received for answer: 'We never teach them any way, sir: a sharp sword will cut in any one's hand.' (Nolan, 107.)

In the Mutiny officers and men of the Bays took to putting 'curb-chains over the right shoulder, for it seems this is a favourite cut of the niggers, and numbers have been disabled by it'. (Maj Smith, 2 D.G., to Capt Wirgman, 10 H., Baker, 39.)

† 17 February, 1843. See Vol. I, p. 231.

Jacob was of course a man who held very strong views on nearly every subject. Major Poore of the 7th Hussars, writing over fifty years later, answered one of his main contentions thus:

'A mounted swordsman should always attack at a gallop, but in no case should he be taught to withdraw the sword. As soon as he has pierced his adversary, the body of the latter will swing round as he passes, and the sword will withdraw with the separation of the horses. . . . It is an acknowledged fact', he added, 'that a point will reach an opponent before a cut.'[7]

Jacob was also answered in most scathing terms by Sir Richard Burton, whose dogmatism was at least as pronounced as his own:

'He knew nothing of the sword', wrote Burton, 'beyond handling it like a broomstick; therefore he would not allow it to be taught to his men, many of whose lives were thus sacrificed to his fatal obstinacy. He utterly condemned the use of the point, which is invaluable throughout India, because the natives neither make it nor learn to guard it. His only reason for this dogmatism was the danger of the thrust by his own inexperienced hand. In a few single combats, after running his man through the body, he had risked being disarmed or dragged from his horse. . . . The superiority of [the point] to the cut is a settled question throughout the civilised world.'[8]

Jacob must have been disconcerted when he learned that at Khushab in 1857 the 3rd Bombay Light Cavalry, which formed part of his cavalry command in the Persian War, (though he was not present at the battle), had practically destroyed an infantry square by for the most part apparently using the point with straight swords![9] (See p. 129.) Looking back on the multitude of evidence collected over the years, it seems that the advocates of the point were more right than their adversaries. Nevertheless there was doubtless much to be said for Major Poore's view that

'the sowar's curved blade is, no doubt, a very effective weapon in the hands of our native cavalry soldiers, and several instances can be quoted as to its having been used by them with deadly effect. . . . It is, however, doubtful whether a cutting sword would be of the same value in the hands of a British soldier, possibly because a native is quicker and more supple in his movements than an Englishman. This is very pronounced when the two races take part in games together.'[10]

In view of the lasting influence which German cavalry performance was to have upon the tactics of the British mounted arm in the years ahead, it is of interest to note what was written by an officer of the 1st Prussian Dragoons of the Guard in describing a combat between his regiment and the 11th Uhlan Regiment of the Austro-Hungarians: a combat between swordsmen and lancers. It took place on the day of the battle of Königgrätz, 3 July, 1866: 'Our men had all been previously carefully instructed to point and never to cut in action. But the nature of the German was against the point, and forgetting all they had been taught, and shouting "Cut him down", they laid about them, aiming chiefly at the heads.'[11]

* * *

Training in the use of the sword started with the recruit being put through 'Extension Motions'. These were designed 'to expand the chest, raise the head, throw back the shoulders and strengthen the muscles of the back'. Formal sword exercise followed when he was shown how to draw, 'recover', carry, slope and return his weapon. He learnt next that the half of the blade nearest the hilt was known as the 'Fort' or strong part and the other half as the 'Feeble' or weak part. This was important to remember especially when guarding against a cut, for 'the strength of the defence decreases in proportion as the Cut is received towards the point' of the sword.

Next the recruit was taught the orders for the 'parade motions' which formed the basis for the use of his weapon in action, and how to react to each of them: 'left and right engage', 'assault' (preparation for making cuts), four cuts (or 'directions of the edge') at cavalry and four at infantry. 'Cut One' at cavalry, for example, was defined as follows: 'Cut horizontally from rear to front . . . the sword resting on the left shoulder, edge to the left, with elbow raised.' Instruction followed as to how to guard cuts from both right and left. For this he was shown the four 'guard' positions. In all cuts and guards the middle knuckles of the sword hand were to be 'in the direction of the edge of the sword'. Only now was the recruit shown the eight positions for delivering the point or thrust (with the nails of the hand always facing downwards), followed by 'pursuing practice' which combined cutting and thrusting.

After becoming proficient on foot in these 'independent practices', or 'loose play' as they were called, using sticks and masks, recruits were given individual and squad practice on horseback, initially at a walk and afterwards at a canter, first with sticks and masks and later with swords. 'Post Practice' was the next stage of training. Each 'Cavalry Riding House' was supplied with numbers of posts to which were attached dummy heads and rings (see illustration). Each post had an arm attached to it to represent a sword,

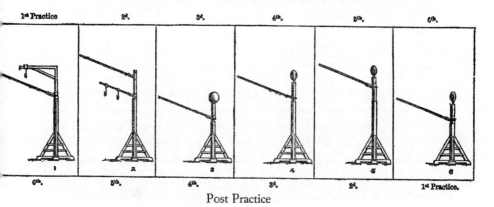

| 1ˢᵗ Practice | 2ᵈ. | 3ᵈ. | 4ᵗʰ. | 5ᵗʰ. | 6ᵗʰ. |

Post Practice

lance or bayonet. This, which was made so as to swivel, had to be turned 'out of the line by some mode of defence' before the budding swordsman could make his own offensive movement.

During the months which all this took, good instructors were drumming into recruits' heads certain principles which it was hoped would have become second nature by the time the moment of truth arrived. For instance a man was taught that, should he give the point too soon so that it was ineffective, he could by a quick turn of the wrist draw the sword's edge along his opponent's face or body. He was told too that the most dangerous quarter from which to be attacked was the left rear. The only hope then was for him to change position. This could be done by a sudden halt so as to allow the enemy to pass thus gaining a chance to press upon *his* left rear; or 'by turning quickly to the left about and thereby having your Right also opposed to his'. If these movements proved impossible it was vital to close up as near as possible to your adversary. If he was permitted to keep a proper distance, his cut would reach while yours would not. When being pursued it was essential to try to keep the enemy horseman on your right rear so that you could use the 'Rear Cut and Point' to check his advance. When attacked by more than one opponent, should you be unable to keep them all on one side of you, it was important to press close upon the left assailants while keeping the right ones at a distance. When attacked by a lancer, it was especially desirable to gain his right rear. Getting horses used to the waving of lances was a great object in training.

Instruction in the use of the lance included lessons in carrying, ordering, shouldering and supporting it when on foot. For mounted fighting, lancers had to practise many different movements such as the 'round wave', points, thrusts and the 'parry'.[12]

*   *   *

The question as to whether the sword or the lance was the better weapon for cavalry continued to be debated, the advocates of the lance almost imperceptibly losing ground. There were those who believed that to wield the lance effectively needed so much skill and practice that whatever virtues it might possess could seldom be realized. There were others who believed that only the front rank should be armed with the lance, and that the rear rank should use the sword. The lance, after all, it was argued, was of little use in the *mêlée*, while its longer reach and moral effect during the initial speedy charge could be devastating. There was one young officer in India during the suppression of the Mutiny who had a good word to say for the lance in action. He found it 'an admirable weapon for Pandies [mutineers]. They lie down on the ground and it is difficult to reach them with a sword, whereas a lance can touch them up anywhere.'[13]

One of the chief sports in which lancers were encouraged to indulge was 'tent-pegging' – the lifting of tent-pegs from the ground with the point of the lance. In India particularly, the officers, and sometimes the men, gained further practice when they went pig-sticking: hunting the wild boar with the lance. A favourite song sometimes sung in the mess, believed to have been Persian in origin, went thus:

'God gave the horse for man to ride,
And steel wherewith to fight,
And wine to swell his soul with pride,
And women for delight;
But a better gift than all these four
Was when he made the fighting boar!'[14]

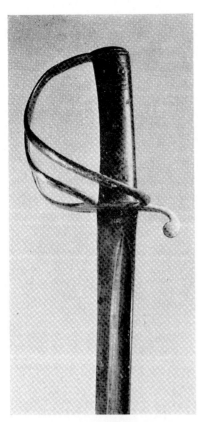

37. (*left*) Cavalry trooper's sword ('Sword, Cavalry, Pattern -/53'), 1853. (See p. 409)

38. (*above*) Heavy cavalry trooper's sword, 1834–1853. (See p. 409.) This example dates from about 1850

39. (*below left*) Cavalry trooper's sword, 1864 pattern. (See p. 410)

40. (*below*) Light cavalry sword, 1829–1853. (See p. 409)

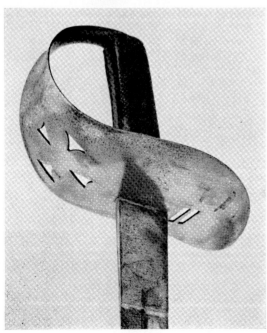

41. .451 calibre Westley Richards breech-loading carbine, 1866. (See p. 419)

42. .451 calibre Westley Richards breech-loading carbine, 1866; action open, left side, showing the operating level which gave the weapon the nickname of 'the monkey-tailed carbine'. (See p. 419)

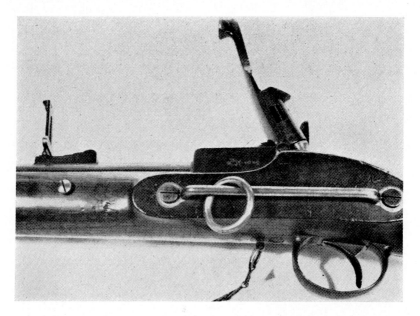

There were always those officers who expected too much of the cavalry and particularly lancers. The experience of a young officer of the Rifle Brigade during manoeuvres at Aldershot in the early 1870s well illustrates this. His company was skirmishing through a hop-pole plantation when they came across thirty or forty of the 9th Lancers,

'their lances entangled in the branches and their spurs in the bracken. Some of them brought their lances down to the charge, which made them quite helpless, as the trees were in rows about a yard apart, and when the lances were down the lancers were committed to that particular lane, and my men roaring with laughter were poking and firing at them from the next lane in absolute security. But I was ordered back by the umpire, Colonel, afterwards Sir Evelyn, Wood, and though I remonstrated it was in vain. Several years afterwards I met the officer commanding the lancers, who said that he was the man who carried out this piece of folly, by order of Colonel Wood himself.'[15]

'As late as 1867 the troops in India had seven different kinds of smoothbore firearms, viz. two muskets, four carbines, and a fusil for serjeants.'
Harmsworth's Universal Encyclopedia[1]

(iv)

Cavalry firearms: pistols – revolvers – carbines

The firearms of cavalry during the twenty years covered by this volume underwent important changes. The pistol which was still in use in some regiments at the end of the Crimean War had changed little since the time of Charles II. Lord Anglesey, who had commanded Wellington's cavalry at Waterloo, described it in 1830 as that 'despicable arm'.[2] It was a large-calibred, muzzle-loading, smooth-bore pattern. Even in the hands of a skilled shot its effective range was only a few yards. Fired from the back of a moving horse it was positively dangerous to everyone except the enemy. About the only recorded occasion on which it proved of any value was at Furruckabad in 1804 where flying Maratha horsemen tried to hide from their pursuers in trees. Men of the 8th Light Dragoons used their pistols to shoot them down. (See Vol. I, p. 67.) It was a grossly inaccurate weapon which few commanding officers ever bothered to teach their men to fire. In 1840 it was withdrawn from most regiments except lancers who did not replace it till 1876. At the time of the Mutiny a type of rifled, muzzle-loading pistol was given to certain regiments in India. In the early 1850s the revolver was introduced from America, and officers quickly adopted it for their own use. Some of the Indian irregular regiments, including the Poona Irregular Horse, as well as the Bengal Yeomanry Cavalry, were issued with it soon afterwards. The effective range of a revolver at that time when fired from a moving horse was not more than ten yards.

The other, more important, cavalry small arm was the carbine, the name given to short-barrelled, small-range versions of both musket and rifle. At the end of the eighteenth century light cavalry began experimenting with rifled carbines. At the same time the heavies adopted the carbine in place of the musket. These carbines were all, of course, muzzle-loading. They were not very efficient weapons, especially in wet weather. It seems that in the field when close to the enemy, they were kept loaded. For instance, Cornet Combe of the 3rd Bombay Light Cavalry wrote in his diary during the Persian War of 1857 that before starting off in the morning after a very rainy day before, his men discharged all their 'loaded carbines ... to make sure of their not being damp – luckily we did, for most of them wouldn't go off, while others fizzed out like squibs.'[3]

The muzzle-loading carbines were very awkward to use from horseback.* Dr C. H. Roads, the leading authority on the subject, has described how

'a trooper had to be able to present and fire his carbine with one hand as the other was fully occupied controlling his mount. ... Reloading was always a very tricky operation. Apart from the risk of losing his rammer, which led to the use of a swivel as a means of ensuring its permanent attachment to the arm, the trooper was in considerable danger of spilling part of the

---

* In India, the Scinde Irregular Horse had double-barrelled smooth-bore carbines as late as 1868, and probably for some years later. (See p. 256.) (Holland and Hozier, I, 189.)

powder charge, dropping the percussion cap or bending his ramrod.'[4]

A carbine loaded at the breech was the obvious answer, and in due course numerous experimental patterns were tried out. But since most cavalry officers were not really interested in efficient firearms – the *arme blanche* was everything to them – the pressure to produce new and better weapons was always slight. Nevertheless, between 1855 and 1867 numerous boards and committees considered a large number of carbines of varying sorts, produced by at least nine different designers, three or four of them Americans. Some of these designs were produced in small numbers for experimental purposes; some were issued to individual or groups of regiments, but most of them were finally rejected. Amongst others there were Sharpe's from America, (of which 6,000 were ordered between 1856 and 1858, and later issued to five Royal cavalry regiments serving in India), Leetch's, Terry's (which looked for a time like staying the course), Green's (of which 2,000 were manufactured but which after eight years of being on the brink of issue remained in store), Prince's, Burton's, Restell's and Manceaux's. In the end the American .451 calibre Westley Richards, which from the shape of its operating lever was known as 'the monkey-tailed' carbine, won the day. In 1864, 20,000 were ordered and by 1867 they had been widely distributed. It was agreed by the Carabiniers, and the 10th and 18th Hussars, to which regiments Westley Richards carbines were first issued, that they were superior to any of their predecessors. The pattern was both shorter and lighter than earlier carbines, being less than three feet in length and weighing only 6 lbs 8 oz compared with an average weight of nearly eight pounds for the old weapons. Though the Westley Richards was not officially declared obsolete until 1881, up to which date the Yeomanry was still using it, it was almost at once overtaken by more sophisticated designs, especially the Snider, one of the earliest issues of which was made to 200 men of the 3rd Dragoon Guards when they went on the Abyssinian expedition of 1867–68 (see p. 256).[5] At home they were issued to the 7th Hussars at the end of 1868.[6] The Snider will be described in Volume III.

None of these breech-loading carbines, some of them excellent weapons, was any more used than had been their muzzle-loading predecessors. Except where there was a particularly keen commanding officer, training in the proper use of the weapon was minimal. It was even said that one lancer regiment when first issued with carbines piled them on the stable barrows and deposited them on a manure heap.[7] The 1876 *Regulations for Cavalry* laid down that the cavalry soldier 'must trust to his sword or lance alone for purposes either of offence or defence. . . . The fire-arm is a weapon which can be used with effect only when he is acting on foot.'[8]

A very few commanding officers thought that more attention should be given to firing practice. One such was Colonel Jenyns of the 13th Hussars who suggested that 'in the cavalry, where men have so little spare time . . . the course of preliminary drills' for recruits should be shortened and 'more actual ball firing substituted'.* Colonel Cameron Shute of the 4th Dragoon Guards agreed that there should be issued more ball ammunition for target practice, although, as he pointed out, 'in cavalry a large proportion of blank ammunition is necessary for the training of horses' so as to accustom them to the noise.[9]

* For many years the annual allowance of ammunition for carbine range practice was limited to 150 rounds per man. (Sheppard, 185.)

10

'The distinction between heavy and light dragoons is but a name.'

VALENTINE BAKER in 1858[1]

(i)

Types of horses – sources – prices

The English Thoroughbred hunter as developed from the pure-bred Arab, combining size with speed and stamina, was the type of horse most favoured by the British cavalry in the nineteenth century. It was generally the envy of continental armies. Its evolution from the very heavy type of Cromwell's day standing over sixteen hands, through the scarcely less heavy type of the first half of the eighteenth century to the hunter of the early nineteenth, (averaging between about fourteen hands, three inches and fifteen hands, two inches), 'may be roughly said to have followed the improvement in roads and communications. The advent of the fast mail coaches of the late eighteenth century coincided with the introduction of horse artillery in our service [see Vol. I, p. 38], and the rise of fox-hunting with the increase of manoeuvring pace in the cavalry.'[2] The illustration facing p. 448 shows a not particularly distinguished officer's charger of the Royal Horse Artillery of about 1861. This rare photograph shows what was perhaps the typical hunter type to be found at that date filling the ranks of the average line regiment.

Unlike the numerous cavalry of a continental army, all concentrated in one place, the British mounted arm, always small in numbers, scattered and stretched from Dublin to Delhi, could never afford to make a clear-cut distinction between heavy cavalry kept exclusively for charging, and light cavalry for reconnaissance and outpost duties. The usual tendency of commanding officers was towards recruiting for their regiments big men on big horses. This was partly because most cavalrymen of all ranks believed that the charge, carried out by more or less heavy soldiers on more or less heavy mounts, shattering and overwhelming whatever opposition was encountered was what really mattered, and that the true functions of light cavalry were contemptible by comparison. But it was also because the light regiments, often being the only ones available in the field, were time and again called upon to fulfil the charging rôle of the heavies. When true light cavalry first came into being in the British army, there had been for a short period numbers of truly lightweight horses ridden by quite small men, but these had gradually decreased, and by the middle of the nineteenth century they were rare. Certain enlightened commanding officers, such as Valentine Baker of the 10th Hussars, tried with some success to reverse in their regiments the trend towards bulk. Baker always made a point, according to the regimental historian, of selecting horses as remounts 'with as much breeding as possible, preferring to depend upon blood for hard continuous work rather than upon size and imposing appearance'.[3]

* * *

At home the provision of remount horses for the army depended entirely upon the regiment going into the open market in competition with all other buyers. The officer detailed by his commanding officer to buy horses ran some risk financially, for he was liable to have his purchases rejected by his colonel, whose responsibility they were. Much skill and experience were therefore essential attributes of such officers. In some regiments the veterinary surgeon was given this vital task. For instance, John Wilkinson, who later became the army's first Principal Veterinary Surgeon, was considered such an excellent judge of horses that when he was the 17th Lancers' 'vet' he bought all the regiment's remounts over many years.[4] Up to about the 1860s purchases were made chiefly at horse fairs, but later the trade became increasingly concentrated into the hands of a few large contractors. The 1859 *Queen's Regulations* laid down that no remount horse was 'to be purchased at an age prior to 1st May of the year in which he becomes four years old . . . nor of an age later than 31st December of the year in which he shall have become six years old.'[5] Before that regulation (and later in spite of it) young three-year-olds were often bought during peacetime. They were usually put out to graze and set to light tasks only until they were approaching five years. This was considered the normal age at which they could begin really hard work.

For some years before the Crimean War the price of three-year-olds had been fixed at £26 5s, except for the Household Cavalry and the Greys who were allowed to spend more. During the war instructions were issued to buy horses from five to nine years old, the price limit being set at £40 for troop horses. 'All were to be in hard, working condition.'[6] This was because life for horses on board transports was pretty tough and it was realized that it paid to embark only animals which were in really hard-working trim if they were to be of immediate use on arrival in a distant country. Looking ahead, it is an interesting fact, as will be shown in a subsequent volume, that this lesson had been forgotten by the time of the Boer War. It is worth noting that when so much else was mismanaged in the Crimean War the old system of buying remounts did at least ensure that they were delivered at ports of embarkation in proper fettle.

Remounts were also purchased abroad. Two weeks before war was declared Captain Nolan – the same who was later killed at Balaklava – set off for Constantinople on an official mission 'to get into the market', as he put it, 'before the French'.[7] He managed to buy 250 Turkish horses, averaging only 14.1 hands, at the bargain price of £16 each. Later on, in Syria, he had to exceed the authorized maximum price of £30 which he had been set, buying 100 horses large enough for British cavalry at an average of £34 a head. None of these was less than four years old. As the war progressed and the demand grew, every conceivable breed was to be found in the allied armies: English hunters, steeple-chasers, drag-horses; French bays from Alsace for the heavy, and 'chevaux de Tarbes' for the light cavalry; Bombay and Herat Arabs; wiry ponies from the Cape; handsome 'Company's stud' from Madras; glossy barbs from Morocco and Algiers; Cossack ponies; angular, well-bred horses from Asia Minor, and the fat, gentle-natured beasts ridden by the Turkish officers.[8]

During war competition in the horse market at home was always severe. In consequence regiments were often reduced to accepting the 'culls', as the inferior left-overs were called, since prices for decent remounts rose well above the official allowances. For some time after the Crimean War these remained much as before: £26 5s for three-year-olds and £30 for four-year-olds. These maximum prices were progressively increased over the next twenty years, never quite keeping up with the ever-growing cost of horses generally. It was calculated in 1872 for example that horses were 33% dearer in that year than in 1866.[9]

'The dead weight which cavalry carries now a
days is what kills horses.'

LIEUTENANT-COLONEL GEORGE DENISON,

in 1868[1]

(ii)

Weights carried by cavalry horses – saddles

When the 5th Lancers were re-embodied in 1858, after their disbandment nearly sixty years before, 'strong, well bred horses of various colours* [were] purchased from dealers in Ireland.' Their average height was fifteen hands, three inches, which was one inch above that laid down in 1857 for the cavalry of the line. The average weight of a lancer† in marching order was about seventeen stone, seven pounds.[2] This of course did not include any of the horse furniture.

The whole question of the weight to be carried by cavalry horses much exercised the authorities throughout the nineteenth century and it was never satisfactorily settled in the twentieth. The conflict between what was thought necessary for the man and how much a horse should carry, if both were to be used to the fullest advantage in war, was perhaps impossible to resolve happily. The Inspector General of the Prussian Cavalry believed that cavalry carrying more than fifteen stone, ten pounds was 'fit for nothing'.[3] In 1891 Surgeon-Major (later Major-General Sir) Frederick Smith, who was to be-

---

* *Queen's Regulations* of 1859 laid down that 'the horses of Regiments of Cavalry are not to be allotted to Troops according to Colour. The Trumpeters are not to be mounted on horses of any particular colour.' (*Q.R.*, 1859, 372). This rule did not of course affect the Greys or the Bays who seem always to have kept to their individual colours. When the Bays returned from India in 1870, they were 'according to traditional practice, remounted on bay horses. To effect this, forty-four animals of that colour were acquired from each of the following units: 1st, 4th, 5th, 6th and 7th Dragoon Guards and the 1st (Royal) Dragoons.' (Whyte and Atteridge, 160.)

One regiment which paid scant attention to the regulation was the 11th Hussars. At a grand review in India in 1872 a local newspaper commented: 'The 11th were . . . certainly the showiest British Cavalry Regiment on the ground, for in that Regiment only were the horses uniform in colour. First a bay squadron, then a squadron mounted entirely on creamly greys of almost uniform shade, and lastly a bay squadron again.' (Williams, *XIH*, 249.)

† His average height was five foot, seven inches.

come Director of Veterinary Services, in a lecture at Aldershot, said that a cavalry horse should not carry more than fourteen stone, three pounds, and that fifteen stone should be the maximum.[4] In spite of these dicta, the actual norm was nearly always over eighteen and often over twenty stone throughout the century, both in the Continental and the British cavalry. Valentine Baker gives the weight of a trooper in the 10th Hussars in 1858 as

	stone	lbs
'Average weight of men	11	0
Men's accoutrements	3	9
Horse equipment	3	11
Total	18	6

Now, when to this is added four days' corn, as must often be the case on service, we get an additional 40 lbs or 2 st 12 lbs making a total of 21 st 4 lbs, under which weight a light cavalry horse is supposed to be capable of doing outpost duty, making forced marches, going at a high rate of speed for long distances, and charging when necessary.'[5]

The chief difficulty was the saddle. It was considered absolutely necessary to make 'the troop saddle pound for pound as heavy as the load of kit it had to carry in order to obtain sufficient strength to stand up to the stresses inevitable on active service'.[6] Further, military saddles, unlike civilian ones, had to be designed to keep the weight of the rider with all his heavy equipment away from the horse's spine. They were built therefore upon a frame made of two arches fitting over the animal's withers and back, joined together by 'sideboards' fitting the shape of the horse. Beneath these sideboards, pads were provided so as to lessen the likelihood of sore backs – a frequent nightmare of all cavalrymen. A blanket, folded in some regiments as many as twelve times, or a horse-cloth was placed beneath the saddle, giving further protection to the back from abrasion by the saddle. A *numnah*, as used in India, increasingly replaced the blanket. It weighed about five and a half pounds and consisted of a thick woollen or felt pad cut so as to fit completely under the saddle.

Unlike the civilian saddle the cavalry model was 'a complication of movable straps and buckles, pilches [saddle covers], woofs [cloths], &c., all made to take to pieces, and put together, like a Chinese puzzle', thereby adding quite a little to its weight. It was beyond Colonel Valentine Baker's comprehension why this method should have been adopted. It was supposed to facilitate cleaning, but as he pointed out in his influential book, *The British Cavalry*, published in 1858, ordinary hunting saddles never got out of order and were easily cleaned although in one piece.[7]

From 1805 until the end of the Crimean War the 'Hungarian' or 'Hussar' saddle, known officially as the Light Cavalry Universal Pattern, was in general use in one form or another by both heavy and light regiments. The illustrations between pages 448 and 449 show what it looked like. Though it became obsolete in 1855–56, the 11th Hussars did not abandon it until 1866.[8] The regiments which were sent out to India at the time of the Mutiny in 1857 and 1858 also appear to have used it exclusively. Officers' saddles were by no means always of the universal pattern, but as the years went by this distinction lessened.

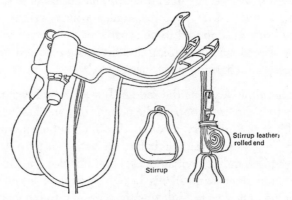

The Universal Pattern saddle of 1856 to 1872:
wood arch with panels

One of the early tasks which the Army Ordnance Department undertook when it replaced the old independent Board of Ordnance as a result of the post-Crimea reforms, was to set up various committees of officers to consider, report and make recommendations upon all horse equipment. The first truly universal saddle was one of the outcomes of their labours. Its form was based largely upon the views of the late Captain Nolan, who was killed at Balaklava (see p. 92). These he had set out in his *Cavalry, Its History and Tactics*, published in 1853. He had had made a prototype from his own designs, and the new model was in many ways similar to it. Valentine Baker's views were also much attended to. His ideal was to reduce the load on the horse to just over fifteen stone, and the Universal Pattern Wood Arch Saddle which eventually emerged weighed only fifteen stone, eight ounces. It was designed to last twelve years, but so good was its construction that some which were made in 1863 are known to have been still in use and in excellent condition fifteen years later. Certain cavalry regiments were still using them, though they were officially obsolete in 1878, as late as 1885. Some were even being issued to Yeomanry regiments during the Boer War. Its design proved to be well in advance of any of the Continental patterns and on the whole was popular with both officers and men. The illustration above shows what it looked like. By 1864 the three regiments of Household Cavalry were the only ones not using it.* In 1872 it was partially replaced by a new Universal Pattern, the Flat Iron Arch Saddle which was a failure since it invariably 'let the pack down on the horse's spine'. Six years later an improved version known as the Universal Pattern Angle Iron Arch Saddle was issued. It will be described in the next volume.

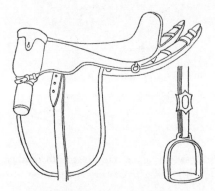

Household Cavalry saddle, 1860

Efforts were made from time to time to cut down the weight of other items of horse furniture (see below). A Board of 1855 wished, for instance, to abolish the shabraque and sheepskin which weighed six or seven pounds, but this desirable reform was resisted by cavalry officers for many years to come. They could not bear to face the disappearance of such decorative, if otherwise profitless, embellishments.[9]

* * *

In India the pre-Mutiny regular regiments generally used the same types of saddles as the Royal regiments. The three Madras regiments, the sole regulars remaining after the 1861 reorganization,

* The illustration on this page shows the 2nd Life Guards saddle of 1860.

continued the same practice. The Bengal and Bombay irregulars before the reorganization used all sorts of saddles or, as in the case of Hodson's Horse when first formed, none at all. In 1859 Probyn's

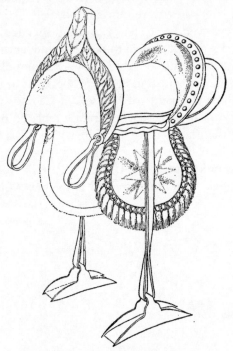

The 'Khatee' or Sikh saddle of the mid-nineteenth century as used by Indian *Silladar* Cavalry Regiments

Horse was using 'the khatee or Sikh saddle'[10] as shown in the illustration. This and similar Indian types were probably still in use many years later. Nevertheless, in the early 1860s the nineteen post-reorganization *silladar* regiments of Bengal *officially* adopted the 1856 Universal Pattern. So, a few years later, did the Scinde Horse.

(iii)

Bridles – horse furniture

The bridles by which cavalry horses were guided comprised basic-
ally a leather headstall, a metal bit passing through the mouth, a curb
and leather reins. They differed little from those of civilian horses,
except in decorative detail. From the Crimea onwards there was a
marked trend away from expensive ornamentation on bridles and
from inessential straps. Early in the nineteenth century the curb
(also confusingly known as the bit), which was pretty severe on the
mouth, was still sometimes used by itself. It consisted of a chain or
strap passing under the lower jaw of the horse and fastened to the
upper ends of the branches of the bit. It acted through the pressure
of the chain or strap on the chin groove. In the eighteenth century
the snaffle, with a mouthpiece which had one or more joints or
links, came into regular military use. Since its action was on the
corners of the mouth it was less painful for the horse; but it had
considerably less controlling power than the curb. Until 1902, when
the elbow bit was introduced combining the action of curb and
snaffle, these two were usually worn together, the combination being
known as a bridoon and the whole bridle as a 'double bridle'. The
illustration on page 430 shows the Universal Pattern bridle which
came into official use in 1860. For some years to come certain regiments still preferred to use their own less simple and more elegant
models, but by the late 1870s, the Universal Pattern was in general
use. Beside the two pairs of reins, one attached to the curb and the
other to the snaffle, the illustration also shows the head collar chain
used for tying the horse up.

*   *   *

Horse furniture, or trappings, as worn in the cavalry, consisted,
with two exceptions, of items which were entirely ornamental. They
also increased the weight which a horse had to carry. Nevertheless

they added to the attractiveness of the mounted arm, and it is not surprising that cavalrymen were loath to abandon them. The two exceptions were the holster coverings worn on the front of the saddle to keep the pistols dry and the valise worn behind the saddle. This was used to hold spare clothing and cleaning materials. It was circular in shape, made of leather or cloth, and generally had the number

UNIVERSAL PATTERN
1860

From 'Some Bridles and Headstalls used by the British Cavalry since the Formation of the Present Standing Army' by Harry Payne, *Cavalry Journal* XIV (1924), p. 312

and initials of the regiment painted on its ends. The chief item of purely decorative horse furniture was the shabraque (or shabrack) which extended along the horse's back from behind the saddle to cover the holsters. In the heavy cavalry the corners of the shabraque were usually cut off square. The hussars had pointed corners, while light dragoons and lancers had rounded ones. Troopers' shabraques were usually lined with heavy leather or rawhide and were often encrusted with 'embroidery, gold or silver lace, regimental devices, crests, titles and battle honours'.[2] By 1857 most of the heavy cavalry had abandoned them, but light cavalry and most officers went on wearing them for many years to come.

'[The horses] were generally looked upon as machines.'

VETERINARY SURGEON MAJOR FREDERICK SMITH

in 1891[1]

(iv)

British cavalrymen's reluctance to dismount – stallions, geldings or mares? – barrack stabling

A besetting sin of the British cavalryman which enlightened officers were at pains to eradicate, but which seems to have persisted until the end of the nineteenth century, was a marked reluctance to dismount. Even as late as the Second Afghan War of 1878 the men of a Hussar regiment were so hampered by their leg gear, overalls and tight riding boots that they were kept in their saddles for long periods when for the good of their horses they ought to have been either leading or resting them.[2] Major Tylden, whose *Horses and Saddlery* is a mine of information upon which the present author has relied enormously, believes that the habit may have originated in part in the days of armour 'when a man had a tremendous weight to hoist into a narrow saddle. . . . Probably', he adds, coming down to the nineteenth century, 'the height of the rear pack with the carbine butt hanging beyond it made a tired man unwilling to go to the trouble of dismounting and mounting again.'[3] Another cause might have been the need for vedettes to remain mounted so as to be able to see better from the greater elevation of their horses' backs. But what was probably the chief reason was given as late as 1891 by a Professor of the Army Veterinary School at Aldershot:

'We have a singular notion in cavalry', he wrote, 'that it is a dishonour for a man to walk or be seen off his horse. The sooner we get rid of such ideas the better for horses' legs and backs. I see no reason why it should not be a recognized thing in our service for men to lead their horses for a part of the way in order to afford the animal the needful rest he requires.'[4]

On the other hand Field-Marshal Sir Evelyn Wood tells of a commanding officer, whose behaviour he held out as not untypical of the 1860s and 1870s. His solicitude 'to keep the Government horses sound' led to his always marching past at 'the walk' and being averse to his precious troopers ever 'being jumped or galloped'.

Wood also says, incidentally, that the troop officers in that regiment invariably cut the horses' tails themselves, this 'duty being considered too important to be entrusted to the private Dragoon'.[5]

*   *   *

As to whether mares, stallions or geldings were best suited to the cavalry, there were conflicting views, stubbornly held. In the middle of the century, as the result of semi-scientific tests, the belief that geldings were inferior in stamina to entire stallions was dying out. From 1848 for instance the Madras cavalry had nothing but geldings. This development was certainly welcomed by most junior officers and men, for although entires were generally better looking and possibly more courageous, they had a significantly higher accident rate and needed more forage. Nor could they be used in close proximity to mares. Lieutenant Blake of the Carabiniers, who in 1858 was temporarily mounted on one of the Indian country-bred troopers 'out of the ranks' of his regiment, found that they were 'vicious brutes, all entire. They are continually screaming, fighting and kicking and are so savage that if they can get you off they will attack you like a wild beast.'[6] A special advantage of geldings was that being more docile they were much easier to break in than were stallions. Further, they did not need heel ropes for tethering. This was important because each set of heel ropes weighed about four pounds – an extra weight for the horse to carry.[7]

*   *   *

Certain not very spectacular improvements in barrack stabling were made during the two decades covered by this volume. Not the least of these was the provision of sheds especially for stable litter which when disposed of indiscriminately was supposed to be a cause of disease. Less easy and inexpensive to provide were the regimental horse infirmaries recommended by Lord Cardigan in 1855.[8]

Florence Nightingale turned her reforming zeal in the early 1860s to the conditions of horses in barracks. 'I do not speak from hearsay', she wrote in 1863, 'but from actual personal acquaintance with horses of the most intimate kind, and I assure you they tell me it is of the utmost consequence to their health and spirits when in the loose box* to have a window to look out of. A small bull's eye will do. I have told Dr Sutherland but he has no feeling.' Dr Sutherland, Miss Nightingale's long-suffering reforming colleague replied in jocular vein: 'We *have* provided such a window and every horse can see out if he chooses to stand on his hind legs with his fore feet against the wall. It is the least exertion he can put himself to.'[9]

'The native animals of the country are of a most inferior description.'

VALENTINE BAKER in 1858

'I don't suppose there is such a good lot of chargers in any other regiment in the service, as ours are all Arabs without exception.'

CAPTAIN HENEAGE, 8th Hussars, in India[1]

(v)

Cavalry horses in India: country-breds — stud-breds — imported Arabs, Capes and Walers

Because of the length of the journey and even more because of the great expense which it would have entailed, Royal cavalry regiments never took their horses with them to India. They had to be remounted on arrival. The chief source was the Company's (and after its demise the Government's) Remount Department, which included official breeding establishments. These had been formed at the end of the eighteenth century because there existed in India very few private enterprise studs of anything like the quality common in Britain and also because the local breeds were usually too small for most military purposes. During the first forty or fifty years of their existence these official studs were inefficient and costly. This was perhaps not surprising since the chiefly native staff was only cursorily trained and under very little control. For instance in the 1850s there was only one young captain responsible for the management

* A stable into which sick horses were put where, not being tied up, they could move about freely.

as well as the veterinary treatment of nearly 1,500 young horses in the Bengal stud, and he had had no formal training whatever.[2]

In 1849 Mr R. G. Hurford, the veterinary surgeon of the 16th Lancers, wrote a letter to the Board of Management of Indian Studs drawing attention to the worthlessness of the stud horse. It was subsequently published and may have been responsible for his appointment as the first Principal Veterinary Surgeon in India in 1866.[3] (See p. 386.) Between that date and the 1880s there came about a marked improvement in both the administrative and scientific management of the studs.

At home and in India individual cavalry officers were apt to consider themselves masters of the veterinary art. In the absence of any representative of the profession on any of the staffs, and holding the humble but qualified regimental 'vet' in some contempt, these officers managed from time to time to persuade headquarters to order the implementation of their pet schemes. One of the Indian equine disorders was *bursattee*, a wet season disease marked by pustular eruptions on the head. Another common complaint known as quittors produced ulcers on the coronet of the hoof. For both of these, though they obviously required different treatments, a certain Captain Apperley recommended the quackish prescription of 'calomel to the point of salivation and black wash to the ulcers', and managed to get this 'valuable recipe' made official. It was, however, resisted by the profession.

Another officer, Major Tapp of the Poona Horse, induced the Adjutant-General of the Bombay army in 1854 to issue a circular directing all veterinary surgeons to practise Tapp's method of producing geldings. The operation entailed the destruction of the stallion's spermatic cord by forcible kneading with finger and thumb, and took even an expert half an hour to perform. The regimental 'vets' had to protest for more than four months before the Commander-in-Chief issued a General Order forbidding this needless and excruciating torture. The historian of the veterinary service points out that 'such an instance of ignorant cruelty could never have occurred had there been a Principal Veterinary Surgeon at the Commander-in-Chief's elbow.'[4]

*   *   *

The hordes of horsemen of the Marathas, Pindaris and other races and tribes in past times had ridden very light indeed. For them the

434

'Country-Breds', which the official studs later tried to 'improve', were just right, but for true cavalry purposes as understood by Europeans they were too slight in size and weight. Their height was usually not much over thirteen and a half hands and their weight was about 780 lbs on average, whereas the European cavalry horse generally weighed not less than 1,000 lbs. Near the end of the nineteenth century a distinguished veterinary surgeon gave a good description of the country-bred mares as they had developed after decades of careful breeding:

> 'Rather light in barrel, not evenly put together, often of an angular and ragged appearance, with small but steel-like bone of joints and limbs. . . . They have wonderful powers of endurance under either tropical sun heat or intense cold, with a light weight, say from 10 to 12 stones in the saddle. . . . After the hardest day's work [they] are never off their feed but always ready for it; moreover they will continue work on the scantiest of feed.'[5]

There were about thirteen distinct breeds of horse in India. Some of them, like the Kathiawar, probably in part descended from the ponies of Tibet, were bigger than the average stud-bred; some of them, like the Marwari from Rajputana, were more carefully bred than most of them.

For some years before the Mutiny, the quality of the horses issued to the regular native regiments, all of which were usually either bred in the official establishments or imported, varied enormously. A subaltern of the Carabiniers, all of whose troop horses were 'what are called stud bred', found that 'beside being bad tempered, they are far from being good horses in any quality, action, speed or endurance.'[6] Nevertheless it was probably true, as Major Merewether of the Scinde Horse said in 1858, that the irregulars, who found their own animals, were mounted 'in an inferior manner to the regulars for the reason that they cannot afford to buy the horses'.[7] Lieutenant-Colonel Harington, commanding a regular regiment, said that his troop horses had sometimes cost as much as 600 rupees (about £50).[8] This was well beyond the means of *silladar* regiments.

These, of course, obtained their horses wherever they could. They were of all sorts. The Scinde Irregular Horse for instance purchased theirs from 'a set of dealers' who had 'established themselves at the headquarters at Jacobabad, who', according to Major Merewether, 'have always horses ready for sale.' They came chiefly from Sind, the Punjab, Afghanistan, Baluchistan and Kutch. 'The purchase is managed by the soldier himself entirely. The commandant merely has the horse brought before him to see if it is fit for the ranks.'[9] In other *silladar* regiments, and later on even in the highly individual Scinde Irregulars, the Commandant became increasingly responsible for the actual buying of the troop horses. In the Central India Horse, as General Watson explains,

'before the introduction of the Waler nearly half these horses were Arabs, purchased . . . in the Arab stables in Bombay. An extra charge of Rs. 50, over and above the regular horse price, was always made for an Arab, who was an expensive animal; and there were always men ready to pay for it. The remainder of the horses were country-breds of the old type. . . . They were, in fact, real Indian horses, hard, wiry, excitable little fellows of all sorts of colours – the dun being very prominent – and for the most part of very high quality; and they were bought at the large fairs held annually at Batesar near Meerut, at Poshkar near Ajmere and at Balotra in Rajputana. . . . In the old days it was not easy to make a profit on the Chanda Fund [Horse Fund: see p. 240]. A horse's length of service was, on an average, ten years. The correct procedure, therefore, was so to adjust the sowar's monthly subscription to the fund that he should subscribe in ten years an amount not less than the average price of a horse. Any excess which he subscribed, plus the price obtained for casters [a horse sold as unfit for use in the ranks], which, however, was negligible, went to the credit side. If he subscribed too little the Chanda fell into debt; if too much the regiment was liable to become unpopular, and recruiting consequently to fall off. In later days, however, when the height of polo ponies was raised to 14.1 and 14.2 [hands] – that is to say, to the same height as our regimental troop horses – many horses were trained and sold as polo ponies, and large profits were made.'[10]

When, during the Abyssinian expedition of 1867–68 (see p. 254), an epidemic broke out in the 3rd Bombay Light Cavalry which eventually caused 367 horse casualties, Sir Robert Napier, before he left India to command the troops, told the Bombay Government that the sum of 200 rupees allowed for each horse dying on service was totally inadequate. He added that 'if it was expected to meet such losses [at that time about seventy had died] the Horse Fund would be entirely absorbed and in fact ruined. . . . As the sum paid in the 3rd Cavalry for remounts averaged upwards of 300 rupees each, these casualties, after deducting the sum allowed by Government, would occasion an outlay of about 10,000 rupees from the Horse Fund, as horses fitted for the Light Cavalry could not be procured in the Bombay market under 350 rupees each.'

A compromise was therefore reached whereby the Government bought the remounts and was later repaid by the regiment 'such portion of the cost as it should reasonably bear'. In the meantime an officer reported from Egypt that 200 suitable Arabs were available at £25 each (about 250 rupees). Some of these were at once bought, thereby for the moment solving a costly problem.[11]

*　　*　　*

From the 1850s onwards a larger proportion of horses was imported into India. English Thoroughbreds were sometimes brought in by individual officers for their personal use, but otherwise they made the passage from England at Government expense for stud purposes only. So also for the same purpose did a few Hackneys and Norfolk Trotters. Cape of Good Hope horses arrived from South Africa in some quantity until the discovery of diamonds in the early 1870s led to a decline in their export. The Cape, in Baker's opinion, was 'the beau ideal of a light cavalry horse; strong, compact, hardy and temperate; and bearing the change to any climate without deteriorating'. As horses were not indigenous to South Africa the original Capes were of Arab or other Eastern origin. Later they were crossed with various breeds including the English Thoroughbred. Baker thought that the Cape horse possessed 'all the good points' of the pure-bred Arab, 'with much greater size; he is equally enduring and more sure-footed.'[12] During the Mutiny when the demand for horses was particularly pressing, the men of the Cape Mounted Riflemen were nearly all put on to collecting Cape horses as remounts and delivering them to the South African ports for shipment to India.[13]

The most numerous of all imports to India were the Walers, originally from New South Wales, but whose name was later used to describe horses bred anywhere in Australasia. They owed their

best qualities, as did also the Cape horses, to the English Thoroughbred, whose excellence in turn came from the pure-bred Arab. Baker
in 1858 found them in size

> 'but little inferior to English horses. They are rather carelessly
> bred. . . . Their characteristics are, large ugly heads, ewe
> necks, good shoulders and quarters, but rather long backs, and
> badly ribbed up. They are generally fiery and timid, and al-
> though in Australia they are considered hardy, I have almost
> invariably seen them fall off quickly in condition when ex-
> posed to the hardships of a campaign.'[14]

Other imports to India included the pure-bred Arabs from
Arabia, who in spite of their small size, proved themselves capable of
carrying fifteen stone and more with apparent ease. Their courage,
stamina, proverbial beauty and, above all happy disposition, endeared them to all who rode them. Wilfred Scawen Blunt, famous
amongst other things as a breeder of Arabs in Sussex at the turn of
the century, believed that 'the Arab horse at his best is so good a
horse that he does not need *improving*.'[15] His bone, according to
Major Tylden, is of the hardest and his feet, in hot climates, are like
iron.[16] Less purely bred varieties came from the Persian Gulf (the
Gulf Arab or Shirazi) and from the Persian interior (the Persian or
Persian Arab). The mounts which the 10th Hussars and the 12th
Lancers brought with them when they arrived in the Crimea from
India in 1855 were all Arabs of one sort or another. 'Quiet, useful
little animals'[17] was one observer's description of the 12th's grey
geldings, while Colonel Hodge of the 4th Dragoon Guards, watching the 10th disembark at Balaklava, thought their 'wild Indian
horses' 'beautiful – all entire Arabs, and in such condition'.[18] But
Mrs Duberly found that when loose they 'fly out, fasten on to, and
tear each other with a tenacity and venom that I should have
supposed only to have existed among women.'[19] In 1859–60 when
the 9th Lancers went home from India, they handed over 100 of
their Arab troop horses to Probyn's Horse. Four years later when
that regiment became the 11th Bengal Lancers, it set up a stud farm
in the Punjab, christened Probynabad after Lieutenant-Colonel
Dighton Probyn, V. C., its Commandant (see p. 224). Here the
earliest stallions were all Arabs.[20]

Another, larger type of horse, also with Arab blood, was the
Turcoman or Turkestan, known by the Russians as the Argamac. It
was defined by an equine authority in the 1870s as the only horse in

Asia 'which comes up to our English standards as a horse rather than a pony'.[21] The very best of the Turcomans sometimes stood sixteen or seventeen hands high, but they were rare and extremely expensive. In the 1870s an high-class entire could fetch as much as £500. Such horses were clearly not for general regimental use.

11

'As a mere picturesque detail, it may be mentioned that in 1861 Light Dragoons disappeared from the British Army.'

SIR JOHN FORTESCUE[1]

(i)

Establishment and effective strengths of the cavalry – increases and decreases – squadron organization – disappearance of Light Dragoons

The effective strength of the Household Cavalry and the cavalry of the line, as well as their official establishments, varied considerably over the two decades covered by this volume. The effective strength was at its lowest just before the Crimea, when it fell to 9,900. Its highest was 17,000 at the beginning of 1859 when the suppression of the Mutiny was coming to an end. In only four out of the twelve years following 1854 was the mounted arm below establishment. This compares very favourably with the figures for the army as a whole, which was above establishment in only one of those years, 1856–57.[2] It is clear that there was little difficulty in recruiting for the cavalry.

The alterations in establishments reflected closely the situation overseas. The moment the sky seemed to be clear of crises, reductions took place. At the end of 1856 and again early in 1857 all regiments at home were reduced. Most cavalry regiments then consisted of about 470 all ranks. In the summer of 1857, when the news of the Mutiny reached home, regiments were augmented from six troops to eight, the number which had been established during the Crimean War but reduced after it. The total strength then became about 620. When the Mutiny was over and done with, considerable reductions again took place.

As always, when Royal regiments went to India, their numbers were substantially increased, but they were no more exempt from modifications there than when at home. The strength of the 7th Hussars, for instance, was fixed in 1860 at 791 of all ranks (616 troopers). Next year, as memories of the Mutiny began to fade, the

440

regiment was reduced to 694 (548 troopers). Seven months later a further small reduction was ordered, chiefly of officers. In 1867 the total of troopers came down to 426, but a sergeant cook, a school-master and a bandmaster were added. The 4th Hussars went to India that autumn with 27 officers, 450 rank and file, 55 women and 71 children.[3]

On the 7th Hussars' return home in May, 1870, the establishment was fixed at seven troops and consisted of:

1 colonel	1 paymaster
1 lieutenant-colonel	1 adjutant
1 major	1 riding master
7 captains	1 quartermaster
3 cornets	1 veterinary surgeon

1 regimental sergeant-major
1 trained bandmaster
1 regimental quartermaster sergeant
7 troop sergeant-majors
1 paymaster-sergeant
1 armourer-sergeant (unless supplied by the Corps of
   Armourers)
1 farrier-major
4 farriers
1 saddler-sergeant
1 hospital-sergeant (unless supplied by the Army Hospital
   Corps)
1 orderly room clerk
1 sergeant-instructor in fencing
1 sergeant cook
21 sergeants
1 trumpet major
7 trumpeters
21 corporals
9 shoeing-smiths
2 saddlers
1 saddletree maker
374 troopers

This made a total for all ranks of 483. The establishment of govern-ment-provided horses was 300. Attached were one surgeon and one assistant-surgeon.* Less than four months later the number of troopers was increased from 374 to 448 and fifty further horses were added.[4] This augmentation reflected the fear inspired by the startling successes of Prussia against France. In April, 1870, indeed, there had been slight reductions in most regiments – the 5th Dragoon Guards, for example, had then lost sixty-five men.[5] But in August, immediately after the battle of Worth, a substantial increase was decreed. This was followed in February, 1871, by yet another.

* * *

Lieutenant-Colonel Valentine Baker of the 10th Hussars, as usual ahead of his time, was the prime mover in a reform which was abandoned after a year's trial. In April, 1868 cavalry regiments were for the first time formed into four squadrons, instead of eight troops, for administrative as well as tactical purposes, that is in barracks as well as in the field. Each squadron had six officers, 131 men and eighty-six horses. There was immediate and strong opposition 'mainly', as the historian of the 10th says, 'from the reluctance of the four junior captains to give up the command of their troops'.[6]

1861 saw the last of the 'light dragoons'. In that year the 3rd, 4th, 13th, 18th, 19th, 20th and 21st Light Dragoons were redesignated hussars. This was, as Fortescue puts it, 'a mere picturesque detail', affecting 'practically nothing except the dress of the officers and men'.[7]

* In 1872, medical officers ceased officially to be part of regimental establishments throughout the army.

(ii)

*Yeomanry cavalry: decreasing employment – aids the
civil power for the last time – establishments – use of
regulars against Fenians in Ireland – fire-fighting –
royal escorts*

The yeomanry cavalry had more difficulty than the regulars in
matching its effective strength with that of its establishment. It is
surprising indeed that during the 1850s and 1860s many of the units
managed to remain in being at all. For the purposes of preserving
law and order the advent of a proper, nationwide police force had
largely removed the need to employ the yeomanry in aid of the civil
power. Smuggling, for instance, which in the past had kept both
regulars and yeomanry busy, was now usually dealt with by the
local police. Further, with the increasing spread of railways and the
telegraph, regular troops could be speedily summoned to deal with
serious civil disturbances.

Nevertheless, there were still rare occasions when the yeomanry
was called out to help in suppressing riots. One such was when the
Wolverhampton and Walsall troops of the Staffordshire Yeomanry
were on duty for five days in 1855 helping to restore order amongst
the miners in the Potteries. As a result of a reduction in wages, the
men rioted at several mines, in some cases destroying the machinery
at the pitheads. Eventually peace was re-established with the help of
a detachment of the Essex Rifles. Again, twelve years later, when 'an
itinerant lecturer against "Popery", called Murphy, had from the
violence of his language caused serious disturbances in Birmingham
and other places', great excitement prevailed in Wolverhampton
when it was learned that he was to visit the town. 'All day long and
until late at night the Hussars and Yeomen patrolled the town and
effectually prevented a riot from developing.'[2]

What was possibly the last occasion when a yeomanry regiment
was called out in aid of the civil power was a food riot which broke
out at Exeter on Guy Fawkes night, 1867. On the requisition of the

mayor and magistrates a detachment of the 1st Devon Yeomanry, numbering 112 officers and men, was called upon to help 200 regular infantrymen and some artillery and rifle Volunteers. 'Early in the evening the Riot Act was read, and a few collisions took place between the mobs and the soldiery, but the presence of the Regulars and Yeomanry', as the Devons' historian puts it, 'had the desired effect of preserving the city from tumult.' Later in the evening

> 'it was thought fit', according to the *Exeter and Devon Gazette*, 'that the Devon Yeomanry Cavalry should make a demonstration in the High Street, and they appeared before the Guildhall in a large body, and with drawn swords. This appeared to be the most unlucky and inauspicious event of the evening. The Yeomanry were evidently very unpopular, and were received with hooting and yells, and showers of fireworks, which the horses did not like, and many in the crowd cut the horses with sticks and canes, and sent them curveting in a very undisciplined fashion. . . . No order was given for the men to draw their swords, and only a few did so, having misunderstood some directions given.'

The regiment remained under arms until two in the morning when the men were 'dismissed to their respective homes; and they were marched out in regular order, and dismissed outside the city, in order that they might not be seen individually in uniform in the town.'[3]

Government treated the yeomanry at the best with indifference during most of the nineteenth century. It was almost entirely due to private and voluntary effort and money that the regiments were kept in being (see Vol. I, pp. 76–82). Lord Dudley, for instance, was said to spend £3,000 or £4,000 a year on maintaining the Staffordshire Yeomanry.[4] There were not many pecuniary advantages for the officers and men. Each was exempt from the horse duty on the animal he used 'for training and exercise'. When 'called out' certain allowances were granted and 'pay as officers and soldiers' was given. Some sort of remuneration was also allowed when, which was seldom, the troops were sent out on training. Officers and men were exempted from serving as parish or special constables.

In 1869 there were in existence forty-eight different 'Corps' (three to five troops) and regiments (six to ten troops). The total of troops was 264, comprising 14,200 officers and men. A troop was supposed to consist of not less than forty and not more than sixty 'Private men, including Farriers'. A squadron comprised two troops.[5] There was a permanent staff of 427, of which thirty-three were adjutants, 280 sergeant-majors and sergeants and forty-four trumpeters.[6] Virtually all of these were seconded from or had been in the cavalry of the line.

Far-reaching reforms affecting the economy and constitution of the yeomanry came about in the early 1870s. An account of these will be given in the next volume.

*   *   *

Increasingly in Ireland the yeomanry was seldom used. Its unpopularity, since officers and men were mostly of the Protestant ascendancy, was great. The regulars, however, found much employment, especially during the Fenian risings of the 1860s. On occasions Fenians enlisted in the ranks to act as 'centres'. Their object was to try to induce the Irishmen in the different regiments to join the movement.

> 'One of these, a man named Boyle O'Reilly, entered the Tenth [Hussars], a remarkably intelligent, well-educated, active young fellow, a man who soon made himself popular with all ranks, and appeared likely to rise. O'Reilly was eventually apprehended . . . and tried, and sentenced to penal servitude and transported. Some years later a ship was sent from America to Australia to assist him and some other Fenians in making their escape, and this was successfully carried out.'[7]

Fire fighting was an activity which, in the absence of sufficient civilian firemen, still sometimes fell to the regulars and the yeomanry. In 1862, for instance, 'E' Troop of the 10th Hussars, which was at Scarborough undergoing musketry instruction, put out a fire in the town. Since their uniforms were much damaged by water, the insurance office made compensation, and gave the men some sort of monetary reward, but it was stipulated that this should be kept secret. 'It was afterwards said that this was owing to the company being managed by Quakers who did not wish it known that any reward had been made to the fighting element of the country.'[8]

There was one other duty which the cavalry of the line sometimes undertook, but from which they were relieved at the end of the period covered by this volume. 1870 was the last year in which the Queen's travelling escorts were furnished by regiments other than the Life Guards and the Royal Horse Guards.[9]

EPILOGUE

'Henceforth, as heretofore, wherever cavalry
meet cavalry *alone*, fire-arms being ignored on
both sides, the victory will be to that side whose
horsemen are the best mounted, most skilled
with their arms, and most ably handled and led.
BUT WHERE CAVALRY ARE OPPOSED
TO INFANTRY, THEIR SUPREMACY IS
A THING OF THE PAST, UNLESS THEY
YIELD TO THE PROGRESS OF THE AGE
– THEMSELVES ADOPT THE RIFLE, AND
ADAPT THEIR TACTICS TO ITS USE.
UNDER THIS NEW ORGANISATION . . .
A WIDER SPHERE OF USEFULNESS AND
ENTERPRISE THAN CAVALRY HAVE
EVER ENJOYED BEFORE, IS JUST OPEN-
ING OUT TO THEM.'

SIR H. M. HAVELOCK in 1867[1]

The Crimean War, one of the two chief conflicts described in this
volume, was a severe test for Britain's small, old-fashioned army. In
the short run it was fortunate that the enemy was imperial Russia,
whose armed forces were not among the most advanced in Europe.
In the longer term the British army suffered from the fact that the
campaign bore very little relation to what the European wars of the
next two decades were to be like. The Russian army of 1854 was
very far from being the Prussian army of 1866 and 1870.

The war was a traumatic experience for Britain, not chiefly
because of the antiquity of her army's weapons and tactics, nor,
certainly, because of any superiority of the Russians in these respects, but because it was demonstrated to the world that her army
lacked the means to survive in an alien environment. This was the
direct result of parliament's parsimony no less than of the inadequate
military thinking which that parsimony imposed.

Both of these stemmed from the fact that the army, as Wellington
put it, was 'an exotic in England; unknown to the old constitution
of the country; required only for the defence of its foreign posses-

446

sions; disliked by the inhabitants.'[2] This was no less true in 1854 than it had been in 1828 when it was written. As soon as the shock of the war had subsided it became true again. The first faint glimmerings of a permanent alteration in the nation's attitudes towards her land forces, with an attendant move towards military professionalism, came about not at all as a result of the Crimean experience. They emerged as a consequence of three wars in which Britain was not involved: the American Civil War of 1861–65, the Austro-Prussian War of 1866 and the Franco-Prussian War of 1870–71. The change was so sluggish that at times it was almost imperceptible. Not the least of the obstacles to its realization were what one modern writer has called 'the twin pillars of Palmerstonian indifference and Gladstonian economy'.[3] Yet in spite of discouragement from on high, there were those in both military and civil circles who realized that there were vital lessons to be learned from these three wars and that it would be fatal to Britain's interests if she failed to profit from them.

It was true that 'on the eve of the American Civil War, the development of British military thought had barely begun.'[4] It was equally true, as the most recent historian of the Staff College has put it, that 'the 1860s constituted a lull or trough during which Britain's military authorities were slow to grasp the significance of developments in the American Civil War and the Austro-Prussian War.'[5] But the 1860s also saw the publication in England of certain controversial books which clearly marked the start of a radical alteration in military notions.* What they preached went well beyond the old approved pattern which, according to A. W. Preston in his illuminating article on 'British Military Thought, 1856–1890', 'seemed to be to look at military history as a great quarry of principles and examples to be judiciously selected to bolster pre-conceived ideas or traditional doctrines.'[6]

In 1864 Colonel Patrick MacDougall, who since 1854 had been superintendent of studies at Sandhurst, published a book called *Modern Warfare as Influenced by Modern Artillery*. It succeeded his more famous *The Theory of War* of 1856 which was 'illustrated by numerous Examples from Military History'. As its title implies the later work was based less than had been its predecessor on distant

---

* Before the publication of the three books discussed below, all of which came out between 1864 and 1868, there had been a dearth of works in English on the general subject of cavalry. Beside Nolan's *Cavalry* (1853) and Beamish's *On the Uses of Cavalry in War* (1855), nothing of any real value had appeared.

history and more on recent developments in the field, especially in America. Of the role of cavalry as he envisaged it he had this to say:

'If the effect of the improved weapons on infantry is to reduce its comparative value, their influence on cavalry must be nearly to destroy its utility altogether as an offensive arm on the field of battle. It will still be available to protect the flanks and rear of a military position, but it can hardly be expected that cavalry can manoeuvre on the ground which separates two hostile armies, without running the risk of utter destruction. In pursuit, or in acting on the communications of an enemy, its value remains much as before, although its losses when opposed to guns or infantry must increase. If this view be correct, heavy cavalry has received its death-blow; and the problem will be to render the organisation of light cavalry more perfect, and to make it more moveable than at present.'[7]

This was revolutionary stuff which cannot have endeared Colonel MacDougall to the average cavalryman.

It was followed in 1867 by an intentionally provocative book called *Three Main Military Questions of the Day* written by Major Sir Henry Marshman Havelock, eldest son of the hero of Lucknow. He, too, had seen service during the Mutiny. At one point he had been given command of a small flying column of mounted infantry, having himself proposed its mounting to make up for the deficiency in cavalry. Later he had commanded the 1st Regiment of Hodson's Horse throughout the Oudh campaign. A modern historian has called him 'a professional reformer notorious for his eccentricity'.[8] In spite of its overcoloured polemical tone, his book contains much sound sense. One of the three questions it deals with is 'Cavalry as affected by Breech-loading Arms'.

'When we come to the Cavalry', says Havelock, 'we find . . . symptoms, only too evident, of an intention to shut the eyes to the manifest direction in which all progress in military practice and art is tending; and a determination . . . to adhere to a tactical system that originated in a state of things which has long passed away. . . .

'Whereas all the rest of the world is watching with an ever-increasing interest the progress of long range and precision in rifled arms great and small, and is eagerly endeavouring to introduce into its cavalry such modifications as this totally changed state of things necessitates, *we* have just succeeded in

43. Near leader, gun team, Royal Horse Artillery, *c.* 1861. (See p. 421)

44. Light Cavalry Universal Pattern Saddle, 1805: the 'Hussar Saddle'. The right-hand photograph shows the underneath. The loose seat is missing. (See p. 426)

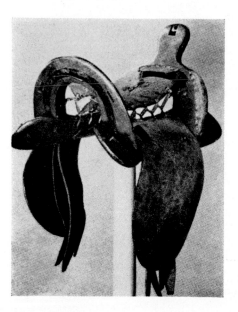

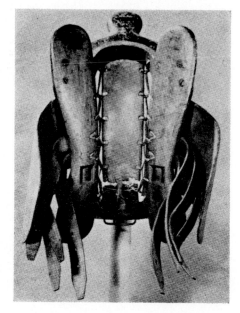

45. Sergeant-Majors Haynes and Borthwick, 7th Hussars, c. 1851. (See p. 426) The saddle shown is of the Light Cavalry Universal Pattern, 1805 type. The two troop horses are, according to Major Tylden, 'a very good type of medium weight general-purpose saddle-horses'.

... virtually abolishing for all good effect the small modicum of rifle instruction which had with infinite labour and fight against prejudice been introduced into our partially rifle-armed cavalry ..., proclaiming aloud that we pin our faith on spurs, lance and sabre.'

Havelock goes on to say that in his view an unprejudiced assessment of the purely cavalry actions in the recently concluded war, in which the Prussians soundly and speedily trounced the Austrians,

'would show, unmistakably, that even more strongly than in America, long range and increased precision, and notably and especially the rapid fire of breechloaders, have, once and for ever, set aside the sway that lance and sabre formerly held undisputed.

'The theory of the representatives of what we may call the "charging" school of cavalry is that it spoils a dragoon to give him any fire-arm but a pistol for the *mêlée*, or a carbine to be used from the saddle in skirmishing; that the proper arms of a cavalry soldier are the lance and sabre ... and that once he is permitted the idea of "shooting" his *morale* is gone. ...

'Till about 1854, when rifled arms began to be generally introduced, a ready forward boldness and dash were the safest as well as the most honourable course for a mounted soldier opposed to infantry. ... He had but at the worst to run the risk of two ill-directed shots, one delivered at 150, the second at or under 30 yards – from a weapon notorious for being quite uncertain beyond 120 yards, and not fully to be depended upon at 50. ...

'Even with [the muzzle-loading musket] a good infantry could, under all but very exceptional circumstances, laugh at the efforts of the best and most devoted cavalry. Waterloo alone was enough to silence any doubt on that point for ever.'

Nevertheless, Havelock admits that cavalry had a considerable moral effect in the days of the inefficient musket. There were numerous examples from history of the panic induced in infantry by 'the terrible whirlwind of a charge'. Yet the casualties actually inflicted by cavalry with sword or lance seldom if ever warranted such panics.

The core of Havelock's argument was that when the precision of long-range, rifled muzzle-loaders and later the rapidity of breech-loading arms replaced the inaccurate slowness of the musket 'the "dangerous ground" of the horseman was increased at once from

200 to 800 and even 1000 yards'. He pointed out, too, that the 'careful individual instruction' which the use of rifled arms made essential raised the infantryman's morale 'above the influence of panic. . . . He had come to understand . . . that the weapon in his hands enabled even one cool determined footman to ridicule and foil the best efforts of the bravest and most skilful dragoon.' He now had time to fire not two but seven or eight shots while the cavalryman was crossing the 'dangerous ground'. This gave him vastly increased self confidence.

Havelock goes on to cite an experiment which had recently been carried out at the School of Musketry at Hythe:

> 'Ten men who had never handled a breech-loader before, except at the preliminary drill, were set to fire ten rounds each with the Snider (converted Enfield) at 500 yards. The whole 100 rounds were fired in one minute and thirty seconds, and seventy per cent of the shots were hits. . . . This experiment was made with targets representing infantry, or only six feet high: with cavalry standing at least two feet higher, probably the hits would have been at least ten per cent more. . . . Reduce the whole effect by a full half to allow for the flurry of action, and the remainder is quite sufficient to bear out any assertion that breech-loading rifles have practically annulled a sabre and lance cavalry.'

He reckoned that a Snider gave a rapidity of fire rather more than four times that of the Enfield.

An important point which Havelock was at pains to drive home was that 'a greater field and scope than in any previous period of the history of war was now opened up to horsemen.' He described how, during the American Civil War, in consequence of their defeat at the first battle of Bull Run and 'the apparent inefficiency of Cavalry against rifled arms', the mounted arm of the Union army, already small, was on the point of being further reduced at the end of 1861 when 'a great change of opinion' took place. This came about 'principally through the stern teachings of adversity – for the Cavalry of General J. E. B. Stuart and the "Mounted Infantry", or Mounted Riflemen, of the daring guerrilla John Morgan, harassed and hunted them to distraction.' The outcome was that the Northern cavalry adopted

> 'the best "repeating" rifles . . . and reduced to an organised system of drill and manoeuvre the practice of fighting with them

on foot, always where possible from behind cover; the horses meanwhile, each held by a mounted man, or never by less than one man to two horses, being kept out of harm's way farther to the rear, but ready to gallop up at a moment's notice to pick up their men, or to meet them half-way in falling back, for any necessary change of position.'

Havelock's conclusion was to press for the addition of a battalion of 500 mounted riflemen to be attached to each cavalry brigade in the British army,* 'so that the hussars and lancers may be kept out of rifle if not of cannon fire, till the decisive moment comes for them to act, and meanwhile be covered in their front by their dismounted rifle skirmishers in great numbers.'[9]

Havelock's book had a considerable success. So did another written by Lieutenant-Colonel George Denison, a Canadian. It appeared in 1868, a year after Havelock's and was called *Modern Cavalry: its Organisation, Armament and Employment in War*. It soon became recognized as an exhaustive and definitive study of the subject. Throughout his book Denison treated cavalry proper and mounted infantrymen almost as if they already existed as two separate branches of the same arm. If anything, he saw the rôle of the mounted infantryman as the more important of the two. Among the suggestions which Denison put forward, mostly based on a deep study of the American war, was that 'Light Dragoons or Mounted Rifles' (treating the two as synonymous and distinguishing both from 'Cavalry of the Line') should carry their carbine 'in a bucket on the offside of the saddle. . . . They should be trained more particularly to its use, and taught the power of accurate firing on foot. . . . If [they] have sabres at all, they should be attached to the saddle and not to the man. . . . They are merely to be used as a reserve arm in extraordinary circumstances, and are *not* to be looked upon as *the weapon* of the dragoon. . . .' He pointed out that nothing could be 'more troublesome, noisy or awkward to a man skirmishing or fighting on foot' than a sword attached to his waist.[10]

The question of mounted infantry became a leading tactical issue in the British army for many years to come. How the controversy

---

* There already existed in the British army a corps of 'mounted infantry', the Cape Mounted Riflemen. But, as Havelock put it, 'what occurs in our remote colonies seldom attracts much attention amongst us.' (Havelock, 47). The men of this South African corps, which will be referred to in volume III, were not true mounted infantry since they fired their double-barrelled rifled carbines for the most part from the saddle.

proceeded will be discussed in the next volume. It is enough here to say that, at home, if not in India, not until after 1888 did *official* doctrine begin, tentatively, to show any interest in the principle of mounted riflemen. Its final adoption on any scale had to wait till the Great Boer War was under way.

Even that far-seeing reformer, Sir Garnet Wolseley, took some years to be converted. In 1869, when he was Assistant Adjutant-General at the Horse Guards he published his famous *Soldier's Pocket-Book for Field Service*. It revealed 'a new and radical attitude towards the question of officer-man relationships in a professional army';[11] but otherwise it said little new about strategy and hardly touched upon the changing nature of war. This is not surprising since such matters were outside its scope. On the use of the mounted branch, Wolseley wrote: 'Whether our cavalry is to be changed into mounted rifles, or to remain as it is at present . . ., it will be . . . an unfortunate day for the English general who is called upon to fight an enemy who has a proportion of good cavalry, whilst he himself has none, being deprived of them in pursuance of some cleverly stated theory.' Of 'Grand charges in force upon infantry', he had this to say:

> 'Unless the infantry has been well shaken by a heavy artillery fire, or is of an inferior quality, or is taken at a disadvantage, such as in the act of deploying, or some other manoeuvre, these grand charges are but waste of men and horses, if made against infantry armed as at present. Circumstances may, however, render it necessary to make this sacrifice for the purpose of gaining time. . . .
>
> 'It is a favourite argument with those, who, basing their opinion on theoretical notions, think that cavalry is a species of anachronism, to point to the smallness of the numbers actually killed by that arm in action.'[12]

These were still Wolseley's views at the time of the appearance of the *Pocket-Book*'s second edition in 1871. But in an essay written in 1872 he propounded the view that cavalry could 'seldom be of much decisive use; whilst the duties of obtaining information . . . protecting the flanks and concealing your movements can be more effectively performed by . . . mounted infantry.'[13]

*   *   *

As part of this volume has tried to show, the fifteen years which followed the war in the Crimea saw the living conditions of the common soldier enormously improved. By 1871, in barracks and hospitals, for instance, a real effort had been made, with mounting success, to increase the cubic space per man. Married quarters had been built at many stations and the married soldiers and their families were no longer compelled to occupy the same rooms as the bachelors. Rations were supplied under the direct superintendence of the commissariat department and their quality was much higher than of old. The awful prospect of nothing but boiled beef had given way to more varied modes of cooking and a wider range of foods. The recruit now received a free kit. The day was past when he had to pay for every article of 'necessaries', when the burden of endless stoppages kept him almost permanently in debt. Now extra free issues of clothing were made annually to every soldier. Those supplies, beyond his 'necessaries', for which he paid were furnished from the public stores. They were of better quality and cheaper than they had ever been before.

Among other advantages enjoyed by the soldier of the early 1870s, which his father had never known, were reading rooms with a free supply of newspapers and periodicals, gymnasia in most barracks, an increased scale of medical comforts and the virtual abolishment of corporal punishment. Most important of all the reforms perhaps were those in the educational field. The standard of teaching, the number and quality of teachers and the frequency of such things as evening lectures had all been much improved both for soldiers and for their children. Life was still tough and hard but the men of 1871 were pampered in comparison with their predecessors of 1851.

Nevertheless, as Samuel Haden, the secretary to the Pensioners Employment Society, said in 1867, it was still true that

'a very small number of men enter Her Majesty's service from choice. They are ignorant of the duties which they are about to undertake. They desire to be soldiers, and are influenced by impressions formed from highly coloured books, or a sanguine imagination that the soldier's life is a very easy, merry existence, and that they must individually do well in it themselves. A large number of recruits are induced to enlist by the blandishments of recruiting serjeants, many of whom grossly misrepresent facts while liberally distributing liquor, and while under the effects of it many men are enlisted.

'The great mass of recruits are men doubtless in difficulties who only enter Her Majesty's service because at the moment they have no other means of existence, and they view the step as a desperate remedy for their case.'[14]

*   *   *

The abolition of purchase of commissions, the institution of short service and the creation of an Army Reserve – the famous Cardwell reforms – constituted a major turning point in the history of the army at home. In India, the changes in military thought and the major reorganization of the army occasioned by the traumatic experience of the Mutiny, marked even more obviously a decisive alteration in direction. The effect of these revolutions upon the cavalry both in Britain and overseas will be considered in the next volume of this work.

APPENDIX

1. (See p. 153)

The 1st Punjab Cavalry became in 1890 Prince Albert Victor's Own Cavalry; in 1903, the 21st Prince Albert Victor's Own Cavalry (Frontier Force); in 1914, 21st Prince Albert Victor's Own Cavalry (Frontier Force) (Daly's Horse). In 1922 it joined with the 3rd Punjab Cavalry which in 1903 had become the 23rd Cavalry (Frontier Force), to make the 11th Prince Albert Victor's Own Cavalry (Frontier Force).

The 2nd Punjab Cavalry became in 1903 the 22nd Cavalry (Frontier Force); in 1914 the 22nd Sam Browne's Cavalry (Frontier Force). In 1922 it joined with the 5th Punjab Cavalry, which in 1903 had become the 25th Cavalry (Frontier Force), to make the 12th Cavalry (Frontier Force).

The 4th Punjab Cavalry was disbanded in the reduction of the Indian Army in 1882. It was never re-raised. If it had been it would have taken the number '24' which was kept vacant for it when the armies were amalgamated in 1903.

2. (See p. 156)

In 1858 Hodson's Horse divided into two regiments. In 1861 these became the 9th and 10th Bengal Cavalry. The 10th, three years later, became the 10th Bengal Lancers, and in 1878, the 10th (The Duke of Cambridge's Own) Regiment of Bengal Lancers. The 9th did not become the 9th Regiment of Bengal Lancers till 1886. In 1903 the two regiments became the 9th Hodson's Horse, and the 10th Duke of Cambridge's Own Lancers (Hodson's Horse). In 1922 they were amalgamated into the 4th Duke of Cambridge's Own Hodson's Horse.

3. (See p. 159)

Lind's Pathan Horse became in 1859 the Mooltani Regiment of Cavalry; in 1860, Cureton's Multani Regiment of Cavalry; in 1861, the 15th Bengal Cavalry; in 1890, the 15th (Cureton's Mooltani) Regiment of Bengal

Lancers; in 1903, the 15th Lancers (Cureton's Mooltanis), and in 1922 it was amalgamated with the 14th Murray's Jat Lancers to make the 20th Lancers.

4. (See p. 164) *List of regiments of irregular cavalry*

Bengal, 1858
  i. European: Bengal Yeomanry Cavalry
               Volunteer Cavalry at Rajshaye
               Calcutta Volunteer Guards (cavalry portion)
 ii. Native: ten regiments of Bengal Irregular Cavalry, and part of one
               other
               Corps of Guides (cavalry portion)
               Sikh Cavalry: four regiments
               Punjab Cavalry: five regiments
               Ramghur battalion (cavalry portion)
               Jodhpore Sikh Horse
               Benares Horse
               Beatson's Horse: two regiments
               Meade's Horse
               Behar Horse
               Rohilcund Horse
               Peshawar Light Horse
               Lahore Light Horse
               Towanah Horse
               Hodson's Horse: two regiments
               Pathan Horse (Jat)
               Mynpoorie Irregular Horse
               Mooltanee Regiment (cavalry portion)
               Bunnoo Horse levies
               Dera Ismael Khan levies
               Hyderabad Contingent: four regiments

Bombay, 1858
  Native: Poona Irregular Horse
            Scinde Irregular Horse: three regiments
            South Mahratta Irregular Horse.
                                      (*R.O.I.A.*, Appx, p. 25).

5. (See pp. 224)

The 1st Sikh Irregular Cavalry became in 1861 the 11th Bengal Cavalry. In 1864 it was converted to Lancers, and in 1876 was renamed The 11th

Appendix

(Prince of Wales' Own) Regiment of Bengal Lancers. In 1903, it became The 11th Prince of Wales' Own Lancers, and in 1914, The 11th (King Edward's Own) Lancers (Probyn's Horse).

The 2nd Sikh Irregular Cavalry, raised in 1857 by Captain P. R. Hockin, became in 1861 the 12th Bengal Cavalry; in 1903 the 12th Cavalry.

Both regiments became The 5th King Edward's Own Probyn's Horse in 1922.

6. (See p. 225)

In 1861 Fane's Horse became the 19th Bengal Cavalry, and three years later, the 19th Regiment of Bengal Lancers. In 1903, it became the 19th Lancers (Fane's Horse), and in 1922 was amalgamated with the 18th in the 19th King George's Own Lancers.

7. *Mortality and Sickness rates of Royal cavalry regiments in India.*

1847 to 1856 (ten years):

Bengal: aggregate strength: 14,681
Annual ratio per 1,000 of mean strength who
were attacked   who died
1,364.9   30.85

Bombay: aggregate strength: 6,559
2,091.78   19.21

Madras: aggregate strength: 5,483
1,389.57   17.87

(*I.S.R.*, I, 1863, 590–601)

8. *Some statistics referring to the 9th Lancers, and the 14th and 15th Hussars in India.*

(1) *9th Lancers.*

1843 to 1859 (seventeen years):*   totals
Average annual strength   652
Average annual deaths   40   672
Average annual number of
men sent home   13   227
Average annual reinforcements:
by transfer   4   65

* Including service in suppressing the Mutiny.

457

Average annual reinforcements:
by drafts   59   1,005

(2) *14th Light Dragoons.*
    1842 to 1860 (eighteen years):*   totals
    Average annual strength   655
    Average annual deaths   30   581
    Average annual number of
    men sent home   19   349
    Average annual reinforcements:
    by transfer   11   198
    Average annual reinforcements:
    by drafts   47   910

(3) *15th Hussars.*
    1840 to 1854 (fourteen years):   totals
    Average annual strength   686
    Average annual deaths   17   257
    Average annual number of
    men sent home   18   269
    Average annual reinforcements:
    by transfer   10   156
    Average annual reinforcements:
    by drafts   47   605
                        (I.S.R., I, 1863, 758, 761)

9. *Casualties from 1860 to 1865 Home & India: in the Royal Regiments of cavalry.*

		Dead	Deserted	Discharged			
(1)	1860	90	586	1,333	Home	Total:	2,334
		191	5	129	India		
(2)	1861	106	420	1,396	Home	Total:	2,207
		186	8	91	India		
(3)	1862	76	265	1,099	Home	Total:	1,602
		105	3	54	India		
(4)	1863	94	403	1,132	Home	Total:	1,791
		84	15	63	India		
(5)	1864	93	339	1,180	Home	Total:	1,786
		96	7	71	India		
(6)	1865	81	399	1,183	Home	Total:	1,855
		117	6	69	India		
		1,319	2,456	7,800			

                        (R.C., 1867, 253–4).

* Including service in suppressing the Mutiny.

The Royal Regiments of

	1851	1852	1853	1854	1855	1856	1857	1858	1859
Household Cav. (1660)	H	H	H	H	H	H	H	H	H
1st D.G. (1685)	H	H	H	H	H/CR	CR	H/I	I	I
2nd D.G. (1685)	H	H	H	H	H	H	H/I	I	I
3rd D.G. (1685)	H	H	H	H	H	H	H/I	I	I
4th D.G. (1685)	H	H	H	H/CR	CR	CR/H	H	H	H
5th D.G. (1685)	H	H	H	H/CR	CR	CR/H	H	H	H
6th D.G. (1685)	H	H	H	H	H/CR	CR/I	I	I	I
7th D.G. (1688)	H	H	H	H	H	H	H	I	I
1st D. (1661)	H	H	H	H/CR	CR	CR/H	H	H	H
2nd D. (1678)	H	H	H	H/CR	CR	CR/H	H	H	H
6th D. (1689)	H	H	H	H/CR	CR	CR/H	H	H/I	I
3rd L.D. (1685)	I	I	I/H	H	H	H	H	H	H
4th L.D. (1685)	H	H	H	H/CR	CR	CR/H	H	H	H
5th L. (1858)								H	H
7th H. (1690)	H	H	H	H	H	H	H/I	I	I
8th H. (1693)	H	H	H	H/CR	CR	CR/H	H/I	I	I
9th L. (1715)	I	I	I	I	I	I	I	I	I/H
10th H. (1715)	I	I	I	I	I/CR	CR/H	H	H	H
11th H. (1715)	H	H	H	H/CR	CR	CR/H	H	H	H
12th L. (1715)	H/A	A	A	A/I	I/CR	CR/H/I	I	I	I
13th H. (1715)	H	H	H	H/CR	CR	CR/H	H	H	H
14th L.D. (1715)	I	I	I	I	I	I	I	I	I
15th H. (1759)	I	I	I	I/H	H	H	H	H	H
16th L. (1759)	H	H	H	H	H	H	H	H	H
17th L. (1759)	H	H	H	H/CR	CR	CR/H	H/I	I	I
18th H. (1759)								H	H
19th H. (1861)									
20th H. (1861)									
21st H. (1759)									

Key: A: South Africa   H: Home (i.e. U.K.)
       C: Canada   I: India (incl. Ethiopia)
       CR: Crimea

Cavalry: Stations from 1851–1871

1860	1861	1862	1863	1864	1865	1866	1867	1868	1869	1870	1871
H	H	H	H	H	H	H	H	H	H	H	H
I	I	I	I	I	I/H	H	H	H	H	H	H
I	I	I	I	I	I	I	I	I	I	H	H
I	I	I	I	I	I	I	I	I/H	H	H	H
H	H	H	H	H	H	H	H	H	H	H	H
H	H	H	H	H	H	H	H	H	H	H	H
I	I/H	H	H	H	H	H	H	H	H	H	H
I	I	I	I	I	I	I	I/H	H	H	H	H
H	H	H	H	H	H	H	H	H	H	H	H
H	H	H	H	H	H	H	H	H	H	H	H
I	I	I	I	I	I	I	I/H	H	H	H	H
H	H	H	H	H	H	H	H	H/I	I	I	I
H	H	H	H	H	H	H	H	H	H	H	H
H	H	H	H	H/I	I	I	I	I	I	I	I
I	I	I	I	I	I	I	I	I	I	I/H	H
I	I	I	I	I/H	H	H	H	H	H	H	H
H	H	H	H	H	H	H	H	H	H	H	H
H	H	H	H	H	H	H	H	H	H	H	H
H	H	H	H	H	H	H/I	I	I	I	I	I
I/H	H	H	H	H	H	H	H	H	H	H	H
H	H	H	H	H	H	H/C	C	C	C/H	H	H
I/H	H	H	H	H	H	H	H	H	H	H	H
H	H	H	H	H	H	H	H	H/I	I	I	I
H	H	H	H	H	H/I	I	I	I	I	I	I
I	I	I	I	I	I/H	H	H	H	H	H	H
H	H	H	H	H/I	I	I	I	I	I	I	I
	I	I	I	I	I	I	I	I	I	I/H	H
		I	I	I	I	I	I	I	I	I	I
		I	I	I	I	I	I	I	I	I	I

ABBREVIATIONS USED IN THE
FOOTNOTES AND SOURCE NOTES

Only those sources which occur more than once
in the footnotes or source notes are included in this list.

Acland-Troyte   [Acland-Troyte, J. E.] *Through the Ranks to a Commission*, 1881

Allgood   [Allgood, Lieut G.] *The China Expedition 1860*, Intelligence Branch, India, 1894

Anderson   Anderson, Maj. M. H. and Anderson, Lieut-Col E. S. J. *The Poona Horse (17th Queen Victoria's Own Cavalry), Part I: The 33rd (Queen Victoria's Own) Light Cavalry 1820–1913*, 1933

Anglesey: *Pearman*   Anglesey, Marquess of (ed.) *Sergeant Pearman's Memoirs . . .*, 1968

Anglesey: *Hodge*   Anglesey, Marquess of (ed.) *Little Hodge*, 1971

Annand   Annand, A. McKenzie (ed.) *Cavalry Surgeon: the Recollections of J. H. Sylvester*, 1971

Anson   Anson, H. S. (ed.) *With H.M. Lancers during the Indian Mutiny: the letters of Brevet-Major O. H. S. G. Anson*, 1896

A.P.R.C.   *Report of the Royal Commission on Army Promotion and Retirement*, 1876

Atkinson   Atkinson, C. T. *History of the Royal Dragoons, 1661–1934*, 1934

Baker   Baker, Valentine *The British Cavalry: with remarks on its practical organisation*, 1858

Baring Pemberton   Baring Pemberton, W. *Battles of the Crimean War*, 1962

Barrack Committee   *Report from the Official Committee on Barrack Accommodation for the Army with the Minutes of Evidence, Appendix and Index*, 1855

Barrett   Barrett, C. R. B. *The 7th (Q.O.) Hussars*, 2 vols, 1914

Barrett: *XIII H*   Barrett, C. R. B. *History of the XIII Hussars*, 2 vols, 1911

Bell   Bell, Maj.-Gen. Sir G. *Rough Notes by an Old Soldier*, II, 1867

Blackwood's   [Anon.] 'The Pursuit of Tantia Topee', *Blackwood's Magazine*, Aug 1860

Blake   MS letters from India to Sir H. Stephenson from Blake, W. G., 6 D.G. (Carabiniers), (the property of James Blake Esq.)

Blood   Blood, Gen. Sir Bindon, *Four Score Years and Ten*, 1933

Abbreviations

Bond	Bond, Brian *The Victorian Army and the Staff College, 1854–1914*, 1972
Bond: *Prelude*	Bond, Brian, 'Prelude to the Cardwell Reforms, 1856–68', *J.U.S.I.*, Vol. 106 [1961]
Bonham-Carter	Bonham Carter, V. *Soldier True: the Life and Times of F-M Sir William Robertson, bt., 1860–1933*, 1963
Boyle	Boyle, Maj. C. A. *History of Probyn's Horse (5th King Edward's Own Lancers)*, 1927
Burne	Burne, Sir Owen Tudor, *Clyde and Strathnairn*, 1895
Cadell	Cadell, Sir Patrick, *The History of the Bombay Army*, 1938
Calthorpe	[Calthorpe, Lieut Hon. J. Gough] *Letters from Head-quarters*, 2 vols, 1857
Cardew	Cardew, Lt F. G. *A Sketch of the Services of the Bengal Native Army to the year 1895*, 1903
Cardigan	Cardigan, Earl of, *Eight Months on Active Service; or a Diary of a General Officer of Cavalry in 1854*, 1856
Cattell	MS *Autobiography of Asst-Surgeon William Cattell* (att. 5 D.G.), the property of R.A.M.C. Historical Museum
Chelsea Board	*Report of the Board of General Officers appointed to inquire into the Statements contained in the Reports of Sir John M'Neill . . . Chelsea*, 1856
Churchill	Churchill, W. S. *History of the English-Speaking Peoples*, 4 vols, 1957
Clode	Clode, Charles M., *The Military Forces of the Crown, their Administration and Government*, 2 vols, 1869
Clothing Regulations, 1862	*Regulations for the Provision of Clothing and Necessaries for the Army*, 1862
Clowes	Clowes, Cornet George C., 8 H., MS letters from the Crimea, 1854–55, the property of Col Henry Clowes
Clowes: India	Clowes, Capt. George C., 8 H., MS letters from India, 1857–1859, the property of Col Henry Clowes
C.M.C.	*Reports of the Commissioners appointed to inquire into the Constitution and Practice of Courts-Martial in the Army, and the Present System of Punishment for Military Offences (Courts-Martial Commission)*, 1869
Coffin	Coffin, Lt K. D., 3 Madras European Regt, to his father, Brig. I. C. Coffin, 20 Apr., 1858, (ed.), Lieut-Col M. E. S. Laws 'Contemporary Account of the Battle of Banda, 1858', *J.A.H.R.*, XXXII (1954), 160–4
Combe	'C.C.' [Charles Combe], 3 Bombay L.C., *Letters from Persia and India, 1856–1859* (privately printed), n.d.
Cornhill	[Anon.] 'Indian Cossacks', *Cornhill Magazine*, VII, 1863
Cruse	Cruse, TS–M, 1 R.D., MS letters to his wife from the Crimea, the property of the author
Daly	Daly, Maj. H. *Memoirs of General Sir Henry Dermot Daly . . .*, 1905
Denholm	Denholm, Anthony, 'Lord de Grey and Army Reform, 1859–1866', *Army Quarterly*, 1971

Abbreviations

Denison	Denison, Lieut-Col G. T., jun. *Modern Cavalry: Its Organisation, Armament and Employment in War*, 1868
Duberly	Duberly, Mrs H. *Journal kept during the Russian War: from the departure of the Army from England in April, 1854, to the fall of Sebastopol*, 1855
Evans	Evans, Maj.-Gen. R. *The Story of the 5th Royal Inniskilling Dragoon Guards*, 1951
Farquharson	Farquharson, K. S. *Reminiscences of Crimean Campaigns and Russian Imprisonment by One of the 'Six Hundred'*, [1883]
Fisher	Fisher (-Rowe), Cornet (later Capt.) Edward R., 4 D.G., *Extracts from Letters written during the Crimean War, 1854–1855*, ed. by his son, Maj. L. R. Fisher-Rowe, (privately printed), Godalming, 1907
Forbes	Forbes, A. *Camps, Quarters and Casual Places*, 1896
Forrest	MS *Letters of William Charles Forrest from the Crimea, 1854–1855*, the property of the National Army Museum
Forrest: *Mutiny*	Forrest, G. W. *A History of the Indian Mutiny reviewed and illustrated from original documents*, 3 vols, 1904–12
Fortescue	Fortescue, J. W. *A History of the British Army*, 13 vols, 1899–1930
Fortescue: *Canteens*	Fortescue, J. W. *A Short Account of Canteens in the British Army*, 1928
Fortescue: *17 L*	Fortescue, J. W. *A History of the 17th Lancers*, 1895
Gimlette	Gimlette, Lieut-Col G. H. D. *A Postscript to the Records of the Indian Mutiny: an attempt to trace the subsequent careers and fate of the rebel Bengal Regiments, 1857–1858*, 1927 [page nos. refer to the original typescript in the present author's possession]
Gough	Gough, General Sir Hugh, *Old Memories*, 1897
Graham	Graham, H. *History of the 16th Light Dragoons, 1759–1912*, 1912
Grey Neville	MS letters of Cornet Grey Neville, 5 D.G., 1854, the property of Mrs L. M. Chesterton
Guides	[Anon.] *History of the Guides, 1846–1922*, 1938
Hamilton	Hamilton, Col H. B. *Historical Record of the 14th (King's) Hussars*, 1901
Hansard: (C)	*Hansard's Parliamentary Debates*, House of Commons
Hansard: (L)	*Hansard's Parliamentary Debates*, House of Lords
Havelock	Havelock, Sir Henry M. bart, *Three Main Military Questions of the Day*, 1867
Heneage	Heneage, Capt. Clement, 8 H., MS letters from the Crimea, 1854–1855 and from India, 1861–62, the property of Mrs B. Walker-Heneage-Vivian
Hibbert	Hibbert, Christopher, *The Destruction of Lord Raglan, a Tragedy of the Crimean War, 1854–1855*, 1961
Hodge papers	The unpublished letters and diaries of Lieut-Col E. C. Hodge, 4 D.G. (In the possession of F. R. Hodge, Esq.)

Hodson	Hodson, G. H. (ed.) *Hodson of Hodson's Horse, or Twelve Years of a Soldier's Life in India*, 1883
Hodson's Horse	Cardew, Maj. F. G. *Hodson's Horse, 1857–1922*, 1928
Holland and Hozier	Holland, Maj. T. J., Bombay Staff Corps and Hozier, Capt. H. M., 3 D.G., *Record of the Expedition to Abyssinia compiled by Order of the Secretary of State for War*, 2 vols, 1870
Hyderabad	Burton, Col R. G. *A History of the Hyderabad Contingent*, 1905
Hyom	MS notebook of Pte Hyom, 10 H., 1847–185? (in the possession of E. A. K. Patrick Esq.)
Incidents	Knollys, H. (ed.) *Incidents in the Sepoy War, 1857–58, compiled from the Private Journals of Gen. Sir Hope Grant*, 1873
I.O.L.	India Office Library
I.S.R.	*Royal Commission on the Sanitary State of the Army in India. Report of the Commissioners . . .*, 1865
Jackson	Jackson, Maj. E. S. *The Inniskilling Dragoons*, 1909
JAHR	*Journal of the Society for Army Historical Research*
Jocelyn	Jocelyn, Col J. R. J. *History of the Royal Artillery (Crimean Period)*, 1911
Journal	MS 'Journal of an Eyewitness of the Central Indian Campaign' [probably an ADC or Secretary to Sir Robt Hamilton], *Mutiny Papers of Sir John Kaye*, India Office Records, H/725 (13) (Home Misc. Series)
JUSI	*Journal of the United Services Institution*
Kinglake	Kinglake, A. W. *The Invasion of the Crimea: its origin and . . . progress down to the death of Lord Raglan*, 8 vols, 1868–87 (various editions)
Knollys	Knollys, H. (ed.), *Life of General Sir Hope Grant*, 2 vols, 1894
Lambrick	Lambrick, H. T. *John Jacob of Jacobabad*, 1960
Layard	Layard, A. H. to Murray, John, 23 Oct 1854, B.M. Add. MSS 38982, f. 321
Liddell	Liddell, Col R. S. *The Memoirs of the Tenth Royal Hussars (Prince of Wales' Own), Historical and Social*, 1891
Lightfoot	Lightfoot, Lieut-Col J. G., Bombay Horse Artillery, MS letters, Jan–Sep, 1858, the property of Miss M. S. Lightfoot
Lowe	Lowe, Thomas, *Central India during the Rebellion of 1857 and 1858 . . .*, 1860
Lucas	MS 'Autobiography of Pte Wm Lucas, 7th Dragoon Guards, 1830–1865', the property of E. A. Lucas, Esq.
Lyttelton	Lyttelton, Gen. Sir Neville, *Eighty Years Soldiering, Politics, Games*, 1927
McCalmont	Callwell, Maj.-Gen. Sir C. E., *The Memoirs of Major-General Sir Hugh McCalmont*, 1924

Abbreviations

MacDougall	MacDougall, Col *Modern Warfare as influenced by Modern Artillery*, 1864
Maclagan	Maclagan, Michael *'Clemency' Canning*, 1962
McNeill and Tulloch	[McNeill, Sir John and Tulloch, Col] *Report of the Commission of Inquiry into the Supplies of the British Army in the Crimea*, [1855]
Malleson	Malleson, Col G. B. *History of the Indian Mutiny 1857–1858, commencing from the close of the second volume of Sir John Kaye's History of the Sepoy War*, 3 vols, 5th ed., 1896
Marshman	Marshman, J. C. *Memoirs of Sir Henry Havelock*, 1860
Maxwell	Maxwell, Capt. E. L. *The History of the XIth King Edward's Own Lancers, Probyn's Horse*, 1914
May	May, Maj. E. S. *Guns and Cavalry: their performances in the past and their prospects in the future*, 1896
M.E.C. (*1*), 1869	*First and Second Reports of the Royal Commission appointed*
M.E.C. (*2*), 1870	*to inquire into the present state of Military Education*, 1869 and 1870
Midshipman	Wood, F-M Sir Evelyn, VC, *From Midshipman to Field Marshal*, 1906
Mitchell	[Mitchell, A.] *Recollections of One of the Light Brigade*, Canterbury, 1885
Mole	[Mole, Edwin] *A King's Hussar, being the Military Memoirs for 25 Years of a Troop Sergeant Major of the 14th (King's) Hussars*, (ed.) Compton, H., 1893
Mouat	Mouat, Fred. J. *The British Soldier in India*, 1859
Moyse-Bartlett	Moyse-Bartlett, Lieut-Col H. *Louis Edward Nolan and his influence on the British Cavalry*, 1971
Murray	Murray, Rev. R. H. *The History of the VIII King's Royal Irish Hussars, 1693–1927*, 2 vols, 1928
Nolan	Nolan, Capt. L. E., 15 H., *Cavalry; Its History and Tactics*, 1853
Oatts	Oatts, Lieut-Col L. B. *I Serve: Regimental History of the 3rd Carabiniers . . .*, 1966
O'Donnell	[O'Donnell, Capt. I.] *1st King's Dragoon Guards . . . 1685 to 1912*, 1913
Ouvry	Ouvry, Col H. A. *Cavalry Experiences and Leaves from my Journal*, 1892
Paget	Paget, Gen. Lord George, *The Light Cavalry Brigade in the Crimea*, 1861
Paget, Leopold	Paget, Maj. Leopold, R.H.A., 'How I helped in the Pursuit of Tantia Topee', Paget, Mrs Leopold *Camp and Cantonments, A Journal of Life in India in 1857–1859, with Some Account of the Way Thither*, 1865
Palmer	Palmer, J. A. B. *The Mutiny Outbreak in 1857*, 1966
Pearse	Pearse, Col H. *The Hearseys*, 1905
Phillips	Phillips, Maj. Edward, 8 H., MS Letters from the Crimea, 1854, the property of Hugh E. Sutton, Esq.

Pomeroy	Pomeroy, Maj. Hon. R. L. *The Story of the 5th Princess Charlotte of Wales' Dragoon Guards*
Poore	Poore, Maj. Robt Poore, 8 H., MS Letters from India, 1857–58, the property of Robt Poore-Saurin-Watts, Esq.
Poore, R. M.	Poore, Maj. R. M., 7 H., 'The New Cavalry Sword and Mounted Swordsmanship', *Cavalry Journal*, III, (1908)
Portal	Portal, Capt. Robt, 4 L.D., *Letters from the Crimea, 1854–1855* (privately printed), Winchester, 1900
Potiphar	Potiphar, Pte F., 9 L., MS narrative, India, 1857–59, the property of L. Potiphar, Esq.
Preston	Preston, A. W., 'British Military Thought, 1856–90', *Army Quarterly*, LXXXIX, No. 1, Oct, 1964
P.R.O.	Public Records Office papers
P.E.S.C.	*Report of the Commissioners appointed to inquire into the System of Purchase and Sale of Commissions in the Army, 1857*
Punjab Cavalry	[Anon.] *History of the 2nd Punjab Cavalry, 1849–1886, 1888*
Q.R.	*The Queen's Regulations and Orders for the Army, 1844, 1857 and 1859*
R.C., 1861	*Report of the Commissioners appointed to inquire into the Present System of Recruiting in the Army, 1861*
R.C., 1867	*Report of the Commissioners appointed to inquire into the Recruiting for the Army, 1867*
RCP	The Crimean Papers of Lord Raglan, the property of Lord Raglan
Revolt	[Malleson, W.] *The Revolt in Central India, 1857–1859, compiled in the Intelligence Branch Div. of the C.O.S., Army HQ, India*, 1908
R.M.C.R., 1855	*Report of the Select Committee on Sandhurst Royal Military College, 1855*
Roads	Roads, C. H. *The British Soldier's Firearm, 1850–1864,* 1964
Roberts	Roberts, F-M Lord, VC., *Forty-one Years in India*, 2 vols, 1897
R.O.I.A., 1859	*Report of the Commissioners appointed to inquire into the Organization of the Indian Army*, 1859
S.C.	*Report of the Commissioners appointed to inquire into the Regulations affecting the Sanitary Condition of the Army, the organisation of Military Hospitals, and the Treatment of the Sick and Wounded; with Evidence and Appendix*, 1858 (known as the 'Royal Sanitary Commission')
Scott Daniell	Scott Daniell, D. *4th Hussar: the Story of the 4th Queen's Own Hussars, 1685–1958*, 1959
Selections	Forrest, G. W. (ed.) *Selections from the Letters, Despatches and other State Papers preserved in the Military Dept of the Govt of India, 1857–1858*, 4 vols, 1893

Sen	Sen, S. N. *Eighteen Fifty-Seven*, 1957
Sepoy War	Kaye, J. W. *A History of the Sepoy War in India*, 1857–58, 3 vols, 5th ed., 1896
Shadwell	Lieut-Gen. Shadwell, *The Life of Colin Campbell, Lord Clyde*, 2 vols, 1881
Shakespear	Shakespear, Capt. C. M. J. D., RHA, Unpublished 'Diary of events and observations during the Turkish campaign of 1854, being an account of what I saw, heard and thought', the property of Mrs L. S. Bickford
Shakespear, letters	Shakespear, Capt. C. M. J. D., RHA, MS letters, 1854, the property of Mrs L. S. Bickford
Sheppard	Sheppard, Maj. E. W. *The Ninth Queen's Royal Lancers, 1715–1936*, 1939
Smith	Smith, Sir Fred. 'Saddles and Saddlery, Bits and Bitting', Lecture, Aldershot Military Society, II, 1891
Smith, *H.R.A.V.C.*	Smith, Sir Fred. *A History of the Royal Army Veterinary Corps 1796–1919*, 1927
Spear	Spear, Percival (Smith, V. A.), *The Oxford History of India, Part III*, 1964 ed.
Stent	Stent, G. C., *Scraps from My Sabretasche, being personal adventures while in the 14th (King's Light) Dragoons*, 1882
Stubbs	Stubbs, Maj.-Gen. F. W., *History of the Organization, Equipment and War Services of the Regiment of Bengal Artillery*, 3 vols, 1877–95
Sutherland	[The Sutherland Report], *General Report of the Commission appointed for Improving the Sanitary Condition of Barracks and Hospitals*, 1861
Sylvester	Sylvester, Asst-Surgeon J. H. *Recollections of the Campaign in Malwa and Central India under Maj.-Gen. Sir Hugh Rose*, Bombay, 1860
Sylvester, diary	Sylvester, Asst-Surgeon J. H., MS diary, India, the property of Miss Beryl A. Sylvester Hodder
Thomson	Anstruther Thomson, Col *Eighty Years' Reminiscences*, 2 vols, 1904
Tisdall	Tisdall, E. E. P. (ed.), *Mrs Duberly's Campaigns*, 1963
Tylden	Tylden, Maj. G. *Horses and Saddlery: an account of the animals used by the British and Commonwealth Armies from the 17th century to the present day with a description of their equipment*, 1965
Tyrrell	Tyrrell, Lieut-Gen. F. H. 'In Piam Memoriam: the Services of the Madras Native Troops in the Suppression of the Mutiny of the Bengal Army', *Imperial and Asiatic Quarterly Review*, July, 1908
Vibart	Vibart, Maj. H. M. *The Military History of the Madras Engineers and Pioneers from 1743 up to the present time*, 2 vols, 1883
Wake	Wake, Joan, *The Brudenells of Deene*, 1953
Walker	Walker, Gen. Sir C. P. Beauchamp, *Days of a Soldier's*

Life, being letters written during Active Service in the Crimean, Chinese, Austro-Prussian (1866) and Franco-German (1870–1871) Wars, 1894

Watson   Watson, Maj.-Gen. W. A. *King George's Own Central India Horse: the story of a local corps*, 1930

Whinyates: Strangways   Whinyates, Col F. A. *From Coruna to Sevastopol: the History of 'C' Battery, 'A' Brigade (late 'C' Troop), R.H.A.*, 1884. [Balaklava chapter by Lt F. Strangways]

Whyte and Atteridge   Whyte, F. and Atteridge, Hilliard A., *A History of the Queen's Bays (the 2nd Dragoon Guards), 1685–1929*, 1930

Wightman   Wightman, Pte J. W., 'One of the "Six Hundred" in the Balaclava Charge', *The Nineteenth Century*, May, 1892

Wilkinson-Latham   Wilkinson-Latham, John, *British Cut and Thrust Weapons*, 1971

Willcox   Willcox, W. T. *The Historical Records of the Fifth (Royal Irish) Lancers . . .*, 1908

Williams: *XI H*   Williams, Capt. G. T. *The Historical Records of the Eleventh Hussars, Prince Albert's Own*, 1908

Wombwell   Wombwell, Lieut George Orby, 17 L., MS diary of the Crimean War, 1854, the property of Capt. V. M. Wombwell

Wolseley   Wolseley, Gen. Visc. 'The Army', Ward, T. H. *The Reign of Queen Victoria*, 1887

Wolseley: *China War*   Wolseley, Lieut-Col G. J. *Narrative of the War with China in 1860*, 1862

Wolseley: *S.P.B.*   Wolseley, Col Sir G. J. *The Soldier's Pocket Book for Field Service*, 2nd ed., 1871

Wood   Wood, Gen. Sir Evelyn, VC, *The Crimea in 1854 and 1894*, 1896

Wood: *Br. Cav.*   Wood, F-M Sir Evelyn, VC, 'British Cavalry, 1853–1903', *Cavalry Journal*, I, (1906)

Woodham-Smith   Woodham-Smith, Cecil, *The Reason Why*, 1953

Yorke   Yorke, Lieut-Col John, commanding 1st Royal Dragoons, MS letters to his sister, the property of the author

SOURCE NOTES

PREFACE (pp. 21–23)

1   Preston, 57
2   Denholm, 64

CHAPTER I (pp. 27–125)

(i)

1   Fortescue, XIII, 30
2   28 May, 30 July 1853, *Punch*
3   Smith, *H.R.A.V.C.*, 127
4   Wood, 149

(ii)

1   Part I, XII
2   Lord John Russell, *Hansard: C,* 1852
3   Craig, G., 'The System of Alliances and the Balance of Power', *New Cambridge Modern History,* X, 1960, 267
4   Churchill, W. S. *A History of the English-Speaking Peoples,* IV, 'The Great Democracies', 1958, 57–8
5   Pomeroy, 167
6   Murray, II, 407
7   4 Apr 1854, Anglesey: *Hodge,* 5
8   See, for example, Atkinson, 325
9   8, 12 Apr 1854, Hodge papers
10   12 May 1854, Yorke
11   Mitchell, 9, 10
12   1 June 1854, Cruse
13   Mitchell, 11–12
14   Capt. W. G. B. Cresswell to Capt. R. Thomson, 10 June 1854, Williams: *XI H,* 181
15   29 May, 17 Jun 1854, Anglesey: *Hodge,* 11, 13
16   12 May 1854, Clowes
17   Farquharson, 5–6
18   Jackson, 157–8
19   Wombwell, 1
20   25 July 1854, Portal
21   29 June 1854, Cruse
22   6 July 1854, Anglesey: *Hodge,* 14
23   Portal, 11

24   Dr Humphry Sandwith to A. H. Layard, 6 Jun 1854, B.M. Add. MSS 38982 f.280

25   *Third Report from the Select Committee on the Army before Sebastopol*, 115

26   26 July 1854, Wombwell, 31

27   Quoted in a letter from F. J. Duberly, brother of Capt. H. Duberly, to Mrs Butt, 24 June 1854. (MS Letter, property of Miss G. M. Biddulph)

28   8 May 1855, *Forrest*

29   18 Jan 1856, Heneage

30   Duberly. See also Tisdall

31   Cardigan, 35, 36, 48

32   Notes made by Capt. Tremayne, quoted in Barrett: *XIII H*, I, 326

33   Raglan to Cardigan, 3 July 1854, P.R.O., K.B.1/265, 26–7

34   Letter from Mrs Duberly, quoted in Tisdall, 47

35   Letter of Capt. S. G. Jenyns, 19 July 1854, Thomson, I, 166

36   31 July 1854, Williams: *XI H*, 182

37   29 July, 17, 22 Aug 1854, Shakespear, Letters

38   Speech of Lord Lyndhurst, 19 June 1854, *Hansard: (L)*, vol. 134, 306–19

39   6 June 1854, Wombwell

40   Lucas, 29

41   9 July 1854, Anglesey: *Hodge*, 16

42   Farquharson, 8

43   3 Aug 1854, Grey Neville

44   Atkinson, 325; 7 Aug 1854, Cruse

45   18 Aug 1854, Anglesey: *Hodge*, 23

46   7 Aug 1854, Cruse

47   7 Aug 1854, Portal, 14

48   18 June 1854, Wombwell

49   11 Aug 1854, Wombwell, 38

50   7 Aug 1854, Portal, 19

51   5 Aug 1854, Anglesey: *Hodge*, 22; 19, 29 Aug 1854, Hodge papers

52   Bell, 203

53   12 Aug 1854, Heneage

54   Paget, 5

55   16 July 1854, Cruse; 26 Jul 1854, Yorke

56   15 July, 8 Aug 1854, Anglesey: *Hodge*, 18, 22

57   12 Aug 1854, Fisher, 12

58   11 July 1854, Grey Neville

59   9, 28 Aug 1854, 22, 24; 24 Aug 1854, Hodge papers; Pomeroy, 172

60   7, 17 Aug 1854, Portal

61   29 July 1854, Shakespear, letters

62   6 Aug 1854, Grey Neville, 3

63   2 July 1854, Cruse

64   Raglan Private Papers (Cefntilla Court) D(1)206; quoted in Hibbert, 31

(iii)

1   Martineau, H. *England and Her Soldiers*, 1859, 71

2   3 Sep 1854, Walker

3   21 Sep 1854, Fisher
4   Portal, quoted in Scott Daniell, 167
5   Murray, II, 411
6   Mitchell, 33–4
7   Paget, 15
8   Murray, II, 411
9   McNeill and Tulloch, 12, 13
10   Wombwell, II, 4
11   Mitchell, 41
12   Diary of Capt. W. A. Godfrey, Rifle Brigade, quoted in Hibbert, 43
13   18 Sep 1854, Portal, 28
14   Bell, 216
15   Quoted in Woodham-Smith, 177
16   Mitchell, 48
17   Cardigan, 75
18   Cardigan, 75
19   Pennington, W. H. in Kelly, Mrs Tom. *From the Fleet in the Fifties*, 1902, 124
20   Mitchell, 49
21   Shakespear, 26–7
22   May, 71
23   Barrett: *XIII H,* 338
24   Gen. Sir R. Palmer (then a cornet of the 11th), in Williams: *XI H,* 190
25   Letters of Pte John Williams, 41 Foot, quoted in Hibbert, 51
26   Fortescue, XIII, 55
27   Paget, 22
28   Shakespear, 29–30
29   Kinglake, III, 286
30   Wombwell, 9
31   Wombwell, 9
32   Paget, 29
33   Quoted in Woodham-Smith, 195

(iv)

1   Hibbert, 101
2   Powell, H., 13 L.D. *Recollections of a Young Soldier during the Crimean War,* 1876, 16
3   25 Sep 1854, Shakespear
4   Walker, 116
5   25 Sep 1854, Shakespear
6   Walker, 116
7   25 Sep 1854, Shakespear
8   25 Sep 1854, Wombwell
9   Walker, 117
10   Calthorpe, I, 217–18
11   Kinglake, III, 90
12   Cardigan, 81

13   1 Oct 1854, Cruse
14   Capt. M. Stocks, quoted in Atkinson, 326
15   1 Oct 1954, Cruse
16   [Anon.] *A Month in the Camp before Sebastopol, by a Non-Combatant,*
      1855, 13
17   'October, 1854' (letter 17), Yorke
18   Jackson, 161
19   *Chelsea Board,* 47

(v)

1   25 Nov 1854, Portal, 71
2   Layard
3   Fortescue, XIII, 92
4   8 Oct 1854, Fisher
5   Kinglake, V (6th ed.) 20, 21
6   Quoted in Woodham-Smith, 200
7   Cardigan, 83
8   7 Oct 54, Shakespear, letters
9   Paget, 65; Layard
10   19 Oct 1854, Cardigan, 86
11   21 Oct 1854, Anglesey: *Hodge,* 39

(vi)

1   Cattell, 14
2   23 Oct 1854, Phillips
3   Walker, 117
4   12 Oct 1854, Fisher
5   21 Oct 1854, Wombwell
6   Stocks quoted in Atkinson, 327
7   Maude, quoted in Woodham-Smith, 211
8   Cattell, 3
9   Farquharson, 31
10   25 Oct 1854, Shakespear
11   2 Nov 1854, Shakespear, letters
12   Paget, 164
13   5 Dec 1854, Yorke
14   Calthorpe, I, 303
15   Paget, 165–6
16   Jocelyn, 199
17   19 Mar 1855, *Hansard: (L),* 733
18   5 Dec 1854, Yorke
19   2 Nov 1854, Shakespear, letters
20   This seems to have been originated by W. H. Russell. In his *Letters to
      the 'Times' from the Crimea,* 1855, the phrase is printed as 'thin red streak
      topped with a line of steel'. Russell claims that he actually wrote 'tipped'.
      In a later, corrected, edition of the letters, entitled *The British Expedition*

to the Crimea, 1877, p. 156, the words are: 'thin red line tipped with steel.' See *Notes and Queries*, 1894–5, 8th S. vi, 379; vii, 57, 115–16, 191. Kinglake writes 'slender red line' (Kinglake, III, 248 (1868)). In his poem 'Tommy', Rudyard Kipling quotes the phrase more than once. E.g.: 'But it's "Thin red line of 'eroes" when the drums begin to roll.' In 1915 Sir Henry Newbolt published a volume called *The Book of the Thin Red Line*.

21 Account of 'an eye-witness' who served with "C" Troop, R.H.A., probably Lieut (later Col) W. A. Fox Strangways, in Whinyates, 133. See also Forbes, 67–82; and Tylden, Maj. G. 'The Heavy Brigade Charge at Balaklava', *J.A.H.R.*, XIX (1940), 98–103

22 Whinyates: Strangways, 128

23 Whinyates: Strangways, 130–1

24 Woodham-Smith, 222

25 Paget, 173

26 Kinglake, V (6th ed.), 89

27 Kinglake, V, 90

28 Kinglake, V, 99

29 Cattell, 11

30 Paget, 175

31 Cattell, 11

32 Moyse-Bartlett, 210

33 Whinyates: Strangways, 130, 136

34 Cattell, 12

35 Whinyates: Strangways, 132

36 General Dacres to Mrs E. Hodge, 8 Dec 1854, Anglesey: *Hodge*, 47

37 5 Dec 1854, Yorke

38 Whinyates: Strangways, 135

39 Maj. Thornhill quoted in May, *Changes and Chances of a Soldier's Life*, 1925, 184

40 Whinyates: Strangways, 143

41 Lt-Col Griffiths, P.R.O. (W.O.44/701)

42 Wood, 113

43 Wood, 113

44 Whinyates: Strangways, 134

45 Wood, 114

46 27 Oct 1854, *Forrest*

47 Cattell, 16–17

48 Kinglake, V, 126

49 Capt. Godman, adjutant, 5 D.G., quoted in May, 92

50 Whinyates: Strangways, 137

51 Godman quoted in May, 92

52 Cattell, 15

53 27 Oct 1854, *Forrest*

54 Lucan to Scarlett, 18 Dec 1854, and fn, Kinglake, V, 418–19

55 Cattell, 14

56 Kinglake, V, 167

57 Cardigan, 88–9

58 Kinglake, V, 170

59   Wightman, 851; Hibbert, 141; Kinglake, V, 176–7
60   Cardigan's answer to Calthorpe (Vol. I, 310); Calthorpe's affidavit, P.R.O., K.B.1/266, 9
61   Kinglake, V, 176–7
62   Cardigan's and Calthorpe's affidavits, P.R.O., K.B.1/266
63   Pomeroy, 174; Atkinson, 331; 26 Oct 1854, Walker
64   Whinyates: Strangways, 202
65   5 Dec 1854, Yorke
66   *Edinburgh Review*, CXXVIII (185), 408

(vii)

1   [Gowing, T.] *A Soldier's Experience or A Voice from the Ranks: showing the Cost of War in Blood and Treasure*. . . . 'By One of the Royal Fusiliers,' 1892, 67; Hutton to Holland, 28 Oct 1854, E.H.N., 'Some Letters of Major Thomas Everard Hutton written after Balaclava', *IV Hussars' Journal*, Oct 1933, 32
2   Kinglake, (1877), V, 184
3   Woodham-Smith, 234
4   Kinglake, (1877), V, 186–7
5   Calthorpe, I, 313
6   Moyse-Bartlett, 125–6
7   Kinglake, (1877), V, 192
8   Kinglake, (1877), V, 200
9   Lucan's speech, 19 Mar 1855, *Hansard: (L)*, 730–52
10   Kinglake, (1877), V, 202
11   30 Nov 1854, Lucan to Raglan, *Raglan Papers*
12   Kinglake, (1877), V, 204
13   27 Oct 1854, Lucan to Raglan, *Raglan Papers*
14   22 Oct 1854, Yorke
15   For instance, see Woodham-Smith, 239
16   Cardigan's memorandum sent to Raglan, 27 Oct 1854, quoted in Kinglake, (1877), V, 210; see also Kinglake, (1877), V, 405 for Cardigan's 'statement' to Kinglake
17   Cardigan, 89; Kinglake, (1877), V, 211, 212
18   Whinyates, 201
19   Explanatory statement for Kinglake made by Lucan, Kinglake, (1877), V, 404
20   Paget, 170
21   Wightman, 852–3
22   Kinglake, (1877), V, 261–2
23   Paget, 178
24   Wombwell
25   Shakespear, letter or newspaper?, [n.d.]
26   Whinyates: Strangways, 161
27   Whinyates: Strangways, 161–2
28   Kinglake, (1877), V, 226
29   Kinglake, (1877), V, 219

30 Baring Pemberton, 97–8
31 26 Oct 1854, Portal
32 Mitchell, 4, 5
33 Kinglake, (1877), V, 247
34 Wombwell, 10–11
35 Cardigan to Howe, 28 Oct 1854, quoted in Wake, 408
36 Wightman, 854
37 Wombwell, 10
38 Thomson, 178
39 29 Oct 1854, Walker
40 Wake, 406
41 26 Oct 1854, Cruse
42 5 Dec 1854, Yorke
43 Kinglake, (1877), V, 294
44 Explanatory statement to Kinglake, Kinglake, (1877), V, 404
45 29 Oct 1854, Walker
46 Mitchell, 79
47 Cardigan, 90
48 25 Oct 1854, Wombwell
49 'Col Tremayne's "Crimean Notes" ', Barrett: *XIII H*, I, 365
50 Thomson, 180
51 Cardigan, 90
52 Affidavit of Capt. Percy Smith, P.R.O., K.B.1/265
53 Cardigan's statement to Kinglake, Kinglake, (1877), V, 408
54 Paget, 207
55 Cardigan's statement to Kinglake, Kinglake, (1877), V, 409
56 'Paper furnished to me by Lord Cardigan', Kinglake, (1877), V, 360–1
57 Extract from Cardigan's evidence in Cardigan *v.* Calthorpe, quoted in Kinglake, (1877), V, 410
58 Kinglake, (1877), V, 253
59 Wightman, 856
60 'Col Douglas's Remarks on My Account of the Battle of Balaclava', Paget, 247–8
61 Paget, 183–4
62 Mitchell, 79
63 Paget, 180–1
64 Paget, 190–2
65 Paget, 206
66 Kinglake, (1877), V, 283
67 27 Oct 1854, Phillips
68 Brandling's account in Whinyates, 165–8
69 'Statement laid before Mr. Kinglake by Lord Cardigan', Kinglake, (1877), V, 405
70 Whinyates, 140
71 Mitchell, 79
72 Barrett: *XIII H*, I, 364
73 Affidavit of James Donoghue, P.R.O., K.B.1/266
74 Cardigan, 91; Kinglake, (1877), V, 337

75   Cardigan, 92
76   Affidavit of TSM F. Short, 4 L.D., P.R.O., K.B.1/266
77   Kinglake, (1877), V, 325
78   Kinglake, (1877), V, 332
79   MS letter from Lieut Arthur M. Earle, 57th Foot, quoted in Baring Pemberton, 112
80   Quoted in Woodham-Smith, 264
81   Whinyates, 201; Kinglake, (1877), V, 326
82   Paget, 199–200
83   Wightman, 856–7
84   18 Nov 1855, Anglesey: *Hodge*, 136
85   Williams: *XI H*, 219
86   Kinglake, (1868), IV, 382
87   Quoted by Kinglake, (1877), V, 287
88   Newcastle Papers
89   General After Orders, 29 Oct 1854, quoted in Cardigan, 109
90   Hallam Lord Tennyson *Alfred Lord Tennyson: A Memoir*, 1897, I, 381, 409–10; Ricks, Christopher (ed.) *The Poems of Tennyson*, 1969, 1034–6
91   5 Mar 1855, Fisher
92   Cardigan's affidavit, P.R.O., K.B.1/265, 22
93   The best recent biography of Cardigan is Compton, Piers *Cardigan of Balaclava*, 1972

(viii)

1   Russell, W. H. *The War from the Death of Lord Raglan to the Evacuation of the Crimea*, 1856, 433; Martineau, Harriet, *England and Her Soldiers*, 1859, 44
2   Mrs Duberly, 125; 31 Oct 1854, Wombwell; Calthorpe, I, 336–7
3   MS letter of Paymaster Henry Dixon, Royal Fusiliers
4   Whinyates, 210–11
5   15 Nov 1854, Anglesey: *Hodge*, 58
6   Capt. Duberly, 8 H, to Mrs Butt, 18 Nov 1854. [Property of Miss G. M. Biddulph]
7   R.C.P. (M.M. 184 Raglan to Newcastle, Private, 28 Nov 1854)
8   18 Nov 1854, Shakespear, letters
9   R.C.P. (M.M. 190 Filder to Trevelyan, 13 Nov 1854)
10   Anglesey: *Hodge*, 29 Nov 1854, 61
11   Lt-Col Low, 4 L.D., McNeill & Tulloch, 15
12   Lt-Col Doherty, 13 L.D., McNeill & Tulloch, 14
13   Assistant Commissary General A. Crookshank to Lucan, 21 Nov 1854, *Chelsea Board*, 42
14   14, 29 Jan 1854, Cruse
15   24 Dec 1854, Portal, 93
16   Raglan to Newcastle, 18 Nov 1854
17   17 Nov 1854, Portal, 65
18   Lt-Col Griffiths, the Greys, *Chelsea Board*, 27
19   Clifford, Henry, V.C. *His Letters and Sketches from the Crimea*, 1956, 105–6

20   Mitchell, 100
21   1 Dec 1854, Phillips
22   3 Jan, 1 Feb 1855, Cruse
23   5 Jan 1855, Wombwell
24   12 Dec 1854, *Forrest*, 13
25   Lucan to Adj.-Gen., 17 Jan 1855, *Chelsea Board*, 15–16
26   21 Dec 1854, Portal, 88
27   Lucan's evidence, *Chelsea Board*, 26, 116
28   22 Dec 1854, Shakespear, letters
29   12 Dec. 1854, Anglesey: *Hodge*, 64
30   8 Jan 1855, Wombwell
31   Whinyates, 221–2
32   19 Jan 1855, Heneage
33   15, 18 Jan 1855, *Forrest*
34   Lucan to Adj.-Gen., 17 Jan 1855, *Chelsea Board*, 16
35   23 Apr 1855, Anglesey: *Hodge*, 80–1
36   Col D. Griffiths in examination, McNeill & Tulloch, 10
37   9 Apr 1855, Portal, 158
38   McNeill and Tulloch
39   McNeill and Tulloch, 36
40   *Chelsea Board*
41   *Chelsea Board*, 187
42   17 Nov 1854, Portal, 65
43   J. B. St C. Crosse's evidence, McNeill and Tulloch, 31
44   28 Dec 1854, Anglesey: *Hodge*, 70
45   3 Jan 1855, Cruse
46   17 Dec 1854, *Forrest*
47   10 Feb 1855, Anglesey: *Hodge*, 86; 16 Feb 1855, Hodge papers
48   Evidence of Asst Surgeon W. Cattell, 5 D.G., McNeill and Tulloch, 27
49   Evidence of Maj. Wardlaw, 1 R.D., McNeill and Tulloch, 8
50   H. Kendall's evidence, McNeill and Tulloch, 29
51   Mitchell, 112
52   22 Dec 1854, *Forrest*
53   19 Nov 1854, Fisher
54   Kinglake, VI, 197
55   Evidence of Surgeon R. Cooper, 4 D.G., McNeill and Tulloch, 21
56   Evidence of Surgeon Kendall, 4 L.D., McNeill and Tulloch, 29
57   Evidence of Surgeon Forteath, 1 R.D., McNeill and Tulloch, 26
58   Evidence of Surgeon R. Cooper, 4 D.G., McNeill and Tulloch, 25
59   Anglesey: *Pearman*, 116
60   16 May 1855, Hodge papers; 29 May 1855, Anglesey: *Hodge*, 109–10
61   9 May 1855, Fisher
62   30 Apr 1855, Portal
63   Thomson, 181
64   1 Jan 1855, Wombwell
65   15 Jan 1855, Anglesey: *Hodge*, 77
66   Paget, 253
67   19 Jan 1855, Heneage

68   26 Jan 1855, Heneage
69   22 Dec 1854, 9 Apr 1855, *Forrest*
70   15 Jan 1855, Portal
71   Kinglake, VI, 393–4
72   9 Feb 1855, Portal
73   2 June 1855, Anglesey: *Hodge*, 110
74   26 Feb 1855, Anglesey: *Hodge*, 91; 26 Feb 1855, Hodge papers
75   2 Apr 1855, Heneage
76   Paget, 91
77   Duberly, 221
78   Paget, 102
79   Paget, 111–12
80   Paget, 117, 19 Sep 1855, Anglesey: *Hodge*
81   8 Nov 1855, Heneage
82   Evans, 73

CHAPTER II (pp. 126–130)

1   12 Feb 1857, Combe
2   12 Feb 1857, Combe
3   Report of Capt. J. Forbes, 10 Feb 1857, quoted in Anderson, 48
4   12 Feb 1857, Combe
5   Report of Capt. Ross B. Moore [n.d.], quoted in Anderson, 50
6   12 Feb 1857, Combe
7   Anon. letter written by an officer of 3rd Bombay L.C. in the *Bombay Telegraph* 'discovered amongst a collection of newspaper cuttings concerning Gen. Sir John Forbes, G.C.B. in the British Museum', quoted in Anderson, 53
8   Ross Moore in Anderson, 50, 51–2
9   Jacob to Capt. Graves, 5 June 1857, quoted in [Currie, Maj. A. P.] *Historical Record of the Services of the 3rd (Queen's Own) Regiment of Bombay Light Cavalry*, 13
10   A good general account of the war and its origins is given in English, Barbara *John Company's Last War: A Victorian Military Adventure*, 1971

CHAPTER III (pp. 131–222)

(i)

1   J. Jacob to his father, Rev. S. L. Jacob, *Lambrick*, 60–1; 25 Dec 1842, Sir Charles Napier's Journal, Napier, William *Life of C. J. Napier*, II, 1857, 270
2   Kaye, Sir J. W. *Lives of Indian Officers*, 1889
3   Fortescue, XIII, 242
4   Lambrick, 350
5   *R.O.I.A.*, 49
6   Palmer, 6
7   Lt-Col T. L. Harington in reply to Viscount Melville, *R.O.I.A.*, 50
8   Spear, 667

(ii)

1   *I.S.R.*, I, 1863, 331
2   Oatts, 136
3   O'Callaghan, Daniel *Scattered Chapters of the Indian Mutiny: the Fatal Falter at Meerut*, [privately printed] 1861, 4
4   Stubbs, III, 251
5   Gough, 3
6   Smyth, Col G. M. 'Mutiny of the 3rd Light Cavalry at Meerut' in Chick, N. A. *Annals of the Indian Rebellion . . .*, 1859, 91
7   Capt. H. C. Craigie to Adjutant, 3 L.C., 23 Apr 1857, *Selections*, I, 228
8   Cornet J. C. E. MacNabb to Mrs MacNabb, 10 May 1857, Cadell, Sir P. 'The Outbreak of the Indian Mutiny', *J.A.H.R.*, XXXIII (1955), 120–2
9   Gough, 21–3
10   Anson, 13
11   Roberts, I, 90
12   Palmer, 107

(iii)

1   Quoted in Maclagan, 83–4
2   Gough, 63
3   Fortescue, XIII, 258
4   Sen, 77
5   Brig. A. Wilson to Adj.-Gen., 31 May 1857, *Selections*, I, 284
6   Sen, 413
7   Roberts, I, 190
8   Grant's Journal, Knollys, I, 2
9   Burne, Maj.-Gen. Sir O. T. *Memories*, 1907, 29
10   Sheppard, 132
11   Knollys, I, 204

(iv)

1   Daly, 141
2   Daly, Gen. Sir H. 'The Punjab Frontier Force', *J.U.S.I.*, XXVIII [1884], 909
3   *Guides*, 36
4   [Anon.] *History of the Siege of Delhi, by an Officer who served there*, 1861, 89

(v)

1   Quoted in Maclagan, 130
2   Dashwood Strettell, Col C. B. 'The 11th P.A.V.O. Cavalry (Frontier Force)', *Cavalry Journal*, XVI, Oct 1926, 420–1
3   Kipling, Rudyard, 'The Lost Legion', *Soldiers Three and Military Tales*, Part II, 1897, 448
4   Daly, 66

5   Daly, 62
6   Daly, 63
7   [Anon.] 'Hodson', *Blackwood's*, Mar 1899, 522
8   Hodson to his brother, 7 Oct 1852, Hodson, 103
9   'One best qualified to judge', 1852, Hodson, xlviii
10   Lieut-Col J. Welchman to Adj.-Gen., 18 Jan 1857, Hodson, 135
11   Hodson to his wife, 17 May 1857, Hodson, 147
12   Hodson to his brother, 19 May 1857, Hodson, 148
13   *Hodson's Horse*, 3
14   Hodson to his wife, 8 Aug 1857, Hodson, 197
15   Letter from Hugh Gough, Oct 1897, quoted in *Hodson's Horse*, 22
16   Hodson, 203–4
17   Daly, 147
18   Anson to Mrs Anson, 20 June 1857, Anson, 23
19   *Incidents*, 71
20   Letter, n.d., quoted in Sheppard, 134–5
21   Roberts, I, 189
22   Roberts, I, 188
23   'M.S. Corres.', *Sepoy War*, II, 580
24   'Letter written ... on the same day by an artillery officer', *Sepoy War*, II, 580
25   See Stubbs, III, 271, 297
26   Gimlette, 235
27   Fortescue, XIII, 299
28   *Cornhill*, 43
29   Figures supplied to Forrest by Roberts, Forrest: *Mutiny*, I, 153
30   Potiphar, 79, 81
31   Lieut McDowell, in *Hodson's Horse*, 36
32   Brig. J. Hope Grant, C.B. to D.A.A.G., 17 Sep 1857, *Selections*, 397–8
33   *Sepoy War*, III, 613

(vi)

1   Quoted in Maclagan, 130
2   Marshman, 280
3   Johnson, Mrs W. T. (ed.) *Twelve Years of A Soldier's Life from the Letters of Major W. T. Johnson*, 1897, 174
4   Marshman, 404

(vii)

1   Ouvry, 138–9
2   Campbell to Canning, 18 Nov 1857, *Selections*, II, 339
3   Gough, 153–6
4   Wardlaw's a/c in *Guides*, 50
5   Malleson, II, 114, 115
6   *Blackwood's*, June 1858, 721–4
7   Oatts, 143

8   Dunlop, R. H. W. *Service and Adventure with the Khakee Ressalah, or Meerut Volunteer Horse . . . 1857–8*, 1858, 68

9   Sheppard, 146

10   6 Dec 1857, Potiphar

11   Canning to Campbell, 29 Dec 1857, Canning Papers, Harewood

12   *Punjab Cavalry*, 9

13   Barrett, II, 38

14   White and Atteridge, 127–9.

15   Seton, Sir James, 'Outram's Division watching Lucknow, 1857–1858: a tactical study', *J.U.S.I.*, XXVIII, 1885, 240

16   Tyrrell, 43

17   Gough, 211–15

18   *Selections*, II, 272

19   Letter to Capt. W. H. Seymour, 8 Mar 1858, Whyte and Atteridge, 140–1

20   *Selections*, III, 510; *Punjab Cavalry*, 10

21   [Anon.] 'The Campaign of 1857–8', *Calcutta Review*, Mar 1859. See also Roberts, I, 407; Fortescue, XIII, 344; Forrest: *Mutiny*, II, 365–6

22   Campbell to Canning, 22 Mar 1858, *Selections*, II, 473

23   Sheppard, 151

(viii)

1   Fortescue, XIII, 401

2   *Cornhill*

3   Oatts, 146

4   Campbell to Grant, 1 June 1858, Knollys, II, 9

5   *Hodson's Horse*, 95–6

6   Daly, 215

7   Daly's report to Brig.-Maj., Cavalry Bde, 14 June 1858, Daly, 215

8   Fortescue, XIII, 388

9   16 Mar 1859, Blake

10   Description of Lieut-Gen. H. Hope Crealock's painting in the 7th Hussars' officers' mess, Barrett, II, 66

(ix)

1   Baker, 11

2   *R.O.I.A.*, Appx, 24

3   O'Donnell, 13

4   Oatts, 155

5   Murray, II, 447

6   Duberly, Mrs Henry, *Campaigning Experiences in Rajpootana and Central India during the Suppression of the Mutiny, 1857–1858*, 1859, 2

7   16 July 1858, Blake

8   Jacob, Maj.-Gen. Sir George Le Grand, *Western India before and during the Mutinies . . .*, 1871, 157

9   Fortescue, XIII, 349

10   Cadell, 200

11   Sylvester Diary, 8 Aug, 5, 7 Oct 1857, 25
12   Durand, H. M. *The Life of Major-General Sir Henry Marion Durand*, I,
      1883, 224–5
13   Sylvester, 30
14   Sylvester, 31
15   Lowe, 83–4
16   Lowe, 83
17   Sylvester Diary, 31
18   Maj. Orr's report in *Hyderabad*, 183
19   Lowe, 102–3
20   Fortescue, XIII, 352

(x)

1   Stent, 187–8
2   Sylvester Diary, 44
3   Lowe, 154
4   Sylvester Diary, 51
5   Lowe, 153
6   Malleson, III, 143
7   'One of the besieged garrison', quoted in Burne, 103
8   *Hyderabad*, 192
9   Rose's Despatch 9 Mar 1858, *London Gazette*, 11 May 1858
10   Annand, 92
11   Malleson, III, 147
12   Sir R. Hamilton to Sir H. Rose, 20 Feb 1858 (Vol. 94 (Outward) 375A),
      quoted in Srivastava, Khushhalilal, *The Revolt of 1857 in Central India-
      Malwa*, 1966
13   21 Jan 1858, Combe
14   16 Mar 1858, Combe
15   Lowe, 229–30
16   Forrest: *Mutiny*, III, 2
17   7 Apr 1858, Combe
18   Stent, 22
19   7 Apr 1858, Combe
20   Stent, 197–205
21   Rose to C.O.S., 30 Apr 1858, *Selections*, IV, xcvi
22   Rose to C.O.S., 30 Apr 1858, *Selections*, IV, xcvii
23   Rose to C.O.S., *Selections*, IV, xcviii
24   Rose to C.O.S., *Selections*, IV, xcviii
25   Rose to Adj.-Gen., Bombay Army, 30 Apr 1858, *London Gazette*, 10 Aug
      1858
26   Annand, 113
27   Annand, 113
28   Stent, 215–16
29   Rose to C.O.S., *Selections*, IV, xcix
30   Stent, 216
31   Rose to C.O.S., *Selections*, IV, c–ci

32 7 Apr 1858, Combe
33 Rose to Maj.-Gen. Sir W. M. Mansfield, C.O.S. of the Army in India, Gwalior, 22 June 1858, *Selections*, IV, 83
34 Annand, 130
35 Rose to Mansfield, *Selections*, IV, 68, 69
36 Quoted in Forrest: *Mutiny*, III, 230
37 Rose to Mansfield, *Selections*, IV, 69
38 Annand, 134
39 Sylvester, 132–3
40 Rose to Mansfield, *Selections*, IV, 69
41 'A cavalry officer, writing to me after the event', quoted in Annand, 135
42 8 May 1858, Combe
43 Sylvester, 134
44 Hamilton, 305
45 Rose to Mansfield, *Selections*, IV, 90
46 Rose to Mansfield, *Selections*, IV, 92
47 Annand, 141
48 Major Forbes to Capt. Todd, Brigade Major, 16 May 1858, *Selections*, IV, 107–8
49 1 June 1858, Combe
50 Quoted in Smyth, Sir John, *The Rebellious Rani*, 1966, 167
51 Rose to Mansfield, *Selections*, IV, 97–8
52 Fortescue, XIII, 368
53 Rose to Mansfield, *Selections*, IV, 103

(xi)

1   Coffin, 161
2   *Revolt*, 172
3   Vibart, 159
4   Vibart, 358
5   Whitlock to Mansfield, 24 Apr 1858, *Selections*, IV, 31, 33
6   Col E. Apthorp (i/c advance guard) to Whitlock, 20 Apr 1858, *Selections*, IV, 35
7   Whitlock to Mansfield, *Selections*, IV, 31
8   Coffin, 163
9   Burne, 125
10 Tyrrell, Lt-Gen. F. H. 'In Piam Memoriam: the Services of the Madras Native Troops in the Suppression of the Mutiny of the Bengal Army', *Imperial and Asiatic Quarterly Review*, July 1908, 61
11 Annand, 202–3

(xii)

1   Maclagan, 221
2   Annand, 153
3   Lowe, 299
4   Edwardes, Michael, *Battles of the Indian Mutiny*, 1963, 178

5   *Journal*, 445
6   16 June 1858, Combe
7   Rose to Mansfield, 13 Oct 1858, *Selections*, IV, 132
8   Rose to Mansfield, *Selections*, IV, 133
9   8 June 1858, *Journal*, 446
10   16 June 1858, Lightfoot
11   Rose to Mansfield, *Selections*, IV, 138
12   Annand, 162
13   21 June 1858, Poore, 134–5
14   Lieut-Col T. N. Hicks to Brig. M. W. Smith, 25 June 1858, *Selections*, IV, 160
15   28 June 1858, Poore, 153–4
16   Brig. M. W. Smith's Report, 25 June 1858, *Selections*, IV, 158
17   21 June 1858, Poore, 136
18   21 June 1858, Poore, 136
19   17 July 1858, Clowes: India, 16
20   Rose to Mansfield, *Selections*, IV, 147, 148
21   Annand, 165
22   *Selections*, IV, 171
23   Rose to Mansfield, *Selections*, IV, 149
24   The best account of the capture of the fort is H. G. Rawlinson's 'Note' in *J.A.H.R.*, VIII (1929), 200
25   Watson, 40–1
26   Watson, 42–3
27   23 June 1858, Combe
28   24 June 1858, Lightfoot
29   Napier to A.A.G., 21 [*sic*] June 1858, *Selections*, IV, 164
30   'An eye-witness, a cavalry officer', quoted in Malleson, III, 230
31   24 June 1858, Lightfoot
32   Napier to A.A.G., *Selections*, IV, 164

(xiii)

1   Paget, Leopold, 444
2   Fortescue, XIII, 381
3   *Revolt*, 205
4   *Blackwood's*, 193
5   Paget, Leopold, 441
6   *Blackwood's*, 175
7   *Blackwood's*, 176
8   Fortescue, XIII, 380
9   Murray, II, 470
10   12 Nov 1858, Clowes: India
11   *Blackwood's*, 191
12   Murray, II, 457
13   21 Aug 1858, Clowes: India
14   12 Nov 1858, Clowes: India
15   Fortescue, *17L*, 158

16   Paget, Leopold, 461
17   *Blackwood's*, 193
18   *Blackwood's*, 178
19   *Revolt*, 226
20   *Blackwood's*, 186
21   *Midshipman*, 131
22   *Midshipman*, 129
23   Norbury, Capt. P. F. 'The Aden Troop', *Cavalry Journal*, VIII (1913), 347
24   *Blackwood's*, 175
25   Annand, 193–4
26   Woodward, E. L. *The Age of Reform, 1815–1870*, 1938, 412–13
27   Preston, Adrian, 'The Indian Army and Indo-British Political and Strategic Relations, 1745–1947', *J.U.S.I., India*, 1971, 367

CHAPTER IV (pp. 223–232)

1   Wolseley: *China War*, 195
2   Fitzmaurice, Lord (Edmond). Lord Granville, 1905, I, 247–9
3   Boyle, 15
4   Boyle, 1–2
5   Mackenzie, Col A. R. D. *Mutiny Memoirs; being personal reminiscences of the great Sepoy Revolt of 1857*, 1891, 136–7
6   Hudson, Gen. Sir H. *History of the 19th King George's Own Lancers, 1858–1921*, 1937, 9
7   Allgood, 25–6
8   Probyn's Report in Allgood, 29
9   Swinhoe, Robert *Narrative of the North China Campaign of 1860*, 1861, 72, 205
10   Rennie, D. F. *The British Arms in North China and Japan*, 1864, 184
11   Tulloch, Maj.-Gen. Sir A. B. *Recollections of Forty Years' Service*, 1903, 100
12   Knollys, H. *Incidents in the China War of 1860 compiled from the Private Journals of General Sir Hope Grant*, 1875, 116
13   Walker, 201
14   Wolseley, Lieut-Col *The Story of a Soldier's Life*, II, 1903, 68–9
15   Wylly, Col H. C. 'An Incident in the China War of 1860', *Cavalry Journal*, XVIII, 1928, 648–50
16   Walrond, T. (ed.) *Letters and Journals of the 8th Earl of Elgin*, 1872, 358
17   Hope Grant to Canning, quoted in Boyle, 22–3
18   Wolseley: *China War*, 195

CHAPTER V (pp. 233–253)

(i)

1   12 Feb 1858, *Hansard:* (*C*), CXLVIII, 1287
2   Maclagan, 243
3   Gen. Order No. 480, 8 Apr 1859

4   Parl. Papers (1860), LI, 23
5   Sir H. Rose to Sir Edward Campbell, 24 Sep 1860, Maclagan, 249
6   Shadwell, II, 409
7   Shadwell, II, 411
8   Gen. Order No. 883, 20 June 1859
9   Mil. letter, 5 May 1860, Parl. Papers (1862), XXXVIII, 189
10   Shadwell, II, 413–14
11   Rose to Campbell, 24 Sep 1860, Maclagan, 249
12   Shadwell, II, 419; Parl. Papers (1860), L, 68
13   Parl. Papers (1860), LI, 431
14   Stanley to Canning, 8 Apr 1859, Maclagan, 251
15   Roberts, I, 484

(ii)

1   *R.O.I.A.*, 47, xiii
2   Holland and Hozier, I, 191
3   *R.O.I.A.*, 1859, 55; Holland and Hozier, I, 187
4   Holland and Hozier, II, 15
5   Watson, 93–8
6   Watson, 101–4
7   Commissioner in Sind to Governor of Bombay, 13 Jan 1859, Martineau, J. *Life of Sir Bartle Frere*, I, 254
8   Quoted in Lambrick, 376
9   *Hansard: (C)*, 14 Apr 1859
10   Lambrick, 377–8
11   Roads, 43; see also Winsbury, J. F. R. 'Jacob's Rifle and a Carbine of the Scinde Irregular Horse', *Bulletin of the Military Historical Society*, XI (Nov 1960), 43
12   Baring Pemberton, 21
13   Lambrick, 385
14   *The Times* (leader), 5 Jan 1859
15   Quoted in Lambrick, 382
16   Lambrick, 382–3
17   Lieut-Col Brian Mahon to Sir Robert Cassels, *The Scinde Horseman*, I, Apr 1938, quoted in Lambrick, 385–6
18   *R.O.I.A.*, 49
19   *R.O.I.A.*, 56
20   *R.O.I.A.*, 48
21   *R.O.I.A.*, Appx V, 210
22   *R.O.I.A.*, Appx V, 213
23   *R.O.I.A.*, 47
24   *R.O.I.A.*, Appx V, 12
25   *R.O.I.A.*, Appx V, 213, 47
26   Cardew, 300–1
27   Holland and Hozier, I, 328, II, 14–15
28   MacMunn, Lieut-Gen. Sir G. *The Indian Mutiny in Perspective*, 1931, 259–60

29   Adj.-Gen.'s Circular No. 117N, 9 Sep 1864

30   Holland and Hozier, II, 15

31   Watson, 101

32   Gen. Orders, May and Sep 1864

33   See Carman, W. Y. *Indian Army Uniforms under the British from the 18th Century to 1947,* 1961, 33–47; Cardew, 334–5

(iii)

1   Roberts, II, 5

2   Fortescue, XIII, 425

3   Elliott, Maj.-Gen. J. G. *The Frontier, 1839–1947,* 1968, 69

4   Quoted in Maxwell, 50

5   Barrett, II, 71–3; Cardew, 311–12

CHAPTER VI (pp. 254–259)

1   Stanley, H. M. *Coomasie and Magdala,* 1874, 451

2   Fortescue, XIII, 471–2

3   *Illustrated London News,* 27 June 1868, 622

4   Holland and Hozier

5   Oatts, 157

6   9 Sep 1867, Napier, Hon. H. D. *Field-Marshal Lord Napier of Magdala: A Memoir,* 1927, 209

7   Holland and Hozier, II, 14, 259

8   Holland and Hozier, II, 332–3

9   Holland and Hozier, II, 14–15

10   Holland and Hozier, II, 61

11   Holland and Hozier, II, 14

12   Napier's despatch to Sec. of State for India, 1 June 1868, Holland and Hozier, II, 473–4

13   [Scott, W. W.] *Letters from Abyssinia during the campaign of 1868 by a Staff Officer,* [privately printed], 1868, 120, 123–4, 131

14   Capt. Holland's Report, 12 May 1868, Holland and Hozier, II, 91

15   Chandler (see below), 153. The best modern accounts of the Abyssinian expedition are: Myatt, F. *The March to Magdala,* 1970, and Chandler, D. F. 'The Expedition to Abyssinia, 1867–8', (ed.) Bond, B. *Victorian Military Campaigns,* 1967, 107–59

CHAPTER VII (pp. 260–364)

(i)

1   Brig.-Gen. George Campbell, *R.C.,* 1867, 39

2   *R.C.,* 1861, 2

3   *R.C.,* 1867, 12

4   *R.C.,* 1861, 180

5   *R.C.,* 1867, 112

6   *R.C.,* 1861, 91

7   R.C., 1867, 58–9
8   Bonham-Carter, 5
9   R.C., 1867, 180
10   R.C., 1861, 21
11   Col H. Graham, R.C., 1867, 7
12   R.C., 1867, 12
13   R.C., 1867, 276
14   Sir J. B. Gibson, R.C., 1867, 156
15   R.C., 1861, 235

(ii)

1   George Townsend, R.C., 1867, 165
2   Col Hope Graham, R.C., 1867, 2
3   R.C., 1867, 6, 25
4   R.C., 1867, 3
5   R.C., 1861, 134
6   R.C., 1861, 12
7   Murray, II, 472
8   Barrett, II, 77
9   R.C., 1867, 115
10   R.C., 1867, 27
11   R.C., 1861, 41
12   R.C., 1861, 90–1
13   Mole, 18–23
14   R.C., 1861, 33
15   R.C., 1867, 95
16   R.C., 1867, 61
17   R.C., 1861, 388
18   R.C., 1861, 235
19   R.C., 1861, 12
20   R.C., 1867, 2
21   Wood: Br. Cav., 150
22   R.C., 1867, 61

(iii)

1   Maj. J. Buckley quoting a man of the Light Division, R.C., 1861, 281
2   R.C., 1867, 150
3   R.C., 1867, 114
4   R.C., 1867, 180
5   R.C., 1867, 21, 38
6   R.C., 1867, 180–1
7   R.C., 1867, 252
8   Samuel Haden, R.C., 1867, 61

(iv)

1   R.C., 1861, 14

2   Mole, 23–4
3   R.C., 1867, 95
4   Mole, 25
5   R.C., 1867, 273
6   R.C., 1861, 198
7   R.C., 1867, 161
8   R.C., 1867, 163
9   R.C., 1867, 14
10   R.C., 1861, 277

(v)

1   R.C., 1861, 21
2   R.C., 1861, 9, 12, 169
3   R.C., 1867, 37
4   R.C., 1861, 171, 242; Bonham-Carter, 12
5   R.C., 1861, 171–2; R.C., 1867, 62
6   R.C., 1861, 280
7   Clode, I, 489
8   Clode, II, 30–1; 30 and 31 Vic. c. 34, 1867
9   Paget, 134
10   Royal Pay Warrant, 1870, 183
11   Poulson, Maj. N. W. 'Medal for Long Service and Good Conduct awarded to the Army (Regular Forces)', Seaby's Medal Bulletin, 1966, 125–6
12   Latham, Brig. H. B. 'The Origin of the Medal for "Distinguished Conduct in the Field" ', J.U.S.I., July 1953, 420–6
13   R.C., 1861, 238
14   R.C., 1867, 117

(vi)

1   R.C., 1861, 236
2   Mole, 27
3   R.C., 1861, 183
4   R.C., 1867, 48
5   R.C., 1867, 114
6   R.C., 1861, 183
7   S.C., lxxvi
8   Report on Gymnastics, 1863, Army Physical Training Corps Museum, Aldershot; The Times, 31 July 1864 (issue of 11 May 1865)
9   Hutton, Lieut A. K.D.G., The Cavalry Swordsman, 1867, 4, 5
10   Oldfield, E. A. L., Lieut-Col History of the Army Physical Training Corps, 1955, 1–9
11   Q.R., 1859, 93
12   Acland-Troyte, 119
13   Q.R., 1859, 93–5
14   R.C., 1867, 83

15   *R.C.*, 1867, 17
16   *Hansard:* (*C*), CLXXXVI, 896–7. Apr 1867

(vii)

1   *R.C.*, 1861, 181
2   *R.C.*, 1861, 27
3   *R.C.*, 1861, 180
4   *R.C.*, 1861, 289
5   *R.C.*, 1861, 285–6
6   *R.C.*, 1861, xii, 303
7   *R.C.*, 1861, 5
8   *R.C.*, 1861, 304
9   *R.C.*, 1861, 240
10   *R.C.*, 1861, 10
11   *R.C.*, 1861, 299–300
12   *R.C.*, 1861, 300
13   Abstract of the *Recommendations of the Principal Commissions and Committees on Army Matters, 1806–1900*, 1901, 60
14   *R.C.*, 1861, 292; but see Q.5845, Q.5847, Q.5848, 301
15   *C.M.C.*, 273–5
16   Scott Claver *Under the Lash*, 1954, 226; *Q.R.*, 228; *C.M.C.*, x
17   *R.C.*, 1861, 259
18   *C.M.C.*, 264–70
19   Acland-Troyte, 157
20   Simmons, Gen. Sir L. 'The Critical Condition of the Army', *Nineteenth Century*, XIV (1883), 175
21   Wolseley, 210
22   *Articles of War*, 1866
23   *C.M.C.*, vii
24   *C.M.C.*, 273–7
25   *R.C.*, 1867, 221; *C.M.C.*, xii
26   *C.M.C.*, 264–70
27   *C.M.C.*, 255–63
28   *C.M.C.*, xii
29   *R.C.*, 1867, 115
30   *R.C.*, 1867, 119
31   *R.C.*, 1867, 96
32   *Q.R.*, 125
33   Sutherland, 58
34   Sutherland, 59
35   *S.C.*, 173
36   *S.C.*, xxviii
37   *Hansard:* (*C*), 19 June 1856
38   Fortescue, xiii, 538–9

(viii)

1   Quoted in Whyte, 30

2   32nd Article of War, added in 1858
3   *M.E.C.*(2), xiii, 2
4   *M.E.C.*(2), 103–5, 40
5   *I.S.R.*, I, 79
6   Denholm, 60
7   *M.E.C.*(2), xii
8   *Q.R.*, 1859, 208
9   *M.E.C.*(2), 104
10   *M.E.C.*(2), 12
11   *M.E.C.*(2), 3
12   *M.E.C.*(2), 2, xxvi
13   *M.E.C.*(2), 50, 40
14   *M.E.C.*(2), 5–12
15   *M.E.C.*(2), 155–6
16   *M.E.C.*(2), 4
17   *M.E.C.*(2), 151–8
18   *M.E.C.*(2), 175–93

(ix)

1   *R.C.*, 1861, 239
2   *Q.R.*, 1859, 207
3   *R.C.*, 1867, 84
4   *R.C.*, 1867, 150
5   Acland-Troyte, 112
6   *R.C.*, 1867, 116
7   *Q.R.*, 1859, 140
8   *R.C.*, 1861, 239
9   *R.C.*, 1867, 116
10   Acland-Troyte, 130–3
11   *Q.R.*, 1859, 124
12   *C.M.C.*, x

(x)

1   *Royal Warrant*, 1854, *Addenda to the Royal Warrant of . . . 1848*, 1855, 94
2   *R.C.*, 1861, 284
3   Sutherland, 49
4   *S.C.*, xxvii
5   *S.C.*, 169
6   Mole, 29–30
7   *S.C.*, 169
8   *S.C.*, xxiii, 169
9   *S.C.*, xxvii
10   *Barrack Committee*, viii
11   McNeill and Tulloch, Appx, 18
12   *S.C.*, lxxvii
13   Acland-Troyte, 30

14 Acland-Troyte, 32
15 Acland-Troyte, 35

(xi)

1   *R.C.*, 1861, 22
2   *S.C.*, lxxx
3   Note by Geo. Ramsay in Clode, II, 568–70
4   *R.C.*, 1861, 274
5   *R.C.*, 1861, 282
6   *Clothing Regulations*, 1862, 44–5
7   Mole, 13
8   *Clothing Regulations*, 1862, 4–5
9   *R.C.*, 1867, 93
10 *R.C.*, 1861, 181
11 Mole, 31–2
12 Baker, 41

(xii)

1   *R.C.*, 1861, 21
2   *Royal Warrant*, June, 1854
3   Note by Geo. Ramsay in Clode, II, 568–70
4   *S.C.*, xxvii–xxviii
5   Carman, W. Y., introduction to 1971 ed. of *Regulations for Dress of General, Staff and Regimental Officers of the Army*, 1846
6   *S.C.*, xxvii, 87, 198
7   *S.C.*, xxvii
8   Evans, 76–7
9   Shakespear, 58
10 Carman, W. Y. *British Military Uniforms from Contemporary Pictures*, 1957, 138
11 *S.C.*, xxviii

(xiii)

1   *S.C.*, ix
2   Miss F. Nightingale's written answer to questions, *S.C.*, 369
3   *S.C.*, vii, viii
4   Statement of Sir Alexander Tulloch, *S.C.*, xiii
5   *S.C.*, xiv, xv
6   *S.C.*, xv
7   Miss F. Nightingale to D. Galton, Woodham-Smith, C. *Florence Nightingale*, 1950, 400
8   *R.C.*, 1867, 84
9   *R.C.*, 1861, 212
10 *Statistical Report on Sickness and Mortality of Troops*, 1853, 20
11 *I.S.R.*, I, lxxxi

493

(xiv)

1 Sutherland, 64
2 *S.C.*, xvi
3 Sutherland, 12
4 *Barrack Committee*, xii
5 Sutherland, 31
6 *S.C.*, 439–42
7 Douglas, Sir G. bart and Ramsay, Sir G. Dalhousie (ed.) *The Panmure Papers . . .*, 1908, I, 95–6
8 Denholm, 63
9 Sutherland, 32
10 Gatacre, Beatrix, *General Gatacre: the Story of the Life and Services of Sir William F. Gatacre, 1843–1906*, 1910, 30
11 *S.C.*, 353
12 *S.C.*, xvii
13 *Barrack Committee*, iv
14 *Barrack Committee*, 94
15 *Barrack Committee*, 79
16 *S.C.*, 174
17 Sutherland, 19
18 Sutherland, 31
19 *R.C.*, 1867, 158
20 Sutherland, 46
21 Acland-Troyte, 38
22 *Hansard: (C)*, 11 May 1858

(xv)

1 *R.C.*, 1861, 281
2 Based on Acland-Troyte, 42–4
3 *R.C.*, 1861, 275

(xvi)

1 *R.C.*, 1867, 119
2 *R.C.*, 1861, 192
3 *R.C.*, 1867, 116–17
4 *Q.R.*, 1859, 248
5 Maj. J. Buckley, *R.C.*, 1861, 279
6 *Q.R.*, 1859, 397
7 Willcox, 161–2
8 *R.C.*, 1867, 157
9 *Official Return of Barracks and Encampments*, 1 Jan 1857; *Barrack Committee*, iv
10 Sutherland, 53
11 *S.C.*, 168
12 Sutherland, 48

13   *Barrack Committee*, iv
14   *Barrack Committee*, 145
15   Whyte and Atteridge, 162
16   *S.C.*, xix
17   Sutherland, 60
18   Fortescue: *Canteens*, 27
19   *Barrack Committee*, v
20   Fortescue: *Canteens*, 28
21   A corporal of the 56th Foot to Col L. Shadwell, *R.C.*, 1867, 30

(xvii)

1   *Hansard:* (*C*), Lord Ebrington, 11 May 1858, Fortescue, 538
2   Sutherland, 85
3   Sutherland, 86
4   Sutherland, 91
5   Sutherland, 93
6   *S.C.*, xviii
7   Sutherland, 94
8   Maj. J. Buckley, *R.C.*, 1861, 277
9   Sutherland, 94
10   *R.C.*, 1861, 277
11   Acland-Troyte, 15–18

(xviii)

1   Memorandum 26 Sep 1853, P.R.O., W.O. (Out-letters (W.O.3)), 326
2   See Daniell, Georgina *Aldershot: A Record of Mrs. Daniell's Work Amongst Soldiers*, 1879; Cole, Lieut-Col H. N. *The Story of Aldershot . . .*, 1951, and Walters, John *Aldershot Review*, 1970

(xix)

1   Clode, II, 290
2   *Royal Warrant*, Part I, Pay, 1866, 94
3   *R.C.*, 1867, 74
4   *Q.R.*, 1859, 177
5   *Q.R.*, 1859, 181
6   *R.C.*, 1867, 115, 216
7   *R.C.*, 1861, 236, 238
8   Clode, II, 290–1
9   *Q.R.*, 1859, 183
10   *R.C.*, 1867, 251
11   *R.C.*, 1867, 59

(xx)

1   *R.C.*, 1867, 165
2   *Royal Warrants*, 1848, 1864

3   *Royal Warrants*, 1848, 1864, 1870
4   *Royal Warrant*, 1876
5   *Royal Warrant*, 1856
6   *R.C.*, 1867, 93

(xxi)

1   *I.S.R.*, I, xi; 18 Feb 1861, Heneage
2   *I.S.R.*, I, lxxxviii
3   *I.S.R.*, I, lxxxi
4   *R.C.*, 1867, 277
5   *I.S.R.*, I, 57
6   Scott Daniell, 217
7   *R.C.*, 1867, 173
8   *I.S.R.*, I, xvii
9   *I.S.R.*, I, xiii, xxix
10 *I.S.R.*, I, xliii
11 *I.S.R.*, I, xxix–xl
12 *I.S.R.*, I, lv
13 *I.S.R.*, I, 201
14 *I.S.R.*, I, 108, 227
15 *I.S.R.*, I, lxvii–lxix
16 *I.S.R.*, I, xli, 234
17 *I.S.R.*, I, 78
18 *I.S.R.*, I, 333
19 *I.S.R.*, I, 197
20 *I.S.R.*, I, 336
21 *I.S.R.*, I, 61
22 Dr F. J. Mouat, *I.S.R.*, I, 330
23 *I.S.R.*, I, 60
24 *I.S.R.*, I, 201
25 Dr W. C. MacLean, *I.S.R.*, I, 143
26 *I.S.R.*, I, 1, [50]
27 *I.S.R.*, I, 56
28 *I.S.R.*, I, lxix, 143
29 *I.S.R.*, I, 190
30 *I.S.R.*, I, liii
31 Tulloch, Maj.-Gen. Sir A. Bruce *Recollections of Forty Years Service,'*
    1903, 43
32 *I.S.R.*, I, 201
33 *I.S.R.*, I, 60
34 *I.S.R.*, I, 57
35 *I.S.R.*, I, lv
36 *I.S.R.*, I, 56
37 *I.S.R.*, I, lv
38 *I.S.R.*, I, 62
39 *R.C.*, 1867, 172, 176
40 *R.C.*, 1867, 150

41 D. Bartlett, *R.C.*, 1861, 207
42 *R.C.*, 1861, 243
43 *I.S.R.*, I, lxix–lxx
44 *I.S.R.*, I, 210

(xxii)

1   *I.S.R.*, I, 154
2   *I.S.R.*, I, 287
3   *I.S.R.*, I, 192
4   Napier, Sir C. *Defects, Civil and Military of the Indian Government,* ed.
    Sir W. F. P. Napier, 1853, 271
5   *I.S.R.*, I, 203
6   *I.S.R.*, I, 78
7   *I.S.R.*, I, 340
8   *I.S.R.*, I, 61
9   *I.S.R.*, I, lix–lx
10 *I.S.R.*, I, 204
11 Maj. J. Buckley, *R.C.*, 1861, 279
12 *I.S.R.*, I, 338, 340
13 *I.S.R.*, I, 61
14 *I.S.R.*, I, 62, 79, 204, 338
15 T. E. Dempster, late Superintending-Surgeon, Bengal Establishment,
    I.S.R., I, 466
16 *I.S.R.*, I, 338, 483
17 *R.C.*, 1867, 176
18 Sheppard, 159

(xxiii)

1   *I.S.R.*, I, 192
2   *I.S.R.*, I, 143
3   Dr Mouat, *I.S.R.*, 333
4   *I.S.R.*, I, lxii, 80
5   *I.S.R.*, I, 209
6   *I.S.R.*, I, 199–200
7   *I.S.R.*, I, 344
8   Lyttelton, Gen. Sir Neville *Eighty Years' Soldiering, Politics, Games,*
    [1927], 79
9   *I.S.R.*, I, xxv
10 *I.S.R.*, I, 80

(xxiv)

1   *I.S.R.*, I, lvii
2   *I.S.R.*, I, 192
3   T. E. Dempster, *I.S.R.*, I, 466
4   *I.S.R.*, I, lvi
5   *I.S.R.*, I, 192

6   *I.S.R.*, I, 202–3, 338
7   Hyom
8   *I.S.R.*, I, lv
9   *I.S.R.*, I, lvii, 466
10   *I.S.R.*, I, lvi–lvii, 78, 202
11   *I.S.R.*, I, 79, 342
12   *I.S.R.*, I, 55
13   Blatchford, R. *My Life in the Army*, [1910], 37
14   *I.S.R.*, I, 206
15   *R.C.*, 1867, 176
16   Hyom
17   *I.S.R.*, I, xxxv, 207
18   *I.S.R.*, I, 58
19   *I.S.R.*, I, 192
20   *I.S.R.*, I, 205
21   *I.S.R.*, I, 79
22   Mouat, 7
23   *I.S.R.*, I, 79
24   *I.S.R.*, I, 63
25   *I.S.R.*, I, lviii
26   Mouat, 23
27   Holland and Hozier, II, 270–1

(xxv)

1   *I.S.R.*, I, 1863, xviii
2   *I.S.R.*, I, 332
3   Dr G. C. Wallich, *I.S.R.*, I, xxii, 335
4   *I.S.R.*, I, lxxvi
5   *I.S.R.*, I, xlii, lxvi
6   *I.S.R.*, I, xxii, xxiii
7   *I.S.R.*, I, 205, 332
8   *I.S.R.*, I, 332
9   *Colonel Sykes' Statistical Journal*, X, 124
10   *I.S.R.*, I, xxii
11   *R.O.I.A.*, 51
12   *R.O.I.A.*, Appx V, 212
13   Gen. Order No. 278, quoted in Cardew, 333
14   Gen. Order No. 101, 1870
15   Gen. Order (C-in-C), 14 Oct 1863
16   Dress Regulations, Bengal, 1868, 1869, 1872 (Adj.-Gen.'s Gen. Order No. 223) and 1874
17   *R.O.I.A.*, 47

CHAPTER VIII (pp. 365–403)

(i)

1   *P.&S.C.*, 180

498

2   *Q.R.*, 1844, 130; *Q.R.*, 1857, 126
3   Mole, 58
4   *McCalmont*, 29
5   *P.&S.C.*, 225
6   *P.&S.C.*, 106
7   10 Oct, 19 Dec 1858, Blake
8   Wood: *Br. Cav.*, 149–52
9   Liddell, 337
10   Wolseley: *S.P.B.*, 1
11   M. J. Higgins ('Jacob Omnium'), *P.&S.C.*, 79
12   *P.&S.C.*, 80
13   *P.&S.C.*, 294
14   Charles Hammersley, army agent, and Maj.-Gen. Scarlett, *P.&S.C.*, 49, 177
15   *P.&S.C.*, 182, 267
16   *Q.R.*, 1859, 135
17   *Q.R.*, 1859, 304
18   *Royal Pay Warrant*, 1866, 33–4
19   *P.&S.C.*, 482; Clode, II, 58
20   *Royal Pay Warrant*, 1870, 54
21   *P.&S.C.*, 178
22   *Report of the Royal Commission on Army Promotion*, 1854, 12

(ii)

1   *P.&S.C.*, 79; 178
2   Standing, Percy C. ' "Purchase" and the Cavalry Arm', *Cavalry Journal*, xix, 1929, 72
3   *P.&S.C.*, 268
4   *P.& S.C.*, 265
5   *P.&S.C.*, 86
6   *P.&S.C.*, 15
7   C. Yorke, 25 Oct 1856, *P.&S.C.*, 395
8   *P.&S.C.*, xxii
9   *P.&S.C.*, 50
10   *P.&S.C.*, 49
11   *P.&S.C.*, 282
12   *P.&S.C.*, 49, 50
13   *McCalmont*, 28, 29, 35
14   *P.&S.C.*, 49
15   *P.&S.C.*, 312
16   *P.&S.C.*, 253
17   Wood: *Br. Cav.*, 149–50
18   *P.&S.C.*, 5, 8
19   *P.&S.C.*, xxv
20   *P.&S.C.*, 313
21   *P.&S.C.*, xxv
22   E. Ellice, *P.&S.C.*, 109

23   *P.&S.C.*, 176
24   *P.&S.C.*, xxii
25   *P.&S.C.*, 177
26   Atkinson, C. T., 138.
27   5 Aug 1871, *Punch*, 43
28   Stacey, C. P. 'Britain's Withdrawal from North America, 1864–71', *Cambridge Historical Review*, XXVI (1955), 185–98
29   The Marquess of Lansdowne (Under-Secretary, War Office), 20 June 1873, *Hansard: (L)*, CCXVI, 1218
30   W.O.32/1014/107 Gen./1609
31   *A.P.R.C.*, xxxiii

(iii)

1   Blatchford, R. *My Life in the Army* [1910], 151; Acland-Troyte, 199
2   *R.C.*, 1867, 60
3   *R.C.*, 1867, 73
4   Secretary-at-War to Treasury, 6 Dec 1845, *P.&S.C.*, 288
5   *R.C.*, 1867, 60
6   *M.E.C.(1)*, 1870, cxlvi
7   *R.C.*, 1867, 60
8   Sir C. Russell questioning Gen. Scarlett, *M.E.C.(1)*, 1870, 231
9   *P.&S.C.*, 183
10   *P.&S.C.*, 218
11   *R.C.*, 1867, 60
12   *M.E.C.(1)*, lxxxiii
13   *Royal Pay Warrant*, 1870, 42, 75–6
14   *R.C.*, 1867, 95
15   Smith, *H.R.A.V.C.*, 115–60

(iv)

1   *M.E.C.(1)*, 1870, 245
2   Memo. by Duke of Wellington, Feb 1849, quoted in *M.E.C.(1)*, 1870, lxviii
3   *R.M.C.R.*, 1855, x
4   S. Herbert to Lord Hardinge, Jan 1854, *M.E.C.(1)*, lxviii
5   *M.E.C.(1)*, 1870, lxix
6   Burne, Maj.-Gen. Sir O. T. Burne, GCIE, KCSI, *Memories*, 1907, 10
7   Quoted in *M.E.C.(1)*, lxxiii
8   Bond, 89; see also Hamilton, Gen. Sir Ian *When I was a Boy*, 1939, 173–9, 222, and *Midshipman*, I, 203–4
9   *M.E.C.(1)*, 1870, lxxxvi
10   *M.E.C.(1)*, 1870, lxix, 215, 218
11   *M.E.C.(1)*, 1870, lxxiii
12   Royal Warrant of 1808, quoted in *Report of Select Committee on Sandhurst . . .*, 1855, iii
13   S. Herbert's Minute, 1 Sep 1859, and Duke of Cambridge's opinion, *M.E.C.(1)*, 1870, 445, 208

14   *M.E.C.*(*1*), 1870, 23
15   *R.M.C.R.*, 1855, V
16   *M.E.C.*(*1*), 1870, xviii–xix
17   Tulloch, Maj.-Gen. Sir A. M. *Recollections of Forty Years' Service*, 1903, 9
18   Thomas, H. *The Story of Sandhurst*, 1961, 117–18
19   *M.E.C.*(*1*), 1870, 178, 179
20   *M.E.C.*(*1*), 1870, lxxiv
21   General Order, Horse Guards, 29 Nov 1858, given in full in *M.E.C.*(*1*), 1870, lxxvi; see also *Q.R.*, 1868, 159–70
22   *R.M.C.R.*, 1855, iii
23   *M.E.C.*(*1*), 1870, 243
24   Bond, 97
25   *M.E.C.*(*1*), 1870, 245
26   Lieut-Gen. W. F. Forster, *M.E.C.*(*1*), 1870, cxvii
27   *M.E.C.*(*1*), 1870, lxxvi
28   Col J. W. Armstrong, *M.E.C.*(*1*), 1870, cxviii
29   *M.E.C.*(*1*), 1870, 246
30   *A.P.R.C.*, 1876, 148
31   *M.E.C.*(*1*), 1870, 234; see also Bond, 88
32   *M.E.C.*(*1*), 1870, lxxxiii
33   *M.E.C.*(*1*), 1870, 242
34   Horse Guards Memorandum, 19 Jan 1859, *M.E.C.*(*1*), 1870, xcii
35   Liddell, 335; Bond, 94, 110–11
36   Army Circular, 16 Jan 1869, *M.E.C.*(*1*), 1870, xcii
37   Liddell, 352
38   *M.E.C.*(*1*), 1870, lxxxvi
39   *M.E.C.*(*1*), 1870, 246

(v)

1   *P. & S.C.*, 37
2   *P. & S.C.*, 24, 26
3   *P. & S.C.*, 26, 36
4   *P. & S.C.*, xxvi, 33
5   *P. & S.C.*, 32, 37
6   *P. & S.C.*, 48
7   *I.S.R.*, I, xix
8   *P. & S.C.*, 48
9   *R.O.I.A.*, 47–8
10   Gen. R. J. H. Vivian, *P.S.C.*, 44
11   *P.S.C.*, 38
12   20 Apr 1856, Combe
13   P. Melvill, *P.S.C.*, 38
14   *P. & S.C.*, 37
15   2, 31 Jul 1858, Blake
16   Blood, 51
17   *I.S.R.*, I, lv; 18 Feb 1861, Heneage
18   Blood, 50

19   2 Jul, 5 Sep 1858, Blake
20   *Addenda to the Royal Warrant, &c. of 1 July 1848*, 1855, 40–3
21   15 Apr 1859, Blake
22   Haley, A. H. *The Crawley Affair*, 1971, 211. See also an excellent account in Hawkey, Arthur *Last Post at Mhow*, 1969

CHAPTER IX (pp. 404–420)

(i)

1   Havelock, 34
2   Liddell, 336, 349
3   'Colonel Jenyn's Non-Pivot Drill', Denison, 341–50
4   Fortescue, XIII, 549
5   Preston, 61–2
6   Knollys, 283, 287
7   *Report of the Commissioners appointed to inquire into the question of Promotion and Retirement in the Higher Ranks of the Army . . .*, 1858, ix

(ii)

1   Nolan, 149
2   Lucas, T. J. *Camp Life and Sport in South Africa*, 1870, 70
3   Brackett, Col *A History of the United States Cavalry*, quoted in Denison, 95
4   Tylden, 219

(iii)

1   Quoted in Landon, Col H. J. 'Cavalry Swordsmanship in 1854', *Cavalry Journal*, II (1907), 463; Williams, Staff-S-M J. E., 6th (Inniskilling) Dragoons, 'Cavalry Swordsmanship', *Cavalry Journal*, I (1906), 471
2   Baker, 46
3   Wilkinson-Latham, 21
4   Baker, 46
5   Wilkinson-Lathan, 102
6   Landon, Col H. J., Inspector of Gymnasia in India, 'Cavalry Swordsmanship in 1854', *Cavalry Journal*, II (1907), 462–4, quoting Jacob to Hale, February 1854, in Pelly, Lewis, *The Views and Opinions of Brigadier-General John Jacob, C.B.*, 1858
7   Poore, R. M., 197
8   Poore, R. M., 195, quoting Burton's remarks on Jacob's *On the Causes of the Defects existing in our Army . . .*, 1855
9   Report of Capt. J. Forbes, 3 Bombay L.C., 10 Feb 1857, Anderson, 49
10 Poore, R. M., 196
11 [Anon.] 'Sword *v*. Lance', *Cavalry Journal*, VII (1912), 439
12 *Instructions for the Sword, Carbine, Pistol and Lance Exercise together with Standing Gun Drill for the Use of the Cavalry*, Adj.-Gen.'s Office, 1865, 10, 16–34, 73–85
13 Captain Aston Warner (later of 20th Hussars) to his brother, 'Lucknow

Cantonments, March 31st, 1858', MS letter in the possession of John A. W. Bush, Esq.

14   Blood, Sir Bindon *Four Score Years and Ten,* 1933, 70
15   Lyttelton, 64

(iv)

1   *Harmsworth's Universal Encyclopedia* (1926), IX, 5604
2   Private Letter Book of Anglesey, 1st Marquess of, 1830, *Plas Newydd Papers,* quoted in Roads, 276
3   12 Feb 1857, Combe
4   Roads, 276
5   Holland and Hozier, II, 61
6   Barrett, II, 74
7   Rogers, Col H. C. B. *The Mounted Troops of the British Army, 1066–1945,* 1959, 214
8   *Regulations for the Instruction and Movements of Cavalry,* 1876, 241
9   *M.E.C.*(2), 199–200. This section is based chiefly on Tylden, Maj. G. 'The Use of Firearms by Cavalry', *J.A.H.R.,* XIX (1940), XXVIII (1950), and Roads, 276–98

CHAPTER X (pp. 421–439)

(i)

1   Baker, 31
2   Tylden, Maj. G. 'The Army Horse', *J.A.H.R.,* XXI (1942), 48–9
3   Liddell, 362
4   Smith, *H.R.A.V.C.,* 133
5   *Q.R.,* 1859, 293
6   Tylden, 21
7   Letter, 20 Mar 1854 from Nolan, in possession of Officers' Mess, 15/19 The King's Royal Hussars, quoted in Moyse-Bartlett, 160
8   Campbell, Lieut-Col C. F. *Letters from Camp to his Relatives during the Siege of Sebastopol,* 1894, 215–17, quoted in Moyse-Bartlett, 173
9   Pain, T. in discussion of lecture by Hozier, Capt. H. M. 'The Breeding of Horses for Military Purposes', *J.U.S.I.,* 1 July 1872, 746

(ii)

1   Denison, 92
2   Willcox, 157
3   Quoted in Tylden, 139
4   Smith, F., Aldershot Lecture 'Weight Carried by the Troop Horse', 1891
5   Baker, 34
6   Tylden, 139
7   Baker, 57
8   Horton, Maj. 'Evolution of a Cavalry Saddle', *Cavalry Journal,* 1909, 359
9   Tylden, 129–43
10   Maxwell, 162

(iii)

1   Denison, 94
2   Tylden, 223

(iv)

1   Smith, quoted in Tylden, 220
2   Bethell, Lieut-Col L. A. ('Pousse Cailloux') 'The Silver Hand of Alexander', *Blackwood's Magazine*, May 1928
3   Tylden, 220
4   Smith, quoted in Tylden, 220
5   Wood: *Br. Cav.*, 148
6   10 Oct 1858, Blake
7   Addington, Capt. Hon. R. A., 8th K.G.O. Light Cavalry, 'The Introduction of Geldings into the Madras Cavalry', *Cavalry Journal*, XV (1925), 64
8   *Barrack Committee*, 46
9   Woodham-Smith, Cecil *Florence Nightingale*, 1950, 398

(v)

1   Baker, 10; 4 Dec 1861, Heneage
2   Smith, *H.R.A.V.C.*, 128
3   Smith, *H.R.A.V.C.*, 127
4   Smith, *H.R.A.V.C.*, 128–9
5   Hallen, Vet.-Col J. H. B., quoted in Gilbey, Sir Walter, *Horse Breeding in India and England and Army Horses Abroad*, 1901, 53
6   10 Oct 1858, Blake
7   *R.O.I.A.*, 55
8   *R.O.I.A.*, 47
9   *R.O.I.A.*, Appx V, II
10   Watson, 99–100
11   Holland and Hozier, I, 373–4
12   Baker, 13, 14
13   Tylden, 60
14   Baker, 12–13
15   W. S. Blunt to Lieut-Gen. Sir F. FitzWygram, 14 Apr 1901, FitzWygram, Lieut-Gen. Sir F. bt, *Horses and Stables*, 5th ed. (1903), re-issue, 1911, 541
16   Tylden, 48
17   Quoted in Tylden, 53
18   Anglesey: *Hodge*, 100, 101
19   Quoted in Farwell, Byron *Queen Victoria's Little Wars*, 1973, 83
20   Maxwell, 28
21   Sidney, S. *The Book of the Horse*, 3rd ed., 1878

CHAPTER XI (pp. 440–445)

(i)

1   Fortescue, XIII, 549–50

2   *R.C.*, 1867, 221, 267; *C.M.C.*, xii
3   Scott Daniell, 214
4   Barrett, II, 76, 77, 79
5   Pomeroy, 184
6   Liddell, 351; Pomeroy, 184
7   Fortescue, XIII, 550

(ii)

1   Benson Freeman, 104
2   Teichman, Maj. O. 'The Yeomanry as an aid to civil power, 1795–1867, II, 1831–1867', *JAHR*, XIX (1940), 142
3   Benson Freeman, Eng.-Com. *The Yeomanry of Devon*, 1927, 110–11
4   Lyttelton, 50
5   *Regulations applicable to Corps of Yeomanry*, 1869
6   Clode, I, 322
7   Liddell, 344
8   Liddell, 332
9   Liddell, 354

EPILOGUE (pp. 446–454)

1   Havelock, 53
2   22 Apr 1828, Wellington, Arthur 1st Duke of, *Despatches, Correspondence and Memoranda (New Series)*, V, 593
3   Denholm, 64
4   Preston, 60
5   Bond, 111
6   Preston, 60
7   MacDougall, Col P. L. *Modern Warfare as Influenced by Modern Artillery*, 1864, 15
8   Preston, 66
9   Havelock, 34, 35, 39, 40, 44, 46, 47, 57–8
10   Denison, 75
11   Preston, 67
12   Wolseley: *S.P.B.*, 244–5, 246
13   Quoted in Preston, 70
14   *R.C.*, 1867, 62

INDEX

Index

Duke of York's School, Chelsea – *see* Royal Military School, (or Asylum) Chelsea

Eden, Capt (prob. Sir Ashley (1831–1887)), 218
education, other ranks', 288–94
Edward VII (1841–1910), 384
Edwardes, Sir Herbert Benjamin (1819–1868), 159
Elgin, James Bruce, 8th Earl of (1811–1863), 223, 226, 231
Ellesmere, Francis Egerton, 1st Earl of (1800–1857), 122
Elliot, Maj-Gen Alexander James Hardy (1825–1909), Scarlett's ADC at Balaklava, 25 Oct., 1854, 68, 70, 73, 74
Elphinstone, John, 13th Baron (1807–1860), 181, 190
Enfield rifle, 136
Erminia, the, schooner, 122
Estcourt, Maj-Gen James Bucknall (1802–1855), 49
Europa, the, catches fire with Inniskilling Dragoons aboard, 1854, 34
Eyre, Maj-Gen Sir Vincent (1811–1881), 164

Fane, Lt Walter, 225
farcy, 38
Farquharson, Tpr K.S., 4LD, 34, 62
Fisher (-Rowe), Capt Edward R. (1832–1909), 4DG, 41, 57, 59, 108, 120
FitzWygram, Col Sir Frederick Wellington John, bt, (1823–1904), 15H 261, 270, 384
Fletcher, Tpr, 104
flogging, 285
Forbes, Capt, Poona IH, 128, 129
Forbes, Maj, 3 Bombay LC, 200–1
forge fund, 241
Forrest, Lt-Col William Charles, 4DG, 116, 119, 122
Forteath, Surgeon Alexander, 1D, 120
Fortescue, Sir John (1859–1933), 23, 57, 146, 174, 202, 217, 251, 254, 287, 405, 442
Fraser, Lt-Gen Sir Charles Craufurd, VC (1830–1895), 177
furloughs, 279–80

Gall, Lt-Col Richard Herbert, 14LD, 185, 191, 202, 290, 339, 349, 354, 356, 357, 359
General Service Enlistment Act, 1856 (India), 134

George IV (1762–1830), 308, 407
Gibbs, Sgt, 14LD, 265–7, 272
Gibsone, Col, 275, 280
Gladstone, William Ewart (1809–1898), 379, 447
glanders, 38
Gleig, Rev George Robert (1796–1888), 288
Goldsworthy, Trumpeter (later Saddler-Sgt), KDG, 230–1
Gordon, Capt Thomas Edward, 14LD, 198
Gordon, Sir William bt (1830–1906), 17L, 217
Gortschakoff [Gorchakov], Prince Mikhail Dmitrievich (1795–1861), 38
Gough, Lt George, 392–3
Gough, F-M Sir Hugh, 1st Viscount (1779–1869), 220, 384
Gough, Gen Sir Hugh Henry, VC (1833–1909), 138, 141, 146, 166–7, 171, 257
Gough, Col Hugh Sutlej (1848–1900), 10H, 394
Graham, Capt, 6DG, 366
Grant, Sir Francis (1803–1878), 148
Grant, Gen Sir James Hope (1808–1875), 149, 157, 161, 169, 174, 175, 231, 393, 406; his pre-Mutiny career, 148; superseded by Sir Colin Campbell in India, 1857, 166; i/c cavalry at siege of Lucknow, 1858, 171–2; joins in charges at Nawabganj, 1858, 176; i/c Anglo-French 'China Expeditionary Force', 1860, 223; at Palikao Bridge, 21 Sep., 1860, 228
Grant, F-M Sir Patrick (1804–1895), 164
Graves, Lt-Col John Crosbie (1820–1882), 3 Bombay LC, 127
Great Britain, the, 179
Greathed, Maj-Gen William Wilberforce Harris (1826–1878), 142, 338, 342, 345, 347, 348, 350, 353, 357, 359
Grey, Sir Henry George, Viscount Howick, 3rd Earl (1802–1894), 377
Grey Neville, Cornet, 5DG, 38, 41
Griffiths, Col Henry Darby (1810–1887) Scots Greys, 72, 114, 117, 409; wounded at Balaklava, 25 Oct., 1854, 69
Gwalior, the Maharajah of, 242

Haden, Samuel, 261, 286, 332, 334, 382, 383, 453
Hamilton, Sir Robert North Collie, bt (1802–1887), 186, 190, 206, 220

Index

Index

Index

Index